INTRODUCTION TO

EXECUTIVE PROTECTION

SECOND EDITION

INTRODUCTION TO

EXECUTIVE PROTECTION

SECOND EDITION

DALE L. JUNE

CRC Press
Taylor & Francis Group
Boca Raton   London   New York

CRC Press is an imprint of the
Taylor & Francis Group, an informa business

CRC Press
Taylor & Francis Group
6000 Broken Sound Parkway NW, Suite 300
Boca Raton, FL 33487-2742

Library of Congress Cataloging-in-Publication Data

June, Dale L.
　　Introduction to executive protection / Dale L. June. -- 2nd ed.
　　　　p. cm.
　　Includes bibliographical references and index.
　　ISBN 978-1-4200-4345-7 (alk. paper)
　　　　1. Executives--Protection. 2. Executives--Crimes against. 3.
Kidnapping--Prevention. 4. Corporations--Security measures. 5. Private security
services. I. Title.

HV8290.J86 2007
658.4'73--dc22　　　　　　　　　　　　　　　　　　　　　　　　　　2007034340

**Visit the Taylor & Francis Web site at
http://www.taylorandfrancis.com**

**and the CRC Press Web site at
http://www.crcpress.com**

Dedication

To Kelly, Casey, Tori, and Katy
For a lifetime of continuous support, love, and inspiration

To Muslima and Mohammed
For unconditional love, unremitting encouragement, and strength

To Jake, Alyessa, Rukhsar, and Sakina
A new generation and reasons for making the world safer

And to all those "brothers and sisters" of the personal protection fraternity who would stand in the line of fire to safeguard another.

IN MEMORIAM
President Gerald R. Ford,
(July 14, 1913—December 26, 2006)
Whom I served with great respect.
A man who believed in "doing the right thing"
for all the right reasons.
He was exactly the right person, for the right job,
at the right time.

Contents

Preface

It is by the presence of mind in untried emergencies
That the native metal of man is tested.

James Russell Lowell (1819–1891)
American literary critic, poet, and diplomat

So the world's people lived in freedom, At ease and happy, till a fiend from hell
Began a series of savage bombings.
They called him Al-Qaeda, a demon grim, Haunting the religion,
Holding the mosques,
Ranging the wastelands, where the wretched fellow made his lair with his monster kin;
Of his philosophy was begotten an evil brood,
Marauding monsters, menacing trolls, gargoyles and fiends who battled in "the Name
of God..."
"...With many an outrage, many a crime
The fierce evil-doer, the foe of good men, stained with blood the homes of the "infidels,"
in the hateful dark, haunting the cities, desert and mountains.
But throne or treasure he might not touch, Finding no favor or grace with God
Great was the grief of the World leaders, their spirit shaken,
While many a Lord gathered in council
Considering long in what way brave and free men best could struggle
Against these terrors of sudden attack ...

... with apologies to "*Beowulf*"

The relevance of this corrupted excerpt from the very ancient Anglo-Saxon epic poem, *Beowulf,* to modern close personal protection and its relationship with international terrorism in the form of Al-Qaeda is to convey the understanding of the common need of specialized protection from evil. When one is vulnerable and safety is compromised, a great anxiety and fear are realized if there is a prominent evil known to take advantage of these vulnerabilities. Having this realization, one must take appropriate action to remedy the situation. The question is whether a remedy can be derived internally or if there is a specific need for outside professional help.

The *Beowulf* reference describes the terror that has stricken the people and leaders of the free world and their discussions of how to defend themselves (their countries) against the terror of suicide bombers, assassinations, and kidnappings that often lead to beheading kidnap victims. In the epic poem, the Danes suffered great atrocities from a grim demon called Grendel. This demon would attack by night and savagely kill any who slept in or near the great banquet hall of the Danes. None of the king's men could stop this demon, so, night after night, without relent, Grendel continued to commit these horrific attacks of terror. For years, the king of the Danes and his council could not figure out how to stop this evil, until a great warrior, Beowulf, offered his service to put an end to this terror. Of course, the king accepted his help, and Beowulf defeated the demon. Ironically, in the modern world, Denmark has again faced the potential attacks of "Grendel" in the form of religious fundamentalists protesting published caricatures of the Muslim prophet Mohammed.

This portion of *Beowulf* makes apparent the fears and vulnerability to evil, which, in turn, demand a proactive plan of how to protect from these evils. In the case of Beowulf, it was the *time* and *need* of a hero to intervene, stepping forward and possessing the skills it takes to provide the protection needed to counteract the treacheries of evil. In many or most cases, evil and terror exist without realistic motives or virtue in any way. They are just there as an obstacle to be avoided or eliminated. These fears, needs, and heroes exist in real life today and are the heart of modern personal protection.

The Beowulf passage describes the "giant Satan" or "the far enemy" (America) as living comfortable and relaxed. When the evil demon, Osama bin Laden and his brood of Al-Qaeda attacked, the world was unprepared and, while new terror was being planned and implemented, the lords (world leaders) gathered in an attempt to figure a solution. Modern protection calls for being constantly prepared, and in preparation there must be included a plan of action should the demons (terrorists) attack again. They attack with suddenness, surprise, and violence. Attacks should always be anticipated and prepared for. "By staying ready, there is no need to get ready."

No matter how great the threat, a protective agent must rise to the occasion to neutralize it for the sake of his protectee. Sudden attacks (which by definition bring terror, fear, and chaos) must always be anticipated with defensive measures in place. This takes a great deal of planning and preparation. It is in times of an attack that a protective agent must not freeze or seek his own safety; he must respond appropriately to safeguard his charge. "It is by the presence of mind in untried emergencies that the native metal of man is tested."

Paraphrasing the last three lines of *Beowulf,* "Many a lord (the protective agents) gathered in council, considering (advance work, anticipation, planning, preparation, and briefings) long (many hours go into preparing and implementing a security plan) in what way brave men (the protective agents) could struggle against these terrors and violence of sudden attack.

Although it is impossible to account and plan for every potential threat, security breach, or scenario that may occur in the personal protection agent's life, it is possible to reduce the chance of malevolence presiding over and claiming the life of the protectee. By having a good protection program in place, we can tip the balance of success in our favor. It is, and will continue to be, a learning of new skills and honing of perfection to stay ahead of our adversaries so as to provide protection to those who cannot protect themselves. We shall improve the odds stacked against the protectee, thereby giving him a better chance of survival and allowing him to live another day. We must constantly strive to meet these objectives. The unpredictable continues to occur!

Acknowledgments

It takes a lifetime to gain the experience and education that we wish we had at age twenty-five. We are where we are today because of the decisions we made, the paths we chose to follow, and the roads we took. Though often when looking back, we may wish the roads were paved and not so bumpy and dusty. In the final , we are each accountable for our own deeds and journeys. However, the people we meet along the way and who spend time in our lives should be credited for their help, guidance, and influence.

The creation of this edition of *Introduction to Executive Protection* is the result of a lifetime of experiences and interlacement with people who have shared the same dreams and positive moments, mutual experiences, and philosophy of life; "We are here to help!" Of course none of this would ever have come about if not for the opportunity and honor to have served as a close personal protector to some of the world's leading dignitaries and finest people, with whom every day was worth a lifetime of adventure, learning and experience, and proof that life is "more than standing and waiting." However, to those who contributed directly to the information contained between these two covers, I want to express a special thank you.

As part of their final exam project, my "Homeland Security and Terrorism" class of 2006 at American InterContinental University, Los Angeles diagrammed several homeland and terrorism questions. Several of these were selected to appear in this book. I would like to acknowledge all of the students who worked so hard—they are our future: Adriana Alvarez, Alejandra Barajas, Gayane Bosnoyan, Jonathan Contreras, Margie Cuevas, Maria Espindola, Jorge L. Estrada, Crystal Franco, Lonette Franklin, Joe Gonzalez, Crystal Juarez, Erick Lara, Yesenia Medrano, Jonette Nettles, Bill Oberle, Kelly Peralta, Anadelys Perez, Maricruz Portillo, Gabriella Quinonez, Louie Ramirez, Amalia Real, Melina Rivera, Damon Robinson, Gloria Rodriquez, Rafael Rodriquez, Ramon Ruiz, Brenda Sanchez, Shante Sanchez, Krizia Santiago, Alba Soto, and Alfredo Tejada.

The late Warren Coffey, my first and greatest mentor, whose positive influence is still at work today. I often hear his words in my voice. (I even tell some of his same old jokes and get the same tired, but respectful, reaction). I now understand what he meant, "Too soon old, too late smart." I still remember my military police brothers of the 110th Military Police Platoon, 7th Corp. Headquarters (Kelly Barracks) in Stuttgart, Germany who gave me my indoctrination into personal protection as part of the commanding general's elite guard. My family of fellow Secret Service agents who inspired dedication to the principles of integrity and professionalism with a legendary willingness to make any and all personal sacrifices all in a days work and who would unhesitatingly "take a bullet" for someone else. Their continuing tradition of excellence and place in history is the yardstick to which most can only dream.

Becky McEldowney-Masterman, of Taylor & Francis, who became my friend and who suggested this second edition. Special thanks go to Lili Darmali-Helin,

Rebecca Weltman, Deborah Weltman, Sarah Perez, Rashanda Montgomery, Yuki Imori, Robert Clements, James Hagidorn, and Sam Taimourzadeh for their security assignment cooperation; and to AIU student Carmen McKnight for her professional photography. An extra acknowledgment to Jeff Miller (www.safehouse.com)—from Special Forces "A" team to protection training and education specialist—for being the highest example of integrity that we in protective services should all envey and srive for.

To many of my students at Henley-Putnam University who inspected, dissected, and analyzed the text material of the first edition of *Introduction to Executive Protection*. Among them are Todd Burke, Jackson K. Chambers, Timothy E. Duprel, Todd A Hoston, David Myhra, Prakash Sharma, and E. Allen Normandy.

Ronald Collins, PhD, a former Secret Service comrade in arms, for his generous contribution regarding the "psychology of security." Gary Stubblefield and Mark Monday for giving what they could, when they could, and for their anti-terrorism efforts, for which they will never receive the credit they richly deserve. To Joseph Bannon, of the Bannon Institute (www.bannoninstitute.com) in Long Beach, California for the Surgical Strike System© of Self-Defense for his always timely inspiration and for all he has done for me and many others. To Nirmalya Bhowmick, Michael Corcoran (PhD) and Sheldon Greaves (PhD) of Henley-Putnam University (www.henley-putnam.edu) for their futuristic foresight and courage to be pioneers. To the Los Angeles Traditional Wing Chung Kung Fu Academy Sifu (master instructor) Eric Oram for the opportunity to study Wing Chun in a direct line from the developer, Buddhist Nun, Ng Mui and under the personal influence of Grand Master William Cheung whom Bruce Lee called "the ultimate martial artist."

We should live our lives so we have no regrets when we die. That has always been my intention but now I have one regret, that the people I have listed are merely a small portion of the people who have inspired, influenced, and helped me.

I acknowledge and thank you all, each and every one. You are all still very much, and will always continue to be, a major part of my life.

Enlightenment comes to those
Who are in the Dark.
For Light can best be seen
When one is in Darkness

Empty the Mind through not Knowing,
Create an Empty Darkness Inside
And the Light will come on.

Such is the Secret of Peace.
Such is the Tool of the Master.

- Sam Taimourzadeh (2007)

Foreword

Warning: Reading this book may cause you to think! That is its intention. If a reader finds inspiration to think of new and better ways to make our world safer, then this book will be considered a success.

In the world of close personal protection ten years is a lifetime. So much has happened since *Introduction to Executive Protection* made its debut nearly ten years ago. The face of terrorism, for example, has changed from "Something that happens 'in a world far, far away,'" and "It could never happen here" to "It could happen to anyone at anytime," and "Where will they strike next?"

This second edition could very easily be titled *More than Standing and Waiting* or *Close Personal Protection 101: Psychology, Philosophy, and Professionalism*, because it goes beyond the primary basics that were the heart of *Introduction to Executive Protection*. This book, though containing most of those basics and concepts, goes further by exploring and discussing the psychology, philosophy, and professionalism of close personal protection.

Introduction to Executive Protection, Second Edition is an initiation into the "fast tracks," "high-level stakes," and "mental challenges" of the world of the potentially dangerous but highly rewarding profession of close personal protection. As a business, close personal protection has come of age with the complexities of an ever-changing and dangerous world. The term itself has become the professional's new way of describing what was once (in the "dark ages" of the last quarter of the twentieth century) termed "executive protection."

Although this book is called an introduction, in reality, it is a step beyond a primer or introduction. Every effort has been made to make the material presented here, while limited, as informative, practical, and entertaining as possible. It offers insights and considerations gained from watching others, listening, learning, and, at times, making mistakes. The material in this book is the result of experience, firsthand knowledge, and personal observation accrued from many years of standing post, owning and operating an executive protective company, and planning and implementing security programs. Especially for this edition, extensive research and sharing of stories with other veterans of the protection wars was conducted to make this book as widely practical and thought-provoking as possible.

It is our philosophy that through the communication of knowledge and suggestions, new ideas and procedures will be born and necessary "break-throughs" will be made. It is not within the means of this new edition of *Introduction to Executive Protection* to be all-encompassing. That would be way beyond the scope of an "introduction" or one solitary book. No one, regardless of his experience or depth of knowledge, could possibly ever know it all. It is a rare, individual protection specialist who does not learn something new about his profession every day. If he does not, he either does not care or he is already dead and is just looking for a place to lie down.

Some of the hard learning experiences gained by the author were the result of his mistakes and those of others that were made without serious consequences. Fortunately we got away with an error without anyone being hurt or seriously endangered. The general dictum is don't make a mistake, it could be deadly and there is no second chance. That dragon will follow you the rest of your life, if you live!

A personal after action analysis usually identifies some activity that occurred that could have been dangerous to the protectee or caused him embarrassment. What was done wrong? What was done right? How can it be improved? It should be resolved and determined to learn from the experience and have zero tolerance for mistakes. The true intent of this book is to share past experiences that may inform and enlighten a student protection specialist so that he might have a successful career without "losing" a protectee or repeating some of the mistakes made by those who have gone before. This book is also intended to reignite passion for the job for the veteran who has seen it all and done it all, but who may experience new surprises if he falls to the Dragon of Complacency.

This book includes some of the important basics that are often neglected or overlooked even in practical application and by some professional schools providing close personal protection instruction. The emphasis here is upon the basic elements of protection, which are as equally important as knowing how and when to shoot straight or to wrestle a man to the ground. It will more accurately cover many of the people points. That is, knowing the technical and practical considerations of the profession is important, but merely by definition, personal protection means working with people on a personal level. Those intrinsically important elements are often overlooked in a person's professional resume. By using actual stories, it is hoped the reader will pick up many things that were learned the hard way. The "hard way" means through experience and trial and error because no one at any of the professional schools ever talked about the practical and common sense things like taking a nap and rest when you can; always keeping a sandwich in your pocket; or going to the bathroom when you have the opportunity, even if you don't feel like you have to go!

An attempt has been made to stay away from the jargon of the industry. If terms and words are unfamiliar and if occupational slang creeps into the narrative there is a convenient glossary of protection definitions in the back of the book for easy reference (Appendix E).

This book is not intended to be a technical checklist or an intensive how-to book, but rather a preface for the professional career that awaits. What follows is intended to be a somewhat detailed, though general, overview of those particular conditions and areas that shape a close personal protection specialist and protection program. In some instances the life of a protection agent has been intentionally painted very dark and forbidding. The reason for that is because an attempt has been made to be as realistic as possible. A person must know what he is getting into and some of the consequences of the life of a protection agent have a real down side. That is not to say that every person engaged in this potentially dangerous, demanding and challenging, yet exciting and rewarding profession will experience any or all of the inauspicious conditions but as it has been said, It ain't all glory!

Insanity has been defined as "doing the same things over and over in the same way and expecting different results." It is insane to think that the status quo will remain as long as there are fanatics, fundamentalists, and racists who believe their way is the only way and will assault, kidnap, and kill any who oppose them. It is to the brave people who choose to oppose those "would-be" assassins, attackers, and antisocial personalities that this book is directed with a hope that there might be one or two pieces of advice or information enabling them to professionally protect all who engage their services and enable them to find new and better ways of doing it.

It is our intention to attempt to take security and protection into the future. I am a futurist. I firmly believe we are in the middle of a "police-security" evolution. The future, as we see it, will find police powers increased to place greater focus on the threats (potential, real, and perceived) of terrorism. Police will become more "militarized"; equipped and trained by the military in methods of "hostage rescue" "bomb disposal," etc. Definitions of terrorism will change to include "street gang" activity, "serial murders, rapes and assaults," and "suspicious actions." There will be a corresponding buildup of police forces to curb growing crime, and the movement of the relationship between police and community will grow ever more distant as the priorities of the police on the street will change from "serving" to "protecting." Thus citizenry will come to rely more and more on "neighborhood" security patrols and private security organizations to perform many of the services of today's police departments. Police will be too preoccupied to respond to "routine" service calls of neighborhood conflicts, "domestic violence," "workplace violence" (unless an incident of violence involving guns, explosives, or other destructive devices have or will be used) and VIP protection.

The first edition of *Introduction to Executive Protection* brought the basic elements of personal security to a new generation of professionals whose chosen calling places them in a unique position. They are in another person's world without being a part of it, yet are expected, nee charged, with providing "a safe, secure environment" in that world. It is an ever-changing environment that could eventually result in two classes of people the "protectors" and the "seekers of protection."

September 11, 2001, brought a new level of security consciousness to the world. It is not a safe place. Terrorism, anthrax, smallpox, "weapons of mass destruction," roadside bombs, schoolyard shootings, and "sniper" are words that now bring fear, worry, and distress. This book hopes to bring a new level of security knowledge to the rising level of concern. Not only will many of the elements of the "How to..." be addressed but hopefully it will be a catalyst for deeper thought necessary to the "homemaker" as well as the protective professional.

It is intended that the readers of this book will be security professionals on all levels, students of psychology and organizational behavior, leadership classes, and others with a concern for security. As the elements of protection are now in a state of evolution, it is hoped that this book will be the beginning of the next generation of security. Universities must begin offering courses in the science of protection; this book will be a pioneer textbook with optimism that it will be the basis for further thought and research. The primary elements of *Executive Protection* will remain because the basics are timeless, but other factors, such as mentioned above, must be considered.

"Would you intentionally take a bullet for someone else?" has been an elementary question I ask in every "protective" class I teach. Interestingly, one woman in an occupational rehabilitation private investigator class and who would never be in a situation where she would need to consider that question, answered it thusly, "It's not the bullet that concerns me. What I would be most fearful of would be, 'Did I do everything I could to prevent the bullet being fired in the first place and did I do all I could to protect my client?'" That answer is perhaps the most astute reply I have received after asking the question of literally thousands of "security professionals" throughout the world. What would your answer be?

This edition takes the reader beyond this is how it has always been done to use your imagination and make it better. This edition is designed to make the reader think.

About the Author

Dale L. June is a former U.S. Secret Service agent assigned to the Presidential Protective Division at the White House with Presidents Nixon, Ford, and Carter, and he served in the Sacramento and San Diego field offices. He is also a former military policeman (110th MP Platoon, Stuttgart, Germany), city police officer (Redding and Sacramento, California); a U.S. Customs intelligence specialist, specializing in organized crime and terrorism; a private investigator and executive protection specialist providing security in the United States and several countries abroad for English and Saudi royalty, VIP's, politicians, and celebrities. He earned his M.A. in criminal justice from George Washington University and his B.A. in public administration from California State University, Sacramento.

June taught executive protection classes to students from Mong Ji University in Korea, lectured similar classes in Mexico, and has been a guest lecturer in other South American and African countries. He has been involved in security and security related matters for his entire adult life. He is a pioneer in private executive protection, founding and managing his own executive protection company (in San Diego) that provided security for many high-ranking persons and corporations long before it became a recognized and necessary profession. June contracted as a security consultant for international businesses in Mexico and Canada. He was also employed as a security specialist for a Fortune 100 company.

He is a member of the National Black Belt Club (Tae Kwon Do) and the Association of Former Agents, U.S. Secret Service. He holds a black belt in the "Quick Defense Personal Self-Defense System" and was inducted into the United States Martial Artists Hall of Fame as "Martial Artist of the Year" in July 2005. He is training and teaching in the "Surgical Strike System™" way of self-defense and is also training to become a certified instructor in Traditional Wing Chun Kung Fu.

June wrote *Introduction to Executive Protection* (1998) and was coauthor, with Carmine Motto, of *Undercover, Second Edition* (1999). He also edited and assisted with Motto's book, *In Crime's Way, A Generation of U.S. Secret Service Adventures* (2000), and is a contributing author and editor of *Protection, Security, and Safeguards* (2000), all published by CRC Press. He has written security-related articles for international security magazines in Canada, the United Kingdom, Mexico, New Zealand, and Germany.

June is an adjunct professor teaching human behavior, psychology, social science, and terrorism courses for National University in Los Angeles, California. He also has taught "Principles of Ethics" and sociology courses for DeVry University and is a full time professor of criminal justice at American InterContinental University, Los Angeles. He has written course lecture material for protective and intelligence curriculum in addition to unarmed defense and defensive tactics for protective personnel. As a cofounder of the California University of Protection-Intelligence Management (CUPIM) (renamed Henley-Putnam University) he has been active with the university since 2000. June sees himself as a "warrior" who loves to read, write, and help those who cannot help (or protect) themselves, especially children, grown-ups, and dogs.

The Shield and the Rose

Aegis. Protection; support; the shield or breastplate of Zeus or Athena; bearing at its center the head of the gorgon (Medusa). In Greek mythology, it possessed the power to terrify and disperse the enemy or to protect friends.[1]

Aegis. Defense; protection; safeguard; shelter.[2]

The Rose (sub rosa). Literally means "under the rose." Speaking confidentially or privately, and nothing about the conversation goes beyond the speaker and listener. In the past, it was not unusual to find a rose suspended over a meeting place or table to remind all present of the obligation to secrecy. The practice is said to have originated with the legend that Cupid once gave Harpocrates, the god of silence, a rose to bribe him not to divulge the love affairs of Venus.[3]

The rose (especially among personal protection agents) is the symbol of silence, which the candidate has faithfully promised and observed. Three rosettes indicate that every (protective agent) has thrice been obligated, to fidelity, to secrecy, and to silence, i.e., fidelity to the protectee, secrecy regarding the agent's responsibilities, and silence as to the proceedings of the protectee, which should never be disclosed to the profane.[4]

The term "sub rosa" comes from the Latin, from the ancient association of the rose with confidentiality. The rose, the queen of flowers, is the symbol of beauty of youth, love, joy, and silence and has long been associated with the Mysteries. In Egypt and Greece, the candidates for initiation into the Mysteries wore roses; and roses were the constant ornaments of the temples during the ceremony of dedication and opening the feasts of the Mysteries. The object of decorating the candidates for initiation with roses is to remind them of that which had been communicated to them as secrets (sub rosa), which they were bound to preserve with inviolable silence. The ritual symbolism of the rose is illustrated on the stone of the Labyrinth of Rhodes (the Island of Flowers). The shape of the rose shows the course followed by initiates, and its rings between the rows of petals symbolize the path leading to the center, where the minotaur awaits.[5]

NOTES

1. *Webster's Encyclopedic Unabridged Dictionary of the English Language.* New York: Gramercy Books, 1996.
2. *Webster's Universal Dictionary and Thesaurus.* Montreal: Tormont Publications, 1993.
3. Ibid.
4. "The Mystical Meaning behind SubRosa." SubRosa Magick, http://subrosamagick. com/Articles/SubRosa.html. September 2005.
5. Ibid.

1 Introduction

An Evolving Necessity in a Changing World

It is not the critic who counts, not the man who points out how the strong man stumbled, or where the doer of deeds could have done better. The credit belongs to the man who is actually in the arena; whose face is marred by dust, sweat and blood; who strives valiantly; who errs and comes short again and again; who knows the great enthusiasms; the great devotions, and spends himself in a worthy cause; who, at best, knows in the end of the triumph of high achievement; and who, at worst, if he fails, at least fails while daring greatly, so that his place shall never be with those cold and timid souls who know neither victory or defeat.

Theodore Roosevelt

As human history was dawning, in the mists of legends and mythology, the weakest would often have a champion or hero who would come forward and place his life at risk to protect the sick, the weak, the intimidated, or those who would be victimized by a "bully," a demon, or, yes, even dragons. Domination and struggles for power are still very evident in cities and societies of today, but in today's world of sudden and violent attacks by a faceless enemy, it is the stronger that have begun to shiver and shake in reaction to terror. The champion of modern times is the mercenary, the soldier of fortune, and the personal protection specialist who will seek out and gladly accept the dangerous responsibility of standing up for those who are incapable of protecting themselves or their loved ones.

Human history is illuminated with instances of conquest, terrorism, assault, vandalism, and assassination. Cave dwellers maintained a fireside watch through the frightful night, and villagers and castle residents were ever-watchful for "the monster" or invader. Centuries later, assassins move with the shadows of the night to deal a hand of death for a singular purpose: to make a "political" statement or deliver a "religious" message.

In the total summation of the history of the world, certain events mark and accelerate the course of man's progress. Those happenings, called a *zeitgeist*—sometimes man-made, sometimes serendipitous—are inevitable and so meaningful and powerful that little else man has done, can do, or will do could in any way compare to the total impact or lasting effect of these main chapters in his universe. The control of fire, development of speech, domestication of animals, and the evolvement of agriculture are the greatest events to shape and alter the world's history.

In the modern world, it is the industrial revolution and the dawning of the age of technology that complete the up-to-date total book on man's highest achievements. Yet the subchapters are often powerful and meaningful in their own way as a microcosm of man's progress. Is it progress, though, when it becomes a necessity and a way of life for those who are often prey for the stalkers, the terrorists, and the assassins to resort to the use of bodyguards and elaborate procedures to protect themselves from harm and possible death? What has changed? Certainly not the need for a personal defender to intervene on the behalf of those who would suffer the arrows, blades, and bullets of the practitioners of the art of bringing injury and death.

A reading of history and literature and a study of assassinations gives us the background of the causes and paths that brought us to this point in time, in which executive protection (now more often referred to as *close personal protection*) is not only necessary but has become a way of life—an acceptable part of society. Many of the assassinations that changed history would never have occurred if certain precautions had been taken. Those same precautions, the basics of protection, are as relevant today as they were when man first sought to gain power and influence through the taking of a rival's life for political or religious purposes.

In the early 1970s, close personal protection was primarily limited to a few governmental agencies having "police" powers. Of course there was the U.S. Secret Service, which created the "science" as a separation from its original duty of enforcing laws pertaining to the integrity of U.S. currency. Along with its mandate to provide protective services, the Secret Service was given the power to arrest any person or group of persons who caused or threatened to cause harm to those protected by the service.

There were other such agencies, but personal protection was secondary to their primary role of policing or law enforcement. The U.S. Marshall's Service, the FBI, and others including the U.S. Department of State, had arrest powers. As agencies of the government, their primary roles are to protect and defend the Constitution of the United States, meaning civil rights and American democracy. These are very well worth protecting with someone's life. Giving of one's life for something as precious as our Constitution and civil rights is an obligation readily accepted and understood by all who wish to live with freedom and democracy. But to place oneself in a position potentially requiring the sacrifice of one's life for another person (who may be someone we dislike or totally disagree with) is a high calling that only a few special people can and will respond to. Those few people who will risk life and limb for the safety and well-being of others have created a niche in professional occupations known as close personal protection agents.

Ten years ago, it was said that the chances of becoming a victim of terrorism were the same as the possibility of being struck by a meteorite. Well, in September 2001, the "meteorite" struck. Terrorism, assault, murder, and exploitation have become the daily fare for Americans living in the most libertarian society in the history of man. Philosophically, it is fitting that people in a free society feel safe in their home, work, and school environments. Practically, however, terrorism, roadside bombs, hostage takeover, workplace violence, and suicide bombers are the terms of the decade. Stalker, serial killer, and sniper increasingly are heard as a frightened world wonders, "Who are these people?" "Who is next?" "What can we do to protect ourselves?" Seemingly, every day there are stories on the nightly news and in daily newspapers of some disaffected or disgruntled individual attacking defenseless school children, fellow employees, or an errant motorist on heavily traveled roadways.

Whatever the cause, whatever the consequences, there are tragic common denominators—people being victimized and killed. The body count continues to pile up on a daily basis, and the public takes refuge behind the security of their triple-locked metal doors and the authority of a police or security officer's badge.

Since the concept of providing a service once known as "bodyguarding" became recognized as a specialized branch of security, it has developed into a highly extraordinary and focused field. It is against all human survival instincts to intentionally place oneself in the direct line of jeopardy for the sake of another person. Yet that is exactly what is expected of the new professionals whose duty it is to be an executive protection specialist or, as it is now more commonly called, close personal protection specialist.

As long as free people live in a democracy, the fear is not of the government but of assault by predators stalking and preying on victims, seemingly at random—the lone wolf or deranged person arriving at a workplace or school with a gun in his pocket and murder in his eye.

The same constitutional guarantees of freedom from an intrusive government, "domestic tranquility," and freedom of choice can and do, in a perverse manner, include the freedom to concede certain individual rights for the sake of living in a crime-free environment. No one in his right mind would ever vote against security measures, and probably would not even argue against them. Yet those who would deny us freedom hide behind the rights and freedoms of the Constitution as a means to destroy it. There will always be those who will use any method, no matter how heinous, to impose their beliefs upon an unprepared and unaware public. We cannot have freedom without security, but it must be balanced. It is possible to surrender 100 percent of our freedom, but it is impossible to have 100 percent security.

It is a matter of choice. Can a person or society continue living under threat of violence and crime from miscreant individuals and groups while enjoying long-established personal and governmental freedoms? Or is there a disposition to willingly compromise a little freedom to eradicate the fear, distrust, and personal invasions that are on the daily menu of radio, television, and newspapers?

To take advantage of our liberties to destroy the freedoms guaranteed to all citizens is beyond the realm of rational thinking. Yet the world has entered an era where the lawless, irrational, and self-proclaimed warriors of God have declared a Jihad (or holy war) against a freedom-loving libertarian government and innocent people. The world they want to destroy gives them the freedom and free will to destroy.

In other words, those people who would attack others simply to satisfy their own motivations have the "constitutional right" to destroy and hide behind their rights in a free society. The Bill of Rights guarantees freedom of speech and religion; protection against unreasonable searches, seizures, and self-incrimination; and the right to a speedy jury trial and a defense attorney. This and the Fourteenth Amendment (the "equal protection" amendment) give terrorists and their ilk the freedom to destroy those rights. The argument is made that once terrorism is eradicated, things will go back to normal. No chance! Terrorism will never be eradicated. It has always been here in one form or another. It may go dormant for a few years, but it will recycle in a generation or two.

Technology has provided us with tools to monitor, respond to, and protect persons and property from unwanted intrusions and hostile actions. Bulletproof glass, security cameras, and a multitude of other technological and psychological gimmicks, gadgets, and procedures are becoming as commonplace as the stalkings, killings, robberies, and violence in the workplace and home that they are intended to prevent.

Police, government agencies, and private security organizations provide the human side of protection by detaining and arresting those who threaten our security or harm us in some way. All of these agencies utilize technological innovations to produce high-tech security. Technology can even monitor our movements within and outside our homes. Cameras are placed on street corners to monitor crime as well as in elevators, businesses, parking lots, and shopping mall walkways. Satellites can identify a vehicle's license number from 100 miles in space. But technology can never replace the "human factor" in the delicate balance between personal security and freedom of movement. A close personal protection agent working with a vulnerable personage is what, in military terms, is deemed "the ultimate weapon"—boot leather on the ground. Reasoning and thought in an ever-changing environment are the advantages a protection agent brings to the security equation.

Man is a creature of society. Human behavior is not ruled by what people simply decide to do or believe. A much stronger force than individualistic choice influences our decisions. An apple falls to the ground as the result of the force of gravity. Similarly, humans react and are influenced by the overall pull of the force of society. The acts of the demented, the criminal, and the socially outcast are changing the course of society. Thus there is a pulling back from basic individualism toward a mainstream of social change, imposing restrictions on fundamental freedoms such as privacy, personal movement, and the right of personal choice. These and similar constraints are the price to be paid by the potential victim of assassination, kidnapping, or assault. It is the responsibility of the protection agent to coordinate the balance between security and freedom of movement.

Security issues have become valid political rallying points, and a fearful society, torn by anxiety about personal safety and a locked-down mentality, turns to technological advances and other devices for answers. Yet a toll is taken for every measure of security and intrusive technology such as surveillance cameras and monitor screens. The loss can be measured in terms of personal privacy, movement, and speech. The employment of close personal protection specialists to provide a measure of security for an individual or group of individuals follows the corollary of American revolutionist, patriot, and essayist Thomas Paine: "The more security one adds, the more his individual freedom of choice and movement is restricted." This has important consequences for both the protectee and the protector. Both must understand and accept this truism and work cooperatively in a mutual partnership.

When security is the point of consideration, preference is usually given to the immediate and intended consequence, with little if any thought given to the unintended consequences.

To combat robberies, banks, post offices, and other institutions including convenience stores and gasoline service stations have initiated the use of bulletproof glass windows at the expense of having personal contact with the clientele. They are also using mechanical devices such as access control units that employ a metal detection sally-port system controlling the entrance to the facility. A green light flashes after entering individuals have been scanned and found to possess no weapons, after which they are allowed entry through a second door. To avoid hiring individuals who have larcenous leanings, many companies require potential and on-board employees to submit to polygraph examinations. In some instances, these same companies have also instituted the use of psychological profiling of employees.

Psychologist Ronald Collins, points out that the desire for security "from a psychological perspective is a reaction to humankind's personal schemas, self-concepts, and adjustments to the realization of their environment." The desire for various formats of security comes from the fear of extinction, whether physical, fiscal, or proprietary.

We have seen images of snipers emerging from the trunk of cars, killing at random, and seemingly disappearing into the fog of early-morning Washington, DC, as well as fuel-laden airplanes turned into high-explosive bombs, skyjacked, and becoming an inferno for those in New York's World Trade Center and the Pentagon, the heart of America's defense. These have created new waves of fear and a renewed look at security concepts.

Many of the events that brought the world to the brink of a possible third world war are merely escalations of trends that have been building for eons. It is essential that close personal protection providers utilize the "four Is": intelligence, integrity, interpersonal skills, and imagination.

Some 30 years ago, the private security industry began an industrial and technological revolution of its own. In those days, if you were to look in the yellow pages (the Internet did not exist in those years) seeking an expert in close personal protection, you would probably be out of luck. You would have to settle for a private eye licensed to carry a gun. Maybe, if you were really threatened and there was sufficient justification (e.g., being a valuable witness), the police might provide personal security for a limited time. Afterward, the protected person was "left on his own" or placed in a witness relocation program. Those instances were extremely rare and the circumstances so limited that, for all intents and purposes, the police could not and would not provide protective services. They were not, and are still not, equipped, staffed, or trained in the fine points of personal security.

The executive protection "industrial revolution" occurred within the past thirty years, primarily because of the rise of various and numerous terrorist activities around the world. During the 1970s, there was a rash of terrorist activities including bombings, kidnappings for ransom of executives of large corporations (and oil ministers of the oil-producing countries), assassinations of corporate personnel and political figures, skyjacking of commercial airliners, attacks on peaceful sporting events such as the 1972 Olympics, and corporate extortions. The targeting of individuals, companies, and commercial and political assets (e.g., corporate executives, commercial airlines, and buildings) by criminal individuals and groups began on a large scale. These actions, although often warlike in terms of the use of weaponry and tactics, were not being committed in a conventional wartime environment. Intended targets were not military and, for the most part, no war (as defined at the time) was being waged between the countries of the aggressors and the countries of the targets. This meant there was little military response relative to the protection of these targets. Simply put, this was not in the purview of the military. Subsequently, public and private agencies, organizations, and individuals began to fill the need.

It was during and after the Iranian revolution in 1979 that close personal security or, executive protection as it became called, emerged as a business. It began as a cottage industry, with a few security specialists from government intelligence and protective agencies providing services to only the very wealthy, such as Iranian expatriates or foreign tourists such as Saudi Arabian princes and Japanese businessmen. It soon ballooned into a billion-dollar professional industry. In the 1980s and 1990s, a different form of terrorism arose. Commonplace events included domestic and workplace violence, celebrity stalkings, random street attacks, carjackings, burglaries, and attacks on executives in their homes (to be held for ransom or to expedite a robbery elsewhere). It was a case of violence begetting violence, creating a climate of fear replacing a spirit of trust. The powerful, rich, and famous became prisoners of their own success, unable to venture out for fear of being attacked and unable to work in a secure environment. This created a niche for men and women willing to provide insulation against those threats. Where there is an exigency, there is a countermeasure. The countermeasure was the evolution of a corps of trained security personnel who recognized the need and came forward, institutionalizing and bringing professionalism to a classic business. Today, if you scan the yellow pages and the Internet, you will find columns of executive protection agencies listed.

With the dawning of the twenty-first century came our modern-day terrorist. Changing tactics, they make each raid more heinous than the last. Suicide bombings, shoe bombs, dirty bombs, anthrax, smallpox viruses, and other weapons of mass destruction are the schemes of the one-sighted terror advocate. Along with international terror and violence, the emergence of domestic and workplace violence, stalking, and an increase in random attacks and robberies have generated a need for trained security personnel to protect potential victims.

The roots of executive protection are government agencies that cover the entire realm of personal security, including working in close proximity to the principal, the use of advance men, security surveillance posts, command posts, and concentric circles of protection (including procedures, systems, and personnel in the protectee's environment). As personal protection companies began to flourish with the dangerous times and terrorist evolution, the founders and personnel were primarily people who had received specialized training from agencies such as the Secret Service, the military services, the State Department, and the U.S. Marshall's Office—agencies that had developed the principles of protection into a high-level element of security for those at risk. Early protection companies founded and staffed by these individuals lent leadership and instruction to the growing industry. The services of these professionals became increasingly in demand as needs for security in many different areas developed. In the end, it comes down to the heart of each highly trained security/protection specialist, who must be willing and committed to examine and dissect evil so as to provide protection to the vulnerable.

With the increase of terror and violence in the 1970s through 1990s, and the war on terror beginning in 2001, the increased demand for specialized protection caused this industry to grow, refine itself, and reach the status of a common and necessary industry that will be needed today and forever, as long as evil exists.

Today it is not enough to merely "being a warm body" standing and waiting for someone or for something to occur to provide "close personal protection." Today's protection agent must be educated in many areas, including psychology, sociology, history, and such related subjects as political science and comparative religions. As society recognizes the growing professionalism of close protective service, new areas of need arise for trained professional consultants who are experts in all aspects of security. These aspects include conducting security surveys and making recommendations for hardening the target, installation of alarm systems, instigation of protective procedures, and provision of close personal protection.

In the end, it comes down to the heart of each highly-trained security protection specialists who is willing and committed to examine and dissect evil, in order to provide protection to the vulnerable. For financial consideration and remuneration or personal allegiance, they will assume the risks and provide protection to those who cannot provide their own security and be willing to "fight the dragons."

For the last thirty years or so, the emphasis has been on *terrorism* and assassination as a tool of terrorism. Throughout history, assassinations have largely been committed by lone individuals acting on a personal (sometimes unknown) agenda. The motivation for such attacks is not always about the specific person but what he represents or the office he holds. To a would-be assassin, the target of the assassination is a symbol of what is wrong in the world, and the assassin believes that his actions will relieve the world of the evil wrought by his victim. It is as true for an executive of a large multinational corporation as it is for the president of the United States, the pope, any head of state, or an employee of a struggling business in a small mill town.

Security may have become more sophisticated and a little more complex but, in general, the old-time concepts of anticipation, planning, and preparation constitute the center around which a good security program is built. There are no magic rituals, just good sound principles such as awareness, never leaving your post, not falling for diversions, and expecting the unexpected!

The total security concept is comparable to an umbrella. When you use an umbrella, you expect the umbrella to protect you from the rain so that you may remain dry, but if the umbrella has a hole, it becomes useless for the task. The same goes for security in personal protection. If there is a hole in the protection plan, the entire plan is useless. For instance, if the principal's home, transportation, and place of business are efficiently and appropriately secure, yet his place of play (e.g., the golf course or the theater) is ineffectively protected due to the lack of proper planning, then all the hard work put into the rest of the security plan is rendered useless, as if nothing at all had been done to protect this person.

Every aspect of protected persons' vulnerabilities must be examined and the appropriate security countermeasures taken so as to make the security of the protectee as efficient as possible, keeping in mind that measures taken should be appropriate to the situation. It also means including all of the people within the protectee's immediate circle, including family, staff, servants, and others. It should include threat assessment, surveys, technology, planning, preparation, and so on.

The concept of security requires the protection agent to take a full account of potential threats to the principal and then develop and implement a plan that addresses, circumvents, or eliminates threats wherever possible, considering all contingencies. This better enables those involved to deal with unforeseen challenges. While this may be complex and involve concentric layers of security, there may also be simple considerations. For instance, the fact that the principal does not wear a seat belt may pose as much of a risk to his safety as the lack of a home security system. Even when a professionally trained security driver is at the wheel, there must be an accounting for the possibility of an accident. The protection agent should make sure that the principal wears the seat belt and keeps the windows rolled up. A Vietnam War hero, Lieutenant Colonel Nick Rowe, was killed in an assassination attack in the Philippines when a round entered his partially open armored car door window. There are no 100 percent perfect security solutions, so it is advised that protection agents remember Murphy's law (whatever can go wrong, will go wrong) and plan accordingly.

Unfortunately, many people who are not properly trained in the finer aspects of the position have entered the close personal protection business. There is more to the job than just being a presence or "just standing and waiting." If nothing were required but a security presence, then the $8.35-an-hour uniformed guard with his whistle, nightstick, radio, and possibly a gun would be sufficient. Uniformed officers are a very necessary and important part of the total security chain. Often working alone and during late hours to protect the people and property in office buildings, construction sites, department stores, and elsewhere, a uniformed officer is a highly visible form of security deterrent, and the job demands courage, integrity, and unique abilities. However, the subtleties of personal protection are such that it takes education, training and experience to develop the necessary skills, reflexes, and intuitions that an untrained person lacks. Every new day brings fresh challenges and new dragons. ("Dragons" will be discussed in a chapter 21.)

Regardless of how long a person has been providing high-level protective services, he will always have an opportunity to learn something new. To develop all the necessary technical skills and social acumen, and to anticipate and plan for all possible intricacies, is virtually impossible and a challenge for even the most experienced and talented protection specialist.

Although a protection specialist must address a familiar routine on a day-to-day basis, he also must be prepared to prevent or mitigate unexpected occurrences and to react in an appropriate manner should the unforeseen occur. Sometimes inattention to the familiar leads to development of circumstances beyond the ordinary.

It is obvious that thousands of human-made and natural dangers can threaten a VIP, a public personality, a high-ranking executive, or a wealthy tourist or organization. Emergencies arise suddenly, without warning. A prudent and wise protection agent and the person or entity being protected must prepare to meet head-on the challenges of the unexpected and face danger, heartbreak, and crisis. The basic principles of protection never slacken; they only become more sophisticated. There will always be aggression and appropriate countermeasures. The attackers will plan an assault, and the defenders will attempt to anticipate and repel the offensive.

A close personal protection specialist must be able to relate and communicate well with people on all levels. He must also be responsive to the total security concerns of the protectee at his business organization. If the protectee is vulnerable because of gaps in the security, then the umbrella of the security program is an exercise in futility. No one can plan for all potential security threats, contingencies, and scenarios. However, a program should be developed that will improve the organization's chance of dealing with even the most unlikely security challenges. The objective of personal protection program planning is to lower the odds against the protectee to a more favorable level.

The progressive protection specialist will avail himself of any opportunity to expand his security horizons and preplan for contingencies that might arise in a range of situations. It is necessary for a protective specialist to develop the necessary confidence and rapport with corporate officials and the principal's inner circle to adequately address and prepare for all potential emergencies.

Personal protection is a sphere in which the participants do not always know when they succeed; they only know when something goes wrong. Of course, success can be measured with each passing day with no "unusual incidents." A protection specialist may be called upon to address and neutralize unexpected security concerns. A working knowledge of the threats posed in several areas must be a part of every protection specialist's expertise.

A recent news story points out the importance of knowing and understanding some of the personal inconveniences that protection agents sometimes must endure. It is apparent from this story that the agents either did not understand the requirements expected of them or were in the business primarily for the money and glory of working with a glamorous celebrity.

Three men hired to guard (a very recognizable music star) have filed a lawsuit claiming they worked long hours and were not paid overtime.... They worked 12- to 16-hour shifts and were required to be on call 24 hours a day during trips with (the star). According to the lawsuit (one agent) worked 12-hour shifts and the threesome claimed they were only paid a "straight salary," missed meals and didn't receive overtime pay.

Obviously, all of the circumstances may not have been reported in the news media or charged in the lawsuit, but a preliminary analysis suggests the agents expected "overtime pay" for working beyond eight hours per day. If indeed that is the case, they should have had it explicitly expressed in their contract. In such cases, it is usually taken for granted that agents are expected to work at least a 12-hour shift at straight salary, especially when the protectee is traveling. Missing meals is no big deal; a circumstance that should be foreseen. The agents should have (and probably could have) kept sandwiches in their pockets. A bottle of water and an "energy bar" can easily fit into an agent's flight bag or briefcase. Being on call 24 hours a day is taken as a given requirement of the position when the protectee is traveling. How else and who else could the "star" call on in the early dawning hours should a need arise?

It is not the intention of this former agent to criticize or second guess the agents in this scenario but, by the tenor of the news article, it would seem they were selfishly more concerned about their own comfort and monetary gain than for the well-being of their client. The news article, and probably the lawsuit, failed to mention that the agents stayed in five-star hotels, had all of their expenses paid, received many other intangible benefits, and were probably paid a large hourly or weekly salary.

The purpose of this book is to introduce the beginner to the occupation of personal protection and hopefully provide him with the tools to understand and appreciate the profession while spelling out the advantages and hardships. This second edition of *Introduction to Executive Protection* will enable the reader to know what is expected of one who is placed in a position of confidence and trust, with responsibility for the safety and life of another.

There is much more to providing a safe, secure environment than having a shadowy figure watching every move you make or every breath you take. The process includes teamwork between the client and the protectors, analytical processing of informational data, ethical conduct, and a knowledge and understanding of the human factors.

This is a book that explores public and private security. It looks at the scope and growth of the personal security industry in the last half of the twentieth century and explores the future of the industry in the twenty-first century and the position client protective services will take as threats to executives, dignitaries, celebrities, and their families increase.

OBJECTIVES OF THIS BOOK

- To become a groundbreaking text used in colleges, universities, and professional academies, developing excellence in personal protection.
- To establish standard principles of conduct and professional codes of ethics for close personal protection practitioners.
- To set forth goals and standards for which the practitioner of close personal protection should strive.
- To identify and discuss elements required for effective close personal protection.
- To inform the reader of the importance of the mechanics of good preparation and planning.
- To establish for the reader the important concepts of critical thinking, confidence, motivation, persistence, mental rehearsals, focusing of attention, and keeping fit.
- To familiarize the reader with the processes of recognition of an assault and analysis of challenges.
- To prepare the reader for the ever-changing face of twenty-first century terrorism and the importance of imaginative security and countermeasures.
- To help the reader determine what is required of a protective agent.
- To introduce the reader to *protection protocol* and why it is important to establish a rapport, but not become overly familiar, with the protectee.

- To emphasize to the reader the importance of realizing the obligations and consequences of his position of confidence and trust.
- To assist the reader in his personal march toward achieving professionalism through education, training, and expertise.
- To allow the reader to appreciate the rapid growth in the security industry over the last three decades and to project future growth.
- To introduce diverse ideas about the proper combination of ethical principles and standards of contemporary practice in a world that is massively devoid of ethical standards in both government and business.
- To provide, through analysis and critical thinking, data and facts so as to arrive at conclusions regarding the relevance of moral and ethical decisions made by protective and security services.
- To provide an opportunity for readers to gain intellectual preparation for making security-protective decisions that will more likely lead to greater good/benefit than to harm.
- To provide readers with a basis for making ethical security decisions through analysis and consideration of intended and unintended, long- and short-term, and physical and emotional consequences.
- To help readers conclude that ethical security procedures are not merely isolated decisions; social consequences are also important.
- To have readers form feelings of confidence, accomplishment, and hope that man will learn to live in an environment that, although ever more dependent on security professionals, maintains private human emotions and ethical considerations.
- To have readers understand the difference between public and private security and prepare an example scenario of how private security relates to public security.
- To identify social and ethical problems created by the presence of personal security and the extent to which these problems have been or could be resolved (i.e., if a protected person openly uses a prohibited drug in the presence of his security personnel).

The past is our window to the future. To acknowledge the past means learning from those who have gone before us. Close personal security has evolved with the demand for services and societal changes. But along the way, there has been a trail littered with unanticipated activities, resulting in mistakes, oversights, and harmful consequences. By studying events and procedures of the past, we can avoid the errors and faults made by others, learn to anticipate the unexpected, and make the unexpected seem routine. It is incumbent that we understand the progression of history as it relates to future possibilities. We cannot remain static in our belief that adverse actions will continue to be performed the way they always have been.

One of the criticisms made by the 9/11 Commission was that "there was a serious lack of imagination" on the part of intelligence agencies in anticipating possible methods of terrorist attacks. There was certainly no serious lack of imagination on the part of the terrorist. By studying the evolution of personal protective security, we can learn to anticipate security needs and requirements of individuals, society, and the human race. We must learn and remember that if it can be imagined and paid for, it can be done!

If we are to understand the complex issues that now define high-level personal protection, the proper starting point for the history of the field is the last four decades of the twentieth century. Since the turbulent and violent years of the sixth decade of that century, close personal protection has evolved from the muscle-bound line-backer mentality of the bodyguard to the martial arts trained bouncer, to executive protection, and now to the highly professional and trained personal protection specialists. What lies ahead?

In the 1970s, terrorism was a real hot button, involving airplanes blown up, kidnappings, bombs thrown into crowded market places, and so forth. The big names in those days were Abu Nidal, Black September, the Jackal, and so forth. Today it is Bin Laden and Al-Qaeda. Who will it be in 20 years? We will win a contemporary war against terrorism no doubt. But will the heightened security alert levels drop to pre-antiterrorist war alert status? Doubtful.

In the immediate aftermath of the World Trade Center and Pentagon bombings, it was readily apparent that lessons learned in the antiterrorist past were no longer sound. The most obvious misconception, of course, was that a terrorist, although willing to die for "the cause," would not intentionally commit an act of self-destruction. The belief was that a terrorist might slip a bomb aboard an airplane, in a piece of luggage or, as in the case of Pan Am flight 103, in a cassette player, but that he would not board the plane himself. In one day of horror, that conviction was laid to rest forever. But should it have been a surprise that a terrorist, knowing he was destined to die in the act, would in fact place himself in the doomed aircraft? Of course not. Suicide bombings were a fact of life in the Middle East for at least fifty years prior to the skyjacking and detonation. By simple deduction, it took no leap of imagination to foresee that it was only a matter of time before the rest of the world would come to know and understand that a terrorist will blow himself up as part of the act.

The second lesson learned immediately after the bombings was that the antiterrorist-related training and information being taught for the last 30 years prior to that horrific day was long outdated and wrong. According to all available data, the passengers on the planes reacted exactly as taught by all the advisories, consultants, and antiterrorism experts. As the terrorists commandeered the planes, the passengers followed the instructions of their captors. From lessons of the past, travelers were taught to do nothing to push the terrorists to violence, to obey all orders, and to cooperate. By following these guidelines, travelers could expect that the plane would be flown to some predetermined location, negotiations would be conducted, and eventually the passengers would be released. Believing in outdated procedures and reacting as expected, everyone on the planes was doomed.

A serious lesson learned from the activities of terrorists around the world is that those incidents are merely dress rehearsals for the storm that could be brewing in the United States. One suicide bomber in a crowded American subway, nightclub, or shopping center, or a daisy chain of improvised explosive devices (IEDs) along a crowded freeway late in the afternoon, would cause extreme psychological damage extending far beyond the actual victims.

This book addresses many of those issues but goes beyond the normal checklist, cookbook approach. We attempt to understand and describe what it means and what it takes to provide a safe, secure environment. To that end, we discuss and examine the following:

- *Human need for security.* Understanding the need (psychology and sociology of security).
- *Motivations* (for the protector, protectee, and the threatening person). To explore the role of personal motivations. Why do some people intentionally choose to put themselves in the line of fire for others? Why do some people decide to have another person, often a stranger, enter their private world in the name of security? And why do others target human beings as the focus of their rage or faulty reasoning?
- *Intuition.* Exploring the "sixth sense" and the role it plays in protection.
- *Requirements.* Elements of education and training; using critical thinking to arrive at reasoned conclusions and to foster new ideas for threat assessment.
- *Team building.* Exploring the concept and dynamics of security and protection as a "team" approach.
- *Ethics.* To examine the role of ethics and morality in personal life and organizational membership.
- *Violence in the workplace.* Working with a dangerous person.
- *How far will security go?*
- *Preparing for any emergency.*
- *Decision-making.* Discussing the anatomy of decision-making and the role of conscience, obligations, and feelings.
- *The power of change.* The effect of change on the individual and organization.
- *Career or job burnout.* How it affects security.
- *The "new" terrorism.* Definition, description, and protection approaches.

Some of the chapters deal with the role of a protection specialist from a psychological perspective. We will talk about history and the archetypical perspective of this profession. It is critical to know the psychological profile of this profession for many reasons. A few of them are as follows:

- This profession is one of the oldest professions known to our civilization.
- One of the significant marks of the professional is the willingness to sacrifice one's own life to protect another. And yet it is very different from being a soldier or policeman.
- It involves assuring the safety of those who live in the spotlight while living one's own life in the shadows.

This knowledge will give a deeper perspective on what it takes to be in the protective service. It also will assist in the process of adjusting to regular life after an individual leaves the profession.

Intuition as a "gut feeling" or "inner knowing" plays a major role for those who are involved in the protective line of work. Intuition provides a higher level of awareness that can make a difference between being safe and alive or wounded and dead.

In recognition of egalitarian correctness, and in fairness to all the distaff persons who are or who would make good protection specialists, and because I attended the "old school" of English grammar, I must acknowledge that I use the pronoun "him" (or conjugations of) rather than "their" or "her" as a matter of convenience when referring to a protectee or protective agent.

This book is called an introduction, but it will also serve as a refresher to the veterans who have advanced skills and to whom the job has become second nature, but who may have lost some of the edge because the challenges have developed into routines that lead to complacency. Surely the "dragons will spring up and get you" if the edge is gone and the senses are not alert and kept keen. It is recommended and hoped that the material presented here might be the keystone of an opportunity for even the most veteran personal protection specialist to expand his security horizons or rekindle and reinvigorate his dedication to awareness and the principles of protection.

This book is also for the person who may, at some point in his life, require the services of a protection specialist. It will provide him with the knowledge of what to expect as the circles of protection enwrap him and keep him safe for one more day.

REVIEW QUESTIONS

1. Describe the conditions leading to an executive protection "industrial revolution."
2. Explain the roots of today's close personal executive protection programs.
3. Why should police experience not be the only criteria for selecting an close personal protection agent?
4. Explain the total security concept of close personal protection.
5. Discuss what is meant by a position of confidence and trust?
6. Explain the objectives of a close personal protection program.

2 Human Need for Security

Protection, Defense, Safety Measures, and Precautions

Fear: terror, dread, horror, fright, panic, alarm, trepidation, and apprehension, worry, concern, anxiety, nightmare, phobia.

The killer is a killer. We are not a nation of killers. It's not the violence that frightens me, it's the fear of violence.

Israeli Foreign Minister Shimon Peres

The Fear, the Horror, the Terror. . . .

Dale L. June

Kill one, frighten a thousand.

Chinese Communist Chairman Mao Tse-Tung

HISTORICAL BACKGROUND

Darkness covered the Earth. Nighttime had fallen, and the human-like beings huddled together for warmth from the winds driving night sounds across the veldt. The roar of a saber-toothed tiger echoed across the scrub brush and tall grass while a pack of hyenas on the opposite side of the tall canyon ripped at the carcass of a freshly fallen antelope. The nearly human creatures dared not move, as their eyes tried to pierce the darkness, looking out for the approach of a stealthy cat or other creature that was sure to pounce on them. Fear created a smell of its own. The only thought, if it could be construed as a thought, through the long fearful night was survival until the next daylight. The clan realized by instinct that safety depended on staying together as a group, forming a circle with the strongest and bravest on the outside of the ring. It was the early dawn of man. During those first millennia, man's only instincts and needs for survival involved food, clothing (for warmth), shelter, sex, and security.

Over time, man experienced a development of his basic biological, physical, social, and psychological needs. By the birth of civilization, man had learned to cultivate the soil, live in communities, and fashion weapons for defense. He began by living in caves and using fire for defense, with the warmth of the fire giving a feeling of security and providing light and protection against hungry beasts. He eventually

15

adopted crude fortifications, houses, and watchmen or guards to sound an alarm in case of attack by wild animals or marauding bands of other humans. Man's need for security kept pace with his other primal needs.

Response to fear is an emotional experience tied to the instinct of survival. According to the Roman poet Lucretius, "Fear was the first thing on Earth to make gods." By putting their faith in gods, the ancient people realized a spiritual measure of security against fear of the unknown and the unexplainable. What could not be explained was explained as the work of the gods. In times of threat or fear, people turned to the gods and asked for safety and protection. Eventually, faith in God(s) led to the formation of religions. Although intended to bring peace, serenity, goodness, and security to all of mankind, religion became corrupted by fanatical constituents seeking to impose their "one true belief" on those with differing views. The thin line between politics and religion became blurred. The Crown and state competed with the cross and the star-crescent for control of property, people, lives, and souls. Wars were fought over territory and the souls of man; Crown versus. Crown, state versus state, and God's "desire" against the "wishes" of God. Lingering elements of those wars are inherent in today's world in the form of groups, sects, and radicals who utilize shocking acts of terror to intimidate, threaten, and kill to satisfy their own egos, cover personal inadequacies, or realize their goals of possessing great power.

VIOLENCE IN SOCIETY

Violence has permeated all societies throughout recorded history. By the very nature of human behavior, violence should be considered inevitable. There is a continuing question with regard to human nurture versus nature as they relate to mankind's predilection for violence. Many behavioral experts and studies of identical twins indicate that violence is a learned condition beginning in childhood.

A *Newsweek* Technology & Science report[1] offers, "A child's slight innate tendency to antisocial behavior can be magnified if parents meet threat with threat, violence with violence." Statistical evidence reveals a high percentage of child-abusing prison inmates were themselves victims of child abuse. But many experts in criminology, sociology, and psychology argue that all individuals have a choice as to whether to participate in criminal or violent behavior. The answer may lie somewhere between these two positions. In any event, violence has been a part of the world since prehistoric times. Every decade has seen a unique brand of "meeting threat with threat, violence with violence." The only differences today are the potential for mass destruction and multimedia coverage of the violence, often spreading fear as it disseminates news of violence.

FEAR OF TERRORISM AND CRIME

FEAR: F—False; E—Evidence; A—Appearing; R—Real.

Veer Sharma

In the United States, although there is a solid tradition of violence and crime, the average person goes blithely about his daily activities with a head-in-the-sand attitude about the magnitude of the potential for becoming a victim. This is rightfully so, for living in a free society means experiencing domestic tranquility and freedom from fear. In the normal stream of daily events, fear of crime and terrorism rates rather low on the average person's scale of priorities. The reason is primarily one of exposure and experience. The approach to living in a cocooned world gives a false sense of security, such as "I'm safe at home (perhaps hiding under the bed?)," with the worries and fears being concentrated on how to pay the rent this month, what to have for the next meal, or whatever the daily routine dictates.

Among average citizens, few have unreasonable worries or fears of being violently attacked—except perhaps elderly shut-ins who never leave home but hear and see the daily violence and body count on television, semi-paranoid conspiracy buffs, and law enforcement officers who have an inherent interest in such matters.

Laughing and joking, or maybe grousing and complaining, people have learned to queue up and wait their turn to be scanned and searched as they enter public buildings, airports, subways, or wherever their chores, errands, or business may take them. It has been shown that people will stay away from self-defense and civil defense preparedness classes, even if they are provided at no cost, while rationalizing, "It will never happen to me!" It has been observed that "an ostrich sticks his head in the sand to get his a** kicked." Only when an "event" occurs that reminds people of the frailty of their position do they concern themselves with the stark realism of becoming a victim. Perhaps that is as it should be. Constant fear and the stress of living in a dangerous environment can have physical as well as mental consequences. It is the overriding fear accompanying a violent criminal act or terrorist action that brings forth demands for more security. Then (for a short period of time) the citizenry is willing to make necessary sacrifices in their daily lives to assure themselves of security and peace of mind.

Fear, as we know, affects different people in various ways. Fear is the motivating factor that prevents sane people from committing insanely dangerous acts and is the stimulant moving them to take some type of preventive action against a perceived or real danger. Fear affects a human's psychological reasoning and interferes with the individual's "normal" psychological mind-set. Fear often leads to irrational action, but this is commensurate with the person's personality.

Police officers, firemen, and soldiers have many things in common, but perhaps the most meaningful is the aspiration to help those who are incapable of helping themselves. Historically, people in distress have turned to men and women who possess a special psychological makeup that gives them the extraordinary faculty to place themselves in danger for the sake of others. Knight, samurai, hired gun, bodyguard, executive protection specialist (or agent) are evolved titles for those unique people. What is that psychological factor? Like most unknown quantities, there may be more questions than answers, because, "Who knows what lies in the psyche of man?"[2]

FEAR—NO GREATER WEAPON

Terrorists seek to send messages in the form of body count or heinousness of an act. Each act of terrorism must be more spectacular, daring, and frightening than the last. There is no greater weapon than fear. Fear results when the victim feels he has no control over his own security. Paralyzing anxiety is that element whereby victims, or potential victims, allow their actions to be influenced by fear. Fear paralysis is sometimes colloquially described as the "deer caught in the headlights" syndrome. Caught on a dark road, lit only by the headlights of an on coming car, a deer will freeze and watch the speeding car all the way up to the inevitable impact.

Even after the bombing of the World Trade Center in 1993, which had already begun to fade into history's memory before the Pearl Harbor-type strike of September 11, 2001, most of the current generation of Americans thought of terrorism as something that occurred only in foreign lands. The belief was, "It could never happen here."

The bombing of the federal building in Oklahoma City by Timothy McVeigh did little to convince Americans that American soil was not impervious to terrorist attack. Because McVeigh was an American and his deed was a singular act of violence, the bombing was soon popularly regarded not as terrorism but as the criminal act of one unbalanced person.

One person can wage a reign of terror! Witness the terror wrought by Theodore Kaczynski, "the unibomber." In 20 years, he killed 3 people and wounded 29 by mailing letter bombs to his intended victims. It was not the fact that he killed 3 and wounded the others that caused so much fear and concern. The fear was a product growing from the unknown.

A similar fear emanated from the unknown sender of anthrax letters on the heels of the bombing attack on the World Trade Center and Pentagon. Prior to September 11, 2001, anthrax was a little-known farm animal disease. Today not only is nearly everyone is familiar with the term, "anthrax" became *le mot du jour* (the word of the day). The still unidentified bioterrorist spreading the anthrax spores may be a single lunatic fringe criminal or perhaps part of a terrorist conspiracy. The number of infected victims is very small, but that is secondary to the results of creating mass fear.

In October 2002, the "Washington area snipers" nearly brought the east coast of the United States to a standstill because of the randomness of their deadly gunfire. The fear the two snipers manifested extended far beyond their victims. Some people who lived in the Washington, DC, area and the Maryland and Virginia suburbs actually packed up and left the area until the snipers were caught! Two men, one rifle, and seemingly invisibility brought new meaning to the term "fear," but they also taught the world that one man operating alone can have as much of a terrifying effect as a small group of suicidal fanatics.

Fear of the unknown and randomness of an act disrupt rational thinking and reasoning. The response to unknown sources of danger often comes as unremitting, uncontrollable panic. Returning to their Florida home from Philadelphia, victim Jeffrey Hopper and his wife were fearful of the sniper who was shooting people at random, so they didn't stop as they drove through Washington, DC. But fate and caution weren't on their side. Mr. Hopper was struck in the abdomen by a bullet from an unseen assailant (the Washington area sniper) as he and his wife walked out of a restaurant in Ashland, Virginia, just north of Richmond. Mr. Hopper, in an understatement said, "It was the worst fear come true."

The questions on everyone's mind were, "Who is the next victim?" "When will he strike again?" "Where will he strike?" "Where is he?" "Who is he, and why is he doing this?" "Isn't anyone safe?" These are valid questions concerning Kaczynski, the Washington area snipers, and other terrorists. But they could also be asked about a serial killer or rapist. The commonality is the fear generated by the seemingly random actions of an unknown entity. Fear is the greatest weapon.

PSYCHOLOGY OF FEAR AND DANGER

Feel the fear, and do it anyway.

Anonymous

You gain strength, courage and confidence by every experience in which you really stop to look fear in the face.... You must do the thing which you think you cannot do. You are able to say to yourself, "I lived through this horror. I can take the next thing that comes along."

Eleanor Roosevelt

It is said that fear was a gift[3] handed down to all creatures by the early gods to enable them to survive in a world filled with dangerous predators. Aristotle said, "Courage is the midpoint between foolhardiness and cowardice." We can speculate that, without the gift of fear, man would never have survived to become the dominate species on Earth. Man was able to develop good judgment and courage to overcome the things causing him fear.

In fact, this is not too different from the main motivation to develop human civilization: we fear discomfort so we store food for more difficult times, we prepare ourselves for dangers like wild animals, but also to defend ourselves from other humans. This fear of discomfort and attachment to comfort has driven humans in their development from a type of smart monkey to a creature that has gained control over nearly all other living beings on this planet. Fear and paranoia, together with attachment, craving and hatred are responsible for wars.[4]

Fear plays a very important part in our daily life, and in human society as a whole. Fear comes in many shapes and forms, but it could be described as: an unpleasant feeling of perceived risk or danger, real or not. It functions to make us alert and ready for action while expecting specific problems.[5]

I must not fear. Fear is the mind-killer. Fear is the little-death that brings total obliteration. I will face my fear. I will permit it to pass over me and through me. And when it has gone past I will turn the inner eye to see its path. Where the fear has gone there will be nothing. Only I will remain.[6]

Throughout history, individuals from every society have sought ways that would enable them to feel confident that they, their friends and loved ones, as well as their possessions would be free from risk or danger. In that, our present society is no different from those that came before; average American citizens today have more confidence in their safety, individual rights, and liberties than citizens of any society of the past. Technology has allowed us to protect our persons, families, and property while we eat and sleep, and even while we are away from our property. On any given day, television, newspapers, and Internet advertisements for security alarm companies promise security and peace of mind for their customers, whether at home or away on vacation. But *just one* well-planned and executed attack will quickly and easily destroy that oblivious confidence. That was made evident on September 11, 2001. But time passes and memories become short and complacent. "The cause of all fear is self-grasping ignorance and all the delusions, such as selfishness, attachment, and anger, which arise from that ignorance, as well as all the unskillful actions motivated by those delusions."[7] In other words, fear is often exaggerated by imagination of the unknown. To maintain the edge of fear, attacks must continue randomly while becoming grander in scope and more horrific in scale.

IMPORTANCE OF UNDERSTANDING FEAR

You don't face your fears, you stand up to them.

Anonymous

Fear is an overpowering emotion appearing as an adrenaline rush that freezes the brain and paralyzes the body. Uncontrolled fear is blind, running in the dark, unleashed panic! Understanding fear and controlling our reactions to it is important if we are to act appropriately in dangerous and threatening situations. Nearly by definition, the profession of close personal protection agent requires acts of unremitting courage. According to Will Rogers, the American humorist, philosopher, political commentator, and cowboy, "Being a hero is about the shortest-lived profession on Earth." Knowing that, a protective agent must, by duty and obligation, react courageously, moving into the zone of danger, taking the heat and shock of a blast, the burning of a bullet, or the sting of blunt weapon or fist. Responding in the expected manner may make him a dead "hero." Failing to act in response to the catalyst of fear, the agent may live on. However, he may "die a thousand deaths" as a coward.

Overcoming this moment of adrenalin overload obviously will be best accomplished by keeping a calm and concentrated mind at the moment you realize that something needs to be done. Clearly, the solution during an actual fearful situation is to control the adrenalin rush and present a strong front (or at least a façade) of courage. To put it in more simple terms, "Don't let them see you sweat." As they say about dogs, "They can smell fear." Recognizing the scent of fear or uncontrollable emotional sweating and tell-tale body language, the source of the fear gains more confidence in his own ability, and his courage overcomes any reservation about being able to conquer his victim.

Regular meditation can be of great help. One of the best ways to really make progress with understanding and changing the functioning of our own mind is to meditate, visualizing "what-if" situations and concentrating on solutions and reactions. If and when the actual crisis arises, the mind will have already been conditioned to do what it must do. The mind will have already visited the situation, calculated the degree of danger, and found a solution. The body will react as directed by the mind. Meditation practice and visualization overcome the weakening defensive mechanism of the adrenalin rush and convert it into protective energy.

Can fear be healthy? Certainly, when it keeps you alert in a very dangerous situation for yourself or others! The early Greek historian Thucydides, writing about the heroes of the Peloponnesian War, recorded, "The bravest are surely those who have the clearest vision of what is before them, glory and danger alike, and yet notwithstanding go out to meet it."

> Our most basic fear is the fear of death, which functions to make us alert in dangerous situations, and can thus be a very healthy emotion. In all cases, we could say that fear is a reaction to something that may happen in the future, be it realistic or not, it is always uncomfortable. And here we find one of the contradictions of fear itself: it should work to keep us from discomfort, yet it is uncomfortable itself.[8]

We define our fear. The range of fear may be narrower in one person than the next. The fear factor in a protection agent must be very high, rating near firefighters, smokejumpers, astronauts, police, and others who must constantly face potentially life-threatening situations. Usually, we think that brave people have no fear. The truth is that they are intimate with fear. In circumstances requiring a positive response against the thing causing the dangerous or fearful emotion, the bravest thing you can do when you are not brave is to pretend courage and act accordingly. To be more explicit, to stand and face a danger, even though survival may be at stake, and to confront the instinct to run away or to be paralyzed like a "deer caught in the headlights," a brave person will suppress his fear and take positive corrective action.

> No matter what you want to do, don't be nervous. You should not let your muscles nor your mind be affected by nerves.... No illusion and no imagination, but to apprehend the actual situation you are in and find a way to deal with it.... No excessive action is needed. Just keep your body and mind relaxed to deal with the outside emergency.
>
> **Bruce Lee**

Fear is a favorite psychological weapon of terrorists (who could be said to be cowards because of their faceless expression of "warfare") against a helpless and apprehensive public. To use the fear-generated adrenalin and gain courage to turn the fear into a weapon against the enemy requires enlisting other emotions while ignoring fear. Anger is a powerful tool and motivator; it is the lion of emotions. Getting angry throws all caution to the wind and drives the respondent into a blind act of bravery. To be even more explicit, anger clouds the state of fear and trumps it.

As fear is based on something that we think may happen in the future, it is clearly a mental process that tries to predict the future—in that sense, the reason for fear is a projection of our mind. One could say that fear is always based on something that has not happened yet and is therefore a fantasy of our mind rather than a fact.

Some people like fear because, in activities such as riding a roller coaster, parachute jumping, and so on, we get an adrenaline rush: a physical reaction to make us alert and ready for action. Some people actually get addicted to this natural drug and get involved in extreme activities. This can easily lead to a need for more dangerous situations more often, so they may tend to take ever-increasing risks—until the parachute does not open or the weather changes while climbing a steep, dangerous mountain slope. In fact, people do not love fear, but they love the release of adrenaline in the blood without anything bad happening to them.

Fear is generally a very uncomfortable feeling. We do not like to be afraid but, still, our fear can keep us from harm when, for example, it makes us hold back when we see a snake or a fast car moving in our direction. So, yes, we need to recognize danger and be alert, but once we are alert, we cannot do much more than whatever we think is best in the situation.

If we let fear take over completely, we can even freeze and become completely helpless. Similarly, many of us have quite irrational fears, of things that do not really pose any threat to us. Therapies for irrational fears work on the same basic principle: discover by experience that the feeling of fear (paranoia) is an exaggeration of what we perceive in the world, and force our rational mind to remain in control.[9]

Most types of fear are related to possible physical or mental pain. Faced with the prospect of physical or mental pain in the future, we probably need to start working to prevent it rather than be frozen in our own miserable predictions and depression. So we should act rather than crawl away.[10]

Fear of the unknown is not the only debilitating fear that must be overcome. Fear of injury can have certain side effects. It may mean a hesitant or slow reaction to something that demands immediate attention. It may mean a meek action when an aggressive manner is required. It can mean the difference between life and death.

"It's not the bullet that concerns me. What I would be most fearful of would be the question, 'Did I do everything I could to prevent the bullet being fired and did I do all I could to protect my client?'"[11] This profound statement is a manifestation of atychiphobia—the fear of failure. It is the fear of failure that sits just over the shoulder of the protective agent. It becomes the driving force that propels him to "step in front of a bullet." The feeling of most professional protective agents is that it is better to be wounded or killed in performance of duty than to be required to explain to a grieving family, a board of directors, or a congressional investigative hearing why "everything possible was not done to prevent the killing of your charge."

ACCEPTANCE OF FEAR

Fear can be controlled and channeled into productive energy.

Do the thing you fear most and the death of fear is certain.

Mark Twain

In the words of Zen Buddhist teacher Suzanne Segal, "The presence of fear means only that fear is present, and nothing more." Meditate with these kinds of thoughts: "I know fear exists, I know it's making my life tougher then it needs to be, but it is not only me that has to deal with it, fear is a problem for all beings, big and small."

Don't be afraid to "look death in the face and spit in his eye." The idea is to allow the worst of your fears—death, injury, incapacitation—to be visualized. Do not allow them to wait in the shadows of your mind. Be in control of it. Fear is something our mind creates, so only our mind can do something about it! Exaggerated fears can have their basis in wrong decisions or experiences.[12]

UNDERSTANDING THE NEED FOR SECURITY— PSYCHOLOGY AND SOCIOLOGY

Anxiety, stress, nervousness, angst, worry, and apprehension are only some of the manifestations brought forth from insecurity. Security is a loving mother tucking her child into bed at night and assuring him that there is no monster under the bed. The need for security is evident in humans at the very earliest moments of life. A newborn has a need to be bundled and cuddled, held close to the mother's breast for warmth and comfort. Studies have proven that a child deprived of the security of family nurture and social interaction will develop fears, insecurities, and unwarranted aggressiveness.

HIERARCHY OF NEEDS

Sociologist Abraham Maslow's Hierarchy of Needs cites several layers of human needs. He identified five categories of needs: physiological, security, belongingness, esteem, and self-actualization. In the pyramidal hierarchy, man's need for security is second only to man's needs for primary physiological sustenance.

Maslow said that as one level of need is met, man will move to the next level and the next until all needs are fulfilled. But if a lower need becomes in demand again, man will drop back to that level until that need is again satisfied. Maslow put forth his hypothesis in 1943 as it related to motivation in the workplace. Since then, other sociologists have adapted mutations of this theory for the workplace, but Maslow's remains the most famous and followed. It easily overlays society in general and describes for us the base needs and desires of social man. The Hierarchy of Needs is a graphic representation of the motivations for the demand for more present-day security in all sectors of society.

UNDERSTANDING MASLOW'S HIERARCHY

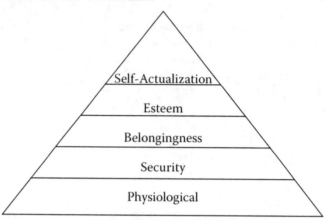

Physiological needs. Air (oxygen), food, water, sex.

Security needs. Freedom from the fear of physical danger and deprivation of basic physiological needs; security, stability, dependency, protection, freedom from fear, anxiety, and chaos, need for structure, order, law, strength in the protector.

Belongingness. Needs of love, affection, and belongingness; people seek to overcome feelings of loneliness and alienation; involves both giving and receiving of love, affection, and belongingness.

Needs of esteem. Self-respect and respect for others; person seeks self-confidence and value as a person; when needs are not met, person feels inferior, weak, helpless, and worthless.

Self-actualization. Person is doing "what he was born to do" and is happy doing it. The person is satisfied that he has met all his other needs and is confident in his ability to maintain.

   A protective agent should be aware of all of Maslow's "needs" to recognize the disparate and shifting changes in his own physiological and mental attitudes as well as the person he is protecting. Through recognition and knowledge of where he and his protectee are in the hierarchy at any one time, the agent can meet those needs and understand mood swings.

SUMMARY

Similar to "whistling in the dark while walking past a graveyard at night," one must be constantly alert and know that danger lies just around the next corner while continuing as though everything is normal. This is a psychological trick for suppressing fear or fooling your emotions into believing that, although danger lurks, it will not overcome your confidence. In other words, expecting danger keeps a person's adrenaline level high enough that when danger exposes itself, there is no unexpected adrenaline rush turning common sense and control into frenzied and uncontrolable hysteria and panic. One of the best methods to control the involuntary fear reaction of panic is to consciously discipline one's mind to think of ways to overcome the threat. In other words, staying alert means staying alive. There are several ways to convince the mind to be alert, but one of the best is to think, "When you least expect it, expect it!"

REVIEW QUESTIONS

1. What is fear and how can it affect a protection agent?
2. Why is fear the greatest weapon?
3. Why is fear considered a gift.
4. Explain Aristotle's definition of courage, "Courage is the midpoint between cowardice and foolhardiness."
5. What should be the limits of ethical, moral, and legal responsibilities of the person providing protection?
6. Explain the following quotation in terms of a protective agent: "The bravest are surely those who have the clearest vision of what is before them, glory and danger alike, and yet notwithstanding go out to meet it."
7. Why should a protective agent be aware of all of Maslow's "needs" to recognize the disparate and shifting changes in his own physiological and mental attitudes as well as the person he is protecting?

NOTES

1. Begley, Sharon. "The Nature of Nurturing." *Newsweek*, March 27, 2000, 65.
2. Paraphrase from the radio show, "The Shadow." The exact quote is, "Who knows what evil lurks in the hearts of men?"
3. de Becker, Gavin. *A Gift of Fear*, reprint ed. New York: Dell, 1998.
4. http://buddhism.kalachakranet.org/fear.html#add (accessed 12/31/05).
5. Ibid.
6. Herbert, Frank. Litany against Fear, incantation in *Dune*. London: Hodder & Stoughton, 2006.
7. From tharpa.com.
8. Ibid.
9. http://buddhism.kalachakranet.org/fear.html#add (accessed 12/31/05).
10. Ibid.
11. See last paragraph of preface.
12. "One Foot in the World," http://www.accesstoinsight.org/lib/authors/desilva/wheel337.html, a long article from the Buddhist Publication Society; "Freedom from Fear," http://www.accesstoinsight.org/lib/authors/thanissaro/fear.html, an article from Ven. Thanisaro.

3 Psychological Perspectives on Security Issues

Know the enemy and know yourself; in a hundred battles you will never be in peril. When you are ignorant of the enemy but know yourself, your chances of winning or losing are equal. If ignorant both of your enemy and of yourself, you are certain in every battle to be in peril.

Sun Tzu

MOTIVATIONS

Why would anyone choose this profession? What is the most satisfying part of this career? Does a protective agent have a passion for this career? What motivates the protective agent to live a potentially frightening and dangerous life? Is it the attraction to the beautiful feeling of adrenaline as it pumps into the brain and changes the chemicals of the mind? Is it the lure of adventure, travel, and monetary rewards?

If the motivation is money, glamour, or public attention, the reasoning is entirely wrong. The protective agent is in the wrong business for all the wrong reasons. The reason to become a police officer should be that the individual wants to be there to help those in need. The same could be said of the protective agent. He should want to be in the business because he has the special talents, skills, and psychological makeup to help those who, for whatever reason, need services only he can provide.

> Most of the people in our society are sheep. They are kind, gentle, productive creatures who can only hurt one another by accident…. Then there are the wolves and the wolves feed on the sheep without mercy…and there are sheepdogs who live to protect the flock and confront the wolf…. If you have no capacity for violence then you are a healthy productive citizen, a sheep. If you have a capacity for violence and no empathy for your fellow citizens, then you have defined an aggressive sociopath, a wolf. But what if you have a capacity for violence, and a deep love for your fellow citizens? What do you have then? A sheepdog, a warrior, someone who is walking the hero's path. Someone who can walk into the heart of darkness, into the universal human phobia, and walk out unscathed.[1]

Entering the field of personal protection requires a special commitment. It means having unique skills and what some would describe as "a measure of insanity" to be willing to put your life on the line for someone else. Many people who enter this field do so for the joy of working with other people in an environment that allows them a certain degree of creativity without being watched over every minute. It requires a person who inspires the utmost confidence in people by performing a function that requires responsibility. Negative reasons for becoming a protective agent are the opportunity to be close to the "glamour" of famous or important people and "the money."

If working strictly for the glamour or money, what psychological motivation is there when the protectee is threatened? What would the agent be protecting—the person or the paycheck? Would he place his life on the line only for the check? How would the agent react if someone else paid him more money not to take protective action? Psychologically, the agent would be reacting only as a mercenary and not for the good of the individual needing protection. Perhaps he might react just a second or two slower, not see the shadow move, or fail to investigate what he rationalizes as a cat in the back yard.

A protection agent has a unique personality. His life is spent in the shadow of someone else, staying within a small perimeter that he knows is a floating bull's-eye. There are more moments of boredom than actual times of glamour, challenge, or danger. Moments of standing and waiting are incalculable, whereas the moments for which he is getting paid—the instant when he must risk his own life for someone else (perhaps even someone he doesn't know or dislikes)—happen infrequently, perhaps only once in a lifetime. It is that one thousandth of a second that defines the agent. Either he reacts bravely and risks everything, or he reacts too slowly (or not at all). If the agent hesitates or thinks too much, he may lose his life as well as the life of the person he is trying to protect. Hesitation kills, and if a protection agent stops to think, it is already too late. He will have lost.

It is a razor's edge between courage and cowardice and foolhardiness. One must not take unnecessary risks or seek dangerous situations merely to gain an adrenaline rush or to impress another person. The protective agent must be aware of the devil of addiction. Fear addiction, like all other addictions, is very wily and stretches its stealthy hand around the unsuspecting as surely as heroin sings a siren song of euphoria. Rightly or wrongly, it has been said that people who work in dangerous professions are "adrenaline junkies" who have become addicted to the euphoric feeling aroused by walking the thin line between death and living "on the edge."

Knowing you have the confidence and the ability to address any dangerous situation is like having a large savings account in a bank. You know it is there but hope you never have to use it. The feeling of confidence may be a delusion until and unless an agent is exposed to the fire of danger. He never knows how he will react until that defining moment where he either freezes, runs away, or takes that "last heroic" action. It is that moment for which he has prepared his life. It is the culmination of all the hours of standing and waiting, the training, the simulations, the what-if mind games, and the stories of his capabilities that he has told himself and others. It all comes together right at that very moment. Is he a hero or a coward?

PSYCHOLOGICAL CORRELATION BETWEEN SECURITY SEEKERS AND SECURITY PROVIDERS[2]

Broad and lengthy discussions can be conducted with regard to the psychological correlation between security seekers (or protectees) and security providers (or protection agents). Sociologist David Kingsley says, "The word 'security' when used by itself is highly abstract." While there are certainly many constants among the varying groups of security seekers and providers (and perhaps better ways of discussing the reciprocal relationship between them), it is fair to say that, although the relationship between seekers and providers is reciprocal, in practical terms it is hardly ever balanced—psychologically or in most other respects.

The need or desire for protection or security indicates that there exists a real or perceived threat to the seeker. And seekers need to admit that adverse conditions exist that they alone cannot counter. Thus, seeking security is a means of self-defense, which is an extension of the basic will to survive. Psychologically, the seeker may experience fear of harm or loss or, at the very least, wish to reduce the possibility of negative occurrences. Here it is key to note three things. First, the motivation is externally generated (or, as some psychologists would more simply say, a *learned phenomenon*). Second, it is determined by the seeker that the threat is not or may not be avoidable. And finally, the seeker chooses to go to an outside source for defense.

An appropriate example is a neighborhood victimized through a rash of robberies. This is an external factor or phenomenon. Rather than move, however, homeowners in the neighborhood begin to utilize home security services and/or request increased police patrols. Here, the homeowners, because of the threat or instance of robbery, determine not to flee but to employ providers (the police, security companies, and so on). In short, when external factors or activities stimulate a psychological response or emotion such as fear, anger, worry, or some other state of unease, the end result is that individuals or groups may become seekers.

Providers may be motivated by external factors to act but, in their role, they willingly assume personal risks at some level. The external factors are secondary motivations to a deeper compulsion. This compulsion, which is internally generated, requires an override or at least a modification of the fundamental tendency to avoid unnecessary danger. There is reference in psychological literature wherein providers are described in large part as thrill seekers and adrenaline junkies. Providers choose work in security fields where there are inherent risks. But of the many constants among providers, the greatest attribute they share is the willingness to help others. In a recent nonscientific study of 200 university criminal justice students, the number one reason for entering law enforcement and personal security was the "compulsive" need or strong wish to help others.

At its roots, the reciprocal relationship between seekers and providers is heartening. It is also often an enabling relationship. Seekers are driven as an extension of their survival instincts, but what compels providers to be there for them is not as clear-cut. Psychologically, seekers and their situations afford providers a sense of purpose. And while there may seem to be imbalance in the value of the relationship in favor of the seekers, it must be reiterated that providers for the most part make a free choice to serve, whereas seekers are forced into their roles. Seekers are made. Perhaps providers are born. Seekers may not always want the providers in their lives, but both manage to maintain a symbiotic relationship.

PSYCHOLOGICAL ASPECTS OF THE PROTECTOR

According to conventional wisdom, no one would intentionally place himself in a position of life threatening danger. However, that is exactly what close personal protection agents must do. Not only do they place themselves in the circle of danger, they must be prepared to step between the danger and the person they are committed to protect. Psychiatrists can debate the psychology of the "why" of this issue for years, but there is a growing society or subculture that is very much dedicated to this proposition of standing in the line of fire.

> The sheep generally do not like the sheepdog. He looks a lot like the wolf. He has fangs and the capacity for violence. The difference, though, is that the sheepdog must not, cannot and will not ever harm the sheep. Any sheepdog who intentionally harms the lowliest little lamb will be punished and removed.... Still, the sheepdog disturbs the sheep. He is a constant reminder that there are wolves in the land...until the wolf shows up. Then the entire flock tries desperately to hide behind one lonely sheepdog.... Understand that there is nothing morally superior about being a sheepdog; it is just what you choose to be. Also understand that a sheepdog is a funny critter: he is always sniffing around out on the perimeter, checking the breeze, barking at things that go bump in the night, and yearning for a righteous battle. That is, the young sheepdogs yearn for a righteous battle. The old sheepdogs are a little older and wiser, but they move to the sound of the guns when needed right along with the young ones.... Here is how the sheep and the sheepdog think differently. The sheep pretend the wolf will never come, but the sheepdog lives for that day.... In nature the sheep, real sheep, are born as sheep. Sheepdogs are born that way, and so are wolves. They didn't have a choice. But you are not a critter. As a human being, you can be whatever you want to be. It is a conscious, moral decision. If you want to be a sheep, then you can be a sheep and that is okay, but you must understand the price you pay. When the wolf comes, you and your loved ones are going to die if there is not a sheepdog there to protect you. If you want to be a wolf, you can be one, but the sheepdogs are going to hunt you down and you will never have rest, safety, trust or love. But if you want to be a sheepdog and walk the warrior's path, then you must make a conscious and moral decision every day to dedicate, equip and prepare yourself to thrive in that toxic, corrosive moment when the wolf comes knocking at the door.[3]

To begin to understand the psychology of what motivates a "perfectly sane" man or woman to practice the potentially dangerous art of "catching bullets" is to know that fear is not influencing your actions. However, if as H.P. Lovecraft said, "the oldest and strongest emotion of mankind is fear, and the oldest and strongest kind of fear is fear of the unknown," how does one reconcile courage and fear when natural instincts are involuntary reactions?

We have discussed the correct mind-set for maintaining physical and mental control in threatening situations, but what of the personality and the psychological profile of the protective agent? What is his psychological motivation to endure high levels of stress from anticipating potential danger, being under constant scrutiny from the protectee and all who he comes into contact with, or the possibility of going from a restful and comfortable manner to a full-faceted life-or-death combat alert or action? What type of individual becomes involved in this kind of profession?

Dr. John A. LaPointe, a licensed clinical and police psychologist, describes them as

... aggressive personality types, who are action-oriented, thrill-seeking individuals that thrive on high stimulation. These individuals often have authority and control issues and score somewhat higher on manic, depression, and psychopathic deviant scales than the general public. They tend to be type "A" personalities that are competitive, driven, and typically impatient. They may be a little obsessive-compulsive. This makes them really good at their jobs but can also cause them a number of interpersonal difficulties (especially personal relationships). There is a noble motivation of wanting to help the public, but they would not remain in the field very long if they were not able to adapt and accept the responsibility of helping others and following some sort of rules which govern their profession.

Where does a protective agent get the psychological strength to not let his fears influence his actions? It begins with character. This moves us into the ethical arena regarding trust, confidence, and honesty—the character of the protective agent. Character is that special extra called upon in times of temptation, duress, hardship, or life-threatening situations. It is making all the right choices for all the right reasons. It is to continue when others have surrendered or given up hope. It is preparing for the worst, while hoping for the best.

In sports, entertainment, or any activity that requires timing, interest, and a best-faith effort, it is said that the performer gets himself psyched or "into the zone." That means bringing the heart rate and blood pressure up, to be stimulated in mind and body by a rush of adrenaline, and becoming mentally prepared for the appropriate action. For a protection agent, psyching is a very important ingredient in his overall preparation. He not only psyches himself through mental preparation but, beginning with physical appearance, confident demeanor, and continuing with a mind-set of being assertive (while not being aggressive), the protective agent may psyche out someone planning a harmful action, or, in other words, stop an attack before it begins

Understanding the motivations, personality, and character of a protectee and using appropriate psychological and communication skills, a protective agent can remain psychologically prepared to react to adverse and harmful actions. An agent must stay within himself, within the moment, and believe the time is always *now*—not three seconds ago or three seconds from now, but now!

MOTIVATIONS

Observation of U.S. Secret Service agents after a presidential election campaign has revealed symptoms similar to combat fatigue. The stress, poor eating and sleeping habits, long hours, and constant travel have taken a serious toll on agents' bodies. But they have maintained professional expertise, mental alertness, and healthy attitudes because of their strength of psychological preparation and character.

"If you are in it for the money, you are serving in the wrong occupation." That is the advice I give criminal justice students who are studying to become law enforcement officers. Many police departments have adopted the Los Angeles police motto, "to protect and serve." A similar but more powerful slogan is, "We are here to help." These should be the two primary reasons a person enters the protective field in addition to being slogans for law enforcement.

"Why are you in this business?" and "Why would you want to place yourself in harms way for someone else?" are two key questions every potential candidate for protective services should be asked, and the reply should be probed in depth. Understanding a protective agent's psychological motivations is important because it helps understand how he may react in a crisis situation.

Thirty-five years after he went absent without leave from a military hospital where he was recovering from a serious wound sustained during World War II, American historian William Manchester explained experiencing a flash of understanding as to why he left the hospital to rejoin his unit, which was going on a dangerous and potentially deadly mission. During the mission, he was again seriously wounded.

> It was an act of love... I had to be with them rather than let them die and me live with the knowledge that I might have saved them. Men, I now know, do not fight for flag or country, for the Marine Corps or glory or any other abstraction. They fight for one another. Any man in combat who lacks comrades who will die for him, or for whom he is willing to die is not a man at all. He is damned.[4]

Placing Manchester's personal observation in context with the motivation of a close personal protection agent, we can come to understand certain types of personalities who want to make a difference, help others who can't help themselves, and protect the weak and intimidated. They are willing to make serious personal sacrifices, without a thought to the personal danger, out of love, compassion, and caring and in the name of fellow human beings. These are the type of people who will be the first to charge through the door, challenge the bully, or take a bullet so someone else won't.

It may prove to be a red flag if, when lives are at stake, the primary motivation is for the money, travel, and adventure. This motivation puts monetary rewards and benefits ahead of the responsibility of protecting a client.

Not too long ago, an Orange County, California, protective and security company[5] won a U.S. government contract to train Iraqi security forces in Jordan. Within a week before the contract was to begin, the government canceled it. The protection company officers were offered a large cash settlement in lieu of the contract. The company refused the offer even though it meant nearly $1 million for the company officers to share. The president and vice president of the company insisted that each person who had committed to the assignment also should receive compensation. Eventually, the government relented and paid enough money for each trainer to be given one month's salary plus reimbursement for all expenses incurred while preparing for the assignment. This meant a serious individual cash loss for the company principals, but their act of character gained them much respect and loyalty from most of their subcontractors.

One subcontractor insisted on receiving more than the settlement share that everyone else thought was not only fair but beyond what the company needed to offer. This individual threatened court action and other legal remedies because his opportunity to make a large payday had been canceled. My reply was to ask, "At what price would he surrender his integrity?" I said I would never hire or work with that person, because money was his prime motivator. He would have become a potential weak security link for the rest of the team members. It would be an easy leap for him to accept more money from an opposing force to possibly sell out his teammates. This man was a mercenary, paid to do a job and willing only for a great amount of money. Renaissance political philosopher Niccolo Machiavelli, in his classic political treatise, "The Prince," warned about the use of mercenaries to protect the prince.

> Mercenaries are useless and dangerous.... For mercenaries are disunited, thirsty for power, undisciplined, and disloyal; they are brave among their friends and cowards before the enemy; they have no fear of God, they do not keep faith with their fellow men; they avoid defeat just as long as they avoid battle; in peacetime you are despoiled by them, and in wartime by the enemy. The reason for all this is that there is no loyalty or inducement to keep them on the field apart from the little they are paid, and this is not enough to make them want to die for you.

This shows one thing: money cannot purchase loyalty, but dedication to a principle and character will.

Even such a pragmatist as Machiavelli postulates that the only secure and trustworthy defenses are those that depend upon one's own strength and virtue. Machiavelli warned Lorenzo de'Medici that putting too much faith and strength in the hands of someone else (such as mercenaries or foreign powers) could have disastrous results. In other words, "Should a (person) place 100 percent confidence in the person he has engaged to protect him, and what should be the limits of ethical, moral, and legal responsibilities of the person providing the protection?"

In October 2001, for the first time in history, warplanes from European alliance nations began patrolling the skies over the United States to help guard against terrorists who might again use airliners as bombs. Possibly our reliance on technology to solve social ills may lead us down the path of abrogation of our own individual rights (so proudly won during the eighteenth, nineteenth, and twentieth centuries). In seeking security through external means, we surrender power. Relying on others to provide our security and safety is to relinquish areas of personal freedom. That is the dilemma faced by anyone who depends on others for security. To what extent does the protector have the right—or moral obligation—to achieve a desired outcome by influencing another actor's (the person being protected) behavior?

We, as citizens in a free and open society, must ensure that individuals who are entrusted to provide security do not misuse, abuse, or convert the power that has been bestowed upon them. Furthermore, we who provide the security for others must treat the power given to us as a sacred trust.

CREATIVITY

Intrinsic personality attributes are distinguishable in high-risk performers of dangerous professions. Creativity is a part of the required psychological makeup of one who provides security or protects a person or place. Being creative is the ability to "imaginate"; to think on your feet, to be flexible, to fashion a defense, or to respond in a unique manner.

No two thumbprints or DNAs are alike. So are no two protective assignments or situations the same. No matter how often a protectee visits any particular venue, the protective agent responsible for securing the site must be creative in imagining and countering new ways an attacker would approach and initiate an attack.

Whenever the president leaves the White House, the Secret Service assumes nothing in its quest for creating the ultimate in a safe environment. Progressive innovation by agents of the Service is testimony to their creative genius. Nothing is ever to be taken for granted. When it comes to high-level protective security, nothing must ever be done simply because "we have always done it this way." Creativity is the manifestation of imagination. If it can be imagined, it can be done. An experienced professional—especially those working in such professions as law enforcement and personal protection—must possess what is called a *creative personality.*

CREATIVE PERSONALITY[6]

Creative individuals are remarkable in their ability to adapt to almost any situation and to make do with whatever is at hand.

1. They work long hours, with great concentration, while projecting an aura of freshness and enthusiasm.
2. What psychologists call the *g factor,* i.e., a core of general intelligence, is high among people who make important creative contributions.
3. Creative people combine playfulness and discipline…. But this playfulness doesn't go very far without its antithesis, a quality of doggedness, endurance, and perseverance.
4. Creative people alternate between imagination and fantasy and a rooted sense of reality. But the whole point of [protective services] is to go beyond what we now consider real and create a new reality.
5. Creative individuals seem to exhibit both traits of extroversion and introversion simultaneously, either preferring to be in the thick of crowds or sitting on the sidelines and observing the passing show.
6. Past accomplishments, no matter how outstanding, are no longer very interesting to them. At the same time, they know that in comparison with others, they have accomplished a great deal.
7. Creative and talented girls are more dominant and tough than other girls, and creative boys are more sensitive and less aggressive than their male peers.
8. Creative people are both rebellious and conservative, but the willingness to take risks, to break with the safety of tradition, is also necessary.
9. Most creative people are very passionate about their work; without passion, we soon lose interest in a difficult task.
10. Creative people's openness and sensitivity often exposes them to suffering and pain, yet also to a great deal of enjoyment.

A close reading and analysis of the above definition of "creative personality" reveals many qualities inherently descriptive and required of the protective agent. Nothing in the protective business is ever static. Ideas and concepts are constantly being created, reviewed, and rendered.

CHALLENGES AND COMPETITION

Facing challenges in the protective services is a powerful motivator. Psychologically, it could be a throwback to being the fastest gun in the West, or possibly to those days of starring on the athletic field. Every day comes a new challenge, with something to be engaged and defeated. It may be a particular logistics problem, an individual or group intent on rendering harm, or perhaps something as mundane as maintaining a high state of awareness while being physically and mentally fatigued. It means needing the "dopamine fix" derived from confronting opposing forces. The test of competition raises the heart rate and elevates the pulse and blood pressure. For many people, especially those engaged in dangerous enterprises, the challenge of competition may have the same serious consequences as an addiction. The need to compete and challenge the odds is a positive reinforcement that lifts a protective agent to the level required to meet his heavy responsibility.

PROBLEM SOLVING—NEW PROJECTS

Every day in the life of a protective agent, new challenges bring new problems and new projects. Doing things in a new or unorthodox way is indicative of a creative personality. If there were no new problems to solve or new projects to complete, the creative personality so strong in a protective agent would soon become mired in the mundane elements he needs to mentally escape. Challenging problems and facing new projects brings the mental release the practitioner desires. It brings the comfort of satisfying an unexplained need or drive of an addiction.

OTHER MOTIVATORS

The idealistic protective agent may not be able to pinpoint the precise motivation that inspires him to place himself in the spotlight of danger for the safety of others, but many conversations with veteran protective agents have provided some insight. Interestingly, the primary motivators are for humanistic and altruistic reasons. Among them are

- *Opportunities for building relationships with interesting people.* The fraternity of protective agents brings together professional people with many similar interests, experiences, and goals. It may be the sharing of working long hours and potentially dangerous assignments or just knowing they may depend on each other for their lives. Either way, the closeness brings them together as a "family."
- *Good work environments.* Working with high-ranking VIPs, celebrities, powerful politicians, and perhaps royalty usually means traveling and staying in five-star hotels, eating the best food, and rubbing elbows with the movers and shakers. A protective agent will be working with people who

are interesting, fascinating, and talented. As a long-time police officer once observed, "It sure beats picking up drunks and scraping blood, guts, gore, hair, and eyeballs off the highway."

- *Travel.* "Join the Navy and see the world" is an old recruiting slogan that can easily be restated, "Be a protective agent and travel the world." Wherever the protectee travels, the protective agent is sure to go.
- *Investing in someone else's life.* What can be more rewarding than knowing that you have done everything possible to keep another person safe and healthy?
- *Self-fulfillment.* There is the prospect of "being all you can be," with a feeling of accomplishment.
- *Be a witness to history.* Working with the world's political, business, and corporate leaders puts a protective agent in a position to be present for historical decisions and actions.
- *Work with dedicated professionals*, with one mission, one goal.
- *Opportunity to meet new people from all cultures and economic levels.* Traveling and conducting protective services puts a protective agent into a world of diversity where he may be working with the highest-ranking people one minute and with the lowest ditch digger the next. Everyone he comes in contact with must be granted dignity and respect.
- *The workplace changes.* It can be either stressful or relaxed.

UNSEEN QUALITIES

What, then, psychologically motivates a protective agent? It is the unseen qualities that make a person want to be a boy or girl scout, a soldier, a policeman, or a fireman. It is the desire and ability to serve mankind and to put the well-being of "the other person" first. It is a form of humanitarianism, seeking to do good for the benefit of others and asking nothing in return. It is the mind-set of the warrior, the Samurai protecting his lord, or a Knight of the Round Table jousting and slaying enemies of the realm. It is an intrinsic desire to help others who are incapable of helping themselves.

PROTECTEE'S MOTIVATION

The necessity of security places fierce pressures on a human and is assuaged in several ways. The expectation of security depends on the level of perceived fear. For some, locking the doors and windows is sufficient security. To others, security means being isolated and/or insulated with layer upon layer of protective gadgets, gizmos, procedures, and people.

A person engages a close personal protection specialist for several reasons, but a primary motive is anxiety about his physical safety. It may be nothing more than a mandated (and necessary) thing occasioned by the person's elected position (i.e., the president of the United States, a corporate executive, or another figurehead or leader). On the other hand, the person requesting the protection may be concerned about a stalker, someone seeking revenge, or another threat. Whatever the reason, the protective agent may be certain that personality issues will exist.

PSYCHOLOGICAL ASPECTS OF THE PROTECTEE

"Every move you make, every breath you take, I'll be watching you" is highly appropriate; the person being protected is constantly under surveillance or being monitored by another person, an electrical device, or cameras. Giving up great amounts of privacy to meet the security requirement may not be a desirable trade-off, but it is generally accepted as the price of doing business. This, coupled with stress induced by the pending unknown hazard, the loss of freedom of movement, and the normal tension of a day's work may have serious consequences on the psychological framework of an individual.

The result could be that the protectee suffers a nervous breakdown or anxiety attack or becomes extremely fearful (bordering on paranoia) of moving about in public and suffers severe bouts of depression. This is extremely unlikely, but the protective agent must be alert to the possibility (see part A of the psychological profile continuum that appears at the end of this section).

The opposite side of that coin is the person who feels an overabundance of courage such that he intentionally visits dangerous places, participates in dangerous activities, and challenges conventional reasoning regarding personal safety. He may develop a mentality of projecting an image of toughness and fearlessness while his protective agents are with him. The bravado displayed when in the presence of protective agents is glaringly absent when the person is alone. Sometimes these individuals will even provoke a fight, knowing that they have solid backup, and will do whatever is necessary to be declared the winner (see B in the continuum).

Then there are those who view protection agents as a necessary nuisance, treat them as nonentities, and are rude and demanding. They fail to communicate with the protective staff and are often demeaning and yet expect the utmost respect, treatment, and service (the key word being service). These types of protectees may use their protection professionals as errand boys to turn on the sprinklers when it's time, retrieve clothing from the cleaners, or to perform other duties expected of other employees. This type of individual is all about power and uses it indiscriminately to bolster his own ego without regard for the feelings of others. In a sense, this person may actually be a narcissistic personality with a self-image that begins with a capital I, and he may explode at any time. Yet, anytime they feel threatened (life threatening or not), they are the first to scream, "Security! Help! Security!" (see C in the continuum).

The opposite of the person described above is one who is unaccustomed to being assertive, is meek, mild, easily intimidated, and introverted, doing whatever the protective agent suggests or asks. He wants to please and to have people think well of him. He is indecisive and looks to the protective agent for advice, even in matters that have no bearing on security. This person is so concerned about not offending anyone that his treatment of the protective agent can be described as being subservient. He addresses the agent as "sir" and never questions anything the agent might say or do (see D in the continuum).

The last two of the above character types are polar extremes in the protective continuum and are usually children, immature young adults, or self-centered individuals whose personal security is not their only problem. These people have serious personality flaws that could partly explain why they need or want protection in the first place. It is good to recognize, know, and understand these types, because the approach to dealing with them varies from one protectee to another.

The majority of protectees are considerate people who acknowledge the presence of the protection agent and respect his duties, responsibilities, and dedication to see that the protectee and his inner circle are safe for one more day. Such people remember that the agent is there for only one reason: to protect him regardless of his race, political affiliation, religious beliefs, or any other label, even different from the agent's own race, affiliations, and beliefs.

Many protectees will share Thanksgiving dinner with the agents (albeit in the kitchen, pantry, or command post) and ensure that they have coffee on a cold, rainy, and wet night. Such a protectee is self-secure, recognizes the dignity of others, and treats them accordingly. This protectee will work with the protective agent as part of a team. He will cooperate with the protective agent and consider all possibilities. Communication is free and open, and it is very easy to develop a good working relationship with him. This particular type of protectee appreciates the partnership between himself and his protective agent(s) (see E in the continuum).

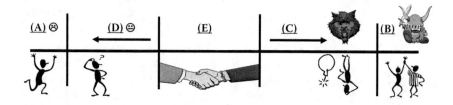

MOTIVES OF THE THREATENING PERSON

> If people honestly thought that they would never be held responsible for their actions, what would stop them from living only for the day?
>
> **Anonymous**

As studies have shown, the antisocial personality—the alienated, the disaffected, or the revenge seeker—who plans an assassination will plan every detail up to and including the actual attack, but not beyond. In their minds, the act of the assassination is the end of their troubles and anything afterward has no meaning. Not only do they not consider the consequences of their act, they do not look to the aftermath. They do not take into account that they may be executed or imprisoned for life. They honestly believe they will never be held responsible for their actions and live only for the present day.

What motivators would cause a person to dedicate his life to only one thing: an attack on someone he has deemed responsible for his own misery and hurt? The reasons are often personal and nonsensical to a clear and rational thinker. But to the assassin, they make perfect sense. Some of the reasons or motivators are:

- *Political.* Perhaps the potential assassin disagrees with the government's policy in foreign affairs, domestic relations, or environmental issues and believes that by killing the head of state, the troublesome policies will change.
- *Religious.* Fanatical believers in a particular religion rationalize, "There is but one God, and he is God. My God is better than your God and to not believe in my God makes you a nonbeliever. God has ordered the death of all nonbelievers."
- *Economic.* The would-be attacker blames his lowly economic state on a political figure, a corporate executive, an attorney, or perhaps a former employer.
- *Revenge.* This involves getting even for a real or imaginary slight, as retribution for something that occurred in the past; for example, "the pretty young supervisor turned down his romantic overtures." The prospective attacker blames others for his wretched state of affairs.
- *Psychological insanity.* The latent attacker suffers from a mental illness that causes delusions, for example, a belief that God or another being has ordered the attack.
- *Legal insanity.* In this case, the perpetrator is unable to distinguish right from wrong at the time he commits the act.

Since the events of September 11, 2001, the common person has come to know the meaning of terrorism. Until that date, the man in the street had merely a passing acquaintance with terrorism from news accounts and events a world away. Even those victims on the doomed planes believed that if they cooperated with the skyjackers, the planes eventually would be flown to a neutral country where negotiations would be held and all but perhaps an unlucky few would be released.

PSYCHOLOGICAL MOTIVATORS FOR TERRORISM

The psychological motivation for terrorism derives from the terrorist's personal dissatisfaction with his life and accomplishments. He finds his *raison d'être* (reason for being) in dedicated terrorist action. Although no clear psychopathy is found among terrorists, there is a nearly universal element in them that can be described as the true believer. Terrorists do not even consider that they may be wrong and that others' views may have some merit. Terrorists tend to project their own antisocial motivations onto others, creating a polarized we versus they outlook. They attribute only evil motives to anyone outside their own group. This enables the terrorists to dehumanize their victims and removes any sense of ambiguity from their minds. The resulting clarity of purpose appeals to those who crave violence to relieve their constant anger. The other common characteristic of the psychologically motivated terrorist is the pronounced need to belong to a group. With some terrorists, group acceptance is a stronger motivator than the stated political objectives of the organization. Such individuals define their social status by group acceptance.

Terrorist groups with strong internal motivations find it necessary to justify the group's existence continuously. A terrorist group must terrorize. As a minimum, it must commit violent acts to maintain group self-esteem and legitimacy. Thus, terrorists sometimes carry out attacks that are objectively nonproductive or even counterproductive to their announced goal.

Another result of psychological motivation is the intensity of group dynamics among terrorists. They tend to demand unanimity and be intolerant of dissent. With the enemy clearly identified and unequivocally evil, pressure to escalate the frequency and intensity of operations is ever present. The need to belong to the group discourages resignations, and the fear of compromise disallows their acceptance. Compromise is *rejected* and terrorist groups lean toward maximalist positions. Having placed themselves beyond the pale, forever unacceptable to ordinary society, they cannot accept compromise. They consider negotiation dishonorable, if not treasonous. This may explain why "terrorist groups are prone to fracturing and why the splinters are frequently more violent than their parent group.

Terrorism Research Center[7]

SUMMARY

We most often refer to motives as *reasons*. Each person has individual reasons for the motivation that moves him toward or away from something. A protective agent has many motivators driving him toward endangering his life for the sake of others. The motives are often undisclosed, even to him. A protective agent may find it difficult to answer the question, "Why did you go into this business?" It must be a passion to dedicate one's own life to the safety of others. There are many rationales but not a single definitive answer.

The simplest answer to the motivations of the person being protected is because he is in fear for his life and is unable to provide his own security. He does not have the knowledge, time, or skill to be concerned about safety issues. Highly practiced and skilled protectors can achieve better success in providing high-level security.

The person who would attack someone, kill a head of state, or render terror among the populace is motivated by politics, religion, economics, or another internal reason that may be known only to, or imagined by, him. This person may be suffering from a mental disease, or he may feel isolated and alienated and desire to rectify all of the wrongs committed against him. His antisocial personality or sociopathy drives him to use his friends and hurt his enemies.

REVIEW QUESTIONS

1. Why would anyone choose this profession?
2. List six personal motivators of your own and explain them.
3. Why does entering the field of personal protection require a special commitment?
4. Should a person place 100 percent confidence in someone he has engaged to protect him? Why or why not?
5. Why is it necessary for a protective agent to be creative?
6. Facing challenges in the protective services is a powerful motivator. Why?
7. Why is it important that a protective agent understand the psychological aspects and consequences of protection to a protectee?

8. Describe the various psychological profiles of a protectee.
9. What are six motivators for an attacker?

NOTES

1. Grossman, Lt. Col. Dave (Ret.). "On Sheep, Wolves, And Sheepdogs." http://hobbes.
   ncsa.uiuc.edu/onsheepwolvesandsheepdogs.html.
2. Collins, Ronald, Ph.D., in an unfinished manuscript, ...In the Name of Security,
   2002.
3. Ibid.
4. LaShan, Lawrence. *The Psychology of War: Comprehending Its Mystique and Its Madness*. Chicago: Noble Press, 1992, 97.
5. http://www.safehouse.com.
6. Csikszentmihalyi, Mihaly. *Psychology Today*, July–August 1996.
7. http://www.youmeworks.com/psychologyofterrorists.html.

4 Assassination!

In the beginning there were two brothers, Cain and Abel ...

Political power grows out of the barrel of a gun.

Chairman Mao Tse-Tung

Assassination. A way of dying; the intentional taking of human life, usually for political or religious motives.

Assassin. A way of living; one acting alone or in consort with others to commit murder, either out of political fervor or religious fanaticism; motivated by desire to gain power, publicity, or renown for self or organization and/or to cause a change in the course of the established order and to settle actual or perceived grievances.

A minor event in time will have a major affect in another time and place. It is possible that every occurrence and event in the past, no matter how minute, has played a role in the making of today as we know it. Therefore, aside from natural disasters such as Hurricane Katrina (2005), the Pakistani earthquake (2005), and the Indian Ocean tsunami (2004), an event as great as an assassination could be one of the most jarring, course-changing, and history-making events. The modern world has undoubtedly been shaped by these human acts of elimination. Governments, religions, the destinies of certain peoples, and the maps of the world have been crafted, in part, by the powerful acts and ramifications of assassinations.

With that in mind, one can clearly see the necessity of fully understanding the role and place of every person in society, the effects that person has on society (and society on that person), and, of how, why, and in what way each person manifests the role that he assumes, or that has been assumed for him. If one has that general understanding, then one can fully assess the consequences of eliminating, replacing, or shifting people. This can best be equated to the common practice of people management in businesses and large corporations. Unfortunately, not every assassin has this basic understanding of people, for rationale and assassination are not always coupled. Generally, assassins are motivated by one goal and are concerned only with the fulfillment of that goal, leaving aside or not comprehending other consequences. Others are left to deal with the situation, and as time passes, the true outcome becomes apparent. These outcomes are irreversible.

Aside from the obvious speculations of what may or may not have happened if the person had not been assassinated, what we do have are the lessons learned from each incident. These lessons have been added to the library of knowledge used to properly fill security gaps so as to protect against future assassinations. Knowing the great impact assassination has had on history, we must realize the importance of protecting against it. Anybody can fall victim to assassination by anyone with any motive. This is probably the most important thought to keep in mind when protecting someone. It matters not how prominent the protected person may be or how routine the situation; a history-making event may occur at any moment.

HISTORY

The term *assassin* comes to us from a group of radical Muslim fanatics operating in Persia (Iran) and Syria for about 200 years, from A.D. 1090 to 1272. They were a secret military and religious order founded by Hasan ibn al-Sabbah (known as "the old man of the mountain" because of his mountain fortress at Alamat, north of Tehran) who killed and terrorized enemies of his extremist faction of Islam. Specifically, their enemies were rival Muslim caliphs (the title of the rulers who succeeded Mohammed as the leader of Islam) and the Christian crusaders who traveled in and invaded the Muslim countries to spread the Christian gospel and to wage war for Christianity.

Al-Sabbah recruited young men (and a very few select women) for his special training camps. The young recruits were drugged into a deep sleep, possibly with the drug hashish. While asleep they were taken to a garden area where, upon awakening, all their wishes were fulfilled with wine, fruit, and attendant women. After being exposed to this wondrous treatment, they were again drugged and returned to the camp. Upon reawakening, they were told they had visited paradise, and if they obeyed the orders and wishes of al-Sabbah, they would be returned to paradise after their missions were complete. (This chapter of history is now being reenacted in similar ways in the recruitment and use of suicide bombers.)

Many of the fanatics took hashish before undertaking to attack their enemies. Because of their use of hashish, they became known as assassins, a term derived from a Medieval Latin word, *assassinus*, taken from the Arabic word for hashish eaters, *hashishin*.[1]

Those who actually committed the assassinations were called *Fedai*, a name now used by Arab guerrillas as *Fedayeen*. A favorite tactic against the opposing Muslims was for the intended assassin to gain employment in the household of his future victim. Sometimes years after gaining trust, the assassin would strike with a dagger, often one blessed by the mysterious Hasan ibn al-Sabbah himself.

The reign of terror of al-Sabbah, his successors, and the assassins came to an end when thousands were slaughtered by the invading Mongol hordes of

Mangu Khan, the third successor to Ghengis Khan. The intent and spirit of those long-deceased followers of the philosophy and decree of Hasan ibn al-Sabbah is ever present and operative to this very day in the person of Osama bin Laden and his fanatical believers, as evidenced by the number of terrorist attacks and assassinations promulgated by groups of dissident fundamentalist Muslims and "insurgents."

The term *assassin* was taken to Europe by the crusaders. Dante used the word in the early fourteenth century to describe a professional secret murder.[2]

Most notable among assassins are the mysterious, black-clad, stealthy Ninja; the highly trained, skilled, and cunning martial arts (Ninjitsu) experts employed by early Japanese shoguns. They usually killed their victims in the dark of night and disappeared as quietly and unseen as they appeared.

Favored weapons of assassins have evolved from crude, sharp instruments such as arrows, spears, knives, and poison to guns and explosives and suicide bomber vests and belts containing explosives with nails, marbles, and ball bearings. Assassinations sometimes have been carried out by lone, often deranged, individuals acting on a moment of opportunity, and sometimes by sophisticated conspiracies following intricate plans.

Assassination as a political or religious tool is as old as history itself. Whenever there have been opposing parties, jealousies, or beliefs, there have been those who would undertake to commit murder to gain power, personal recognition, or alter the direction of human affairs. History is dotted with assassinations and intrigues involving political murder or violence against a ruling head or potential heir to political power. The assumption of a position of power or influence brings with it prestige, wealth, love, adoration, hate, jealousy, fear, and the ever-present threat of assassination.

Some assassinations have had little impact outside the lives of the subjects of the assassination. Most, however, have had social, religious, and political consequences that have, for better or worse, altered the mainstream of civilization.

POLITICAL ASSASSINATION

One of the earliest recorded historical political assassinations of significance entails the violent stabbing of Julius Caesar by his friends and fellow senators on the steps of the Roman senate (March 15, 44 B.C.). Caesar had been warned and was aware that he faced the possibility of assassination during the Ides of March, but he chose to conduct business as usual, in what has come to be a mentality of martyrdom in potential assassin victims: "If they are going to get me, they will." Shortly after he claimed the title of dictator for life, he was killed by those who feared that his consolidation of power and control of the military forces was leading to tyranny. The friends of Caesar (for it is believed that there were more friends than enemies involved in his killing) foresaw a tightening of political control that would greatly diminish individual freedoms and signal the end of the republic.[3]

Caesar's nephew, Caesar Augustus, succeeded him. By political maneuvering, annexation of conquered lands, popular support, and control of the Roman Legions, Augustus assumed the title of imperator (emperor), thus ending the Roman Republic and beginning the Roman Empire that was to endure, in various forms, for nearly 1,000 years.

A sampling of Western civilization's history and literature silhouettes a dark side to the royal line of descent through the ages. The royal courts of the world were built on marriages of convenience, invasion, conquest, and elimination of rivals through imprisonment, public executions, and mysterious assassinations. Power was gained and lost through intrigues and death, often starting costly wars that drained human lives and economies and setting a precedent for future generations.

In literature, the stories of Shakespeare, for example, bring to us many instances of royal assassination and intrigue and a momentary glimpse into the mind of the assassin who has but one goal and cannot see the ramifications beyond the act. Macbeth is a sterling literary example of assassination by an amateur for the sole purpose of dispatching the rightful king and gaining the throne.

On his way to stab and kill the sleeping King Duncan, Macbeth stops to think about the plan, looks ahead to being king, and reflects on the consequence and his own hesitancy to kill. "If it were done when 'tis done, then 'twere well it were done quickly."[4] He shows no remorse (common in the antisocial personality, the serial killer, and assassin) but has a dominant anxiety or trepidation only of discovery.

He looks forward to being king but doesn't wish to have to commit the act of murder to fulfill his and Lady Macbeth's desire. Yet he goes to commit the act willingly. He wishes the deed (the killing) was behind him and he was already the monarch. He naturally assumes he will be made king, as people will proclaim him a hero. As he continues the soliloquy, Macbeth has a very clear sense of the moral wrong he is about to commit but driven by his own vaulting ambition, which is too strong an urge to disregard or allow him to reconsider his murderous intent: "I have no spur to prick the sides of my intent but only vaulting ambition which o'erleaps itself and falls on th' other."[5] (The martyr syndrome is very common in the profile of assassins and suicide bombers.) He is remorseless for the death of King Duncan, yet he knows it will cause great sorrow and pity for the family of Duncan, and he will forever be damned. But it is for his own earthly enrichment that he seeks to assassinate the king and take the crown, reconciling his behavior with his ambition, which is more compelling than his sympathy or remorse for the king's subjects or his own soul. His faulty reasoning justifies the killing, but he has no plans beyond becoming king, and he cannot see the unfortunate consequences or the resulting war that will ultimately lead to his death.

This allusion to Macbeth reveals the heated passion an assassin may have about the act he is about to commit. He is focused with only one goal in mind. Some residual consequences may be momentarily considered, such as the knowledge of committing murder, the possible acknowledgment of causing the immediate turmoil that will follow, or the possibility of failing, but reasoning nothing beyond that.

It shows that an assassin, suicide bomber, or terrorist may not think about the complex web of possibilities that could come out of his act. It would be impossible to fully predict every conceivable scenario that would result from an assassination without a dedicated committee of math professors working out the odds. Even then, the future remains unpredictable. It is safe to say that the rationale of a lone assassin is dangerously blind to the realities of the act he is about to commit.

The danger of such historical and literary irrationality lies in its oneness with today's world of political and religious upheaval, including violence, terrorism, kidnapping, and assassination. It is the same view held by today's fanatical groups that want the world to be one way (theirs), and if that is not attainable, they believe that the world is better off destroyed for the good of all, in the name of God.

Thoughts and actions such as those not only affect groups, governments, and countries but the entire living world. That is the result of adhering to a single-minded goal, without concern for any but one's own agenda, in congruence with the Macbeth quotation. Macbeth is so blind with ambition that he does not realize his act of assassination is the sole cause of his fate, which is death. The same or similar rationale may apply to modern assassins and suicide bombers who are so focused on the act of assassination and murder for personal reasons (or for the good of God) that they cannot foresee its effect on their own mortality, or any other consequences. This represents blind ambition of the most extreme and dangerous type.

In real life, as in literature, there has been a fascination with assassination, because those participants seeking to carry out the killing generally do not even consider the wrongfulness of the act but are driven only by their perception that the world will be better off. Between the years 1881 and 1914, anarchists (people who believe that no government is better than any government) murdered several world heads of state. Among those assassinated were Alexander II of Russia (1881), Empress Elizabeth of Austria-Hungry (1898), King Umberto of Italy (1900), President William McKinley of the United States (1901), and Premier Jose Canaljas of Spain (1912), to name just a few.[6] A list of the people assassinated by the jealous, the insane, the racist, or for no clear purpose would fill several volumes.[7]

For many reasons, special holidays commemorating historical events play an important role in personal protection. Heightened emotions and expectations arise on those dates, particularly for those acknowledging the holiday but also for people in general. A group of people or a lone assassin may want to connect a cause to a particular holiday to make a point, thereby gaining the most possible attention and making certain that the day is memorialized. Some holidays are revered and sacred to some people, bringing out a greater conviction for their cause, which may inspire the act they are about to commit.

When it comes down to it, in very realistic terms, holidays cause distractions. Large groups of people may gather, offering a *raison d'être* (excuse) for a murderer to be there, possibly poised for an attack while blending in with the crowd. A protection agent must be fully aware of all these potential threats and prepare for any scenario. The agent must maintain the highest level of caution and awareness and have proper security arrangements, with the appropriate protection plan in place, during a holiday protection job.

ASSASSINATION OF THE ARCHDUKE OF AUSTRIA

The shooting of the Archduke of Austria, Franz-Ferdinand, and his wife, the Duchess of Hohenberg, on the streets of Sarajevo, Bosnia, on June 28, 1914 (a Serbian holiday) is remembered as the event that ignited World War I. The assassination (as most assassinations) could have been averted if certain precautions had been observed, but the world war probably would have eventually occurred anyway because of other unavoidable circumstances. The assassination, however, will always be memorialized as the flashpoint.

Franz-Ferdinand had been warned that it was critically dangerous to visit Sarajevo because of the impending trouble in the continuing conflict between Serbia and Bosnia, along with the resentment against the occupying Austrians. The archduke, in a historically stereotypical, political foolish, and prideful decision, with no consideration of the consequences (martyr mentality), chose to ignore all the warnings and intelligence indicators, electing instead to follow his itinerary and make his publicly announced and previously arranged appearances.

Several assassination attempts had been made against dignitaries of the archduke's Hapsberg family in the immediate past, but on the occasion of his visit to the Bosnian city, no special security arrangements were taken, even though the date was an important Serbian patriotic festival day. The visit on that particular day was taken by the Serbians as an obvious affront, chosen specifically to offend and infuriate them.

As Franz-Ferdinand and the duchess left city hall and walked to their motorcade, an observer asked a nearby policeman in which car the archduke would be riding. The obliging officer pointed out the exact car. The citizen immediately threw a bomb in the direction of the car as the archduke and his entourage approached. The archduke and his wife escaped injury, although several others were wounded, some critically.

Plans called for the archduke to travel four miles in an open car with no extra police protection, even after the bombing! In what apparently was the only realistic security decision made that day, Franz-Ferdinand asked that the route to his next appearance be changed.[8] However, everyone neglected to tell his driver! As the motorcade proceeded, the military governor realized the driver was using the original route. He shouted and commanded the driver to stop and alter the route immediately. Was it a coincidence the driver stopped the car in front of and near the assassin, who shot point-blank into the car, instantly killing Franz-Ferdinand and the Duchess of Hohenberg? The assassin, Gavrilo Princip, was grabbed, wrestled to the ground, and taken into immediate custody.

The assassination of Archduke Franz Ferdinand was caused by a complete security debacle. The errors made on that day suggest that no one was consulted regarding security, and does not appear that any security arrangements were made.

The first mistake in the line of errors was to insist on visiting Sarajevo despite warnings of critical danger and tossing aside the imperative intelligence and common knowledge of the conflict in the area. Visiting a nation occupied by your own country should make anyone a little concerned with safety, but the archduke put aside the resentment of the people toward him—another mistake! It could have still been possible to thwart an ambush had he replaced his publicly announced itinerary with new, undisclosed arrangements—but he did not. The third gross error would be scheduling the archduke's visit on a Serbian patriotic holiday. Any modern-day security personnel would see this as a doomed visit at that point.

The policeman who pointed out the archduke's car to a curious citizen (bomber) apparently lacked any insight or had no concern for the situation. The officer could be blamed for his apparent lapse of common sense, but Ferdinand's personal security staff should have made proper arrangements with the local police. The lack of advance security arrangements rendered the policeman a regular civilian spectator.

After the bombing attack, the archduke, duchess, and entourage should have had an escape plan and followed it instantly. The visit should have been declared too dangerous to continue and aborted immediately without discussion. Had that occurred, the royal couple might have survived, and we can only guess how history would have been changed.

The lack of proper communication was the nail in the coffin. Having suitable communications within the entourage might have allowed the route change to reach the driver. In some cases, the driver is the last defense against the odds. Notwithstanding any conspiracy theory, this last incident was the extra mistake it took for the archduke and duchess to become historical figures. Any of these mistakes alone could have been enough to allow an assassination to take place. The couple were lucky to have avoided earlier attacks, given the heightened animosity toward the archduke, especially for arriving on the Serbian holiday. They were lucky that the bomb did not kill them or injure their driver. By the time they realized their final mistake, luck had unfortunately run out. One should never depend on luck for survival.

The assassination might have been only a small footnote in history and taken its place in relative obscurity alongside many other obscure political assassination events, but the occurrence, timed with several other factors and circumstances, sparked a world war. Within months, the whole of Europe was engulfed in the "war to end all wars," and the world would be changed forever.

AMERICAN ASSASSINATIONS OF THE 1960s— AMERICA'S DECADE OF VIOLENCE

Most memorable in the long list of historical assassinations to many Americans is the tragic killing of President John F. Kennedy. His death brought the term *assassination* home to the living rooms of even those who had no previous interest in the far-away world of politics. For four days, every television set and radio in America was tuned to the live broadcast coverage of the events in Dallas and Washington, D.C., as a nation (and the world) mourned the death of a president. That singular moment and subsequent events were of such historical and unprecedented magnitude that every topic of conversation centered on the assassination and related incidents, including speculation concerning conspiracies, international plots, and intrigues. Nearly a half century later, all who lived through those days can recall exactly where they were, what they were doing, and what they said when the awful news interrupted regular programming.

The assassination made America aware of the ever-present danger of presidential assassination, even though America had experienced three previous presidential ones and four unsuccessful attempts. The shooting of President Kennedy by Lee Harvey Oswald on November 22, 1963, ended America's post–World War II and Korean War decade of peace and innocence and rolled the nation into its most violent chapter in nearly half a century. There were other assassinations, rioting, looting, and burning that year of 1963, but the assassination of the president marked the beginning of a public consciousness of our contemporary escalating lawlessness and violence. It was, of course, not the cause of the coming violence, but it was a watershed day as the news of the next decades continued to shock, horrify, anger, and forever change the world. It was a combination of the power of television and a continuum of ever-increasing, shocking violence that popularized assassination.

After that date, America and the world have experienced violence, terrorism, and assassination at an unprecedented rate. Murder, terrorism, kidnapping, and violence have escalated beyond anything that could have been predicted by social scientists, historians, or prognosticators. Riots in the cities, airline skyjackings, bombings, kidnappings of corporate executives, stalking, and attacks against public figures and celebrities have become popular; rising crime rates and random killings have dominated the social landscape. There can be no direct correlation, but the assassination of President Kennedy certainly marked the beginning of the pattern of violence that soon became a part of every day's news, police reports, and the human experience. From 1963 until 1981, there were six major assassinations (including President Kennedy's) in the United States, three other attempts on the life of the president, and one against a presidential candidate.

The first of several politically related killings during the violent 1960s to have a national impact occurred on June 12, 1963. While national attention was focused on the civil rights movement, related civil disobedience, and racial upheaval in Jackson, Mississippi, civil rights leader and Mississippi State Field Secretary for the National Association for the Advancement of Colored People (NAACP) Medger Evers was fatally shot in an ambush on the front lawn of his home. He was killed by a local businessman, Byron De La Beckwith, who was not brought to justice for over 30 years. On February 5, 1994, a jury found De La Beckwith guilty of the murder of Evers.

The doggedness of a president can be his downfall. For President Kennedy, that was the case. He was cautioned that his life would be in danger while making the trip to Dallas, but he chose the fatalist route and went as scheduled in spite of the threat (reminiscent of the "if they want to get me they will" syndrome mentioned earlier with the assassination of Caesar).

Dallas, Texas, November 22, 1963, is a place and date that will forever be remembered as when and where an assassin's bullet ended America's "Camelot." The presidential motorcade passed a solitary building, the Texas Schoolbook Depository, which overlooked the motorcade route. Suddenly, the president pitched forward as a bullet fired from that building struck the back of his head. Texas Govenor John Connelly was also wounded. Secret Service Agent Clint Hill raced forward from the Secret Service follow-up car and jumped onto the rear of the presidential limousine, preventing the first lady from crawling out of the car. Farther back in the motorcade, Agent Rufus Youngblood climbed over the front seat of the vice-president's car, into the rear seat area, and shielded Vice President Lyndon Johnson from harm with his own body. Agent Youngblood later remarked, "I wasn't sure if the sound I heard was gunshots or not, but I reacted as though it were. I jumped over the seat and covered Mr. Johnson, but I remember thinking that if it weren't shots, I'd be fired as soon as I unwrapped my body from Mr. Johnson's lap."

As the motorcade raced to the hospital, the assassin, Lee Harvey Oswald, escaped from the building but was captured in a movie theater later that day, after also killing Dallas police officer J. D. Tippit. Oswald was himself assassinated a few days later by a local nightclub owner and police hanger-on, Jack Ruby, in the basement of the Dallas police department as he was being transferred to a more secure location. Ruby was a part of the crowd of news media and onlookers that had been allowed into the police basement to witness the transfer. Ruby later died of cancer. Conspiracy theories abound to this day.

Black activist and leader of a Black Muslim faction, Malcolm X was killed by members of an opposing Black Muslim group as he addressed a rally at New York City's Audubon Ballroom on February 21, 1965. He had received death threats and experienced a premonition of being assassinated, but he continued with his agenda as planned. His security men were stationed nearby, flanking him on the stage. When a disturbance, involving a fight and the release of a smoke bomb, broke out several rows into the audience, the security men diverted their attention to it and moved in to quell the fight and remove the smoke bomb. The diversion left Malcolm X standing at center stage, completely unprotected. Three gunmen stood up from the front row and shot him to death. After the shooting, witnesses described seeing the men arriving in the hall and taking the front row seats long before the scheduled time of the event.

Malcom X's personal security men should not have been responsible for crowd control. They fell for an old diversionary tactic and wrongly responded to the source of the problem rather than covering and evacuating their protectee. A group of security personnel, police, or others should have been assigned the duties of disturbance response in an outside-perimeter ring of protection. Malcolm X was left alone to be killed. A plan should have been in place ahead of time to deal with what happened that day. This is another fine example of where proper planning and proactive thinking is indispensable and must occur whenever and wherever the protectee goes, regardless of how routine the circumstances may be.

In a really bizarre Alfred Hitchcock or Stephen King type of twist to the story, a weekly publication, the *Village Voice*, reported (March 26, 1998) that one of Malcolm X's killers, Muhammed Abdul Aziz (formerly known as Norman 3X Butler), was appointed by Nation of Islam leader, Louis Farrakhan, to be Farrakhan's East Coast director of security. According to the newspaper, he was also named to be the head of Mosque 7 in Harlem, formerly led by Malcolm X.

In 1967, the American Nazi Party was very strong, led by its charismatic founder and president, George Lincoln Rockwell. Rockwell was killed on August 25, 1967, in Arlington, Virginia. A former member of Rockwell's Nazi Party, disgruntled over being ousted from the party for believing Rockwell was not radical enough, assassinated him. The American Nazi Party, organized by Rockwell in 1956, was quickly growing and gaining influence as a hate group. Because of the several large, violent big city racial riots of the 1960s involving civil rights and social conditions of black Americans, hate was easily the most marketable emotion of the day. The remarkable aspect of Rockwell's assassination was that it was committed by a fellow hatemonger and not by a target of Rockwell's special brand of bigotry, antisemitism, and racial prejudice. After Rockwell's death, the party quickly sank to a secondary status and, although it still exists, its growth and influence quickly waned.

On April 4, 1968, a sniper shot Dr. Martin Luther King, Jr., as he appeared in full view on a motel balcony in Memphis, Tennessee. In one of the greatest manhunts in history, including a time-consuming and arduous manual search of FBI fingerprint files, James Earl Ray, traveling under the name of Ramon George Sneyd, was arrested in Great Britain and charged with the murder. Ray immediately confessed and pled guilty without any court testimony being given.

Several questions were raised in the 1990s by many, including the King family, regarding Ray's guilt or innocence and the possible role of a conspiracy. The shooting and escape were arguably beyond the sophistication of Ray, a bumbling and ineffective petty criminal prior to the assassination. However, those doubts were never addressed in court because of legal maneuvering and Ray's poor health and death on April 23, 1998. Until his death, Ray, 70 years old and suffering from liver and kidney disease, maintained his innocence and argued that he was setup by persons unknown to him. Three days after pleading guilty and receiving his 99-year sentence, Ray recanted his guilty plea and asked for a new trial. He stated that he was setup to take the blame by a mysterious figure known to him as "Raoul." But a new trial was denied for lack of evidence.

In March 1998, an investigation by the district attorney's office in Memphis ruled that Ray did not warrant a new trial, because no new credible information had been developed that would indicate involvement by anyone other than Ray. In an interesting side note, in 1979, the congressional House Assassination Committee investigating the assassinations of the 1960s concluded, "There is a likelihood that James Early Ray assassinated Dr. Martin Luther King as a result of a conspiracy."

After successfully campaigning for the democratic presidential nomination in California on June 5, 1968, President Kennedy's brother, Robert Kennedy (accompanied by two bodyguards, Olympic decathlon champion Rafer Johnson and former professional football defensive tackle Roosevelt Greer), was gunned down in Los Angeles in the kitchen of the Ambassador Hotel. He was assassinated by Sirhan Sirhan, a Jordanian-born Arab immigrant living in Los Angeles. Senator Kennedy and his group took an unplanned detour through the kitchen because of the pressing crowd in the large ballroom where the victory was proclaimed. No precautions were taken to exclude members of the public from the kitchen, so it was crowded with hotel staff, well-wishers, onlookers, and an assassin.

Working his way through the crowd to get as close to the senator as he could, Sirhan pulled his gun and, reaching his extended arm over the heads of people in front of him, began shooting at Senator Kennedy from a few feet away. Kennedy's security bodyguards, pinned in by the crowd, were helpless to prevent the shooting. The senator was shot to death, and Sirhan Sirhan was quickly subdued, wrestled to the ground, and taken into custody. Sirhan is currently serving a life sentence in a California State Prison.

ATTACKS ON THE OFFICE OF THE PRESIDENT—1970s TO 1980s

George Wallace, the governor of Alabama, was a candidate for the democratic presidential nomination in 1972 when he was speaking in the parking lot of a shopping center in Landover, Maryland. In the space of two seconds, five shots were fired from the handgun of Arthur Bremer, a loner who was standing in the crowd. The governor and Secret Service Agent Nick Zarvos were wounded. In the confusion, it took several minutes to get an ambulance and medical care through the crowd to Mr. Wallace and Agent Zarvos. Preplanning had allowed for the positioning of the ambulance, but no one foresaw the problem of moving the ambulance through the crowd. During the investigation of Bremer's background, it was learned from his rather extensive diary that he had previously stalked President Nixon, including a trip to Ottawa, Canada, but had changed his focus of attention because Secret Service and Royal Canadian Mounted Police security around the president was too tight.

The Secret Service agents protecting President Gerald Ford expertly and incredibly saved the president's life on two separate assassination attempts within a two-week period. Both attempts were committed by woman, making them the only women in history to attempt the assassination of an American president. (This emphasizes that anyone can be an assassin.)

The first attempt occurred while the president was taking a walking shortcut through Sacramento's Capitol Park. Taking an unplanned route is a random, spontaneous act, which may or may not be a good protective tactic. A potential attacker may be thrown off by the unexpected move, but it may offer the possibility of an attack of opportunity. Such was the case of a "woman in red" who was prepared to attack the president on that route. This further proves that an attack or ambush can occur at any moment. Quick thinking and unhesitating action by Secret Service Agent Larry Buendorf saved the president that day.

As he left the Senator Hotel in Sacramento, California, President Gerald Ford began to walk to the state capitol building and took a shortcut through the peaceful and beautiful Capitol Park. A woman dressed in a red cape and hood suddenly stepped out from the crowd and, at point-blank range, pointed a military .45 caliber pistol directly at the president. Acting quickly and instinctively, Agent Buendorf, who was within an arm's length of the president and the woman, grabbed the gun, placing the web of his hand between the gun's hammer and firing pin, thus preventing it from firing. After being subdued, the lady in red kept repeating, in disbelief, "I can't believe it didn't go off." It was later learned that the assailant, Lynette "Squeaky" Fromme, a follower of convicted insane mass murderer Charles Manson, was unfamiliar with the operation of the gun and had neglected to put a round into the firing chamber. This was the first time in American history that a woman had attempted to assassinate a president.

One may think that, after saving the president's life and thwarting an assassination attempt, it would be natural to relax, thinking the worst is over. After all, what are the odds of an American president being attacked twice? But in President Ford's case, the odds were very low. Two weeks later, another assassination attempt took place. The Secret Service had protocols to follow and did so like clockwork, saving the president's life again. A protection agent can never let his guard down or allow his awareness to fade, as the improbable may occur.

President Ford was approaching his waiting motorcade in San Francisco when shots rang out from the crowd across the street. Sara Jane Moore then became the second woman in history to attempt to assassinate a president. Secret Service agents shoved President Ford into his armored car, and he sped away unharmed. Moore, a middle-aged woman, was quickly and easily subdued and wrestled to the ground by onlookers. Lynette Fromme and Sara Jane Moore are currently spending their lives in federal prison.

With memories of all the assassination and assassination attempts of the previous eighteen years still fresh in the public's mind, the world was again reminded that an assassin can spring from anywhere. President Ronald Reagan had completed a speech at the Washington Hilton Hotel, only two miles from the White House. As he exited the hotel, he was accompanied by the usual Secret Service personnel and several staff members and was walking to his limousine, which was parked only a few feet from the hotel door. As long as there has been a Washington Hilton, presidents have come and gone using the same entrance and exit. Business trips of the president to the Hilton are almost as commonplace and probably even more frequent than presidential trips to Capitol Hill.

Between the hotel door and the parked limousine, there has always been a small reserved space for members of the press corps. Only news media displaying proper press credentials are authorized to be in that area. In the crush of press angling for the best spots, and with a possibly lax attitude of the staff and press, and even possibly because the police saw the visit as entirely routine, no one noticed John Hinckley as he slipped into the area with no press credentials—but with a gun in his pocket.

When the president was just a few feet from his limousine, Hinckley drew his handgun and began firing rapidly. The president's press secretary, James Brady, was critically wounded in the head and suffered brain damage. Secret Service Agent Timothy McCarthy turned in the direction of the shots and stepped in front of the president, taking a round in the stomach. The president was pushed into his bullet-proof car, which sped away. Newsmen, police, and Secret Service agents subdued Hinckley. While driving toward the White House, it was discovered that the president had also sustained a wound to the abdomen.

Whenever the president leaves the White House, medical and hospital staffs are alerted in advance in case of possible injury to the president. The speeding limousine with the wounded president was diverted to George Washington University Hospital. The medical staff was prepared for the arrival and performed immediate life-saving surgery.

In video recordings of the shooting, a D.C. Metropolitan Police officer who was assisting the Secret Service with crowd control near the press area is seen watching the president rather than the crowd! The first commandment of crowd control during a presidential movement is, "Watch the crowd, not the president." Any attempts on the life of the president will come from the crowd, not the presidential party! The officer is then seen grabbing presidential Chief of Staff Michael Deaver and ducking down behind him for cover! This is in no way meant to demean the officer but to emphasize the importance of training. Agent McCarthy deliberately turned his body toward the location of the shots and in front of the president; the untrained officer reacted instinctively for self-preservation.

The attempt to assassinate President Reagan had a visible effect on security protocols. Before this occurrence, the procedure for moving a president between his car and a building was to have him walk in full public view with Secret Service personnel surrounding him. That is how John Hinckley got a somewhat of a clear shot at him (or at least was able to discharge his weapon five times). Fortunately, the rapid response by Secret Service agents successfully covered the president and evacuated him safely to the hospital. Since the Hinckley assassination attempt, presidential motorcade arrivals and departures have been in covered areas. If no secluded and secure place is available, a large tent with controlled entrances is erected, and the presidential limousine is parked inside, hidden from view of all but authorized persons.

Another great lesson was learned by agents responsible for the president. The agent who conducted the advance was, of course, at the scene. When gunfire broke out, the agent was carrying his briefcase in his hand. He maintained his grip on the briefcase and was therefore unable to draw his weapon. An after-action investigation and experiments concluded that a person carrying something when an emergency occurs will continue grasping that article and not think about dropping it. The conclusion, of course, is that a protective agent should keep his hands free.

The would-be assassin, John Hinckley, son of an Oklahoma oilman, was found to be mentally ill and incarcerated in the criminally insane ward at St. Elizabeth's Hospital in Washington, D.C., where such people have been institutionalized since the early 1800s. It is anticipated that Hinckley will remain incarcerated in the hospital or similar surroundings for the rest of his life. However, in 2005, a federal judge allowed Hinckley to spend unsupervised time with his family away from the hospital.

HISTORICAL PRESIDENTIAL ATTACKS

Whether it is America's frontier mentality or just a condition of office, the U.S. presidency has attracted a large share of mad outsiders who, either acting alone or in consort with others, have undertaken to murder the president. From the time the first president, George Washington, came into office in 1789 through the term of the forty-third president, George W. Bush, the United States has seen four presidents assassinated and seven attempts. That is quite a high percentage for one of the world's leading "civilized" nations!

Every day, letters and telephone calls are received at the White House making either direct or implied threats against the president's life by those who would wish him harm. Each letter and telephone call is thoroughly investigated by the Secret Service. An evaluation is made of the potential risk factors and threat level. If necessary, appropriate protective measures are taken, but there remain those who would attack the president without warning.

President Andrew Jackson was visiting the capitol building on January 30, 1835, to attend the funeral services for Representative Warren R. Davis of South Carolina, who had died in office. The president was approached by an unemployed English house painter, Richard W. Lawrence. Lawrence pulled a pistol from under his coat and, from a distance of about thirteen feet, aimed it at Jackson's chest and pulled the trigger. For a reason never fully determined or explained, the pistol failed to fire. The cap exploded, but the charge failed to ignite. Perhaps the notorious Washington, DC humidity had dampened the powder. Lawrence pulled a second pistol and, at point-blank range pointed it at President Jackson's chest. For an also unexplained reason, the second pistol failed to fire. The cap again discharged, but the main charge failed!

President Jackson had a combative nature, and his fiery, red-haired temper was aroused. He lifted his hickory cane (the president's nickname was "Old Hickory") and lunged to strike Lawrence, but a young army officer restrained the 68-year-old president before he could inflict much damage. Congressman Davy Crockett and some others jumped upon Lawrence,[9] who was arrested and later stood trial. At the trial, the prosecutor was Francis Scott Key, famous for penning the poem that became America's National Anthem, *The Star Spangled Banner*. Lawrence at first blamed Jackson for his father's death in England. After it was proven that Lawrence had not been in England since he immigrated to the United States with his parents at age 12, he changed his story, claimed to be a member of the English royal family, and insisted that the death of Jackson would help him regain his rightful heritage.

Prosecutor Key cooperated with the defense and crafted an insanity defense based on the assumption that if the accused suffered from the disease of delusion, and if the deed were a direct result of the disease, he should be acquitted. This legal assumption was founded on the precedent of a case in England 35 years before, when a person named Hadfield was acquitted, by reason of delusional insanity, of attempting to shoot King George III.[10] Lawrence was found not guilty by reason of insanity and sentenced to a life term in St. Elizabeth's Hospital, Washington, DC's, newly built institute for the insane.

Jackson had received more than 500 letters threatening his life, but he paid them no heed. He said, "I try to live my life as if death might come at any moment." Both of Lawrence's pistols, new dueling weapons, were tested, and they fired perfectly every time! At that time, it was calculated that the odds of both pistols misfiring were 1 in 125,000.[11]

In one of life's ironies, late in the afternoon on April 14, 1865, President Abraham Lincoln signed a bill into law that created a federal law enforcement agency to investigate crimes against the currency of the United States—most notably counterfeiting. At that time, immediately after the Civil War, nearly one-third of all currency in circulation was counterfeit. President Lincoln's bill authorized the creation of the United States Secret Service. In the future, the Secret Service would be assigned the responsibility of protecting U.S. presidents.

In the evening of that fateful day, which was to change the course of history, President Lincoln was accompanied by Washington, DC, Metropolitan Police Officer John Parker to Ford's Theatre to view the play, "Our American Cousin." Two stories are common regarding Parker's actions that night. One version says that Parker had a drinking problem, and during the play he stole away to have a drink. The second version has Parker moving away from the president's box so he could obtain a seat with a better view of the play. In either case, the president was left unattended by security, allowing John Wilkes Booth to enter the theater through a rear door, make his way to the unguarded president's box, and shoot President Lincoln in the back of his head.

Booth escaped but was shot twelve days later in a Virginia barn. The investigation following the assassination uncovered a very complex conspiracy to kill the president, the vice president, and the secretary of state. Four people, including Dr. Samuel A. Mudd, whose only known involvement was treating Booth's broken leg, were sentenced to life in prison. Four others, including Mary E. Surratt, the first woman in American history to be hanged, were condemned to death and were hanged on July 7, 1865, only 24 hours after the pronouncement of their sentence.

Justice was swift in those days. Less than two months after the assassination, the legal case was closed by hanging! There still exist conspiracy theories and assertions that innocent people (such as Dr. Mudd) were wrongly accused and sentenced while the real guilty people (e.g., John Wilkes Booth) escaped. This and the attempted assassination of President Truman nearly 100 years later are the only known and recognized conspiracies to kill a U.S. president.

On July 2, 1881 (only thirteen years after the death of President Lincoln), President James A. Garfield was approached from behind and shot in Washington, DC's railway station by a truly demented person and disappointed office seeker, Charles Julius Guiteau. Guiteau came from a family with a history of relatives who were said to be "a little weak in the upper story" or "foolish." There was, for example, cousin Abigail. They called her "foolish Abby," as she would cozy up to visitors and whisper into their ears, "Do you love Jesus?" until someone would lead her away. She died in a mental institution. Then there was cousin Augustus, who came completely unwired as the result of a soured business deal. He also died in an insane asylum. There was Uncle Francis, who suffered a great emotional hurt as the victim of a cruel hoax perpetrated by the love of his life and her real lover. That totally deranged him.[12] Charles Guiteau's mother died when he was seven, and he was raised by his father, who was a successful banker but a strict and cruel disciplinarian. He would often beat the friendless and lonesome Charles in a fruitless attempt to cure his son's speech defect. The father had one other eccentricity: he was a religious fanatic who believed the second coming of Jesus had occurred during the Roman conquest of Jerusalem in A.D. 70, and no one noticed. He thought that because he was a believer, he was entitled to everlasting life and that he was immortal.[13]

Today, Guiteau would be considered a letter writer and a homeless street person. He was virtually penniless, sleeping in daily boarding houses and skipping out when the rent was due. His clothing was tattered and dirty. His stockings, having long ago worn out, were gone. He wrote speeches for Horace Greeley in his unsuccessful attempt to become president. The speeches were rambling and incoherent. He would have hundreds of them printed and would stand on the corner and pass them out to passers-by. He also would give long rambling sermons to anyone who would stop to listen.

When Garfield became president, Guiteau simply removed Greeley's name from his speeches and inserted Garfield's. Believing that the newly inaugurated president would appoint him to a high ranking, responsible position in his administration (such as ambassador to Austria), Guiteau began visiting the White House and State Department on a daily basis. He would walk in, talk to the secretary-receptionist, and leave a copy of his speech as he would a business card. If he were to attempt to do that today, he would be interviewed at the Northwest Gate of the White House by a Secret Service agent trained and experienced in interviewing White House visitors who show an overly special and possibly threatening interest in the president. It would be very possible and most likely that, after a conversation with him, the agent would summon "Mr. Wheels" (the "wagon") and transport him to St. E's (Saint Elizabeth's Hospital) for further evaluation. It would also be very probable that the agent would initiate a full field investigation to determine the degree of danger to the president posed by Mr. Guiteau.

One night "God" told Guiteau that Garfield had to be "removed." Guiteau began sending letters to the White House making very plain threats to the president. In modern days, Guiteau would be arrested at this stage for threatening the life of the president, indicted, and possibly sentenced to a mental institution until he was no longer deemed a threat. However, in 1881, he was not arrested. He borrowed $10.00 from an acquaintance and bought a .44 caliber pistol (with an ivory handle, because it "looked dignified"). For several weeks, Guiteau stalked Garfield, waiting for the opportunity to get close enough to shoot him. Guiteau had no experience with firearms, and the only time he practiced with his new pistol, he was nearly knocked over by the unexpected recoil. He realized he had to be very close to the president to kill him.

Guiteau also sought out the local jail in Washington, DC, to ascertain whether it was strong enough to repel the thousands of people he felt would surely storm the prison to lynch him. But he also believed that the masses would come to realize he was a great hero and patriot and that he would be honored. From the daily Washington newspaper, he learned that the president would be leaving from the train station for summer vacation. Guiteau arrived at the train station well before the president and concealed himself in the women's waiting room, where he could see all the entrances. The president arrived accompanied only by his two sons, Harry and Jim, and his friend James G. Blain. Walking directly up to the back of the president, Guiteau drew the pistol from under his coat and shot twice, mortally wounding President Garfield. On September 19, 1881, Garfield died, only six and a half months after taking office! Today the wounds would not have been fatal. In those days no good medical treatment was readily available or standing by and the wound eventually took its toll. Guiteau went to the hangman chanting a childish poem he had written, "I am going to the Lordy."[14]

Twenty years later, on September 6, 1901, President William McKinley was attending a reception in a hall at the Pan-American exposition in Buffalo, New York. During the reception, the president was greeting and shaking hands with a line of well wishers. In the line, a lone figure, with his hand wrapped in a bandage, stood waiting to greet the president. Concealed in the bandage of Polish immigrant Leon Czolgoz was a pistol with which he intended to shoot the president.

No one seemed to notice or question the circumstances of the bandage or the unusual appearance of the man waiting nervously in the reception line. As the president extended his hand to shake the hand that was about to kill him, Czolgoz stuck his hand out and shot the president twice in the abdomen. Czolgoz was seized, arrested, tried, convicted of the murder, and then executed in New York's Attica prison (near Buffalo). He was found to belong to a group of anarchists who believed in the assassination of rulers, but no evidence of a conspiracy was determined. Ironically, two Secret Service agents were in attendance at the reception and were waiting in line to greet the president, but they were not in an official capacity and at that time had no responsibility for President McKinley's safety. McKinley died on September 14, 1901. Upon his death, as Theodore Roosevelt came into office, Congress charged the Secret Service with the duty of protecting the president.

On October 14, 1912, then former President Theodore Roosevelt was again campaigning for the office as a candidate of a third party (the Bull Moose or Progressive Party) and was making a campaign appearance in Milwaukee, Wisconsin. As he left the Hotel Gilpatrick en route to the convention hall where he was to give his speech,

Roosevelt was accompanied by an unofficial bodyguard, Colonel Cecil A. Logan, a former hunting companion. Logan carried a pistol in his pocket. Colonel Logan attended Roosevelt to his car and then started to walk back to the second car in the motorcade. Roosevelt saw that a crowd had assembled to witness his departure from the hotel. The former president stood up in the open-top car to wave to the crowd and acknowledge their applause and support.

Suddenly, the sound of a shot pierced the gathering darkness! Roosevelt was jolted backward and clutched his chest. He had been shot with a pistol from about 30 feet away by John F. Schrank, a part-time bartender from New York City who stood in the second row of the crowd. A Roosevelt aide and people in the crowd immediately set upon Schrank, beating him and holding him for the police. The crowd brought Schrank before Roosevelt, who merely looked at him and ordered him taken away. Only the thickness of Mr. Roosevelt's rather lengthy and folded speech and his iron eyeglass case in his jacket pocket prevented the shot from being fatal. The bullet entered his chest, breaking a rib, and lodged just short of his right lung. The former president spit into his hand and saw no blood, revealing to him that a lung had not been struck. With characteristic fortitude, he continued to his scheduled appearance and allowed medical treatment only at the conclusion of his speech, an hour and a half later.

Schrank said he wanted to kill Roosevelt not because he had a personal dislike for him, but because he thought a presidential third term was unconstitutional, and he was defending the anti–third term tradition that had been established by previous presidents. He later claimed that the ghost of President William McKinley had visited him and accused Roosevelt of assassinating him. Schrank said McKinley wanted him to avenge his death.[15] In a letter to the people of the United States, Schrank explained his reasons for the attempted assassination:

TO THE PEOPLE OF THE UNITED STATES

Sept. 15, 1901—1:30 a.m. in a dream I saw President McKinley sit up in his coffin pointing at a man in a monk's attire, in whom I recognized Theodore Roosevelt.

The dead President said "this is my murderer, avenge my death."

Sept. 14, 1912—1:30 a.m.: While writing a poem, someone tapped me on the shoulder and said "Let not a murderer take the president's chair, avenge my death." I could directly see Mr. McKinley's features.

Before the Almighty God I swear that the above written is nothing but the truth.

So long as Japan could rise to be one of the greatest powers of the world despite her serving a tradition more than 2,000 years old, as General Nogi so nobly demonstrated, it is my duty of the U.S.A. to uphold the third term tradition. Let every third termer be regarded as a traitor to the American cause. Let it be the right and duty of every citizen to forcibly remove a third termer. To prevent is better than to defend. Never let a third term emblem appear on an official ballot.

I am willing to die for my country. God has called me to be his instrument, so help me God.

Eine feste Berg ist unser Gott (A mighty fortress is our God)

INNOCENT GUILTY

Schrank was declared insane and spent the rest of his life incarcerated in a Wisconsin mental institution. In 1940, President Franklin Roosevelt broke the anti–third term tradition with his third election, and in 1944 he was elected to a fourth term. Schrank (an early term-limit advocate) lived to see the beginning of the third term.

Many years later, in 1933, a few weeks before an unsuccessful attempt had been made against his own life, Franklin Roosevelt related to his vice president–elect, John Nance Garner, "I remember T. R. saying to me, 'The only real danger from an assassin is from one who does not care whether he loses his own life in the act or not. Most of the crazy ones can be spotted first'."[16]

It is said, "Theodore Roosevelt often went for brisk walks about Washington while president, accompanied by only a single Secret Service agent. Sometimes he packed a pistol, telling one friend, 'I should have some chance of shooting the assassin before he could shoot me, if he were near me'."[17] Mr. Roosevelt was correct about an assassin who doesn't care about losing his own life, but his bluster of walking with only one Secret Service agent, carrying a gun to shoot any assassins, and being able to spot a crazy first was erroneous and dangerous. Was there not a lesson to be learned from Charles Guiteau and the fact that he shot President Garfield in the back?

President-elect Franklin Roosevelt was the target of an assassin in Miami, Florida, on February 15, 1933. Mr. Roosevelt had concluded a twelve-day fishing vacation and was being given a crowded reception at Miami's Bayfront Park. He was in the lead car of the three-car motorcade, sitting atop the rear seat in the open-top convertible, from which he gave a short acknowledgment speech. He was accompanied in the car by Miami Mayor R. B. Gauthier, sitting beside him, Gus Gennerich, his personal bodyguard sitting in the right front seat, and Marvin H. McIntyre, a former newsman assisting in coordinating press relations. A follow-up car containing Secret Service agents was several feet back, and approximately 75 feet behind was the third car. Upon culmination of Mr. Roosevelt's speech, a reporter jumped onto the car and asked the president–elect to give the speech again for the camera. Roosevelt refused and slid down onto the car seat.

As he slid down, the president was approached by Chicago Mayor Anton "Tony" Cermak. The two shook hands and spoke for a few minutes, setting up a meeting for a later time. The mayor moved away a few feet and was talking to a nearby Secret Service man, Robert Clark, when another (unidentified) person boarded the car and stood on the running board and discussed a long telegram with Roosevelt. Suddenly there was a shot, followed instantly by four more. The presiden–elect was uninjured, but he witnessed Mayor Cermak being wounded in the chest and Clark being grazed in the hand by the same bullet.

There was the usual considerable confusion, shouts, screams of pain, and terror as the Secret Service attempted to get Mr. Roosevelt's car started and away from the area. Roosevelt ordered the car to stop, pick up the wounded mayor, and transport him to the hospital (where he died about two weeks later from gangrene). It was later observed that it was fortunate the car had moved those approximate 30 feet before it stopped to pick up the mayor, because the area was quickly engulfed by the crowd plummeting the shooter, making it extremely difficult to get the other two cars away.

The assassin, Italian immigrant Guiseppe Zangara, was captured by the angry crowd and had nearly all his clothing torn off. He had stood on a bench several rows back in the crowd to shoot at the president–elect. He had planned on getting closer to Roosevelt, but the front rows were filled when he arrived at the park, well in advance of the president-to-be. Lillian Cross, a 48-year-old wife of a local doctor, was nearly pushed off the same bench as Zangara jumped up with a gun in his hand. She was a diminutive woman weighing just 98 pounds but slightly taller than the 5-foot Zangara. She saw the gun and realized what he was about to do. She grabbed his arm and pushed the gun hand up, ruining his aim. In addition to Mayor Cermak, four other victims were wounded, including William Sinnot, a New York City policeman assigned to Roosevelt's security detail.

Zangara was described by the newspapers of the day as standing barely an inch over 5 feet tall, and he was proportionately narrow of body. Similarly unimpressive was he by the standards that normally measure human importance. Negatives described his general condition. No longer youthful at age 33, a bricklayer by trade, he was unemployed, unmarried, uneducated, unfriendly (therefore friendless), unmoneyed—and most decidedly unwell. Zangara gave a full statement about his desire to kill the president-elect. 'I want to make it clear I do not hate Mr. Roosevelt personally, I hate all presidents, no matter from what country they come, and I hate all officials and everybody who is rich.'"[18] On March 20, 1933 (a month and a half after the shooting), Zangara was executed in Florida's electric chair. Zangara failed to alter American history, and probably world history (as the death of Mr. Roosevelt most assuredly would have done), but Mayor Cermak's name was forever linked with President Roosevelt.

Two New York resident Puerto Rican nationals seeking independence for Puerto Rico, conspired to kill President Harry S. Truman at the Blair House, across the street from the White House. They had no specific plan except to go to Blair House and shoot the president. They did not even know if the president was in the house or where he was located. They had no particular experience in the use of weapons and were only vaguely familiar with the handguns they had recently purchased, having never even fired them in practice.

On November 1, 1950, President Truman was taking an early afternoon nap in an upstairs bedroom that faced Pennsylvania Avenue. The Trumans were living at Blair House because the White House was undergoing extensive renovation. At about 11:30 P.M., Oscar Collazo and Greselio Torresola, members of the Puerto Rican Revolutionary Nationalist Party, left the cheap hotel room they had rented the day before, on their arrival from New York City. (Believing they would not be returning to New York, they had purchased one-way train tickets.) Both men calmly walked along Pennsylvania Avenue until they came to Blair House, not exactly sure where it was. They split up and approached the president's temporary home from separate directions.

Walking up to the uniformed White House police officer's guard booth at about 12:15 A.M., Torresola promptly shot and killed Officer Leslie Coffelt. Collazo aimed his first shot at the back of Officer Donald Birdzall, but the gun did not fire. In an exchange of shots, Collazo shot Birdzall in the knee. In the ensuing gun battle, two other police officers were wounded. Officer Birdzall, although wounded in the knee, ran into the busy afternoon traffic to the middle of Pennsylvania Avenue as he engaged the hostile attackers with his return gunfire. His actions drew the attacker's gunfire away from Blair House, and he was wounded again in the opposite knee. Torresola was killed in the exchange, and Collazo was critically wounded.

Meanwhile, upstairs in Blair House, President Truman raised up and looked out of the window to see what the commotion was all about. Secret Service Agent Stu Stout, stationed outside the bedroom door, rushed in and made the president get down. Then, armed with a Thompson submachine gun, he went back outside the bedroom doorway to stand in the hallway facing the stairs in case any attackers made it that far. Agent Stout was later questioned by Mrs. Truman as to why he did not respond to the attack downstairs with his friends. The news media and the public also criticized him for not rushing to the aid of his coworkers. The Secret Service defended his response as the only action he should have taken, because his duty and responsibility was to respond to and protect the president, not to rush to what could have been a diversion. Mr. Stout was then credited and well remembered for his proper and heroic actions.

President Truman felt that the attempt on his life was a part of the political way of life and offered, "A president has to expect such things." Mr. Truman kept all his scheduled appointments that afternoon, including a visit to Arlington National Cemetery and took his customary walk the next morning. Collazo was convicted of attempted murder and was sentenced to die in the electric chair. President Truman later commuted the sentence to life in prison.

LESSONS LEARNED

It is true of the early presidents that the security measures in place, if any, were notably deficient. That, of course, is what supplies us with the lessons that spawned real proactive protection. President Jackson was lucky the first pistol misfired and blessed that the second one did the same. The potential assassin, Lawrence, should not have been able to get so close to the president. The president should have been covered up immediately and the assailant tackled before his gun came out of his pocket. There is no way he should have been able to reach for a second gun and fire without hindrance.

President Lincoln was left unprotected by a policeman more interested in the play or going for a drink than the president's safety. In contemporary times, Booth would have never made it into the building with a gun. President Garfield was approached from behind and shot in the back by a man who repeatedly wrote and visited the White House. This man was obviously disturbed yet was never detained and questioned. At that time, there was no protocol to deal with that sort of thing. This is another lesson learned and bolstered the creation of the deep collage of protocols now in place to deal with this element of security.

Certainly, our presidents often move in unplanned and/or secret comings and goings. President McKinley was assassinated by an obviously nervous man with an oversized bandage, waiting to shake the president's hand. The president did not have trained men by his side protecting him from such a blatant attack. President Franklin Roosevelt was standing up, alone in his open-top car when shot at from the crowd.

When Franklin Roosevelt was elected, the Secret Service was in place to protect him. Some kinks still needed to be worked out, but he was not hurt while under attack. His agents should have been closer to him, guarding him or shielding him from the crowd. His driver should have had the car running and ready to move the whole time the president was in or near it. As demonstrated by the attack against President Reagan several years later, it is unlikely today that the presidential vehicle would stop to pick up the wounded while possibly still under attack.

President Roosevelt's would-be assassin was a man who apparently did not care for any person of prominence. He could just as well have gone after any powerful or rich person, but on that day he went after the president. There are many people like that in the world, but not all will pull the trigger. Spotting one who would is the challenge.

By the time Harry Truman was president, the Secret Service had gained more experience and honed their form. While guards were fending off assailants outside of Blair House, where President Truman was staying, his Secret Service agent stayed by his side. The assassins blatantly attacked the house, starting a gun battle in the street. Some attackers will go to any lengths to commit their act, sometimes going for the impossible works. That is why you must always expect the unexpected. Luckily for President Truman, he had dedicated guards who bravely fought off the attackers, stopping them and their plan.

Assassination attempts against U.S. presidents, successful or not, have supplied building blocks for the ever-changing needs of professional protection. Out of bad will come good, out of mistakes will come lessons. Such are the facts of life. We must review history so that we may recognize when it is repeating itself and apply a refined, appropriate response.

The importance of studying past assassinations is self-evident. Just by reading, in chronological order, accounts of the assassination attempts, one can see the change in the way presidential protection has evolved. These attacks have "ring of protection" written all over them. We can see how the art of the rings of protection and crowd control evolved just by looking at these early attacks. The need for understanding behavioral psychology is also an imperative development that arose from the study of these attacks.

There is no way of actually learning how to protect someone unless you know the many ways, shapes, and forms of an attack and how they actually occur. It is a strange twist of life that from the most devastating events or mistakes come the most valuable lessons. If we did not study past assassinations, we would be reinventing the wheel over and over, making the same mistakes and therefore never progressing. Before setting out to do something, it is wise to see how it was done before so as to see how to improve upon that which is to be done again. They who have died have not died in vein, for in their death they have shown how to protect the next man. Change is inevitable, so we must acknowledge and learn from what just happened to keep up with change—always trying to stay one step ahead.

RELIGIOUS ASSASSINATIONS

From early history, religious assassinations have been as consequential as political assassinations. In the year A.D. 64 or 67, the first pope, St. Peter, was put to death by the Romans. They crucified him by hanging him upside down. The next fourteen popes succeeding Peter also were put to death by the Romans. Involved in political disputes with the powerful families of Europe, and with no secular protection after the death of Charlemagne, nearly twenty popes met violent and untimely deaths. During the Middle or Dark Ages, popes were variously killed in their sleep, imprisoned, and starved, and one, Leo X, was the victim of an attempted poisoning. But since the days of the Renaissance, popes have usually lived quietly and peacefully, tending to affairs of the church and bringing messages of peace to the world.

Religious assassinations that changed the face of religion and perhaps modern history have included the early seventh century poisoning of Hassan bin Ali Abi Talib (a Shiite), grandson of the Prophet (Mohammed), by his own wife, Joada Binte Ass-us, who sought to endear herself with the ruling Caliph, Maviah (Mu'awiya) (a Sunni). She had been convinced and promised, by Marwan, the Royal Governor of Medina, acting on behalf of Mu'awiya, that if she killed Hassan she would be married to Mu'awiya's son, Yezid, and be in line to rule as queen when Yezid acceded to the Caliphate. However, Mu'awiya induced Marwan (who owed allegiance to Mu'awiya) to believe that if Joada would murder Hassan, Yezid could also be vulnerable to her. She was received and honored at Marwan's royal palace in Medina. As she was seated in the chair of honor, the floor collapsed into a pit under the floor, where she was stoned to death. Naturally, Mu'awiya was absent when the reception, stoning, and killing were being done by Marwan and/or his followers.

However, unbeknown to Joada, there was an ironic second part to the intrigue and scheme to kill Hassan. Mu'awiya had a pact with Hassan that he very dearly wished to end in his own favor. The agreement was that should Hassan outlive Mu'awiya, he, Hassan and not Mu'awiya's son, Yazid, would succeed to the Caliphate. Consequently, to ensure and hasten Hassan's early death, Mu'awiya plotted with Marwan to entice Joada to kill Hassan. In the ensuing years, through warfare with far superior numbers, Yazid, who had become Caliph after Mu'awiya's death, killed Hussein, Hassan's younger brother, his family save for one son, and all of Hussein's followers (of about 250) in a major ten-day battle at Karbala (in modern day Iraq).

A generation earlier, Hassan and Hussein's father, Ali bin Abi Talib, the cousin and son-in-law of Mohammed, was also assassinated. He was killed while in prayer by a former follower who was now aligned against him as a member of a dissident faction that believed Ali had made some unsatisfactory political decisions. Ali was killed with a sword that had been covered with poison. When Ali entered the Mosque to pray, the assassin lurked inside in the shadows. As Ali knelt down and prostrated himself in the normal Muslim prayer position, the assassin stole upon Ali and struck him on the head with the poisoned sword. The blow was not instantly fatal, and Ali did not die from the wound; rather, he died two days later from the poison that spread though his entire body.

According to the Muslim Shiite belief, Allah (God) appointed Ali as Mohammed's successor as God's messenger and Caliph (ruler) through Mohammed and that subsequent Imams (leaders) should be direct descendants of Mohammed. Muslim Sunnis believe that Abu Baakar (who seized power upon the death of Mohammed) was the rightful leader of Islam and that subsequent Imams should be elected by popular vote. Those disagreements were partly responsible for the split of Islam into the major divisions of Sunni and Shiite sects, which are still at odds today and manifested in incidents of terrorist activity and often open warfare. Of course, in the modern world of Islam, as in any other religion, while the Sunni and Shiite beliefs are the major primary branches, there are many smaller yet often vocal, radical, and conflicting offshoots and splinter factions of orthodox fundamentalists, heretics, liberals, or moderns. Such a fragment was the group of fanatical assassins led by Hasan ibn Al-Sabbah 1,000 years ago.

Sometimes the line between political and religious motivations is very thin, blurred, or indistinguishable, as the current political and religious struggles in Iraq attest. Another reasonable example is in Northern Ireland, where political and religious differences have their genesis in the creation of the Church of England by King Henry VIII nearly 500 years ago.

Henry broke from the Roman Catholic Church in a religious and political fight with the pope so he might divorce his first wife, Catherine of Aragon (from very Catholic Spain) and marry Ann Boleyn. Although the king had been a staunch supporter of the church, his desire for a male heir drove him to seek a divorce from the aging Catherine, who had failed to produce a male heir. Henry believed that the young and beautiful Ann Boleyn would produce the heir that he so desperately coveted. The church refused to sanction a divorce or grant an annulment, not necessarily on religious grounds but because the pope needed the political support of Catherine's nephew, Charles V, emperor of the Holy Roman Empire. Although Henry had previously been honored by the pope with the title of "Defender of the Faith," he was excommunicated from the Roman Catholic Church. This forced him to nationalize the church in England and become the head of the Protestant Church of England. King Henry annulled his marriage to Catherine and married Ann Boleyn. Ann did not produce a male heir but was the mother of a daughter who, in later years, was to become Queen Elizabeth I.[19] During her reign, Queen Elizabeth signed the death warrant for the beheading of her rival, Mary, Queen of Scots, after she had been declared guilty of plotting with spies and assassins to overthrow or possibly even to assassinate Elizabeth. In modern times, religious (and political) assassinations are common in a troubled political and religiously divided world.

"Just an old man in a loincloth in distant India: Yet when he died, humanity wept." This was the observation of a newspaper correspondent at the death of Mahatma Gandhi. The tragedy occurred in New Delhi as the gaunt old man walked to a prayer meeting and was engulfed by one of history's great ironies—a lifelong pacifist and promoter of nonviolence struck down by an assassin's bullet.[20]

On August 14, 1947, at 5:12 P.M., seventy-nine year-old Mahatma Mohandas Gandhi, the spiritual leader of nonviolence (and inspirational role model for Dr. Martin Luther King, Jr., and others in America's civil rights movement), who led India to independence from Great Britain, was assassinated by a Hindu nationalist in New Delhi. The assassin, Nathuram Godse, killed Gandhi with three pistol shots to the chest as he walked to an evening prayer meeting. The motive was to kill Gandhi, a Hindu, for his pacifist attitude toward Muslims—in particular for going along with Britain's partition of India into the separate nations of India (Hindu) and Pakistan (Muslim).

It was one of those shining Delhi evenings, not at all warm but alight with the promise of spring. I felt well and happy and grateful to be here. Bob and I stood idly talking, I do not remember about what, and watching the Mahatma advance toward us over the grass, leaning lightly on two of 'the girls,' with two or three other members of his 'family' (family or followers) behind them. I read afterward that he had sandals on his feet, but I did not see them. To me it looked as if he walked barefoot on the grass. It was not a warm evening, and he was wrapped in homespun shawls. He passed by us on the other side and turned to ascend the four or five brick steps which led to the terrace or prayer-ground.

Here, as usual, there was a clump of people, some of whom were standing and some of whom had gone on their knees or bent low before him. Bob and I turned to watch—we were perhaps ten feet away from the steps—but the clump of people cut off our view of the Mahatma now; he was so small. Then I heard four small, dull, dark explosions. 'What's that?' I said to Bob in sudden horror. 'I don't know,' he said. I remember that he grew pale in an instant. 'Not the Mahatma!' I said, and then I knew.

The room with the glass doors and windows, by the rose garden at the end of the arbor, had a crowd of people around it. Many were weeping. The police were endeavoring to make them leave. Bob could not tell me anything except that the Mahatma had been taken inside that room. On the following day he told me that he had seen him carried away and that the khadi which he wore was heavily stained with blood.[21]

Nathuram Godse was hanged on November 15, 1949. Another conspirator, Narayan Apte, the mastermind of the plot, was hanged beside him. Four other men, including Nathuram Godse's brother, Gopal Godse, were sentenced to life in prison. Gopal Godse was released on parole in 1967 and died in November 2005. In the last years of his life, he supported himself and his small family by selling books and giving interviews about how he and the others plotted to kill Gandhi.

"Yes! I Killed Mohandas Gandhi and I am Glad I Did It!" Gopal Godse said. Godse described his brother, Nathuram Godse, walking to the gallows alongside Narayan Apte, with the two gloating about the clear winter light filtering into the Punjab prison yard—"Bestowed on us by our Motherland at this heavenly juncture."

Of a previous, failed attempt on January 20, 1948, ten days before the actual assassination, "I gave my consent immediately," Gopal Godse said about his brother asking him to join the conspiracy and when talking about his own role in the assassination. On the failed attempt, the conspirators detonated explosives in a wall at the

New Delhi house with a view to drawing people away from Gandhi, but they stopped short of tossing a grenade at their intended victim for fear of killing bystanders.

> You know, I had mixed feelings. I knew I was going to lose a brother; and I had no doubt that I was going to be arrested and share his fate. On the other hand, our target had been fulfilled. We had done away with somebody who was not only satisfied with the creation of Pakistan; he wanted to see Pakistan progress; he was in fact the father of Pakistan.
>
> So if you ask me, did I feel any repentance, my reply is no—not in the least. We had taken the decision fully knowing what we were doing. We knew if we allowed this person to live any longer, he would do more and more harm to Hindus, and that we could not allow it.
>
> So you see, it is not as if we had gone to New Delhi to steal Gandhi's watch—that would have been a sinful, dirty thing. But that was not the case. We killed with a motive, to serve the highest interests of our people.[22]

In 1970, knife-wielding Benjamin Mendoza attacked Pope Paul VI in Manila, Philippines, opening a small chest wound in the pontiff.[23] In February 1980, Pope John Paul II was scheduled to make an appearance before approximately 100,000 people in a sports stadium in Karachi, Pakistan. Approximately 30 minutes before the pope was due to arrive, a grenade-carrying man was killed by the exploding device he had smuggled into the stadium.[24] It was speculated that he was going to attempt to kill the pope. However, even with these modern-day attempts against the life of a pope, no one was prepared for the act of Mehmet Ali Agea in Rome at about 5:10 P.M. on May 13, 1981.

Pope John Paul II was being slowly driven through the large crowd gathered for his weekly public audience in the Vatican's St. Peter's Square. He was standing up in the back of his vehicle acknowledging the crowd when suddenly, from a few rows back in the crowd, lone gunman and avowed and convicted Muslim terrorist Mehmet Ali Agea shot the pope five times with a .9 mm pistol. John Paul was struck twice in the abdomen, twice in the right arm, and once in the left hand. Agea, who had escaped from a Turkish prison, had threatened to kill the pope two years earlier when the pope visited Turkey.[25]

One of the pope's special security men, Alois Estermann, of the elite Swiss Guards, ignored the bullets being directed at the pope and flung his body onto the wounded pontiff to shelter him from further infliction of harm. Seventeen years later, on May 4, 1998, His Holiness promoted Estermann to be commander of the Swiss Guard. Approximately nine hours after receiving the appointment, violence was again brought to the vicinity of the pope. Estermann and his wife were shot to death in their apartment in the Vatican by a young, 23-year-old fellow guardsman, Cedric Tornay, who then placed his gun in his mouth and killed himself. This solitary incident raises the question of "who watches the watchers?"

In 2006, Mehmet Ali Agea was released from prison for the attempted assassination but was rearrested on other charges and is still serving time in a Turkish prison.

Israeli Prime Minister Yitzhak Rabin was assassinated at a peace rally on November 4, 1995, in Tel Aviv's Kings of Israel Square. He was walking to his car after the rally when he was shot in the arm and back by Yigal Amir, a law student at Bar Ilan University. Amir confessed to the assassination and reportedly told investigators, "I acted alone on God's orders and I have no regrets." Amir awaited Rabin in the parking lot adjacent to the square, close to Rabin's official limousine, where he shot Rabin twice with a Beretta 84F semiautomatic pistol .380 ACP. During the act, Amir also injured Yoram Rubin, a security agent, with another shot. Amir was caught at the scene. Upon hearing that Yitzhak Rabin died, the assassin told the police he was "satisfied."

Asked where he got his ideas, Yigal Amir told the magistrate that he drew on the Halacha, which is the Jewish legal code. "According to the Halacha, you can kill the enemy," Amir said. "My whole life, I learned Halacha. When you kill in war, it is an act that is allowed."

Amir was sentenced to life imprisonment plus six additional years in prison for injuring Rubin. In the verdict, the judges wrote:

> Every murder is an abominable act, but the act before us is more abominable seven-fold, because not only has the accused not expressed regret or sorrow, but he also seeks to show that he is at peace with himself over the act that he perpetrated. He who so calmly cuts short another's life, only proves the depth of wretchedness to which [his] values have fallen, and thus he does not merit any regard whatsoever, except pity, because he has lost his humanity.[26]

Five years later, in an unauthorized interview, Amir said he killed Rabin to stop peace moves with the Palestinians. He was asked whether he had any regrets about the assassination. "Yes," replied the handcuffed former law student, who is serving a life sentence. "Why didn't I do it earlier? I should have done it before Oslo 2. I didn't do it for any personal reasons," said Amir. "I have nothing against Rabin."

PSYCHOLOGICAL PROFILE OF THE ASSASSIN[27]

Attackers, assassins, stalkers, and it seems even mass murderers and serial killers may have several factors in common. The most noteworthy is that they likely can be diagnosed as antisocial personalities. They are incapable of remorse, shame, or guilt and will usually blame others for their insensibilities and shortcomings. They may harbor feelings of repressed hate or resentment toward a parent. The potential assassin's feelings about his mother may not be overt and, most often, if she is present in his life, he is overly protective of or insensitive to her. Often the mother has abandoned the child either through death (frequently suicide) or disappearance. Usually an only child, he is raised by an overbearing, demanding single mother or other relative, never experiencing the close personal feelings of love and the closeness of family. If the father is present in the household, he is either unwilling or unable to provide an image of strength and love and is a very poor role model for the child. Sometimes the father is a demanding and strict disciplinarian, often beating or abusing the child and expecting more from the child than he is capable of giving or being. As a child, the future attacker spends most of his time alone, left to devise pastimes of his own creation. He makes few if any friends through his lifetime and is incapable of forming close personal relationships, especially with members of the opposite sex.

David G. Hubbard conducted a psychiatric study of airplane hijackers in 1971. His study revealed that skyjackers (attackers, assassins, stalkers, mass murderers, and serial killers) shared several common traits: a violent father, often an alcoholic; a deeply religious mother, often a religious zealot; a sexually shy, timid, and passive personality; younger sisters toward whom the skyjackers acted protectively; and poor achievement, financial failure, and limited earning potential. Those traits, however, are shared by many people who do not hijack airplanes (or become attackers, assassins, stalkers, mass murderers, and serial killers). Thus, profiles of mentally unstable hijackers would seem to be of little if any use in detecting a potential hijacker (attacker, assassin, stalker, mass murderer, or serial killer) in advance. [28]

As though he needs to validate himself and explain or rationalize his course of action, the assassin, at least the amateur, will frequently maintain a diary or other extensive writings. Many are prolific writers, producing boxes of material that, to another person, will be rambling and incoherent, sometimes making sense and at other times being utterly confusing and incomprehensible. Yet to the writer, his written work makes perfect sense, even if read at times when he is seemingly normal.

His writing helps explain his motives and what is driving him. It becomes a course of rationalization. Sometimes the writings will be mailed, in the form of letters, to the focus of his attention, public figures or institutions, and newspaper editors. But just as often, the writings remain a part of his secret life. If read from the beginning, the writings will trace a picture of his mental collapse from a troubled individual to a cold, scheming assassin who is convinced that his problems will be erased by an act of murder. The writings often take on a very skewed identity with a political or religious movement. Deeply believing in a political cause or religious affirmation, the assassin believes his murderous actions will cleanse his soul and guarantee his ascension into heaven or paradise, and he will be publicly hailed and recognized as the instrument of a new world order.

An attacker of a public figure has a deep-seated need for recognition, and he thinks he will receive it solely by some act that will draw attention through great shock value. He must complete some act that will bring him the favorable attention he craves. That was indeed the case with John Hinckley, who attempted to kill President Reagan because he felt he would receive the attention of the target of his demented affection, Oscar winning-actress Jody Foster.

Sometimes the assassin or attacker (especially in a workplace setting) may even belong to an organization or group, but his feelings of alienation prevent him from really belonging. On the surface, these people appear normal and lead respectable lives, although in lonely desperation. That appearance of normalcy enhances their dangerousness. They give no indication or clues to friends (if they have any), relatives, or neighbors of their rage and intentions. Often, after a violent assault or assassination, the interviewed neighbors will state, "He was a nice person. Very quiet, kept to himself, never any problems!"

The quiet personality (at least in private) rapidly deteriorates from the calm and very orderly façade to rage, violence, and confusion (often indicated by the writings).

His work habits are erratic. He blames his inability to hold a job on his superiors, who are always bossing him and telling him what to do. The rage and contempt felt for his superiors often leads the killer to commit some type of workplace violence, most likely toward a supervisor or executive of the business, or his blame may be focused on a public figure. If the potential killer has recently been laid off or fired from his job, he is very likely to express his rage in a murderous rampage.

The three most psychologically traumatic times in a person's life are the death of a loved one, a divorce, and loss of employment. Should the person harbor any character traits of the sociopath (antisocial personality), and should any or all of the psychological traumas occur, he is very likely to pose an extremely dangerous threat to those he feels are responsible for his personal dilemma. The target of his repressed feelings could be a former spouse, a former supervisor, an executive, or the president of the United States!

There is a very thin line between admiration or love and hate or rage. The unstable person may be a strong, even ardent admirer of a famous person or celebrity, usually a movie or television personality. He may exchange eye contact or share a handshake and a few spoken words with the famous person. In the mind of the individual, that is an indication of the bonding and love the celebrity holds for him. The individual begins sending letters and making telephone calls to the celebrity, maybe even sending gifts, all the while visualizing the celebrity returning the burning, unrequited love. When the calls and letters go unanswered and the gifts are returned, the love turns to rage and hate. The individual feels humiliated and embarrassed. He swears and is determined to avenge his feelings. What began as following the celebrity to share time and events soon degenerates into a deadly game of stalking with the intent to harm or kill the object of his misplaced affection.

A trait common to assassins, serial killers, and terrorists is a total absence of remorse. The only regret they may have is if they fail to accomplish their mission. When convicted terrorist Ramzi Ahmed Yousef was sentenced to spend the rest of his life plus 245 years in prison for his role in the 1993 bombing of the New York World Trade Center, he was quoted by the news media as telling the judge, "I am a terrorist and proud of it."

The typical assassin makes long-range plans up to the attack, with every activity or occupation being a means of preparing for and accomplishing his chosen antisocial goal. The focus of his life is the anticipation and planning of his exploit. Once the act is committed, he has little or no plan of escape. Of course, that is part of the recognition factor. He prepares for death and notoriety, never anticipating that the ending will be anything other than what he wanted, but in many cases expecting to be exalted and praised. In Iraq, Afghanistan, Israel, and the surrounding countries, many suicide bombers have been proclaimed heroic martyrs; their pictures are prominently displayed on public walls, and often the family of the bomber is rewarded with cash.

A number of key observations about assassins and their behaviors have emerged from the U.S. Secret Service Exceptional Case Study Project (ECSP). The first is that targeted violence is the end result of an understandable, and often discernible, process of thinking and behavior. Assassinations, attacks, and near attacks almost without exception were neither impulsive nor spontaneous acts. The notion of attacking a public official or public figure did not leap into the mind of a person standing, for example, at a political rally attended by the president. Assassins were not impelled into immediate violent action by sudden new thoughts that popped into their heads. Rather, ideas of assassination developed over weeks and months, even years. For some would-be attackers, such thinking organizes their lives, providing a sense of meaning and purpose or an ending point when they believe their emotional pain will cease. For others, thinking about assassination is compartmentalized. Some potential assassins engage in ongoing internal discussions about their attacks while maintaining outward appearances of normality and regularity. In every case, however, assassination was the end result of an understandable process involving the attacker's pattern of thoughts, decisions, behaviors, and actions that preceded the attack.[29]

A professional assassin (or in the street vernacular, a "hit man"), on the other hand, will not even attempt to undertake the job until every last-minute problem has been eliminated and his chances of escape are assured. Although he has the same psychological profile as the amateur, his motives are usually monetary rather than emotional. A professional assassin is dangerous in that he will spend the same amount of time and effort thinking through, anticipating, and planning as his counterpart, the security specialist whose job it is to prevent the attack. Each tries to neutralize the other in advance of the performance. A professional tries to eliminate all mistakes and plans for all contingencies, not wishing attention or wanting to risk his life or freedom, whereas the nonprofessional makes mistakes and does little planning beyond the commission of his deed.

PROFESSIONAL ASSASSIN

It is very possible that the protective agent's opposition could include a professional assassin. If this is ever the case, the agent will need all the good luck and information he can get.

If the assassin's target is protected by security personnel, he is either going to disable or go around their security. The most dangerous aspect of a professional assassin is that he knows how to find and interpret information about the agent's client. This is quite possibly where the battle will be won or lost. The effectiveness of a professional assassin depends on how much useful data he can gather on the target. The protection responsibility includes learning to spot surveillance and making it as difficult as possible for the opposition to collect information.

Professional assassins do not go on suicide missions and are not political or religious fanatics. What makes a professional killer dangerous are the same qualities that make a good protection agent: dedication, training, skill, and detached professionalism.

PROFILE OF A PROFESSIONAL ASSASSIN

Professional assassins do not skulk around with long trench coats, do not all look alike, and so on. In fact, the better they can blend in, the more effective they are. They may appear to be just the businessman next door. Also, they rarely choose their profession. Instead, they tend to gravitate toward it, maybe through youthful psychological and physical abuse experiences, or they may come up through military special forces or special police units. True professionals, as opposed to simple criminals that kill, are

- Physically fit, mentally and emotionally strong
- Reliable, honorable in their own way or according to their own codes
- Often literate and well educated, with good connections, resources, and intelligence
- Often working in sales or other jobs where travel would not seem unusual
- Often adrenaline junkies who like the element of personal danger; they may not like the actual killing (although some do get extra pleasure from killing) but enjoy the setup, preparation, and the hunt

Some of the skills possessed by a professional killer are

- Combat shooting and expert marksmanship
- Evasive driving
- Surveillance skills
- Skill with improvised weapons
- Proficient in a variety of martial arts
- Patience

An amateur and professional assassin are the same animal but on different rungs of the evolutionary ladder. The sole focus of the amateur is on the act he is to commit and envisioning his expected outcome. His planning does not go beyond that act, without regard for himself other than the belief of self-gain in the form of recognition on a grand scale, making his mark in the world. He makes no assurance of his own escape and may be willing to die for his cause, making him a dangerous adversary. Consumed by his evil objective, he does extensive planning, similar to the professional. Although his motives may vary, they are generally guided by emotion. That emotional attachment makes him prone to mistakes. For the professional, it is business or a job for financial gain. He meticulously does his planning to successfully carry out the job without recognition and to assure his escape. If he feels it is too dangerous, he may opt to turn the job down. The most dangerous aspect for the professional is the fact that he will spend the time to find the weakness in the security around his target, becoming the equal but mirror-image opposite of the security agent. It is a constant marathon between security specialist and assassin, trying to be one step ahead of the other.

A professional may not always act alone. He may have a team backing him, maybe for the getaway or diversionary tactics. Perhaps the highest level of assassinations have been conducted by governments, using the military or another type of secretive service to kill single persons, small groups of people, or even entire sections of populations.

ASSASSINATION MYTHS AND ECSP FINDINGS[30]

Three beliefs about assassination have been widely held and perpetuated in the popular culture: (1) there is a profile of the assassin, (2) assassinations are the result of mental illness or derangement, and (3) those who make threats pose the greatest risk. These beliefs, however, were largely unsupported by data from the ECSP and do not withstand critical thinking about assassination behaviors. Because these beliefs are untrue, they are now known to be myths.

Myth 1: There is a profile of "the assassin."

Many believe in a profile of the American assassin. In actuality, public-figure attackers and near-lethal approacher do not fit any one descriptive or demographic profile (or even several descriptive or demographic profiles). American assassins and attackers have been both men and women. They have ranged in age from 16 to 73. They have varied in educational background, employment history, marital status, and other demographic and background characteristics.

While there is no assassin profile, there are common behaviors and activities in which assassins and near-assassins have engaged before their attacks. Mounting an attack on a prominent person requires a number of pre-incident decisions, behaviors, and activities. A potential assassin must choose a target, figure out where the target is going to be, decide on and secure a weapon, survey security, develop a plan of attack, and consider whether to escape (and if so, how). While not every public-figure attacker and near-attacker engaged in all of these activities and behaviors, most engaged in several of them (Fein and Vossekuil 1998, 1999).

Myth 2: Assassination is a product of mental illness or derangement.

Many believe that an attack on a public figure is a deranged action, without rational or understandable motives and, by extension, that perpetrators of this type of crime must be mentally ill. In most cases, however, mental illness did not appear to be a primary cause of assassination behavior. Attacks on persons of prominent public status were actions chosen by persons who saw assassination as a way to achieve goals or solve problems. Mental illness rarely played a major role in assassination behaviors. Most near-lethal approachers, and the great majority of attackers and assassins, were not mentally ill. Although almost all had some type of broadly defined psychological or emotional problem, relatively few suffered from serious mental illnesses that caused their attack behaviors.

Myth 3: Explicit threateners are the persons most likely to carry out attacks.

Much thinking about assassination links threateners and attackers, as if the two categories are one. Many people assume that those who make threats (that is, those who communicate verbally or in writing their intent to harm their targets) are the ones who also pose threats. However, fewer than one tenth of all 83 attackers and near-attackers communicated a direct threat about their targets either to the target or to a law enforcement agency prior to their attack. In actuality, persons who pose threats (that is, those whose behavior indicates they are thinking about, planning, and/or building capacity for an attack) most often do not make threats, especially explicit threats.[31]

SUMMARY

Assassination as a political and religious (or in many instances, personal) tool to effect an agenda of some type of change has always been and will continue to be a fact of life (or death). An executive protection agent must always recognize, guard against, and prepare for it.

REVIEW QUESTIONS

1. Describe the impact of assassination on the course of history.
2. Imagine how the world would be different if the assassinations discussed in this chapter had never occurred.
3. Discuss the impact on history of the world if the most ruthless dictators of all time had been assassinated as they were assuming power.
4. How does the excerpt from Macbeth relate to the mind of a contemporary assassin?
5. Explain how the assassination of Archduke Franz-Ferdinand could have been avoided, or at least delayed. What mistakes did the Duke and others make regarding his security on that day?
6. The assassination of Franz-Ferdinand occurred on a Serbian holiday. Regarding executive protection, why is it important to be aware of special holidays?
7. What were the six major American assassinations of the 1960s?
8. How could the assassinations of Robert Kennedy, Martin Luther King, Jr., and Malcolm X have been prevented? What mistakes were made, making the assassinations possible?
9. Describe the assassination attempts against American presidents. What lessons were learned from each?
10. Why is it important to study past assassinations?
11. Why is it important to know the psychological profile of assassins? What are the differences between an amateur assassin and a professional hit man?

NOTES

1. *Webster's Universal Dictionary and Thesaurus*. Montreal, Quebec: Tormont Publications, 1993.
2. Ibid.
3. Roberts, J. M. *A Concise History of the World*. New York: Oxford University Press, 1995.
4. Shakespeare, William. Macbeth, act 1, scene 7.
5. Ibid.
6. *Compton's Interactive Encyclopedia for Windows*. Millin Publishing, 1995.
7. One such book for recommended reading is George Featherling, *The Book of Assassins*. Edison, NJ: Castle Books, 2006.
8. Roberts, J. M. *A Concise History of the World*.
9. Burke, David. *Old Hickory—A Life of Andrew Jackson*. New York: Dial Press, 1977.
10. Hastings, Donald W. "The Psychiatry of Presidential Assassination" *Lancet* 85 (July 1965).

11. Ibid.
12. Peskin, Allen. *Garfield*. Kent, OH: Kent State University Press, 1978.
13. Ibid.
14. Ibid.
15. Gardner, Joseph L. *Departing Glory: Theodore Roosevelt as Ex-President*. New York: Charles Scribner's Sons, 1973.
16. Miller, Nathan. *F.D.R.: An Intimate History*. Garden City, NY: Doubleday, 1983.
17. Ibid.
18. Davis, Kenneth S. *F.D.R.: The New York Years 1928–1933*. New York: Random House, 1977.
19. Ibid.
20. "The Assassination of Gandhi, 1948" www.eyewitnesstohistory.com, 2005.
21. Sheean, Vincent. *Lead, Kindly Light*. New York: Random House, 1949. Quoted in Ashe, Geoffrey, *Gandhi*. New York: Stein and Day, 1968; "The Assassination of Gandhi, 1948." www.eyewitnesstohistory.com, 2005.
22. *New York Times* on the Web, March 2, 1998, http://www.nytimes.com.
23. *U.S. News and World Report*, May 25, 1981, 90, 25.
24. Ibid.
25. *Los Angeles Times*, May 14, 1981.
26. CNN, April 1, 2006.
27. This information is from a compilation of unpublished material and actual experience collected from various sources by the author and others involved in protective services. Much of the material resulted from interviewing several psychologists and psychiatrists and appeared in an unpublished paper, An Examination of Motiveless Murder, written by the author in 1975.
28. Hudson, Rex A. *The Sociology and Psychology of Terrorism: Who Becomes a Terrorist and Why?* Washington, DC: Federal Research Division, Library of Congress, 1999, http://lcweb.loc.gov/rr/frd/.
29. Vossekuil, Bryan, Borum, Randy, Fein, Robert, and Reddy, Marisa, Preventing Targeted Violence Against Judicial Officials and Courts, http://www.secretservice.gov/ntac_aapss.shtml (accessed March 28, 2006).
30. U.S. Secret Service Exceptional Case Study Project (ECSP), a study of all 83 persons in the United States known to have attacked, or approached to attack, a prominent public official or figure between 1949 and 1996. The ECSP was an operationally focused study. That is, it was principally designed not to examine scientifically or theoretically interesting questions but, rather, to generate behavioral information that investigators and others with protective responsibilities could use to conduct more effective assessments and prevent targeted attacks. Accordingly, the central questions of the study focused on identifying patterns of thinking and behavior among attackers and near-attackers in the days, weeks, and months before their assaults or near-lethal approaches.
31. Vossekuil, B. et al., "Preventing Targeted Violence Against Judicial Officials and Courts."

5 Close Personal Protection
What It Is, What It Is Not

Have Gun, Will Travel
Reads the Card of a Man,
A Knight without Armor in a Savage Land...

Theme Song, 1950's television series, "Paladin"

It is more than standing and waiting.
It ain't all glory and glamour.
We do not seek medals, or marching bands, or even praise. There will never be
parades, or ceremonies, even if we fall. We know that what we do, if done well, will
be forever unknown. We ask only that, in the dark of the night, when you are afraid,
remember we are there to watch over and to protect you.

George Hrabovsky, Henley-Putnam University

WHAT IS CLOSE PERSONAL PROTECTION?

In the late 1990s, executive protection become a corporate household word and catch-all phrase describing risk management, deterrence, and security. The idea of executive protection (close personal protection) includes all the principles of protection such as determination of actual and potential vulnerabilities, careful analysis and planning, preparation, implementation of a well-conceived plan, advance security arrangements, and total awareness to provide a safe secure environment. Close personal protection (CPP) is a security program designed around the lifestyle, family, and environment of the individual being protected. It is much, much more than "standing and waiting." It means anticipating, preparing, and planning for any contingency that would place the person being protected in a life-threatening position.

Close personal protection is a general description for professionals providing close proximity personal security to a person who is likely to be targeted by those who would inflict harm. The definition of the phrase executive protection has taken on many meanings through years of misuse by both amateurs and professionals who have no real idea, or only a general understanding, of what executive protection really entails. Executive protection has become a misnomer today because close personal protection, planning, and awareness programs are not limited to executives but are available and applicable to anyone with a need, real or perceived, for personal security; thus the descriptive designation of close personal protection.

The protective agent is responsible for the security, safety, health, and well-being of the principal. Planning, preparation, and anticipation are the keys to minimizing risk to the principal. It is not a job of confrontation but rather a planned response to an unavoidable situation. The object is to deter an attack or avoid a confrontation rather than expose the protectee to danger. The goal in close personal protection is to remove one's client from harm's way.

Close protection covers many areas, from establishing an area of security and perimeter defense to moving formations that shield the protectee with the bodies of the men and women sworn to provide the required protection. The best way to establish protection is to form circles or multiple layers of security around him. The objective is to create a defense that will prevent anyone from gaining a position wherein he is able to injure or kill the person being protected and those within his inner circle.

There are four sacred commandments for protecting the principal:

1. Be aware of everything occurring in a 360° circle around the person being protected. This accounts for the term *circles of protection*.
2. The first circle must remain within arm's reach of the protectee. Allowing a greater distance than an arm's length only invites intrusion by a potential attacker and will allow him the range to inflict injury or death.
3. Never leave the area of responsibility around the principal. Moving out of position will be like leaving a gap in dental work. The space is empty, and germs (the attacker) can easily infiltrate the protective shield.
4. Cover and evacuate. In the event of an incident of danger, the mandate is to cover the protectee—provide a shield for him with the protection agents' bodies—and evacuate him to a safer location.

HISTORICAL ROOTS—PERSONAL PROTECTION–PRIVATE SECURITY

Some methods of defending against assassination have been as bizarre as the method or reasoning of the assassination itself. For example, Mithridates VI (120 to 63 B.C.) was king of the tiny kingdom of Pontus, in early Asia Minor, near the Black Sea. As a great enemy of Rome, he was paranoid about being poisoned. To defend himself against this manner of secretive and most probably very painful death, he dosed himself over a long period of time with ever-increasing quantities of various deadly poisons, gradually building a tolerance and immunity to them. In 63 B.C, the conquering Romans defeated the army of Mithridates in a great battle. Rather than accept surrender to his hated and sworn enemies, he chose death. However, in an ironic twist of fate, he could not go quietly to meet death by taking poison but had to fling himself onto his sword.[1]

Since the very beginning of the socialization of man, intended targets of assassins have utilized more practical and less drastic measures to protect themselves. Primarily, they employed bodyguards who would sacrifice their own lives in defense of the employing patron. The Japanese shoguns, for example, employed contingents of ninja and samurai to protect them from other shogun ninja. The beefeaters, yeomen of the royal guards of Britain, have secured royalty for hundreds of years. Even the pope protects against assassination by surrounding himself with dedicated members of the Swiss Guard. The president of the United States, since 1901, has been protected by the Secret Service.

During the Middle Ages, adventure-seeking knights traveled the countryside enlisting in causes and defending the rights, property, and lives of less-capable citizens. These knights (who, with a real stretch of the imagination, could be considered forerunners of the present-day protection-for-hire practitioners, bodyguards, and protection specialists) were called *knight-errants* or *paladins*. Their loyalties were purchased for a fee, entitling the employer to utilize the knight's specialized skills with weapons and in combat to ensure his security. It was very typical for a knight-errant to be employed by several noblemen and causes in the course of a year or lifetime.

The knight's role in medieval society, up until the eleventh century, was largely acting as a warrior or mercenary for hire. After the church's religious campaigns in the late eleventh century, to crack down on the violence running rampant throughout western Europe, the knight's identity as a warrior adopted a distinctly religious flavor. His primary tasks—in theory, at least—were defense of the church and the poor. The knight's double-edged sword represented truth and loyalty, and his shield defense of the church.[2] The knight of today (a protective agent) carries on this tradition, but his clients are no longer the church and the poor, but the rich and famous. His double-edged sword is the power of knowledge and experience.

CHIVALRY OF KNIGHTS AND PROTECTIVE AGENTS

"Knights must have two hearts, one as hard as a diamond, the other as soft and pliant as warm wax,"[3] the Lady of the Lake told the knight Sir Lancelot. A chivalrous knight was expected to achieve individual glory in war as well as uphold virtues ranging from loyalty and humility to self-sacrifice and faith in Christian beliefs. He was expected to be courteous, loyal to his lady love, gifted in the arts of dance, conversation, and music, and able to play a good game of chess.[4] Is it a coincidence that the protective agent of today must be versed in these same virtues and other similar attributes?

HISTORICAL ANTECEDENTS

It may well be that today's society, because of the high terrorist threat, rampant violence, availability of drugs, and a soaring crime rate, has in subtle ways been reverting to precautions, procedures, and even personal protection reminiscent of the Middle Ages and the knight-errant. Homes, businesses, even entire communities are being built surrounded by walls, fences, guards, electronic alarms, and closed-circuit television, much like castles and towns in the Dark Ages, when moats, drawbridges, walls, and sentries protected the inhabitants.

Niccolo Machiavelli (1469–1527) (most notable for his political essay "The Prince") was responsible, at the height of the Renaissance, for replacing the mercenaries who had been hired to defend the city of Florence with a citizen's militia.[5] He was concerned that Italy's political weakness was directly attributable to the presence of large numbers of foreign troops. His citizen's militia was also responsible for protecting the city and its inhabitants from within. They were concerned with many of the same citizen problems as today: lawlessness, disruption, and violence.

They were, although not necessarily historically recognized as such, the precursors to today's municipal police.

More modern policing and private security began in the early 1800s in England. Great Britain's home secretary, Sir Robert Peel, with many others, recognized the need for a professional civilian police force to counter the lawlessness that was so pervasive in cities of that time. For hundreds of years before, there had been a position of *reeve*, providing enforcement of the king's law and collecting taxes in the shires (counties). The holder of this position became known as the *shire-reeve* or *sheriff*. The position eventually became mostly ceremonial, with very little power to quell the rampant violence, roving gangs, robberies, and total social chaos. Peel initiated and passed through Parliament legislation that created the first municipal-type police department. Adopting Secretary Peel's name, the police became known as *peelers*. This name, however, was unappealing (pun intended), and they soon came to be called *bobbies*, a name that today is known and respected throughout the world.

Unfortunately, as in modern times, the limited resources of the police could not cope with the rapidly rising crime rate and also perform the primary mission of crime prevention. As a consequence, citizen groups were empowered to supplement the police. The new groups hired out their services to merchants and the wealthy on a private basis to maintain a watch over the property and merchandise during the hours (mostly nighttime) when the owner could not be present. Thus began the concept of private security. In colonial America, individuals were hired to patrol the streets of the settlements and cities at night, always on the alert for prowlers, Indian attacks, and fire. These private citizens became known as night watchmen.

As police in the cities and sheriff departments in the unincorporated towns or counties were established, it became evident that their efforts were inadequate in the lawless West and great open spaces. Railroads and stage lines hired their own police and security. They carried badges and guns and enforced the laws as they related to the railroad or stagecoach line that hired them. The term *riding shotgun* comes from the practice of having a shotgun-carrying guard riding on the stagecoaches to protect against hostile Indian attacks and stagecoach robbers.

PINKERTONS

No discussion of personal protection would be complete without mentioning Allen Pinkerton. Colonel Allen Pinkerton, a Civil War spy and intelligence officer for the Union, formed the first private investigative and security company to operate in the United States on a full-time basis in Chicago, Illinois, in 1851. He initially founded the company as a private security agency to help protect the railroads. In some areas, where the government had little or no ability to conduct investigations, render security, enforce laws, or "provide for domestic tranquility," it was the Pinkerton Company that performed these essential duties. In the absence of a federal law enforcement agency or representative, the Pinkertons soon established a reputation as their own law enforcement agency, taking jurisdiction wherever there was a need, carrying guns and badges like police and sheriffs.

The company saw growth and strength under Pinkerton's son, Robert, who foresaw the tremendous potential in the private security and bodyguard business. Even with the eventual arrival of sworn law enforcement personnel and a criminal justice system, there remained plenty of work for private companies such as Pinkerton's, which had also naturally branched out into private investigative matters. Pinkerton and his men, with a squad of Secret Service agents, on November 7, 1876, watched over (or *bodyguarded*) the grave of the slain President Lincoln when rumors of a conspiracy to steal the body arose. The conspiracy involved two individuals, Jack Hughes and Terence Mullen, members of a counterfeiting gang who planned to steal the president's body and exchange it for the release of an imprisoned fellow gang member, Ben Boyd. The conspirators escaped in the darkness when a Pinkerton man accidentally discharged his firearm.[6] Today, of course, Pinkerton Consulting and Investigations is one of the largest private security and investigation companies in the world.

EXECUTIVE, VIP, AND CELEBRITY PROTECTION

The history of close personal protection as we know it today has had a relatively short life. If we are to understand the complex issues that define high-level personal protection today, the proper starting point for the history of the field is the last four decades of the twentieth century. Since the turbulent and violent years of the 1960s, close personal protection has evolved from the muscle-bound linebacker-mentality bodyguard to the martial arts trained bouncer, to executive protection, and now to the highly professional and trained personal protection specialists. What lies ahead?

Once the concept of providing a service, known as bodyguarding, became recognized as a specialized branch of security, it developed into a highly extraordinary field. It is against all human instincts of survival to intentionally place oneself in direct line of jeopardy for the sake of another person. Yet that is exactly what is expected of the new professionals whose duty is to be a personal protection specialist.

In the early to mid-1970s, after several corporate executive kidnappings, terrorist acts (which included assassinations), and general threats against the corporate world, major companies (especially international companies at first) began looking seriously at providing bodyguards for vital and vulnerable executives. Celebrities and public figures soon saw a need for a personal security agent to protect them from the very public they wanted to recognize and idolize them. Again, the police could not provide this function because of limited manpower and money. In many jurisdictions, the official law enforcement community was also legally restricted.

For a company to provide private security to its personnel, it had to either establish an in-house position or contract to a private entity. The best the typical private security company could offer was security guards who were trained to sit or stand at a particular post, or sometimes to patrol a specific route and check locks and doors, and to report any unusual activity. A company representative, often a personal secretary or human resources person, usually filled the position by looking in the telephone yellow pages under private investigators and locating one who also did bodyguarding. That probably meant a former policeman who was licensed to carry a firearm. There were limited choices. The private eye/bodyguard usually had no specialized training in the complex factors of executive protection. The bodyguard might be armed and trained in some method of martial arts, but many guards received all their training and experience as bouncers in nightclubs, playing college or professional football, weightlifting or body building, or were just big, mean, and tough.

With the onset of the Iranian Revolution (1978–1979), a small but very significant change began in the security business. Notice was made of the increasing numbers of Iranian expatriates immigrating, or escaping, to the United States. Many of these immigrants were wealthy and influential people back in their own country. Out of fear, they created a niche for professional executive protection specialists. Well-trained and experienced protective personnel of agencies such as the Secret Service, the FBI, the Naval Investigative Service, the U.S. Marshall's Office, and other agencies left their jobs and founded businesses whose specialty was executive protection. Many of the businesses found success. Today, executive protection has gained a place in the corporate and business worlds as well as in the entertainment industry.

BODYGUARDS VERSUS EXECUTIVE PROTECTION

BODYGUARDS

Assassination of royalty was a common event and it was a customary thing for kings to have bodyguards sleep in their bed. King Henry VIII of England (known to have had six wives) routinely slept with bodyguards in the royal bed. King James survived two kidnappings and four violent attempts on his life. Such experiences did nothing to cause King James to break with the normal procedure of always keeping his bodyguards close at hand. In sharing his bed with royal bodyguards, King James was only following the normal practice of the royalty of his time....[7]

It is now very rare, if indeed it is ever practiced, for a bodyguard to share a bed with the person he is assigned to protect as a matter of standard professional performance. But keeping bodyguards close at hand is surely a very much accepted practice for those who cannot defend themselves and lead lives conducive to becoming a victim of stalkers, molesters, rogues, robbers, kidnappers, or terrorists. There have been many changes in the role of the protector through the years, and these changes can be expected to continue.

The terminology used to describe the discipline of protection has also undergone significant changes in recent years. Today, most personnel in the protection field no longer use the term bodyguard. Terms such as personal protection agent, personal protection specialist, and others are now the preferred designations. This has come about for several reasons:

1. To increase the professional stature of the protection agent
2. To distance today's protectors from the hired-thug image that many people have of bodyguards
3. To remind people that body takes away the living human image of the person being protected, and he is being protected, not guarded

4. To bring the image of the protector more in line with his responsibilities
5. To illustrate a movement toward a more realistic description of the full range of services provided by a person designated to neutralize danger
6. To show that providing a full protective service is "more than standing and waiting"

Bodyguard. The name conjures conflicting stereotypical images. On the one hand, a stereotypical bodyguard may be a hulking man. His suit is one size too small, and he is crude, mentally impaired, and sometimes overzealous but a totally dedicated and loyal constant companion to the "boss" (although faithfulness and dedication sometimes change over monetary considerations or when personal loyalties are swayed). On the other hand, when one thinks of bodyguard, because of media and literary glorification, the mind might think of fictional private eyes such as Mike Hammer and Magnum, protecting a glamorous "doll" with a .45, muscle, and brawn. Of course, we have seen this movie and television version many times, especially in older movies and pulp fiction. The image of a bodyguard was also softened somewhat in a movie, *The Bodyguard*, which depicted Kevin Costner as a former Secret Service agent in the role of the new generation of personal protection specialists. The differences between a bodyguard and a close personal protection specialist are in education, training, and skills. A bodyguard relies more on size, combative skills, and intimidation than on planning, anticipation, and preparedness.

In an actual incident, a movie production company hired an executive protection company to provide security during business hours (usually from noon until 2:00 or 3:00 A.M.) for the company president. There were no real threats to the president, but he wanted to have security "just in case." In case of what never became clear, because he was a very nondescript person in a very nondescript building, and the only people who ever visited him were his friends, family, and a few respected business associates, it is believed that this particular executive was nearly a D on the executive protection continuum (see chapter 3) and wanted to have a personal protection agent present merely for show, to emphasize or exaggerate his importance. After several months of paying high hourly wages to the professionals to watch the entrance, the president hired a bodyguard at a much lower rate to stand watch inside the office.

This particular guard, "Bobby Jim the Bodyguard" (a stereotypical image), would have been more in his element working the defensive line for any National Football League team. He was big, and he looked mean. His first day in the office, he wore a black suit (a size too small), a dark shirt, a pastel tie, and dark sunglasses. He stood with his arms folded across his chest, near the center of the office where everyone entering the office had to walk past him. People who were there for nothing more than a discussion of the movie business were greatly intimidated.

After the first day, Bobby Jim assumed a semisitting position on a high-back chair at the rear of the office, but in the center where guests could easily read the meaning of his scowl. When asked about his training, qualifications, and experience, he said that he had worked as a road security bodyguard for a touring rap musical group.

One Sunday afternoon, the client called the protection company, said he wanted to go to a restaurant several miles away, and requested a protective specialist to accompany him and his wife as a precaution. Upon arrival at the production company office, Bobby Jim met the executive protection specialist. Bobby Jim said he would be riding in the right front seat of the company president's limousine and the specialist was to follow in his own car. The bodyguard said he didn't know where the restaurant was, but the limousine driver had a map.

While driving on the main expressway to the restaurant, the driver would suddenly change lanes without signaling, allowing other cars to get between the limousine and the specialist's car. At other times, the driver would put his signal on and not change lanes. It was all very confusing and dangerous.

The restaurant was positioned in the back of a small strip mall shopping center, with the main entrance door around the building from the street. After driving around and looking for a parking place, the driver drove the limousine down a short dead-end alley and parked. The security specialist quickly parked his car in an available parking slot and ran to the limousine. He found the driver-side door and right front door of the car open, the car engine running, and the principal and his wife sitting in the back seat. The driver and bodyguard were nowhere to be seen.

After about five minutes, the driver and bodyguard returned. They said they had found the main entrance to the restaurant, around the side of the building. The walkway to the door was paved with very rough cobblestone. The principal had to cross that route with crutches, because he had only limited use of his legs and would not be seen in a wheelchair. This was a very long, difficult trip, taking several minutes, during which the principal became exhausted, hot, and sweaty enough to need to change his shirt before sitting down to dinner.

After the principal was finally seated, the bodyguard and agent returned to the limousine. The protection specialist questioned the bodyguard about why the car with the principal and his wife had been left unattended in a dead-end alley. Bobby Jim's reply was that he and the driver had to find the door, and they assumed the specialist would be at the limousine after parking his car.

The disgusted specialist left to take up a position outside the restaurant where he could watch the surroundings and observe the area of the principal. From there he could also see the bodyguard and driver sitting in the back seat of the limousine. They were drinking sodas, reading the newspaper, and watching the limousine television set. The windows were open in the car, and the air conditioner was running with the engine turned off.

The specialist checked the restaurant area and found a rear entrance that was easily accessible from the limousine. It was a matter of a mere 50 steps from the limo to the principal's chair inside the restaurant. It would have taken just a minor effort to take the principal inside using this entrance. Upon departure, though, the bodyguard still insisted on again using the front entrance rather that the rear door, because he didn't want the principal to have to exit through the kitchen. He said it was his policy to never use the kitchen, because it was too dangerous. He expressed the idea that maybe the principal could slip on a wet floor or some spilled food. This part was sound thinking. However, in this instance, the floor was dry. The kitchen had long been cleaned and closed, and there was a rubber mat that could have been moved to cover the small kitchen floor area where the principal would have walked.

Every proven tenet of protection was broken during this trip. If there had been any viable threats, including a crime of opportunity such as an armed robbery, the principal and his wife and the rest of the party would have been highly vulnerable. The principles of protection don't change with time; they are only observed more closely and improved upon by professionals. But even an amateur wannabe like Bobby Jim the Bodyguard could have taken the following precautions:

1. He should have driven his own car to the restaurant in the afternoon (he had time) to check and time and routes, locate the restaurant and its entrances, and so on. He could have even left five minutes ahead of the limousine and done at least a primary advance to locate entrances and parking places.
2. He should never have relied on a hired driver to locate the restaurant.
3. He and the driver should never have left the limousine unattended, with the engine running, doors open, and the principal inside.
4. He should never have assumed that someone else would arrive to cover him.
5. He should have located the rear entrance, a direct route into the restaurant.
6. He should have taken a surveillance position where he could observe anyone who approached the principal inside the restaurant.
7. He and the driver should not have moved to the back seat to read the newspaper and drink sodas. They risked battery failure by running the air conditioner and television with the engine shut off.
8. He should have been more alert. He could have become the victim of an opportunistic passer-by.
9. He should have been flexible enough to consider a departure through the kitchen exit, since it was the shortest, most direct route.
10. He should have been flogged and keel hauled, or at least fired, right on the spot!

EXECUTIVE OR CLOSE PERSONAL PROTECTION

A new title, executive protection specialist, and then close personal protection agent, replaced the term bodyguard with a new image connoting professionalism, training, and integrity. The private eye/bodyguard has given way to highly trained and educated specialists who are as comfortable in a corporate boardroom or mingling with presidents and kings as they are in the violent world of the streets.

The new generation of personal protection provides security to a living person. By literal definition, a body is someone no longer living. With that definition, a bodyguard is someone guarding a body, dead and gone. The goal of personal protection is to keep a protectee safe and alive. Therefore, to professional protection specialists, if a charge becomes a body, they have failed in their protective mission. Only once in a long career of providing close personal protection has this author ever been involved in real bodyguarding.

In that instance, in a still-unsolved San Diego, California, 1980's murder case, the swing-shift foreman at a local aerospace manufacturing plant returned home alone from work at around midnight on a Friday. He parked his car in the driveway and started to walk toward his house. When just a few feet from the car, he was gunned down from ambush. During the course of the weekend, the family and mortuary where the deceased's body was taken received anonymous telephone calls stating that the body of the foreman was going to be "snatched." The dead man's employer retained the writer's company to provide security to several other officials of the company, and also to assign two people to guard the body, around the clock, in the mortuary.

Business had been good for the mortuary that weekend. Three other bodies lay in open caskets in other rooms of the funeral home. The protective agents' assignment was to sit in an area adjacent to the foreman's casket during the night, when no one else was present, and to prevent any attempt to steal into the mortuary to desecrate or take the body.

The mission was a success. There were no other attacks against corporate executives, and no one attempted to take the body. But sitting beside an occupied casket all night in a dimly lit, cool, and quiet mortuary with the scent of flowers in the air and soft organ music in the background was enough bodyguarding for the two executive protection agents.

ORIGINS OF EXECUTIVE PROTECTION

The term *executive protection* comes from the early 1970s, when the U.S. Secret Service created a new division called the Executive Protection Service (EPS) to protect embassies and visiting foreign dignitaries. The term, meaning an elite program of security for the very wealthy or powerful, caught on and became a catchphrase of corporations, government service, and elite personalities. As the time of the 1970s was one of terrorist activity and domestic upheaval, with the war in Vietnam starting to wind down and domestic crime rising, a need developed for a specialized security professional to provide protection to corporate executives, VIPs, celebrities, and some political dignitaries. Initially, very few executive protection specialists were available for hire in the private sector. If a corporation or an individual desired or needed the services of a special bodyguard (as they were called in the early days), a former or off-duty police officer with the right to carry a concealed firearm was called into service. Thus, a career path was born for those who wished to put themselves in danger for the safety and security of others.

With the proliferation of private security companies over the past 20 years, executive protection became a generic term for many things. Every security alarm company and every guard company developed an executive protection package. Some security companies viewed it as installing alarm systems, closed-circuit cameras and monitors, and even strategic lighting in an executive's residence and/or corporate premises. Some saw executive protection as developing complex systems and procedures to safeguard an office or a building. To others, it meant learning high-speed and evasive driving techniques. Of course, the provision of bodyguards was probably the most widely accepted idea of executive protection. Executive protection actually embraced all these concepts.

Since that time, the role of executive protection programs has evolved into a large industry incorporating many principles of security and protection beyond the imagination of the early bodyguards. As the definition of executive protection implies, when providing a safe secure environment, many factors must be considered. These include security surveys (residential, business, and travel); advance planning, preparation, and implementation; psychological and physical concerns of the protected as well as the protectors; adapting to changing and variable circumstances; electronic and technological eavesdropping; environmental security engineering; threat assessment and workplace violence; defensive tactics (unarmed combat); loss prevention; security awareness of the persons within the circle of the person being protected; and a veritable range of other topics.

The executive protection specialist, now becoming better known as a close personal protection specialist, is considered to be at the top of the food chain or pecking order of security personnel. He is expected to be well versed in every aspect of security, to have a range of knowledge comparable to the *Encyclopedia Britannica,* and to be physically capable of performing miracles.

The role of the executive protection specialist is to bring together all variables—including personnel, practices, and procedures—to provide optimal security. There is no such thing as 100 percent security unless the person being secured is entombed in thick metal, concrete, and lead under several feet of earth. The objective of the protection specialist is to bring the odds more into the favor of the person being protected. Both experts and novices acknowledge that it is impossible to guarantee 100 percent security (even at the White House), but effective security-protection programs are calculated to bring the odds more in favor of the person being protected. That is the intended end result of personal protection—to bring the odds down and to deter any opportunistic attack while discouraging all but the most determined or professional attackers, assassins, or terrorists.

How is the individual to be protected? Where is he to be protected? What is he to be protected from? What are the consequences, if any, of the protection? What kind of protection will he receive? These questions are the responsibility of the protection specialist working with a principal or his representative. To answer these questions, a comprehensive analytical security survey is the first required step. The survey should identify potential dangers and recommend specific countermeasures. It must include all areas of vulnerability. The principal is at risk in only three places: home, work, and travel. Of course, he is always either at home, at work, or traveling.

Planning and implementation of the program are the steps that follow final preparation of the security survey. Planning a security program incorporates the entire living, working, and travel environments of those being protected, affording the best possible security while providing the widest latitude of personal freedom and least possible lifestyle disruption. Implementing the program begins with making the individual aware of potential hazards and having him accept the recommendations identified in the survey. Included with the recommendations should be an estimated cost breakdown, the advantages and disadvantages of the planned program, and necessary equipment. Security briefings should be conducted regularly for all personnel who have constant contact with the individual concerned, including family members, household staff, secretaries, clerks, and others. Each person must think about security and be aware of the dangers and risks.

HEROES? OR JUST ANOTHER DAY AT WORK?

In an interview for A&E's History Channel, U.S. Secret Service Agent Larry Buendorff explained his reactions on the day in Sacramento when he stepped between intended assassin Lynette Fromme and President Ford.

> All of a sudden, I saw a hand coming up very low with an object in it. Not really thinking about it, I just stepped in front of him (the president) to stop it. Because coming the way it was coming, it could have struck him in some way, but in my case I stepped out. The minute I hit that weapon I knew it was a gun. Why I didn't say "gun" I don't know. But I yelled out, forty-five! and pulled the gun out of her hand. I had a hold of two or three of her fingers in my left hand and the gun in my right hand. I remember pulling the gun into my chest. And now I am pushing her away from the president.... The rest of the agents did exactly what they should be doing, they covered the president and evacuated him.... I turned the weapon over to another agent and went back to work. It happened pretty fast!

> A lot of things go on in your mind afterwards about what might have happened. Initially, you make the moves much like an athlete makes a move, if you are playing basketball, if your guy moves left, you move left, if he moves right you move right. These moves are automatic from our training, so when something like this occurs, you just do it.

> I had no hesitation to do what I had to do. You never think of losing, you only think of winning. You don't think, "If I do this, it might cost my life." That is not what you think about. You think, "You know, I can successfully do this. That's what I am trained to do and it will work. If I do all the things the right way and I pay attention to what I am doing, everything will come out right."

In the same venue, President Ford described the incident from his perspective.

> There were people lined up on the path on either side. I was shaking hands with various people who wanted to say hello and shake hands. As soon as we moved toward the capitol, I noticed a lady, dressed in a very bright red dress, who kept moving slowly with me but didn't put her hand out to shake my hand. And as we got closer and closer to the steps of the state capitol, I went to shake a hand and here was a hand that had a gun in it. Obviously the person was about to pull the trigger.

TAKING A BULLET ...

> It's not the bullet that concerns me. What I would be most fearful of would be, "Did I do everything I could to prevent the bullet being fired, and did I do all I could to protect my client?"

Would you intentionally take a bullet for someone else? Secret Service Agent Timothy McCarthy did, that day in front of the Washington Hilton when he intentionally turned his body in a spread-eagle position between the shooter, John Hinckley, and President Reagan, taking a round in the stomach. Likewise, Agent Nick Zarvos received a round in his throat while protecting presidential candidate George Wallace.

Reference was made in an earlier chapter to the Washington, DC police officer who actually grabbed presidential chief of staff Michael Deaver and ducked down behind him. This in no way was meant to cast aspersions on that officer for acting instinctively. The intent was to demonstrate that what is all in a day's work for some in the fine art of close personal protection (i.e., being willing to take a bullet for someone else) is not everyone's cup of tea.

WHY PROTECTION?

Assault, murder, and exploitation have become the daily fare for Americans living in the most libertarian society in history. Terrorism, hostage takeover, workplace violence, and suicide bombers are the words of the decade. Stalker, serial killer, and sniper are heard increasingly as a frightened world wonders, "Who are these people?" "Who is next?" "What can we do to protect ourselves?" Seemingly every day, stories in the nightly news and daily newspapers tell of some disaffected or disgruntled individual attacking defenseless school children, fellow employees, or an errant motorist on heavily traveled roadways. In a free society, there should be a right to live without fear.

Thirty-five or forty years ago, one did not see armed police and soldiers patrolling airports in Europe (except in Spain, which was operating under the dictatorship of Generalissimo Francisco Franco). Yet now is it not only accepted, it is the model for the rest of the world. As the second year of the twenty-first century passed into history, not only were armed soldiers patrolling our airports, aircraft from NATO member nations were patrolling the skies over America. This was the first (and hopefully the only) time American airspace was overflown by foreign military warplanes. Not one civilian aircraft was in the air over America.

In early September 2006, this writer had an occasion to be at the Los Angeles International Airport. He observed several police officers, in full SWAT combat gear and carrying M-16s, very conspicuously standing guard throughout the airport. There were also several squads of military personnel conducting secondary searches of baggage at the boarding gates.

What are the real hazards and dangers? After the world-changing events of the terrorist skyjacking and bombing of the World Trade Center and the Pentagon in 2001, the threat of terrorism anywhere in the world must be considered to be a very serious danger. If we take the more common and contemporary definition of terrorism to mean being stalked, harassed, robbed, and victimized by criminals and vandals, or if we think terrorism means to be kidnapped and held in life-threatening situations for ransom or elaborate extortion schemes, we must look only at society and this morning's newspaper to see that, yes, there is a high threat of victimization, and there are reasons to be concerned about personal security.

Workplace violence is rapidly becoming the number one cause of injury and death in the work environment. Because of the unusually high number of postal employees who have avenged an actual or perceived grievance with a gun, "going postal" is now a slang term that means settling a dispute or taking revenge in the workplace by violent means. It has also taken on a meaning of just going crazy. A firing, an unsatisfactory personnel action or job evaluation, or even being passed over for a promotion may precipitate workplace violence. Many rampages in work environments have been initiated by a jilted lover who shoots the former paramour, an estranged spouse, or a victim of his unwelcome advances.

STALKING—EROTOMANIA

Working with a psychiatric patient in 1921, French psychiatrist, Dr. Gaeton de Clarembaults identified a condition now called De Clarembaults's syndrome and more commonly known as erotomania. The syndrome is characterized by obsessive romantic interest in a person. A person with the disorder imagines a romantic relationship with a targeted individual even though no such interaction has taken place. An erotomanic person will obsess over the target, sending cards or letters, gifts, and flowers that express romantic interest, and he may even attempt to confront the target directly.[8]

> The term erotomania is usually associated with a stalker who has severe mental problems, including delusions. The perpetrator may actually believe the victim knows and loves him or her. These stalkers expect the target to play the role the stalker has determined, and when threats or intimidation does not work, they may resort to violence.[9]

Instances of erotomania and stalking are becoming commonplace, especially with entertainment and professional sports celebrities. Celebrities have long known the fear, inconvenience, and even danger created by stalkers. Many famous people have become aware of and troubled by pursuers, who, while professing love, have attacked, scarred, maimed, or killed the objects of their attention. Often, a well-meaning but overly enthusiastic fan in the beginning wishes nothing more than to spend time with the object of his adoration. But sometimes the innocent interest degenerates into demands and threats. The thin line between love and hate is very delicate, and the fan who today wishes the celebrity well may cross the line and become tomorrow's deadly threat out of jealousy or having been shunned, ignored, or even embarrassed. Sometimes the stalker has mental problems and sees himself as the savior of the source of his misdirected affections. This stalker will know every intimate detail of his victim's life and will most probably have many photographs of the victim, taken without the victim's knowledge.

Beatle John Lennon was killed outside his home in New York City by a former fan and former mental patient, Mark David Chapman, who had stalked Lennon for days. A Los Angeles case involved well-known and successful movie producer and director Stephen Spielberg, who was stalked and threatened by another man. The stalker professed love for Mr. Spielberg and intended to kidnap him, tie him up, and rape him in front of the producer's family. Fortunately, the stalker was arrested before he could bring harm to Mr. Spielberg or his family. When the stalker was arrested at the producer's residence, after he had climbed over a high security fence, he possessed handcuffs and other paraphernalia to carry out his intentions. The stalker, a body builder, was convicted and is now serving a long term in state prison.

In a classic case of the erotomania syndrome, and a stalking that ended with a deadly encounter, the stalker, Robert Bardo, killed actress Rebecca Schaeffer. In the beginning, Schaeffer answered a fan mail letter from Bardo with "With love," which

Bardo interpreted as a message that Schaeffer actually loved him. Bardo pursued Schaeffer with letters, gifts, and flowers. When she seemingly ignored him, the gifts were returned, and he was denied entrance to the studio where she was working, he felt rebuffed and sulked. Then he decided to take more direct action. Learning Schaeffer's home address (from a private investigator who obtained a copy of her driver's license), Bardo went to her home. When Schaeffer answered the door, he shot and killed her.[10]

PRINCIPLES OF PROTECTION

Whatever the cause, whatever the consequences, there are common denominators— people being victimized and killed. The body count continues to pile up on a daily basis, and the public takes refuge behind the security of their triple-locked metal doors and the authority of a police or security officer's badge.

> The idea of executive protection includes all the principles of protection such as deter- mination of actual and potential vulnerabilities, careful analysis and planning, imple- mentation of a well-conceived security plan, advance security arrangements, violence prevention and response, and total awareness to provide a "safe secure environment."[11]

There is much more to providing a "safe secure environment" than having a shadowy figure watching every move you make or every breath you take. The process includes teamwork between the client and the protectors, analytical processing of informa- tion, ethical conduct, and knowledge and understanding of the human factors.

It is impossible to develop and implement a security plan that will guarantee no threats and client invulnerability. A successful protection plan should employ avail- able resources, implement proper strategies and tactics, and account for contingencies. However, the objective of a security/executive protection plan is not to supply the most detailed, rigid, and complex security scheme; it should be flexible enough to allow the client to engage in necessary activities under the safest possible circumstances.

The theories and reasons for personal protection have remained basically the same since one person took up a stick to protect another. The primary principle of protective services is to protect the principal or protectee from all potential hazards by reducing risks from the following:

1. Intentional injury
2. Unintentional injury
3. Embarrassment
4. Unauthorized release of information, including the principal's schedule

Intentional injury means harm inflicted by those who would commit an overt act to bring great bodily injury, most probably death, to their selected target—the person requiring security. Intentional injury includes using force or violence to render the greatest possible damage, such as assassination, serious injury, or kidnapping.

In addition to the threat of intentional criminal injury, extortion, robbery, and kidnapping, unintentional injury can't be overlooked. An innocent but overly enthusiastic well-wisher may cause an individual to fall, safety regulations may be disregarded, or a preventable accident might occur. Personal protection programs must recognize these threats and address them accordingly.

Protection against unintentional injury is self-evident as preventing injury from accidents, falls, or an overzealous fan or friendly well-wisher. President Ford was notorious for slipping and falling. It is not that he was constantly falling down, but when he did slip, it was caught by national news cameras. Fortunately, in these cases, a Secret Service agent was in close proximity and caught him before he crashed to the ground and injured himself. President Nixon was often so absorbed in his thinking that it was not unusual to see him stand up and turn right into a wall or another person standing behind him. President Clinton slipped and fell on a slippery sidewalk and injured his leg. He was on crutches for two months.

Sometimes an unintentional injury comes from a fan or enthusiastic well-wisher who merely shakes the hand of the politician, VIP, or celebrity too hard. Hazards such as loose carpet, television cables strung across a studio floor, sidewalks slippery from rain or snow, even an unexpected step must be considered and assumed as potential sources of injury. Of course accidents do occur but the potential must be anticipated and minimized. Carpets, cables, and wiring must be checked and taped down; slippery walkways must be sanded or cleaned.

One of the most serious unintentional injuries recorded in our time was the September 1997 accidental death of Princess Diana of Great Britain. In an effort to elude pursuing cameramen, the driver of the princess's limousine and their flash bulb cameras reached speeds approaching 120 mph as he sped through a tunnel with a speed limit of 35 mph!

To protect a person from embarrassment can mean something as simple as utilizing restrooms out of public view. Keeping the protectee from public appearances counter to his beliefs and image can save him from having to give embarrassing explanations. For example, if the protectee is an avid animal rights activist, do not take him (unless he insists) to a sports lounge decorated with big game trophy heads, mounted animals, and skins.

Protecting against unauthorized disclosure of information about the protectee could conceivably keep embarrassing personal information from being compromised. It also prevents strategic or tactical information from falling into the hands of those who would do harm to the protectee. Assisting the protectee in maintaining his schedule is extremely important in eliminating the embarrassment of late arrivals at planned functions. It may deter a planned attack or an attack of opportunity by placing the protectee where there is a feeling of expectancy and heightened anticipation. Furthermore, it eliminates the need to speed or drive recklessly between engagements.

Keeping all communications with and about the protectee confidential (including itinerary and schedule) inspires trust and confidence. A philosophy of "what is seen here, what is heard here, stays here" should not be compromised. To members of a certain organized crime group, the policy is known as *omerta*, a code of silence. Protectees expect total and unquestioned loyalty when it comes to maintaining privacy of information.

Keeping information confidential is a very significant part of the reputation, principles, beliefs, and tradition of the U.S. Secret Service. It might even be considered the "secret" part of the service. In an annual directive to all present and former Secret Service personnel, in December 1997, the then director of the Secret Service, Lewis Merletti, included a reminder of that credo:

> Each of you is keenly aware that a vital element of the success of our protective mission is the ability to develop a working relationship with our protectees. The success in achieving that relationship is largely dependent upon our ability to maintain an environment of mutual trust and confidence. The trust and confidence we currently enjoy result from the selfless, dedicated service of our predecessors.

> Providing information to any source regarding any aspect of the personal lives of our protectees has a negative impact on the Service's relationship with our protectees. An atmosphere of professionalism is crucial to maintain our integrity in the performance of our mission. Our need for confidentiality has long been recognized.

> I am asking each of you to refrain from discussing any information or activity associated with our protectees regardless of its content or significance. We must never compromise our tradition of excellence. I ask that we all remember our commission book oath as "being worthy of trust and confidence." This is a confidence that should continue forever.[12]

Confidence and trust are the highest of all respects that can be bestowed on a person. It is like placing a raw, exposed beating heart into one's hands for them either to crush and breathe bacterium onto it, or to hold it with care and to place it in a sterile and protected environment. As some would say, "I lay my guts before you in confidence and trust." In personal protection, the confidence and trust one places in the protector's hands is the full responsibility of one's safety and one's life—the ultimate responsibility. Being worthy of confidence and trust also means integrity, honesty, trustworthiness, ethical, of good character, morally incorruptible, and so on.

Protection agents, by virtue of their role, are in close contact or proximity to their clients. They most likely come in contact with the clients' friends, families, and associates. They may be at the clients' homes, workplaces, and even social affairs. And yet the sole reason the protection agent is there is to ensure the personal safety of the client. The access necessarily afforded to a protection agent requires the trust and confidence of the client. The position of confidence and trust by definition means not only that the agent is self-assured, honest, and discreet but just as importantly the client is sure of the integrity of the agent and that the agent will not disclose the client's private matters. The protective agent will also respect the protectee's property and privacy. Confidence means keeping everything seen and heard as confidential and private.

A protection specialist is often called on to provide safeguards of information for associates, staff, and family. This may mean a review of procedures, an electronic "countermeasure" sweep and physical search for hidden listening devices and recorders, checking telephone lines for taps, and identifying and proposing other means of safe communication.

PREPARE FOR ANY EVENTUALITY

With technological advances, security is only limited by two factors—imagination and finances. What can be conceived and paid for can be implemented in the total protection package. The simplest yet most important feature of security, however, is common sense and preparedness. That is, to borrow the Boy Scout slogan, "Be prepared." Be prepared for emergencies, anticipate danger, and be aware of threatening situations.

Being prepared for any situation lends an aura of confidence and anticipation to the protective defense. When a potential attacker, whether via a planned assault or an opportunistic attempt, sees a protective shield that is well prepared, confident, and alert, he may be deterred and change his mind about launching the attack.

DETERRENCE

Deterrence is an important ingredient in the protection-security mix. Because of deterrence (or prevention), it can be said of personal protection, "You never know when you are successful, only when you fail." The corollary is that, if your program is well planned and executed and there are no attacks on the principal or his environment, then your assignment has been successfully completed. You will never know what attacks were thwarted. However, if an attack does occur in spite of all precautions, either something was wrong and a weakness was exploited, or the attacker was determined and could not be deterred.

HOW MUCH PROTECTION IS ADEQUATE, AND WHEN DOES ADEQUATE BECOME EXCESSIVE?

An interesting question is, "How much is enough, and how much is too much?" What if the protectee is protected by only one person, security arrangements are only partially carried out, and the protective agent is also the limousine driver, baggage carrier, and total staff person? If nothing happens to place the protectee in danger, and he is not attacked, the conclusion could be that there was sufficient security. On the other hand, what if the protectee is protected by a whole platoon of Special Forces troopers, Navy Seals, an armored tank division, Secret Service trained personnel, and a troop of Boy Scouts? If an attack occurs anyway, can it be reasoned that there was insufficient security? Of course, the proper approach is to attempt to reach a satisfactory balance.

In truth, most security is inadequate. It is inadequate purely because nothing is impenetrable. Paradoxically, protection is excessive if the client finds it onerous, or if it interferes too much with his quality of life. Unfortunately, security can never be truly invisible. Close personal protection straddles a fine line and that line is one drawn first and foremost by the protectee.

An effective protection program is generally successful without the participants even knowing about the success. Such was the case of Arthur Bremmer, who followed President Richard Nixon to Ottawa, Canada, in 1972. He wrote in his diary that he was going to shoot the president but, when he saw the close attention of the Secret Service and the Royal Canadian Mounted Police, he changed his mind because he felt he could not get close enough to complete the plan.

Sometimes, because of deterrence, nothing apparently happens. If the protective detail has done its job, deterrence will be a very effective tool. Failure is measured when an attack is actually attempted, even though the protectee escaped harm. After working six months for a Fortune 500 company, one executive protection specialist providing close personal protection to the company president was told that the position was being eliminated as a cost-saving measure because "nothing ever happened to warrant the protection." Could it have been that nothing happened because of the presence and deterrent factor of professional security?

HARDENING THE TARGET

Deterrence is accomplished through a process known as *hardening the target*. Hardening the target is implemented in many ways. Simply stated, it means making the focus of the potential attacker's interest more difficult to reach. That in effect is what protection programs aim to accomplish. Sometimes it doesn't have to be an elaborate plan of bells, whistles, and sirens but something as uncomplicated as a low-profile approach (e.g., varying a schedule, using alternating routes, and presenting a face of alertness and readiness). But it is also more complex. It is integration and intertwining of several measures, circumstances, people, and technology. In other words, target hardening involves people, procedures, and equipment.

The protectee, his family, staff and management, rank-and-file employees, and the protection specialists are all part of the people equation of hardening the target and deterrence. Procedures in the form of instructions provide direction for those involved in the security process and outline the proper response to any adverse activity or questionable situation. Equipment and technology may be in the form of access controls, physical and psychological barriers, closed-circuit television, lighting systems, intercoms, signs, and intrusion alarm systems—anything that can be imagined and paid for.

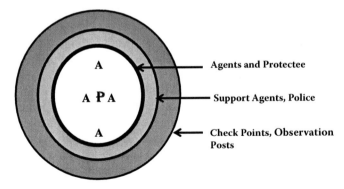

Surrounding the protectee with rings of protection provides a great measure of security within his environment. Personal protection programs center on the person being protected and expand outward in a series of concentric circles. In an ideal situation, one would have at least three rings of protection (similar to a bulls-eye target), but there may be many more than that.

The innermost circle (the bull's-eye) begins with the individual protectee himself. He must be aware that there are criminals who would harm him or his family or compromise his business for real or perceived gain, or that there is a potential and real threat posed by noncriminal means. Sometimes this is as difficult to accomplish as it is to provide the actual protection. Many executives and VIPs refuse to believe someone would even consider harming them. Inside the circle are those persons closest to and most trusted by the individual. This means family, friends, staff, and security personnel working in close proximity to the protectee.

Occasionally, a principal (protectee) will resent the protective shield around him because it hinders his freedom of movement or infringes on his privacy. His attitude may be the cavalier one of "whatever happens, happens," or he may be blinded by the belief, "It could never happen to me." In some extreme situations, the martyr syndrome may be present: "If they are going to get me, they'll get me." Those principals are very difficult to work with, because their cooperation, although necessary, is given only reluctantly. This type of principal is usually a person who has been assigned a protective detail as a result of regulations (such as the children of a president) or a corporate executive who believes he is capable of controlling any situation, even to the point of risking his life.

A Los Angeles executive protection company had the president of a large multinational company as a client, and this person was a stereotypical chief executive officer (CEO) who felt she could handle anything. This mission was, for very good reason, called the assignment from hell.

The CEO had reluctantly accepted protection because an employee of one of the subsidiaries she was going to visit had made statements that were interpreted as threatening. She used loud profanity toward her staff and everyone else who came into contact with her. She was as hardboiled as a Marine drill instructor. Nothing could soothe or please her! For example, the protective detail followed her at a discrete distance early one morning when she took a walk on the streets of a large American city with a friend, a very recognizable television personality. During the walk, she and her friend spotted the protective agents following them. They then began to play games to lose the agents. They would hide behind parked cars, cross the street several times, and walk down alleys, until they finally decided it was time to return to the hotel. Upon returning to her hotel, she was extremely irritated and said that no one told the security detail to follow. She called them imbeciles, kooks, and boobs. She could not be convinced that this action was part of the security responsibility she was paying for or that they were there to intercede if an opportunistic street thug accosted her—or in the unlikely event that she suffered a medical emergency such as a heart attack. Furthermore, being with an extremely recognizable and famous person, she was even more vulnerable, because her companion attracted attention walking on a very public street.

In spite of her antics, she was afforded the very best protection possible, and she eventually left town without incident. It was a great relief to the men when she dismissed them and said that she didn't think she would need the protective detail any longer.

Generally, a person receiving the protection is very gracious and cooperative, asking for and following advice. He recognizes the necessity for the security and that it is for his own benefit. He is the center of attention in his interior ring, with only a few trusted individuals including staff, family, and the close proximity security experts. The sole responsibility of the inner ring of security is to protect the principal.

The second ring is the ring of protection afforded by the personnel working on all sides of the protectee. They provide coverage, usually within arm's reach. Whatever direction the protectee turns, there is someone between him and an attacker or even a friendly well-wisher. This ring is constantly looking for known threats, suspicious persons, furtive movements that may signal an attack, weapons, or something that just doesn't fit.

The third and forth circles of the protection program are composed of security personnel or uniformed police officers who have responsibility for access control and surveillance points. They staff the inner and outer perimeters of the principal's location, maintaining vigilance and allowing only authorized personnel to enter. The outer rings can also include checkpoints, staff personnel, and even representatives of the press who might spot and recognize a threatening situation.

Another ring is environmental. The use of psychological and physical barriers can be an effective deterrent. These include alarm systems (including closed-circuit television), strong doors, locks, hedges, fences, and restricted areas, and even the strategic placement of certain members of the audience or crowd. For example, placing school children near and in front of the speaker's platform will prevent a person from getting too close to the protectee. The staff advance person will also like the arrangement, because it looks good for the news cameras.

Finally, the last circle incorporates knowledge and assessment. This means being aware of every potential threat and having the ability to identify, analyze, and anticipate situations that would be detrimental to the person being protected. It also means being aware of alternatives and secondary measures that, if necessary, could be instantaneously activated to enhance the protective endeavor.

WHO ARE THE PRINCIPALS OR PROTECTEES?

Anyone can be a protectee and use the services of a protection specialist. Most generally, it is a political figure, member of royalty, or a celebrity such as a movie or television star. It can be a highly visible captain of industry. It can be a foreign tourist shopping and sightseeing. It can be a wife who is a victim of domestic violence, or even a federally protected witness. In other words, it can be anyone utilizing the services of a professional trained in the complexities of keeping another person or entity safe from embarrassment, injury, or death.

Sometimes a protectee will use close personal protection as a status symbol. There may be no particular threat or even no threat at all, as in the instance of the production company president who employed Bobby Jim the Bodyguard. But the ancillary services performed by the security personnel, such as advance work, logistics, and problem solving, give the protectee a feeling of exaggerated importance, especially in his circle of business contacts.

SUMMARY

Executive or close personal protection is more than a buzzword. It is a common-sense approach to protecting a certain individual or group, incorporating awareness, personnel, procedures, and sophisticated systems. The protection specialist is responsible for the security, safety, health and well-being of the principal. Planning, preparation, and anticipation are the keys to minimizing risk. More simply stated, close personal protection is more than standing and waiting for danger; it is a planned program of awareness and prevention to safeguard a potential victim.

Close personal protection is not a job of confrontation but rather a planned response to an unavoidable situation. The objective is to deter an attack or avoid a confrontation rather than expose a protectee to danger. Attacks happen with suddenness, surprise, and violence. The goal of close personal protection is to remove one's principal from harm's way. This can usually be accomplished by giving close attention to risk assessment (anticipation and evaluation) and advance work (planning and preparation).

The role of close personal protection in the overall security plan is to provide a "safe secure environment" to those persons, places, or things requiring close personal protection. It can be likened to the ultimate weapon against those who would bring harm to people who cannot defend themselves.

REVIEW QUESTIONS

1. Draw parallels between home security in the Middle Ages and contemporary times.
2. Describe the differences between bodyguard, executive protection specialist, and close personal protection agent.
3. What mistakes did Bobby Jim the Bodyguard make, and how could they have been harmful to his protectee?
4. Define close personal protection. What are its purpose and intent?
5. Explain the concept of the protectee environment.
6. Describe a survey report. How is it used in planning a protection program?
7. Define workplace violence.
8. What harm do stalkers pose?
9. Discuss the primary theory of protective services. Who is to be protected, and what is he to be protected from? Explain.
10. How does the Boy Scout slogan, "be prepared," relate to executive protection?
11. Explain the importance of deterrence.
12. What is hardening the target? Give examples.
13. Explain the theory of concentric circles. What constitutes each ring?
14. What does the term close proximity mean?
15. Who are the recipients of close personal protection?

NOTES

1. *Webster's Universal Dictionary and Thesaurus*. Montreal, Quebec: Tormont Publications, 1993.
2. http://www.pbs.org/wnet/warriorchallenge/knights/profile_job.html.
3. "The strength of the shield; the sensitivity of the rose."
4. http://www.pbs.org/wnet/warriorchallenge/knights/profile_job.html.
5. Ibid.
6. Neal, Harry Edward. *The Story of The Secret Service*. New York: Grosset & Dunlap, 1971.
7. American Institute of Executive Protection, Condensed History of Close Protection, . . .
8. http://www.angelfire.com/extreme/lawenforcement/execprotection/hx.html.
8. Hill, Anita. *Speaking Truth to Power*. New York: Doubleday, 1997.
9. Gosselin, Denise Kindschi. *Hard Hands; An Introduction to the Crimes of Family Violence*. Upper Saddle River, NJ: Pearson-Prentice Hall, 2005.
10. Landau, Elaine. *Stalking*. New York: Franklin Watts, 1996.
11. June, Dale L. *Protection, Security and Safeguards*. Boca Raton, FL: CRC Press, 2000, 54.
12. Merletti, Lewis, director, U.S. Secret Service, 1997.

6 Preparing for the Big Dance
The Advance

I will prepare myself and when opportunity comes, I'll be ready.

A. Lincoln

Question: What does an advance man need to know?
Answer: Everything!

Mirror, mirror on the wall, please tell me who is the most prepared of all.

THE ADVANCE

Do you think you would attend a formal function—the dance of the year, the one big event you have had in your mind for the last year, anticipating the event and planning every little detail—without proper preparation? You would be sure to know the correct day and time, secure tickets, and determine the location of the event and how to get there. You would have your tuxedo pressed and waiting, and you would perform your personal hygiene rituals. In other words, you would anticipate the event, make your plans, and have everything in readiness.

You have an appointment tomorrow with a very important client at 2:00 P.M., at an address in an unfamiliar part of town. You are not exactly sure of the directions, where you will leave your car, or how to find the exact office. You can wait until the next day, guessing how much time it will take to drive there, find a parking place, and wander around in the building until you find the office, probably stressing the whole time. But it would be much better to know exactly how much time is needed to drive to the appointment, the routes of travel, where to park the car, the exact location of the appointed office, and who will meet you there. With those concerns resolved, the stress level is greatly reduced and the focus can be on the business at hand. That is the same situation an executive, VIP, celebrity, or tourist often finds himself in as he travels. A highly placed business executive, a notable politician, a celebrity, and even a tourist all have one thing in common—an increased vulnerability to harm from stalkers, disgruntled workers, criminals, even well-meaning but overly enthusiastic fans. At home or work, they are more relaxed and stress free, as their vulnerability can be reduced to an acceptable level through psychological and physical barriers such as alarm systems, closed circuit television, manned checkpoints, walls, fences, and central access systems.

For some bizarre reason, it is not unusual to encounter a traveling businessman or visiting tourist who believes he is immune to local crime. He will visit nightclubs and wander (sometimes partially or fully under the influence of alcohol) in parts of the city that he would never ever consider visiting in his own. The hotel may be a very exclusive enclave in a high-crime rate area, yet the unaware traveler may believe he can safely walk the streets alone at 2:00 A.M. Or he may believe he can simply give a taxi driver an address, and the driver will take him there via the shortest and safest route.

The most dangerous time in a person's life is when he is traveling, whether across town, across the nation, or around the world. In unknown territory, the chance of victimization increases, calling for extra precautions and advance preparation. Aside from the primary concerns of his business (or vacation) routine, he must also be concerned about the normal problems of personal security, travel arrangements, logistics and whatever troublesome problems might arise. With his mind preoccupied with business purposes, he cannot afford the time or effort to be concerned about irksome things that are better left to someone more expert in those particular fields.

The single most important, yet difficult and complex, aspect of close personal protection is preparing for everything. Predetermining the necessary information and making appropriate arrangements ahead of the scheduled appointment is a process known as "advancing the location." Solid advance work is required to prepare for effective and successful protection of a person or place in anticipation of anything that man or nature can create. A summary of the things an advance agent must do and know would be reflected in three primary categories—anticipation, planning, and preparation:

ANTICIPATE ...

1. Anything that could, would, or might happen to endanger the safety of the person, place, or thing being protected
2. Everything you can do to prevent something happening to endanger the person, place, or thing being protected
3. Anyone who might target the person, place, or thing and cause harm

PLAN ...

1. The itinerary of the person to be protected
2. The method and means of providing the protection
3. Alternative plans
4. Emergency contingencies
5. The logistics and special instructions for all participants in the protective assignment
6. Everything!

PREPARE ...

Visit each site and learn all there is to know about the location—all of the people, the timings, the entrances and exits, heating and air conditioning ducts, electrical maintenance, facilities, emergency response, parking, the weather, location of the sun... everything!

WHAT IS AN ADVANCE?

Advance security work will prevent accidental injury, embarrassment, planned assault and harassment by friendly or hostile persons and assist the VIP in maintaining his schedule. Advance planning is preparation. The keyword is anticipation. Anticipate, plan, and prepare.

Remember an attacker may be well prepared and attacks well planned. Attackers have an unfair advantage; they select the time, place and method of an attack. A sound security advance will deter all but the most determined attacker and reduce the vulnerability of the traveler to a more favorable level.

A well-planned security response and effective countermeasures may mean the difference between life and death. The plan may save the life of the security personnel as well as the protectee because, as statistics have borne out, in over 90 percent of cases in which an attack has resulted in death of the protectee, the security personnel have also been killed! Sometimes the protective personnel can be killed or injured in an accident. That was evident in the Princess Diana crash.

The time to stop an attack is before it happens. The only way to do that is through prevention. Prevention is the result of planning, anticipation, and preparation. That means carefully planning the traveler's movements, anticipating all possible adverse events that could occur, and taking steps to counter them. When an attack occurs, it is too late to take preventive measures. If a tough guy suddenly jumps directly in front of you and demands, "Gimme all your mother (physical act) loving money," and he has a gun in his hand—or if a group of terrorists with Uzies begin to spray the area with 9 mm rounds—the only thought is survival and a wish that better anticipation, planning, and prevention had been provided.

In other words, high-level protection requires a through analysis of the potential problems, liaison with appropriate hosts or agencies, and a definitive mobile protective cocoon provided by a capable, skilled advance man. An advance is a method of incorporating all the necessary ingredients for making a protectee's environment as secure as possible. This procedure includes knowing the principal's itinerary, logistics, and venues; the people he will meet, interface, and travel with; and so on. In essence, it is understanding and anticipating everything in advance.

The *staff advance person* concept became popular with politicians, celebrities, and VIPs during the 1960 presidential campaign of John F. Kennedy. The Secret Service and other professional security agencies pioneered the security advance long before, but it was adopted during the Kennedy campaign as a staff advance practice and was proven to be a highly effective tool and efficient method of preparing a location for the arrival of the principal. Today, most professional security organizations and government agencies use an *advance person* to prepare the way for individuals considered to be at risk, and many VIPs, celebrities, and politicians engage a *staff representative* to conduct a nonsecurity-related advance. In the private sector, it has become commonplace (but not recommended or ideal) for the security advance person to also be responsible for the nonsecurity-related advance.

As the term advance person implies, the advance is conducted by someone who travels ahead of the VIP. An advance consists of carefully making a personal inspection of all areas a principal will visit and determining what facilities are available, finding potential problem areas, understanding restrictions, checking secured and unsecured areas, and meeting with personnel involved (e.g., the host committee).

A good advance man is the person to whom the traveling dignitary and accompanying protective personal, staff, even family members turn for answers. He takes care of all travel arrangements, from hotel reservations to special dinner menus. But he also needs to incorporate these nettling nonsecurity needs with good security preparation.

Advance security planning can make the difference between a properly organized and enjoyable trip and a trip disrupted by pressing crowds and hecklers. It also can prevent a serious criminal attack. Good advance preparation relieves the traveler of problems and results in a sound security plan. An advance man should always ask the question, what if? If the right what-if questions can be anticipated, asked, and answered, the result can be a satisfactory, successful, and safe trip. Conducting and completing an advance calls for common sense and imagination.

WHAT IS COMMON SENSE?—USING YOUR BRAIN

1. Ordinary—usual
2. Practical—workable, suitable
3. Good sense—intelligible
4. Good judgment—reasonable decisions, discretion

"Common sense isn't so common" is an old yet apparently true saying. Often, it seems, people become so wrapped up in ambiguity, standardization, bureaucratic hyperbole, and/or legal jargon that they lose sight of the real purpose of their mission and complicate matters simply by failing to consider logical and practical concerns. Instead, they may fall into the trap of "that's how we have always done things" or make decisions based on political correctness. An advance agent must marshal all his common sense and imagination to find the most expedient and workable means and methods of performing his tasks so the principal can move about freely without glitches, confusion, or misdirection.

WHAT IS IMAGINATION?

1. Creative ability
2. Ideas!
3. Resourcefulness
4. Analytical thought
5. Ensuring that you account for all significant consequences
6. Utilizing reasoning, logic, experience, and training
7. The ability to ask and answer what-if questions

Imagination, imagination, and more imagination: if it can be imagined and paid for, nothing is impossible, especially with regard to security. An advance protective agent must continually ask what if? The process becomes a mind game of creating scenarios and inventing counters to each one. Nothing is too far-fetched or improbable—some antagonist will likely think of the same scenario and take overt action to fulfill it.

If it can be imagined via what-if reasoning, the protective advance agent must take the next step and anticipate that it possibly, if not probably, will occur. In this anticipation, the advance agent must take every step to neutralize the vulnerability of his protective charge. In a larger sense, that is exactly the focus of the advance agent's job of anticipation, planning, and preparation. Anticipate everything, plan for anything, and prepare for all things. To paraphrase Murphy's law, "If anything can go wrong (or happen), it will go wrong (or happen)."

Going into battle, a general must have three plans: the strategic (long-range planning), the tactical (for immediate use), and an alternative (in the event circumstances change, warranting a fallback or failsafe maneuver). A protective agent assumes the role of the "general" in formulating the tactical, strategic, and alternative plans for the safe movement of his principal.

The *battlefield* (the venues of the events the principal will attend) must be thoroughly reconnoitered to ensure a complete knowledge of the landscape with its advantages and pitfalls. With this knowledge, the battle plan (defense) is crafted. Offensive, defensive, and fallback options are considered until an effective plan is in place. The potential movements and positioning of the enemy are anticipated with counterplanning, subterfuge, and preparation. Yet the plan must be flexible enough to accommodate the wishes and demands of the principal.

Unless the principal is a stay-at-home type or a shut in, he will want to maintain business as usual in terms of exposure to the public, adoring fans, and/or employees. This is the sand in the gas tank of good security. The advance agent must provide a workable security plan while considering the wishes and itinerary of the person being protected. The advance agent must plan and do everything within his range of authority and responsibility, but he must also maintain a flexible posture to accommodate the good relations among the principal, staff, hosts, and public.

Experience has shown that a belligerent, "I am the expert" attitude on the part of the protective agent will result in minimal cooperation from those whose support and cooperation is most critical. To maintain good working relations, an advance agent must practice diplomacy, tact, and sometimes gentle persuasion to be accommodating while providing the best security allowable under circumstances that are not entirely under his control.

ANTICIPATE, PLAN, AND PREPARE

ANTICIPATION

Surprise, surprise, surprise! No one involved in the risky business of providing protective services for an individual, agency, or corporate entity likes even small surprises. Every conceivable scenario must be visualized, every nook and cranny searched, and every locked door opened to reveal the other side (and then relocked). A door may have a sign that reads, Danger! High Voltage! Do Not Enter! Even so, it must be opened and inspected for safety violations, possible sabotage, or someone hiding inside. Every countermeasure must be employed, and every person must be checked, verified and vouched for. Anticipation is the art of (seemingly) supersensory detection of detrimental occurrences before they happen and taking restrictive action.

An advance person should anticipate the whims and wishes of the protectee and make available information regarding local activities and facilities, including the theater (availability of tickets and performance times) and local points of interest, and even provide scrapes and snippets of local color and history. Anticipate everything and plan for it.

PLANNING

An advance man must plan for any eventuality! This means anticipating everything that could happen and plotting a course of action to respond. For a simple example, all carpeting and cables must be soundly taped down. Walkways must be inspected for cracks and loose stones that could cause the VIP to stumble or fall. In the extreme case, a protectee may be attacked or suffer a medical emergency. When the advance is completed, the advance man will have set security post positions and security personnel assignments, determined locations and routes (including the walking path of the principal), and put everything in place. At this point, he must conduct a mental dress rehearsal. He should physically and mentally give the entire operation a complete walk-through, looking for every possible element that could go wrong. He looks for places a sniper could lie in wait. He looks for weaknesses in crowd control. He times and measures every step the principal will take. He even obtains weather forecasts and railroad train crossing times. He may even consider the position of the sun and how its angles could affect the positioning of the VIP and security posts. The VIP and his security personnel would be handicapped and perhaps ineffective if their vision were affected by brilliant sunlight.

PREPARATION

Once the advance man decides that everything is in place and nothing can go wrong, he should assume that something will go wrong. He must try to find that something and prevent it. He must go over the entire sequence and locations, again and again if time allows, putting himself in several roles and seeing the picture from the viewpoints of everyone else involved. He should even assume the mind-set of an attacker to anticipate the means and methods of an attack.

CONDUCTING A PROTECTIVE ADVANCE

The initial advance begins with obtaining the VIP's itinerary. The schedule should be carefully reviewed to determine whether sufficient information has been furnished to make complete advance arrangements. It should include places to be visited, dates and time of travel, length of visit, time of arrival and departure, methods of transportation, reasons for travel (business or pleasure), names, addresses, and telephone numbers of local contacts or officials sponsoring the visit, and what publicity or media coverage is expected.

If the information is incomplete, as it often is, the person doing the advance must obtain the missing data. Frequently, some of the desired information can be obtained only while conducting the advance. And most often, much the information is subject to change, sometimes at the last minute. If the protectee has been in that location before, it is good policy to review previous advance reports. A good security plan revises, builds on, and updates plans created by other security teams. As good as a plan appears, it can always be improved upon because, referring back to Murphy's law, "anything that can go wrong, will."

If travel is by commercial aircraft, arrangements should be made with the airline so check-in procedures, including boarding passes and security screening, can be completed without bringing the VIP into contact with regular passengers. The airline customer service representative can allow the VIP to proceed directly from his vehicle to the boarding area and possibly be preboarded, or otherwise taken to a VIP lounge and boarded after the other passengers. The latter is usually preferable, but in either case, the VIP's seat must be selected and reserved in advance.

When choosing a seat, as in all arrangements, the VIP's wishes must be considered. But security concerns come first. For good security, seat the VIP by the window, with family, accompanying security personnel, and other staff surrounding him. This maintains a circle, or buffer, of security. If sufficient manpower is available, security personnel might be seated at different locations throughout the plane (perhaps in the midsection and back in the very last aisle seat) where they can readily see anything unusual. Their responsibility is to monitor other passengers and to take preemptive action should a threatening situation develop. In terrorist skyjacking incidents, it has been observed that some terrorists may not reveal themselves at the onset of the event. Consequently agents not assigned to close proximity with the protectee should take their seats as though they were just average travelers, maintain a very low profile, and avoid drawing attention to the fact they are security personnel.

The VIP's luggage should be taken to the airport and checked in and cleared with security, and any special requests or instructions should be discussed with the airline representative prior to the VIP's arrival at the airport. The advance man should also be contact airport security, especially if those accompanying the VIP are armed. There are usually special procedures to be met and forms to complete if any personnel are armed. It is the advance man's responsibility to ascertain the correct procedures well in advance of departure. All airports have standard procedures, but procedures may vary among different airports and airlines. One can avoid enormous embarrassment and potential trouble by clearing all regulations before arrival at the airport. Airport security can also assist in streamlining the procedures at the screening point. If the VIP is a popular or controversial person, security might escort him to the boarding area or recommend a more private route to the aircraft.

Upon arrival at the VIP's destination, the advance man should make arrangements for ground transportation and baggage pickup, allowing the VIP to proceed directly to a waiting vehicle for a quick exit. Again, airline representatives and airport security can provide significant assistance. It is best to designate a protection agent for the task of baggage retrieval and transport.

The next item on the advance man's agenda should be lodging. If the VIP is staying at a hotel, he should be checked in before arrival. The advance man should possess the room key so the executive can proceed directly to his room, bypassing the lobby area. Hotel security should be notified, and escape routes and fire extinguishers should be located. Emergency telephone numbers, including fire, police, and ambulance, should be obtained. In addition, any special instructions concerning housekeeping (e.g., when the maid or bellman enters the room) should be discussed with the proper hotel representative.

When staying at a private residence, the advance man should determine the means of ingress and egress between the neighborhood and the residence, noting any alternative entry and exit routes. Parking spaces should be located that will least disrupt or otherwise affect the neighborhood. Any local ordinances relative to street parking should be predetermined. For instance, some communities allow street parking only to residents with special permits, between 5:00 P.M. and 5:00 A.M. and on weekends. Or perhaps parking is allowed only on alternate days or at special times of day. Some cities ban overnight parking on the street to facilitate street cleaning or snow removal. Whatever the unique parking regulation, one must comply with it or obtain a special dispensation.

Whether patronizing a restaurant, traveling to the location of a speech or presentation, or even visiting a private residence, the planning procedure remains the same. Select the most direct but safest routes (noting any potential hazards). Locate, select, and reserve parking facilities. Locate the best entrance and exit (including emergency and alternate exits) to the building. Contact representatives of the site to be visited or the host committee. Determine the name of the person or persons who will meet and greet the protectee. Select good surveillance and access control posts, establishing manpower requirements and procedures and formulating *post orders* for the agents assigned to the security posts. Establish liaison and formulate any special planning with the police, fire department, and paramedics.

Do not place the protectee in front of or near windows. An assassin could easily employ a sniper rifle to shoot through the window or throw a bomb from the street. The protectee should be seated where he is sheltered from outside view and protected if a bomb is thrown through a window. If the room has clear windows, they should be covered with nontransparent curtains or blinds.

An advance man most often has to arrange ground transportation for the protectee. It is always best to have one of your own as the limo driver. He knows the principal, is familiar with the staff and family, and is trained in the principles of protection in addition to being an experienced driver. He is also less likely to be intimidated by, or in awe of, the protectee's status or celebrity.

In the event one of your own is not available, the next best option is to hire a local protection specialist or an off-duty policeman (see chapters 10 and 13). The advantage is that a local person knows the city, streets, social scene or atmosphere, restaurants, and so on. He also can help in obtaining protective intelligence via his contacts.

The least favored (but most frequently used) method of obtaining a car and driver is to hire a local limousine service. The upside is that the driver will know the city and area and may have local contacts such as ticket vendors, restaurants, dry cleaners, or whatever.

The downside, however, far outweighs the upside. The driver will not be familiar with the concepts of security, and he may feel that his priorities are more important than security concerns. He may be overly impressed with his position and use his influence to impress others. He may discuss his job with people who have no need to know the principal's identity, schedule, or itinerary. He also may not be trusted to keep confidential information to himself. And, of course, the person may be a security risk. He may have a drinking problem. He may be psychotic. He may not be worthy of confidence and trust. When working with a driver who is not security trained and experienced, do not discuss any personal or business matters within his hearing. Keep all conversations with him strictly business or inconsequential.

To engage a local for-hire limousine and driver, choose a service at random. Have an official of the company provide the name of the driver, his date and place of birth, his social security number, and his driver's license number. It is also advisable to inspect the car and obtain the vehicle identification number as well as the license plate number. When the driver reports in, examine his documents (driver's license and social security card) and compare for his assignment information with that obtained from the company. Also make sure the vehicle is the same one that was previously inspected. If anyone other than the expected driver reports for duty, either dismiss him and obtain another driver (same procedure) or call the limousine service and determine the same information about the new driver and compare it with his documents. Do not call the company with a telephone number provided by the new driver. Use a number you personally obtained.

When using a hired driver and limousine, conduct at least a visual search of the vehicle, looking for recording devices as well as explosives each time the car and driver have been away from the assignment (e.g., overnight).

The advance man should, if the dignitary's public profile dictates, contact the local police authorities to find out if they have any information about threats, planned demonstrations, or any person or group that could pose a danger. Also, the police can assist in route planning and traffic and crowd control if necessary. Sometimes police assistance is not required, but it is usually good policy to advise the police that a certain dignitary or executive will be in their jurisdiction.

Local hospitals should be located and the best routes and transportation to them determined. In most instances (except with the president and vice president, in which case it is mandatory), it is a discretionary decision as to whether to make prior contact with hospital authorities. It is sometimes desirable to ascertain what facilities are available at the hospital. Information (names, addresses, and map coordinates) about hospitals closest to a visited site should be included in the advance survey report. Many advance men include the address of medical treatment centers and directions to them on the same page as the site address.

The next area to be addressed is liaison with the host organization or local contact person. The advance person should work very closely with the host committee. There is usually one primary individual who either controls the event details or has considerable influence in directing the nonsecurity arrangements. The host committee presents the program; it is the responsibility of the security advance man to work within those parameters to ensure the principal's security while maintaining the wholeness and intent of the event. Changes in the program will be suggested by the advance man only when the principal's security may be compromised by the proposed events or some aspect of the affair may have an influence on security arrangements. A schedule of events and the names of participants, special guests, committee members, and officials involved in the program should be obtained. The host committee and assisting staff should be interviewed regarding any foreseen problems. They should also be advised that if they hear even unconfirmed rumors about potential problems or threats, these should be reported to the advance man immediately.

The advance man should not overlook facilities for the personal comfort and convenience of the VIP. These include food, water, refreshments, rest, lavatory, and telephone. Arrangements should be made for a holding room for the principal. This is a room, usually located somewhere between the motorcade arrival point and the point where the principal makes his appearance. It can be considered a convenience room for final preparation before the public appearance. The room should be in a secured area, with its integrity intact. If the principal arrives early, he will wait in this room until the appointed presentation. In some instances, the room may be equipped with a closed-circuit television monitor showing the events in the venue where the protectee will be appearing. The holding room is usually a highly appropriate place for the principal to receive a final briefing relating to the event and to meet and greet those responsible for it.

The job of the advance man is never complete, and he has no time to rest until the visit is over, the VIP has safely gone to his next stop, and the *after-action* or final survey report is prepared.

SITUATION REPORTS

Technology and communications have forever changed the means and methods of transferring information. With the latest developments in telephone and digital camera technology, it is now possible for an advance agent to produce nearly up-to-the-second situation reports to a protective detail long before they arrive on the scene. The protective agents working with the principal can actually see and become familiarized with the arrival point and other pertinent locations so that, on their arrival, there is immediate recognition of the site.

The advance agent can use his camera phone and computer to produce unlimited photographs to supplement the information he has produced in his advance report. Simply making a walk-through, the advance agent clicks off images of the location, downloads them to his computer, and almost instantly sends them to the detail.

DIAGRAMS, MAPS, PHOTOS—THEIR ROLE IN THE SECURITY PROCESS

Maps and diagrams are very important to the overall effectiveness and coordination of the advance and can be transmitted in the same manner as the photographs. Maps depict the location of all sites, the routes to and from them, and the locations of ancillary facilities with which the protective detail may need familiarity, such as police stations, hospitals, auditoriums, churches, and others.

ROLE OF PROTECTIVE INTELLIGENCE IN AN ADVANCE

Protective intelligence is being aware of and understanding people and situations that could have an impact on the health and safety of the principal. Upon arrival at a distant city, one of the first things an advance agent must do is learn the latest news and weather. While he is writing his reports or working on the plan for the trip, the advance agent should have the television or radio tuned to a local news channel. He can learn the character of the city and traffic problem areas and listen to weather forecasts. He will become aware of local issues, planned demonstrations, the political climate, and other information that could affect his security plan.

The advance agent must be aware of situations such as a crime being committed in the areas the principal will visit. A dangerous situation (e.g., an armed robbery, a drive-by shooting, or a hostage taking) having nothing to do with the movements of the principal may occur just as the principal is about to arrive or depart a location. Situations such as these must be anticipated, considered, and planned for. The advance agent must know if there are construction projects or civil utility malfunctions that could in some way impede or affect the safe movement of his principal.

Threat intelligence comes from many different sources. When arriving in a new city, the first sources of information are the local daily newspaper, radio, and television. The local news will usually describe problems the VIP may encounter, such as demonstrations (friendly, unfriendly, or having nothing to do with him). But other factors could have an adverse effect, such as planned road closings and construction, parades, sporting events, and so forth. The news will also provide information about local trouble spots, high crime rate areas, local celebrities and celebrations, controversial issues, and social problems.

If the principal is a high-profile or controversial person, someone may have expressed dissatisfaction with him and may wish to harm him. The advance agent must attempt to determine if this is the case and take preemptive cautions. In essence, protective intelligence means knowing all there is to know about people, circumstances, and situations that will impact safe movement of the principal.

ROLE OF TECHNICAL SURVEILLANCE COUNTERMEASURES IN AN ADVANCE

Technical countermeasures and sweeps for listening and transmitting devices must be done in all areas where the principal will expect privacy. This means the residence, hotel suite, conference rooms, holding rooms, and so on. After the countermeasures are complete, the advance agent must assign someone to maintain security over the area. If manpower is limited and it is not possible to place a person at every secured area, sprinkle talcum powder on the floor in out-of-the-way places to detect the footprints of any intruder.

PSYCHOLOGICAL PERSPECTIVES OF AN ADVANCE

Beyond the usual preparation of venue analysis, planning, and implementation, the "warfare" of protection vs. accident, assault, and assassination depends very much on the psychological aspects of prevention. Psychologically, a \$4.00 lock on a \$1 million mansion will be deterrent enough to at least keep out honest people. The same concept relates to a properly conducted security advance. If everything that can be anticipated and done is anticipated and done, the psychological edge belongs to the protective agent as he brings the odds of a successful assignment more into his favor.

A well-executed advance brings other psychological advantages to the protective agent. He can tune his attention to his protective duties with full confidence that he has addressed every imaginable aspect critical to his mission. Conversely, his opposite counterpart, intent on harming the principal, will be psychologically deflated, if not defeated or deterred, when he recognizes the totality of preparedness against his dreadful deeds.

Psychologically, the principal will also recognize the advantages of well-developed advance preparation. He will feel he is in the care of a protective agent who is knowledgeable, caring, and professional. He will observe the well-planned organization and the smoothness of the entire operation, all leading to confidence in his protective agent(s).

WRITING AN ADVANCE SECURITY SURVEY REPORT

PURPOSE

The purpose of an advance survey report is to make a record of the advance, provide details of the assignment to protective personnel, provide a medium for formulating assignments and special instructions, and resolving anticipated problems. The more information that is detailed, the better the odds are for deterring any adverse activity.

After security preparations are complete, a limited survey report detailing itinerary, telephone numbers, special instructions, and hotel room assignments for the protectee should be forwarded to the VIP and his administrative office. Those outside the protective channels should not receive a copy of the security advance report, but it is suggested that the principal or his staff receive a "sterilized" version pertaining to the event along with protectee instructions and logistics. The survey should be as explicit as possible in detailing special instructions or information such as including the names and telephone numbers of the people the protectee is to meet. The survey report for the VIP's office does not require, nor should it include, information pertaining to security preparations and protective agent instructions.

Very often, other security personnel will not arrive at a location until the protectee arrives, or immediately before. An advance report (accompanied with photos, maps, diagrams, and so forth) provides an immediate local orientation, giving instructions to the agents and informing them of what to expect. A survey report details points of contact and provides general information relevant to involved personnel. The document should be treated as confidential material and given out on a need-to-know basis only.

In making a record of the advance, there will be a permanent account of security preparations in the event a hostile or adverse action occurs. The survey also becomes a source of information for future advances and trips to the same location.

FORMAT

The format of the survey varies from agency to agency but the form and substance is generally similar to the following:

Type of advance. This advance survey report is made by Agent Blank for the visit of Mr. Principal and his wife and family to a named site on specific dates. It was conducted on the dates beginning when the advance commenced and when it was completed.

Itinerary. The proposed and scheduled times of the Principal's movements includes arrival and departure dates and times, name of person who will meet and greet the protectee, the mode of travel (car, commercial or charter flight, limousine provided and driven by whom, and so on). The itinerary can cover several days and locations.

Logistics. How and when personnel, equipment, and other items are moved to each location, and reporting times. This section may also include provisions for meals and lodging and any special transportation needs.

Routes. Provides exact time and distance between locations and directions for the motorcade. In effect, it is a narrative map. It makes note of any expected detours, anticipated traffic conditions, drawbridges and railroad crossings, and anything unusual the motorcade will likely encounter. Maps may be attached to the report.

Special instructions. Provides information and anything relevant to the safe conduct of the principal. This section may also provide information necessary for the protective personnel, such as radio frequencies, location of special equipment (e.g., fire extinguishers, bomb disposal), special eating provisions, breaks, and so forth.

Post assignments. Assignments of protective personnel by name and location. Included in post assignments is the operation and location of the command post that will control the operation and be the logistical center for all communications and equipment.

Telephone numbers. This section provides the names and telephone numbers, including pager and fax numbers, of contacts and emergency numbers. It is especially important to include police, fire, and paramedic information.

Identification. Provides samples and description of any special identification methods (lapel pins, badges, tags, logos) worn by personnel who need to enter the secured areas or must have close access to the principal.

Intelligence. Any information regarding threats, potential danger points, descriptions (and photos, if available) of persons who may pose a problem, and risk assessment. This section may also provide special instructions of who to contact or ways of dealing with the perceived and anticipated problem.

Emergency facilities. Emergency medical facilities and hospitals, including names, locations (street addresses and map coordinates), emergency and administration telephone numbers, and person(s) to contact.

OTHER DUTIES OF AN ADVANCE MAN

A good advance man will address considerations beyond good security. There is no question that he will be asked a million questions by the principal, his family and staff, other security personnel, the police, even host committee members. He must have the answers to any and all questions that arise.

He should prepare a large city map pinpointing all locations the VIP will visit. Sometimes a protectee will ask for a map for his personal orientation to the city, especially if he is a foreign visitor. Also marked on the map should be the locations of shopping centers, with specialty stores, entertainment and sport venues, and sight-seeing attractions.

The advance agent should familiarize himself with the culture and any special needs of the VIP, such as medicine, newspapers, special meals, and so on. If the VIP is Jewish, it is advisable to locate restaurants that serve kosher food. If the VIP is Muslim, locate restaurants or caterers who serve halal meals (meats that are blessed before slaughter).

The role of the advance man is perhaps the most critical of the entire protective team. He is responsible for the planning and conduct of the protective function. He must anticipate every conceivable attack scenario and take measures to prevent it.

He must anticipate every desire of the protectee and have a solution immediately at hand. The advance man is also responsible to the rest of the protective team for any questions they may have. He is the person who acts as liaison between staff, host committee, and ancillary support such as police, fire, paramedics, and others. A good advance man needs to know everything and be everything to everyone!

WHAT IF IT IS NOT POSSIBLE TO HAVE AN ADVANCE MAN?

In the private sector, it is not always possible to have a full support staff. Sometimes the executive protection specialist has to operate alone. He becomes the driver, close proximity security, and advance man. To operate in this manner is not only difficult, it is tempting the gods of the principles of protection.

In a special assignment, an executive protection agent was cast in all three roles for the former defense minister and one of the founding fathers of Israel, Abba Eban (now deceased) and his wife. Eban was an 85-year-old, average-appearing individual who could walk among the masses (outside of Israel) and go unrecognized. In fact, his name, outside of certain circles of people who remember all this great person accomplished in his lifetime, is not even well known. To put his accomplishments into perspective, if Thomas Jefferson were alive at the same time as Eban, he and Eban would make great dinner guests together.

Eban was the defense minister of Israel during the Israeli-Arab Six-Day War of 1967 and was considered the number one target for assassination for several years thereafter. In 1970, he visited the United States and was given full Secret Service protection equivalent to that of the president of the United States, plus his full contingent of Israeli security men.

When he returned to the United States in 1996, only his wife accompanied him. The Ebans arrived in Los Angeles on a Sunday night and went directly to their hotel, where they were already checked in. The next day, they met a security specialist at their suite and informed him that they wanted to leave immediately for a luncheon appointment at Universal Studios. On the way out, their security-advance man-driver quickly confirmed the directions to Universal Studios with the hotel doorman!

Arriving at the studio offices, clearance had to be made at the security gate with an officer who had no knowledge of the visit (or even who Eban was). Eban remained waiting in the car for clearance until the officer confirmed the appointment and pointed out the office building where the appointment was set. They searched for a parking place near the office building, because Eban had difficulty walking very far; he was recovering from a broken leg and still occasionally used a cane. The car was parked in a red no-parking zone, risking an encounter with ticket-giving, car-towing parking enforcement officers.

After escorting the Ebans to the appointed office building, it was learned that the person they were to meet was in the cafeteria across the street. Eventually, the Ebans made their expected lunch appointment. The entire experience was an embarrassment to the protection specialist, reflected poorly on him and his company, and of course caused considerable inconvenience for the Ebans. (While the Ebans were lunching with their host, the advance agent-driver returned to the car and parked it in an authorized parking spot, no ticket was issued, and the car was not towed by the ever-vigilant parking enforcement officers.)

When the Ebans were again safely in the car for the return trip, they were told that it would be beneficial if they could provide more advance notice of their itinerary. Subsequently, all routes and locations were checked during the protective agent's off-duty hours or slack time to better prepare for the Ebans' journeys away from the hotel. The rest of the trip, which lasted a week, went very well and was uneventful.

Sometimes a brief advance is all that is possible because of time factors or a lack of personnel, but some action and planning is better than arriving at a location with absolutely no knowledge of what to expect. An advance may be nothing more than a drive-by to determine entrances, parking availability, even where the principal can exit the car.

A spontaneous stop, such as former President Clinton's famous drive-ins for hamburgers at a busy fast-food franchise, allows no opportunity for advance preparation. This is usually safe, because there is also no opportunity for an organized, planned attack. However, vigilance must be maintained, because some person may seize the opportunity to render a spur-of-the-moment attack.

TERRORIST ADVANCE

ATTACKER'S VIEWPOINT

Time, effort, education, training, and experience are components of a good protective advance agent. He works long and diligently to ensure that every aspect of his principal's security is covered. If one minor detail is overlooked, it can mean the difference between a tragic ending and a successful venture. With all his checklists, cooperation and support from team members and staff, and so forth, the advance agent is normally confident that he has done everything possible to bring the odds more into his favor and create a secure environment. However, he very well may overlook one extremely important factor—there may be an unseen set of eyes watching him and mirroring all his movements.

Mirror Image

Throughout the entire advance operation, but especially during the preparation phase, an advance man must anticipate that he is under surveillance by a not-so-friendly person or group. Keeping this in mind, the advance agent should conduct his own countersurveillance, looking for signs that someone may be watching with more than curious intent and mirroring his plan.

The mirror image (i.e., seeing an advance from the opposing view) is a recently recognized and quite likely possibility. An attacker (or terrorist group) plans and conducts what may be considered a mirror advance. Whatever the protective advance agent is doing to anticipate, plan, and prepare is reflected directly by attacker's plans and preparations.

A summary of the things a mirroring solitary attacker or a terrorist group agent must do and know would fall into three primary categories: (1) research (surveillance and countersurveillance) and reconnaissance (intelligence gathering that mirrors the anticipation portion of the protective agent's advance), (2) planning (making a plan to counter the plan of the protective agent), and (3) execution of the plan (exploiting any weakness in the protective agent's anticipation, planning, and preparation).

A terrorist attack begins long before it is actually initiated. The attack may have been conceived weeks, months, or years in advance. Once a target has been selected, for whatever reason, preparation begins with surveillance and intelligence gathering. Terrorists are as well informed about the potential target—perhaps better informed than their counterpart, the protection specialist.

Mirror Effect

Learning the methods through which terrorists act increases the chance of intercepting an attack and mitigating it prior to execution. To do this we must assume the terrorists' profile and examine a potential target's environment. This includes adopting a terrorist's perspective in assessing technical systems, security loopholes, and operational processes, thereby providing a snapshot of an environment's vulnerability. In other words, as a potential attacker watches, learns from, and mirrors the protective agent's activities, the protection personnel should also mirror the preparation of the attacker (counterintelligence).

The attacker's intelligence gathering begins with obtaining all possible data regarding the target. Over a period of several months, the data gathering will include site visits by the terrorist or sympathizer, either on a public tour posing as a tourist or surreptitiously. He will obtain photographs, maps, and blueprints. Research will include reading news accounts, review of public records, and interviews (friendly conversations) with appropriate people such as security officers, employees, neighbors, and associates. In short, the terrorist will conduct a full investigation mirroring the activities of the protection specialist. He will track the movements of the target to determine routes, timing, patterns, lifestyle, strengths, and weaknesses. He may also track the activities of any security personnel and observe their arrangements. Over a period of months, the terrorist will engage in planning, preparation, and anticipation very similar to the activities of a security consultant or protection specialist.

After the surveillance information and intelligence materials are obtained, the planning phase begins. The surveillance and intelligence gathering will actually continue right up to the moment of the attack, as there may be last-minute changes in the target's itinerary or routine. Terrorists are very meticulous about planning the assault. Just like the protection specialist, they leave nothing to chance and overlook nothing. Alternative plans, routes, methods, and equipment will all be considered and included in the overall plan. The preparation aspect involves briefings, rehearsing and "walking through" either at the actual site or a "mock-up," obtaining weapons, false identification, passports, appropriate clothing and/or uniforms, and training with any special equipment.

The terrorist organization conducts a risk analysis very similar to the planning and preparation of the protective team. In selecting a potential target, the terrorist will balance the benefits against the risks and the costs involved in the operation. The attack will occur if the benefits equal or outweigh the risks and the costs. The benefits the terrorists seek are the accomplishment of specific that result from the strike. These goals may include political concessions or religious recognition, publicity, money, increased membership, and release of prisoners that were captured during earlier terrorist incursions.

As the protection specialist views risk levels and the potential for an attack from a position of defense or deterrence, the terrorist views the risk from a perspective of the likelihood of success. The risks a terrorist weighs are demise of the organization through death or capture of attack participants, adverse or unfavorable publicity, loss of popular support, and the very real possibility of the group splintering. The cost to the terrorist organization may be too high a price to pay for some particular aggressions. There may be monetary or logistic reversals that cannot be recouped. The capture or death of the terrorist is a price some groups are unwilling to pay, but the loss of the organization's esprit or morale could be devastating it.

Well-coordinated terrorist attacks have a high percentage of success, because the planner of the operation will attempt to anticipate every relevant contingency including risk analysis or assessment, operation management, leadership and staffing, escape routes and methods, synchronized split-second timing, and reliable communication and equipment. The planner and coordinator of the terrorist event knows that something can and will go wrong, especially if the target's security force has done its job properly. If the chances of success are reduced by an effective security plan, the attack will be delayed or cancelled until a weakness can be ascertained. When evaluating the risks and threats posed by the target's security contingent, the pertinent question asked by the terrorist planner is, what if?

Terrorist acts are calculated, sophisticated, and, most of all, well planned. Therefore, such acts require extensive preparation, not unlike that of a military operation. The key to a successful terrorist action or campaign requires:

1. Target identification—selecting a target for its vulnerability, shock, and strategic value
2. Intelligence acquisition (open source, surveillance, and informants)
3. Target surveillance to confirm or refute the intelligence
4. Assessment of target attack plan
5. Assessment of resources and equipment acquisition
6. Rehearsal or training of the attack, including traveling to an unfamiliar environment and blending in with the target's surroundings
7. Planning and testing of the escape route
8. The execution and its desired impact

Regardless of the type of attack, terrorists may take a year or more to plan their mission. In most cases, the execution is the shortest phase of the mission, taking split seconds for the detonation of a bomb to a few hours for a hijacking or sabotage. In most cases, when explosives, arms, or other means are introduced, it is already too late for the protection agent to prevent an attack. Obviously, most attack plans try to avoid any contact with law enforcement and security. In fact, the optimal attack is the one that encounters the fewest obstacles.[1] Terrorist intelligence is as sophisticated as governmental or private intelligence, and sometimes more so.

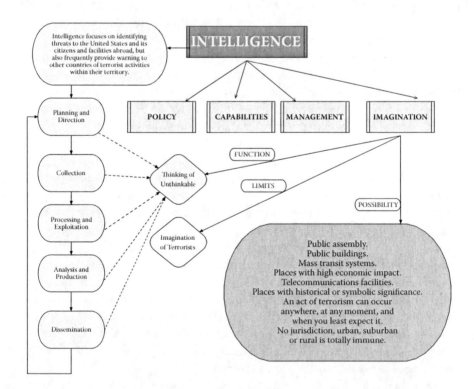

Diagram by American Intercontinental Student.

FIRST STAGE—RESEARCH, RECONNAISSANCE, SURVEILLANCE/COUNTERSURVEILLANCE

An attacker knowing, or surmising, what a protective agent and his team are planning will always give him the advantage. He knows when, where, and how the attack will be made. After all plans and counterplans are set, the attacker has the first move. To obtain all the intelligence data necessary, the attacker will normally engage in tactics of reconnaissance, research and surveillance.

RECONNAISSANCE AND RESEARCH

Reconnaissance means "a search for useful information; a survey." In military terms, it means the same as to reconnoiter, "to inspect, observe, or survey the enemy, the enemy's strength or position in order to gain information for strategic and tactical purposes; to examine or survey." In more generic terms, and in language more familiar to the protective agent, the opposition is conducting his own intelligence gathering and surveying all the advance agent is doing. The potential attacker, in theory, is mirroring the advance agent and preparing his own counterplan. In doing so, he

- Mirrors intelligence agent (anticipation, planning, and preparation)
- Follows same methods and criteria (contacts, intelligence, timing, checklists)
- Reads same books, receives similar training, follows the same procedures (finding out all there is to know)
- Uses the same equipment and expertise in electronic countermeasures as law enforcement
- Conducts spy versus spy versus spy operations ad infinitum (plan, counterplan; establish alternatives and make decisions)
- Collects precise information about the target, which may be a person, place, or thing
- In the case of assassination or kidnapping, gathers specific information about the target:[2]
  - His name, age, residence, social status
  - His work
  - Time of his departure to work and return
  - The routes he takes
  - How he spends his free time
  - His friends, relatives, and visitors and their addresses
  - His car(s)
  - His wife's work and whether he visits her there
  - His children and whether he visits their school
  - Whether he has a girlfriend, her address, and when he visits her
  - The physician who treats him
  - The stores where he shops
  - Places he spends vacations and holidays
  - His house entrances, exits, and surrounding streets

- Ways of sneaking into his house
- Whether he is armed and how many guards he has
- How well trained and disciplined the guards are

In other words, the attacker studies people, timings, entrances and exits, heating and air conditioning ducts, electrical maintenance, facilities, emergency responses, parking, the weather, angle of the sun... everything!

OTHER THINGS TO KNOW

From the Outside

- Width of the streets and in which direction they run
- Common transportation means (e.g., auto, bus, helicopter)
- The area's physical layout and setting
- Traffic signals and pedestrian areas
- Security personnel centers and nearby government agencies
- Economic characteristics of the area
- Traffic congestion times and railroad crossing times

From the Inside

- Amount and location of lighting
- Characteristics of the area (residence, leveled, industrial, rural, trees, physical and psychological barriers
- Number of people inside
- Number and location of guard posts
- Number and names of leaders
- Number of floors and rooms
- Telephone lines and location of switchboard or telephone wiring room
- Electrical lines into and out of the location

In other words, the successful attacker must know... everything!

SURVEILLANCE AND COUNTERSURVEILLANCE

Surveillance involves the observation of a person or targeted location for the purpose of developing information. It means to keep a steady watch, to look at something or someone with the intention of determining the person's activity and intentions. Surveillance is a highly valuable tool, because it involves actual observation/listening. There are three types of surveillance:

- *Moving.* Following the subject wherever he goes.
- *Fixed.* Observation of meetings and events occurring within limited areas.
- *Combination.* Having some form of fixed coverage at point of surveillance initiation so no one else moves when the subject begins to move; the moving coverage begins at some point along the route subject is sure to take.

A protective advance agent must consider the possibility of being under surveillance. It has been said (and proven) that the "good guys" are the easiest to surveil because of their mind-set of being a good guy, doing nothing suspicious or wrong. This conditioned frame of mind allows an advance agent to go about his duties without being concerned that he could be showing his security plans and arrangements to unknown and unseen persons. An ostrich sticks his head in the sand only to get his a** kicked.

Terrorists have been schooled in surveillance, quite often exceeding the countersurveillance training of a protective agent. Beyond mirroring and learning all about the protective advance agent's preparations, a prospective attacker needs to conduct surveillance and research to

- Know all that is known about the subject.
- Discover what is not yet known.
- Share information with team members.

A conscientious protective agent must always remember that he is not living in a vacuum and recognize the probability that his every move is being recorded. He should conduct his affairs as though he knows he is being watched, because he probably is. To conduct his own countersurveillance, a protective agent should mirror terrorist countersurveillance measures. Terrorists are very security conscious and often are aware of how law enforcement agencies conduct surveillances.

Countersurveillance

- Be vigilant for surveillance. Always be aware of your surroundings. Be conscious of where you are, who is in the area, and what everyone is doing. Look for persons who are seemingly out of place or engaged in innocuous actions.
- Be suspicious of vehicles and people you see in different locations on several occasions.
- Look suspicious people directly in the eye. Perhaps walk toward them while looking directly at their faces.
- Use reflective surfaces to see surroundings (e.g., windows and mirrors).
- Stop and pick up dropped objects or tie your shoelaces while looking around for furtive moves by people in the immediate area.
- Retrace your steps or drive in erratic manner; turn around and walk in the direction just covered, then unexpectedly turn around and walk back. Drive down one-way alleys or short streets, make sudden U-turns, stop and wait at a yellow traffic light and start just before it turns red.
- Confront people on the street and accuse them of following you.
- Tell a police officer a particular person is following you. Have the officer confront the person.
- Use public transportation (on and off).
- Use associates to detect surveillance; have them watch and detect people leaving a certain location.
- Use public restrooms; stay inside for long periods.

- Most countersurveillance movements are abnormal. The countersurveillant (the person under surveillance) may be doing some kinds of things an average person doesn't do, such as driving the wrong way on a one-way street, jumping on and off buses, changing his appearance, and confronting people on the street.

The fact that a subject has been conducting countersurveillance can be useful information because, as they say in police work or in legal terms, he displayed a consciousness of guilt or he knew what he was doing was wrong.

SECOND STAGE—PLANNING

After receiving information about the target, an operational plan is created. The following should be considered:[3]

- The type of weapon(s) required
- Number of required members and their training
- Alternative plans
- Type of operation from a tactical perspective (is it a loud or silent elimination process?)
- Date and time of the specified operation
- The target of the operation (is it one individual or many?)
- Team meeting place prior to operation
- Team meeting place after the operation, how to withdraw the team, and withdrawal routes
- Anticipated difficulties that the team may encounter

THIRD STAGE—EXECUTION[4]

- To discover any unexpected element that may impair the operation, it is necessary to rehearse the operation in a place similar to that of the real maneuver.
- The rehearsal may take place shortly before the execution, after which the operation is executed at the time and place specified.
- After execution of the operation, a complete evaluation is made. At the end, a full report is given to organization leaders.

IMPORTANT RECOMMENDATIONS

1. The operation should be appropriate to the participant's physical and mental abilities and capabilities.
2. The participants should be volunteers, not draftees.
3. Roles should be assigned according to the member's physical and moral abilities.
4. Equipment for the execution of the operation should be taken to the proper location in a timely fashion and hidden in a convenient place.

5. The members should be well disguised and placed in a location nearby the operation.
6. Shortly before the operation, reconnaissance should be repeated to confirm that nothing unexpected has occurred.
7. Team members should not be told all about the operation until shortly before executing it so as to avoid leaks. Information is given on a need-to-know basis.
8. Weapons should be tested prior to the operation.
9. The place and time should not be unsuitable for the operation.
10. When using a pistol or rifle, a bullet should already be in the firing chamber (duh!).

AFTER THE OPERATION

- Conduct a debriefing and evaluation (after-action or final survey report):
  - Determine what was right and what went wrong.
  - Make personnel evaluations (according to assignment).
- Reward each member who succeeded in his role; each who failed or was weak should be dismissed (terminated with prejudice).
- Hide or send abroad those who executed the operation.
- Hide the weapons used in the operation.
- Burn all documents, maps, and drawings related to the operation. Remove all traces of burning.

SUMMARY

Looking at all venues, possibilities, and contingencies has been discussed in previous paragraphs. However, it cannot be overemphasized that an advance agent must know and anticipate everything. (See the advance checklist in Appendix C.) We train for the expected, but we educate for the unexpected. An advance agent who has learned the details about a city, location, or situation will be able to respond properly in any circumstance or answer any question that might arise. Merely obtaining contact telephone numbers and walking through a location does not guarantee good security or an effective advance. The advance agent must know the terrain like his own back yard and familiarize himself with every nook and cranny, every person who should or should not be there, and any unexplained absences or fixtures out of place.

After his advance is complete, the advance agent should be nearly able to walk through the areas with his eyes closed. He should at least know every minute detail and anticipate things he cannot control. "No stone too small to turn over; no rock too large to look under; and nothing to overlook."

The advance man has the responsibility squarely on his shoulders for the safe and trouble-free conduct during a VIP's visit. Anything he can do to make the visit a smooth, clocklike operation will help ensure the likelihood of a safe trip. A good advance man must know everything from the simple location of a parking spot to the most complex security antiterrorist countermeasures. He formulates his security arrangements through insightful anticipation, careful planning, and thorough preparation. He asks "what if" and works out all possible solutions to all what-ifs.

A good protective advance isn't complete until the advance agent has considered the likelihood of his activities being mirrored as he prepares for the "big dance."

The protective agent's "dance partner" or counterpart (the attacker) plans his routine as meticulously as the protective agent prepares his advance. For him, nothing is left to chance. The success or failure of his mission rests entirely on how well he has obtained information, planned the operation, and executed his plan.

On both sides of the looking glass, the operation depends on anticipation, planning, and preparation. In other words, the protective agent and his adversary, the attacker, must know and be aware of *everything!*

REVIEW QUESTIONS

1. Explain "advancing the location."
2. What is the "most dangerous time of a person's life"? Explain why.
3. What is an advance? Explain the three major elements.
4. What is meant by asking "what if?"
5. Describe advancing a VIP's trip by commercial airline.
6. Describe advancing a VIP's temporary residence.
7. Describe advancing a VIP's speaking engagement at a convention hall and a television studio.
8. Why is it important to know local parking regulations?
9. Describe the procedure for selecting a driver.
10. What should an advance man anticipate?
11. Why is it relevant to know if there are other protective assignments working in the general vicinity?
12. What are some good sources for local intelligence data?
13. Why contact the local police?
14. Describe a holding room. Include its purpose and importance.
15. Why is an advance survey report important? Why should an after-action or final survey report be written?
16. Prepare a sample advance survey report.
17. Describe some other duties of an advance agent. Why do those duties fall to him?
18. Why is it so difficult, even dangerous, to operate a protective assignment without an advance man?
19. Explain mirroring.

NOTES

1. Tomer, Benito. Chameleon Associates, LLC. www.chameleonassociates.com.
2. Al-Qaeda manual.
3. Ibid.
4. Ibid.

7 Protective Intelligence
Identifying the Potentially Dangerous Subject

Not all information is intelligence, but all intelligence is information.

We must "get into the opponent's decision loop and move through it faster." When we do so, we will win. When we win, we are secure.

Col. John Boyd, twentieth-century military strategist (1927–1997)

We enjoy the comfort of opinions without the discomfort of thought.

J. F. Kennedy

If you are talking, you are not listening; if you are not listening, you are not learning.

Dale L. June

Intelligence is derived from information or raw data but is not "intelligence" until it has been "analyzed." Analysis means assimilating information to its "lowest common denominator" and rendering it useful for the intended purpose. It is a way to establish a basis for rational decision making and planning. [Protective] intelligence analysts, in looking to make sound judgments and predictions, are always under the obligation of "making sense" of complex issues. Intelligence is basing a conclusion upon the facts; not making the facts fit the conclusion.[1]

INTRODUCTION

"He was always a very quiet, stay-to-himself private person, a good neighbor, but we never socialized and, in fact, I hardly ever saw him. He is the last person you would think would do something like this." If this sounds familiar, it is because this type of statement is frequently reported in the aftermath of workplace violence, an assassination attempt, or another outrageous act of man-made violence.

Less frequently reported but just as telling is, "It doesn't surprise me. I always thought he was a ticking time bomb, just waiting to explode. He was wound tighter than a cheap alarm clock, always unfriendly, never smiling, always 'grousing' about something. He just seemed, you know, 'different,' sulking, always by himself, a loner."

Then we sometimes hear, "He was so pleasant, maybe a little depressed, but he said that one day he would 'make it big.' He was always working on some angle."

These are after-the-fact observations. In many cases, the attack or violent act might have been prevented if the early warning signs had been recognized or if particular personality traits had been correctly interpreted. What follows is not meant to describe a complete psychological profile or turn readers into diagnosticians. But this chapter can serve as a general guideline for the novice or layman on how to recognize issues inherent in situations involving a volatile and potentially dangerous person. He may be a coworker, neighbor, or even family member. A second purpose is to describe to security professionals how to spot a potentially dangerous person in a crowd. A third objective is to allow readers to recognize and evaluate characteristics of a sociopathic (antisocial) personality who may intend to hurt or embarrass a protectee. This discussion also focuses on methods used by the aggressive person to bring violent conduct to a workplace setting.

IDENTIFYING THE HUMAN DANGER FACTOR

A protection specialist should develop skills for analyzing information derived from media coverage and other available resources and look for motivation indicators that will provide an edge when making a risk assessment and planning security coverage.

There are early warning signs or red flags (indicators) that, if recognized as possible warnings of violence, may herald a coming hurricane. Coworkers and immediate supervisors are in the best position to recognize initial unacceptable behavior and potential problem areas. It is critical to train coworkers, supervisors, and managers in appropriate ways of dealing with potentially threatening situations and to recognize and report a shift in attitude, possible substance abuse, and other anomalies before they can escalate.

An early symptom of aberrant employee behavior is an increasingly poor history of attendance and dependability. For example, a person might have an excellent record of dependable and appropriate service over a period of time, but, "Recently, he has been late with assignments, fails to meet deadlines, arrives late to work, leaves early, or does not show up at all because of sickness or some other excuse." Taking sick days off, missing deadlines, and not completing assignments may be unusual if the person has never taken any time off for sickness or missed a work assignment or deadline, even when walking around with pneumonia.

Another out-of-character behavior may consist of expressing direct or implied threats and/or intimidation, which may lead up to an actual incident of violence. The protection agent must become familiar with certain common behaviors among potentially dangerous people. Historically, perpetrators have displayed obvious unacceptable behavior, unusual or bizarre demeanor, and emotional instability that somehow went unrecognized, even by those closest to them. Perhaps the perpetrator's personality slowly changes from gregarious individual to a sulking, vindictive person. He begins reading gun magazines, taking shooting lessons at a local firing range, and talks about "getting even someday" or mentions that "they are out to get" him. He becomes secretive, laughs at or takes offense at meaningless comments, and so on.

It is theorized that at the root of most emotional motivations toward anger and violence is distress or depression. A good rule of thumb to remember is, "Depression equals anger; paranoia equals fear; fear and anger equal violence." Depression leaves a person weepy and gloomy; anger makes the person feel empowered. Anger (the lion of emotions) becomes the means of escaping feelings brought about by depression.

A quiet, downhearted person may suddenly erupt into rage and destructive violence, usually with no warning or readily apparent motive. For weeks, or perhaps months or years, he has maintained his own counsel, keeping to himself and often disengaging himself from office activities other than his assigned duties. He may have no effective support system, such as a family or social contact, outside of the workplace. If he has a family, he may retreat from them or direct his frustration and anger toward them. "There is a strong relationship between job stress and incidents of harassment and violence in the workplace and home. Over twenty-five percent of violent incidents in the workplace are carried over from domestic violence. The violence cycle continues as workplace problems are carried over to the home."[2]

Stress, anxiety, and boredom are constant companions, infecting him with resentment and suppressed anger over real or imagined slights such as being passed over for promotion or being assigned meaningless jobs. His isolation and resentment fester over time until the bubble bursts and his actions, so out of character, result in human misery, pain, and perhaps death. The typical potentially dangerous person's behavior can be diagramed as shown in the following figure.

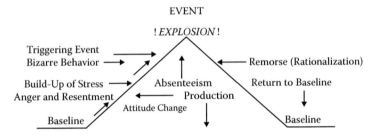

Working up to the vortex of his stress, anger, and resentment may take several months or years, allowing the transformation to be easily overlooked by those (e.g., friends, family, coworkers, and supervisors) who should take note of the changing pattern. After the violent act, these people can retrospectively identify various levels of progression leading up to the event.

Drastic Changes in Habits

He exhibits symptoms of burnout such as drastic changes in his work performance, appearance, attitude, and demeanor; changing from being a "hard charger" or "heavy hitter" to a "round to it." ("I'll do it when I get around to it."). He was once punctual, meeting deadlines and always at work either on time or early, often staying late, maybe working on weekends. However, at some point he begins a trend toward absenteeism, lowered productivity, and a lack of dependability.

His attitude toward his work and coworkers changes to anger and resentment, often complaining and nit picking or moaning about trivial matters, expressing impatience with coworkers, and displaying paranoiac allusions about supervisors. His paranoid behavior drives him to act secretively and defensively, often to the point of overt hostile actions or becoming argumentative and physically aggressive. Perhaps he focuses his aggression or special interest on another employee, manager, or supervisor. He begins to hear voices, see images, or imagine someone or something is out to get him.

TALK ABOUT GUNS, WEAPONS, VIOLENCE, OR GETTING EVEN

He never had much, if any, interest in guns, other weapons, or "combatives" (martial arts), but within the last year or so he began talking about them, reading gun magazines at work, and talking about hunting or other gun- or defense-related topics. He exhibits inappropriate anger or explosiveness, focusing attention on one person or organization, sometimes speaking of suicide or hurting someone. He may compile a criminal record for violence, assault, or other aggressive behavior and begins (or continues) to abuse drugs or alcohol.

EMOTIONAL TRAUMA

He may have experienced trauma in his life such as a divorce, job termination, financial hardship, or the death of a loved one. The person could display episodes of depression, alienation, or isolation. Without a supportive circle and understanding people in his life, he becomes a loner, changing his personal habits, hygiene, and attitude toward life (perhaps drifting into depression, which could lead to anger and hostility). His mood swings often are apparent, ranging from empowerment to feeling unappreciated.

Over time, if not treated, he may build up resentment, hostility, and paranoia, eventually erupting into an act of violence. After the act, he may not show remorse, shame, or guilt, but usually those emotions, especially remorse, will replace the devastating passion that drove him. He may not feel guilt or remorse but may rationalize his actions as something driven by others.

PROTECTIVE INTELLIGENCE INVESTIGATION

Intelligence is raw data (information) after it has been deciphered, examined, analyzed, and exposed to the light of critical assessment and transformed into a usable form for either strategic or tactical planning. Every day, the Secret Service receives hundreds of letters, telephone calls, and other communications addressed to the president of the United States. The writers and callers may be only concerned citizens who simply want to engage in their democratic constitutional right of free speech and to express advice, compliments, and complaints to the president. But a minority of the correspondence goes beyond the realm of plain exercise of free speech. Every bit of communication is routinely inspected for implied, potential, and real threats. Each word is scrutinized for double meanings that can spell anger, suicidal thoughts, warnings, and intentions. If reasonable and logical thinking indicates that the correspondent might present a clear and plain danger, an investigation is warranted.

The first step, naturally, is to identify the letter writer or caller. Usual procedure calls for comparing the words, phrases, style, tenor, and tone with other correspondence received previously. Often, a match can be made that will lead the investigator to an identification. Forensic or scientific examination of the ink, paper, envelope, postmark, and so on can often lead to determining the source. Once an identification is made, further background checking must be conducted to determine the level of threat posed by the correspondent. For example, one writer may make extremely viable-sounding threats, such as, "I am going to kill (the protectee). He is a (profane words). I am coming and will (shoot, stab, or whatever) him."

Background investigation reveals the subject has a military background and is qualified in several types of weapons, is proficient with explosives, and has other relevant aggressive expertise. Perhaps he has a criminal record and has been under psychiatric care. To further instigate the person to violence, he has recently been abandoned by his wife, lost his job, and is in deep financial debt. This person sounds like a very likely candidate of being capable of fulfilling his threats. He would be classified as a 1-A threat level.

On the other hand, a personal visit to the person may reveal him to be a bedridden paraplegic, destined to live within the confines of his bedroom, always attached to his oxygen bottle. His threat level suddenly drops to a 4-F level. More often than not, a serious attacker will not be known or heard from until the instant he triggers his plan. But just because a person makes his threat known does not mean he is incapable of carrying out his scheme. In other words, nothing must ever be taken for granted when it comes to determining threat levels posed by those who wish harm to a protectee. In over 50 years of Secret Service protective intelligence, not once has a presidential attacker made his intentions known in advance. But to say it has not happened doesn't mean it will not. Every threat must be taken seriously.

INTELLIGENCE ANALYST

The process of taking raw data and obtaining useful intelligence from it involves careful analysis and is an integral part of protective intelligence work. Intelligence is derived from information or raw data but does not become intelligence until it is viewed from a perspective of critical thinking or, in other words, until it has been analyzed. Analysis means digesting information or data to its lowest common denominator and rendering it useful for the intended purpose. It is viewing a particular set of circumstances from a number of sources and perspectives to form an inference and premise based on analysis, reasoning, logic, training, and experience. Intelligence decision-making is a way to consider all significant consequences (long-term/short-term, subtle/obvious, direct/indirect, physical/emotional, intended/unintended, immediately obvious/not revealed for a long time) while establishing a basis for rational planning and strategic and tactical action. The summation or conclusions are rooted in reasonable deductions from all available information and consideration of the reliability of the source and the weight of the information, with the result of proving or disproving the data. In other words, analysis is another term for critical thinking.

Opinions are like noses—everyone has one. The formation of opinions comes from many sources, internal and external stimuli, influences of others, conscious and unconscious bias, facts and rumors, and experience. Opinions are thoughts. Opinions are not like facts. Facts are indisputable and cannot be changed. They have been proven by laws of nature, physics, math, and common acceptance. Opinions, on the other hand, are subject to feelings, moods, prejudices, and wrongful conclusions. An analyst bases his conclusions on his opinions only after closely examining all the data, information, and knowledge. We know that rumors are nearly always unfounded or, if grounded in fact, distorted beyond the original truth. Therefore, conclusions based on rumors are unreliable. In addition, feelings are unreliable for determining the trustworthiness of decisions based strictly on hunches, intuition, or the physical and/or emotional state of the person making the decision.

In an example of how feelings are unreliable for making judgments, a young "wannabe" gang member or a simple bully walks down the street and, for no apparent reason, strikes an old lady in the face with his fist. As the old lady falls out of her wheelchair or drops her cane, she begins bleeding profusely from the nose and mouth. When asked why he struck the woman, the young punk replies, "Because I felt like it." He did not consider the feelings of the other person or the consequences of his action. He was directed by his feelings. Therefore, we might say that opinions formed merely on feelings are mostly unreliable.

Opinions are often clouded by the error of the double standard. In other words, better ye than me. It is often referred to as the not in my backyard syndrome. This means that a matter affecting someone else might be a minor matter, but if it affects the holder of the opinion, it becomes a major matter. If a person has a close personal or emotional interest in a matter, his judgment or opinion is prejudiced by his personal interest.

An analyst cannot base his decision on feelings. It is permissible to express an opinion, especially in a conclusion, but the opinion must be sustained by facts, reasonable deduction, and thoughtful consideration.

Does the analysis tell the whole truth and nothing but the truth? The rule of contradiction states that nothing can be true and false at the same time, in the same place in the same way. Like in a true/false test, if one word in the question is wrong, the answer to the question will be false. Leaving out words, poor word selection, misleading words, and context can change the entire meaning of a statement, leading to erroneous implications, distorted meaning, and false information. An analyst has an ethical duty to be honest and truthful. Manipulating language to hide facts, present false data, or leave out unfavorable information is dishonest and will very likely have adverse consequences, either for the analyst, his organization, the subject of the report, or all of these.

The analyst must regard the interests of anyone who will be affected by the report. His moral duty is to report facts without allowing his prejudices, biases, or presentation to color the facts and skew the conclusions. It is in the best interest of no one to form a conclusion and then write the facts to fit the conclusion. A good rule is to let the conclusion fit the facts, not the facts fit the conclusion. Anything else can be correctly viewed as being one-sided and on the level of lying.

PSYCHOLOGICAL PERSPECTIVES

Certain psychological pathologies have security implications. By looking into an opponent's mind, we can gain a better understanding of his behavior and how to control or prevent a behavior from developing into an actual assault. The protective agent should understand the importance of identifying aberrant human behavior and foreseeing its consequences. He needs to work with mental health professionals and local officials to develop means of mitigating the actions of potentially dangerous, mentally ill persons. The protection agent must learn to recognize the dangerous person, assess the degree of danger, and develop methods and procedures for working with dangerous people.

The experienced protection professional learns to understand the importance of reading nuances of body language and unspoken words and develops a familiarity with available mental health services and general legal requirements for the detention or hospitalization of a mentally ill person.

People having personality disorders believe they are correct, and the rest of the world is wrong. They fail to recognize that they have the problem. The actions of such people are what could be understood as *bipolarism*, not as in manic depression but as instability. One minute they are calm and low key, and the next instant they are raging with anger, fear, and anxiety. People in their presence generally do not know how to approach this type of person because of this mood instability. Being around people like this is often referred to as "walking on eggshells." If they feel mistreated or misunderstood, they may suddenly experience a mood swing and become a raging lunatic, completely out of control of their emotions.

An experienced protective agent soon learns to recognize and deal with various psychological personalities and disorders. It becomes a matter of reading body language, listening to words and expressions used during an outburst, or observing how the person of interest manipulates others. Of course, not all potentially dangerous people display recognizable or diagnosable symptoms of a psychiatric disorder. A person may have the symptoms but not the inclination toward violence. That is the fine line a protective intelligence agent must walk. He must be careful not to label someone and later find that he misread the person. Many apparent psychiatric disorders are not disorders at all; they may simply be part of the person's developed personality.

ANTISOCIAL PERSONALITY DISORDER

A notorious example of an antisocial personality is serial killer Ted Bundy. This type of personality can be colloquially described as a *glad-hander* or a *backslapper*. To a person's face, he is the picture of sociability. Smiling and charming, he will easily and quickly win the confidence of other people. Greeting someone with a smile, a handshake, and a pat on the back, he will quickly put the other person at ease and make him feel warm and comfortable in his presence. In actuality, he is a remorseless *backstabber* who can exhibit temperamental and threatening behavior over real or imagined grievances against others. They are either charming and cunning for their own purposes, but can be surly and uncaring. Often they alternate between the two extremes, depending on the current mood or need. A narcissistic person having no sense of personal responsibility and lacking insight and compassion, he is highly egocentric and does everything out of self-interest. The antisocial personality is typified by several criteria:

1. Such people lack of empathy for others. They cannot put themselves in the shoes of others and feel what they feel. They generally feel no remorse about the effects of their actions on others and are often unfeeling, standoffish or cynical, and contemptuous of the feelings, rights, and suffering of others. They may rationalize or even feel justified in having hurt or mistreated others. They do not possess the ability to confess to wrongdoing or to apologize for hurting others; in fact, they may take perverse pleasure in it. When others show what is perceived as weakness or emotional hurt, the antisocial personality will play to that weakness and exploit it. They tend to bully and blame others for their own inadequacies. They may blame the victim for being stupid or deserving of what he got, believing, "It's his fault, I had to hurt him. He knew I like to be the first one to the coffee pot in the morning."

2. Possessing an arrogant and unjustified inflated opinion of themselves, they often are unemployed because they know it all and believe they should be in a supervisory position. They feel believe themselves to be constantly bossed by an incompetent or inferior supervisor who is not qualified to be in charge. They are cocky and self-assured when there is no reason for such high self-esteem, which may be recognized by others. They use charm in dealing with the opposite sex, potential employers, and victims. They are capable of "conning" others for profit or fun, using technical terms, jargon, or slang words to impress others, with no thought of the consequences. Because of this arrogance, they believe their actions to be justified, giving them the right to use force to achieve their goals.

3. Functioning under the assumption that friends should be used and competitors destroyed, they are aggressive toward those who show fear but dutiful and unassertive to those they fear or who have power over them. They often hide their resentment until it is convenient to will ruin or destroy their competition.

4. With this type of personality, actions are rationalized as entitlements or rights, even though they often trample the entitlements and rights of others with total disregard. As long as they feel their rights are maintained, they will remain under control, gregarious, smiling, and happy. But when they feel overlooked, offended, or slighted, or someone becomes a threat (either to them or their rights), they lose control and let their aggressive, angry impulses take over. After carrying out some act of rudeness, cruelty, or intolerance, they may be asked, "Why did you do that?" The answer will simply be, "Because I felt like it," displaying total disregard for what the offended or harmed person feels. They come to believe they are innocent victims of some imagined injustice and have a right to defend themselves and their perceived rights. They believe that anyone who gets in their way is guilty of some encroachment and must be fought (or in some cases killed) in self-defense. They often develop unreasonable paranoia and suspect or feel certain that they are being watched or persecuted.

5. Experiencing unpleasant moods (often complaining of stress, boredom, and depression), they may be impulsive, ill-tempered, and belligerent, as indicated by repeated verbal or physical assaults. They are often dangerously indifferent to their own safety and the safety of others. This indifference

can lead to risky behavior, frequenting dangerous places, and associating with others with whom they can experience high-risk sex and drug or alcohol abuse.

6. Consistent in their irresponsibility in all aspects of life, they fail to hold jobs (as pointed out above), pay debts, pay child support, and meet other routine responsibilities. They are inconsiderate and abusive in sexual partnerships and may have a history of being sexually promiscuous (or celibate as a way of keeping a "clean spirit"). They may never have sustained a truly loving relationship with a partner of either sex. If a parent, they will be negligent in this relationship as well, often verbally and physically abusing the child. Their own childhoods may include abuse and neglect, unstable or erratic parenting, and either too lax or too stringent parental discipline. They are typically indifferent to having hurt, abused, or otherwise mistreated someone else and have a record of failure to be self-supporting. They may be destitute or homeless and may have spent considerable time in prison.

POWER SYNDROME

The power syndrome is sometimes referred to as the Napoleon complex. To overcome their feelings of impotence and ineffectiveness, afflicted people exaggerate their own importance and, if given a little authority, they translate the "power of the position" into a weapon against those they resent and dislike, turning their feelings of resentment, scorn, and insecurity into aggressive, often violent, behavior. They are jealous of (as they see them) powerful and potentially dangerous adversaries. Feelings of jealousy combined with inherent insecurity frequently breed hatred and violent behavior. Violent behavior can give the illusion of power. People become elated when feelings of weakness and helplessness are replaced by feelings of power. Power elation drives them to consummate acts of violence, degradation, and control over others, whereas depression makes them feel weak and powerless.

Anger and depression are joined. Anger, like elation, is active, strong, and masculine and can make a person feel very good. Depression is passive, weakness, tearful, and feminine. Depression makes a person feel empty, alone, and resentful. Conversion of depressed feelings into angry ones is a short therapeutic step for alleviating despair. Depressed persons are frequently angry people who are driven to acts of hatred and violence. Violent behavior is the acting out of feelings that make them feel powerful and good. Commonly this is seen as cyclical. An explosive temper and mood changes between anger and passiveness may be a sign of manic depression or bipolar syndrome in its conventional sense.

INTERMITTENT RAGE DISORDER

Sometimes a person suddenly blows up, exploding in rage. This often is colloquially referred to as "flying off the handle." This person may have an explosive emotional makeup but generally appears as docile, even subservient, until he can no longer control the impulse to express anger. All people have negative and destructive emotional impulses, but the ability to control these impulses is critical. An effective analogy would be a large pressure cooker in which water continues to boil and build up steam. At some point, it must be released or the pot explodes. When it does explode, everyone and everything nearby becomes a target of the boiler contents. The same can be said of a human with IRD; anyone in his vicinity becomes a target.

"Road rage" is sometimes suggested as a type of IRD. The IRD person goes along on cruise control until that awful instant when another driver cuts him off and moves ahead of him or gives him a "social salute" with one-fifth of a hand. Over-reacting in uncontrollable rage, the IRD person may drive his car into the offender's or in some other way seek vengeance.

In some rare instances, the IRD could be caused by a physical aliment having nothing to do with the person's emotional makeup. Neurosarcoidosis, though extremely rare, is one such disease. It attacks the central nervous system, making the person a threat to himself and others. The neurosarcoidosis-afflicted person may be gentle and well in control then suddenly, and with no visible symptoms, verbally and physically attack anyone in his presence.[3]

ALIENATION OR ISOLATION

Isolation may be a distant cousin of depression. The person harbors feelings of lone-liness, helplessness, and dissatisfaction, and possibly desperation. He feels he has little control or decision-making power in his work world and his life. His life is controlled by higher-ups. It may be the boss, his family, or circumstances setting him apart from others. He builds a protective cocoon or emotional wall around himself until, eventually, he is driven to some act of desperation, often violent.

BORDERLINE PERSONALITY DISORDER

For people with borderline personality disorder, every day is a "bad-hair day." Some-thing or someone always causes them to misfire. These people are self-destructive with suicidal tendencies and often will commit some act to sabotage themselves as they near a goal, be it employment, education, or family centered. Recurrent job losses, interrupted education, and broken marriages are common. In other words, their usual personality is chronic instability.

Indicative of this behavior is an emotional instability and unpleasant mood most of the time, which is manifested in anger, panic, and despair. Their profound anger at inappropriate times makes it difficult for them to control sudden outbursts of anger, temper, and physical clashes. They are prone to extreme sarcasm, bitterness, and verbal outbursts. They may experience stress-related feelings of suspiciousness and the belief that they are being harassed, persecuted, or treated unfairly. Often, their self-destructive behavior leads them to slash themselves with razor blades.

MAJOR DEPRESSIVE EPISODE

Three major traumas in a person's life that can bring about a major depressive episode are divorce, the death of a loved one, and loss of employment. This may result in anger and the belief that "somebody must pay." Manifestations of this problem include weep-ing, distress, agitation, somber and unreasonable concerns about health problems, anx-iety attacks, phobias, and, often, drug and/or alcohol abuse. Occasionally, the person will burst through the depression and weepy feeling (especially after alcohol abuse, which for no known reason usually leads to anger and violence) to become a frenzied storm of anger (anger produces power) directed at his environment and anyone in it.

Schizophrenia, including Paranoia

Paranoid schizophrenia is perhaps the most potentially dangerous mental personality, because the afflicted person may suffer from hallucinations and/or delusions that "everyone" is a potential threat. He may take a preemptive action to hurt others before being hurt. The most common and dangerous of the delusions are those in which the person believes he is being attacked, watched, harassed, cheated, persecuted, or conspired against. He may believe that his feelings, thoughts, and impulses are under the control of some external force or person. This personality illness must be considered potentially harmful to the object of the schizophrenic's interest.

IDENTIFYING THE DANGEROUS PERSON IN A CROWD

The most useful observation is often that something doesn't fit, is out of place, or does not belong. "If it doesn't belong, it is wrong." An unsmiling, unfriendly looking person in a crowd of well-wishers, for example, may seem out of place. For example, a very pale person wearing heavy clothing in a tropical or subtropical setting may have traveled from a colder region to see the protectee. This is a possible cause for concern. A person who seems be an innocent presence at all public functions the protectee attends may be a stalker or someone intent on harmful action. A person sweating nervously or uncontrollably when others are not might be a concern. A person jamming his hands deep into his pockets when everyone else in the crowd is waving and extending their hands to the protectee might be holding a gun or other weapon.

These are a few indicators that may reveal a potentially harmful personality. Each must be weighed in the full context of the assessment and evaluated on its own merits.

Assessments

A. Five Categories of Probability
   1. *Virtually certain.* This is the most likely. There is always a possibility of something not occurring, but the chance is so infinitesimal that it is considered in thousandths of a percentage.
   2. *Highly probable.* Very likely.
   3. *Moderately probable.*
   4. *Improbable.*
   5. *Unknown and undeterminable.*

B. Four Areas of Consideration
   1. Evaluate the occurrence (what is the likelihood that it will happen).
   2. Determine the impact of an occurrence.
   3. Identify the countermeasures necessary to reduce the threat.
   4. Implement effective security controls.

WRITTEN THREAT ANALYSIS

As with the spoken word, when using written communication, it is not only what is stated but how it is stated! The writer translates his thinking, action, and emotion into an experience of feeling. Feeling comes from expression and sincerity. An angry report will be slashed with exclamation points; short, stabbing sentences; and slashing, angry words. A humorous or friendly communication will use words in a light, playful manner.

In the above paragraph, note the use of the words slashing and stabbing to describe an angry report. (Can you not see Norman Bates in the Alfred Hitchcock thriller, *Psycho*, as he plunges the butcher knife again and again through the steamy shower curtain? The viewer never sees the knife actually striking the surprised victim, but he feels her shock and helplessness as the blood begins to trickle into the water spiraling down the drain.) That is the definitive use of slashing and stabbing. The writer is no longer watching. He is part of the action. He feels it! He experiences it! He is it!

This type of writing is identified with psychopathic personalities exemplified in serial killers, perpetrators of workplace violence, and stalking cases leading to homicide.

Word repetition is a commonality of many threatening-letter writers. It indicates a limited vocabulary and hints of amateurism and carelessness. Frequently, a writer will use a favorite catch word or phrase over and over and will not edit out anything he has written.

Voice, Tenor, and Tone

Careful consideration must be given to the tenor and tone of the article. The *tenor* refers to the inflection or "sound" of the writing. The *tone* of the wording refers to the mood or emotions of the writer. It gives a manner of voice. Is the writer angry? Is he being reflective? Is he excited and trying to excite the reader? Is he being expressive, moving the language into a crescendo of demonstrative emotion, gradually increasing in loudness and intensity, working toward a climax? Is he telling the story in a professor's monotone or a show-business monologue? Is he simply announcing the events as they unfold, in a businesslike manner, or is the writing incoherent and rambling?

What is being told may be based on actual experience; not necessarily the writer's experience, but someone's. If the objective is to galvanize an action or stir the emotions, the writer will use short, powerful words or phrases! Coming in rapid succession! Or piled onto the next! Not stopping for a breath! Punctuating them with exclamation points!!! It's a boxer using a series of quick sledgehammer jabs to the solar plexus, emphasizing his intent to knock out the opponent. Very much like this paragraph! Take that! And that! And this! Even the words in the last phrase connote violence.

A monotone is page after page of seemingly nondescript or passive-voice sentences woven together in a manner that informs but not necessarily excites. The sentences are marked with an ordinary period rather than the exciting exclamation point. Depressed persons and the mentally ill usually write that way.

MOTIVATION

There are several motives for writing threatening letters. Motivation is relative to topic selection. An essay or letter is usually written to advance one's opinion, feelings, or establish a position in a social matter. To many people, writing is a form of therapy. The correspondence may be a threat, an implied threat, or just a method of "venting." Writing requires a certain amount of passion. It is left to the reader to identify that passion.

TOPIC

The writer simply engages his imagination, selecting a topic in which he has a special interest, and expresses himself. Topic selection is closely tied to the feelings, thoughts, interests, and knowledge of the author. A letter may have a religious theme, indicating that the intended recipient is sinful, lusting, a harlot, and so on. This type of writer is usually very prolific. To him, the words are messages from God, revealed to him as His commands and wishes, but his letters are usually nonsensical, disjointed, and rambling. To create fear, the writer must include bits of information that demonstrate his knowledge about the reader. The writer seeks out data and facts from documents, surveys, and interviews. He may even be an insider.

JARGON

Jargon provides a clue about the background of the writer. For example the expression "yardbird" refers to a person working in a train yard, a "screw" is a prison guard, and so forth. Every job or occupation has its own special language, known as jargon. Many writers have a fixation and will focus on a specific topic. For example, a religious fanatic will ramble about the wages of sin, the wickedness of sex, and everlasting damnation.

Flowery words are used by egocentric persons who think they are being profound. Such words connote a sense of insincerity. They are used by flatterers, con artists, and anyone who is trying to convey his message by overwhelming the reader with his intellect. The writer most clearly will use words and vocabulary that best fits his style, personality, maturity level, and education.

ENDING

The first order of business is to read the entire piece, making sure to grasp its content. The next step is to apply critical thinking skills for analysis. New thoughts and ideas may emerge. Words should be checked for subtle meanings to reveal the unconscious or hidden messages.

On the second and third readings, lend an eye on looking for critical mistakes and mechanical errors. These could include such little words as: and, but, like, however, whereas, inasmuch, for example, and others; spelling mistakes; misused words, punctuation, and capitalization; and improper grammar. All of these words and mistakes help form a pattern that could identify the writer.

It is not unusual for the threat—be it overt, implied, or conditional—to not be unrevealed until the end of the message. Sometimes this may necessitate reading pages and pages of unconnected thoughts and reasoning. Even the closing signature line may contain the threat; e.g., "Yours in Death," "We'll soon meet in Hell," or "Best wishes for a beautiful funeral."

SUMMARY

There is no such thing as a *specific profile* of a potentially violent person. We can look for and analyze commonalities, but this is not a perfect science. Each person travels a different path with emotions, ideology, environment, social settings, and psychological mind-sets that give him a unique personality. Circumstances, mental conditioning, and social framework form that personality. Most personalities are healthy and present no danger to anyone. On the other hand, some personality traits can drive an individual to commit an act to either direct attention to himself or bring injury to innocent people. Being able to identify and correctly interpret the meaning of certain personal actions and demeanors can mean the difference between a life-saving decision and ignoring the warning signs until it is too late.

Anticipate… Plan… Prepare.

REVIEW QUESTIONS

1. Describe indicators or "red flags" of a potential workplace violent aggressor.
2. What is "intelligence"?
3. Why should intelligence be based on fact, not feelings?
4. Explain the role of opinion in determining a person's threat level.
5. What are the steps to identifying a letter writer, and how would you determine his threat level?
6. Why should a protection (security) specialist be familiar with psychological pathologies, and what are the symptoms of a psychological pathology?
7. Describe the five categories of probability when making an assessment.
8. What four areas of consideration must be addressed when making an assessment?
9. Explain the method(s) of analyzing written communications and determining the writer's potential threat level.
10. Is it more prudent to attempt to create a profile or to look for commonalities in constructing a picture and determining the threat level, of a letter writer?

NOTES

1. From a university course outline, "Analysis of Raw Intelligence," by Dale L. June.
2. From data according to the National Institute for Occupational Safety and Health.
3. The author had a client (a trained medical doctor and family practitioner) who was diagnosed with neurosarcoidosis. She hired personal protection agents to keep her from harming others. Obviously, she had to give up her medical practice. Sometimes, at

night, she would have to be chained or handcuffed to the bed so she would not sneak out and hurt someone. The author never witnessed any of those episodes, but they were described by the client.

8 Working the Principal
More Than Standing and Waiting

𝕻ersonal 𝕻rotection - 𝕿he 𝕾trength of the 𝕾hield; 𝕾ensitibity of the 𝕽ose[1]

Yea, though I walk through the valley of the shadow of death, I shall fear no evil.

People would ask me, "What do you do for a living?" I would say, "I travel a lot, mostly see airports and hotels; and spend a lot of time standing and waiting..." Semper Peratus (Always Ready).

Dale L. June

KNOW THE PROTECTEE

"Know your principal" is one of the primary rules of protection. Working with a protectee is a lot like a marriage. The better you know the person, the smoother the relationship. In a total protective environment, the protective agent begins the day with the principal in the morning, takes him to work, returns him home at night, sees him go to bed, and watches over him during the night. In fact, protective agents spend more time with protective assignments than with their own wives and families. Getting to know the work and family environment of the protectee is as important as knowing the threat level of potential harm. It is easier to understand, anticipate, and neutralize the threat if there are no unknowns and if the business and family protective shield is also in place and enforced. If the protectee's concerns and needs are known and can be anticipated, the association will be friendly, cordial, and mutually rewarding most of the time.

When first assigned to a protectee, it is incumbent upon the protective agent to ascertain as much information about the protectee as possible. The protectee himself will often provide a good deal of information, or he may designate a staff member as primary contact for whatever information is necessary. It is important to know the schedule of the protectee, the location of his appointments, the names of staff and family, contact telephone numbers (24 hours a day), and any known medical problems such as heart trouble, seizures, allergies, and disabilities. In the event of a medical emergency, the protectee's blood type should be known, especially if it is rare.

General information about the protectee and his business usually can be obtained from company brochures or stock reports, often obtainable in the office lobby. If these are not available, then a trip to the local library for a little research is in order. Good sources of information regarding corporations and corporate personnel are directories from Dunn & Bradstreet and Standard & Poor's, found in the reference section of most libraries.

If there are also security concerns about the family, much of the same basic information is needed. Where does the wife work? What are her organizational associations? Where do the children go to school? What are the arrangements for taking them to school and picking them up? (See Terrorist Advance Checklist in chapter 6.)

It is not always appropriate to determine what information is necessary at the initial meeting with the protectee. In fact, most initial meetings with the protectee are nothing more than introductory. Most details and arrangements are usually developed through a senior staff member. As the information is compiled, it should be recorded in a secured notebook and shared only with working security personnel on a need-to-know basis.

CLIENT PROFILING

> What enables the wise sovereign and the good general to strike and conquer, and achieve things beyond the reach of ordinary men, is foreknowledge.
>
> **Sun Tzu,** *The Art of War*

Knowledge is power, and information is the best weapon. When working with a protectee, it is important to profile the principal thoroughly. Consider all known personality traits of the protectee. Is he abrasive? Combative? Timid? Does he have a tendency to attract trouble? A protectee with an outsized ego may invite trouble from outsiders, or he may challenge the judgment of the protection agent, resulting in head-butting. This creates an assignment from Hell in which no one wins. Consider the principal's attitude. A callous or reckless attitude can lead to security problems. A protectee's prejudices can be dangerous, as they are deeply ingrained and will forcefully surface during times of stress. Beliefs, opinions, and convictions can also lead to problems. A client may believe that he can trust someone, or that he is not in danger, but that may not be the case. Remember, it is not necessary to like the protectee or his politics to work together efficiently. What is necessary is to remember that the protection agent has a responsibility to provide the very best, good-faith security effort to the protectee.

UNDERSTANDING THE PRINCIPAL AND YOUR RELATIONSHIP

Although the protective agent may have the requisite training, education, and technical abilities necessary for employment in the profession, there is no substitute for being able to maintain a proper relationship with the principal. The first step is to understand that your principal may not be in favor of having someone follow his every movement. Whether you are assigned to this person for a few hours or a long term, you should have a clear understanding of what the principal expects of you.

Understand that your principal will not do everything recommended for his security. There may be exceptions to this rule, but they are usually short lived. Everyone must decide for himself what level of risk he is willing to take, and your protectee is no exception. Convincing your principal to cancel all public appearances and ride in a low-profile, fully armored vehicle when he ventures out of his fortress and into public is most likely beyond the realm of possibilities. An agent must understand and adapt to what the principal believes to be acceptable security for himself and his family.

Therein lies one of the challenges of the protectee service profession. The protective service agent must not only have the knowledge of proper security procedures, he must possess the ability to communicate this knowledge to the principal in a way that is likely to produce the desired results. Further compounding the communications gap is that the protective agent may be unable to speak directly with the principal; instead, he may be required to present suggestions to a staff member or assistant (maybe even through an interpreter).

PROTECTEE AND A PROTECTION AGENT HAVE A SPECIAL RELATIONSHIP

A protectee and a protection agent have a special relationship for many different reasons. The primary reason is that the protectee is relying on the protection agent to keep the protectee and his family, coworkers, and property out of harm's way. For a protection agent to adequately protect his charge, he must be intimately involved in the clients' lives. The protection agent must be aware of the protectee's personal habits, lifestyle, and travel arrangements, all of which must be planned so as to develop the best possible protection program given the particular situation and available resources.

Knowing he is being targeted for violence can be stressful and difficult for a protectee. It is important for the protection agent to understand this when dealing with the client on a day-to-day basis.

The protectee is in a challenging position when hiring a protection agent. He is being threatened by violence, and the protection agent's mere presence is a constant reminder of that threat. A protectee must place an enormous amount of trust in his protection agent. The protection agent may be present during business meetings, family outings, and other parts of the protectee's everyday life. Additionally, protection agents may be present to help their clients avoid embarrassing situations.

The overall relationship must be one based on trust, professionalism, discretion, and competency. Protection agents are trusted to fulfill their duties in a professional way. Protection agents must also keep family and business matters confidential. The protectee requires nothing less than a competent professional who can keep him safe while allowing him to lead as normal a life as possible.

"You are in their world, but you are not part of it." This sound piece of advice cannot be overemphasized. A protective agent has one mission or goal, and that is to provide "a safe secure environment." In his position at the side or in the vicinity of the person he is protecting, the protective agent is often found attending social events, political rallies, stockholder meetings, and maybe even costume balls. He may attend polo matches or be present in high-stakes gambling forays in grand casinos. It is not unusual to mix with political dignitaries, entertainment or sports figures, royalty, or simply the high-born rich and famous.

The protective agent can become accustomed to living in the Ritz-Carlton where his protectee is staying, attending charity affairs and calmly plucking shrimp off a silver platter held by a service attendent. This is several social levels above staying at the "Don't-Tell Motel," which offers hourly rates, eating the humble burger, fries, and apple pie served by a waitress named Flo.

Appearing at the charity affair as a guest, the protective agent can never forget that the only difference between him and the service maid is the role they are filling. Both are *employees* hired to perform a specific task. As an employee, the protective agent works at the whim of the employer and can be discharged at any time and for any reason (with or without cause). In the private sector, a protective agent might be fired for no other reason than the person being protected feels the agent is getting too close or becoming too familiar. In the public sector, the agent cannot be fired, but he can be quickly and quietly reassigned.

Employer–employee (protectee–protective agent) relationships can be best described in terms of *impersonal* relationships as defined by Verderber and Verderber[2] as "an impersonal relationship is one in which a person relates to the other merely because the other fills a role or satisfies an immediate need." When the need is fulfilled, the relationship ends.

A personal protection agent–protectee relationship should not happen. A *personal relationship*, according to Verderber and Verderber[3] "is one in which people share large amounts of information with each other and meet each others interpersonal needs." The key term in that definition is *interpersonal needs*. Although a great deal of information is shared between the agent and his charge, the information is best kept on a need-to-know or professional basis. When the protector and protectee are close together, sometimes day and night and under various circumstances, they may allow an inappropriate level of bonding to occur. When one person, usually the protective agent, assumes that a personal relationship exists, a line is crossed, and the agent may begin to believe he is of their world, not just in it. At this point, the protectee begins to feel that the agent is getting too close or too familiar. The line between love and hate is very thin.

WHAT DOES IT MEAN TO GET TOO CLOSE TO THE PROTECTEE?

From history, reality, and popular myth, we understand that getting too close to the client is an occupational hazard. In the scope of human experience, we have learned from psychological and sociological studies that having mixed company work closely together, either by design or accident, may lead to compromising situations. Even same-sex situations involving closeness and sharing of common experience will lead to close bonding or intimacy. Intimacy in this sense does not necessarily mean in a sexual manner but, rather, a personal closeness. The relationship between the protectee and the protector is a special one. To an extent, it is based on trust, and yet shared power and control. When someone is obligated for another's safety and well-being, personal relationships will form. This is called psychological transference. All of this can be intoxicating and lead to poor judgment and unprofessional conduct. "Good judgment comes from experience, and often, experience comes from bad judgment."[4] Getting too close to the protectee creates problems. There is a distinct loss of objectivity that is necessary to make difficult decisions.

FEELINGS, NOTHING MORE THAN ...

"The heart is deceitful above all things and beyond cure. Who can understand it?"[5] We know, intellectually, that feelings cannot be trusted. Where trust prevails, personal feelings (often in a sense of gratitude or obligation) should be expected. However, feelings always should be held in check. We should strive to maintain a balance. If personal feelings cloud judgment, the equation is out of kilter, and we have a problem. Feelings are intangible and, for most humans, difficult to control. Even balanced scales are never truly at equilibrium; they vibrate imperceptibly, but vibrate they do.

It is not exactly the same, but a relationship that, in the eyes of the beholder, has become personal can be likened to the characteristics of the delusion called *erotomania*. In this delusion, one person begins to believe the other person, usually of a higher status, is in love with him. When a protective agent assumes that a personal relationship exists, he is probably deluding himself; in all likelihood, it is a one-way relationship that can (and must) be quickly ended by the protectee.

In one such case, the agent was fired because he crossed over from impersonal relationship to personal. This person (taking on characteristics of erotomania) would not accept the firing because he "knew" the family really loved him. In time, he became a resolute stalker, following the family, making telephone calls, and actually presenting himself at the family's front door. He never accepted that the family was frightened of him. He is now serving time in state prison for the murder of the person he was supposed to protect. The line between love and hate is very thin indeed.

Of course, on the other hand, a protectee may cross the line and begin believing the agent is in love with him. There are examples of love that was reciprocated and ended with "...and they lived happily ever after," but they are few. Usually, the story has a more tragic or traumatic ending for one or both participants.

"Being in their world but not a part of it" can have other consequences, nearly as unfavorable or harmful. A protective agent can easily become accustomed to the high life, living in rich surroundings, enjoying the best food and drink, and being introduced to famous and beautiful people. It becomes an artificial way of life and lasts only as long as his relationship with the protectee. When the job is finished, the agent must remember that he has a wife and two children and lives in a middle-class neighborhood where he has to mow his own lawn, pay the mortgage, watch football on television, drink beer, and listen to his tired wife complain about the children's dentist bills. This is the highest level of entertainment, celebrity, and refreshment he will see in his private life.

People of a foreign background often note how difficult it is to live in two cultures—their own and American. The protective agent can find himself in the same situation, living in two cultures: the high life and as a middle-class husband, father, and homeowner. If any relationship suffers, it probably will be the one involving the family and home. It takes a steady hand to guide oneself through a course of such temptations as the agent finds in the world of the protectee. That is why the relationship between the agent and his protectee must operate on only one level, employer-employee, and that relationship must remain as impersonal as possible.

WORKING IN CLOSE PROXIMITY

The protective agent's primary responsibility is to protect the principal! The single most important aspect of that obligation is the advance. The higher-profile and most dangerous position, however, belongs to protective agents working close proximity to the protectees.

Close proximity[6] means working immediate to the person being protected. It is the innermost circle of the concentric protective circles in the secure environment. Usually within an arm's reach of the protectee, the inner-circle agent (the ninth circle in a ten-circle bull's-eye target), in an emergency such as an assault against the protectee, is expected to cover the protectee with his own body and evacuate him to a safer location. This maneuver is called, appropriately enough, cover and evacuate.

There are slogans or mottos for everyone. The Boy Scouts have "Be prepared" (although it is equally applicable to protection). The police (courtesy of the Los Angeles Police Department) have "To protect and serve." Security officers have "Observe and report," and the dominant truth of all is Spiderman's "With great power comes great responsibility," from creator Stan Lee. All of these slogans fit or are styled for close personal protection. But the primary slogan of protection agents must be "Cover and evacuate."

In a defensive position like personal protection, the reaction immediately required is for the protectee (the tenth ring in a bulls-eye target) to shield himself from the impending danger. The second reaction is to evacuate him to a safer place. This advice should be tattooed onto the brain of every personal protection agent. With the rush of excitement and the brain's physiological acceleration during an attack, the natural instinct might very well be to "duck and cover;" that is, to duck behind something (or someone) to provide cover from the shooting or blasting. There is no time to think and reason. Covering and evacuating must be an instantaneous natural response.

How is the protectee covered and evacuated? The agent closest to him doubles him over forward (to create a smaller target and to protect vulnerable body areas) by wrapping his (the agent's) closest arm around the protectee's middle, pushing the client's head down with the other arm, and positioning his own body between the threat and the protectee. Keeping the arm and hand that pushed the protectee's head down on the protectee's outside shoulder, the agent pushes and steers, at a run, the protectee away from the area to a more secure location. The second proximity agent on the opposite side of the protectee does the same from his side, but he also grabs the arm and shoulder of the first agent, building a "security fence" around the protectee. If there are third and fourth agents, the third clears an evacuation path through the crowd while the fourth delays the threat and/or protects the rear of the formation.

One evening, a U.S. president was attending a fundraiser in a large hotel reception room. As the president moved through the crowd, shaking hands and speaking with each of the estimated 1,000 people in attendance, the room lights suddenly and unexpectedly went out. The room was plunged into total darkness for a brief few seconds before power was quickly restored. When the lights came on, the president was on the floor with five Secret Service agents piled on and standing around him. They quickly raised him up and moved him out of the room until it was ascertained that the lights were accidentally turned off when someone brushed against the light switch, and there was no actual threat or danger. (In this case, the advance agent should have determined ahead of time that the light switch was in a vulnerable location and secured it, perhaps with tape, so it could not have been turned off accidentally.)

The inner circle protective agents (numbering one to four, or possibly five) surround the protectee and provide a shield from all directions. They never leave the presence of the principal when he is in a crowd. As the crowd moves closer to the protectee, the protective shield moves closer to the principal. The agents move from arm's length (standard when walking from one location to another and the crowd is at a safe distance) to nearly touching the principal when the crowd gets close. At times, they may even link hands or elbows.

If there is a full complement of security (which is very rare unless the protectee is on the high end of the economic and risk scales) the principal is surrounded as follows. One agent, usually the senior agent or agent in charge, walks on the right side (if the agent is right-handed), possibly a half step to the rear, always within an arm's length or closer. He can communicate with the protectee as they walk. He can whisper cautions, such as "watch your step" or "a step down." The right hand is usually extended toward the front and down, providing nonverbal communication to the crowd that says, "Please step back." He is in a position to easily come back, brush aside his unbuttoned suit coat, and pull his weapon, if necessary. His left hand is near the middle of the protectee's back, where he can guide the principal if necessary. It is best to avoid touching the person of the principal if possible. The agent is in a position to instantly cover the protectee. His field of vision is to the front and immediate right.

Another agent is in a similar position on the left side of the protectee. His field of vision is to the front and left side. A third agent walks in front, an arm's length away. His field of vision is to the front, left, and right. And a fourth agent walks to the rear, nearly walking backward, to protect the back side. The fifth agent is the point man, usually the advance agent who already knows the exact route, expected hazards, and everything! He walks a few steps in front of the lead agent. His responsibility is to open the crowd, watch for danger, and lead the protectee to his destination. He is the first to enter the elevators, round the corners, and enter a room.

This manner of walking with a protectee is called a *diamond* or *box* formation. The name is unimportant. What is important are the assigned responsibilities and awareness of accompanying agents. In this formation, the protectee is protected on

FIGURE 8.1   Detail leader briefing the protective team and answering questions. Photo by Carmen McKnight.

FIGURE 8.2   Preparing to leave the building where protectee attended an international women's conference. Not seen in the photograph is the point or lead agent. All points (front, sides, and rear) are covered. Photo by Carmen McKnight.

FIGURE 8.3   Attacker with knife suddenly strikes. Photo by Carmen McKnight.

all sides. If he should suddenly decide to change directions, to shake hands with an old friend or to answer a question from the press, the agent on that side simply becomes the leader and all agents rotate with the principal, maintaining close 360° coverage.

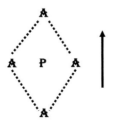

- The diamond formation is used in close quarters or when moving through a busy, crowed area.

- It is the most common of all formations.
- Agents are usually within "arm's reach" of the principal.

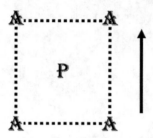

- The box formation is used in private areas and wide-open spaces.
- It is intended to give the principal privacy and personal space.

Elevator Entry

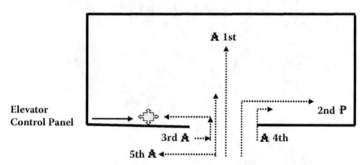

It is usually considered good manners to open a door for someone and let him go first, or to step aside at an elevator to let another person enter first. That is not true when working a principal! Keeping in mind an old saying, "the pioneers take all the arrows," a protective agent precedes the protectee through the door and into the room. The agent quickly scans the room, looking for anything or anyone that would present an immediate threat. Whenever the principal enters an elevator, a protective agent should be the first to enter, or they should enter almost simultaneously. If the doors close quickly or the elevator drops unexpectedly, there will be at least one protective agent on the elevator with the protectee.

If only one protective agent accompanies the principal, he would walk on the left or right side of the principal. If the agent is left-handed, he would walk on the left side of the protectee, with his right hand near the back of the principal and his left hand in a position to reach for his weapon. A right-handed agent would assume the same position on the right side of the principal. With the trailing hand near the principal's back, the agent could quickly and forcefully push him away while stepping into the line of fire (as Secret Service Agent Timothy McCarthy did when John Hinckley shot at President Reagan). A one-man security detail is very risky because of the many areas that have to be watched.

ONE PROTECTION AGENT

If at all possible, the "rule of two" applies. This means that every protective detail should have a minimum of two agents to work with the principal.

TWO PROTECTION AGENTS

• Within arm's reach of principal

THREE PROTECTION AGENTS

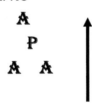

• Within arm's reach of principal

REACTIONS

If an overzealous fan or well-wisher shaking the principal's hand gripes it too tightly and does not let it go, the closest agent must respond and break the grip. This is accomplished by placing the agent's arm over the protectee's arm and hand and gripping the hand-shaker's hand. The agent then slides his other hand over the gripped hands, takes the thumb of the well-wisher in his own, and forces it up and away from the protectee's hand. If the hand-shaker resists and squeezes harder, the agent then will place a well aimed but restrained stomp of the heel of his foot across the bridge of the offender's foot. The agent continues smiling, looks the person in the face, and says "excuse me" as the maneuver is executed. The hands will be released, and the agent and protectee will continue moving on as though nothing happened. By the time the surprised fan recovers, there will be other people and space between him and the protectee. If the fan complains, the stomp can be explained and apologized away as an accidental and incidental movement with no malicious intent.

If an object is thrown at the principal, the covering agent seeing the object bats it down and away from the protectee with his hands, then executes the *cover and evacuate* maneuver. The thrown object should never be batted back into the air or caught! If the object is an explosive, it can detonate in the air, causing more extensive damage than if it were thrown or batted backward and toward the ground.

If an explosive device is thrown, covering agents should push the protectee to the floor, with his head away from the bomb. (His feet should be toward the explosive. If, in the chaos following the spotting of the explosive, this position is impossible in the rush to get the protectee down, the agents should at least instantly move the protectee into a prone or supine position.) Agents then place their own bodies between the explosion and the protectee. Quickly after the explosion, the agents should cover and evacuate the principal, keeping their bodies between him and the source of the explosion. While covering the protectee in this manner, agents should be alert for a follow-up attack, e.g., someone nearby with a gun. The agents would shield the protectee while bringing their own weapons into a position of defense. The agent nearest the explosive would have to throw his own body over the bomb to limit the extent of the explosive damage. Needless to say, that would probably be his last heroic action.

An agent sighting a weapon (gun or knife or similar instrument) will shout out, "Gun!" or "Knife!" and take instant action. He will immediately cover the protectee or step in front so as to take the shot or thrust. If he is within an arm's length of the assailant, he will attempt to knock or direct the weapon down and away from the principal or grab the weapon hand and pull it into his own body (as Secret Service Agent Larry Buendorff did with Lynette Fromme when she attempted to shoot President Ford). The remaining agents will immediately cover and evacuate the principal. He must be removed without delay to a safer location in case other attackers are waiting for an opportunity to strike. Most of the time, it is best to rush the protectee to his waiting car and speed away. (See figures 8.4–8.20.)

FIGURE 8.4   Agent closest to attacker (within arms reach) intercepts the attack and shouts, "Knife!"

FIGURE 8.5   Agent, applying appropriate restraint, disarms the attacker and hold's him for the police. Photo by Carmen McKnight.

FIGURE 8.6   Photo by Carmen McKnight.

FIGURE 8.7   Photo by Carmen McKnight.

FIGURE 8.8   Protectee is not injured but nearly faints as protective agents prepare to cover and evacuate. Photo by Carmen McKnight.

FIGURE 8.9 Covering and evacuation of the protectee. Note positioning of agents and placement of hands. Photo by Carmen McKnight.

FIGURE 8.10 Placing the protectee in the car preparing for departure. Note the watchful eyes and awareness of the protection team. The driver is already in place with the car running but in "park." Photo by Carmen McKnight.

FIGURE 8.11   A representative from an African country arrives at an international women's conference. She is accompanied by a her son, also a security agent from her own country, and a private protective detail. Note the presence of female protective agents. This particular protective team consisted entirely of females. Photo by Carmen McKnight.

FIGURE 8.12   As young teenage girls approach to ask for autographs, the protective team responds to intercept them and to cover the protectee. Photo by Carmen McKnight.

FIGURE 8.13   The protectee consents to give the girls an autograph and to spend a moment talking. The protective team carefully watches every movement. Photo by Carmen McKnight.

FIGURE 8.14 Arrival at the main entrance door to the conference. The close proximity agent will open the door and precede the protectee into the conference hall, followed by the remaining team. Photo by Carmen McKnight.

FIGURE 8.15 What is wrong with this picture? The protective agent is walking on the side of the protectee closest to the wall of a building. There is no threat coming from the wall. The proper placement of the agent is on the outside of the protectee, which places her in a position to react to danger from the open side. Photo by Carmen McKnight.

FIGURE 8.16 The protective detail forms a 360 degree protective circle around the protectee.

FIGURE 8.17 The details maintain total alertness on all sides.

FIGURE 8.18   The detail maintains a close ring around the protectee.

FIGURE 8.19   The shift leader has his hand near the middle of the protectees back, but is careful not to touch her.

FIGURE 8.20 In the event of an attack he can easily direct her in the direction she should go or push her out of harm's way.

Walking on a public street presents an assortment of challenges. If the passers-by on the sidewalk are spread out and paying no attention to the principal, the protective formation could spread out; it is always best to not draw attention. Again, if the crowd moves closer, then the protective shield naturally draws in closer. But the protection agents must also be aware of vehicle activity on the street, people in building windows and doorways, and potential threats from above. It is not a stretch of the imagination to expect to encounter potentially hazardous activity that is completely unrelated to the protectee's presence on the street. A crime, such as a robbery, could be occurring, and the protectee could unwittingly walk directly into it. He could be shot or taken hostage. A cardinal rule of protection is to be constantly alert for irregular or unusual conditions and activities. While walking with a protectee, the protective agents must always be scanning the passers-by and looking to detect any security or safety hazards.

Passing vehicles present an ever-present threat. In most major cities, drive-by shootings are everyday occurrences. In over 90 percent of the cases, an innocent bystander is shot. In some cities across the world, bombs thrown from passing car windows have been a threat and have caused considerable damage. Sometimes a vehicle is laden with explosives and detonated as the protectee goes by. And, of course, vehicles are used for kidnappings.

In one case, a protective detail was accompanying the nephew of the king of an important Middle Eastern country at about 9:00 P.M. There was only a small crowd on the street of La Jolla (San Diego), California, on that warm summer night, so the entourage was spread out, with the prince in the center. Suddenly, a speeding older-model van (with curtained windows) braked to a squealing stop in a parking spot immediately near the walking group. At the same time, the side door quickly slid open, and several people jumped out. Anticipating the worst, expecting the incident to be a kidnapping attempt, the protective detail quickly pulled their guns, moved close to the prince, and encircled him. The group responded to totally protect the prince. To everyone's relief, the people in the van were making a coincidental stop at the location, and it was quickly ascertained that no threat existed. But to all the people in the prince's group, it was a reminder of how suddenly a quiet, peaceful walk can turn into a hostile and violent encounter.

DECEPTIVE TACTICS

Deceptive tactics are challenges to the imagination and experience of the protective detail. In the instance of celebrities or other well-known and easily recognized protectees, it is sometimes necessary and prudent to use deceptive tactics to confuse, sidetrack, or throw off anyone tracking, surveilling, or attempting to maintain or initiate contact with the protectee. In this category are overzealous fans, stalkers, assassins, or terrorists, and (of course) those camera-toting magazine freelancers who have a love-hate relationship with the protectee: the *paparazzi*. There is literally no end to the deceptive tactics that may be utilized. The only limitations are the ability to imagine varying scenarios, the planning necessary to successfully execute the ruse, and the willingness and cooperation of the protectee.

Many celebrities use a pseudonym. Their travel bookings, hotel and restaurant reservations, and even real estate listings may be under the false name. It is not uncommon for television news personnel, for example, to use only part of their correct name. Some will use a married name or maiden name.

A common deceptive practice is the use of a double for the protectee. A person with the same general physical features as the protectee uses makeup, hair styling (or a wig), and clothing for the deception and travels in an official-looking vehicle or motorcade to draw the attention of anyone wishing to follow the principal. In the meantime, the real protectee (possibly in disguise) travels in a common-looking vehicle or secondary motorcade with little or no fanfare.

Many well-known celebrities dress in dowdy clothing and wear no makeup while flitting about town in an old, unwashed, beat-up sedan with faded paint. However, the car is more likely to be a year-old, luxury-type four-wheel-drive or SUV. The idea is to drive a vehicle that blends in with other cars in the area. Casualness draws little interest. Of course, the protective personnel likewise assume a casual posture with regard to their clothing and outward attitude toward the principal, appearing more like a companion, close personal friend, or business associate than an on-duty security professional.

One well-known television personality was seriously concerned about a former employee who was stalking her and making threats because she refused to lend him a large sum of money. The former employee knew everything about the celebrity, who had to use utmost caution when traveling about. She purchased a new car that the stalker would not recognize. She then would have someone else park the new car ahead of time at a location where she could quickly change cars and leave the more familiar one behind. With the older car in a secured garage where the former employee could not see or approach it, she would drive away and conduct her business (accompanied by a protection specialist, of course) in relative safety.

One day, she drove the old car (a year-old Mercedes) to her second residence on the beach in Santa Barbara (one that the stalker knew about). She parked in a conspicuous place in front, entered the residence, walked through the house, exited the rear door, and drove away in the new car. She managed to have a full day of business and pleasure alone while the protective specialist waited at the house as though he were on a fixed post, waiting for his protectee. At the end of the day, the principal returned and entered the house through the back door, and she and the security person left in the old car as though she had been visiting inside all day. After that, the harassing phone calls and threats soon stopped. The end of the threats had nothing to do with the deceptive ploy; it merely coincided with a restraining order and the possibility of arrest for stalking and extortion. But it was a very good tactic to sidetrack the pursuer.

WORKING A PRINCIPAL IN A CROWD

Working a principal in a crowd is very difficult. The risk factors increase so greatly that if there were a way of measuring them, like with a danger thermometer, the mercury would burst off the scale and out the end. The protectee is close to the crowd, individually speaking with as many people as possible, signing autographs, posing for photographs, and touching and shaking hands. He is very exposed and vulnerable. There are hands reaching toward him, some extending a pen, a note pad, or autograph book for his signature. Some people are holding babies (or is that a weapon wrapped in blankets!). There are umbrellas with long, spiked tips. Sometimes people are wearing long raincoats or overcoats. What is under the coats or in the pockets? Does anyone have his hands in his pocket? Cameras are clicking and whirring, and flashbulbs are going off near the face and eyes of the protective agents, momentarily causing "flash blindness." There is pushing and shoving and shouting. Everyone is calling out to the protectee and shouting his name, trying to get his attention for an autograph, photograph, or magic touch of a handshake.

Even a friendly crowd can have its risks. If the protectee is a famous and popular person, everyone wants to shake his hand or touch him. Sometimes the press of the crowd can close in on the protectee, leaving very little room to move. The circle of protection closes very tightly around the protectee, requiring the protective agents to link arms and hands to prevent the crowd from overwhelming him. Sometimes the protective agents have to lean against and shove the crowd back, all the while maintaining touch with the protectee, allowing no one inside the circle, watching, and pushing hands away. An agent must watch faces and hands in the crowd—especially the hands. In such circumstances, hands are reaching from all angles to just touch the person of the protectee. Hands over the top, hands reaching between other hands, hands extended past the protective agent, hands pushing and pulling! The hands are grabbing and pulling.

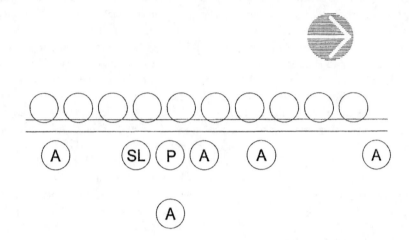

FIGURE 8.21   Fenceline situation. Agents (A) precede the principal (P). Along the fence-line looking for potential threatening persons. The principal is closely followed by the shift leader. (SL). The agent directly in front of the principal works very close to the principal looking at the faces and hands of the poeple along the fenceline who want to touch or shake hands with the principal. An agent trails along the fenceline while another agent surveys the whole scenario from the rear.

Watching the hands is very important. Nothing can happen unless the hands are holding a weapon or other device that could harm the protectee. In addition to guns or knives, also look out for pointed objects, pepper spray, and chemicals (such as acid) that could be thrown or rubbed in the face and eyes of the protectee. Anything can be used as a weapon. Look for it! The face and eyes of the attacker sometimes offer an early warning. In a friendly and happy crowd, look for the person who is unsmiling, even scowling. This person may maneuver to get close. He may be spotted working his way through the crowd, focusing on the protectee, paying no heed to the crowd. The attack could come from several rows deep. The attacker (as in the cases of Sirhan Sirhan, Arthur Bremer, and John Hinckley) extends his arm and hand, holding the gun up over the crowd, and begins firing! His total appearance may be different from the rest of the crowd. He may be wearing a hat down over his eyes; he may have a disheveled or dirty appearance; he may be wearing a coat when it is not appropriate; he may be sweating; he may look dour and serious while everyone else is laughing and having a good time. Look for the unusual, anything that doesn't fit. But that is speaking in generalities! An attacker could be well dressed and smiling as he plunges a long knife into the protectee. A suicide bomber could be wearing bulky clothing to cover the explosive and nail-loaded vest or belt while waiting for the protectee to come within range. The bomber might be clean-shaven to show his clean spirit to God.

While the agent dresses appropriately for the occasion, it should be borne in mind that even a friendly crowd presents special challenges. Therefore, it is wise to wear less than your best suit when there is a chance the protectee will dive into the

Head Table or Banquet Setting   **Stage Setting**

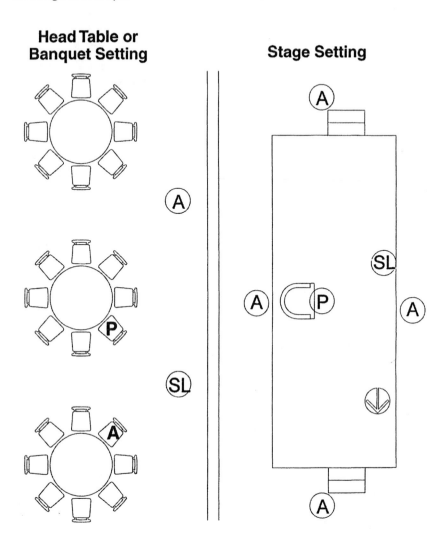

FIGURE 8.22   Agent positioning at a head table or banquet and a stage setting. An agent (A) is posted at each entrace of the stage with another agent positioned backstage or behind the curtain if one is present. The shift leader (SL) or another agent is positioned either directly in front of or on stage near the principal (P). The responsibility of the shift leader sitting on stage or near the protectee is to monitor the entire room while staying alert for any duress indicators from the principal and to respond to the protectee if needed.

crowd. Looking good and looking professional are important, but to have an expensive suit ruined by an overzealous crowd can be harmful to the health and welfare of the wallet and credit rating. Save the tailored designer diplomat-looking suits for those occasions when a power appearance is important. When working a crowd, wear an older, less-expensive suit, because the clawing hands may take a souvenir, such as a pocket.

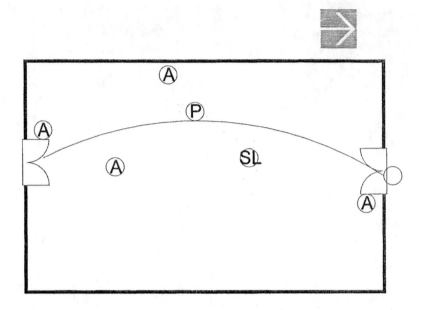

FIGURE 8.23 Receiving line. An agent (A) stands approximately an arm's length behind the principal (P). Other agents are positioned to observe the persons in the receiving line as it proceeds past the principal. The shift leader (SL) assumes a position near the receiving line in front of the principal.

Many protective agents have what they call a midnight or rainy-day suit. It is usually older, maybe getting a little worn, and on it's way to replacement. This suit is usually worn on the midnight shift when no one else is around; the agent may have to walk across dew-covered grass, vacuum the command post, or perform other duties that could possibly ruin a good suit. The agent would not want a new or very expensive suit to be exposed to the midnight conditions. The agent should wear this midnight suit when a close crowd or a great deal of physical movement is anticipated. It is not so shocking when an older replaceable suit is torn in the crowd melee.

The same suggestion holds for the wearing of jewelry. Many an agent has lost an expensive watch in a crowd situation. Watches having linking bracelets or snap-type bands are easily torn from the wrist, and there is nothing the agent can do. He may not even notice when the watch is grabbed. It is best to wear a watch with a leather or nylon strap or band and a buckle-type fastener. Large rings with stones can get caught in clothing or hung up on something, so if wearing a ring is important, it should be something simple, like a wedding ring. If the agent is wearing glasses, they should be secured by some method to prevent them from falling or being pulled off. Sunglasses should likewise be secured or quickly put into a pocket.

Sunglasses are the trademark of the stereotypical protective agent. Some bodyguards use the glasses as a prop to enhance their image. In actuality, sunglasses have a very real and practical purpose. They should be worn only out of doors. Sunglasses reduce glare, improving the protective agent's ability to see. They also prevent someone from seeing exactly where the agent is looking. When moving to the inside of a building, sunglasses should be removed just before crossing the door threshold. This allows the eyes to adjust to the different lighting conditions more quickly. The glasses then should be hastily stowed in a pocket, leaving the hands free to react to any circumstance. When departing the building, the glasses should be put back on just prior to crossing the exit threshold, again making it easier and faster for the eyes to adjust to outside conditions.

PROTECTIVE TEAM—SINGULAR

It is extremely difficult for a one-person protective "team" to provide 24-hour security coverage. But it is very common. Long after the protectee has retired for the night (which in itself may be very late), the protective agent may still have a few hours of work to complete. This may include making arrangements for the next day, writing reports, returning telephone calls, checking and confirming flight schedules, and whatever administrative duties are required. Then the agent must be up and ready to go at least an hour before the protectee to make sure everything is properly prepared for the day. What about arrangements for the protectee's breakfast, and how about the limousine and driver? Are they in place and ready to go? Are there any schedule changes? Has any new information been obtained, or have situations developed that would impact the safe movement of the protectee?

A very wealthy individual retained an executive protective company to provide two executive protection agents to accompany him on a nearly month-long vacation to Europe and other exotic places. The client expected 24-hour coverage, yet he also expected both agents to be with him and his group on their nightly outings to nightclubs, sometimes until daylight. The client and his friends were free to go to bed and sleep all day, which they did. But, alas, the security agents had to maintain their protective responsibilities during the daytime, allowing very little time for sleep. For the entire month, the agents managed only a few hours of sleep each day, grabbing a nap whenever they could, all the while being alert for any harmful activity.

On a one- or two-person protective assignment, personal contact with the protectee is usually very close, and the protectee comes to expect duties beyond the protective responsibilities of the protective agent. There are (probably literally) 1,000 different errands and "little" things that the protectee insists be done for him.

For example, many protectees prefer a morning newspaper delivered to their hotel room with the breakfast room service. The protective agent must arrange to have the paper delivered (or have a staff person do it, if one is available). The protective agent should accompany the room service delivery into the protectee's suite. A former government official, now in private business, wants a local newspaper delivered to his room the first thing in the morning but also expects a copy of the *New York Times, Los Angeles Times, USA Today,* and *Wall Street Journal* to be waiting for him on the back seat of the limousine.

It is not uncommon for a protectee to expect such common courtesies as sending a shirt out to be pressed, help carrying the luggage to the limousine, or even passing along instructions to service personnel. It is the duty of the protective agent to know and anticipate such trivialities; he should even know the five-day outlook of expected weather conditions. All these things have nothing to do with security, but they are important to a good working relationship.

PROTECTING CHILDREN, TEENAGERS, AND WIVES—FAMILY PROTECTION DETAILS

A man's wife and family are often included in a protective assignment. The basic principles of protection remain the same, no matter the sex or age of the person being protected, but there are unique differences in the way the principles are applied; there may be different protocols and relationships.

WIFE

The wife of a protectee may not have as high a profile as her husband, but she very often deserves and requires equal protection. Whenever possible, of course, it is best to have a female protective agent(s) assigned to the wife for all the obvious reasons relating to privacy and for going into public areas such as shopping malls, hair salons, meetings, and so on. In those instances, a female agent naturally would more readily blend into the environment than would a male. However, in the absence of a female agent, a male agent must be aware of situational differences and potential "tar pits" he may encounter that would not exist if he were working with a male protectee. A male agent working with a wife must recognize and respect her need for more privacy. There will be moments when a male agent should divert his eyes or provide more spatial distance. He must recognize that a woman's conversation with other women may be more intimate than a man's and make an extra effort to remain out of earshot.

Even with nothing more in mind than providing the best good-faith effort of protection, a male agent must be especially aware of his positioning and eye contact with a female protectee. If she has even the smallest feeling of discomfort with the way an agent looks at her, she may misinterpret his intentions as unprofessional. A protection agent may spend more time with a protectee's wife than with his own, and she may spend more time with the agent than with her husband. Closeness creates intimacy, and an agent must maintain a very strict professional line and never cross it. If, and, or when a protectee's wife slips her hand onto the agents arm or takes his hand for support, the physical contact must be taken only for what it is. Courtesy, respect, and professional conduct are extremely important when working with a female protectee. Misinterpreting or misunderstanding a word or gesture can create a problem that leads to the agent's dismissal.

CHILDREN TO AGE TWELVE

Working with young children presents a wide assortment of challenges that are not necessarily related to protection. The job description has been cynically referred to as "babysitter with a gun." But it takes a very special individual to render protective services while having the tenderness to relate to a young boy or girl. The agent must walk a very thin tightrope because of the many emotional pitfalls he must navigate.

He may become a surrogate father, substituting for the real father who is too busy to spend time with the youngster. He may play catch with a football or baseball, maybe kick a soccer ball, or even have tea parties or dress-up dolls. The child will form a very close bond with the agent, and the agent may also feel the bond. This bonding can be very devastating when it is time for the agent to move on. The child may feel like he is losing a parent, and the agent likewise may have strong feelings of emotional loss.

Behavioral questions and disciplinary problems that arise must be handled with good judgment. It is best to have the parents handle these questions, but if the parent is absent or too busy, the resolution will fall to the agent by default. This then becomes a very dicey problem. It is not the agent's position or within his authority to discipline his charge. Very often, it is also difficult to take the matter to the parent, who may reflect the blame for the bad behavior back onto the agent or even ignore the agent's concerns.

TEENAGERS

By any measure, teenagers are a special category. From the moment the clock turns their age from 12 to 13, and until they turn 20, boys and girls go through many metamorphoses; one moment they are the little boy or girl, lost and unsure, the next a mature and confident young person. Under normal circumstances, a teenager must face many problems and questions while searching for his identity. Add to the equation the requirement of living under the supervision and perhaps control of a protective agent, and the teenager will have to face the teen years under very trying circumstances.

The role of the protective agent takes on many facets beyond his protective responsibilities. It should not be that way, and neither should the agent encourage anything beyond his assigned duties. He should work to establish good rapport and understanding with the teenager, including behavior parameters. At times, the teenager will ask for help with his homework, sit quietly and engage the agent in conversation, or ask questions about life in general. He might ask questions about everything from teenage skin problems and how to be popular, to boy-girl relationships and social conduct. A prudent and wise agent will steer the questions away from most such topics and any other sensitive questions relating to sex, politics, or religion. If the teenager insists on talking about such topics, the agent should answer diplomatically and refer him to his parents, a teacher, a minister, or someone more qualified to discuss such matters.

Then there are the teenage troublemakers. They may be involved with drugs and alcohol and perhaps have little respect for others. They may be getting into fights or going to clubs and meeting a stranger for a one-night hook-up. This type of teenage protectee will attempt to ditch the protective agent, playing games like going into a building and exiting a side door, getting lost in a crowd, or having a companion divert the agent's attention while he goes out the back door. There are any numbers of ways a teen will attempt to elude his protective detail or deceive him.

There are no magic formulas or textbook answers on how to handle these nettling problems. An agent should try to communicate the seriousness of the circumstances to the teen and attempt to make him understand the consequences of his actions and how he could get kidnapped, hurt, or killed. In terms the teenager can understand, the agent should council him that the agent is there for the teen's own good, that the agent is not the enemy, and that the teen should not attempt to elude the one person who is dedicated to his safety. In the final analysis, the agent should try to win the teen's trust and cooperation as he would with any other protectee.

All persons, including a rebellious teenager, should be treated with dignity and respect. This may include calling the young man or lady "sir" or "miss." This will gain respect, and the agent can request the teenager to address him as "mister" or "sir." The agent must always remember that he is not a parent or buddy; he is an employee with a specific mission—to protect and keep the child or teenager safe.

PROTECTIVE ETIQUETTE

Etiquette is more than the "be nice" graces taught in the third grade by "Ms Manners." Etiquette means social skills: communication, demeanor, association, and, yes, even the manner of dress.

When discussing social skills, we mean areas of interpersonal action that indicate a well-bred, civilized person, including manners, conversation skills, and inoffensive behavior. Etiquette is knowing when to say please and thank you, and "may I help you with that?" In other words, it is saying and doing the right thing at the right time for all the right reasons. Etiquette implies courtesy. As previously stated, "Courtesy is more than good manners, it is a way of showing respect to others."

Communication comes in many forms and styles. Verbal communication includes much beyond the actual spoken words. It includes tenor and tone of the voice, inflections, jargon, and slang. The voice can indicate the mood of the speaker, his level of training, education, and experience. It can show surprise, shock, questioning, demands and orders, anger, and sympathy. It can be loud and boisterous or soft, soothing, and influential. Because we communicate on two levels, the spoken word (or "fact level") and through emotional intensity, we first absorb or decode the words and their actual meaning then interpret the emotional or unspoken meaning.

Good communication etiquette requires choosing words carefully to fit the appropriate setting and emotional level. It means using verbal skills equivalent to the social, educational, and emotional level of the speaker and listener. Learning to speak suitably is only half of the equation of effective communication. The other half is listening.

The listening requirement for good communication etiquette means listening actively, letting the speaker know you understand and are interpreting his words as he means them. This means listening on a nonverbal or emotional level as well as fact gathering. An adage says, "If you are talking, you are not listening; if you are not listening, you are not learning."

If you are busy talking and thinking of your reply, it is the same as interrupting and is considered rude and poor etiquette. At the same time, you are also missing emotional signals or body language that will allow you to address the real meaning and emotions of the speaker.

Etiquette is also apparent in the demeanor of a person. Demeanor means the way he carries himself, his movements, and his conduct. A protective agent carries himself with a confidence that shows in his walk, his standing posture, and his over-all carriage. Slumping or standing droop-shouldered indicates tiredness or lack of interest. Standing tall with "shoulders back, chest out, belly in" shows the observer that the agent is attentive, interested, and capable. His body movements are appropriate to the occasion, with hand gestures and facial expression in congruence with the setting and occurrence. Asymmetrical (or incompatible) body movements with the time, setting, and occurrence may be interpreted as being rude, crude, and of very poor etiquette.

An interesting yet often overlooked aspect of etiquette is association. A protective agent has his own friends, cohorts, peers, and social circle. It is considered not only rude but in poor judgment and bad etiquette to form relationships and associations with friends, peers, and cohorts of the person being protected. This can result in many serious consequences because, as stated earlier, "You are in their world, not a part of it." The people within the protectee's circle are best left with a totally impersonal relationship; make a favorable impression and leave it there. As the old saying goes, "Familiarity breeds contempt." It is best to remember that the mission of the protective agent is to maintain a safe secure environment, not to socialize and associate with friends of the protectee. A person being protected does not want his *employees* associating with his friends, guests, family, and business acquaintances.

The manner of dress says much of a person. "If you look good, you feel good; if you feel good, you do good." Dressing appropriately for an occasion tells the protectee that his protective agent is respectful of his considerations and settings. Customarily, a protective agent is expected to wear dark, conservative clothing—nothing loud or garish that would draw attention to him. On the other hand, when attending a beach function, golfing, or other informal events, the agent is expected to dress accordingly. It is also wise to not dress above the protectee. That is, don't overdress. Select suits, ties, and footwear that are just a notch below the style and quality of the protectee's apparel.

PROTOCOL

Good manners and etiquette necessitate certain rules of protocol when working with a protectee. Another word for *protocol* is *custom*, or a way of doing something. It is customary to address certain people by their current or last retained title. For example, a military general would be addressed as "General (whatever his name)"; a political figure by his position, such as Congresswoman or Congressman, Senator, or Mr. Mayor; and a judge by Judge or Your Honor.

In other circumstances, if there is no specific title, make reference as Mr., Mrs., or Ms. There is nothing wrong (actually it is encouraged) to use the old stand-by, calling a person either sir or ma'am. Some adults find it difficult to refer to a junior person as sir or ma'am, but a professional will not stumble over this small matter. The protectee might suggest or instruct that he be referenced by name. In that case, this is permissible.

It is up to the discretion of the protective agent to determine the proper physical distance between himself and the person he is protecting. The rule of thumb is "within an arm's reach" but, depending on the circumstances, it may be prudent to allow a much larger space. Ordinarily, people don't like having their space "invaded." Whenever possible, allow as much space between the person you are protecting and yourself as good judgment will allow. In two words, don't overcrowd him.

As a manner of respect, do not touch the protectee except in crowded situations where it is necessary to guide him or keep him from being touched by the crowd. In the instance of a female protectee, do not put your hand on her back, again unless it is absolutely necessary for good protection.

It is a matter of good protocol to not interfere in any way with any conversation or discussion in which the protectee is engaged. The protective agent, if he is close enough to hear the conversation, should pretend disinterest and most probably look away as if he were more interested in observing the activity surrounding the area. If the protective agent's advice is sought, he should be either noncommittal or neutral. The only area in which the agent should be considered enough of an expert to give advice is in the realm of security and possible risks to the protectee. The protective agent should never lie to the protectee, provide false threat assessments to frighten the protectee and ensure his own job security, or understate a potential threat.

SECURITY POSTS

A basic principle of protection is "never abandon your post or leave your protectee." This axiom should be tattooed on the forehead of every protective agent. Well, not really tattooed on the forehead, but on the brain, right beside "cover and evacuate." The agent should be able to remain at his post without wandering away. Some post assignments are truly boring (with a capital B!), and it is so easy to step a few feet away, then another few feet. In no time, the protective agent has wandered far enough from his post to allow a security breach that he may be unable to stop or detect.

Protective Agent "Wayward Willie" had a case of wandering feet; he just couldn't stand in one place. His company had a long-term contract with a popular television game show to provide audience screening (making sure no one came into the studio carrying, guns, knives, contraband material, or anything that could be used to cause injury) and to provide security for the stars of the show. Willie would work his screening assignment flawlessly and with merit. He was very good with the public, and nothing ever got by him. After the audience was all screened and in place, Willie then would be assigned a position somewhere backstage where he could become part of the protective circle around the show production and could prevent mishap to the stars.

But there was a serious problem. Without fail, Willie would begin to drift and wander. Before long, he would be far removed from his position, even when he was assigned to work in close proximity to the stars. Very frequently, he would be found somewhere near the stage area, often beyond the line of cables, cameras, and crew and would come into the visual area of the cameras. Willie was very popular with cast, crew, and his own coworkers. Even the big-name stars of the show called him by his first name and spent time with him in lively and laughing dialogue.

The common question was, "Where is Willie? Where has he gone now?" Everyone covered for him. Over time, though, his dereliction of duty began to wear on the producers, who would see him on the edges of their camera shots. When a new taping season began, the protective company was in place as usual, performing the audience screening routine. The cast and crew were the same, performing as in past seasons. But Willie was nowhere to be found or seen. The producers of the show had requested that he not be retained for another season.

The military has a general order that states, "Do not leave your post until properly relieved." That general order remains in full effect for security personnel. Never, ever leave your post until directed by a supervisor—unless, of course, it is required to shelter the protectee in an emergency situation. It may not be unusual for a principal to spot a protective agent and direct him to perform an errand. Decline as diplomatically as possible and offer to communicate with a supervisor or someone else who can complete the task without jeopardizing or compromising the security area. When directed to abandon the security post by a staff member, the same diplomatic answer is appropriate—even if the staff member angrily shouts, "I am ordering *you* to do it!"

Should a fight, fire, disturbance, or gunshots occur, only the protective agent(s) working in close proximity to the protectee should respond to the protectee. The posted agents must hold their post until directed to leave. The altercation or other disturbance may be nothing but a ruse to distract a post agent so an assault can be initiated.

Security posts are part of the second and third rings of protection around the protectee. There are several types of security posts with varying functions. A security post is an established area of responsibility assigned to a protective agent as a screening point to observe or regulate access to the secured areas.

CHECKPOINT

The checkpoint or choke point (as those waiting to be processed through may call it) is usually the busiest and most important post. Everyone who has an authorized reason or purpose to be in the restricted zone must pass through this location. It controls the number of people in the area of the protectee and restricts their movement. Everyone must be cleared to enter by security personnel tending the site. All suspicious acting persons are screened and noted. If there is reasonable cause to prohibit their entrance, they are prevented from entering. A checkpoint is usually established at some location where all must pass. It is usually setup in a hallway, doorway entrance, admission gate, or stairwell. One or two protective agents, with a host organization representative (sometimes including a local uniformed or plainclothes police officer), usually staff the checkpoint to verify identification and invitations and to inspect all entrants for weapons. Usually, the checkpoint is equipped with a metal detector—either a handheld wand or the larger, more sensitive type found at airports. All persons must pass through the metal detector with all bags, backpacks, cameras, packages, and other handheld items being physically searched and examined.

SURVEILLANCE POST

A surveillance post is established, as the name implies, to observe a specific area and the people in it. While being as inconspicuous as possible (although at times a high-profile visibility is effective and necessary), the surveillance posts pay particular attention to anything that could be harmful or embarrassing to the protectee and to anything that is abnormal, unusual, or out of place. Should anything be seen or detected that could impact the welfare of the principal, it should either be resolved (without leaving the post unattended) or reported to a command post or team member who can respond to investigate and negate the circumstance.

A surveillance post manned by a protection agent forms part of the second ring of security. It is established within a secured area, usually within areas the protectee will be present. The secured area is established and restricted by ropes, barricades, and locked doors. Upon establishing the secured area, it is searched for explosive devices and other items that do not belong or are considered to be potentially hazardous. If anything is discovered, it is removed. The surveillance agents assume their posts and become operational as the search gets underway. Agents accompanying the principal assume fixed surveillance posts in the vicinity of the protectee. There are two types of surveillance posts, roving and stationary (sometimes referred to as a *fixed* post).

1. The roving post may be walking and patrolling the entire secure area, usually with no particular assignment except to observe people and things and to respond to assist the fixed posts if necessary. Or the post may be in a car, patrolling the perimeter of the secured area, making contact with suspicious persons, or investigating unusual activity. In some extreme cases (such as a high-profile protectee like the president), the observation post may be located in a helicopter, scanning the entire procedure from overhead.
2. The stationary (fixed) post may be located anywhere to observe and maintain the integrity of the security zone. It may be at the entrance or exit to a room, on a highway overpass or underpass, on a rooftop, in a hotel corridor, or at strategic locations throughout the building and room where the principal will be in attendance. It may be on the balcony of a hotel.

A U.S. vice president was visiting Los Angeles ("on a dark and stormy night") and was staying in the presidential suite of a (very) high-rise hotel. The suite was located at least 30 stories above the ground floor. The supervising shift leader that night assigned a freshly appointed (and relatively inexperienced) agent to the vice president's protective detail, to the balcony outside the vice president's suite. He explained that the post was important and necessary to prevent a terrorist from rappelling down the side of the building to gain entrance to the vice president's rooms. The young agent reasoned, without convincing, that it would be more practical to have the position located on the roof, a floor above. He did not see the smiles or share in the laughter of the other agents as he spent a good share of the entire midnight shift on the balcony, braced tightly against the wall, an eternity above the ground. It must have been a successful deterrent, however, because not one terrorist scaled down the side of the building that night! Or any time since, as far as they know.

SURVEILLANCE POST GENERAL INSTRUCTIONS

An agent assuming a surveillance post must know and be aware of many things. Some are very obvious, some a little more subtle. Naturally, the agent must know who his supervisor is and who the principal is and be able to recognize him. He should also know members of the family and key staff. He should be aware of the principal's schedule, knowing arrival and departure times. Of course, the agent should be aware of the principal's location within the secured area. It is the responsibility of the command post to notify the posts of any movements of the principal and to keep them informed of the principal's location. The post agent must know and recognize the current form of immediate identification in use by other protective personnel and people authorized to enter the secured zone for that particular site. Is it a recognizable lapel pin, picture identification card, or something else?

The agent must also know the locations of the other surveillance posts and the activities planned for the adjacent posts as well as his own responsible area. Each post will have specific instructions and equipment unique to that particular post. The agent must be familiar with his post directives and the operation of all emergency equipment. Of course, the agent must not vacate his post until directed by the command post or until properly relieved by another agent. When relieved by another agent, he must fully brief the relieving agent about the post coverage and operation.

SPECIALTY POSTS

When working with a principal, certain special assignments require a protective agent or strict oversight.

1. *Luggage.* Being responsible for the luggage is a very critical assignment. Upon departure from the residence, for example, the bags should be locked and distinctive seals placed over or across the opening. If the bag is opened, the seal will be broken and provide a good, quick indicator of possible tampering. All protectee and protective agent baggage should be escorted and monitored until it is placed into the care and control of the airline personnel. Upon retrieving the luggage at the destination, the seals should be checked before removing the bag from the airport. If the bag has been opened, it should be fluoroscoped if possible, then physically examined and searched to determine that nothing has been placed in the bag or removed.

2. *Protective intelligence response.* If a suspicious person is encountered or threats are received by the checkpoint or surveillance posts, the protective intelligence response agent will be notified. He will react to interview the suspicious person, possibly escort him out, or otherwise resolve the situation so the post agent can return to his normal duties.

3. *Relief.* When the advance man determines the number and location of posts, he should also determine the number of relief personnel needed. The relief agent(s) should be briefed on the requirements of each post and be able to

fill in on a routine or emergency basis. Relief is utilized to give the post agents a break for meals, refreshment, or bathroom. When not relieving a post, he should assume a walking or roving post or be available in the security room or command post to assist at any location.

4. *Security room.* This is a break room utilized by "off-post" agents. The agent's spare equipment or other amenities such as meals and drinks are maintained in this room. It may or may not be staffed at all times. If it is not staffed, it should be secured.

5. *Command post.* This is the nerve center or *command module* of the whole operation! It is usually a 24-hour operations control center. At an event site, it is a centrally located, fixed post used to provide communication, equipment, information, and directives. The command post is a conduit for all information, receiving and disseminating pertinent information to all appropriate areas. Someone who is experienced and familiar with the entire procedure should operate the command post. At the time he is briefed by the advance agent, the command post agent(s) should have a complete walkthrough so he will be familiar with the posting and what particular problems the agents on post are likely to incur. He will oversee, direct, and coordinate the security function with all other elements of the protective assignment. He may be in communication with the host organization, staff, support personnel, and the local police and fire departments. He may have direct contact with the protectee. He maintains a radio log of all the protectee's movements and fields all communications and inquiries. In generic terms, he is the supervisor or administrator responsible for the successful execution of the protection assignment.

The command post is generally equipped with everything necessary to maintain the security and safety of the principal. The equipment and resource material may include (but certainly is not limited to) closed-circuit television monitors; telephones (cellular and land line); appropriate telephone numbers and directories; first-aid kit and resuscitator; maps and diagrams; notebooks containing special orders, directives, memoranda, and photos of the principal, his family, and staff; duplicate car and room keys; flashlights and radios; spare batteries and a charger; emergency lighting designed to come on when power is turned off; binoculars; and computers and copy and fax machines.

The command post is a professional place of business that is very critical to the successful administration of the protection program. It should be maintained as a business operation. It should be kept clean and orderly. If the command post is located in or near the residence of the protectee, always expect him to drop in at any time. If a temporary command post is established at a principal's temporary residence (e.g., in a hotel) it should be near the principal's suite but not adjacent to it. It should be between the principal's suite and any general traffic areas but, if possible, away from the general traffic areas. If maid service or room service people have access to the command post, it should be only at specified times and when their activities can be monitored. When an outsider such as hotel staff is present, all sensitive material should be covered, and conversation concerning the protectee and others should be restrained.

Because of its 24 hour operation and security, the command post may be utilized as a short-term depository for protectee and agent valuables, packages, equipment, briefcases, and so on. Have all money and valuables including (passports and other documents) placed in an envelope and sealed. Write the owner's name on the envelope. All packages should be stapled shut or sealed and all briefcases and suitcases locked. All deliveries, mail, packages, official or unofficial inquiries, and so on should be directed to and received by the command post before being delivered.

Some principals place a telephone and fax for receiving official after-hours messages in the command post. These messages should be logged and delivered to the principal according to his instructions.

SUMMARY

When working a protectee, it is important to know as much about the person and the background of his or her business as possible. (See Appendix.) Good manners, etiquette, and professional protocol are important and should be maintained at all times. Professionalism comes with many faces but, in the protective arts, professionalism must mean the highest standards possible in areas from education and training to interpersonal relationships.

It is very easy for a protective agent to cross the line and begin to believe he is a buddy, pal, or confidential advisor to his protectee. But he has to remember that he is an employee, and the relationship must stay at that level. Once the line of employer/employee is crossed, the relationship can never be the same, and the loser will be the agent. The protectee will feel overcrowded and that the agent (employee) is getting too close or too familiar. People come into our lives and they go out. Keeping the relationship impersonal will result in better communication, belief, trust, and confidence in the protective agent. The protectee will feel the agent is professional, with no personal emotional involvement and that personal prejudice, bias, or emotion will not cloud his security decisions.

Etiquette and protocol play very large roles in the relationship between a protective agent and a protectee. Etiquette shows courtesy, good manners, social grace, and respect. It is evident in the manner of speech, actions, dress, and consideration of others. Protocol calls for completing a task in certain prescribed or customary ways.

The rules of protocol and etiquette dictate how one addresses the protectee (in a respectful yet nonfamiliar way), how one walks with him, and where he sits in the car. At times, an agent should appear to ignore personal conversations between the protectee and others within his confidential circle. It is important to show good taste and social grace.

For the agents working in close proximity, the watch words are: be prepared for and expect any emergency, do not fall for diversionary tactics, sound off to alert others to the danger, react to cover and evacuate the principal, and, if working an outer ring of protection (fixed posts), never abandon or wander away from the assigned position.

REVIEW QUESTIONS

1. Explain close proximity.
2. What is the meaning of cover and evacuate? How is it important?
3. What meaning do the following slogans or mottos have for personal protection:
   - Be prepared
   - To protect and serve
   - Observe and report
   - With great power comes great responsibility

4. Define and explain working a principal.
5. Describe the working formations and each agent's responsibility.
6. Why should an agent precede a principal around a corner, through a door, and onto an elevator?
7. Objects are being thrown at the protectee. What is the correct response?
8. Why should agents be alert for a secondary attack?
9. What particular attention should be paid while walking on a public street? What is the agent positioning?
10. Describe some types of deceptive tactics. Under what conditions should they be considered and used?
11. Why is working a protectee in a crowd so difficult and dangerous? What particular things should be looked for?
12. Why are sunglasses a valuable part of an agent's equipment? Explain the proper usage.
13. Why is the wearing of an expensive suit and jewelry discouraged?
14. What information should an agent have about a protectee?
15. How does providing protection by a singular agent differ from a full team?
16. Describe a surveillance post and specialty posts. What are their respective responsibilities?
17. Explain the extra importance of a command post.
18. Why should you develop a profile of your client?
19. How can a client's prejudices and attitudes pose a danger?
20. What are some special problems you might face in protecting politicians?
21. What are some special problems you might face in protecting corporate executives?
22. What are some special problems you might face in protecting diplomats or foreign nationals?
23. What are some special problems you might face in protecting celebrities?

NOTES

1. Copyright date June 1994.
2. Verderber, Kathleen S. and Verderber, Rudolph F. *Inter-Act: Interpersonal Communication Concepts, Skills, and Contexts,* 9th ed. Belmont, CA: Wadsworth-Thompson Learning, 2001, 72.
3. Ibid, 73.
4. Rita Mae Brown (b. 1944), American writer.
5. Jeremiah 17:9, King James Bible. http://www.biblegateway.com/quicksearch/?quicksearch=heart+deceitful&qs_version=31
6. The term is actually redundant. *Close* means near; *proximity* means nearness. But the phrase *close proximity,* in protective service jargon, means, "within arm's reach of the person being protected."

9 Principal's Home, Work, and Play

There are only three places a protectee is vulnerable: At home, at work, or in transit.

Be it ever so humble, there is no place like a fortified, monitored, alarmed, and guarded home ... or business.

Cynical close personal protection specialist

ESTATE SECURITY

If the most dangerous time in a person's life is when he travels, the safest time and place is (or should be) at home. Home and hearth; warm, comforting, and secure feelings. That is the way it was when the world of the high-powered protectee extended no farther than his bedroom, house, or lawn. But now, after acquiring fame, glory, renown, wealth, and power, the meaning of a secure home has drastically changed.

Home invasion robberies and burglaries are at an all-time high. The continuing and constant threat of stalkers and terrorist kidnappings and/or murder ensures that the physical home environment has evolved backward from unlocked doors and "strangers are welcome" back to the Middle Ages with its fortifications and thick walls, armed guards, and watchdogs (or geese) that sounded an alarm at the approach of strangers.

It is very typical for today's protectee home to be located in a gate-guarded community, with a uniformed security officer allowing entrance only with a code word, personal identification number, or magnetic card, through a gate or a raised a crossing bar. High walls or foliage surrounds the perimeter of the homeowner's property (the castle grounds). Entrance is gained through a remotely controlled gate (replacing the moat and drawbridge) and monitored with cameras and intercom systems. Inside, the house is alarmed with the latest bells and whistles (replacing the geese) and with armed security professionals (like sentries carrying spears on the castle walls) monitoring the estate through closed-circuit television (CCTV). The only thing that has changed in 500 years is the technology of securing the "king's" property.

A protectee's house, residence, or estate should be the hardest target for an invader to penetrate and the place where a principal (and his family) can feel safe and relax, free of worry about personal injury, kidnapping, invasion, and burglary. But there are no guarantees and, as in all security, there can only be best-faith attempts and strong deterrent efforts to prevent uninvited and unauthorized intrusion. Even places like the White House cannot be guaranteed 100 percent safe against encroachment. It is protected by a tall, steel fence, alarmed grounds, strategically placed and imaginative lighting, and the ever-present watchful eyes of the Secret Service uniformed division officers and special agents. Counter sniper teams on constant surveillance on the roof to use whatever means necessary to stop airborn intrusion or a sniper hidden in a Washington DC apartment facing the White House. Cameras with pan, tilt, and zoom capability are constantly monitoring the fence and grounds. Even so, some (usually deranged) persons frequently attempt to climb the fence and make a dash to the president's residence or office. On two unrelated occasions, a person has attempted to land an airplane either on or in the house. There are also people who enter the White House by joining the daily public tour and try to slip away for their own nefarious purposes. When stopped, as they always are, they usually attempt to claim to be just a tourist who got separated from the tour and became lost. But the Secret Service has procedures in place to safeguard against the possibility of someone innocently getting separated and lost.

Just as at the White House and with personal security, the goal of estate security is to bring the odds of transgression more in favor of the resident. This is accomplished by maintaining the same system of concentric circles. The series of circles includes planning, people, procedures, systems (alarms), and barriers. Physical security is limited by only two factors: imagination and finance.

The technology is available to provide the very highest in sophisticated electronic protection. What can be imagined and paid for can be implemented. On the exterior and grounds of the estate are seismic alarms that are buried in the ground to detect the footsteps of an intruder. There are photoelectric beams and microwaves that can be positioned to go into alarm when broken or disturbed. The beams and alarms can be joined with lights and cameras to come on instantly to detect and monitor the movements of anyone walking, creeping, crawling, or running on the property. The CCTV cameras are connected to VCRs that record an entire 24-hour period. The tapes are usually retained at least for a week and are available for review should the necessity arise. There are cameras that take instant still photographs that can be used for identification purposes. Then, of course, there are computers to receive, store, and analyze all data. A very good and effective system is a loud, screaming siren alarm system connected to a very powerful strobe light system inside the residence. An intruder would find it highly disorienting if he were in a dark house and then the siren and strobe lights came on. If you can imagine it, it is available and can be installed.

Beyond the limitation of imagination, installation of complex, sophisticated electrical equipment is restricted by the budget. It is very expensive to purchase the hardware (CCTV, VCRs, beams, control panels, monitors, and power supplies) and software (computers and appropriate programs) and to have it installed. The expense can jump into the high thousands of dollars very quickly. When planning and engineering an alarm and associated systems, the cost should be taken into consideration, with the systems being integrated into an efficient combination that provides maximum coverage while minimizing costs.

The principle of providing protection around an estate is the same as the moving concentric circles around a protectee as he travels. The systems are arranged in layers or circles within circles to form a greater deterrence. The challenge to security equipment specialists is to provide a target that is difficult to penetrate and affords little opportunity for an authorized or unwanted person to gain entrance. The intent is to discourage an intruder so that he selects another target down the street. Estate security, in other words, is a series of concentric circles consisting of planning, technological systems, procedures, barriers, and people.

PLANNING

Planning begins with conducting a thorough, ongoing, security survey, identifying and noting all possible weaknesses, vulnerabilities, and possible points of infiltration. The survey must be a constant ongoing process, because conditions change. Lighting goes out, and equipment malfunctions and deteriorates. If equipment is not maintained, it eventually becomes a possible weakness, inviting to a person wishing to make more than a neighborly visit.

The survey begins with a physical inspection of the grounds, premises, and house. Beginning at the property boundary line, the inspection looks for holes and gaps in the fence or hedge. Walking in ever-tightening circles around the property, the inspecting security specialist determines areas requiring attention and notes the best possible positioning for security systems hardware. Electrical wiring, telephone communication lines, and plumbing safeguards must be installed and enclosed in tamper-proof containers or placed underground. All lines and plumbing, if possible, should be underground, with the control boxes in a secured area and locked. There should be an alternative power source, such as a fully fueled generator, located in a secured area. The generator should be test run on a routine basis, with extra fuel stored in safe containers. Doors, gates, locks, fences, and windows must be repaired or installed where appropriate.

The human factor of the survey includes interviews or conversations with family members and domestic and household staff to determine routines and to learn of any particular areas of concern. These conversations and the ensuing information are very important, because the security systems and procedures must accommodate the lifestyle of the household members.

After all the required information has been obtained, it is analyzed, with the resulting conclusions being the basis for the formulation of the overall physical security plan integrating alarms, lights, cameras, and activities.

PHYSICAL AND PSYCHOLOGICAL BARRIERS

Physical barriers include anything the intruder must go over or around to gain entrance. The outside circle, the perimeter, consists of fences and gates, walls and hedges, and trees or shrubbery. The fences should be of a style that will prevent entrance in that location. The most common type of fence consists of vertical steel bars, approximately six to eight inches apart and eight to ten feet tall. At the top, there is a decorative spike or, in some instances, razor wire. Trees, plants, shrubbery, and hedges might be planted along the fence line to add privacy to security. The greenery should have thorns, spikes, thistles, or barbs and briers (e.g., roses, cactus, and berry bushes) that will discourage anyone from attempting to climb over the fence and through the hedge. A barbed-wire fence can be very effectively added and camouflaged in the shrubbery.

At the driveway gate entrance, a speed bump could be installed in the driveway to force a vehicle to slow down or even stop before approaching the gate. The gate must be heavily reinforced to prevent ramming. A telephone speaker and CCTV camera should be mounted where the driver must exit the car for admittance and identification. The lens of the camera should have zoom capability to view the guest closely enough for identification. A still camera should be focused to take instant photographs of the visitor and his vehicle, including the license number, for a permanent record or further identification purposes.

A protective agent in a command post monitors all approaches to the gate. When the still camera takes a picture of the visitor, it is instantly transmitted to the agent's computer monitor to be printed as a hard copy. After determining that the visitor is authorized entrance (by visual identification and voice contact through the telephone speaker), the monitoring agent remotely opens the gate then quickly closes it to prevent a *tailgating* entrance by an unauthorized person. Some estates require a security person to be physically present at the gate to identify visitors and control the gate openings and closings.

Inside the perimeter, strategic landscaping hides the cameras and electric eye beams that overlap into zones of protection. The well-placed trees and shrubs, and even the swimming pool and outdoor furniture, provide simple barriers an intruder must dodge.

Psychological barriers are open areas like a well-lighted lawn or patio. Gravel driveways and surrounding areas are good because of the noise made when someone walks on them. A highly visible camera adds to the deterrent effect of psychological barriers. Motion detectors with floodlights that come on when someone attempts to cross a specific zone will dissuade all but the most determined and skilled.

A highly placed executive from a well-known company was staying at a remote country resort hotel in San Diego, far removed from the sights and sounds of the city. The nights were quiet, and there was very little activity after the executive retired for the night. The threat level was very low, he was not a controversial figure, and people outside his business and social circle did not know him (or even care who he was). At the rear of the executive's residence was a wide gravel driveway monitored by motion sensor lights that would flood the area with bright light whenever the photoelectric beams were disrupted.

Two of the midnight shift protective agents were former Navy Seals. Every night around 2:00 or 3:00 A.M., both agents would attempt to cross the zone without making any noise or making the light come on. They were successful in approximately 75 percent of their attempts. Both agents eventually returned to active military duty. The object lesson learned from their nightly exercise was that nothing is to be taken for granted and that technological systems can be thwarted.

Psychological and physical barriers may be combined into a deterrent so intimidating that no one, regardless of his intent, will attempt to transgress. In olden days when the West was being opened to settlers and pioneers, a form of defense was to circle the wagons when the resisting Indians attacked a wagon train, thus creating a nearly impenetrable fortress or barricade. That was the theory in 1971, when several hundred thousand angry anti-Vietnam War demonstrators, radicals, and rabble rousers invaded Washington, DC, during the so-called "Days of Rage." Their intent was to completely shut down the government until they could be heard. There were rumors and intelligence information to the effect that the protesters were planning to invade the White House. In defense of the White House, city transit buses were parked tightly bumper to bumper in a close and tight ring around the White House complex. The barrier was so formidable that there was no attempt to storm the White House. Either it was a very effective deterrent or invasion plans were changed or merely rumors.

TECHNOLOGICAL SYSTEMS

Supplemental to the human element are the bells, whistles, lights, and sirens circle of protection technology—the "toy factory" of the industry. There is no limit to the technology hardware available and the configurations in which it may be applied. The system can include infrared beams, lights, seismic sensors, cameras, and intercom systems, to name just a few. Installation of the intrusion detectors, fire alarms, CCTV, and other equipment affords 24-hour-a-day monitoring inside and outside the residence.

Whatever the arrangement or equipment utilized, the protective principles remain the same. The system should be designed so that one type of system overlaps another, and the covered area and premises should be "zoned out." *Zoning* means that, if an alarm is registered, a quick glimpse of the monitoring control panel will instantly inform the protective agent of the exact location of the potential security violation. Also, zoning provides for periodic disabling of certain sectors to allow for resident movement and freedom. Overlapping and integrating the systems increases the capability of any particular portion to support another, extending and increasing the effectiveness of the whole system. For example, the lights and cameras instantly activate and trace the movements of the violator in whatever sector an alarm is activated.

RESIDENTIAL BUILDING

The heart of the estate rings of protection is the residential building itself. All doors, windows, and locks must be in good order and secured. Each door, window, and other opening should be alarmed with special glass-breaking detectors. Windows made of polycarbonate or similar transparent yet nonbreakable materials add an extra layer of strength. Bushes and greenery having thorns, barbs, and briers may be planted near and under windows and around anything that could be used for climbing to the second floor or through a window.

Smoke, fire, and heat detectors must be strategically located and communicate to the protective agent in a special command post. Tests have indicated that the best location for smoke detectors is in the center of a room, because smoke circulates throughout a room. If the detector is located in a corner near the bedroom door (where most detectors are placed), the entering smoke may escape detection until the room is filled with it.

In the interior of the residence, the homeowner might have a *safe room* constructed. The room is fortified and reinforced. It should contain emergency equipment such as a food and water supply, an independent lighting system, and communications devices (e.g., cellular telephones and a radio monitored in the protective agents command post). Perhaps it should be located at an off-residence site such as the protectee's business place. The room could contain a safe with all the important family papers, valuables, and so on. The room entrance should have an alarm and be secured whenever no family member is present. The protectee and his family could seek temporary refuge in the safe room should an attack be made against the residence. A secret escape door should be installed if possible.

PROCEDURES

An invisible yet effective circle of protection consists of procedures. The chosen method of permitting admittance to the estate or residence has a deterrent effect on all unauthorized visitors. The security specialist, working with the protectee, should establish a set of regulations and guidelines for receiving visitors, deliveries, service and repairmen, and mail and packages. A system of maintaining a log to register all entering and departing visitors to the property must be maintained. Any unexpected delivery men or similar visitors must wait outside the gate until their purpose, identification, and intent has been verified. The procedures should be strictly enforced, routinely reviewed, and reconsidered to sustain their effectiveness.

All personnel responsible for enforcement of the admittance procedures should remain alert to overly inquisitive people and those attempting to gain entrance for no legitimate or authorized reason. Whenever there is an unusual occurrence, such as an attempted penetration or an overly inquisitive person, a report recording the occasion must be prepared and filed. The events and person(s) should be investigated to determine any potential risk factor. Repeat occurrences could signify a planned attack of some nature against the protectee or his family.

PEOPLE

The innermost of all the circles is the intimate surroundings of the protectee. He and his family, friends, and business and domestic staff are an important and integral part of the internal security program. Their awareness and alertness to such things as strangers; persons asking questions about the protectee, his security, and his schedule; and any unusual occurrences is crucial. Anything that arouses their suspicion should be brought to the attention of the protection specialist immediately. A continuing, friendly, ongoing dialogue and open communication with the family and staff must be a high priority to the security people. Protective personnel must establish a good working relationship with the domestic staff as well as the professional staff. The staff is a great source for pertinent information that otherwise might not be communicated to security. They know of any pending trips (to the grocery store, the doctor, or out of town). The household staff knows the household schedule and times the protectee will depart for work and other locations. They know when and what guests are expected. They usually know all delivery persons and are aware of any expected gifts or packages. They are usually good sources of information regarding the location of emergency power switches, cutoff valves, and so forth.

Working within all these circles is perhaps the most crucial component of all... the protection personnel. They provide the element that ties it all together. They should be stationed around the estate at strategic locations where they can maintain full physical surveillance of the residence and not rely exclusively on the technological equipment. Should any untoward activity occur, they are placed where they can readily respond to neutralize the activity or proceed directly to the protectee.

Usually operating out of a centrally located command post (a room that might be set aside by the homeowner), the protective agents monitor and respond to all alarm systems, enforce regulations for admittance, and provide whatever assistance the protectee should need. The command post is equipped with the control panel for the alarm systems, CCTV monitors, telephones, radios and extra batteries, emergency and rescue equipment (fire extinguishers and first aid gear), operating procedure manuals, and office equipment. A home away from home for the protective agents, the command post should be maintained, equipped, and supported like a professional business operation.

OFFICE SECURITY

The concept of protectee insulation as a deterrent is as effective a tool in the workplace as it is at a residence or while traveling. As many barriers and procedures as practical and possible should be placed between the potentially targeted executive and an intruder. A secure work environment begins at the entrance to the business property. That usually means the parking facility. Many corporations, agencies, and film studios arrange for employee parking to be in a structure or outdoor lot that has public access. From the first World Trade Center bombing in New York, in 1993, we learned how easy it is for a dissident or terrorist group to plant a bomb in such an open and freely accessed building.

If security for the person or group of individuals exists in the workplace, it should commence in the parking area. It is not unusual for the protective personnel to be responsible for the safety and well-being of the protectee(s) only in the workplace because, very often, the threat is from a former employee who might have no way of knowing where the executive lives. Some public figures, like entertainers, have protection only at the studio, because they are most concerned about the crunch of fans who want to get close to the celebrity.

One or more representatives of the protective team should be positioned in the parking area well before the expected arrival of the protectee. They will monitor the arrival and parking of all employees and others in the facility. If the protectee has a designated parking space, it should not have his name on it. If the parking space is designated by a sign that displays a name, it should not be the protectee's real name. In the case of a young and attractive (and very popular) television series star, her parking place was marked with the name of a former high school male companion. The protective assignment began with the prepositioning of at least one, and usually two, protection agents in the vicinity of her parking place. The agents would meet the lady and escort her to her dressing room in the studio. From the time of her arrival until she departed at the end of the day, the agents would escort her wherever she went. At the end of the day, the agents would see her safely back to her car and out into the public street. One agent would follow her in his car until a few blocks from her residence to make sure no fans were also following.

As a protectee arrives in the parking lot, the protective agent(s) will meet and accompany him to his office. All protective personnel should be alert to someone suddenly sitting up in a vehicle or exiting the trunk or passenger area with a weapon or explosive device. If possible (and practical), the parking structure should be continuously monitored, either by a security presence or CCTV. Inside parking, with limited natural lighting, should have sufficient artificial lighting to eliminate all shadowy hiding places.

The protective agents will be objects of wonder and curiosity to the employees who are not aware of the circumstances or even the reason for the sudden appearance of "strangers in dark suits" who seemingly do nothing except "just standing there." It is a management decision as to the amount of information provided to the rank and file. All protective agents should maintain their professional attention and project an image of professionalism and company dedication. They should be friendly yet firm in enforcing policies and procedures. They will be highly visible, just by the fact of their presence, yet it is important to maintain a low profile and not interfere in any way with the routine of the employees or the operation of the business.

Access Control

The key to controlling workplace violence from an outsider (or former employee) is to control access to the office or place of business. Limiting and monitoring access will tell employees and outside personnel that the business considers workplace security to be a high priority. Monitored CCTV cameras should be mounted in the elevators, stairwells, and main doors leading into the business. Entry into the work facility is gained from an electronically controlled lock on the door. A visitor must speak with a receptionist or security person before gaining entrance. Authorized employees gain entrance by swiping[1] a magnetized reader card near a contact point of the door and/or entering a numerical combination.

Inside the office space, a counter (sometimes with a bulletproof and smash-resistant glass partition) should separate the reception area from the main business section. All visitors must sign a visitor's log after determination of their identification and authorization for being in the facility. The offices of core executives should be well away from the main entrance to the office or business. A protective agent should be positioned in the area of the executive offices. Depending on the threat level, an agent might be stationed in the hallway near the elevators or main entrance. All entrances and exits to business premises should have access restricted either through a monitoring process such as CCTV and electronic locks or by having a protective agent (or company security officer) in place. If a particular threat exists and is known, such as a former employee harboring a grudge or seeking revenge, a full physical description and photograph (if available) should be distributed to all protective personnel. This information is usually available from human resources department records.

The primary role of a protection agent in access control is to monitor all incoming personnel traffic, being vigilant for suspicious persons or designated threats. Sometimes a screening device such as a metal detector augments his position. Prior to the arrival of the protection agents, the business may not have any security awareness, and access is readily and easily gained by anyone. In those cases, such as a public building, the focus should be placed closer to the object of any potential threats. A security and risk survey, or even a general review of the premises and procedures, will provide indicators of vulnerabilities. These susceptible areas and recommendations for correction should be directed to the executive in charge (often at his request) or to a designated representative.

CORPORATE SECRETS, INDUSTRIAL ESPIONAGE, AND THEFT

In a corporate or business environment, the law of unintended consequences may be an operating side effect of personal executive protection. The law is basically defined as the secondary (and fully unexpected) result of a planned feat. An executive protection agent, positioned in strategic areas of the business, may be well situated to observe or overhear conversations relating to corporate theft, trade secrets, and espionage.

Industrial espionage is the penetration of corporate secrets. It is not always like the images of shadowy figures, clandestine meetings, and unmarked cash in numbered bank accounts so readily portrayed in popular fiction. For the most part, industrial espionage is nothing more than the innocent interchange of conversation at gatherings where security-naïve employees engage in shop talk, giving no thought to proprietary information or who may be listening. A conversation in a public cafeteria, restaurant, business building lobby, or elevator may concern the company progress, setbacks, and solutions on a particular project. The speakers may be inadvertently sharing business information. Even employee gossip and rumors are subjects of interest to competing businesses, and market checkout-counter magazines will pay for good rumors. Bits and pieces of information quickly become information to be exploited by those who have an interest.

Employee theft may be observed on the monitoring television cameras, or it may be detected by the executive protective agent as he performs his protective function. It is estimated that approximately one-third of businesses that fail do so as a result of internal theft and related crimes. Theft of intellectual property, resources, services, and time may be occurring simply because the person committing the crime has not considered the seriousness of his act and does not realize he is in reality stealing from the company.

Instances of loose lips and misappropriation of company resources discovered and observed by an executive protection agent should be discussed with the appropriate executive in the business. Corrective recommendations and alternative procedures should be offered with the sensitive information. An amazing and interesting phenomenon has been observed by corporate executives in a position to monitor statistical items such as inventory and profit and loss. When protection agents are assigned to locations throughout the business to provide protection from unwanted intruders, their mere presence measurably reduces the amount of internal theft, there is a lower absenteeism rate, and productivity and profit increase! That is the law of unintended consequences at work!

Computer Security

Computer security is relevant to executive protection in that most, if not all business (and residential) security systems, access controls, and personnel file data bases are computer controlled. When conducting a security survey the vulnerability of the computers must be considered. A hacker could easily infiltrate the system and destroy or corrupt all access codes and information. A computer equipped or connected with a telephone line to a modem in any way is vulnerable to penetration and data theft. If the computer contains confidential or critical data, the modem–telephone line must be disconnected and /or the computer turned off at the end of each business day or when left unattended.

An executive protection company was retained to do an electronic counter measure sweep and search of the headquarters building of a large international business. The sweep also included a physical inspection of the entire three floors of office space. That included opening all electrical outlets, inspecting telephones, searching behind furniture, in file cabinets, in the ceiling and everywhere else a camera or transmitting devise could be located. The most notable and very common discovery was that approximately two-thirds of all the computers in the business were left on overnight. Many of the computers even were left open with files, reports, and data on the monitor. The next time (six months later) when the sweeps were again conducted, not one computer had been left on!

The first step in computer security, naturally, is to verify, to the extent possible, the trustworthiness of the personnel having access to the computer information. It is impossible to be absolutely certain that an employee might not misuse the critical information stored in the computer, but by allowing only trusted employees to have access on a need to know basis will greatly reduce the possibility of unauthorized usage. Computer entry to specific data can be controlled by code word software that utilizes tiered systems that restricts access to personnel having a prescribed code or password. Most password security systems (including intruder alarm systems as well as computer systems) have a user log-in record that maintains an archive of the date and time the system and information was accessed and by whom. A system can be defined to automatically shut down after a prescribed number of unsuccessful attempts. The number of attempts is commonly limited to three.

Security Awareness

An executive's security is the responsibility of himself, his close associates, family, staff, employees, and (of course) his executive protective team. The protection agents are the professionals and must take the initiative and be the leaders in a common objective—to keep the protectee safe, well, and alive. The means to achieving that common goal is good sense and security awareness. Proper security awareness can prevent a great degree of trouble. The executive protection agents are expected to be cognizant of any security risks at all times and to be fully alert and capable of taking preemptive action or reactive measures. Yet, on the other hand, the protectee and his entourage (including family, friends, and employees) can greatly enhance the protective team effort by taking certain precautions. With a little effort, thought, and awareness, protectees and others can greatly reduce their chances of being involved in a damaging security incident.

Security awareness is a matter of training, education, and attitude. Whenever the opportune moment presents itself, protective agents should encourage the protectee to learn some basics of self-protection and security awareness. Security awareness training and education begins with an initial briefing of the protectee and his staff. They should be given an orientation covering relevant security precautions, what to expect in relation to the security function, and how their cooperation and involvement can strengthen the total team security effort. A positive attitude toward security and the protection effort by the people who populate the protectee's milieu is contagious and should carry over to all who have a concern about the well-being of the protectee. Upon being introduced to the protective concepts and total consequences, all personnel, including the protectee, should begin to think security.

Thinking security never ends. A number of factors require constant concern for the security of the protectee and others. These include evolving circumstances as new threats develop. The ever-changing schedule, itinerary, and agenda of events could place the protectee in a social or political circumstance that leaves him in harm's way through the negligence or unmindful interest of someone oblivious to the protective concerns. To help them avoid adverse security incidents, protectees should do the following:

- Avoid predictable patterns of movement or activity. To whatever degree possible, vary departure and arrival times at home and work. Before leaving a safe location (home, office, restaurant) take a brief moment to look around the immediate vicinity and attempt to identify anything out of the ordinary, such as strange cars or vans (especially vans, because they make good kidnap vehicles and surveillance posts). If something seems out of place, or if something is amiss or just does not seem right, do not leave.
- Avoid wearing and carrying exorbitant jewelry, clothing, or other highly distinguishable and expensive accessories.
- Use alternate routes and avoid, as much as possible, routes that involve natural choke points or delays such as long traffic lights, construction, and narrow and lightly traveled roads. Try to avoid rush-hour traffic and use the most expeditious route. Tune the car radio to a station that provides frequent traffic updates and conditions. Drive with the car doors locked and the windows rolled up. Have an alarm installed in the vehicle, and have the alarm annunciate to a pager or other device at a central monitoring location.
- Park in secured and monitored parking zones whenever possible, and vary the parking spaces used. Do not park in a reserved parking spot with the name of the user posted for all to see. Use a common, nondescript vehicle that is similar to all the other cars parked in the vicinity. Avoid the use of "ego" license plates. The license plate numbers should be a standard state-issued and numbered plate to avoid easy identification.
- Try to make a quick brief inspection of the car before entering it. Especially look in the back seat area and the space between the seats to make sure no one is hiding inside the car. Also make a determination that nothing has

been placed in the gas tank intake or accessible wheel wells. It is a very simple task for someone to just walk past the car and, while unnoticed by anyone, place a bomb (packed in a metal soap dish with a magnet attached) in the gas tank area or wheel wells. If anything looks out of the ordinary or abnormal, do not attempt to remove it or start the vehicle. Simply walk away and call for assistance.

• Establish communication between home and company facilities and all vehicles. Vehicles should be equipped with a cellular telephone with preprogrammed emergency numbers to be utilized in the event of a crisis.

SAFETY

Safeguarding an executive or his business enterprise from *unintentional* injury can be interpreted to mean protecting him (and his business assets) from liability resulting from safety violations and hazards as well as physical injury. Safety concerns are a recognized component of the security survey. It should not be a surprise that many corporate executives assign a high priority to safety (and liability), because it directly impacts the financial bottom line through corporate profits, productivity, absenteeism, and a better workplace morale. When an injury occurs, the executive or his company must pay. If the injury incapacitates the employee and he is prevented from working, the company will be responsible for workmen's compensation, and the likelihood of litigation is a constant threat. Any unsafe condition must be corrected as soon as it is discovered. A safety risk can also jeopardize the well-being of the protected executive.

Safety cannot be assumed. The protection agent should make a daily routine survey of the working environment at the beginning of his shift. In addition to looking for security risks, he should also be alert for and correct safety problems that could cause injury. Safety dangers can include slippery sidewalks or driveways and frayed or overloaded electrical cords and cables. Noting and reporting or correcting safety hazards in a timely manner prevents accidents and tragic consequences. Certain categories of dangers apply to almost every job situation, including oil, grease, coffee, and other liquid spills that make a floor slippery and can cause slips and falls. The protection specialist should make sure fire doors and emergency exits are kept clear and unlocked and correct anything that could provide a potential physical hazard to the protectee or expose him to civil liability should someone else be injured.

Accidents are unplanned tragedies that can be prevented. As in preventing *intentional* injury to a principal, the protection agent must maintain the same high level of alertness, awareness, and attention to detail. Do not take an attitude of "it won't happen to me" or "it couldn't happen to my principal," because it can and will.

SAFETY CONSCIOUSNESS

Safety consciousness, awareness, and training should begin as soon as a new employee starts on the job. Often, the protection specialist is expected and called on to provide the new employee with an orientation in all aspects of safety and how to protect himself from debilitating accidents. The education of employees includes using statistics, posters, billboards, flyers, and even the company newsletter to emphasize the importance of good safety sense.

The new employee should reflect the corporate attitude regarding safety. A positive attitude toward safety procedures by supervisors, management, and experienced workers is contagious and carries over to the new personnel. *Thinking safety* never ends. Many factors require safety consciousness to be part and parcel of every day on the job. The protection agent must keep himself informed of developments that may impact the safety (and security) of his protectee in the workplace environment. Some of the circumstances and reasons the executive protection specialist cannot become complacent are

1. New hazards develop with the changing workplace.
2. New safety rules are created by management, court cases, and insurance companies.
3. Government regulations change.
4. Personal concerns change.

NATURAL AND HUMAN-MADE DISASTERS

Included in the corporate responsibilities of a protection agent is a response to natural and man-made disasters. No one can control Mother Nature to eliminate floods, tornadoes, hurricanes, earthquakes, and fire. But the effects at least can be mitigated. Natural disasters should be anticipated by being in a state of constant readiness to salvage lives and property. Some natural disasters (such as hurricanes, tornadoes, floods, and typhoons) can be predicted, seen, and prepared for. Man-made disasters (bombings, acts of war, arson) and some natural calamities (such as earthquakes) usually cannot be predicted, but the level of preparedness can remain at the same high degree. Protection personnel are expected to have an emergency operations plan in force to address any natural or man-made disaster.

EMERGENCY OPERATIONS PLAN

In cooperation with the protectee, his designee, or corporate planners, the executive protection specialist may be called upon, or he may volunteer his expertise, to program and initiate an emergency operations plan that could save lives and corporate assets. The plan should be general enough to allow flexibility according to the type of emergency, yet it should be specific in identifying responsibilities and procedures. The plan will

1. Designate or determine a crisis management team that will bear authority and management responsibility in a typical disaster-type emergency. Primary and alternative designees should be specifically noted, trained, and drilled in their reactive responsibilities.
2. Establish an early warning device and system for all personnel (conduct monthly or bimonthly practice and drill). Battery backup sirens, alarms, and "runners" are the usual modes of alarm notification.

3. Plan an evacuation procedure. A diagram of evacuation routes should be conspicuously located in all offices and near elevators and stairwells. It the event of fire or an emergency with potential power failure, the elevators should not be used. All personnel should be familiarized with primary and alternate evacuation routes.

4. Establish an employee training and education program, including emergency medical service, reaction to emergency situations, and disaster preparedness.

5. Develop a plan for mobilization and control of critical supplies and security of all personnel, records, and sensitive material. Designate responsibility to a crisis management team or specific personnel who can be trusted to perform under trying circumstances.

6. Activate the emergency control center. This is usually located in a safe environment with effective communication capabilities. In some instances, this site may be at a location away from the primary position. Arrangements must be made for the rapid relocation of personnel, critical equipment, and sensitive material.

7. Plan and prepare potential shelter and relocation areas treating injured and maintaining a personnel count.

8. Have a stock of emergency food, water, tools (e.g., shovels, axes, and rope), medical supplies, lights, blankets, generators, and emergency communications equipment located in strategic spots. Personnel must know the locations and have access to the equipment supply.

9. Maintain ongoing liaison with local governmental authorities. This should include local civil defense and National Guard units; power, water, light, and hazardous material departments; fire departments; police; and emergency hospitals and care and treatment centers.

SUMMARY

At home and away, the physical security environment of the protectee can be amplified by specific security arrangements. Controlling access to the premises is perhaps the most significant consideration. Technical equipment supplements the strategic placement of man-made and natural barriers, but it can be thwarted and even incapacitated. The human element (including protection agents, the protectee, and his surrounding friends, family, and staff) enhances the total security ring. But it is incumbent upon all involved personnel to maintain a heightened degree of security knowledge and awareness.

At home or away at a place of business, a protectee is susceptible to vulnerabilities that can have major effects on him, his personal life, his business, his employees, and the financial position of his commercial endeavors. He expects the protection specialist to recognize and reduce those vulnerabilities. Anything that involves security and safety should be within the purview of an alert and conscientious protection agent. A protection specialist who performs his duties with an eye to the total security and safety of a protectee is a very valuable resource and an asset to the overall well-being of the protectee, whether at home or in the business community.

REVIEW QUESTIONS

1. Discuss the security limitations of imagination and finances.
2. Design an exterior home security system.
3. What is the purpose of a security survey? What is included and how is it conducted?
4. What are physical barriers? Give examples. What are psychological barriers? Give examples.
5. Explain how technological systems interact with physical and psychological barriers.
6. Explain *zoning*.
7. What features within a home are of security concern?
8. How do *procedures* figure in the security circle?
9. Explain how the law of unintended consequences has a positive effect on a business when executive protection personnel are present.
10. How can executive protection agents help protect against loss of company secrets and guard against industrial espionage?
11. What is an executive protection agent's role in corporate security awareness?
12. Give examples of how a protectee can help protect himself.
13. How can an executive protection agent protect the company personnel from unintentional injury?
14. Natural and environmental dangers are a unique challenge to the executive protection agent. What are his responsibilities in meeting that challenge?
15. How can a corporation best utilize an executive protection agent in protecting its bottom line?

NOTE

1. Not so long ago, to swipe something meant to steal it.

10 Cars and Driving

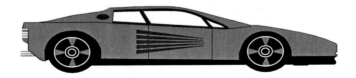

"Drive!" he said.

Keep it between the ditches, and don't hit the car in front of you!

(Lesson number one)

Many skills are required to become an effective, driving, multitasking protective agent. These skills are undervalued by the philosophy of "keeping it between the ditches," which can lead one to believe that all a driver must do is drive like everyone else on the road—talking on the telephone, listening to a CD or the radio, reading a newspaper (or map directions), or perhaps eating a donut and drinking a cup of coffee. In actuality, driving is only a small portion of the overall responsibilities of a "driver."

It could be a shiny new limousine or a Porsche, a Mercedes, or a Lamborghini. Whatever it is, it belongs to your protectee, and you are the designated driver! That is an awesome and critical responsibility. Just get in and drive? Ah, hah, "therein lies the rub." If only it were that easy or simple! Many car designers and manufacturers seem to take pleasure in hiding and designing buttons and switches such that a normal human being cannot find them. Just getting into some of the new high-tech cars is sometimes enough to test even the most knowledgeable car devotee or highly trained astronaut. It may not require an engineering degree to open the door, with its alarms, combinations, and locks, but the interior control panel will certainly be cause for anxiety. Simple things like a light switch, the windshield wipers, the ignition key, and the brake release are usually disguised as something else. Trying to find and operate them without an orientation can be extraordinarily confusing.

An protection agent was called to drive the teenage son of a VIP. The assignment was nothing more than to drive and keep an eye on the teenager and his girlfriend as they experienced their first real date—dinner, a stage play, and an after-show dessert at a local café in the "wilds" of Hollywood. As soon as he arrived at the principal's residence, about an hour after sunset, the agent was handed a set of keys and told to drive. Without even a moment to familiarize himself with the car, they were off for a night of adventure. It turned into a night of misadventure for the agent until he learned to operate a car with all the knobs, switches, and lights of a space shuttle.

The first indication that it was going to be a long night was when the teenager handed the keys to the agent in the driveway and said, "Here is the remote." It was a night darker than a stack of black cats in a coal mine, and the indicators on the remote could not be read in the ambient light. It took a few rounds of opening the hood, then the trunk and the hood again, before the front door opened. After another try or two, the rear doors opened. Inside the car, there were so many buttons, knobs, switches, lights, and controls that the agent felt like a first-time B-57 bomber pilot just trying to find the slot to put the ignition key. Eventually, with a few bucks, jumps, and starts, all was ready, and they set off to the first stop.

While waiting for the couple, the agent began to experiment and check out some of the gadgets. In too short of a time, he saw the boy and girl exiting the restaurant. Confidently, he drove to the entrance and started to exit the car. Then he realized, to his utter dismay and consternation, he was locked in, and his passengers were locked out! The doors were all locked, and he could not find the right button to unlock them. The teenagers were no help either, because it was "Daddy's" car, and neither knew how to operate the buttons. Finally, the embarrassed agent figured out that the doors automatically unlocked when he turned off the engine. After that, the date proceeded and a "good time was had by all," with only minor difficulties such as a radio that could not be shut off, an air conditioner that seemed to have only one setting (very cold), and headlamps that apparently had a mind of their own!

When learning to drive, before even taking the car out onto the road, the first requirement is to learn about the vehicle's instrumentation so things can be switched on, operated, and adjusted without looking. There are so many variables in driving and so many unpredictable occurrences that a driver must anticipate (e.g., a dog or child runs into the street or the moment the driver looks down to find the windshield wiper control, the car in front suddenly stops) that the least of the driver's concerns should not be about how to adjust the radio, air conditioner, or headlights. Becoming familiar with the equipment is a requirement in a profession in which someone's safety depends on the skills of the protector.

Add the elements of darkness and an impatient principal who also may not be totally familiar with the operation of the car, and the result can be an experiment consisting of "push, pull, readjust, swear, and pray." Things really start getting dicey and exciting when the windshield suddenly becomes fogged, and visibility is limited to the interior of the car. In that case, the way to clear the fog is to turn the defroster fan on high and the temperature down to cold. The cold air should quickly clear the window (if the right gadgets can be found to operate the controls). All the while, the executive protection agent will try to reassure the protectee, but who will mutter something like "...can't get good help," "...what kind of driver?" "...anybody can turn off the G** d***** cold air!" "...shoudda taken the limousine," or something a little stronger. But eventually the vehicle will be under way. All that is left to do once the car is actually operational is to concentrate on the driving while mentally identifying all the gismos and gadgets and preparing for the next crisis, when the passenger asks for the radio or more heat. At that point, the driver can focus on the instruction, "keep it between the ditches, and don't hit the car in front of you."

That sage piece of advice was the only prior instruction one young Secret Service agent received several years ago, on his third day on the job as an agent. It was during a presidential campaign that strained the manpower resources of the service to its limits. Every agent, even if he had just been sworn in, was considered available for any assignment at any time.

A popular candidate took his campaign to Sacramento, California, and surrounding suburbs. Just before the arrival of the candidate, the special agent in charge informed the "still wet behind the ears" rookie agent that he was going to be the candidate's driver. The surprised agent inquired of his boss, "What should I do?" The impatient senior agent simply stated, "Lesson number one! Don't forget it! Follow the car in front of you, don't hit it, and keep your car between the ditches!" Fortunately, the new agent had had prior experience in tactical driving as a police officer in Sacramento. Aside from some nervousness about driving a potential president of the United States, the agent's assignment went very well. He did not get lost, he did not hit the car in front, and the streets of Sacramento had no ditches—only curbs, and he avoided them. As part of his formal training a few months later, the young agent received much more instruction in the fine art of limousine and follow-up car driving. In fact, two or three years later, he became a driver for the president and other high-ranking executives and VIPs.

The philosophy of "keep it between the ditches, follow the car in front of you, and don't hit it" would be adequate for today's average driver, who is only concerned with driving from point A to point B. However, it is not sufficient for ensuring the safety of a protected person. When a protective agent is providing for the safety of a principal while driving, he must be trained to handle a variety of threats.

A protection agent must drive the vehicle but also be observant of the constantly changing surroundings. He must be cognizant of the surroundings and observe evolving threatening or dangerous situations. Constant situational awareness is imperative. A driver could have the best emergency driving skills in the business, but, if he is unable to recognize and respond to a developing threat, the emergency driving skills will be meaningless. A protection agent must be as aware of his surroundings while in a vehicle as while on foot. Situational awareness requires the agent to observe things that lie beyond the vehicles that are immediately adjacent to the principal's vehicle. "Follow the car in front of you, don't hit it and keep your car between the ditches" implies that the driver need only observe his immediate surroundings and avoid accidents. But many other things can threaten the principal's safety.

Being familiar with a vehicle's operation is just as important as being familiar with one's weapon. Anyone in a profession that involves carrying a firearm must be capable of manipulating and reloading the weapon without looking. This skill enables the armed professional to keep his eyes on the threat without being vulnerable to an ambush or outflanked during a gunfight. The same applies to knowing one's vehicle. A professional should not be preoccupied with functions that can be committed to muscle memory. By training oneself not to be distracted by equipment functions, the protection agent can focus on his surroundings and respond to any threat.

Learning to drive properly is a requirement. One must learn good habits and practice. It is like the old story of the child with a violin case tucked under his arm, walking down a street in New York City. He inquired of a passerby, "Hey! Yo! Mister, how do I get to Carnegie Hall?" The well-dressed and proper gentleman replied, "Practice! Practice! Practice!"

A car, even a new and expensive one, must be maintained in the very best mechanical condition. A major mechanical failure or accident may occur at the most inopportune time. (There is never a good time to experience a breakdown.) Even the limousine of the president of the United States has an occasional malfunction.

It was a very hot mid-summer day, well over 100°. It was 11:45 A.M., about two minutes before Air Force One was scheduled to touch down on the runway at Laredo, Texas. The president's driver (the same agent whose first lesson in driving the principal had occurred a few years earlier, in Sacramento), following standard protocol, turned on the rear seat area air conditioner as he waited in the limousine on the ramp with the rest of the motorcade. The motorcade consisted of a pilot car with an agent and a Laredo police officer driving, a lead car for the advance agent and the chief of police with an officer driving, the presidential limousine, the agent's follow-up car, three or four staff cars, a convertible for the traveling press pool, a press bus for the remainder of the media contingent, and finally a Laredo police car.

As Air Force One made its final approach and its wheels touched down on the runway, the presidential limousine began to spew overheated radiator coolant, creating a cloud of steam that signaled the end of the road for the car for that day. (Actually, the car was disabled for about two weeks because a special part had to be manufactured to correct the overheating problem.)

Reacting quickly, the driver-agent (and a presidential mechanic who always traveled with the limousines) pushed the car out of the motorcade and sought a substitute. The only one available was the press convertible, a "hot" supercharged "four on the floor" Oldsmobile. It had glass pack mufflers, and it rumbled and shook, ready to race, even at idle. The car was on loan from a young Nebraska airman who was assigned to the airbase in Laredo. In that year, the University of Nebraska had the number one college football team in the nation, and the Texas Longhorns were number two. Both bumpers of the car bore stickers proclaiming, "Nebraska #1" and "Go Big Red." The car also had Nebraska license plates. The car had been selected only because a convertible was required, and this apparently was the only available convertible in that part of Texas.

The agent driver quickly attached magnetic presidential seals to the car doors, proclaiming the car Limousine One, and tried to familiarize himself with it. He checked both side-view mirrors, adjusted the rear-view mirror, the seat, and his seatbelt. (These procedures must always be followed, including fastening the seatbelt.) He quickly thanked his father, who had insisted that he learn to drive a car with standard transmission and to "make smooth starts and stops, use the clutch and gas pedal together, and never let the car jerk, even when going very slow." He also remembered and mentally recited the advice from his first Secret Service boss (keep it between the ditches, and don't hit the car in front of you). With the president standing in the back seat area and holding on to the front seat with a white knuckle grip, the motorcade moved along the parade route on the streets of Laredo as though it were common for the presidential limousine to be such a sporty, supercharged, roaring and rumbling convertible.

Much to the driver's relief, the assignment went without further problems or disruptions, and the president even joked about a "cornhusker's car" in Longhorn country. The only one more pleased was the airman who had reluctantly offered his prized possession for the occasion. He later received an autographed photograph from the president with a letter expressing a "grateful thank you for your unselfish contribution to my recent visit to Laredo."

Nothing is as irritating and annoying to a principal as a driver who accelerates and decelerates in a herky-jerky motion. A car must start and stop in a smooth, flowing manner. Even a smooth-running, properly tuned and maintained car with an automatic transmission (especially a high-powered one) may have a tendency to jump when set in gear. The driver should learn to be "two footed." When placing the car in gear, the left foot must be on the brake and the right on the gas. As the car moves forward, the left foot should ease off the brake. This makes for a smooth startup. To come to a smooth stop, the stop should be anticipated and planned. The right foot comes off the accelerator, allowing the car to decelerate, and the brake is applied gradually and smoothly.

When in motion, the car should be driven in as straight a line as possible. An excellent way to determine if the car is being driven in a straight line is to look at its tracks on a wet road. Look into the rear-view mirror. The tracks of the vehicle will show if the car is wandering. Do not change lanes without first checking the mirrors and looking for other vehicles in the blind spot. Use the turn signal and execute the lane change only when it positively can be made safely. Turns must also be smooth. Allow ample time to turn without doing a "two-wheeler." A passenger notices rather quickly if he is suddenly thrown to the side of the car by centrifugal force.

The principal is quite vulnerable while traveling in a car. The driver must be constantly alert, visually scanning the roadway several hundred yards in all directions. He must avoid staring at the lane dividing lines or the area directly in front of the vehicle, as this can cause "highway hypnosis" and sleepiness. The driver must avoid conversation, because this distracts his attention from the safe operation of the vehicle. He should watch for sudden changes in traffic conditions and hazards such as oil slicks, mufflers dropped from other cars, sand, bricks, and other highway debris. He should expect anything from potholes to mattresses! He should also anticipate intentional threats (i.e., an ambush) and allow sufficient maneuvering space to avoid them.

The driver should also observe some subtle courtesies that benefit the principal. For example, when picking up or discharging the passenger, park the car approximately 12 to 18 inches from the curb. This allows the passenger to comfortably step out of the car, even if there is a high curb. Entering the car is also easier. At times, the curb may be too high to allow the door to open properly. Leaving some distance between the car and the curb will avoid the problem.

Unless he is the only protective agent on hand, the driver should not leave the car to open the door for the protectee or other passengers. Opening the door is the responsibility of a second agent, who usually rides in the right front seat. The principal's door should not be opened until the protective agent has visually scanned the area and determined that there is no imminent danger. This usually takes about half a minute, so it is appropriately named "the rule of 30 seconds."

If a full complement of protective agents is available and the protectee risk assessment warrants it, additional agents will be working the fenders of the limousine. As the supervisor makes his 30-second observation, the agent working the right front fender moves to the rear door to shield the exiting protectee. Whoever opens the door must do so and then reposition himself to provide a shield between the principal and onlookers.

Getting in and out of the back seat of a car is very awkward, especially for a woman wearing a dress or skirt. As the protective agent opens the door, he should divert his eyes to observe other activity in the area and place his body in a position to block the view of any onlookers.

When stopping at an intersection, the driver should position the car so the occupants of any adjacent vehicle cannot see into the principal's car. This usually means stopping a few feet before the intersection line. A good rule of thumb is to place the front bumper of the principal's car approximately even with the middle of the rear door of an adjacent car. This discourages passengers in the adjacent car from gawking at the principal and avoids placing him in a vulnerable situation.

A professional hit man once described one of his many kills. "I stopped beside him at a red traffic light. I rolled my window down and looked at him and smiled as I pointed my sawed-off shotgun toward him. He never knew what hit him. I was surprised at the results. I wasn't surprised I killed him, but what surprised me was that my shot took his head completely off."[1]

When the principal's car comes to a stop behind another car, the driver should stay back far enough that he can see where the rear wheels of the other car meet the concrete. This provides sufficient maneuvering room but is close enough to prevent another car from cutting in and pinning the limo down.

When driving on an open road or expressway, try to stay in the second lane from the outside. Driving in the inside or outside lane raises the possibility of being trapped if maneuvering room becomes limited. The driver must be constantly aware of the vehicles and drivers around him. If another driver appears to be aggressive or moves his car into a dangerous position, speed up, slow down, or change lanes to avoid contact with the aggressive driver. Never attempt to bluff or intimidate another driver. He may become angry and do something that endangers the principal and his party. Do not worry about who has the right of way. Cemeteries are full of people who were right—dead right.

Protective agents must be constantly vigilant for attempts to cut off and stop the principal's car. A vehicle that suddenly pulls out of a driveway or alley may be initiating a kidnap or assassination attempt. The protective agent driver must take immediate evasive action by swerving around the vehicle and increasing speed or by changing direction.

It is common for traffic to become jammed on a busy expressway when slow or stopped vehicles block the lanes. As soon as the principal's driver recognizes the slowdown, he should move to a lane next to the highway shoulder. To avoid being blocked in, leave at least one car length between your car and the car in front and maintain access to the shoulder lane.

Attackers have been known to use several cars in an attempt to cut off a protectee's vehicle. They follow the principal's car until one attacker can move in front of him. A second car then moves alongside, and possibly a third pulls up directly behind him. The front car slows down and stops, forcing the principal's car to do the same. The principal's driver can take evasive action by suddenly braking, letting the car on the side pass by, and then suddenly swerving into the space vacated by the car on the side. But evasive tactics will work only if the driver anticipates the situation and takes instantaneous preemptive action.

The driver's responsibility is to control the car and to observe other traffic. When the passenger is getting into or out of the car, the driver should leave the car in park. After the passenger and secondary agent are securely in the car (with seatbelts buckled) or have stepped a safe distance away from the car, then the driver will place the car in drive. Many protective agents have had a foot run over by a limousine because the driver was not paying attention and moved the vehicle before the protectee and protective agent had moved safely away. The driver should never leave the car until it is parked in a secure area or unless he has been instructed to do so.

The driver should never, ever, under any circumstances, smoke in the car. A nonsmoking principal will detect the odor immediately and be offended and probably angry. Unless the principal asks the driver to turn on the radio, it should remain off when the principal is in the car. If the radio is set to a specific frequency, it probably is the principal's favorite, so do not change it unless instructed to do so.

The driver is responsible for keeping the car clean, fueled, and properly equipped. A fire extinguisher and first aid kit should be in the passenger compartment where they can be easily and readily accessed and used by the driver in the event of an emergency. They should never be stored in the trunk of the car where they could be inaccessible, especially if the principal's car were rear ended. In case of emergencies or in the event the protectee wants to be driven somewhere in the middle of the night, the car should be refueled at the end of the day or whenever the fuel gauge reads between one-half and three-quarters of a tank.

It is the driver's responsibility to know travel routes. If time allows, the routes should be pre-run. That means driving over the route and noting the time, distance, and any potential trouble areas such as overpasses and underpasses, construction, and traffic conditions (at varying times). Also, the driver or another agent should map the route and write down the exact directions, including distance between turns, describing the route in detail from the point of origin to the event site. He should describe the turns as right or left, also giving the compass directions and street names.

The route should be divided into zones or checkpoints. While the motorcade is in progress, the limousine can report locations to the command post by these zones or checkpoints. While "running the routes," the driver should also note hospitals and emergency clinics, police stations, service stations, and other buildings and services of interest. Arriving at the intended destination, the driver should locate turnaround and parking facilities.

Sometimes the protectee drives his own car while the protective agent follows along in a separate one. Give him general instructions on how to drive as an agent would while working with a follow-up vehicle. Instruct him to drive in the middle lanes during less-congested traffic times and in the outside lanes during periods of heavy traffic. Tell the principal to signal for lane changes and allow enough time for you to initiate the change and block any traffic that could come between the vehicles. When stopped, have the principal allow enough room to maneuver his vehicle in case of an emergency and to avoid pulling up directly beside another vehicle. In the event of an attack, the principal should immediately drive away from the attack location and avoid stopping until some distance away or until the danger is no longer present. Instructions to the principal should be simple and limited so he will not be paralyzed by too many instructions, which could cloud his judgment during an attack.

When parking, the principal should be aware of several things. First, the vehicle must be parked in secure locations, away from pedestrian traffic. If a secure location is unavailable, a highly visible area, or one monitored by security cameras, would be recommended. The principal must roll up the windows, lock the doors, and set the vehicle alarm when leaving it unattended. The principal should note the condition of the vehicle so as to notice any tampering that occurs in his absence.

At the beginning of the protection assignment, the agent must inspect the principal's vehicle and photograph it to check its condition, locate any possible surveillance equipment, and inspect for any signs of tampering. Once the vehicle has been inspected and the agent has determined its condition, he should inspect the vehicle whenever it has been left in a vulnerable situation, such as outdoors during the night. The protection agent should inspect the vehicle for signs of tampering, tracking devices, and explosives. They should be easy to find after the agent has conducted the initial vehicle inspection.

Photographs should include all areas of the car. Frequent comparison of the vehicle and the photographs will assist in detecting any tampering or changes, loose wiring, etc.

Instinct is an important human trait. Instinct is enhanced throughout our lives as we gain experience learning more about others and ourselves. If the little hairs on the back of a police officer or agent's neck begin to stand up during an incident or when talking to a possible suspect, it is time to become extra attentive. In some cases, taking decisive offensive action prior to an attack can keep the potential attacker off balance and prevent the assault. The same is true when a protection agent is driving a principal. If training, experience, and instinct tell a driver that something is wrong or an attack is about to happen, he must act without hesitation. It is better to err on the side of caution, with both the principal and protection agent going home safely, than to ignore that gut feeling and have a terrible result.

WHAT IF ... ?

What if... while driving the protectee, an attack situation is observed approximately 100 yards ahead? Without hesitation, take immediate action to identify the type of threat and find a route away from the attack location. Communicate with the follow-up vehicle to make those agents aware of the situation and details about the attack location. When taking an alternative route, also look for possible secondary attack sites; the first attack may have been a diversion designed to channel the principal to another attack location. The follow-up agents and the principal's driver all must be prepared to take defensive action if an actual attack occurs. The primary goal is to get the principal to a secure location.

What if... two motorcycles approach the principal's car from behind, they split off, and one goes on each side of the principal's car? Once the agent recognizes the situation, he should slow down enough to allow the motorcycles to pass. This action will determine whether the motorcycles are an actual threat to the principal, based on the motorcyclists' response to the braking of the vehicle. If they remain alongside the principal's car and continue to pose a threat, steer the car to force one of the cyclists to swerve or veer off. If they continue down the road, notice any identifying characteristics of the riders and motorcycles just in case they appear again.

What if... an agent is driving the principal on a narrow street, and the street ahead is blocked by a car? When approaching the blocking vehicle, look for side streets that could be used to leave the area. If there is no other way out, to back the car to the nearest exit street. If no side streets are available, stop the vehicle well behind the blocking one to avoid entering the ambush "kill zone." Place the car in low gear and prepare for a ramming. With steady pressure on the gas, strike the blocking car just to the front of the front wheel or just beyond the back of the rear wheel and push it aside. After passing the blocking car, accelerate and evacuate the location.

What if... a protective agent is driving a principal down a narrow road, a car in front stops suddenly, and another car is immediately behind? Stop as quickly as possible to allow as much room as possible between the protectee's vehicle and the vehicle in front. Watch both of the other vehicles and their occupants for signs of an attack. At the same time, observe traffic and watch for an opportunity to pass the front vehicle and escape both of them. If there is not enough room on the roadway to pass but there is sufficient room on a shoulder, sidewalk, or open field, do not hesitate to use that route to pass the stopped car. When doing so, tell the principal to lie down in the seat in case shots are fired in the event of an attack. The basic idea, threat or not, is to avoid being trapped in a static location where an attack can take place.

What if... the protectee has a set itinerary and gives it to his driver agent three days in advance? With this much notice, there is plenty of time to become familiar with the area. Familiarization includes finding the local police stations, fire stations, hospitals, road construction delays, and detours and identifying traffic areas. It is also important to meet with the local police department to identify crime-prone areas and other locations to avoid. Survey the routes and locations to be traveled to ensure the safest routes and ensure that the principal remains on schedule.

What if... while stopped at a traffic light in a lightly populated part of town, the light changes and the principal's car starts to move, but a pedestrian hurrying across the street trips and falls in front of the car, sprains his ankle, and is unable to stand? The first priority is to stay inside the vehicle, especially if the principal is present. Focus on the surrounding area and look for a possible ambush situation developing. Keep watching the pedestrian and consider him a possible threat; he may have a weapon. If he produces a weapon, do not hesitate to hit him with the vehicle to escape the area and protect the principal. If there are no vehicles behind or there is enough room, you can back away from the intersection without having to hit the injured man. Regardless of whether an ambush presents itself, drive away from the location. Sometimes the principal will order the driver to stop and attend the fallen person. In that case, discretion dictates doing so, but remain fully alert to the possibility of attack.

What if... the agent and protectee are crossing a narrow, single-lane bridge in a rural area? As they start across the bridge, a large tractor with a wagonload of sugar cane or hay enters from the other end. As the agent starts to back up, a large truck with fifty armed men enters from that end. A deep gorge lies on both sides of the bridge. The tractor and trailer are not vehicles that can be vulnerable to being rammed. The driver should exit the vehicle and determine if the men in the truck are hostile or threatening and/or if he can persuade the truck driver or farmer on the tractor to back up. If the men in the truck and the tractor is a part of the ambush, the only option left for the agent and protectee is to, as a veteran army sergeant said, "Put their heads between their legs and kiss their a**es goodbye, because their a** is grass, and the hostile men are giant lawnmowers."

The reader is reminded that the above are only what-if scenarios, and there are many other possible problems and solutions. Every situation must be measured and gauged according to its own elements, with the solution being in the best interest of the principal.

FOLLOW-UP

A follow-up vehicle in a protection assignment is one more moving part that the agent driving the principal must keep an eye on, as close coordination between the two vehicles is required. A protection agent must already have good situational awareness while driving the principal. Additionally, the agent must know the routes well enough to communicate with the follow-up vehicle to coordinate both vehicles' movements properly and effectively. If the principal's driver is preoccupied with only "keeping it between the ditches," he will not achieve the goal of coordinated protective movements between the two vehicles.

The entire protective group functions as a team, but no two individuals operate as closely as the two drivers. The follow-up or "follow car" refers to the car driven immediately behind the principal's car. Teamwork and communication between the limousine driver and follow-up must be well coordinated and smooth. The two drivers must think as one and perform flawlessly. Driving at speeds of up to 50 or 60 mph with only a few feet (sometimes only half a car length) between the cars (so no other car can come between them and cut off the follow-up) leaves little room for mistakes. It requires a high level of response, reflex, anticipation, and awareness.

In one case, a U.S. president was visiting Warsaw, Poland. The motorcade passed through the city's center square. It is estimated that more than 1 million cheering and shouting people were jammed into the square to catch a glimpse of the Americans and their president. The Polish police preceded the presidential limousine, which was followed by the American Secret Service follow-up car. As the motorcade departed the airport, the Polish police attempted to cut off the American follow-up and force their version of a follow-up car (with no American Secret Service agents, only Polish police in it) between the presidential limousine and the American Secret Service agents. The American follow-up driver maintained a distance of approximately twelve to eighteen inches between the limousine and the follow-up, preventing the Polish police car from moving in.

The follow-up driver and the limousine driver drove as one. They maintained eye contact through the limousine side-view mirror and communicated via quick finger and hand movements. As the motorcade entered into the city square, the crowd of people surged forward and nearly surrounded the slowly moving motorcade. To prevent even one person from getting between the limousine and the follow-up car, the agent driver moved the follow-up car into direct contact with the limousine. The front bumper of the follow-up was firmly against the rear bumper of the limousine as they moved through the crowd. The cars remained so close that the follow-up driver and crew could not see the limo's turn signals or brake lights. After the motorcade ended and the cars were safely parked at the temporary presidential residence, an examination of the two cars revealed scratch marks on the limousine bumper caused by the follow-up license plate frame. The veteran limousine driver said that, in all his years of driving the president, he had never before been involved in such precise driving.

Within a month or two of that trip to Eastern Europe, the presidential limousine was equipped with a small set of lights between the center of the rear window and the trunk hinge. A small green light would come on when the limousine accelerator was pushed, and a small red light would come on when the brakes were touched. The lights were placed such that if the two cars ever again were driven as close as they were on that trip, the follow-up driver would be able to read the go and stop lights.

The driver of the principal's car signals for lane changes, stops, and turns to assist the follow-up driver. The signals must be given far enough in advance to allow the follow-up driver to open the lane by making the lane change first (when it is clear and safe). As the follow-up completes the lane change, the limousine driver eases the car into the new lane. When making turns, the follow-up makes a wide turn to block traffic, to provide a safe turn buffer zone, and to prevent another car from ramming into the exposed side of the principal's car. (See figures 10.1 and 10.2.)

The follow-up driver needs to watch all sides of the car. He must keep his eyes on the principal's car and react to any sudden move or signaled changes. He must be aware of traffic to the left, right, and rear to keep anyone from overtaking and driving alongside the principal. If another vehicle moves alongside, the follow-up driver must keep him from getting too close to the principal. The follow-up is usually driven either about half a car width to the left of the limousine to provide a view ahead for the driver and to prevent other cars from passing, or about a half a car width to the right to provide a view ahead for the senior agent or shift leader riding in the right front seat. (See figures 10.3, 10.4, and 10.5.)

A one- or two-man detail, of course, will not have the luxury or necessity of a follow-up vehicle, because those agents will be riding with the protectee. But a detail consisting of three or more accompanying protective agents requires the use of a second car.

The second or follow-up car serves a number of functions. The first, of course, is transportation for the other protective agents and, in the case of the Secret Service, a doctor. If there is a full complement of agents, they do not just pile into the follow-up car willy-nilly; they follow a preconceived plan.

The senior agent or shift supervisor rides in the right front passenger seat. The working agents are assigned numbers corresponding to positions on the limousine. Number one is the left rear door area; number two is the right rear door area; number three is the left front fender area and, of course, number four is the right front fender area. Consequently, the agents are assigned seating positions in the follow-up that will allow them to speedily and easily exit the car to assume their positions alongside the limousine whenever the situation demands.

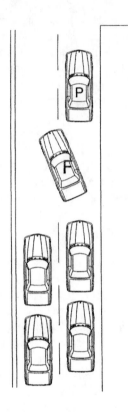

FIGURE 10.1 Changing lanes. The principal's car (P) signals for a lane change. The follow-up (F) signals when the lane is clear to make a safe change then pulls diagonally into the next lane, blocking oncoming traffic. After the follow-up has secured the lane, the principal's car completes the lane change.

Safety must be a concern when exiting a moving vehicle. While anticipating an exit, the agent should think and mentally review the safety procedure for jumping from the car, which may be traveling at up to seven miles per hour. One second of carelessness could result in serious injury. The first command from the shift leader is usually, "One and two up and hit it!" This is followed by, "Three and four up and go!" The agents must move as soon as instructed. The outside foot strikes the pavement first. It is suggested that the agent wear shoes with good arch supports and rubber heels. This makes the transfer from a moving vehicle to the stationary roadway easier and safer. As the feet hit the ground running, the hands are pushed or removed from the door of the car. Two cautions or caveats must be kept in mind: watch for objects in the roadway, and be careful of snagging clothes, rings, or watches on the car!

Numbers two and four exit from the right side of the follow-up, and one and three exit from the left. The first two out are two and one, followed by four and three. Exit from the follow-up is usually done at parade speed, i.e., two to five miles per hour. The duty of the agents positioned along the moving limousine is to prevent any onlooker from rushing to the car or throwing anything at it. As the agents move with the car, they must have fingertip contact with the vehicle so they will always know their position relative to the car. The agent's eyes must be focused on the passing crowd and not the car. It is very embarrassing (not to mention other possible

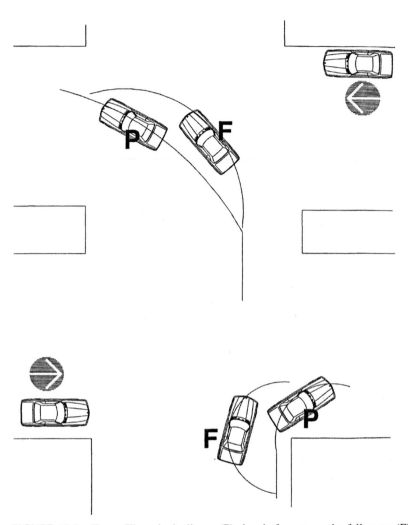

FIGURE 10.2 Turns. The principal's car (P) signals for a turn. the follow-up (F) signals the turn, then makes a wide turn blocking and protecting the side of the principal's car from oncoming traffic.

problems) to be running down the street, watching the crowd, and unaware that the limousine has stopped or, worse, turned down a side street, leaving the poor "out of touch" agent on his own. Touching the car will also prevent the agent from getting too close and possibly injuring himself. It can be extremely painful to be running beside the limousine and get a foot caught under the wheel.

As the limousine and follow-up approach the stop, the limousine stops directly where the advance agent is pointing or at a designated spot where the principal can step out directly onto the walkway. The follow-up is parked approximately two feet to the rear and about half a car width to the left into the traffic lane or right side of the limousine (depending on which side is the traffic lane). The objective is to keep

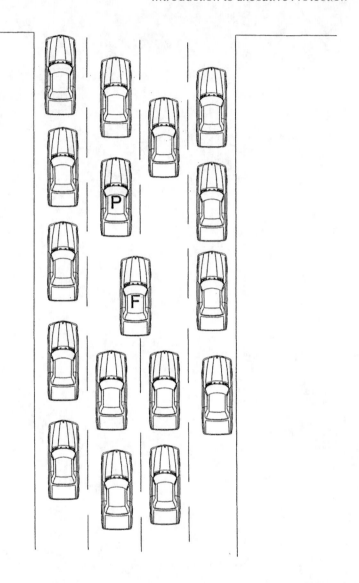

FIGURE 10.3   Follow-up car in center lane. The follow-up car (F) remains approximately one-half to two-thirds of a car length behind the principals car and approximately half a car width to teh right. preventing any other car from getting between teh vehicles and from coming directly alongside. The principal (P) rides in the eight rear seat.

another car from parking between the two cars, or to have someone run between the cars and protect the limousine from oncoming traffic. If there is a staff car, it is parked in the lane of traffic beside the limousine, approximately even with the rear door.

The first priority is the right (passenger) side of the limousine. When the number of protective agents is less than the full complement, a follow-up agent will

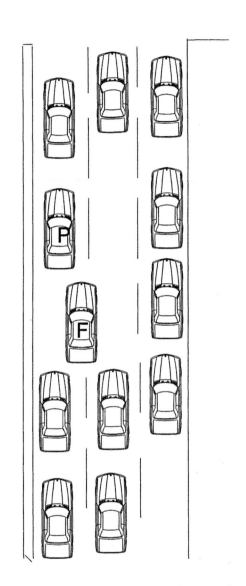

FIGURE 10.4 Follow-up car in center lane. The follow-up car (F) remains approximately one-half to two-thirds of a car length behind the principals car and approximately half a car width to teh right. preventing any other car from getting between teh vehicles and from coming directly alongside. The principal (P) rides in the eight rear seat.

cover the principal's doors first (the proper sequence being relative to importance: right rear, left rear, right front, then left front), depending on the number of available agents. Then, of course, as the principal exits the car and begins walking to his destination, the protective agents are naturally in a position to shield him in the prescribed manner.

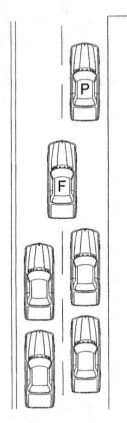

FIGURE 10.5 Follow-up car in curb lane. The follow-up car (F) is approximately one-half to two-thirds of a car length behind the principal's car and approximately half a car width to the left, preventing any other car from getting between the vehicles and from coming directly alongside. The principal (P) rides in the right rear seat.

The supervisor or shift leader assumes his position near the protectee's right (or left elbow) area. The advance agent meets him and leads what will be a diamond-shaped formation. He is followed by agent number two (from the right rear door area) point. On the right side of the formation is agent number one (from the left rear door). Number four (from the right front fender) assumes the left side of the diamond. Trailing and covering the rear is agent number three, from the left front fender area.

As the protectee and covering agents move safely away from the cars, the drivers (who have kept the engines running and the cars in "park" while remaining alert) will reposition the vehicles for departure.

A second function of the follow-up car is to transport equipment that is necessary for performance of the protective agents under any scenario. The first aid kit (including eye wash, in case acid or an eye irritant such as tear gas or CS gas is thrown) and fire extinguisher are readily available.

During the angry antiwar protests of the early 1970s, spray bottles filled with brake fluid (a nontoxic form of paint remover) were kept in the front seat area of the presidential limousine and follow-up car in case the demonstrators splashed paint onto the windshields. The driver and supervisor in the front passenger seat could spray the windshield from their seated position while maintaining their responsibilities inside the car. The paint and brake fluid would then be removed with the windshield wipers.

Other equipment includes a bolt cutter (in case demonstrators or terrorists chain or lock gates) and a crowbar (for a range of purposes such as prying open a jammed door). Additional equipment includes gas masks and antitoxins for gas attacks and tear gas canisters for defensive purposes. There also are route maps and area maps, a radio communication system (the driver and supervisor should wear an earpiece connected to the radio), spare mobile radios and extra batteries, a cellular telephone, jumper cables, towels, blankets, flares, flashlights with extra batteries, foul-weather gear, and a shotgun with extra ammunition. Protective equipment in the follow-up falls into five general categories: health, fire and safety, weapons, convenience, and accidents. Because of the extra equipment in the follow-up vehicle, it is often referred to as "the war wagon," a name alluding to a John Wayne movie.

Another important and common function of the follow-up car is its use as a mobile command post. With its equipment and radio communication gear, the follow-up is a natural command post. The agents can work from the car, using it as a resting and break room when relieved from post. The relief agents and the supervisor in charge can maintain a complete operation from the car.

The follow-up car is also very important for its role as a secondary car or backup for the principal's vehicle. If the principal's car becomes inoperative for any reason, he can ride in the follow-up car.

The last primary function of the follow-up is as a defense against vehicular assault. By blocking traffic and protecting the principal's car on turns, preventing other cars from closely following or ramming the principal's car, the follow-up serves a defensive function.

In selecting (if the option is available) a follow-up car, several criteria should be considered. The car must be powerful enough to reach high speeds in a short time and capable of speeds commensurate with the principal's car. Of course, with some of the high-octane cars available as "toys" for some protectees, an equally fast and powerful car may not be available.

A young member of a royal family was vacationing in Geneva, Switzerland, where he had an opportunity to attend an auto show. A bright red Lamborghini Countach with flawless white leather interior struck his fancy. He immediately laid down the cash to purchase it. The next day, he wanted to try it out. His protective agents dutifully followed him in a rented BMW. Before the agents could leave Geneva, the young man in his sporty new car was in France, trying to figure how to get the car out of second gear! That is perhaps an extreme and only slightly exaggerated example. But, for the most part, the protectee's car and the follow-up are compatible, and instances of the protectee running away from his protection are very rare.

A lot of equipment and several protective agents are assigned to a standard working protective assignment. A properly equipped and ready follow-up must have sufficient cargo and passenger space. Every inch of space is converted for some functional purpose. A modern follow-up could be considered very "James Bondish." For example, Uzi .9-mm semiautomatic (or automatic) guns are stored in the hollowed-out backs of the front seats and covered with breakaway Velcro®. The seat cushions are easily removed to provide access to the storage compartment underneath, and the side panels are removed to provide even more hidden equipment storage. Every available inch of the car is used for something.

The follow-up vehicle of choice fits the needs and purposes of a particular protective assignment. The ideal follow-up must be all utilitarian; sporty, fast and powerful, capable of carrying large payloads, and strong enough to withstand ramming. But it should not appear threatening or militaristic like an adapted version of the Humvee. With the ever-increasing popularity of, and improvements in, four-wheel-drive sport utility vehicles, a customized rendition of this fashionable transport would be a preferred choice. A modern SUV is as common a sight in trendy Beverly Hills and international society as it is in the heartland of America.

Unfortunately, in less than the ideal situation, the follow-up may be a standard sedan, a station wagon, or what ever mode of transportation available. It is not uncommon in many (or most) private protective assignments for the protective agents to use their own cars or a rented vehicle.

VEHICLE SECURITY

At times, the principal's vehicle and the follow-up have to be left unattended. It is imperative that certain security precautions be observed. Both vehicles should be equipped with alarm systems that annunciate at the command post or a protective agent's cell phone in addition to the local audible alarm. Even if the vehicles are parked in a locked garage on a gated and secured estate, they should be locked and the alarms set in a readiness position. At night, the cars should be parked in a well-lighted area and monitored with cameras if possible.

When away from the home compound, the cars should be parked in a secure facility. If a secure facility is not available, park the cars only in well-lit areas, and lock the doors and windows. If the cars are left unattended, do not start the engine until you visually check under and around the car, the exhaust pipe, the wheel wells, gas intake nozzle, and under the hood for any unusual devices or signs of tampering. The hood-locking device must be located and controlled from inside the car, and the gas tank intake should have a locking cap with a cover that also is controlled from inside the car.

Maintenance and service must be performed at a known and reliable service station or dealership. All maintenance records should be retained. If possible, always use the same mechanics. After being serviced, give the cars a thorough physical inspection, looking for any unusual devices or anything other than the normal equipment. Photographs of all sections of the car should have been taken during the first overall inspection. These photographs can be used to compare all parts of the car after it is returned to service.

When traveling by vehicle, always keep the doors locked and the windows rolled up. It is the driver's responsibility to lock the doors and raise the windows while driving a protectee. The driver of the limousine and the follow-up (along with all the other protective agents) should be on the lookout and alert for vehicles that appear to be following the entourage. The route and schedule should be varied each day. The driver should know the locations of emergency services (fire, police, and medical) and plan to avoid congested areas as much as possible. However, travel should be over a well-traveled, public route.

Drivers should never pick up or stop to assist apparent stranded motorists. If a roadblock is encountered, do not stop unless it is manned by official uniformed police officers. A system of communication between drivers should be established in the event anything goes awry. If it does, the drivers should immediately head for the nearest police station or public area and notify the authorities.

SUMMARY

Moving the protectee by vehicle is a very complicated and potentially risky procedure. The duty of driving the car is not to be taken lightly. The driver must be totally aware of many things at one time. He should familiarize himself with the operation of the vehicle and the primary and alternative routes of travel. He must constantly scan the traffic area around him and make immediate adjustments to evolving traffic conditions. The driver should refrain from making jackrabbit starts and all stops, and turns must be done as though he were carrying a load of nitroglycerin and the slightest jarring or tipping would send him to the heavenly highway. When making stops, the driver should always leave room to maneuver around any car in front and park so that no adjacent car occupant can stare at the protectee.

While observing good protectee protocol (e.g., no unnecessary talking, no smoking), the driver should remain in the car until instructed to leave and let the protective agent open the protectee's door. The driver should control the door locks and should keep them locked at all times except when the supervisor is ready to open the protectee's door.

Communication and coordination between the driver of the principal's car and the follow-up car must be closely synchronized. They are a team but must operate and think as one person. The purpose of the follow-up is to transport protective personnel and equipment, provide defense against a vehicular assault, act as a mobile command post, and function as a spare car if the protectee's car becomes inoperable.

Any type of vehicle can be utilized as a limousine or follow-up, but the criteria should match the purpose of the transportation within the limitations of what is available. The purpose, of course, is to provide safe transportation and support for the principal. In some circumstances, when the protectee has used a unique form of transportation, a follow-up bicycle, horse, or boat has performed the same duties as a follow-up car.

All protective agents should anticipate the time when they will be commanded to "drive!" If possible, the agent should sit in the protectee's car and familiarize himself with its control panel and operation. Safe operation of the protectee's car and the follow-up vehicle should be considered as important as the operation of any protective equipment. A protective agent should prepare himself for this opportunity and practice, practice, practice, because there is much more to protective driving than, "Don't hit the car in front of you, and keep it between the ditches."

REVIEW QUESTIONS

1. Why is it important to familiarize oneself with a car before driving a protectee in it?
2. Describe the composition of a standard motorcade.
3. Why should a driver learn to drive with two feet?

4. Why is a protectee particularly vulnerable while in a car?
5. What are subtle courtesies a driver can perform for the convenience and safety of the principal?
6. Why should opening the protectee's or second passenger's door not be the driver's responsibility?
7. What should be the interval between the principal's car and the car in front, when in motion, and when coming to a stop at a traffic signal or stop sign.
8. Explain the driver's protocol with regard to conversation, smoking, and playing the radio.
9. What is a follow-up car and why is it significant? Detail its uses and equipment.
10. A limousine driver and the follow-up driver must work as a team. How do they effect turns and lane changes?
11. Why must agents "working the fenders" have fingertip control or contact?
12. What kind of vehicle is best suited for a follow-up car?
13. What type of vehicle is usually used as a follow-up car in private protection?

NOTE

1. Kuklinski, Richard. *The Ice Man Tapes: Confessions of a Mafia Hitman.* Home Box Office, 2002.

11 Ambushes
Recognizing and Reacting

Swearing, Shouting, Shooting, Smoke, Explosions, Confusion, and Violence

Ambush attacks occur with suddenness, surprise, and (often) extremely violent actions. Not surprisingly, they can involve shooting, explosions, smoke, shouting, and swearing. When an attack occurs, it is too late to take preventive measures. When the attack comes, it will come totally out of the blue, with split-second timing and incomprehensible violence. A key component of the attack is intimidation, allowing the victim no time or ability to resist.

RECOGNIZING INDICATORS OF A POSSIBLE AMBUSH ATTACK

"Unit eight, we have a report of a large street fight in progress at the Nova Housing Tract development on Third Avenue, just south of Broadway. Check it out and advise."

"10-4—unit eight."

"Unit eight, also be advised you are the only unit available for another 20 minutes because of shift change."

"Unit 8—check that!"

It was 10:55 P.M. on a very hot night. The northern California days and nights had been hot all summer. The ambient temperature was not all that was hot. The city, and the rest of the country, was experiencing what had become known as "a long, hot summer." Racial tensions were running high, and many cities were imploding from racial distrust, riots, fires, looting, and anti–Vietnam War demonstrations.

The police overlap shift had been at work since 10:00 P.M, but now the regular shift had drifted to the station for relief of shifts. Unit eight, normally assigned to the mid-south patrol section of the city, was being sent to cover what would normally be unit six's call, but unit six was already at the station involved in the shift change from swing to graveyard.

Six minutes later, at Third and Broadway,

"KMA, this is unit eight. We are at the reported scene. It is very quiet, no one on the street, just a couple of streetlights are out. We don't even see lights in the apartments."

"10-4, unit eight. You are clear. Return to your own district."

Then, seconds later came a "thump, thump, thump." The driver turned to his partner, "What was that?"

"Bullets. They are shooting at us," the partner calmly replied.

The driver, just as calm and unexcited said, "What bullets? Who? And what are you doing getting down there on the floor?"

"Those are real bullets and they are shooting at us! Get us out of here!"

217

"Bullets? You mean people are shooting at us? Why didn't you say so?" The fact that someone would purposely shoot at a police car still was not sinking in.

"Uh, KMA, this is unit eight. We're getting the hell out of here! They're shooting at us!"

Obviously, that was a long time ago, many lifetimes away, and laughable now. But it is a true story. The sniper was never found, and the city police car had three bullet holes in the passenger side door panel, near the window. The point to be made here is that, unless the brain is aware of possibilities, it will not register unlikely or unfamiliar events as actualities. Those officers were lucky. They were not killed or injured. But the cold, hard fact remains that they failed to observe or recognize that something totally unrelated was afoot and about to happen.

Not taken into account was the fact that someone had telephoned the police dispatcher and reported a large street fight in progress, the officers were driving into a known racial and gang hotbed, the streets were deserted where normally there would be a great deal of activity, the street lights were out, and there were no lights in the apartments. All of this was coincidentally occurring at the shift change, when it was known the police were at minimal strength. Today's police are better informed from experience to not only recognize the indicators of a possible attack but also to recognize that it is possible, and perhaps likely, that a police car or someone will be ambushed.

RECOGNIZING ELEMENTS OF AN AMBUSH ATTACK

An ambush is commonly defined as, "a violent and sudden attack launched from a hidden position by a person or persons intending to injure or kill a specific individual or component such as a protective detail, a military unit, or other unsuspecting entity." Recognizing an attack as it begins to unfold is an important and sometimes daunting task that is essential to both protective agents and their principal. By identifying these elements, certain safeguards or further assessments can be put into place to avoid or dissuade such an attack. Recognizing an ambush attack is an expression that should not be taken lightly. Most people or novices would view this as seeing a man with a gun hiding and lying in wait or watching a car coming to a screeching halt, with masked men jumping out.

To train for comprehending an attack means asking certain questions such as: "Who am I looking for?" "What am I looking for?" "When will it happen?" "Where will it happen?" Even though there may be no readily definitive answer to these questions, an agent is preparing himself mentally for a reaction or response that could save his or his principal's life—if lucky, maybe his actions will save all their lives.

Ideally, an agent will detect and prevent an ambusher's attack in its earliest phases—during the surveillance or information-gathering stage—by conducting some type of countersurveillance or having some knowledge of the victim's potential attackers. Preplanning and being ready for the unexpected means knowing what the norm is and detecting what is out of place. It is looking and seeing things by interpreting their hidden message. "If it doesn't belong, it is wrong."

Recognizing an attack before it develops can have many benefits. Among the most important of these is the ability to overcome the natural "freeze" response. Other benefits include the ability to meet the attack with a plan of action so a protection detail can respond effectively. Seeing it as it is coming, or before it commences, provides a significant tactical advantage to the person being attacked; it allows him to seize the initiative. If a protective agent sees an attack coming, physical reaction times will be lessened, and plans can be put into effect. An attacker in the open, coming toward a principal or a protective agent with evil intent, conceivably can be stopped dead in his tracks with a loud warning. The least amount of physical force is always the optimal solution. Regardless of whether verbal techniques are sufficient or physical techniques are needed, the rule applies.

A verbal confrontation, however, will not do the job in an ambush attack, so a physical response is necessary. In this case, preplanned ambush response measures need to be implemented so the element of surprise does not work to the advantage of the attacker. In a sudden, unexpected attack from a hidden location, the unprepared victim may not even realize what is going on until it is too late. In a surprise situation, even the most highly trained person may have a natural freeze response when an attack is initiated. The freeze response refers to the initial state of shock a victim feels once he realizes that he is being attacked. In a fight that lasts only seconds, failure to react immediately can prove deadly. However, if the potential victim is aware of his surroundings and understands the situation, he can respond without succumbing to inaction. Being aware of the hidden violence in the world and anticipating an attack allows the potential victim to shake off that natural response.

A group intent on committing a kidnapping does not come stealthily in the dark of night, nor does it always attempt to lure the victim into a trap. Historically, the best-planned and possibly rehearsed attacks have occurred mostly in the morning, in the form of a vehicle ambush. Attacking a victim by means of a vehicle ambush has proven to be an extremely successful technique. Generally, either the victim's car is halted by a blockade or the attacker's vehicle maneuvers into a position that causes the victim's car to swerve off the road or stop. The stoppage is so sudden and swift that the victim is completely surprised, usually having the first impression that the attack is merely the result of an inattentive driver causing a traffic jam or mishap. When the trap or ambush is sprung, the victim is either isolated, quickly pulled from his vehicle, and forced into the kidnapper's car or he is assassinated on the spot.

The attackers have a twofold advantage over the victim and the protective detail. The first advantage, as usual, is the fact the attackers employ the element of surprise: they control the location, the time, the method, and the mode of escape, having the option of either killing or kidnapping the victim. The attackers will already have an aggressive mind-set for the kidnap and will be physically ready, with weapons drawn. The second advantage is the fact the protective personnel must recognize and react to the attack by either attempting to drive out of the situation or responding with belated and limited firepower while assuming the responsibility of mitigating the risks to innocent bystanders. (Attackers will have no such concerns.)

Many factors can be involved when the driver simply stops and surrenders. A protection agent must be aware of those elements and guard against them by mentally preparing himself and the potential victim (the protectee) for a surprise vehicle ambush. Being mentally unprepared and physically inattentive are the foremost reasons for falling victim so easily. An unwillingness to recognize the situation and to believe what is really happening is difficult for some people, and they simply may not know what to do or how to react. There must be an instantaneous acceptance of the event with a determination to resist, and it must be accompanied by a positive countermeasure. An effective counterforce is to use the victim's car as an offensive weapon by attacking the kidnapper's position with a strategic ramming of the road-block or aggressor's car.

The driver of the protectee's vehicle should not attempt to drive around the road-block, nor should he attempt to ram it broadside. He must also avoid side-to side contact, which will have little effect except to place the driver and protectee in a direct line of fire. In aggressive driving countermeasures, the first consideration is escape. In the city, street curbs might have to be cleared. To jump a curb, the curb must not be approached directly head on but at a 45° angle at speeds up to 15 mph. There will be no loss of control at the lower speed or at that angle. A larger angle could result in damage to the tires, and a higher speed could cause the vehicle to roll.

When anticipating ramming the attacker's roadblock, the protectee's car should come nearly to a stop and be placed in low gear while maintaining a high engine rpm to avoid stalling. This may result in the attackers momentarily relaxing, incorrectly believing that the driver is about to surrender. The driver aims his vehicle at the rear wheel area, rear corner area, or front wheel area of the offending roadblock vehicle. The ramming vehicle is accelerated forward into the blocking vehicle. The driver must continue accelerating and not slow down, pushing through the attacker's vehicle with power and momentum. As the other car is spun away, the ramming car picks up speed in a higher gear and drives away. Offensively charging the attacker's car will have a maximum shock effect on the attackers and may cause them to lose control of their weapons, and their vehicle may be disabled.

Tests have found that the best ramming speed is approximately 25 to 35 mph. A slower speed will not provide enough power to push through the blocking vehicle, and a higher speed may cause the ramming vehicle driver to lose control. The ram must be done squarely with the front or back of the ramming vehicle. A glancing blow will not be powerful enough to push aside the attacker's car, and it could send the ramming car into a spin or totally out of control. The driver and protectee must be mentally prepared to ram the car into a roadblock, which is counter to all normal instincts. They must be prepared for the impact and belted in because of the physical shock of striking the other vehicle.

When an attacker attempts to force the protectee's car to the side or to a stop, especially when traveling at normal driving speeds, a practical tactic is to brake suddenly, causing the attacker's car to pass the protectee's car. The protectee driver can then accelerate and ram the attacker's car or, even better, make a quick turnaround and drive away. It is best to escape as quickly as possible, with as little engagement as possible.

Other factors that could invite a vehicle attack include mechanical failure, poor driving, improper timing, and just plain bad luck. It is incumbent upon the protection agent to have all equipment in good working order and to always be mentally prepared for any confrontations.

To synopsize, other than watching for the obvious "man with a gun hiding in the bushes," there are no definitive guidelines or rules that the protective specialist can follow to spot a pending ambush. Comprehending an attack is an art that requires practice, patience, and mental prepardness. It is all about perception. Awareness and discernment is a deadly game of cat and mouse that the protective specialist cannot afford to lose. It is a game in which the opponents are ever-changing, and the only way to win is by being flexible and mentally alert.

A properly run and mentally aware protection detail will be able to meet an attack in its earliest steps and implement plans to get its principal out of the area and to harden the target against attack. Attacks can be recognized by looking for things that may not belong (e.g., a person dressed improperly for the weather or a car parked where it should not be). There must be a constant lookout for such warning signs. Recognizing an attack as it unfolds is the difference between proactive counteraction and a delayed response.

Proactive counteraction may or may not make the actual confrontation less dangerous, but it does blunt the sword of the attacker. He expects to be the aggressor and to meet little resistance. He expects to have power over the situation. "Within the context of conflict, it is often perceived that whoever has the power will be the winner." The attacker was counteracted, and his power was stripped away by his opponent, so the balance of control shifted to the defending party.

The importance of early attack recognition cannot be calculated, and a violent person is dangerous under any circumstances. An ambush attack by such an individual or group can be catastrophic. Psychological reactions on the victim's side can range from a quick freeze reaction to not even realizing what is going on, which gives the attacker a huge advantage. That advantage must be eroded by proper vigilance on the side of the protection detail and the protectee. If an attack is recognized, it may be thwarted before it becomes physical.

While working with a protectee, an officer or protective agent should be running numerous what-if scenarios through his head. This will enable him to be more prepared for whatever. Failure to stay alert or consider all possible types of situations can be deadly. Failure of the potential victim to recognize an approaching attack will give the ambushers an edge and a better chance to fight and escape. The victim and security personnel must listen to their inner voices and what they feel and think inside (intuition), because sometimes this is the strongest indicator that an attack is coming. A perception or feeling that something is going to happen is often correct. Not only does the victim have to be psychologically alert, he also needs to be open to new approaches to handling the attack if the usual way doesn't work. He should be mentally prepared to react "right here, right now" and be able to act swiftly and with violence.

NO SURPRISES! ANTICIPATION, RECOGNITION, REACTION

ANTICIPATION

Assassinations and kidnappings from ambush are not random acts of violence. They require weeks of intense planning. An attack begins long before the actual ambush. Therefore, the first portion of an attack is actually the intelligence-gathering and preplanning stages.

Intelligence gathering means surveillance to map and time the activities of the victim. This phase will last as long as necessary for the attackers to be certain of their target's movements. Humans being what they are, one can never be totally sure that the victim will behave in a set way. But with sufficient surveillance, an attacker can gauge with a high degree of probability that the victim will usually behave in a routine manner. It is here that the victim's security antenna and anticipation should be finely tuned. He should watch for surveillance, use deductive reasoning regarding a "coincidence" of any unusual activity in his vicinity, and gather his own intelligence appropriate to his security and the possible threat level of an attack against him. He should remain abreast of news reports of any unusual activity or other incidents and compile sufficient information to calculate and assess the threat potential. He should, in other words, prepare himself mentally and physically for an attack.

The victim is at a disadvantage even if he is mentally and physically well prepared. The ambushing attackers will have planned every move and calculated the attack to commence and be carried out with astonishing shock and speed. In a kidnapping attack, the purpose is to render the victim helpless as quickly as possible and escape the area with little or no attention from passersby. Sometimes the attackers will have no concern about stealth but will commence the attack with "shock and awe" and guns blazing. The intent will be to kill the principal and as many of his staff and protection agents as possible, in as short a period of time as possible, and then to escape. The hit-and-run assassination ambush plan is designed to strike at the most surprising moment, when the victim may be momentarily exposed and vulnerable.

Attackers depend on shock value and gaining rapid control of the victim. Occurring with sudden speed, the attack will take the victim unaware and may cause him to react very slowly, until he recognizes what is happening. That time lag is usually enough for the attackers to fulfill their mission. It has been observed that the surprise of the sudden and violent attack has actually led victims to surrender long before they recognizes the predicament. Victims have actually been known to exit their vehicle to "see what is the matter" or to utter, "What the …?"

OBSERVATIONAL AWARENESS

Observation means seeing, recognizing, and reacting. The word observation often and mistakenly is substituted with watching, looking, seeing, and surveillance. We see or watch something while looking at or making a surveillance of it. But a true observation is more far-reaching. We see with our eyes, and the image is transported to our brain, where it is translated into something accepted through recognition. This process of recognition relies on many factors, such as experience, education and training, physical and emotional conditioning, social norms, instinct and intuition, and perhaps environmental and biological factors.

Seeing and recognizing are only two-thirds of the observation equation. What good does it do to see and recognize something if there is no reaction? Reaction should be an instantaneous reflex initiated by the element that has been recognized, but, unfortunately, there may be a delay time as the brain attempts to classify and segregate the images and issue instructions for the appropriate response. If there is a short circuit, the process time can have tragic results, such as fear paralysis in the face of danger.

Recognizing and reacting are about perception. Perception means interpreting the definition of what you have observed and having a critical viewpoint with skills for assessing the situation. It may be a gut reaction, a feeling, or a hair-raising intuition. In many ways, recognizing an attack and preparing for one are the same things, and practice is required. By working with diverse people in diverse situations on a daily basis, you can develop a sense of what is normal and what is out of place. This training and practice allows you to develop a sixth sense (perception) for when something is not right. This is the essence of recognizing an attack.

FACTORS AFFECTING PERCEPTION

"Perception is seeing the things you don't see," but many factors may affect the extent of perception.

- *Experience.* Experience is based on past events, the things we have been exposed to, and the things we have seen and done. Every encounter is an opportunity to learn and gain. One episode of an event brings knowledge, understanding, and know-how. Experiences, in other words, may be defined as the building blocks of future recognizable events.
- *Education and training.* A sequence of events will be more easily and quickly recognized, analyzed, and addressed by a person of higher education, or at least one who is educated and trained in the particular field or occupation.
- *Bias and prejudice.* Preconceived thoughts and feelings will render a person incapable of seeing others, events, and places as anything other than what he wants to see or thinks he sees. Prejudice will color a person's perception.
- *Pain and physical state of the observer.* If an observer is experiencing pain, a fever, or another abnormality, even a common cold, his concentration will be more focused on personal comfort than his surroundings.
- *Complacency.* Routine and sameness encourage mistakes in observation and reaction and make it easy to overlook subtle changes. For example, it has been established that the most vulnerable time for an ambush victim is in the early morning hours while he is in transit and at close range, usually between his home and office or within 3.5 miles of home. There are a few reasons for this.
    1. Primarily because the victim has a set routine, leaving home at nearly the same time every morning, there may be few people in the area to witness the attack, and there are usually a limited number of streets and roadways (usually only one or two, at most) by which the person can leave his residence.
    2. Being close to home, in a familiar and friendly environment, the potential victim and his protection agents have a tendency to become complacent, dropping their guard.
- *Other factors.* Perception is also affected by (1) the distance from the threat (a close object is more likely to attract attention than something occurring a

long distance away), (2) a sound and how it relates to previous experiences (a loud noise will more readily attract attention and be identified), (3) movement (a moving object is more readily seen than a stationary one), and (4) size (obviously, a large object will be seen before a small object).

ACTION

The success or failure of an ambush depends on several factors. The first is how the victim acts, reacts, or fails to act. In a fight-or-flight situation, the brain sends signals to the rest of the body, preparing it to respond in a manner that will provide safety. There is an overflow of adrenaline, the heart rate increases, blood pressure goes up, and breathing becomes rapid. Many signals are flashing from the brain, possibly causing a short circuit that compels the body to begin shutting down, forcing a failure to recognize the true danger or a collapse into surrender. On the other hand, the prepared brain quickly assesses the situation, sends signals to prepare for defensive action, and does not ask whether to act at all but instead reacts aggressively.

INDICATORS OF A PENDING AMBUSH ATTACK

It is rather apparent that early detection of a possible attack greatly enhances the chance of escape. In a motorcade, in a private vehicle, or as a pedestrian, the intended victim can decide to back up or go forward, increase or decrease speed, alter direction, or, as a last resort, prepare for action. There is no sure-fire, failsafe method of detecting an attack, but there are indicators to be recognized, considered, and evaluated. Among such indicators are

- *Being channeled.* The road narrows naturally or by a man-made obstacle, causing a bottleneck that the victim's vehicle must navigate and closing off escape routes. This allows the ambushers an opportunity to direct the victim's vehicle into the desired attack zone.
- *Absence of populace in the area.* Local people may become aware of a pending attack and vacate the area.
- *Slow-moving or stopped trucks or cars.* These may appear immediately in front of the intended victim's car or possibly emerge from an alley or street to block the traffic flow, or there may be a vehicle following very close to the victim.
- *Blind spots.* Blind spots occur when the victim is rounding a curve or otherwise does not have an opportunity for effective observation and awareness. One might observe limited or no lighting where there is usually normal illumination.
- *Construction crews.* A large construction truck, tractor, or van and a crew, in uniform or not, that seems out of place or not actually working.
- *Obstacles.* The victim's car may be forced to stop by a railroad crossing gate, a traffic signal, or other congestion.

- *Shouting, swearing, shooting, smoke, and explosions.* Attackers are not going to a tea-party social, and they are not especially interested in following the rules of etiquette. They have one mission: to render the victim helpless or dead as quickly as possible and to escape.
- *Observation or surveillance.* People loitering in the area, a person on a utility pole who may be talking on a radio or telephone, motorcycles following close or pulling up alongside the victim could be indicators.
- *Abnormal activities.* Watch for things that are different, out of place, or unusual; things that "just do not fit."
- *The presence of cars, vans and other vehicles in the area where they are not usually present.* Vans make excellent observation, blocking, and kidnap vehicles. The presence of such a van in the area may indicate that someone is either under surveillance or will be kidnapped.
- *False accidents.* This can be in the form of pedestrian or cyclist who pretends to be struck or injured by the victim's vehicle, or another vehicle crashing into the victim's—anything to make the victim stop.

Obviously these are not all the indicators of a pending or actual attack. Indicators are limited only by the imagination of the attackers and protective agents.

PREPARE FOR REALITIES

Recognizing an attack is a mind game that calls for mature judgment, that is a psychological perspective based on alertness, awareness of environmental conditions, setting and mind-set, and a general consciousness of all possibilities. In the preceding police ambush story, the officers failed to recognize the possibility of a setup or an ambush because their minds were fixed on the dispatcher's description of "a large street fight in progress." Driving to the scene, their thoughts focused on the fight and what tactics they would employ. Would they only "observe and report" or take some immediate action knowing that backup was at least 20 minutes away? Even when the shooting started, they did not hear gunfire or see anyone in the area; their minds were still transiting to relief that there was no large crowd or fight in progress—the only "reality" their minds could interpret.

REACTION

The victim (and his security) must be mentally conditioned to react immediately, swiftly, and with violence. Response becomes a reflex action. This calls for preplanning, anticipation, mental awareness, and conscious alertness. Getting into the correct mind-set for recognizing the reality of an attack takes drill and practice, preparation for the unexpected, and resistance to psychological shock.

AMBUSH!

A successful ambusher never attacks unless he feels sure of winning. Security agents must be aware of the successful ambusher's key rules.[1] Incidentally, the security agent must not fail to see the mirror image of his own preparation in these key rules.

1. Always have a good plan providing for every course of action of the enemy.
2. Always select an unlikely ambush spot.
3. Always put around-the-clock surveillance on the objective and the area of the attack.
4. Always obtain as much information about the target as possible.
5. Always rehearse the elements of the ambush attack.
6. Always achieve close control through rehearsals and effective communications.
7. Always vary the ambush techniques and design so that there is not a set or consistent pattern.
8. Always have patience. It may be necessary to occupy an ambush position well ahead of time.
9. Always have effective camouflage (cover and concealment); an effective ambush cannot be achieved if men, weapons, and equipment are not properly concealed.
10. Always strike suddenly and with violence.
11. Always withdraw quickly and by various routes.
12. Always have all-around security.

The following are some scenarios that may or may not be precursors to an ambush attack. It is obvious from these and similar scenarios that recognizing an ambush or attack may be difficult. They do, however, stress the point of the importance of countersurveillance and very vigilant awareness.

1. A pedestrian jumps in front of your car and is accidentally hit.
2. A bicycle rider "falls" in front of your car.
3. A baby carriage is pushed in front of your car.
4. A motorcycle moves alongside your car.
5. A construction flagman stops your car.
6. Another vehicle (or other obstacle) blocks your progress.
7. Something else impedes the progression of your vehicle.

RESPONSE TO AN AMBUSH

An ambush attack must be instantaneously reacted to without waiting for orders. A prompt, decisive initial reaction will greatly reduce the effectiveness of the ambush. An analysis of the above factors (and past attacks) indicates, naturally, that the first step in launching an ambush attack is to stop the principal's car just before or at the moment of attack. Therefore, it is reasonable to attempt to avoid stopping and to keep moving at all costs. The driver should quickly decide whether to back away, move around the blockage, or drive on through. In less time than an eye blink, he must select his best option and pursue it, in one movement. A rule of thumb is to drive through the ambush if possible, because it limits the time in the kill zone.

If an ambush is suspected or there are indicators of the possibility of a roadside bomb, a good evasive maneuver is to suddenly speed up to pass the bomb location before it can be set off, or to suddenly slow down, throwing off the timing of the detonation. Extensive textbooks and training courses are available that describe evasive maneuvers such as ramming, turning, and positioning. It is beyond the scope of this chapter to delve deeply into each aspect of defensive driving; however, each is mentioned below to familiarize the student with possible options.

> *Ramming.* As the name implies, this means refusing to stop and running through the blockage. In some cases, where it is clearly impossible to evade a roadblock or ram through it, a driver may opt to drive around it or to ram any relatively frail-looking building on either side of the street. If the car can be driven completely inside, the driver and passengers may have a chance to escape through the rear of the building.... In any event, the crash will create confusion and much noise. In many cases, the ambushers will retreat because they have not planned for such a scenario.
>
> *Turning.* Sudden twists and turnarounds in a "bootleggers" or "J" turn make it difficult for the ambushers to continue their pursuit or to employ accurate firepower. Sudden turns into a motorcyclist or ambusher's car may dissuade the attack. It is against all instincts to intentionally drive into another vehicle, but it can be a lifesaver.
>
> *Positioning.* Suddenly braking, allowing the attacker's car to pass, may work if the attackers attempt to drive alongside the principal's car. Forcing the attacker's car to pass on the right side means that gunfire from one of the attackers—the one in front—will be blocked by the driver of the car.

SUMMARY

There are no hard and fast rules for recognizing a pending ambush attack. If there is anything close to a simple rule, it is to recognize or view any unusual or peculiar act as a sign of potential danger. Anything happening that is not an everyday occurrence should be viewed as a potential attack situation. Attacks vary with the imagination and modus operandi of the attacker. Recognition comes with awareness, experience, observation, and intuition. Reaction to an ambush or attack must come immediately or reflexively. You cannot always be sure.

Recognizing an attack is a matter of perception and of heeding intuition and feelings. If a feeling (or intuition) sends up red flares, listen to it! Intuition (or extrasensory perception) is the sixth sense that is sometimes stronger than the five normal senses of taste, hearing, smell, touch, and seeing. Perception is the ability to utilize unconscious recognition of an intangible message being sent to the brain with no explainable stimulus.

Recognizing an attack means knowing the area being traveled and recognizing things that are out of order or that do not fit. This could mean unusual activities, lack of activity, channeling, blockages, the creation of blind spots, or the elimination of escape routes.

Recognizing an attack means being mentally aware and consciously alert for any possibility, including a motorcycle moving up alongside the victim's vehicle, fake accidents, and stopped vehicles or other obstructions in the roadway. Being prepared for the unexpected reduces the surprise and psychological shock of the sudden violence created by the ambushers.

REVIEW QUESTIONS

1. Describe the first few seconds of an attack.
2. How can you mentally prepare for an ambush attack?
3. Why would someone intentionally stop his car and inquire, "What the…?" allowing himself to be easily kidnapped."
4. What is an ambush and what is its intent?
5. What are the indicators of a pending ambush?
6. How should a person under an ambush attack react?
7. Describe three ways for escaping an ambush attack.
8. Why are perception and observation important in recognizing an ambush?
9. What does the phrase, "If it doesn't belong, it is wrong," mean in reference to recognizing an ambush?

NOTE

1. A major portion of this section (in italics or otherwise noted) is presented with thanks to my good friends Gary Stubblefield and Mark Monday from their book, Killing Zone. Boulder, CO: Paladin Press, 1994.

12 ABCs of Medicine

Treat him as best you can with common sense and do no harm.

Take two aspirin and call me in the morning.

Conventional non-emergency advice

MEDICAL EMERGENCIES[1]

A protection agent has many roles. Among them are security specialist or protector, trip and logistics planner, confidant, friend, and emergency medical responder. Many things can befall a protectee that have nothing to do with the activities of terrorists, crazies, or anyone who would want to intentionally harm him. In spite of the very best preventive measures taken by a protection agent, accidents, injuries, and other life-threatening medical emergencies occur.

Every year, in just the United States, more than 180,000 people die from heart attacks, 163,000 from strokes, and more than 140,000 from injuries.[2] Many of them die needlessly because of a lack of adequate and available emergency medical treatment. Many of those deaths can be prevented if certain procedures are taken immediately. Therefore, it is important that protection personnel have at least a minimal working knowledge of first aid. While it is not necessary for a protection agent to have passed an emergency medical technician (EMT) course, it is highly recommended.

The following material can in no way approximate the degree of training inclusive in EMT or other advanced training and is intended to serve only as a very condensed version of emergency techniques and procedures that may provide a rescuer with the tools to save a life. It is intended only to introduce the protection agent to some of the emergencies that he is likely to encounter in the course of routine duties. Proper preparation for and response to an emergency could very well save a life. It is incumbent upon the protection agent to acquire the skills necessary to professionally and adequately perform his job. Emergency medical response is a great part of that professionalism.

Whether at the White House, a hunting preserve in Texas, or a houseboat vacation on Lake Shasta in northern California, in instances of injury or sudden illness (e.g., heart attack, stroke, or gunshot wound), everyone expects the protection agent to provide the correct medical response until the emergency has been stabilized and the victim is in the care of professionals. The initial actions of those at the scene of the medical emergency could save the life of the victim.

Emergency medical response (EMR) is sometimes referred to as *ten-minute medicine*. Lifesaving procedures such as cardiopulmonary resuscitation (CPR, or *rescue breathing*) and control of bleeding, if applied immediately, can sustain life beyond the ten-minute absolute time limit after which a person is considered brain dead and clinically deceased.

Emergency medical services are required immediately, when there is no time to wait for the arrival of an ambulance and medical technicians. Emergency medical treatment is initiated in response to an unforeseen illness or injury. A first responder (the person or persons initially responding to the emergency) should meet certain objectives:

- Promptly identify and respond to the emergency situation.
- Use proper emergency medical care and life-support systems to sustain life.
- Transport the victim to the nearest medical facility for more extensive treatment.

Following an unexpected injury or illness, there is usually a time of total confusion, stress, and excitement. Anyone responding to the emergency must approach it in a calm, assured manner. His demeanor will be contagious to bystanders and the victim. If he appears confident and in charge, he will lend assurance to everyone, including the victim, that things will shortly be all right. Several things should be done immediately and concurrently at the scene of the medical emergency:

- Before beginning any lifesaving procedures, it is recommended that the first person on the scene call 911 (or direct someone to make the call) to initiate professional emergency medical services (EMS) such as a rescue squad or ambulance.
- Make sure the victim is in a safe area to prevent further injuries to the victim, attending personnel, or even onlookers. If there are electrical lines down, they should be secured. At the scene of an automobile accident, reroute or stop passing traffic. If there is gunfire, provide blocking barriers. If in a burning building or at the scene of a dangerous chemical spill, remove the victim to safer ground.
- Win the victim's confidence and alleviate some of his anxiety, especially in a heart attack or trauma victim. Speak softly and reassuringly. Minimize the degree of injury and convince him that he will soon be all right. A victim will be suffering great pain catalyzed by thoughts and fears of impending death. The psychological aspect of the victim must be considered of great importance. If he believes the injury or physical attack can be treated and he will be restored, he will respond with a positive attitude that could forestall the onset of secondary trauma such as shock.
- There have been cases in which a gunshot victim has lost entire portions of his body and totally recovered. On the other hand, there are also recorded cases of a victim suffering a small and easily treated wound, say from a small-caliber gun like a .22, who believed he was dying and did in fact die.

If a victim thinks to himself, "Oh my God, I've been shot! I'm gonna die!" he probably will unless he is becomes convinced that he will soon be OK. It is considered very poor treatment to approach the victim with, "Wow, you've been shot, just look at that hole! You could drive a truck through there! Shall I call anyone? Next of kin? A priest?"

- Identify the victim's problems and establish which ones require immediate attention. This procedure is termed "patient assessment" or the *primary survey*. The assessment is made by physically examining the victim. The primary survey is extremely important because it entails checking for and controlling immediate life-threatening problems such as a clogged airway, absence of breathing, stoppage of blood circulation, or loss of blood. The secondary assessment looks for other serious but not immediately life-threatening injuries such as broken bones or burns.

The patient assessment must be calm, unhurried, and systematic. Therefore, it is important to perform the examination in specific steps so no important information is missed. Begin at the top of the head, examining the right side and front middle, and continue to the bottoms of the feet. The same procedure is followed on the left side and middle, then the back.

The physical examination is divided into four steps:

1. Primary survey, including vital signs (breathing [respiration] and pulse).
2. Resuscitation—restore breathing by CPR (rescue breathing) if necessary.
3. Secondary survey.
4. Provide needed emergency care.

Obtain information about the victim that may not be readily available later in the hospital (i.e., observations about the environment and what caused the injury, illness, or trauma). This information could be important to treating physicians. Include the time of the accident or onset of illness, what treatment was given, condition and appearance of the victim, and his pulse, respiration, and temperature when treatment began.

PRIMARY SURVEY

A primary survey is a physical examination of the victim designed to locate and identify immediately life-threatening conditions. Before moving the victim, determine if there could be a head, neck, or spinal area injury that might be exacerbated by movement. If such an injury is suspected, do not move the victim until those areas have been immobilized! The primary survey may have to be done in very awkward or uncomfortable positions but, nevertheless, the following areas must be immediately examined, especially if the victim is not breathing, his skin is very pale, or his lips and fingernails are beginning to turn blue. Immediately check the "ABCS": A, airway; B, bleeding; C, circulation; S, shock.

Airway. Is it open? If not, why? Are blood, secretions, and so on blocking it? Gently tilt the head back and lift the chin; this often will be sufficient to open the airway. If tilting the head back does not open the airway, open the victim's mouth and look for the obstruction. Do not attempt to put a finger down his throat to remove a blockage, as this may only push the object deeper into the throat. If head, neck, or spinal injuries are suspected, do not tilt the head. Is the victim breathing? What is the quality of respiration (rate, depth, regularity, and apparent ease)? To check breathing, look, listen, and feel for it. Look for the chest to rise and fall, place your ear near the victim's mouth, listen for breathing, and feel for exhaled air. A victim may not be breathing even though there is movement in the chest. Consequently, listening and feeling are important for checking a victim's breathing.

Bleeding. Is there a major external hemorrhage? Does the patient appear to be in shock? Head wounds and cuts normally involve substantial of bleeding even if the wound is very small. It is not unusual, however, to have only minimal bleeding from a gunshot, puncture, or knife wound unless a vein or artery is cut or a major organ is ruptured. Internal bleeding may very rapidly lead to shock. During the primary survey, is the victim coughing up or vomiting blood? Is there swelling, bruises, or hardness or tenderness of the abdomen or other areas? Check for skull, chest, and stomach wounds. Also look at the back area for entrance or exit wounds that would not be detected in a frontal exam.

Circulation. Does the patient have a pulse (heartbeat)? What is the quality of the pulse (rate, regularity, strength)? To check the pulse, place two fingers (not a thumb) over the carotid artery (between the Adam's apple area of the throat and the main neck muscle) and feel for a beat. Check the color of the lips, fingernails, and toenails. If they are pink and respond with color when pinched, they are receiving blood. But if they begin to turn blue or do not return to the normal color after pinching, circulation has stopped.

Shock. Does the patient exhibit symptoms of shock or potential shock? Shock is characterized by a weak and irregular pulse; cold, clammy, pale, or bluish skin; rapid and shallow breathing; and confusion, anxiety, or loss of consciousness. If not treated immediately, shock can lead to death, even in the case of minor wounds. Shock is a very common secondary reaction to traumatic injury, such as a broken bone (especially a compound fracture, when the victim can readily see the broken skin, a protruding bone, and blood in the area). A victim may even go into shock from hitting his thumb with a hammer. The pain may be so intense that, coupled with a visual stimulus, the brain begins to shut down, causing the person to slip into shock. Shock can also result from a blow to the neurological system (the head, neck, or spinal area). Those areas must be carefully examined to prevent further injury. Are there any signs or symptoms that might indicate damage to the central nervous system? The circumstances of the injury are important when determining the possibility of such injuries. Is the person unconscious from a fall, other type of accident, or blow to the head, neck, or spine? Is the head, neck, or spine in an abnormal position? Are there lumps or bruises on the head, eyes, or face? Is there bleeding from the mouth, nose, or ears? There may be headaches, nausea, and vomiting. Vision may be blurred and speech slurred, and perhaps there is difficulty in breathing. There may be dizziness, confusion, loss of balance, seizures, and even a loss of consciousness.

SECONDARY SURVEY

Begin at the head and check the victim all over for injuries that could be significant but not readily visible. Be sure to check front, back, and sides. Identify and correct any life-threatening problems. This assessment should be done rapidly but surely and confidently. The examining responder should talk to the victim and reassure him during the entire procedure. If he is conscious, the victim should be queried about any locations of pain and discomfort. *Caution:* while making the assessment, do not fail to provide whatever urgent treatment the circumstances dictate. For example, be sure to clear an obstructed airway immediately. During the secondary survey, the victim may begin struggling for air or stop breathing, become unconscious, go into shock, or begin hemorrhaging. If any of these occur, follow appropriate emergency procedures.

PROVIDING NEEDED EMERGENCY CARE

RESCUE BREATHING RESUSCITATION

If a victim still is not breathing after the airway is cleared, the rescuer (the protection agent) must restore breathing by cardiopulmonary resuscitation and cardiac compression. A brain can be damaged after as little as three to five minutes without blood and oxygen. The victim will be brain dead after seven minutes and clinically dead after ten minutes. (Thus, the term "ten-minute medicine," often used to describe the critical period when lifesaving procedures must be instituted.) While emergency medical technician training is not required of an executive protection agent, CPR should be mandatory.

To perform CPR (also called "rescue breathing")

1. Lay the victim flat on his back.
2. Check for breathing.
3. Open the airway. Open the mouth and check for obstructions. Tilt the head back and lift the chin.
4. If the victim is still not breathing, begin rescue breathing.
5. Pinch the victim's nose shut and place your mouth over the victim's lips, creating a tight seal. Give two quick breaths, watching for the chest to rise. Repeat. (If and whenever possible, use a barrier device such as a resuscitation mask to protect against ingesting the victim's saliva or other liquid and to protect from infectious bacteria—but do not delay rescue breathing if a barrier device is not immediately available.)
6. Check for pulse with two fingers on the carotid artery.

7. If there is no pulse, begin chest compressions. If there is a pulse, continue rescue breathing with one breath every 4 to 5 seconds. Check for a pulse after 12 breaths.

8. To begin chest compressions, place one hand on the victim by locating two fingers in the notch where the breastbone meets the ribs. Place the other hand at the edge of those fingers, on the heart side of the victim. (The location should be approximately 1 inch above the breastbone notch.) Interlace the fingers of both hands and begin compressions.

9. Press down firmly, forcing the breastbone to depress approximately 1.5 to 2 inches, then release, lifting only the finger part of the hands—leave the heel of your hand in place on the breastbone. Administer 12 to 15 compressions at the count of "one, one thousand, two, one thousand, three…."

10. Repeat the rescue breathing of two breaths and chest compressions at the rate of 2:15. If there are two rescuers, the breathing/chest compression should be 1:5.

11. Check the pulse after every fourth cycle of breaths and compressions.

12. Continue until the victim regains a pulse and is breathing on his own or until help arrives.

13. If there is a pulse but the victim is not breathing, perform rescue breathing at the rate of 1 breath every 5 seconds, and check for breathing after every 12 breaths.

14. Monitor the victim until he is fully stabilized.

CONTROL OF BLEEDING

If the bleeding is from an extremity (an arm or leg), elevate it and apply direct pressure over the wound. Use a clean cloth, gauze sponge, or terrycloth towel, if available, to apply pressure on the wound. If the cloth becomes saturated with blood, do not remove it. Simply apply a second cloth bandage over the first. If no cloth is available, apply pressure using your hand. If the wound has a projectile protruding from it or was caused by a bullet, do not attempt to remove it. Simply apply pressure around the missile. Sometimes the skin must be pinched and held together.

If the wound is in the chest cavity area (front or back) or the abdomen, the blood being discharged may be pinkish and frothy. This is an indication that air is getting into the body through the wound and could cause an immediate breathing problem. That type of wound, known as a "sucking" chest wound, must be sealed airtight. Anything that will prevent air from seeping through can be utilized in an emergency to stop the inward airflow. Plastic or rubberized cloth, a piece of aluminum foil, or even the rescuer's hand can be placed over the wound to seal it off. Be sure to take the same precautions in the back area as well.

If elevation and direct pressure fail to stop the bleeding, some vital pressure points can be closed off by pressing on them. Pressure points are locations where arteries carrying blood from the heart can be squeezed to stop the flow. Locate the pressure point nearest to the wound and between it and the heart and apply pressure until the blood flow stops. As a last resort, apply a tourniquet between the wound and the heart.

In all instances involving bleeding, after the bleeding stops and breathing and circulation are restored, treat the victim for shock.

TREATMENT FOR SHOCK

Position the victim on his back with his feet elevated approximately 12 inches. Cover him to prevent chilling, and make him comfortable. Do not administer liquid or food, as this may cause vomiting and block the airway. Also do not position the head on a pillow, as this could also cause the airway to close.

Anaphylactic shock is an extreme allergic reaction to an insect bite, a bee sting, or certain foods and drugs. It can be fatal if not immediately treated. The symptoms include the following:

- Skin irritation, itching, and possibly hives (a skin rash and possible swelling)
- Reddish and flushed face and warm skin
- Swollen face and/or tongue
- Dizziness and increased heart rate, difficulty breathing
- Nausea, vomiting, and/or stomach cramps
- Loss of consciousness

Treat an afflicted person in the same manner as for regular shock. If available, apply medication formulated specifically for allergic reactions. A shot or dose of epinephrine may be administered. If it is suspected or known that a potential victim suffers from an allergic reaction, especially to insects and bees, it is prudent to have epinephrine (and proper instructions for administration) included in a medical kit. A commercial preparation called an Ana-Kit is available at your local pharmacy. However, it can be obtained only with a prescription.

CHOKING

The universal sign for choking is grabbing the throat area with two hands. Choking is usually caused by the ingestion of a large piece of food that becomes stuck in the throat. Ask the victim if he can speak. If he can, he may be experiencing a heart attack, which has some symptoms resembling those of a choking victim. In the case of a possible heart attack, the choking rescue should not be attempted, as it will only increase the discomfort and risk.

If the victim's gag or cough reflex cannot dislodge the food item, he will be unable to breathe, will be experiencing fear, and may begin to develop bluish skin and bulging eyes. If treatment is not immediately begun to relieve the choking, he may become unconscious or have a seizure. The best method for dislodging the blockage is the Heimlich maneuver. This very simple maneuver can be quickly and easily accomplished with very little practice.

Simply stand close behind the victim and wrap your arms around him. Make a fist with one hand and place it in the middle of the abdomen, just above the navel and below the ribs. Clasp the fisted hand with the other hand and give five quick, strong thrusts inward and upward. If that does not remove the blockage, repeat until the airway opens.

If the victim becomes unconscious and stops breathing, place him on his back and commence rescue breathing and, if necessary, chest compressions.

HEART ATTACK

If the victim can speak, cough, or make a noise through his mouth but is beginning to sweat, has a shortness of breath or difficulty breathing; has pain radiating to the arm, neck, or jaw; begins to feel nausea or vomits; and is experiencing dizziness and rapid or irregular pulse, he may be experiencing a heart attack. Loosen any tight clothing and make the victim comfortable. Keep him warm with a blanket or extra loose clothing. Monitor his breathing and pulse. If he stops breathing or his heart stops beating, begin CPR immediately. Speak to the victim in quiet, calm, and reassuring tones. Attempt to calm others who are present or have them leave. Do not give the victim anything to eat or drink except for appropriate prescription medicine or an aspirin under his tongue. Place him in a comfortable recovery position. This position places the victim on his stomach, with one leg partially bent and the arm of the same side bent with the hand resting near the face. The opposite leg and arm rest in a relaxed, straight position.

One can recognize a heart attack by the following usual symptoms:

- Sudden crushing and squeezing pain in the chest or a tightness of breath that lasts approximately ten minutes or more. The pain often starts in the center of the chest and radiates to the jaw, neck, back, and arms, especially the left arm. The arm may begin to feel numb as though it were "asleep."
- The heartbeat may become irregular or stop, with an accompanying shortness of breath and dizziness.
- Heavy sweating (beginning around the mouth area), nausea, and vomiting accompanied by fear and anxiety about death.
- Loss of consciousness.

STROKE

A stroke is the result of blood flow to the brain being interrupted as a result of a blocked or pinched artery. It causes sudden weakness or numbness in the face, arm, or leg on one side of the body. The victim will experience sudden difficulty in seeing and may lose vision in (often) one eye. There will be an accompanying loss of speech or difficulty in speaking, and he will have difficulty understanding others. A severe headache will strike and cause dizziness, loss of balance, and consciousness.

If the victim becomes unconscious and is not breathing, administer CPR. If he is breathing, place him in the recovery position and keep him warm. If he is conscious, make him comfortable, in a reclining position, with his head and shoulders slightly elevated. Offer him reassurance. Do not provide him with anything to eat or drink, as it could cause him to vomit and form an airway blockage. If he does begin to vomit, turn him onto his side to keep the airway open.

HEAT STROKE AND HEAT EXHAUSTION

Heat stroke and heat exhaustion result from performing strenuous exercise in very hot or humid conditions. The body is deprived of its ability to cool itself and may stop sweating. There is a shortage of water in the body caused by excessive sweating and/or dehydration. These conditions are common in long-distance runners, tennis players, and others who exercise very vigorously and refuse to stop for refreshment. While he was president, Jimmy Carter participated in a 10-km road race near Camp David, in the mountains of Maryland, on a hot and humid day. He ignored the early warning signs and collapsed with heat exhaustion.

Sometimes the conditions appear without the victim even feeling like he has been sweating. In very low humidity, the sweat dries instantly. This leaves the victim's clothing and skin dry, giving him the false sense that he is not losing water. These conditions can be avoided with proper hydration (taking liquid) before and during the activity. By the time we feel thirsty, the dehydration process has already begun. In heat stroke (the most serious condition), the body's core temperature soars to 104°F or higher. The skin becomes hot and dry, and the pulse and breathing become labored and fast. Confusion, seizures, and loss of consciousness come on very quickly.

Normal body temperature must be restored as quickly as possible. Move the victim to a cooler environment and remove any unnecessary clothing. Put cool, wet towels on his forehead, behind his neck, and on his body. Place a cooling fan where it can blow over the victim, and continue to sprinkle, splash, or sponge cool water (never an alcohol rubdown) on the victim's skin. Do not give him food or drink until his temperature has stabilized.

Treatment for heat exhaustion is very similar. If the victim is conscious and can swallow without difficulty, administer a saltwater drink in proportions of one teaspoon of salt per quart of water. Never give an alcoholic or caffeinated drink. Make victims of heat stroke and heat exhaustion comfortable and allow them rest. When they have sufficiently recovered, provide more liquid, such as an electrolyte drink, to replace the fluid and lost minerals.

BURNS

If the victim is unconscious, is not breathing, and has no pulse, begin rescue breathing and CPR immediately. Remove clothing and jewelry from the burned area before swelling complicates the task and causes secondary problems. Burned arms and legs can be elevated to prevent or reduce swelling. Keep the burned area clean and avoid breathing or coughing on it. If the burned area is small (six to eight inches in diameter), cover it loosely with a cool, wet cloth or towel. If possible, let cool running water run over the burn or hold it in a bowl of cool water for approximately ten minutes or until the pain subsides.

For larger burns, place a light, clean, dry cloth or sheet over the burned area. If the cloth becomes soaked with fluid from the burn, place another cloth over it. If the victim remains conscious, he may be given small sips of water to avoid dehydration, but he should be monitored in the event he becomes unconscious or begins to vomit.

Do not apply ointments, butter, lotions, baking soda, ice, or any other substances that could infect the burned area. Do not attempt to wash the area with cotton balls or apply anything (e.g., adhesive bandages) that will adhere to the burn. If blistering occurs, do not break the blisters.

There are four degrees of burns:

- *First degree.* This is the most common, consisting of a searing of the top layer of skin. It is usually not serious but is usually very painful. Sunburn is a common example of a first-degree burn. It is characterized by a reddening of the injured area.
- *Second degree.* This is more serious and very painful. The burn injures the top two layers of skin and produces redness, swelling, and blistering. Some sunburns have risen to this degree.
- *Third degree.* Initially these are painless, because the burn has extended through all layers of the skin and nerve endings. The burn area appears as charred or white skin.
- *Fourth degree.* This is extremely serious and life-threatening. The burning extends through all layers of skin and into the tissues and organs.

The above-listed conditions are by no means all-inclusive of the medical emergencies that may be encountered by a protection agent. They are only some of the most common yet most serious afflictions that, left untreated, could result in death of the victim. It is a personal responsibility of the protection agent to obtain training and instruction in providing emergency medical treatment and to be able to respond when the life of an accident or illness victim depends on his abilities. When in doubt, use good common sense, apply the ABCs, and do nothing that could cause further harm to the victim.

MEDICAL KIT

It is not possible to have on hand all of the equipment necessary to treat every type of injury and illness. It is not expected that a layman such as a protection agent will have access to more exotic equipment such as defibrillators, but common supplies should be readily available. A well-stocked emergency medical kit should include, as a minimum, the following:

- Gauze bandages and rolls of gauze in all sizes, including "band-aids" and the very large, absorbent gauze sponges
- Rolls of adhesive tape and bandaging tape
- Large (sling-size) triangular bandages
- Cold or instant ice packs (chemical packs)
- Clean towels
- A space blanket (emergency thermal blanket)

- Nurse's shears
- Assorted disinfectants, ointments, and painkillers[3]
- A small flashlight
- A small roll of aluminum foil
- Inflatable casts for broken arms and legs
- Snake and insect bite kits (Ana-Kit)
- An emergency medical handbook
- Diarrhea medication[3]

Emergency medical care must be part of any protection specialist's training and experience. Cardiopulmonary resuscitation and the ability to restore breathing and control bleeding are required lifesaving procedures. The immediate application of the ABCs of first aid can mean the difference between life and death.

SUMMARY

1. Check and open the Airway (rescue breathing and CPR).
2. Control and stop Bleeding (direct pressure, pressure points, or tourniquet).
3. Check and restore Circulation (cardiac compression, CPR).
4. Treat for Shock.

REVIEW QUESTIONS

1. Explain, "Treat him with common sense and do no harm."
2. Why is EMT training very highly recommended for a protection specialist?
3. Why is CPR training a requirement for a protection agent?
4. Explain the initial steps in responding to a medical emergency.
5. Why is the rescuer's demeanor so important?
6. What are the ABCs of medicine? Describe patient assessment.
7. Explain the term ten-minute medicine.
8. Explain rescue breathing.
9. When is CPR begun?
10. Explain the importance of an emergency medical kit to a protection agent. What should it contain?

NOTES

1. The information in this section is based on material taught in a standard EMT course. The author received his EMT training at Concord General Hospital, Concord, Massachusetts.
2. National Safety Council. *Basic Life Support: Healthcare and Professional Rescuers.* New York: McGraw-Hill, 2007.
3. Keep all medication, sprays, disinfectants, and ointments away from children, and be aware of the expiration date.

13 Legal Considerations

Badges? We ain't got no badges. We don't need no badges! I don't have to show you any stinking badges!

Gold Hat, in *The Treasure of the Sierra Madre* (1948)

It is a fine line you must walk without a shield.
...to protect and serve

Los Angeles Police motto

PUBLIC AGENCIES AND PRIVATE ENTERPRISE

Many "protective" companies have been created by people who spent 15 minutes sharing a cup of coffee and a doughnut with a law enforcement officer and believe they know how to be protection specialists. They could not be farther from reality! Even a 15 to 20-year police veteran will not have the necessary training and skills for close personal protection. It takes years of specialized training and experience to become fully proficient in the nuances of personal protection.

Many police departments have a small unit, such as an intelligence division or a SWAT unit, that can offer a few specialists to assist the Secret Service when the president or other dignitaries visit their jurisdiction. Some of the larger cities (e.g., New York, Chicago, San Francisco, and Los Angeles), because many high-ranking government officials visit the city, have divisions dedicated to providing protective services, but they are restricted to officially authorized persons, that is VIPs and government officials.

A private-sector protection agent must know the limits of his authority, his responsibility to obtain the proper credentials (licenses), and the differences and similarities between private security and public law enforcement. Law enforcement, personal protection, and other members of the security community deal with similar concepts, but there are differences. Law enforcement agencies deal with a wide range of crimes and other political landmines. In contrast, personal protection and security agents are charged with protecting individuals and structures, which is a much more focused level of protection.

A police background makes a good beginning, because it provides excellent training to develop people skills, gain street smarts, and learn that some things are never as they seem. People skills; powers of observation, recognition, analysis, and comprehension; and the ability to react to an evolving situation, so necessary to police work, are also employed by close personal protection professionals. However, policing and working the street are not the same as working with elite personalities in government, politics, entertainment, big business, and society. While personal protection demands many of the talents learned in police work, such as expertise with weapons, some combative expertise, and awareness, it also requires diplomacy, finesse, and patience, and even proper protocols and etiquette.

Police skills may offer a foundation to build on, but police experience should not be the only criterion for selecting a personal protection agent, as the job of personal protection requires specialized training far beyond the scope of standard police work. Individuals with police experience may possess skills that are critical to a protection agent. However, police officers' competencies, abilities, and experiences will vary. The skills and the roles demanded of a personal protection agent are beyond those of most police officers.

Primarily, police officers enforce laws to protect people and property. They work within a specific city or jurisdiction and in a particular job such as traffic control, beat patrol, detective work, and so on. Police officers have a great deal of contact with various types of individuals, and they receive some specialized training with a range of weapons and even in some martial arts. However, they generally are not required to work directly for high-profile individuals within the often delicate, socio-political environments in which corporate executives, celebrities, and heads of state function. Police officers who are inexperienced in working closely with people in high and powerful positions may be shy, reserved, and reluctant to engage in a necessary repartee with the principal, and they may not respond properly to simple but possibly threatening gestures. On the other hand, some officers may be at the other extreme of the behavioral continuum. They may be full of excitement and emotional "dynamite," fully prepared to pounce upon anyone and everyone who approaches the protectee. They may attempt to show off their paramilitary warrior mentality by taking unnecessary risks or confronting and challenging everyone outside the protectee's circle as though they were the nastiest, dirtiest, slimeball assassins alive, intent only on approaching the protectee to shove a shank into him. The effectiveness of a personal protection agent may be judged as much on his ability to talk to a client and make him feel safe and comfortable as his ability to shoot or physically take down an assailant.

PUBLIC AND PRIVATE AGENCIES

Police agencies represent a political entity such as a city, state, or federal government. Their mission statements proclaim them to be public servants, trained to "protect and serve." Law enforcement officers must follow specific paramilitary rules and procedures. Law enforcement officers are peace officers 24 hours a day. They are held to a higher standard on and off duty. The police officer has arrest authority, and the protective agent doesn't. The police officer also determines whether she will arrest and jail someone. If a crime is committed in the officer's presence, or if she is aware that a felony has been committed and she has probable cause to believe a particular person committed the crime, the police officer *must* make an arrest. A private protection agent, having no arrest authority, is not required to make an arrest. If she does, the arrest is considered a citizen's arrest.

Law enforcement officers are mandated by the state to undergo a certain number of hours of training each year. Police are trained and conditioned to respond to the source of the problem and not to the person under attack. Although police training and experience are vital assets, they do not completely meet the training requirements of a protection specialist. More is needed in this multifaceted profession. Personal protection, of course, is a specialized industry requiring specialized and unique training. Police are primarily reactive, meaning that they react to the source of the problem. In contrast, personal protection agents know that the best response is to the protectee rather than the cause of the attack or disturbance. Personal protection is proactive or preventive, meaning that it is nonconfrontational, and great efforts are made to anticipate and avoid incidents.

Both private security and law enforcement grew out of the need for security for the people. They differ in how that security is provided. Law enforcement officers actively go out and seek people who are breaking the law. Tactics include undercover operations, street patrols, and seeking assistance from the public. A municipal law enforcement agency covers a large area and uses its officers to perform a broad range of duties in that area. Officers do everything from investigating homicides to giving out parking tickets, and they often do it all in the same night. The power to arrest anyone at anytime, as long as a severe enough offense is committed, allows them to do this. Private protection agents can place someone under citizen's arrest, but they must wait for the police to complete the process.

An analysis of the law enforcement and personal protection fields shows that each industry is unique, with many similarities and differences. Both fields of expertise, with their distinct methods of conducting business, require separate skills, but they have the same goal: preserving life and minimizing loss. The mind-set of the police officer is simply not the same as for the citizen protective agent. The job of a police officer is to keep the peace while adhering to constitutional procedures. Protective agents, not being representative of the government, are not restricted by constitutional concerns, but they must work within the narrow borders of reasonable and necessary force and/or intrusion while being a protective force. The law enforcement community is reactive and offensive, reacting to citizen complaints, actively searching out lawbreakers, and investigating suspicious circumstances. Police usually work in a specific and condensed geographical area with emphasis placed on (naturally) law enforcement, street crimes, and calls for assistance. When confronting unknown individuals, typically after a crime has been committed, the situation can be unpredictable, so this industry relies heavily on its hard skills (i.e., driving, the use of weapons, and defensive and come-a-long techniques) to keep officers safe and to do an effective job. Because of these hard skills (plus professionalism, discipline, and training) and the daily risks that they face, law enforcement is often thought of as the superior profession.

The personal protection industry, on the other hand, takes on a more proactive and defensive approach, with emphasis placed on deterrence and prevention. Protection agents are typically employed by corporations, businesses, or private citizens. They work within a smaller area of responsibility than their partners in public law enforcement. Protective industry personnel usually work to secure an area, system, or individual from violent attack from an unknown, outside source. Because there is wide variation in the missions of the protection industry, these individuals rely more heavily on soft skills (interpersonal and communication, advance planning, specialized practices and procedures, technology, access controls, security doors, lighting, and others) to prevent an attack.

Private protection groups and public law enforcement are often closely intertwined. Over the years, because of budgetary and other factors, state and local law enforcement agencies have been short on specialized personnel, which increases their work load and decreases their ability to provide personal protective services. Private industry is viewed as an easier and more efficient solution. Governmental law enforcement (on all levels) is faced with constitutional issues, inadequate resources, a lack of protective industry knowledge, and the inability to provide protective services over a geographical range that may cross international borders.

The idea of private protection and public law enforcement grew out of a common need for security, but over the years the two paths split into separate concepts. Law enforcement turned to making sure laws are obeyed, but the private security industry diverged into protecting people, places, and things.

The concept of private protection in the modern world is still evolving. In the past, an off-duty or retired police officer could have done the job, but this is no longer true. In the post–September 11 world, "the inventory of security concerns is always growing and perpetually changing." While executive protection, at its base, has always been employed to protect a person or thing, this is also changing. The concept is becoming more refined, and the new version includes highly trained professionals with not only the required physical capabilities but also other skills specifically tailored to protecting a client. These include threat assessment, knowledge of the law, and experience in the industry.

The concept of how to protect a client is evolving into a science. Studying threats and determining the safest way to move a client from one place to another involves skills that must be learned. The protector needs extra training, aptitude, and special abilities to get the job done. Colleges and universities can no longer ignore the need for education and training in specialties such as proximity personal protection. To do the job right, a protector needs to know a little about a lot or a lot about a lot.

Whereas the concept of personal protection is much the same as that of law enforcement, there are differences. Law enforcement and the security industry have very different powers and mandates. Law enforcement has a broad mandate to investigate crimes, apprehend criminals, and generally to keep order in a city, across state lines, or on the border. To keep up with all that needs to be done, law enforcement casts a broad net by separating manpower into specialties and partnering with the community. However, a law enforcement agency does not operate in a vacuum; it is a public entity, which means that it is subject to the changing winds of politics. Agencies must work hard to get funding and to keep the public happy. This idea is expressed clearly in the San Francisco Police Department's mission statement, "We maintain open communication with all the communities we serve. Their input helps determine police policies, priorities and strategies."

The world of personal protection is privately funded, which simplifies things for the average protection agent. Security employees do, however, face a job that can be as dangerous as law enforcement, and some do it with little or no training.

This reveals a glaring difference between protective security and law enforcement—the training and compensation gap. The overall security industry is segmented into many different levels of competence and responsibility, from the untrained to the highly trained. Wages reflect this difference, and low-level guards work for low wages while highly trained security workers, such as close protection specialists, are well compensated for assuming the extra responsibility.

Conceptually, personal protection, security, and law enforcement have the same goal—to protect the public. However, differences are evident in terms of the areas in which they operate and the niches they fill. Law enforcement is a large chain of organizations dealing with the big picture, large-scale crimes and trends, whereas security and personal protection concentrate on their clients, providing a more focused level of protection.

Often, the protection agent's job, in the private sector, is like a high-wire act, performing without a net. He walks a very thin line because his job is only quasi-official. His duties and responsibilities are limited to protecting the life and property of those who engage him and pay for his services. He must provide protection to an individual or entity, with all the commensurate accountability, but without any legal sanction or backing. He has no statutory authority, no charter mandate, and no badge or shield.

The protection specialist often works side by side with the police, sometimes depending on their support. At other times, he must depend entirely on his wiliness and wit. For example, something as simple as parking a motorcade or principal's limousine at the airport can require real ingenuity. Without the cooperation of the airport police, the protection agent is just like every other "Joe Citizen," trying to find a parking space and picking up his friends and loved ones as close to the arrival point as possible. He is continually reminded that the "white zone is for immediate loading and unloading of passengers only." While keeping one eye open for the ticket-book officer and his tow truck, the protection agent must also remain on the lookout for his principal, get him into the car, and retrieve his baggage, all while never leaving the car parked (or double parked) illegally!

LEGAL RESTRICTIONS

The authority to engage in contract personal protection (unless working exclusively for one person or corporation as an employee) is governed by the political jurisdictions in which an agent works. He must meet some basic requirements of the city, county, and state.

Some states have no regulations governing personal protection except as it is generically described and included in the category of security guard companies. Some states require a license and administer a test that appears to be designed more to raise funds for the state than to determine what a person knows about close-quarter protection and the private security business. The tests and licensing are usually very expensive and have very little to do with personal protection. Of course, licensing is important, as it helps to regulate the entire security business and ensure that the trust inherent in the profession is not misplaced.

Some state jurisdictions require protection specialists to obtain a "security guard card" that authorizes him to work in the profession. The card is required of all uniformed security guards. The card is obtained after taking a two-hour course and passing a written exam—with answers provided! The questions on the test have nothing to do with the personal protection industry.

Another requirement is aimed at those who wish to work as independent contractors or operate a close personal protection business rather than working for a single full-time employer. That requirement is to obtain a private patrol operator's license, which is geared to running a security patrol business. Some states still require an executive protection specialist to also obtain a private investigator's license. After passing all the state tests and obtaining the proper licenses, one still must (if running his own business) obtain a city or county business license, or both.

Being a protection agent usually requires the right to carry a concealed weapon. Concealed weapon permits are issued by the chief of police or sheriff of the city or county in which the permit holder resides. The requirements vary in each jurisdiction. In many localities, it is extremely difficult to obtain that important document, but in others it is simply a matter of submitting an application. Some counties in California require a state-issued permit to carry an exposed weapon before the chief of police or sheriff can issue the concealed weapons permit.

To obtain all the required licenses in California, it costs approximately $1,100 before one can begin to work as a licensed private protection specialist. It is a misdemeanor to work in that capacity without all the proper licenses.

Some states require at least a minimum of $500,000 liability insurance, including an "errors and omissions" provision, for close personal protection companies. The insurance is very expensive and difficult to obtain, because it is based on the salary of employees carrying firearms. At the same time, an off-duty police officer may hire out his services with no other state or locally mandated regulations.

CONFLICTS OF INTEREST?

An off-duty police officer working as a security specialist or a personal protection agent raises some interesting ethical and legal questions and involves the possibility of a conflict of interest. If, as in most police jurisdictions, a police officer is authorized (or required) to carry his weapon at all times because he "is on duty 24 hours a day," when is he off duty and able to work as a private agent? When working as a private entity is he still duty bound to effect an arrest if a crime (even a misdemeanor or minor infraction) occurs in his presence? What if his protective responsibility commits a crime or engages in questionable activities? Must the off-duty officer report the activity? If the crime has nothing to do with his private protective duties, must he still make the arrest? What if he observes his client committing a felony? What happens to his protective responsibility if he involves himself with an arrest?

Do his arrest powers become the same as those of a full-time private protection agent? Is he required (or forbidden to) report and use information gained while working in a private capacity for public purposes? If an incident arises in which force is used, is his "official duty" entity (the police department or the city, county, or state) liable for his actions as if he were on duty? Are his actions in the normal course of his employment?

In some cities, the police work a twelve-hour shift, three days a week. This, then, allows them to work part-time for a private protection company, or as in many cases, run their own company. The question becomes very clear: is the officer working for a police department as a full-time officer, or is he a part-time officer working at the police department in between his full-time job as a private protection agent?

These questions are not aimed at being antipolice; they are legitimate questions that a police jurisdiction and the off-duty police officer must address and resolve before engaging in activities that may result in legal actions.

Several years ago, a protection security agent had the experience of working as a bank robbery suppression agent for a major banking company in a large city. This was an extremely dangerous job because of the high incidence of take-over robberies wherein several robbers with semiautomatic weapons would crash into the bank, demand that all of the patrons lie on the floor, and even take hostages while grabbing as much cash as they could scoop up and carry. The teams assembled for robbery suppression consisted of current off-duty and retired police officers and former federal agents.

A suppression agent assigned to partner with this particular protection security agent was an active city police detective. He would report for work at his department early in the morning and sign out in the field, then he would report to work as a suppression agent. After working all day at the bank, he would return to his departmental office and sign off. The conflict of interest in this case is quite obvious. Here was a sworn police officer working as a bank robbery suppression agent for a private security company while drawing full-time pay as a police detective. There were several ethical, moral, and legal questions in this case. He was drawing pay from two jobs at the same time. Having placed himself in danger at a bank where shoot-outs were common, where would liability lie if he were shot or if he shot someone?

Another conflict of interest case including the police and private security involved an officer working in the police chief's office of a major city. When a person requiring protective agents would call the police department seeking referrals, this enterprising officer provided the caller with the telephone number of a "highly respected and professional executive protection company." The caller would then dial the number given by the officer. The number rang at another telephone in the same office, where the same officer answered the call with, "ABC Protection Company, Special Agent John Doe." Yes, the officer was running his own protection company out of the chief of police's office!

SIMILARITIES

Public law enforcement and private executive protection have common responsibilities and considerations, as follows:

- *Prevention of criminal acts against the person of the protectee.* Preventing murder, assault, robbery, and violence against the person of the protectee are the reasons for the presence of a close personal protection specialist. It is his duty and function to provide sufficient protection to deter or prevent the occurrence of an attack against his principal. The police role is related in that, if the police or responsible law enforcement agency becomes aware of any planned or overt action against the person of the principal, they work with the protection agent to make an appropriate response. Or, even in the absence of a known threat, the police and protection agent cooperate to prevent any harmful action directed toward the protectee.

- *Protection of the life and property of the protectee.* Protection agents have the overall responsibility of protecting the life of the person they are hired to protect. When an attack occurs, the executive protection specialist must make every effort to neutralize the danger. Law enforcement agencies are charged with protecting the life and property of all persons, not the life of a VIP exclusively. But in the event of a threat, an attempted assault, or an assassination attempt, the police have the jurisdiction and responsibility to assist in taking preventive measures.

- *Investigate threats and risks against the protectee.* When a threat, verbal or written, implied or overt, is received, it must be investigated (by police and the executive protection agency) to ascertain the degree of danger it presents. The investigating agent determines and assigns the risk factors. After completely investigating the circumstances of the threat (which may include the possibility of a personal interview with the person making the threat) and looking at his capability to carry out the threat, protective measures will be employed to counter the threat.

- *Respond to emergencies.* Whatever the emergency (an assault, a medical problem, a fire), the executive protection agent and the police move to neutralize the situation as quickly as possible. When an emergency involving the safety of the protectee occurs, the protection agent's response is to the protectee, not to the source of the emergency. After the safety of the protectee is assured, the source of the emergency is addressed. If an emergency can be addressed without leaving the proximity of the principal, then it should be handled as quickly and efficiently as possible. For example, if an agent standing in the vicinity of the protectee observes a person in the crowd experiencing a heart attack, he can, without compromising his position, respond by radioing for assistance. It is part of the police's responsibility to respond to the emergency.

- *Detecting threats, risks, and vulnerabilities.* Everyone involved in the total security effort must be always vigilant and watchful for an activity, circumstance, or even equipment failure that could signal an immediate danger to the principal.

- *Deterrence* of any adverse action against the protectee. A strong and visible protective and police presence will deter all but the most determined attacker.

Both security and law enforcement officers handle some of the same things during the course of the day. These include handling disputes, taking reports, and keeping people safe.

LEGAL CONSEQUENCES

Protection specialists must understand the legal consequences of their actions or inaction. Laws vary from jurisdiction to jurisdiction. It is incumbent upon the specialist to make himself aware of the local or state regulations. Some of the laws it is necessary to know included the following:

- *Carrying a concealed weapon.* Some states have reciprocal recognition of other states' issuance of a concealed weapon permit. Other states require an individual license for their own state. Carrying a concealed weapon without a permit issued by a legal jurisdiction (usually a local police department or county sheriff's department) constitutes a misdemeanor in most states. In some localities it may be defined as a felony.
- *Use of force.* Legally, a protection agent may use whatever force is necessary and reasonable for effective self-defense and the protection of his principal. Anything beyond reasonable and necessary force is considered excessive force. Excessive force is always one level above reasonable and necessary. When force is used, the totality of circumstances must be articulated to justify why it was necessary and to what extent it was reasonable. Excessive force can never be justified. There are five levels in the escalation of necessary and reasonable force:

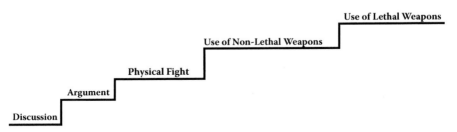

The discussion state is the first stage of contact, where nothing is wrong and two parties are talking in a normal conversational tone. There is no threat, and all parties are calm. Turning up the heat in terms of rising voices, temperatures, heart, and pulse rate, the next step is a loud, shouting argument. Reasoning and logic go out the window. The apparent thinking is, "He who shouts louder wins." If you can't win with "in your face" shouting and screaming, the next rung on the ladder is just a short step up to physical fighting. "Wrestle them to the ground and hold 'em!"

Sometime during the fighting and wrestling in the "mud, the blood, and the beer,"[1] one party or the other (or both) will resort to the use of nonlethal weapons such as flashlights, batons, mace, or flowerpots—whatever is not bolted or nailed down. When a life is endangered and the only way to save the threatened is to move to the next option, you reach the fifth and final step: the use of lethal weapons.

It cannot be stressed enough that the use of a firearm should be considered the very last alternative. Company policy, state and federal law, and court cases dictate the circumstances for the use of deadly force such as dispensed by a firearm. Never use unnecessary force or any force except in the defense of self or others. A gun is a defensive weapon and should never be removed from the holster except to defend the life of yourself or others who are in immediate danger. The three major rules of gun safety are (1) all guns are always loaded, (2) never point a gun at anyone or anything unless you intend to kill (or stop) it, and (3) all guns are always loaded!

Those are rules of gun safety, but a common error made by police officers when they shoot and kill an offender is to say, "I was afraid for my life and shot to kill." They shoot the offender in "center mass" (as they were trained) and when asked (especially in court), "Did you intend to kill the offender?" The (incorrect) answer is, "Yes, I was afraid for my life." The correct answer should be: "I was afraid for my life and shot him as I was trained, but my intent was to stop him, not to kill him." The intent should always be "to stop him, not kill him." This could be a mitigating circumstance when liability is being assessed.

It is important to know what liabilities are incurred if the use of force is necessary. What are the civil and criminal penalties such as lawsuit, fine, or a jail sentence if you are found liable for use of unnecessary force? Simply displaying a gun unnecessarily can be defined as assault with a deadly weapon, which is a felony.

RECOMMENDATIONS FOR PROTECTION AGENTS

When contacting and dealing with a potential problem person, several recommendations perhaps will make the task a little easier and avoid a legal confrontation.

1. Maintain a calm, confident attitude at all times, under all conditions and circumstances. As tempers and voices rise, the first tactic should be to deescalate the situation through the use of reasoning, logic, understanding, and humor.
2. Speak in a quiet but firm, nonabusive and nonthreatening manner at all times. The agent who blusters, threatens, brags, and curses is only trying to compensate for shaky confidence and cover up fear and doubt. Abusive language and threatening gestures may be interpreted as verbal or physical assault.
3. Always give the impression of being in control of the situation.
4. Always leave a way out for the person you are dealing with. Do not force or goad him into a fight. Leave an option open for the person to save face before friends and onlookers. Unfortunately, this may not always work with a violent, drunk, or mentally ill and totally unreasonable person. In those instances, more traditional and physical methods may be necessary for control of the person. Nonetheless, note a word of caution. When restraining a person, be certain before laying hands on him that the action is justified and reasonable. If it is not, the action can be construed as an assault, making the agent susceptible to civil or criminal charges.

5. Stay away from the good old Bobby Jim approach. Be straightforward and firm, yet friendly, and give the impression that the situation will be resolved in the favor of the agent and cooperation is the best option.
6. Never, ever, lose your temper, and never take the situation personally. A transgressor's anger and threatening demeanor, although directed toward the agent, is usually with some other external or internal source. Control the emotions of the moment before they escalate into a physical confrontation that might require lethal force.

The way a protection agent approaches people, his attitude, and his physical appearance are all important to the psychological impression he gives. The agent who has to fight every suspect or offender he comes into contact with is not an example of the desired protective agent image and is risking legal sanctions.

One of the weapons mankind seems to forget is that the use of language and mind control can be just as effective in controlling a dangerous and threatening situation. This means that most situations can be resolved using reason if the proper verbal commands are utilized and alternative solutions are presented early enough. Hence, your voice and language become a "weapon." A defensive weapon that is very effective and available to everyone is the use of psychology or the power of the human brain. Protection agents can employ a low-key, self-confident manner to avoid the use of force under most circumstances. In all the years of providing presidential protection, a Secret Service agent has never, ever had to pull his weapon and shoot an attacker!

In one case, a protection agent had completed his assignment for the day and returned to his hotel room, changed clothes, and secured his weapon in his locked briefcase in his room. He then walked to his car in the darkened hotel garage. After placing some articles in the back seat, he turned to enter the car. Suddenly, seemingly from nowhere, a young tough with a gun confronted the agent and menacingly demanded, "Gimme me all your mother (physical loving) money!" With no weapon available (which probably would have had tragic consequences), the agent relied on his wits and confident manner (which was actually a big cover-up of his concern for the gun the teenaged robber held in his shaking hand). He convinced the ruffian that he was attempting to rob the wrong person. When the kid realized that the agent was serious, he actually turned around and ran from the garage, to the great relief of his intended victim!

SUMMARY

It is the private sector that personal protection of individuals developed into a professional business. Whereas governmental agencies have "peace officer" status and the power to arrest, private agencies hold no similar power and must refrain from making an arrest, except as a private citizen and only under circumstances of extreme emergency.

Simply stated, police police. They are a public law enforcement creation, deriving powers and authority from a political entity such as a city, state, or federal legislature. The police are sworn "to protect and serve" and, as part of their official oath, "to defend and protect the Constitution of the United States." That means to maintain the peace and public order, protect people and property from violation, investigate crimes against people and property, and apprehend or arrest those who transgress against people and the laws prescribed by the governing jurisdiction. In other words, they enforce the law and arrest the lawbreakers.

Law enforcement agencies are reactive, responding to calls of help and violations of law. When a law is violated or someone's life or property is threatened, a police officer is duty bound to make an arrest if the person committing the violation is known.

Law enforcement is confrontational almost by definition. Police are trained to be aggressive and assertive. They are proactive as well as reactive. Police initiate contacts with persons on the street and in the community, taking information, making directives, and investigating matters that have occurred or may transpire. They are responsive in nature, with a primary intent of protecting the people from criminal activities and helping those in need. The police function is usually most effective when it is very high profile.

Notwithstanding the deterrence factor, a personal protection group functions best when it maintains a very low profile, not drawing attention. This is the recommended approach. Personal protection is most effective when it is nonconfrontational.

Personal protection, being private security, is defensive. Prevention and deterrence are the keys. A protection specialist (or agent) takes no overt action toward someone except when his protectee is threatened. Then the action is limited to defensive measures. A private protection agent has no expectation or obligation to affect an arrest after observing a violation of law. On the contrary, making a citizen's arrest is discouraged and should be viewed as a last resort. The protection agent may, however, have at least a moral obligation and legal responsibility to report a violation to a police agency.

Regardless of the entity that employs a protection specialist, the specialist must know the limits and source of his authority. Civil and criminal penalties can be incurred for violation of laws and regulations. Acting beyond the scope of authority and reasonable and necessary force can be cause for punitive action against the executive protection specialist and his employing agency.

REVIEW QUESTIONS

1. Describe the differences between a police agency and a private close personal protection agency regarding arrest powers.
2. How is law enforcement "confrontational by definition"?
3. Describe how a police function is most successful when it is high profile and how a protection agent should maintain a low profile and avoid confrontation.
4. What is the purpose of close personal protection licensing?
5. Explain the possible conflict of interest of an off-duty police officer working a private, close personal protection assignment. What are possible liabilities?
6. How do the duties of a law enforcement agency and a private executive protection agency overlap or have similarities?
7. Explain the executive protection agent's authority to carry a concealed weapon.
8. Explain the executive protection agent's authority to use force. What are the restrictions?

9. What is the importance of the psychological impression given by a protection agent? How does it relate to his legal posture?

NOTE

1. Cash, Johnny, "A Boy Named Sue."

14 Requirements, Character, and Conduct

"Character counts."

A good protective agent looks and acts like a good agent.

What lies behind us and what lies before us are tiny matters compared to what lies within us.

Ralph Waldo Emerson

REQUIREMENTS OF A SPECIALIST—PROTECTIVE AGENT

Individual character traits deemed important by an employing protection agency are what separate the employables from the wannabes. It is no secret that the best protection agents are selected from the most highly qualified applicants. Experience in the military and/or a law enforcement agency is an advantage. A college degree (at least a bachelor's degree) is required by many agencies. A degree is not necessarily a requirement in the private sector, where the intangibles of personal character are considered of primary importance.

PERSONAL CHARACTERISTICS

The most sought after and valued personal qualities of a personal protection agent (and leader, because protection agents are leaders) are the following:

- Intelligence, integrity, imagination and interpersonal and leadership skills
- Self-motivation and innovation, enthusiasm and resourcefulness, adaptability and flexibility, worthiness of confidence and trust, ethicality, and the ability to be a team player
- An ability to analyze data to develop a logical framework of strategic and tactical planning
- The ability to grasp the seriousness of assignments and situations and the role each person plays in the overall mission, while appreciating and maintaining the sense of humor necessary to encourage fellow employees' morality and productivity
- The ability to relate well with persons of varying talents, motivations, and interests, and with diverse cultures and social and economic positions
- The ability to communicate on all levels, both orally and in writing
- The ability to conduct interviews and research

- The ability to work with highly placed individuals in politics, entertainment, and business
- The ability to manage subordinates and support personnel, including protectees' staff and employees, by positive reinforcement
- Advocacy of continuing education and professional training to develop the full potential of himself and others
- Basic computer and word processing skills
- The ability to maintain a helpful, friendly, and professional attitude and demeanor under trying and adverse conditions
- The ability to respond appropriately in emergency situations
- Unselfishness and a willingness to take risks for the safety of others

A few months after the publication of the first edition of *Introduction to Executive Protection,* I had occasion to be visiting a former Secret Service colleague who was the owner and operator of his own personal protection company in Los Angeles. While I was in the office, a young man came in to apply for a job as an executive protection agent. My friend interviewed him and read his resume, which was very impressive. For an outside opinion, my friend asked me to read the resume and interview the applicant.

When I got to the part about personal characteristics, I stopped reading and began to interview the young man. I emphasized the need for honesty, integrity, and trustworthiness. He went on to explain how he had earned respect and gained all of the characteristics listed above in previous assignments and in the military. He claimed those character traits in his resume. I opened a copy of my book, which my friend kept in his office, to the page discussing personal characteristics in the chapter titled, "Requirements, Character, and Conduct." I pointed out to him (and my friend) that his resume was copied directly from that chapter and those pages. Obviously, the young man quickly left the office without the job.

SUPERVISORY AND MANAGERIAL QUALITIES

A protection agent is unique, regardless of his total experience or ranking with other agents, because his position dictates certain personality traits similar to those of an effective manager and supervisor:

1. *Assertiveness.* Protection agents must be take-charge types, able to positively and assuredly affirm their ideas and thinking. They must speak with confidence and, when it is necessary disagree with people, be able to sustain their argument with facts and clear reasoning.
2. *Emotional stability.* In a high-profile position like executive protection, an agent must do his best to remain calm and collected, no matter how stressful, chaotic, or demanding the situation. When a conflict arises, he must maintain patience, tact, and tolerance. His job performance must remain at expected levels in high-pressure situations. In the face of disappointment or failure, he does not attempt to blame others or indulge in self-pity.

3. *Self-knowledge.* A protection agent must be aware of and recognize his limits, strengths, and weaknesses. He must have confidence in himself and his abilities.

4. *Inner directedness.* Good protection agents are self-motivated and set the standards that bring out the best in themselves and others. They constantly do a good job, performing beyond merely expected limits, even when it is possible to get by with less. They are resourceful and able to improvise when a situation develops for which there is no predetermined solution. They do not need to wait to be told what to do or how to respond, and they do not pass problems on to someone else.

5. *Personality.* A protection agent has a personality that allows him to relate well with other people. He can laugh at himself and accept his mistakes and those of others, especially if the mistake is not costly. He is enthusiastic and expressive, demanding as much of himself as he does of others, and is capable of viewing a situation from the viewpoint of others.

6. *Communication.* Of necessity, a protection agent must be able to effectively communicate his directives and requirements and, if questioned, can articulate clear and well-organized answers and explanations.

7. *Leadership.* From the protectee to the lowest-ranking staff person, everyone looks to the agent as the source of leadership, especially in crisis situations. The agent must set a standard that others respect. In a crisis situation he must remain calm, collected, and resourceful to find a solution. He must be able to generate ideas, plans, and suggestions that will win the enthusiasm and support of others while not being patronizing or demeaning to those who are critical of his suggestions. He can criticize others and avoid placing himself in an inferior position, retaining their respect and cooperation.

8. *Productivity.* He provides high-quality performance beyond what is expected.

9. *Planning.* A protection agent is expected to plan the secure environment surrounding a protectee, analyze the requirements, set realistic and obtainable goals, and see the plan to its conclusion. He consistently prepares well-organized schedules and logistics, performing his duties in a timely fashion and meeting deadlines, even in sensitive situations.

10. *Decision making.* A protection agent is expected to make quick decisions and accept the consequences. He can make up his mind independently, without waiting for unnecessary input from others, especially in time-sensitive and crisis situations. He attempts to obtain as much information as possible before arriving at a conclusion or decision but is capable of making the decision as quickly as necessary.[2]

There are no actual physical size requirements for the job, but the appearance of a protection agent is extremely important, because it sets the tone for how he is perceived. Each agency may have unofficial criteria regarding height and weight, but protective agents come in a vast assortment of packages (however, the agent's weight should be commensurate with his height). Most are just average looking, and in fact the more average looking the better. Like a camouflaged U.S. Special Forces trooper, a good protective agent blends into the scenery; his presence is subtly felt rather than overt. One objective of the protective ring is to project a strong protective element yet not draw attention to oneself. It is important for an agent to be able to be lost in a crowd. The center of attention must remain the protectee.

Naturally, a protective agent must possess important traits beyond physical appearance. Mental stability is a foremost qualification. It takes a special personality with sound judgment and good strong moral character to work with many types of people under conditions that push the envelope of physical endurance and entail nearly inconceivable mental stress. On one long-term protective assignment, which really was not that taxing, it became apparent that some protective agents simply could not work midnight shifts. The protection firm hired a protective agent because he was a young retired deputy sheriff. (He said his retirement was based on a lower-back injury that rendered him incapable of working as an officer but did not disqualify him from executive protection work.) After about two weeks on assignment in a large city approximately 100 miles from home, he suddenly could not take the stress any longer. At around noon one day, the detail leader received a frenzied telephone call from the agent's partner and roommate. He said, "Get down here quick, you have to see this! 'Mike' is acting crazy!" It seems the poor roommate, who had known "Mike" for only the first two weeks of the assignment, was awakened from a deep sleep by the screams and antics of his partner. "Mike" was completely naked, jumping up and down on the bed, flaying his arms about, and screaming, "I can't take it any longer! I can't take it any longer! All I ever work is midnights! Midnights! Midnights! I want a change!" He got his change. That afternoon, he was in his car and on the freeway home. It was later determined that a bad back was not the only reason for his early retirement from the sheriff's department; mental stability had a lot to do with it.

But possessing certain personality traits and being of sound mind and moral character are only a few of the basic requirements. A good protection agent must manage his personal life and problems while maintaining an efficient and professional persona. Several attributes, although somewhat intangible, are (or should be) qualifying factors for the position of protection specialist.

HUMOR

A sense of humor is very important in an agent, because sometimes you have to be able to laugh at yourself. Humor relieves tension in stressful situations. A protective agent must take his job seriously, but not himself. He must be able to recognize the importance and seriousness of the situation presented to him while laughing about the occasional trivial burdens he must shoulder.

A good example was when the CEO of the previously discussed "assignment from Hell" (chapter 5) berated her protective detail for following along on her daily walk even though they were not specifically instructed to do so. A sense of humor allowed the agents to accept her tirade, laugh it off as just another self-important, ego-inflated, manic reaction, and continue to provide her with professional security. A good sense of humor often ameliorates a very stressful situation.

PHYSICAL CONDITION

It is important that the protective agent be in good physical condition. Physical conditioning has the extra benefit of stimulating mental prowess and confidence, enabling the agent to address and resolve a conflict or problem. He may be called upon, in less than a heartbeat, to go from a rather relaxed posture to a full in-your-face stance. Then again, an agent may have to engage in vigorous physical exertion for an extended period of time, such as running beside the protectees car for miles in the New York City summer heat and humidity.

Good physical fitness is as important to appearance as it is to endurance and good health. We all know (and unhappily may be one of) them: the "out-of-shape, where do I sit down," unprofessional-appearing agent. After a certain stage in life, gravity begins to take its toll, and we experience a decline in fitness. The gut begins to hang over the belt, the suits feel a little too tight, and the shirts become too restrictive. It becomes harder to move quickly, and the body generally begins a slow but inevitable deterioration. But good physical conditioning and proper eating will delay that bulge in the middle. A solid, muscular or wiry build denotes a professional and separates him from agents who are overweight, out-of-shape, and struggling.

MENTAL AGILITY

A properly trained and capable protective agent must have the ability to be flexible and think on his feet. That is, he must be able to resolve problems quickly. He must recognize a developing situation, analyze it, and deal with it instantly. He must be able to think for himself and have good self-direction. He cannot ask for specific instructions in every instance. He must make his own decisions. Does the situation pose a threat? What are the alternatives? What are the consequences of action or inaction? What action should be taken? Failure to recognize complexities leads to indecision and inaction. Uncertainty can inhibit action that could save a life or prevent a terrible accident.

In a humorous vein, quick thinking probably saved a Secret Service agent from a few days suspension without pay, or worse. It happened on the graveyard shift one night at Camp David. After a grueling week that strained the agent's limits of endurance, the president decided to go to Camp David immediately, without giving agents (or himself) time off. During the late hours (around 3:00 A.M.), the assistant agent in charge of the Presidential Protective Division, who was notorious for "sneaking up" on posts, decided to make a walk-around check of all the posts. As he very quietly approached one post, it appeared that the agent had momentarily nodded off. He was sitting down (his first mistake), his head was bent down toward his chest, his eyes were closed, and his hands were folded across his chest. As the senior agent approached, instinct alerted the post agent. He quickly opened his eyes, summarized the situation, and recognized his boss. Without a second's delay, he looked skyward, raised his hands in a gesture of supplication, and uttered, "amen."

FAMILY

Where would a protection agent be without an understanding and cooperative wife or significant other and a supportive family? Probably writing textbooks, greeting card verses, and resumes someplace. Possibly he would be teaching in some small college somewhere.

First you miss a birthday, then an anniversary, then a major holiday. The list goes on. There never seems to be time for that little league game you promised your son you would attend. When was the dance recital or school play? Missed it! What about the weekend or vacation alone with your spouse? Maybe next week or next year! How about the baby's first steps? Hope she got it on tape! Making plans more than just a few minutes in advance seems nearly impossible. Wives, families, and even friends and neighbors have a difficult time realizing that a protective agent's time is never his own, and his life is not his or his family's. His life is controlled by and dedicated to his protectee.

Having a supportive and understanding family is extremely important; you sometimes will have to leave the country and spend time away from them. You will need to keep your head clear and focused on the job at hand, not about the issues your family has about your profession. Confidence does not just come from within. Confidence also springs from a good support system.

FORBEARANCE (PATIENCE)

A necessary trait of the protection agent is patience. It is said that to be a dedicated professional in the protective field, "one needs to have the forbearance to watch a giant redwood tree grow and to see the grass grow tall and turn green then back to brown." Boredom is one of the closest companions of a protective agent. Working shifts of eight, twelve, or even fifteen or sixteen hours, just standing and waiting for a protectee or watching a certain area as a post assignment, can become very boring very quickly. On an assignment, patience is important because, at times, boredom will develop while you are "just standing and waiting" for the principal. Spending hours alone with no one to talk to (except yourself, the occasional passing cat or dog, or a servant who exchanges a word or two before moving on) would test anyone's patience.

The Secret Service rotates or "pushes" posts regularly, usually every half an hour. This relieves the stress of boredom, but more importantly it provides a fresh set of eyes. After watching the same thing for a long time, the eyes and brain begin to ignore subtle changes occurring before them. It can be disastrous when we fail to see subtle things and weave them together, fail to recognize patterns, and become unable to react to or understand meaning of these things. A relief will spot the changes more quickly.

Patience goes a long way in having tolerance for other people and their eccentricities, imperfections, and shortcomings. A protection agent is expected to hold very high physical, mental, and moral standards. He must demand this of himself, but he cannot expect or demand that his protectee have the same rigid standards. His client may be frail, indecisive, habitually late, or demanding and inconsiderate. Whatever the particular idiosyncrasy of the protectee, the protective agent must have forbearance and toleration, never showing even a hint of impatience.

TEAM PLAYERS

"One is the loneliest number...." Teams can simply do more than an individual. Personal protection is a position that requires a concerted effort by all participants. There is a reason why those involved in providing protective services are called a *protection team*. A definition of teamwork is "the effort of many working together to achieve a common goal." With this in mind, teamwork is an essential part of any group, project, or effort to solve a common problem or reach a desired success level. We all know teamwork is one of the most important roles. Effective protection is a combination of the efforts of all the participants. You must be able to read the thoughts and movements of the other agents. Each person must be able to do the jobs of everyone on the team. That way, if one man is taken out of the situation, any other can step in. That is effective teamwork.

SELF-INITIATIVE

A self-starter is able to individually motivate himself to complete any task that arises. He does not need a supervisor to explain every detail of his assignment and direct him as to how and when to respond. He sees a need and jumps in to see that the condition is rectified. He constantly attempts to find ways to improve the protective curtain. Even when standing at the most innocuous and boring post, he will seek ways to rebuff any attempts to penetrate his area of responsibility.

CHARACTER

> I have a dream that my little children will one day live in a nation where they will not be judged by the color of their skin, but by the content of their character.
>
> **Dr. Martin Luther King, Jr.**

"Upon these fields of friendly strife are sown the seeds that upon other fields on other days will bear the fruits of victory," observed General Douglas MacArthur in a speech at West Point's football stadium. He was addressing the physical and mental aspects of training and development of a group of individuals into a team (soldiers) able to surmount adversity through planning, hard work, respect, and determination. It is a standard football cliché to say, "The team came back from way behind to win the game because they had character." But is sports (football in particular) really the best analogy for character? Surely it means that they never gave up and continued to put forth the best effort in spite of their position and perhaps overwhelming odds. But character goes far beyond the gridiron and athletic fields.

What is character? People do not define character; character defines the person. Defining components of good character are the following:

Compassion. Giving understanding, empathy, and nonmalfeasance (avoiding doing injury to others)
Courage. Not letting your actions be influenced by your fears
Courtesy. More than good manners; a way to show respect to others

Fairness. Treating all with whom you come into contact with equality, without bias or prejudice

Forgiveness. Showing mercy, extending absolution, and giving acquittal and exoneration

Honesty. Uprightness, morality, and honor

Integrity. Trustworthy, worthy of confidence and trust

Justice. Evaluation of situations according to merit, without prejudice, and giving each person his due

Kindliness. Being compassionate and humane

Loyalty. Devotion, faithfulness, and allegiance

Prudence. Practical wisdom, discretion, making good judgments

Social responsibility. Meeting obligations of good citizenship, being charitable and public-spirited

Temperance. Moderation and restraint of one's desires and passions

Tolerance. Withstanding unpleasantness, unfortunate circumstances, and disadvantages

Truthfulness. Candor, honesty, and veracity

Character has been identified as virtue. An honest man, a man of good character, is free from corruption and cannot be deterred by negative influences. Someone who cannot be corrupted and manipulated by others or circumstances knows the meaning of honesty. This person is a man of integrity; he is acquainted with great personal honesty in oneself and treatment of others. Character builds one's reputation and devotion to others. Devotion begins in the family, work, friends, and colleagues. Good character should be taught at an early age and practiced for a lifetime. It is not an ascribed status; it is an achieved quality. Loyalty and trustworthiness add to a person's reputation of virtue and character.

A person is of good character if he respects other people's privacy and freedom. He is polite to all and tolerant and accepting of differences. The ability to listen to varying opinions and be aware of the needs of others is an element of character. Being open to different viewpoints and not ignore another's opinion shows strength of character. A person of character meets the demands of duty, responsibilities, and obligations; is accountable; and refrains from using excuses. A responsible person will face the job and do it as best as he can and will make the maximum effort to finish what he started.

Caring is a very important component of character. A person who really cares and feels an emotional response to the pain or pleasure of others is kind, expresses gratitude, and helps people in need has developed emotional or empathetic character.

Character is the sum of one's distinctive behavior, qualities, and moral and ethical constitution. These two traits can be expressed in many positive ways. For reasons of convenience and comprehension, these factors have been summarized as the "six pillars of character": trustworthiness, respect, responsibility, fairness, caring, and citizenship.[3]

Character is knowing the good, loving the good, and doing the good.

Thomas Lickona

Professional Conduct

The professional image and conduct of the protective agent are extremely important. He is constantly being observed and evaluated by someone—the client, the staff, contacts, the public, and coworkers. The protective agent is measured by all who see him. His appearance and conduct often determine the mind-set of those watching the agent. The train of thought is similar to, "Wow! If that is security, I don't think I would like to tangle with him. He looks like he knows what he is doing." Or the thought could be, "That is security? Ha! He don't look so tough. I think I could take him." It is like the "fastest gun in the West syndrome," in which everyone mentally measures the gunfighter and believes he can outdraw him. Outsiders often take the same measure of the protective agent and compare themselves to him.

Personal and professional conduct is an especially important aspect of professional protection and must be observed and enforced. Some professional appearance and personal conduct rules should never be compromised. Most are self-evident. They are also good guidelines to follow in both professional business and private life.

The respect, or lack thereof, earned by the protective agent directly correlates to his appearance and conduct. Being seen drinking (or drunk) and carousing in a hotel bar at any time diminishes respect for the agent. Cooperation from other agencies, staff, and host committees is much easier to obtain if the protective agent presents a professional image and his personal conduct is above reproach.

Alcohol

The rules regarding the use of alcohol should be at the very top of everyone's list! It is always best to refrain from using alcohol at all. If you do drink alcohol, never do so within 12 hours of the beginning of the work assignment. First, the odor of alcohol on the breath is not only offensive, it tells everyone that the protective agent may not be reliable, his judgment could be impaired, and his reactions may be hampered. Second, alcohol is a depressant, causing the body to slow down and need sleep. The physical demands of the job without alcohol are strenuous enough; when the toll is augmented by the use of alcohol, the result is a security agent who is less than fully responsive and less than totally effective.

It is much easier to beg off from an assignment, explaining you have had a few drinks, than to accept the assignment and explain to an investigating authority why the incident (or accident) occurred and why there was alcohol in your system. Three independent tests were conducted on Princess Diana's driver after the tragic crash in that tunnel in Paris. All three tests determined that the driver was beyond the legal limit. No matter what his past reputation, experience, and capabilities, he will always be remembered as a primary cause of her death because he "had been drinking."

Appearance

The physical appearance of the protective agent, while not intimidating, must engender feelings of respect. He must be well groomed and properly attired for the occasion. His hair should be conservatively cut and held in place with a dependable, odorless hair spray, with no radical styling or color. Any facial hair should be well shaved or very neatly trimmed, and any after-shave lotion used must be odorless. Hands and face should be washed and fingernails cleaned—perhaps manicured.

The dress of the protective agent is usually a conservative, dark business suit, white shirt, and conservative tie. In most instances, a totally black suit, while not highly inappropriate, is not recommended. Many people identify black suits with funerals. A black suit should be softened with thin pinstripes. It gives an aura of strength and professional dress. The shoes, while comfortable, should be polished and match the style of the clothing.

Sometimes a suit is not appropriate, so the protective agent must know the itinerary and dress accordingly. A western barbecue, for example, most probably would require jeans, boots, and a western shirt and jacket. On one occasion, an executive protection agent and his coworkers changed clothes five times in the course of one day because of the many different functions of the client. Sometimes the wishes of the client have to be considered. On one formal occasion in the White House, a Secret Service agent wore a blue tuxedo shirt with his tuxedo. The First Lady told him, "Go home and change your costume!"

ATTITUDE

Nobody likes a surly, grouchy, impertinent, or belligerent person. If that is the attitude and demeanor of the protective agent, he will alienate himself from those he has to work with, and he will receive little cooperation and no respect. His attitude will reflect poorly on his protectee and garner hostile feelings toward himself and the principal. A professional will be self-confident and assured but friendly, diplomatic, and helpful. His attitude, while not necessarily being charismatic, is "can do, will do." He accepts the least desirable assignment without complaint, because "somebody has to do it."

Proper manners and etiquette reflect a good attitude and earn respect and cooperation. It is just as easy to say, "Please stay back," "Please let us through," and "Excuse me" as it is to say "Get outta da way" or "Let us through." "Please" and "thank you" are still the magic words they were in kindergarten and are the most powerful phrases in any language.

COOPERATION

One cannot work as a protective agent if he cannot cooperate with his fellow workers and everyone around him. He must also be able to solicit and obtain the cooperation of others. It is not a one-way ride. Cooperation must flow both ways. Cooperation means compromise and getting along with others. It is sharing and caring. It should have been learned in kindergarten! In reality, a protective agent might often have conflicts with the staff advance person or members of the host committee, because their concerns are often at cross-purposes with the protective mission. The staff advance man or the host committee will want the protectee to receive as much exposure as possible, whereas the protective advance man wants to limit the vulnerability inherent in maximum exposure. The protective agent must be willing to make concessions in a spirit of cooperation and bend to the circumstances, as long as the secure environment of the protectee is not compromised.

COURTESY

Courtesy begets respect! Politeness and kindness are not out of fashion. It is always best to treat people with dignity and consideration. When he said, "Speak softly and carry a big stick," President Theodore Roosevelt could have been speaking to a protective agent. Kind words and a gentle manner constitute the sheath for the sword of authority and influence. There is an old country saying, "You catch more flies with honey than with vinegar." If you want people to cooperate with you, show them courtesy; they will give you what you want, and you will gain their respect.

DEMEANOR

This does not mean that the less cooperation you have, "da meaner" you get. It means the way you carry yourself and what your behavior says about you. A useful personality trait is the ability, through body language and other nonverbal communication, to communicate that you are confident, alert, enthusiastic, and entirely in control of the situation. Demeanor often will tell observers about the relationship between the protectee and his security agent. It will say the agent will go to extremes if necessary for his protectee, or it will say the agent is in it only for the money and reflected glory. A lackadaisical demeanor will invite aggression toward the protectee and create a lack of respect for his protective shield.

DEPENDABILITY

The agent is someone to be counted on; on time, every time. He is always in the proper position and responsive to any situations and capable of being in control. A client, VIP, or principal will look to his agents to resolve any nettling situation and to always be nearby whenever and for whatever the need may be. Clients like to know that assigned tasks will be carried out to their satisfaction, without any hesitation or lapse of confidence.

DIPLOMACY

Working with staff and some host committees can be difficult. It is their job to make sure "the boss" receives maximum exposure and is seen under the most favorable conditions. Their goals and the intent of security are often in direct conflict. To satisfy both requirements takes tact and finesse. Diplomacy is the art of convincing someone to do what you want and have him believe it was his idea.

DISCIPLINE

The correct term is self-discipline. For it is self-discipline that makes a person capable of standing in one place, sometimes for hours; to be on time; and to respond without anger to a protectee or family member. Self-discipline makes us put forth the extra effort expected by our public. Discipline is the little internal mechanism that helps us stay awake and alert after hours on duty or when working with little or no sleep.

Sometimes, staying awake requires more than discipline or the internal alarm clock. Little techniques can be employed to help get through those graveyard hours. One that is employed often requires holding a key ring with the keys held lightly between the thumb and forefinger. As the person begins to doze off, his fingers relax, and the keys are dropped, bringing him back to alertness. (This is even useful in that boring math class that doesn't make any sense anyway. But in that case, substitute a pen or pencil for the key ring.)

Sometimes, just relaxing for an instant and letting the self-discipline lapse can cause a tired person to instantly nap off. In once case, an agent was standing post at an ocean side presidential vacation compound at 2:00 A.M. He was bundled up in a warm parka and maintaining a long vigil, walking around and playing "what-if" mind games, visualizing possible responses to varying scenarios. He saw his relief coming and recognized the approaching agent, who was approximately 50 steps away. The agent on post stopped walking and leaned against a wall while waiting for his relief. The next thing he realized was his relief grabbing him by the throat and jabbing a simulated knife into his neck. The posted agent had had no warning of the onset of sleep. It was an occurrence of a momentary relaxation of self-discipline.

DISCRETION

Play it by ear is a phrase often heard in the Secret Service and other types of executive protection when the situation is changing constantly. Discretion means having the freedom and ability to make good decisions when there is no time to wait for someone else to provide advice and direction. Making wise decisions often calls for looking at all alternatives. In the final analysis, it is the good judgment of the protective agent that determines the proper course. Extend the same good judgment when working with people. People skills require a great degree of discretion. Good working relationships begin with respect, and that respect is earned through trust, compromise, and judicious discretion.

EDIBLES—EATING HABITS

Never let them see you eat! Do not consume food or beverages, chew gum, or smoke in the presence of the principal or the public unless the situation requires it. Of course, if the protectee is eating in a restaurant and this is the only opportunity for a protective agent to eat, he should do so, but usually at a different table (where he can observe the area of the protectee). When ordering, order something that can be prepared quickly and eaten before the principal has finished. Never order any food that is messy or difficult to eat, such as barbecued ribs or crab legs! When invited by a host or hostess to eat, either politely decline or be as discrete as possible. Don't take large amounts of food or overload your plate as though it were your first meal in several hours (which it may be) or as if it were intended to be your last meal. Take amounts commensurate with good taste (pun again intended), then retreat from the public view. Sometimes it is possible (or even necessary) to make other arrangements for meals. Always keep a sandwich, energy bar, or similar snack in a pocket or nearby briefcase when you might expect to miss a meal. Missing meals and working long hours is nearly standard fare and must be accepted as the price of doing business.

Chewing gum and smoking are strictly forbidden. If standing a post away from public view and there is no contact with the principal, staff, visitors, or others, chewing gum may be permissible. Smoking is another matter. Smoking while standing a post in the dark provides a telltale sign for anyone watching and attempting to locate security personnel. The smell of the smoke is another giveaway. What to do with the finished butt? Throw it on the ground? In a short while, there will be many of them littering the grounds.

HONESTY

There should never be any doubt about the protective agent's honesty and character. He must be beyond reproach. Being "worthy of confidence and trust" are among the words inscribed in a Secret Service agent's *Commission Book*. Those words deftly define the integrity demanded and expected of a protective agent. His client (protectee) must have the assurance he can be trusted to maintain secrets and handle large amounts of cash, expensive jewelry, and other valuables. The philosophy to keep in mind is, "If it is not yours, don't touch it." That means everything! Honesty relates to truthfulness as well. Never, ever lie. One lie will erode the protective agent's credibility and shake the confidence the protectee must have in his security. Honesty is like pregnancy—you either are, or you are not. A woman cannot be half pregnant; the same is true with honesty. You are either honest or you are not.

There is another old reminder about honesty and stealing: "He who takes what ain't hizzen, ends up in prizzen." It may not be grammatically correct or properly spelled, but the message is very clear.

"Secret Service Arrests Man Seeking Job as Celebrity Bodyguard," read the headline in the *Los Angeles Times*.[4] The person behind this story may have had all the credentials (apparently self-made) he thought he needed to apply for a part-time second job with a Hollywood celebrity protection company, but he lacked many other very important things—character, honesty, and integrity. The man previously worked as a protective agent for celebrities and was experienced in the field. When applying for a job to protect a very high-profile Hollywood acting couple, he arrived in a flashy car with tinted windows and police lights. He claimed to be an agent with the Homeland Security Department and produced credentials allegedly from that agency. The protection company he applied to felt his application was a little strange and notified the Secret Service. After an investigation of the person, he was arrested for impersonating a federal officer and could be spending the next three years in prison.

KNOW YOUR LIMITATIONS

"A man has got to know his limits."

Clint Eastwood (as Dirty Harry)

Do not take unnecessary risks. There will be times when the protectee expects you to do something that is simply beyond the capability of a protective agent. If the consequence of attempting the activity would cause injury or death, do not attempt it.

Sometimes the protectee will insist. If there is no way to decline or discourage him, at least mitigate the circumstances and attempt to reduce the risk.

A nephew of the king of a Middle Eastern country was vacationing in Barbados. He and his entourage had been partying all day aboard a yacht anchored a little over a quarter mile off shore. Late in the afternoon the prince decided everyone would swim ashore. The protective agent accompanying the group very strongly recommended against it. The protective agent was not a strong swimmer and had been suffering the effects of seasickness all day. There were also other members of the party who had limited swimming ability and most had been drinking alcohol. The prince and several others jumped overboard anyway and began the swim. After instructing the captain of the yacht to follow the swimmers as close to the shore as posible, the protective agent also jumped in and began the swim to shore.

About half way in, one of the friends of the prince began to flounder and call for help. He could never have made it to shore. The prince and the protective agent (who was also struggling but found strength somewhere) responded to the floundering swimmer who began to clash with the two men who were trying to help him. Somehow they managed to keep him afloat and got him to shore. The three collapsed at the waterline, totally exhausted from the ordeal. The remaining members of the group also narrowly managed to reach shore.

A tragic ending was averted by some strange miracle. When he had recovered sufficiently, the protective agent angrily scolded the prince and told him to never place the group in such needless danger again. The young nobleman clearly understood! Know your limitations!

Sometimes it is physically impossible to work because of illness or fatigue. Recognize those limitations and make arrangements for a replacement. Attempting to work while suffering with a fever (or seasickness) limits your ability to properly provide the service required. Inadequate or impaired ability could result in miscalculations and mistakes, concluding in accident, injury, or death.

KNOWLEDGE

I can give you knowledge, but I can't make you think….

Unknown

It is a given that a protective agent must be well educated and trained in his specialty. But that alone is insufficient. He must be well read, informed, and educated in all fields. It is important to keep abreast of current events in the news, because the principal will discuss local, national, and world affairs. An informed and well-thought out reply will enhance the standing of the protective agent. It is also extremely important to be current in local history, geography, and knowledge of community figures.

Education plus experience equals knowledge and wisdom.

LOYALTY

Loyalty to the employer, coworkers, and protectee is intrinsic to character and integrity. Loyalty is based on more than the monetary gain a person receives for providing his services. It is an intangible that others count on. Without loyalty, there could be no trust.

PERCEPTION

Being able to anticipate and instantly recognize potential dangers that might harm a principal is only a part of the total package. One must also perceive the needs and concerns of the protectee. Being able to resolve such concerns before they are expressed affords the protectee peace of mind and assurance that the protective agent is well aware of all conditions that might affect his secure environment. Typically, it is said that man has five senses: touch, taste, smell, seeing, and hearing. It is the contention here that man has seven senses—the previous five plus perception and balance.

Perception is the ability to "see what is not seen." It is a feeling, a hunch, or an intuition—maybe a gut feeling. Perception is that feeling when the small hairs of your neck star to prickle. There is no scientific evidence, but it has been learned through experience that when an extrasensory feeling such as perception is trying to say something, it is best to listen and investigate or both.

"The world is a matter of balance and circles." When anything is out of balance, it must go in a cycle to be restored. "What goes around, comes around." A protective agent spotting something out of sync must rely on all his senses (including perception) to find why it is out of balance and what it will take to reinstate homeostasis (balance). "What doesn't belong is wrong."

PROVIDE GOOD SERVICE

No matter who the client or principal, he deserves the best possible service. There should be only one type of service—professional! When occupied in a vocation responsible for the health, safety, well-being, and life of an individual or corporate entity, it should be criminal to provide less than the best service or conduct oneself haphazardly. It could very well be conceived as criminal if an incident arose and was addressed unsatisfactorily because of negligence, omission, or error.

IMAGE

Project an image that includes all of the above. The protective agent is always being observed and evaluated by someone—the client, staff, professional contacts, the public, and coworkers. Always assume you are on camera and being videotaped. "If you can see the lens, it can see you." (And it most probably will. And, considering today's advanced technology, you may not see the lens.) The image of the protective agent reflects on everyone. It can set the tone of how the security detail and the client are perceived. A professional image can deter an attack or confrontation. Sloppiness sends the message, "I don't care." A neat, clean, aware, professional image sends out an aura of confidence and transmits a message that says, "I care, and I can handle any situation."

POLICE AND PROTECTIVE AGENT IMAGES AS "WARRIORS"

Police officers and protective agents confront not an "enemy" but individuals who are protected by the Bill of Rights. Confusing the police and protection functions with the warrior mentality can lead to dangerous and unintended consequences, such as unnecessary assaults, shootings, and killings.

… problems stem in part from an outdated and dangerous image of policing (or personal protection) as a he-man occupation with the primary requirements for success a thick neck and a taste for physical violence…. As long as the warrior image remains, policing [and personal protection] will draw the wrong kind of applicants, reward the wrong kind of behavior, and fail to provide the kind of services that communities now demand.[5]

In a recent survey of 808 Texas law enforcement agencies conducted by the state commission on standards and training, "physical ability" was rated the least important among ten dimensions of "being a successful peace officer." It rated slightly below "appearance." Other dimensions included "initiative," "dependability," and "interpersonal skills." The highest-ranking characteristic was "integrity.[6]

Although tests for general physical fitness might be appropriate for police officer applicants, the selection process should emphasize the skills and characteristics needed for community police officers [and protection agents]—communication, problem solving, empathy, and the ability to successfully interact with members of diverse cultures. Job analysis data tells us that these skills are far more important for successfully performing the duties of a community police officer [and protection agent].

The warrior image of policing also contributes to problems of excessive force, corruption, and other forms of misconduct, by fueling a climate that tolerates brutality, enforces the code of silence, and punishes those who seek to challenge the "brotherhood…." Finally, the warrior image of policing epitomizes the paramilitary style that communities nationwide (and protection agencies) are rejecting in favor of a more community-oriented approach. It will also require redesigning traditional recruitment practices to ensure that the right kinds of people enter policing [and close personal protection].[7]

With all of that said and understood, we must also understand that a protective agent or police officer must have a warrior's outlook of the world—that it is a dangerous place, and often there is the thin line between safety and danger. A trait of a good warrior is that he possesses the four I's of intelligence, integrity, interpersonal skills, and imagination. This type of warrior mentality trumps the warrior image of the hulking, quasi military, them-versus-us personality.

PROTECTIVE AGENT IMAGE AS A KNIGHT

"A knight without armor in a savage land reads the card of a man…"[8] aptly describes the modern knight—a protective agent. His chivalry (good manners and mannerisms), willingness to face the dangers brought to his lord (the protectee), and strength of character set him apart from the common man in the street.

KNIGHTS AND WARRIORS

It has come to pass that modern-day protection agents have assumed many of the traits of the bygone "double-hearted" knight and warrior. Agents prepare for battle by performing rituals of physical fitness, combat readiness, and proficiency with weapons while upholding virtues of loyalty, humility, and willingness to make any necessary sacrifice. They seek to turn the odds of victory in their favor by knowing the lay of the land and everything they can learn about the aggressor. At times like these, their hearts are "as hard as a diamond."

In other moments, the protective agent (warrior-knight) will stoop to wipe a tear from a youngster's face or play football or dolls with the child of his protective responsibility. In some cases, the child may actually be his protective responsibility. This ability to turn a heart "as hard as a diamond" into one that is "as soft and pliant as warm wax" likens the protective agent to his past brethren, the knights and warriors. Alluding to the knight and warrior as role models or self-images may not be a perfect representation as seen by some segments of society, and it might lend a degree of legitimacy to those who would misuse their position of power and strength with excessive force over others. On the other hand, if viewing a warrior and a knight as someone who believed in good over evil, help for the oppressed, and sacrifice to the death in the name of saving someone else's life, then a protective agent can easily and justifiably refer to himself as a modern knight or warrior.

PROTECTIVE AGENT EQUIPMENT

It's not as high tech or astounding as Batman's utility belt, but the equipment the average protection agent carries is just as utilitarian. The agent usually carries a small but powerful flashlight to be used, of course, should the electrical power be interrupted. It is also used to check dark corners, under tables, and elsewhere for bombs, listening devices, and anything else that should not be present. He also carries a compact radio or cell phone with an earpiece and a surveillance mike (a small one-piece microphone and speaker fitting inside the ear), a notebook and pen or pencil, small change for parking meters, sunglasses, handcuffs or plastic restraints, breath mints or refresher, a weapon and extra ammunition, a pocket knife, and an optional small canister of pepper spray or mace. The cell phone typically has all the bells and whistles of Internet, video recording, and other features.

The agent's briefcase is his utility belt, for it contains everything he needs for several days on the road or on assignment. It contains all the proper forms to complete his paperwork, such as invoice forms, schedules, envelopes and stamps, and emergency telephone contact numbers. There is a foul-weather jacket or poncho folded very compactly; a set of small screwdrivers and wrenches for opening electrical faceplates for inspection; a larger flashlight and extra batteries; a tube of sunscreen and lip balm; a package of pain reliever such as ibuprofen; two or three energy or similar high-calorie nutrient bars; extra pens and pencils; a small measuring tape or ruler; spare car keys; gloves; passport; calculator; extra business cards; a disposable razor and travel toothbrush; a small first aid kit with band-aids, a disinfectant, an insect or spider and snake bite and bee sting kit; a needle and thread; paper clips and safety pins; and anything else that will assist him in his duty or render a little comfort and relief.

WEAPONS

Executive protection agents working for private protection companies most often carry weapons of their own choosing. It is usually a matter of preference and what the agent personally finds comfortable. Only a very few are still stubborn enough to cling to the old five- or six-shot .357 revolver. Today the demand is for more firepower. Many agents have switched to the Glock .40 calibre pistol. It is compact and lightweight. It is accurate and easily concealed. Some agents prefer a 9-mm handgun. For many years, agents of the U.S. Secret Service carried a 2.5-inch barrel Smith & Wesson .357 combat magnum revolver with a special-load 110-grain bullet. However, the Service has switched to a semiautomatic pistol as standard issue to all agents and uniformed personnel. After extensive research, they selected the 9-mm SIG-Sauer P228 with special 9-mm ammunition developed by Remington exclusively to meet the requirements of the Secret Service. For off-duty personal protection, agents are authorized to carry the SIG-Sauer .380 P230.

When choosing a personal-duty handgun, the protective agent must consider several factors. The weapon must have stopping power yet must not have penetration through a human body. If a weapon is fired in a protective assignment, it probably will be in a crowd situation. Therefore, the bullet must not pass through the intended target and possibly wound a second or more persons. The pistol must be accurate, lightweight, comfortable in the hand, easily gripped, and readily concealed. Most shooting done in close quarters is instinctive point shooting without the use of sights. However, the agent's handgun should be equipped with tritium night sights. The ammunition should have high knock-down power, such as provided by the Hydra-Shock bullet.

CARRYING A CONCEALED WEAPON

The handgun of choice must be easily concealed yet readily available. A properly fitting holster is very important. It is best to select a holster that fits inside the pants and is secured behind the belt loop, directly on the side of the trousers. If that location is not comfortable or if the hand cannot easily and naturally retrieve the weapon, the belt loop should be relocated. An extra belt loop can be added to keep the holster from sliding toward the back. The gun is placed behind the belt loop to keep it from sliding around or pulling forward when the weapon is drawn. The weapon should fit snugly against the side of the body and not protrude or snag when covered with a suit coat. The placement and fit of the handgun should be such that it is hidden even when just a plain tee shirt is worn over it. Some people prefer a shoulder holster or a "small of the back holster." These have benefits, but they are not practical for close operation with a protectee, and the gun cannot be easily and quickly drawn. The holster should securely hold the weapon to prevent it from falling out when the agent is running or engaged in a physical activity such as close engagement in a large, surging crowd.

Some assignments require special ingenuity to conceal a weapon. When a protectee spends a day at the beach, the protective agent can wrap his weapon in a towel, carry it in a paper bag, or even keep it in a cooler. (That's a thought—keeping a "heater" in a "cooler.") It is quite common these days to see a fanny pack being used to conceal a weapon. It fact, it has become so common that anyone wearing a fanny pack is suspect and automatically assumed to be carrying a weapon. Many fanny packs on the market today are designed expressly for carrying a handgun.

SHOTGUNS AND OTHER WEAPONS

Many security posts (e.g., in the backyard of a protectee, near a front driveway gate, or even in the interior of a residence) require or should be equipped with a backup weapon such as a shotgun. For close quarters such as the examples mentioned, a shotgun must be the weapon of preference. The standard shotgun selected by the Secret Service is the Remington model 870. The preferred type has a 14-inch barrel with a pistol grip and folding stock. It is compact and, with the magazine extension, holds seven rounds of no. 4 buckshot. A shotgun loaded with rifled slugs has tremendous stopping power and can be accurate up to 200 yard. (Because of their effectiveness and limited range, some states require deer hunters to use shotguns with rifled slugs.)

Another effective weapon for close quarters is the 9-mm Uzi select fire (semi-automatic/automatic) submachine gun. With the stock folded and its short barrel, it is very compact and can be carried in a briefcase. The magazine holds 30 rounds of ammunition. This weapon (especially with the short barrel) is not available to the general public.

PERSONAL BODY ARMOR

A piece of equipment that should be included in every protection agent's inventory is lightweight body armor, "bulletproof vest." The wearing of body armor is required by most police departments and has been proven to be worth the inconvenience and cost, as many lives have been saved by the armor. If a protective agent chooses not to wear the vest (after all, they are hot, a little bulky, and somewhat restrictive), it is suggested that a high-profile protectee wear a vest when appearing in public. A properly fitting lightweight vest is not obtrusive and could well be worth the appearance of gaining a little weight (maybe ten pounds). A wraparound level 4A vest with Kevlar layers has been proven to stop shotgun rifle slugs at close range. There may be traumatic bruising, but that is far better than the alternative! Recently, a Los Angeles County deputy sheriff was shot in the chest at close range with a .30 calibre AK assault rifle. Fortunately, he was wearing his departmental mandated vest. He suffered only minor bruising.

PERSONAL CONDUCT—PROTECTEE PROTOCOL

Certain standards of decorum must be observed when working close proximity with a protectee or his family. As a protective agent, you are only an observer, a guest in the protectee's world, not a part of his world or social circle. After working very closely with a protectee and his family, spending time in his home, traveling with him and being familiar with all the events in his life, it is very easy to become comfortable and at ease, almost like being at home. It is perhaps natural that a form of bonding occurs that leads to being overly familiar. Don't fall into that trap! Remember, you are not a close personal friend; rather, you are an employee, like the maid, the gardener, or family cook. As a security specialist, your status may be higher than that of the maid, but as an employee, you can (and will) be replaced very easily and quickly—probably quicker and easier than the maid, cook, or gardener! Always assume you are replaceable, because you are!

Always maintain a professional barrier, that is an employee-employer relationship between yourself and the protectee. Your area of competence is security and protective policies. Those are the only areas in which it is proper to offer advice. If your advice or opinion is solicited in any other area, do not pretend to be an expert. Avoid a direct answer or attempt to deflect the question with a humorous retort if appropriate. On the other hand, never ask the protectee for advice, stock tips, special favors, autographs, photographs, or gratuities. Ask him for information only when it relates to his security, such as itinerary, threats, suspicious people or incidents, and so forth.

One young and attractive television game show hostess and situation comedy star remarked to her regular studio-based protective agents that whenever she traveled to another city, the network would not send the regular agents with her. She complained that the fill-in agents hired locally would persistently hound her for autographs and photographs in poses with each agent.

Do not use the protectee's telephone, business machines, or supplies for personal reasons. Obtain his permission before using the telephone, copy machine, or fax, and use them for business purposes only. If he gives permission, never, ever abuse the privilege! Some employers have been known to withhold payment in the amount of telephone calls made by the protective staff. Some have even fired their security personnel and replaced them with other, more professional and cost-conscious agents.

Treat the protectee, his family, and staff (including domestic service) with dignity and respect. Observe all rules of good manners and etiquette. An appropriate saying to remember is, "Familiarity breeds contempt." Do not become overly familiar or too personal. Maintain an invisible barrier or even an air of mystery. The protectee needs only job-related information.

Treat the protectee's property with respect and care. During the dark hours of a night shift, it is so easy to take a short cut across the grass, through the flowers, and over the hedge. There is no one to see the footprints, the trampled flowers or hedge, or the broken water sprinkler. But the darkness does not last forever! The next day, the protectee will notice. He won't be happy. You will hear from him.

When entering the residence or office, be sure the bottoms of your shoes are clean. Walking across someone's expensive white carpet with dirty or muddy shoes is no way to make a favorable impression. Several clients have demanded that all shoes be removed at the door prior to entering the home. Note: Be sure to wear socks that don't have holes in them, with a toe coming out!

A client will probably own a very expensive car—maybe several. Handle the car as if you were making the payments. Drive it carefully. Never make jackrabbit starts, gun it to see what it will do, or squeal the tires when rounding a corner. A car is part of the client's family; treat it as such.

"If it is not yours, don't touch it" is a rule to remember when having access to the client's papers, books, or personal items. Do not read or disturb anything on his desk, bookshelves, or tables. If a protectee even suspects that his personal or business notes, papers, memos, or belongings have been rifled, he will lose confidence and trust in his security personnel. This is a fundamental rule; never compromise the principal's confidence, trust, or security. Some protectees will test their agents by purposely leaving money, jewelry, or sensitive papers in a certain place or position then check it to see if it has been removed or tampered with.

Do not engage the protectee in unnecessary conversation. Let him initiate small talk, and respond only to the topic. Never volunteer personal matters. It is no concern to him, unless he asks about your family's health, what school your son or daughter attends, what movie you saw last night, and so on.

It is a very poor practice to discuss prior assignments, other clients, or another client's business. If you need to use an example to make a specific point regarding security, state it in very general terms. Mention no names, businesses, or circumstances that would lead your protectee to identify the person or incident you are describing. It is obvious. If you talk about other clients, you will talk about your current one. Clients do not like that. Everything you see, hear, or encounter must remain confidential. The client must maintain the confidence that his security agent will not discuss him or his business with future clients. A protective agent should never discuss previous clients with the current client, because it undermines trust and confidence. A protective agent is privy to the private world of the principal. If the protective agent talks about his previous clients, the trust of the current client could be undermined, because he does not know whether a conversation with a future client will revolve around him.

Trust and confidence needs to be maintained, because the protective agent's job includes calling for him to make hotel reservations and airline flights, and even being with the client when he goes to the doctor. If the trust is not there, the agent may not be allowed to do those things, creating a security gap. A lack of trust could even lead to the agent being fired.

Always assume that any conversation you have (even off the record) with media, staff, personnel, or others will be reported and taken out of context because it will be. Television crews have sound recording people accompanying them whenever they are at the scene of a news event. They may just be standing around, but you can be assured that the sound recording equipment is on and recording every bit of information. The large microphones they carry look innocent enough, but say something inappropriate, and it's "gotcha." Never tell off-color, racist, ethnic, or sexist jokes. They will always come back to haunt you. A number of former public figures are now unemployed because they told a joke or story that someone found offensive, and it was reported by the news media.

One agent learned that lesson the hard way but, fortunately, no one else found out about it. The agent was working with a high-profile public figure. There was a large contingent of press accompanying the person. As they were walking into the site where the protectee would be speaking, the agent made several "aside" comments to another agent. Later, a television producer friend of the agent called him and said, "Listen, I have something on tape you might be interested in." She then replayed the agent's entire conversation, which had been inadvertently recorded by a cameraman and crew accompanying the protectee. Fortunately for the agent, the producer kept the comments private.

"Anything you say can and will be used against you" is a lot more than a Miranda rights (Fifth Amendment) warning! Always assume you are being recorded, even if you see no camera or microphone. You probably are! Even if you are not being recorded, your conversations will somehow find their way into print, broadcast on "News at Eleven," or at least reported back to your employer. Never say anything derogatory or disparaging about your assignment, the people you work with, or especially the people you work for. Be loyal to your protectee. Do not demean him to anyone. Always speak in an affirmative and positive manner; someone is always listening and watching.

A protection company had a client, a wealthy and powerful chief executive officer of a very noteworthy company. He had CCTV cameras monitoring his property, and the agent on duty in the command post could observe the entire estate from that position. There is nothing unusual about that; it is very common and even recommended. What was not common (and was little known) that he also had hidden cameras and microphones installed in the command post so he could visually and audibly monitor the agent working in the command post at any time, from his living room, study or bedroom!

Deport yourself in a manner that gains the respect and good will of the client, his employees, visitors, and even neighbors. Never swear, curse, or use offensive language. Guard against and enforce infractions of horseplay and other disturbances (laughter, loud talk, and even a loud radio or cell phone).

Do not smoke in the protectee's presence or in his house, car, or office. If you must smoke (though highly discouraged), do it only out in the open air where it will offend no one. When you are finished with the cigarette, field strip it, that is tear the paper open, toss the remaining tobacco into the wind, and roll the paper up into a small ball. Discard the paper ball and filter in a trash can. Then either brush your teeth or use a breath mint or spray to freshen your breath. Remember that clothing retains the smell of cigarette smoke, which may offend the protectee.

Establish procedures that will only minimally disrupt the protectee's routine. Your position is to be a shadow. The protectee should be able to maintain as normal a lifestyle as possible under the circumstances. He sets the itinerary and places to visit; the protective agent is responsible for setting and establishing a secure environment around the protectee's wishes. Learn his personal habits, such as when he rises in the morning, when he wants to leave for work, how late he stays at work, when he retires for the night, and so forth. Plan security around his habits. He should not have to change his routine to suit the protective agent's wishes. Rather, it is the protective agent who must be flexible and adapt to the lifestyle of the protectee.

Maintain a very low profile and do not draw attention to yourself. Do not overdress the principal. Some protectee's will wear $100 ties, $500 shirts, and $2,000 suits. (What security person can afford that?) The protective agents should dress appropriately and professionally but not so as to draw attention away from the protectee. Some protectees have very fragile egos and do not like to have someone (especially an employee) steal the spotlight.

When making security or safety recommendations to the protectee or staff, be prepared to explain your reasoning. Do not exaggerate the threat level, and do not frighten the protectee, his family, staff, or other employees. Be truthful and straight-forward, and explain the potential risks and hazards. Do not overestimate or underestimate the threat. Keep the protectee (or his designated representative) fully apprised of all threats and planned countermeasures.

If the protectee is paying for meals at a restaurant or assuming other expenses, order a conservatively priced meal (something nutritious that is not messy). It is really in poor taste (that pun again) and classless to order the most expensive item on the menu, such as the largest steak or a lobster. You are spending someone else's money, so be thrifty! If given money or authorization to provide tips, extend only the correct and proper amount, usually 15 percent.

Never overguard the principal. Give him room to breathe. No one likes his personal space invaded. The proper distance between the security agent and the principal varies with the situation. The closer the crowd, the closer the agent should be. In an area where there is little threat and no one crowding around, allow more space.

When the principal is engaged in a telephone call, conversation, or other private and personal matters, the protective agent should move a discrete distance away. Do not seem to be listening to the business being discussed. If it is not possible to move away, at least turn away and appear to direct your attention elsewhere.

If the principal is shopping, allow him to have a feeling of independence. Do not monitor or comment on any purchase. If your opinion is solicited regarding color or size, be diplomatic and tactful. When it is time to pay for a purchase and the principal opens his wallet or checkbook or takes out a credit card, move away and do not look at the wallet or checkbook, or even at extended cash. Also provide enough space to allow the protectee and clerk to discuss the price and payment in private. Even though a protectee is powerful and (most probably) wealthy, his credit card occasionally may be "maxed out" and declined by the store. In that instance, it is best if the protective agent is far enough away to avoid overhearing the conversation and spare the protectee any embarrassment.

WORKING WITH THE PRESS—MEDIA RELATIONS

Whether the principal is a VIP, celebrity, political figure, controversial or renowned individual, or other famous person, there is a common denominator. He is newsworthy! Whenever he makes a public appearance, gives a speech, or makes a pronouncement, the news media will be well represented. There are cameramen, soundmen, and reporters from network or local television and radio, and there are representatives from the print media (newspapers and magazines) as well. They all will be jockeying for the best positions to shout their questions or get the best camera angle.

In chapter 3, the personality of a protective agents is described as

...aggressive personality types who are action-oriented, thrill-seeking individuals that thrive on high stimulation. These individuals often have authority and control issues and score somewhat higher on manic, depression, and psychopathic deviant scales than the general public. They tend to be type "A" personalities that are competitive, driven, and typically impatient. They may be a little obsessive-compulsive. This makes them really good at their jobs but can also cause them a number of interpersonal difficulties (especially personal relationships). There is a noble motivation of wanting to help the public, but they would not remain in the field very long if they were not able to adapt and accept the responsibility of helping others and following some sort of rules which govern their profession.

This personality type also exactly fits a newsperson. By definition, this can result in personality clashes as well as a conflict between the mission of the news media and that of the protective agent. An agent must recognize and understand the competing goals and personality types and act accordingly. To understand and accept the media dictates reasonable compromise.

The media and the security team operate as two diametrically opposed factions. The press wants to have unlimited and up-close access, but the protective agent wants to maintain the highest level of security. A third factor to consider is that the principal and his staff desire favorable press attention along with full security protection. These diverse elements make for a dilemma that the protective team must resolve. Common sense, compromise, and good planning usually result in a workable arrangement.

An advance man should anticipate and make arrangements for the location of the press. It is usually best to establish a special press area in the vicinity of the principal's arrival and departure and at the speech or presentation site, where the press can record and photograph the event without interference from spectators. The entrance to the press area should be controlled (either by police, a protective agent, or an authorized representative), allowing only credentialed press inside and checking credentials, camera bags, and the assortment of equipment carried along by the press. The person responsible for monitoring the press entrance should maintain vigilance in case someone or something was overlooked. (Remember John Hinkley, the attempted assassin of President Reagan?)

The news representatives are not the enemy. They are often aggressive and pushy, and sometimes obnoxious, but they are also just doing a job. If proper arrangements are made, the press will cooperate and even assist in the security function. They may spot an unauthorized person in their midst and bring attention to him. The press may be placed in a position to provide a buffer zone between the crowd and the client, preventing an approach by someone who wishes to harm the protectee.

When working with the news media, keep several caveats in mind.

1. The business of news people is the news. They are professionals in their field and should be treated as such, with respect and dignity. Any queries from the press must be handled with diplomacy and tact. Do not simply state "no comment," but also refrain from imparting information to the media unless specifically authorized. It is best to be as candid and truthful as possible without divulging any information that would in any way compromise the principal or his security. Generally, it is not the role of a protection specialist to communicate information to the press. When it is

unavoidable, be friendly but noncommittal. Any attempts to mislead, lie, or deceive will undoubtedly result in highly unfavorable publicity for the protective agent and his protectee.

2. It is important that all inquiries be directed to one designated spokesman. Most principals will have a business manager, press liaison person, or aide who will disseminate all information to the press, to ensure complete and accurate data, and who will be responsible for any "misquotation."

3. Do not pose for photographs. Avoid being in any photographs if possible. A photograph can be used as intelligence data by someone planning harm to the principal and can aid in identifying protective personnel and procedures.

4. Never ask for favors from the press. One favor begets another. Do not show or provide favoritism to one news person or organization over another. The less-favored person or organization will eventually find a means to retaliate. It will be embarrassing at least and possibly damaging.

5. Do not refer to the news professionals as "newsies." It is a derogatory term. It will probably offend and anger someone and could result in some type of unfavorable action. It is good to establish a working relationship, rapport, and communication with the press, but it should be businesslike and professional. Do not discuss the protectee, his schedule, his business, the protective assignment, or anything else relating to the principal in the presence of the press. Joking, "horseplay," profanity, and other unprofessional conduct by the protective agent will be recorded and reported.

WORKING WITH THE HOST COMMITTEE

Host committee is a generic name given to the supervisory members of a sponsoring organization, event, or location the principal visits. The event may be a speaking engagement, dinner, reception, or fund-raiser, or even the Academy Awards. Whatever the function or location, there will be a contact person or group responsible for organizing the event.

This person or group will work with the security people and lend assistance when necessary and possible. The host is friendly with the principal and will want to expose him to all of the guests at the function. Sometimes the host's enthusiasm translates into a security risk. For example, the host may wish the protectee to meet and greet all the attendees. If there is no way to screen them or shelter the principal, it is quite possible that someone with a grievance may gain close proximity to the principal and bring him harm. If the host's arrangements and planning are contrary to good security, use tact and diplomacy in neutralizing the position. It is advisable to not alienate the host or coworkers. The host and security can find grounds for compromise, but it must weigh favorably on the side of security.

Working with the host, it is possible to strategically locate and establish insulating barriers. The placement of tables, dais, and crowd are factors that should be considered when positioning the protectee. Sometimes it is appropriate to place the band, children, or other groups in front of the protectee, between him and the crowd. This prevents someone in the crowd from dashing toward him.

Someone from the host committee should be responsible for operating a *trouble desk* that maintains a list of all the invited guests. The duty of the trouble desk, which should be located outside the secured area, is to authenticate, through personal knowledge or photographic identification, anyone who arrives without a ticket or invitation and to resolve any questions or conflicts an arriving guest might have. A host representative should also assist in screening the incoming crowd at the security checkpoint (usually at entrance doors).

SUMMARY

When working closely with a principal, follow the rules of good manners and etiquette. Be aware of and sensitive to his needs and wishes. Be professional in all situations, and maintain as low a profile as possible. Honesty, integrity, and good character are requisites for the position of close personal protection agent. Remember to ask, "Who watches the watchers?" They could be watching you.

REVIEW QUESTIONS

1. Why is it important for an executive protection agent to be able to "get lost in a crowd"?
2. Explain the importance of a sense of humor to an executive protection agent.
3. Why is a supportive, understanding family one of the prime requirements of an executive protection agent?
4. Explain the role of patience and the concept of teamwork to an executive protection assignment.
5. Comment on and discuss the criteria of professional and personal conduct.
6. Explain the relevance of a protection agent's briefcase.
7. Why are shoulder and "small of the back" holsters poor choices for work in close personal protection?
8. Discuss the advantages and disadvantages of wearing body armor.
9. What does it mean to say, "You are not a part of the protectee's world"?
10. Aside from the protective responsibility, what is the proper role and relationship of the protection agent and his protectee.
11. Why should you not brag and talk about previous assignments? After all, the protectee should know about the agent's prior experience and how good an agent he is, right?
12. Why is it important to establish security procedures around the protectee's lifestyle rather than having him alter his routine or plans to accommodate the protective requirement?
13. Explain the significance of proper dress.
14. Explain the principle of "overguarding" the principal. Why is it a poor procedure?
15. Discuss the proper professional relationship with the press.
16. Why is there a conflict between the mission of the press and the goals of protection? What are their similarities?
17. "Who watches the watchers?"

NOTES

1. Frankena, William K. *Ethics*, 2nd ed. Upper Saddle River, NJ: Prentice Hall, 1973, 91. Quoted in Thiroux, Jacques P. *Ethics: Theory and Practice*, 7th ed. Upper Saddle River, NJ: Prentice Hall, 2001, 4.
2. Adopted from a management and supervision instruction memo of an indeterminate source.
3. Josephson, Michael. "The Six Pillars of Character." Character Counts, http://www.charactercounts.org.
4. *Los Angeles Times,* September 15, 2006, B-5.
5. Lonsway, Kimberly A. "Dismantling the Warrior Image: The Role of Women in Community Policing." National Center for Women & Policing, www.feminist.org/police.
6. Survey Report on the Activities of Texas Law Enforcement Agencies (July, 2000). Texas Commission on Law Enforcement Officer Standards and Education. Available at www.tcleose.state.tx.us and cited in Lonsway, "Dismantling the Warrior Image."
7. Lonsway, "Dismantling the Warrior Image."
8. Theme song, 1950's television show "Have Gun, Will Travel."

15 Codes to Live By

Do unto others as they would want to have done unto them.

Choose the course that gives the greater good or the lesser harm.

The choices people make between right and wrong.

Greater love hath no man than this; that a man lay down his life for his friends.

John 15:13, *King James Bible*

Honor never grows old, and honor rejoices the heart of age. It does so because honor is, finally, about defending those noble and worthy things that deserve defending, even if it comes at a high cost. In our time, that may mean social disapproval, public scorn, hardship, persecution, or as always, even death itself. The question remains: What is worth defending? What is worth dying for? What is worth living for?

William J. Bennett, in a lecture to the U.S. Naval Academy, November 24, 1997

ETHICS

Ethics, the moral expression of integrity, trustworthiness, empathy, and understanding, is decision making for the greater good of the individual, society, and mankind. Protective services require integrity (strict personal honesty and all the components of character), trustworthiness, and human interaction. Ethics are about how people's actions, traditions, and beliefs create certain situations and how conflicts are resolved. Personal protection and ethics are about people. The incorporation of the study of ethics as part of life prepares us to come to grips with problems of living in a social, security-concerned environment.

> To be moral one must not just act in accordance with duty; one must act for duty's sake. An action is right if it conforms to a moral rule that the (agent) must follow if he is to act rationally.
>
> **Immanuel Kant**

> Every free action is produced by the concurrence of two causes: one moral, i.e. the will that determines the act; the other physical, i.e. the power that executes it.
>
> **Jean Jacques Rousseau**

Understanding the meaning of the phrases "choose the course that gives the greater good or the lesser harm" and "the choices people make between right and wrong" is the key to determining appropriate courses of action. Ethical principles are applied to choices and decisions that arise in professional, personal, and social lives and reflect our values in a democratic society. Ideal ethical principles include "oughts," conscience, obligations, and appropriateness.

Oughts are the way things should be. They are the paradigm we strive for but seldom attain. The "first principle of moral ethics" states, "We ought to desire only that which is good for us and nothing else." The reverse side of that golden coin says, "We also ought to desire only what is good for others and nothing else."[1] The key words in this definition are ought and desire. A protective agent ought to desire only what is good for his protectee and nothing else. It is the agent's duty to assure "only the best" for his protectee.

Conscience is that little voice in our head that tells us when we have done wrong. People without a conscience have little or no guilt, remorse, or shame. We make our conscience feel better by rationalization, justification, apology, and confession. A protective agent should have a strong conscience but must avoid being so overly sensitive that he is hindered by feelings of remorse and guilt for things he cannot control or influence. On the other hand, guilt over "losing" a protectee will haunt him forever, and his guilt will never be resolved regardless of how many times he apologizes or how much he rationalizes and attempts to justify his failure.

Obligations are results of relationships. One cannot have a relationship without obligations. When a protection agent takes on the responsibility of his protective duties, he has a legal obligation (usually in the form of a formal contract) and a moral obligation to provide his best good-faith effort. Upon assuming his duties, his obligation binds him to service of his client until such time as his services are no longer required. Service to the client and the business relationship means a responsibility to maintain a secure environment and related duties that will ensure the health and safety of the protectee. We all have obligations, and we ought to treat everyone with whom we come into contact with dignity and respect.

Appropriateness simply means "doing the right thing at the right time, in the right way, for all the right reasons."

CODE OF ETHICS

Popular cultures, most professional corporations, military institutions, governmental agencies, and businesses are guided by specific rules enumerated in formal ethical codes of conduct. Inclusive in such codes are ideals and virtues as fairness, courtesy, tolerance, compassion, loyalty, forgiveness, kindliness, integrity, truthfulness, honesty, social responsibility, prudence, justice, temperance, and courage. All are indicative of solid character, reputation, and beneficence (doing good acts for their own sake).

Codes of ethics spell out personality characteristics indicative of solid character, reputation, and beneficence sworn and adhered to by professionals dedicated to the propositions of service, honesty, good faith, and competence.

To be more specific, the role and conduct of the executive protection specialist are spelled out in the "Personal Protection Specialist's Code of Ethics."

PERSONAL PROTECTION SPECIALIST'S CODE OF ETHICS©[2]

- As a personal protection specialist, I am charged with the responsibility for the security, safety, health, and well-being of another human being. In keeping with these obligations, I pledge my honor, reputation, and, if necessary, my life.
- I swear to hold to the highest standards of honesty, courtesy, integrity, and moral character in performance of my duties. I will stay physically fit and mentally strong.
- I will conduct myself in a manner commensurate with the expectations of my position of confidence and trust. I will exhibit patience, understanding, compassion, loyalty, and courage.
- I shall always maintain a professional employee–employer relationship between myself and those I am assigned to protect.
- I will treat all persons with dignity and respect. I will treat the property of those I am assigned to protect with care and hold as confidential and private all personal and professional information I am privileged to hear and see.
- I will not engage in unnecessary conversation, nor will I ever discuss prior assignments, other clients, or their businesses.
- I will deport myself in a manner that will gain the respect and good will of my client, his family, staff, and acquaintances.
- I will establish procedures that will only minimally disrupt the client's lifestyle and personal routine while maintaining a posture that does not draw attention to myself or my charge.
- I will be diligent and dependable, observing truth, accuracy, and discretion while discharging my responsibilities without permitting my personal feelings, prejudices, attitudes, animosities, or friendships to influence my judgment.
- I will remain aware of my personal and professional responsibilities and will use my special knowledge, training, and skills for the security, safety, health, and well-being of those I am charged with protecting.
- I swear to high ethical and moral convictions and will perform my obligations with truthfulness, respect, integrity, and trustworthiness. I hold these virtues as self-evident, for I am a personal protection specialist.

DEFINITION OF THE CODE OF ETHICS

"As a personal protection specialist" (This is my occupation, profession, passion.)

"I am charged" (It is my responsibility, my duty.)

"with the responsibility" (accountability, obligation, and charge)

"for the security, safety, health, and well-being" (a guard to those who have no protection)

"of another human being." (man, woman, or child)

"In keeping with these obligations," (It is my duty to fulfill my responsibilities as charged.)

"I pledge my honor, reputation, and, if necessary, my life. (I am willing to make any sacrifice.)

"I swear" (I give an oath, dedication, and affirmation.)

"to hold to the highest standards of honesty, courtesy, integrity, and moral character" (ethical, brave, and respectful)

"in performance of my duties." (as well as in my private life)

"I will stay physically fit and mentally strong." (Physical conditioning and mental soundness are basic requirements.)

"I will conduct myself in a manner commensurate with the expectations of my position of confidence and trust." (The protection specialist is held in high esteem and often privy to proprietary and top secret information. As such, he must always display a demeanor and conduct beyond question and continue to be "worthy of confidence and trust.")

"I will exhibit patience, understanding, compassion, loyalty and courage." (the human side of the protection specialist)

"I shall always maintain a professional employee–employer relationship between myself and those I am assigned to protect." (The protection specialist is an employee, not a pal, relative, or associate of the person being protected. As an employee, he is expected to conduct himself accordingly and never cross the line.)

"I will treat all persons with dignity and respect." (Everyone is entitled to be treated fairly and respectfully as a fellow human, regardless of his political, economic, or social standing.)

"I will treat the property of those I am assigned to protect with care" (If it is not yours, do not touch it! If you must touch, do not bend, staple, or mutilate.)

"and hold as confidential and private all personal and professional information I am privileged to hear and see." (What you see and hear stays where you saw and heard it.)

"I will not engage in unnecessary conversation" (No one likes someone who talks excessively, unnecessarily, and pointlessly. Let the person being protected initiate the conversation.)

"nor will I ever discuss prior assignments, other protectees, or their businesses." (To do so will lead the person being protected to believe you will talk about him and his business, lowering the level of "confidence and trust.")

"I will deport myself in a manner that will gain the respect and good will of my protectee, his family, staff, and acquaintances." (Good will is like a bank deposit; it is good to have when needed and it makes the duties easier.)

"I will establish procedures that will only minimally disrupt the protectee's lifestyle and personal routine" (Security is an inconvenience, and security procedures, while necessary, may not be consistent with the protectee's wishes for privacy and personal habits.)

"while maintaining a posture that does not draw attention to myself or my charge." (Low key and "hidden in plain sight." High profile draws attention of everyone, including those who would harm the person being protected.)

"I will be diligent and dependable, observing truth, accuracy, and discretion while discharging my responsibilities" (I will pay attention to detail, be "on time all the time," and successfully accomplish all duties using good judgment, without being deceptive or false.)

"without permitting my personal feelings, prejudices, attitudes, animosities, or friendships to influence my judgment." (There will be times when the protectee may be of a different race, religion, or political affiliation; he may be antisocial, demanding, and difficult to please. The protection specialist must overlook all of this and carry on his responsibilities regardless of his personal feelings toward the protectee.)

"I will remain aware of my personal and professional responsibilities" (Do not lapse into complacency, forgetfulness, or irresponsibility; stay alert to all possible circumstances at all times.)

"and will use my special knowledge, training, and skills for the security, safety, health, and well-being of those I am charged with protecting." (This is your reason for being a protection specialist and obtaining the necessary knowledge and skills to successfully complete your duties and responsibilities.)

"I swear to high ethical and moral convictions and will perform my obligations with truthfulness, respect, integrity, and trustworthiness." (I take an oath to maintain the set and prescribed standards my position demands.)

"I hold these virtues as self-evident, for I am a personal protection specialist." (Beyond question, this is what I know, do, and expect, because that is what I am.)

SAMURAI CODE

Bushido (the Way of the Warrior), established centuries ago, is a universal code of personal conduct as relevant for today's living as it was when Samurai were the elite class of warriors (or protectors) for Japanese shoguns and royalty. A professional close protection agent should embrace these concepts and make them a way of life.

Honesty and Justice—Gi

Be exactly honest throughout your dealings with all people. Believe in justice, not from other people, but from yourself. To the true Samurai, there are no shades of gray in the matter of honesty and loyalty. There is only right and wrong.

Polite Courtesy—Rei

Samurai have no reason to be cruel. They do not need to prove their strength. A Samurai is courteous even to his enemies. Without this outward show of respect, we are nothing more than animals.

Heroic Courage—Yu

Rise up above the masses of people who are afraid to act. Hiding like a turtle in a shell is not living at all. A Samurai must have heroic courage. It is absolutely risky. It is dangerous. It is living life completely, fully, and wonderfully. Heroic courage is not blind. It is intelligent and strong. Replace fear with respect and caution.

Honor—Meiyo

A true Samurai has only one judge of honor and this is himself. Decisions you make and how these decisions are carried out are a reflection of who you truly are. You cannot hide from yourself.

Compassion—Jin

Through intense training, the Samurai becomes quick and strong. He is not as other men. He develops a power that must be used for the good of all. He has compassion. He helps people at every opportunity. If an opportunity does not arise, he goes out of his way to find one.

Complete Sincerity—Makoto

When a Samurai has said he will perform an action, it is as good as done. Nothing will stop him from completing what he has said he will do. He does not have to give his word. He does not have to promise. Speaking and doing are the same action.

Duty and Loyalty—Chugo

For the Samurai, having done something or said something, he knows he owns that thing. He is responsible for it and all the consequences that follow. A Samurai is immensely loyal to those in his care. To those for whom he is responsible, he remains fiercely true.

HONESTY AND INTEGRITY—A VALUES CONVERSATION[3]

It is impossible to spend any time in law enforcement, the military [or personal protection] without hearing about at least two values: honesty and integrity. We hear about these values early in our careers. Virtually every presenter at an academy graduation will incorporate those words into his or her speech. Honesty and integrity are powerful, and they mean more to us than mere words. Still, do we really understand what honesty and integrity mean? More importantly, how do we live our lives with both of these values in them?

In my opinion, dictionary definitions mean very little. In this industry, we use these terms so often they sound clichéd. As such, they have lost their meaning. Worse yet, I imagine that most of us explore these concepts only superficially. Perhaps we only scratch the surface, because we don't understand the material. It is likely we're just too embarrassed to admit it.

So, how are we to lead our lives with honesty and integrity, when we aren't really sure what these qualities are? Personally and professionally, I have noted that most people cannot tell the difference between honesty and integrity. We use the terms synonymously. Although inevitably intertwined, honesty and integrity are demonstrably different.

One cannot have integrity without honesty; yet, one can be honest and have no integrity. Personal intentions apply, but integrity matters only when we share it with others. Honesty may be individual, but integrity is applied to our relationships.

Honesty and truth are elements of integrity. Integrity, however, is often not as sound, solid, or steadfast as we wish it were. One merely need ask others for the definitions of these words, and we will find this conversation is as clear as mud. In the end, both values are only as important as they relate to trust. Trust must be shared. As I mention often, whether the trust be public or personal, life is about relationships. Without trust, real relationships do not exist.

DEFINITIONS

To illustrate my point, we'll start with Merriam-Webster's definitions:

> *Honesty:* 1. obsolete: *chastity*; 2 a: fairness and straightforwardness of con-
> duct; b. adherence to the facts: *sincerity.* Synonyms*: honesty, honor,*
> *integrity, probity* mean uprightness of character or actions. Honesty
> implies a refusal to lie, steal, or deceive in any way. *Honor* suggests an
> active or anxious regard for the standards of one's profession, calling,
> or position. *Integrity* implies trustworthiness and incorruptibility to a
> degree that one is incapable of being false to a trust, responsibility, or
> pledge. *Probity* implies tried and proven honesty or integrity. [4]
> *Integrity:* 2. firm adherence to a code of especially moral or artistic values;
> *incorruptibility; 3.* an unimpaired condition; soundness; 3. the quality
> or state of being complete or undivided; *completeness.* Synonym*,* see
> *honesty.* [5]

If *honesty* and *integrity* are synonymous, how are they different?

CONNOTATIONS

At the Sherman Block Supervisory Leadership Institute (SB-SLI),[6] where I serve as an auditor, we discuss honesty and integrity *ad nauseam.* To attend SB-SLI, one must be a sergeant for at least two years. Just to attend SLI, the selection process is very competitive. Selection and graduation are considered quite prestigious. Students must volunteer to be selected, and not everyone is chosen.

Yet consistently, in my own class and those I have audited, I watch in awe and dismay as SB-SLI students struggle with these two terms. Dismally, we demonstrate a distinct and disappointing lack of compassion for them. For me, at least, it is hardly encouraging, watching sergeants struggle in this way. I fear we cannot teach what we do not understand. More importantly, I feel we cannot live in a manner, which we cannot explain.

In my humble opinion, honesty means commitment to the truth, particularly at personal cost. True honesty is measured by a difficulty factor. The harder it is for one to tell the truth, the more trustworthy one becomes by the telling of it.

The truth is invaluable, when measured by selflessness. We can be trusted, but only by admitting our mistakes. When we do this, we sacrifice our safety. We must never forget that all of us make mistakes. We are human. Yet, when it comes to mistakes, we are deplorably ruthless when it comes to confessing the sins of others. At times, we even seem to enjoy holding others accountable. Nothing is easier than pointing the finger at someone else. So how many of us will "cowboy up" when that finger is pointed in our direction, especially when life, finances, and reputations hang in the balance? Why is it so easy for us to be such hypocrites?

WALKING THE TALK

Without personal cost, honesty is easy. We can tell the truth, if we don't have to sacrifice. So, what if the truth can harm us? What if the truth endangers our position? What if the truth includes revealing facts that are less than flattering? Will we tell the truth then? Aren't these the specific scenarios, when telling the truth is most important?

The selfish part of our human nature motivates us to lie, to escape negative consequences. The more negative we perceive the consequence to be, the more likely we will lie. We believe we are protecting ourselves. Self-preservation is the very foundation of selfishness.

As selfish youngsters, we all considered lying. In truth, we did it! If we met success the first time we lied, we were encouraged to do it again. That's why lying is so dangerous. Lying is based on fear. We are afraid that we will be rejected, if we tell the truth.

When we tell the truth fearlessly, even at personal cost, we can be trusted. For goodness' sake, we are human! We're never perfect. Still trust is necessary in good relationships, and trust is critical to this industry. If we cannot be placed in faith and confidence, we are useless. Everything unravels and comes apart. That's how honesty relates to integrity. Honesty breeds trust. Together, both give birth to integrity. Trust completes our relationships.

MORE THAN THE SUM OF OUR PARTS

Integrity is about completeness. If honesty is keeping the truth, then integrity is keeping our word. To whom do we give our word? Are we bound by our word, thus fulfilling the expectations of our relationships?

Integrity is a commitment to a comprehensive, all-encompassing value system, and ultimately, how we measure our character. We either commit, or we don't. To measure integrity in others, we must begin with an honest self-evaluation. We ought not make promises we cannot keep. Promises are not meant to be broken. Oaths are not necessary for men of integrity.

In truth, self-evaluation is where we fail most often. Yet without it, there is no integrity. Unfortunately, our integrity is attacked constantly. Convenience, comfort, and complacency abet such attacks. If we are not careful, we don't even realize the attack is coming.

ENTROPY

Rarely is our integrity threatened in one fell swoop, as if it were a brand-new building suddenly demolished with a wrecking ball. Usually, human character is eroded by a series of seemingly insignificant acts or omissions that together, combine to create a person who is unrecognizable in the mirror.

Our character edifice is whittled away, after being subjected to worldly threats, both real and imagined, as we weather the elements. Ultimately, situational ethics cause us to rationalize away this behavior. Moral relativism does not help us relate to each other. If we are fortunate, life will humble us. With humility, we may come to understand that what ever we try to protect, by compromising our integrity, is hardly worth saving.

Most dangerously, when we get away with such behavior, the more frequent it becomes. We must be vigilant to avoid it. Vigilance demands we admit our own flaws first. By admitting our humanity, we can earn the trust of other humans.

PERSONAL VALUES AND PERSONAL PROTECTION

We cannot protect if we cannot be trusted. Trust is born by our telling the truth unabashedly, humbly, and fearlessly. I would never consider having someone protect me, if he or she could not be trusted.

Ironically, I have found that others are able to forgive us, provided we admit our mistakes in the first place. When we lie, we fatally assume others will not forgive us, or that somehow they are incapable of forgiving.

I wouldn't want to work under those conditions. Good relationships preclude negative fantasies. Integrity is only significant as it relates to other people. People are important and life is about relationships. Without people with whom to share it, integrity *is* just a word.

Most truths are so naked, that people feel sorry for them and cover them up, at least a little bit.

Edward R. Murrow (1908–1965)

LAW ENFORCEMENT CODE OF ETHICS

Another code of ethics that a professional personal protection agent must understand and follow was developed by the International Association of Chiefs of Police (IACP). This code, while directed to the law enforcement officer, is also highly relevant to the modern protection agent who embodies traits of honesty, trustworthiness, integrity, fairness, tolerance, empathy, respect, responsibility, loyalty, accountability, and self-control (self-discipline).

> As a law enforcement officer, my fundamental duty is to: serve the community; safeguard lives and property; protect the innocent against deception, the weak against oppression or intimidation and the peaceful against violence or disorder; and respect the constitutional rights of all to liberty, equality, and justice.

> I will keep my private life unsullied as an example to all and will behave in a manner that does not bring discredit to me or to my agency. I will maintain courageous calm in the face of danger, scorn, or ridicule; develop self-restraint; and be constantly mindful of the welfare of others. Honest in thought and deed both in my personal and official life, I will be exemplary in obeying the law and the regulations of my department. Whatever I see or hear of a confidential nature or that is confided to me in my official capacity will be kept secret unless revelation is necessary in the performance of my duty.

> I will never act officiously or permit personal feelings, prejudices, political beliefs, aspirations, animosities or friendships to influence my decisions. With no compromise for crime and with relentless prosecution of criminals, I will enforce the law courteously and appropriately without favor, malice, or ill will, never employing unnecessary force or violence and never accepting gratuities.

> I recognize the badge of my office as a symbol of public faith, and I accept it as a public trust to be held so long as I am true to the ethics of police service. I will never engage in acts of corruption or bribery nor will I will ever condone such acts by other police officers. I will cooperate with all legally authorized agencies and their representatives in the pursuit of justice.

> I know that I alone am responsible for my own standard of professional performance and will take every reasonable opportunity to enhance and improve my level of knowledge and competence.

> I will constantly strive to achieve these objectives and ideals, dedicating myself before God to my chosen profession... law enforcement.

This code, while using terms such as law enforcement officer, enforce the law, prosecution of criminals, and chosen profession... law enforcement, can very easily be adopted by a protection agent by substituting appropriate wording to symbolize his own personal and professional ethics.

SUMMARY

Many professions, businesses, and organizations swear to a code of ethics. The codes are specifically written for each different occupation, yet they have certain similarities. By occupational definition, truth, trust, confidence, courage, and a willingness to make necessary sacrifices are woven into the code of ethics of a close personal protection agent.

REVIEW QUESTIONS

1. Define *ethics*.
2. Explain, in your own words, the meaning of the quotations by Immanuel Kant and Jean Jacques Rousseau found on the first page of this chapter.
3. Why should there be a Close Personal Protection Code of Ethics for protection agents?
4. Explain the reference to the Samurai Code and why such an old code of ethics is still relevant.
5. What are obligations and why should they be honored, even at personal expense?
6. Explain the difference between "oughts" or "shoulds" and "is" or "reality."
7. In your own words, explain honesty and integrity.
8. Write your own personal code of ethics.

NOTES

1. Ruggiero, Vincent Ryan. *Thinking Critically about Ethical Issues*, 5th ed. Mountain View, CA: Mayfield Publishing, 2001.
2. Copyright D. L. June, October 2001. This code, written and copyrighted by Dale L. June, may be reproduced and used for purposes of ethical training of protective agents.
3. This essay was written by E. Alan Normandy, a lieutenant in the South San Francisco Police Department and a student at Henley-Putnam University.
4. http://www.m-w.com/dictionary/honesty.
5. http://www.m-w.com/dictionary/integrity6.
6. http://www.post.ca.gov/training/sbsli.

16 Professionalism and Success

Believe in your best, think your best, study your best, have a goal for your best, never be satisfied with less than your best, try your best—and in the long run, things will work out for the best....

Henry Ford

When you are not training or studying, someone, somewhere is, and when you meet, he will defeat you ...

Bruce Lee

MUNDANCY OF EXCELLENCE[1]

An amateur will practice over and over until he gets it right. A professional will practice over and over until he can't do it wrong.

Anonymous (National Football League advertisement)

On the surface, to include mundancy and excellence in the same sentence is a contradiction in terms. A popular dictionary tells us that mundane means commonplace, everyday, ordinary, and routine, whereas excellence indicates superior merit, rare achievement, and outstanding quality. Yet, it seems appropriate to describe a protective agent in these exact terms simultaneously. For a professional protection agent to reach and maintain the level of quality required of her position and expected by her protectee, she must practice "mundancy of excellence." To a professional, there is only one standard and that is "gold." She cannot think in terms other than excellence. Professionalism begins with the fine points of excellence. According to William Frankena, "Whatever is good will also probably involve 'some kind or degree of excellence.'"1 Therefore, excellence to a professional is ordinary, commonplace, and routine, or in other words, mundane.

On any given day, if you ask ten people to define *professionalism* and *success*, you'll get 50 different definitions and a lot of hemming, hawing, and you-knows. Hundreds of books have been written about professionalism and "secrets of success" by outstanding people like Vince Lombardi, John Wooden, and inspirational writers and speakers of all ilks. With all of this in mind, I will try to be courageous enough to offer my observations of what it takes to be a successful professional.

Professionalism has often been described as receiving money or payment for performing a specific skill with uncommon talent. However, in the real world of conflicting viewpoints, competition, and idealism, there is more to being a professional than making money. A professional is considered to be at the top of the game or his profession. He is there because he is blessed or gifted with certain qualities and an adeptness that others don't have. There is a dedication to develop his special aptitudes to the highest degree and to work, learn, train, and practice to be among the corps of elite individuals in a selected field. A professional is expected to recognize the nuances of the job and to perform the required duties at a supreme level of proficiency and skill for extended periods of time.

Webster's New Twentieth Century Dictionary defines professional as one "worthy of the high standards of a profession" and as "having much experience and great skill in a specified role." Professionalism encompasses a person's attitude, appearance, and personality. There is also more to being a professional than simply possessing the right set of expertise, talent, knowledge, and competence. Contrary to popular belief, especially among professional athletes and entertainers with their "show me the money" attitude, professionalism is a complex description of a person maintaining all of the above traits but also possessing the intangibles of dedication, loyalty, and integrity.

PROFESSIONAL ATTITUDE

Especially important to being a professional is a disposition to do whatever it takes to effectively accomplish the task. A professional's attitude is positive. It is being efficient in all dealings. This businesslike attitude transmits assurance that responsibilities are not being taken lightly. This is not to say that conducting oneself with dignity means being dour or always solemn. It is possible to be cheerful, pleasant, and friendly and still remain businesslike. On the other hand, levity and horseplay at inappropriate times reflect poorly and diminish respect. A professional's attitude is also that of a team player. In the instance of a protection agent, he must have the trust and respect of his fellow agents as well as that of his client. This trust is a constant challenge toward organizational and individual improvement. The team's goals are adopted as one's own.

The professional does not necessarily forfeit his own personal goals but, as an integral instrument of the organization, he places the objectives of the organization above his own. The professional must devote himself to total honesty in all his personal and career dealings. This dedication to an attitude of honesty must never waver or falter. A professional is willing and capable of making the personal sacrifices so often demanded in the interest of his team or his protectee. For example, there is no downtime when working a protective assignment. Every moment is dedicated to the safe pursuit of protectee convenience and security.

When not actually involved in the physical protection of the protectee, a professional will remain immersed in the ancillary duties and anxieties of his responsibility until the task comes to a satisfactory conclusion. A professional goes farther than doing only that which is expected. He will take the extra steps beyond expectation and anticipation to accomplish what is necessary without mistakes. "A professional," according to Frederick Forsyth in *Day of the Jackal*,[2] "does not act out of fervour and is therefore more calm and less likely to make elementary errors." In other words, a professional is capable of living up to his obligations with nearly instinctive precision and imagination; planning, even scripting and rehearsing each detail; anticipating all contingencies and preparing, mentally and physically, to meet the challenges of ever-changing circumstances. That may mean a willingness to work long hours of overtime (sometimes without extra compensation) or to travel away from home for extended periods of time with very short notice. It may mean covering the same ground again and again to determine and correct any flaws, oversights, or inconsistencies.

PROFESSIONAL APPEARANCE

The outward appearance of a professional reflects his inner qualities. One's physical image is an important asset in commanding respect. The Scottish poet Robert Burns said, "If only God would give us the gift to see ourselves as others see us." This certainly would be true of protection agents and the impressions they project. There may be occasions when thousands see a protection agent through news coverage of his protectee. How the public judges the agent is based primarily on a visual impression. If the agent is sharply dressed, is clean-shaven, and has neatly groomed hair, he engenders a feeling of certainty and respect. Physical appearances alone, however, do not make an individual a professional. He must have a strong belief in his own competence and display that confidence to all. Everyone has periods of depression and gets tired, worried, or discouraged. Every protection agent can readily recall missing a holiday, anniversary, birthday, or other special occasion because he had to work or travel. A professional must conceal his feelings and disappointments. He exhibits a confident, courteous, and enthusiastic manner to those he works with, to his client, and to the public. Remaining calm and poised under stress is vitally important and indicative of a professional.

PROFESSIONAL PERSONALITY

The personality of a professional must be unique. The ability to communicate with and get along with all types of people is imperative. He needs to believe he is worthy of the high standards of his profession but manifest no air of superiority. He takes constructive criticism and uses it to improve his methods of working with others, and he does this without resentment. He remains unexcitable and even-tempered. An executive protection agent's personality should be one of quiet efficiency—of getting the job done well and having no need or desire for public notoriety. He does not expect reward or great acclaim for performing the duties required of him.

A professional is accomplished in interpersonal relations as well as the technical aspects of his particular vocation. Traditionally, the public holds protection agents in high esteem, believing them to be gentlemen and highly trained individuals, physically and psychologically prepared for any eventuality. They are worthy of confidence and trust.

Most protectees expect a protection agent to possess good communication and people skills commensurate with the responsibility of the position and a base of knowledge in topics beyond their vocation. A professional will refrain from using occupational jargon or slang and technical language when communicating with those outside of his occupation. A professional's appearance, character, and demeanor often (rightly or wrongly) communicate unspoken volumes about his commitment and capability. A professional maintains high personal, moral, and occupational standards and is continually seeking to improve his command of his craft, his knowledge, and his range of expertise. He accomplishes this by working hard while diplomatically and intelligently maintaining the required protocols to appropriately represent himself, his organization and protectee, and sometimes his government!

KEYS TO PROFESSIONALISM AND SUCCESS

It is important that a protection agent remain knowledgeable and physically capable of performing his duties at the highest level. That means continuous and ongoing training and education. An effective running or other workout program and any martial arts or "unarmed defense" practice will provide appropriate physical training. Security associations and magazines provide the latest information relative to security equipment, technology, and procedures. A professional protection specialist should attend security association meetings to exchange information and stay abreast of the changes in the profession. He should subscribe to magazines that feature articles about the security industry, covering everything from access control and fire prevention to procedures and practices. Most security magazine subscriptions are free to security professionals.

TRAINING, EDUCATION, AND EXPERIENCE TRIAL

The evolution of modern close personal protection specialists owes a debt to the U.S. Secret Service for providing a model for the professional protective agent. Agents belonging to various government protection agencies have maintained a professional image over many years and are highly educated before beginning their professional training. Operators in the private security industry have not always been so educated and trained.

Security in the twenty-first century must adjust with changes in society. Workplace violence, terrorism, corporate theft, and a host of other security-related threats, from within and abroad, will undoubtedly increase, making the security field a growing industry. More sophisticated measures used by terrorists, who in many cases have more technological and financial resources available, make training very important to the security industry. The protection agent, to function properly, must change with the times and conditions and present himself in a professional manner. Agents should cross-train in the different security fields to stay competitive and updated in their field. Training, education, and experience are everything!

Today's close protection specialist is highly trained and sophisticated and protects clients by preventing trouble rather than relying on an *ad hoc* response during a crisis. Education, training, competence, and expertise are hallmarks of professionals. So are personal standards, codes of conduct, ethics, morals, and an understanding of the consequences of both action and inaction.

Close personal protection as a profession is still in its infancy as it pertains to recognition of high standards, educational requirements, and personal conduct. We are over the learning curve relating to methods, but the bar of professionalism is still being raised.

Vires per Eruditionem—Strength through Education[3]

In the early 1960s, only a handful of colleges and universities offered degrees in police science and administration. Police departments did not require their officers to be college educated. It was considered sufficient if the officer held a high school diploma or GED. Often, military service could be substituted for educational requirements.

With the passing of years, society, the sophistication of crime, and the complexities of the criminal justice system (law enforcement, the courts, and corrections) have evolved into forces demanding professionalism in the law enforcement community. Colleges and universities have responded with upgraded curricula, renaming them *criminal justice* programs.

TWENTY-FIRST CENTURY EDUCATIONAL PIONEERS

Today, criminal justice programs are common, and police departments and other law enforcement agencies recruit criminal justice majors with bachelor's and master's degrees. The state of personal protection and intelligence services has begun the same type of evolution. Occupations from *bodyguards* to *executive protection* to *close personal protection specialists* require professionals. By definition, professionalism includes education. These fields of specialization are expected to grow at a dizzying rate. The demand will soon outstrip the supply of well-educated and trained professional protection specialists. A career in the protective and intelligence services is rewarding in many ways; it offers monetary incentives, world travel, prestige, adventure, and countless other benefits whose value cannot always be measured. The most important, though, is knowing that, at the end of the day, your actions and conduct have made the client's life a little easier, allowed him to carry out his normal activities, and perhaps even made the difference between life and death. To reach the level of competence expected of a professional demands formal education and training, whetted by experience.

Even before the attacks on the World Trade Center and Pentagon on September 11, 2001, recognizing a growing need for professional security specialists, colleges and universities began offering courses in security management, risk assessment, and other security-related topics designed to graduate security professionals. Since the bombings and the creation of a cabinet-level Department of Homeland Security, a few universities have begun to offer courses in homeland security, but those courses do not yet recognize or include the importance of close personal protection in overall security operations.

Close personal protection (also known as *executive protection*) is a professional and recognized occupation that has gained its place in the business world as well as the entertainment industry, where agents protect celebrities, VIPs, and political figures. Security-experienced personnel (not necessarily educators) staff training venues, and the subject matter is restricted to and focused on training exclusively in the art of protection. It is left to the students to obtain a fully rounded education elsewhere.

One pioneer and leader in this specialized field of education is the Henley-Putnam University[4] (formerly named the California University of Protection and Intelligence Management). Students from law enforcement, military, intelligence, and private sectors can obtain bachelor's and master's degrees in management of personal protection, intelligence management, or terrorism and counterterrorism.

Henley-Putnam University came into being after more than twelve years of planning and research to contribute to the professional development of the protection, intelligence, and counterterrorism fields. The founders designed the university to meet the strategic security industry's establishment of higher educational standards—and in keeping with that intent, hired only faculty with real-world experience in their respective fields. According to Nirmalya Bhowmick, founder and chairman of Henley-Putnam, "The ultimate purpose of our education and training is to enhance the knowledge of prevention and deterrence of terrorism and assassinations for professionals whose primary mission is the protection of human life. It is evident to all that the need for such training is rapidly growing."

The university's management team chose the name Henley-Putnam University as a tribute to historical figures Colonel David Henley (General Washington's chief intelligence officer in the War of Independence) and General Israel Putnam, to whom is attributed the command, "Don't fire until you see the whites of their eyes" at the battle of Bunker Hill. This name reflects the spirit of the school. It allows them to tell the story of Henley and Putnam, who were among the first intelligence officers in U.S. history. Few people are aware of the vital role that intelligence played in the defeat of the British by America's first spymaster, George Washington.

Henley-Putnam University is the premier university for higher education in the advancing fields of protection, intelligence, and counterterrorism. The university received accreditation for its undergraduate and graduate degree programs in 2007, from the Accrediting Commission of the Distance Education and Training Council (DETC). The DETC is recognized by the U.S. Secretary of Education and by the Council for Higher Education Accreditation.

Greg Von Gehr, Henley-Putnam CEO said, "With the accomplishment of DETC accreditation, we officially join the ranks of the best distance learning colleges and universities in the United States. Police officers, intelligence professionals and military personnel involved in the strategic security industry now have an education option with much more rigor and credibility, delivered by a faculty rich with real world experience from the military, police, CIA, FBI, Secret Service, and many other similar agencies."

As far as it is known at the time of this writing, this is the only university in the world authorized by a state (California) educational agency to award bachelor's and master's degrees in specialized areas of the protective-intelligence services and to be awarded accreditation.

Programs feature on-line classes in academic and practical applications ranging from basic to advanced close personal protection, intelligence methods, and management and counterterrorism.

Headquartered in San Jose, California, the university administration and staff are passionate about "passing the torch to a new generation." The university demands that its faculty meet rigorous educational and occupational standards and be dedicated to one purpose: providing the necessary leadership to inspire students to use their imaginations, motivations, and dedication to explore means, methods, and procedures for providing the best in protective and intelligence management and counterterrorism. The university administration, staff, and faculty believe that working toward a democratic world of freedom and liberty through education, while sustaining the highest levels of security, is the best way to pass the torch.

The founder of the university, Nirmalya Bhowmick, sees specific and general university education as the solution to national security training needs. He said, "We plan on fulfilling training ideals and raising standards. We have set high standards for our instructors and graduates. Each instructor, having met certain educational requirements, has a solid commitment to providing the best training and education possible. It is a question of personal ethics to teach to the highest standards from beginning to end—for the entry-level beginner as well as the professional experienced veteran."

TRAINING, EDUCATION, EXPERIENCE

It has been said that freedom and strength flow through education. "The security of a nation is the education of its youth." Education is a pillar of the training, experience, and education triangle. Training and experience are nearly synonymous in that training means *practical instruction*, and experience refers to *education gained by seeing and doing*. Naturally, both are important factors in any endeavor, especially one as potentially dangerous as close personal protection. But it is education, the third element of the equation triangle (the process of learning and training) that forms the base of a well-rounded personal protection specialist.

Training teaches how and when to react; education teaches how to think; experience equals reaction plus thought. We enjoy the comfort of opinions without the discomfort of thought.

John F. Kennedy

One piece of advice I have given my children for many years is, "If you are talking, you are not listening; if you are not listening, you are not learning." Talking is easy, but thinking is very difficult; it requires focus, motivation, purpose, intention, and good sense. Knowledge, experience, and maturity make wisdom. A very wise mentor of mine, who enjoyed speaking in parables to make people think, once said, "Wisdom is like social security." I didn't get it and said so. His simple answer was,

"You'll get it at sixty-five." What he meant was that wisdom comes with maturity and is the "grandfather" of training, education, and experience.

> To know wisdom and instruction; to perceive the words of understanding; to receive the instruction of wisdom, justice, and judgment, and equity; to give subtlety to the simple, to the young man knowledge and discretion. A wise man will hear, and will increase learning; and a man of understanding shall attain unto wise counsels: To understand a proverb, and the interpretation; the words of the wise, and their dark sayings. The fear of [ignorance] is the beginning of knowledge: but fools despise wisdom and instruction.
>
> **Proverbs, chapter 1**

For every problem there is a solution. Finding a solution takes thinking. Logic plus facts makes a winnable argument. Loud arguing and emotional reasoning accomplish nothing beyond setting the stage for a fight. Solving a problem takes looking at the "givens" and adding thinking and reasonable logic to arrive at a solution or a new idea. (Tenth-grade geometry!)

A close personal protection agent relies on his brain.

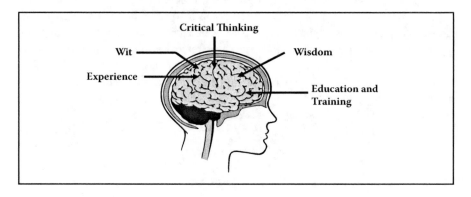

I can give you knowledge, but I can't make you think.

Anonymous

Problem solving may require thinking creatively and beyond the ordinary or expected. The process of creative thinking begins with being a keen observer, identifying a problem, and understanding it. As stated elsewhere, observation means being a good watcher, listener, and learner. Knowing what others have done and how they resolved problems allows for adapting their solutions and ideas to your current problem while trusting your own intuition, gut feelings, and hunches and being an innovator. "Running water does not stagnate," is a metaphor for, "Don't wait until the problem has become unmanageable or until someone else comes forward with a solution." You can often solve a problem by simply doing something. Do not fall into the tar pit of being a "do nothing" person. An old, childish rhyme sums up the person who encounters a problem and is so fixated on it that he doesn't seek the solution, "When in worry, when in doubt, flap your arms and run about."

Fuzzy problem solving comes from that type of fuzzy thinking. Creative problem solving begins with a feeling (emotion or intuition), a hunch, a gut reaction or thought, or an idea. It may be a result of "multiple perception" when, suddenly seeing the problem in a new light, the answer seems to appear from thin air. Creative thinking is the offspring of intuition and emotion. The problem solver breaks out of his comfort zone and puts fuzzy thinking behind him, pouring emotion, intellect, and intuition into the solution.

CRITICAL THINKING

Critical thinking is analysis through the asking of questions and the employment of deductive reasoning. It is a basic tool of investigators, researchers, writers, students, and professionals. When all facts and circumstances are gathered and organized, the critical thinker (through logic and deduction) is able to arrive at a conclusion commensurate with the facts. Critical-thinking tools include emotional feelings, visual images, bodily sensations, reproducible patterns, and analogies. A good critical thinker can translate these tools into thoughts, expressing insight that can give rise to new ideas in others' minds.

Critical thinking is the ability to view a particular set of circumstances from a number of perspectives and form an inference based on analysis, reasoning, logic, experience, and training. It is synonymous with ensuring that you account for all significant consequences by developing the habit of using your imagination. Critical thinkers are called "imaginators," having the ability to look at something and see more than the physical representation. For example, a critically thinking protection agent will look at an empty football stadium and see thousands of people, each having the potential to harm his protectee. He will visualize his protectee standing at a podium on the 50-yard line and ask himself, "If given this assignment, how would I best protect him?" His answer would lie in how he was able to imagine all scenarios and reasonably deduct logical solutions. In literature, Sherlock Holmes (created by Sir Arthur Conan Doyle) is famous for his deductive reasoning in solving the "unsolvable" mystery. Yet it is no mystery how he arrived at his conclusions. He viewed a problem from all possible perspectives; asked himself every question related to the facts; weighed in with his training, education, and experience; and, with a "small leap of imagination," analyzed each possible inference to arrive at the final solution.

In summary, critical thinking means analysis—the breaking down of the total problem into smaller fragments, with each component being thoroughly examined in relation to other factors and evolving a reasonable (and provable) hypothesis. The process of arriving at what could reasonably be termed "probable cause" or "a likely solution" includes a set of facts, circumstances, or statements received through physical collection of all data and communication. After seeing, hearing, or reading the information, the receiver begins a process of mental analysis, consideration, and thoughtful deduction until he arrives at a conclusion. The critica-thinking process includes mentally (or in writing) asking the following questions:

1. What was the data (article, movie, book, statement, information, or data) all about?
2. What parts of it were the most important?
3. What are the key elements or ideas?
4. What opinions, if any, did it contain?
5. What is my opinion of it?
6. What element makes it unique?
7. What is the value of this information, or what is my evaluation of it?
8. What was the particular slant or spin of the information?
9. Does the writer or presenter have a hidden agenda? If so, what is it?
10. What message was the speaker or writer trying to convey?
11. Should this information be blindly and strictly adhered to and totally believed because an expert or figure of authority generated it?
12. What are the *givens* (i.e., indisputable facts that do not have to be proven)?
13. What is the source of the information? What is the assessment of the source?
14. What is the credibility and weight of the information?
15. Does this parallel or resemble anything I have already learned?
16. If it does resemble something I have already learned, how do they fit together?
17. How can I paraphrase the information in my own terms?
18. How would I sum up the information in one sentence? How would I synopsize the meaning of this information and explain it to others in more common terminology?
19. Do I still have any unanswered questions? What are they? Where and how do they fit?
20. Does the information raise new questions? How would I answer them?
21. What specifics should I focus on? How can I view them in a different light?
22. How much of the information is true and factual? What is false or mere filler?
23. Is the information vague or specific? For example, "There were several people in the room" as opposed to "There were 45 people—23 men, and 22 women—in the Forever Rest Hotel, room 254."
24. If the information is vague, is there a specific reason for that?
25. Is the information easily understood, or are there double entendres, jargon, or slang that confuse the reader?
26. Are there unsustained statements made or unanswered questions?
27. What other findings, ideas, or conclusions have others arrived at?
28. How are my findings and conclusions different? Why?
29. What are all the alternatives or what are some solutions?
30. What are all the consequences of this information? Have I looked at all the consequences?
31. Are there any "absolute" words (e.g., *always, never, perpetually*) that can be disputed?
32. Is the information based on fact or someone's opinion? What part is fact? Is the factual information supported by evidence? What is editorial or merely opinion?
33. What part of this information is grounded in rumor, gossip, or innuendo?

34. What is the source of the information thinking or feeling? What is (was) the source's mind-set?
35. If I heard this information in a conversation with the source, how would I respond?
36. Does this information persuade me one way or another?
37. What effect does the media, personal prejudices, or outside influence have on my thoughts?
38. What is being done with the information? How can it be used?
39. What should be done? What are the next steps? What followup is required?
40. How does this information fit into the big picture? Am I seeing the full view?
41. Can I take this information and argue it from both sides?
42. What is the proper order of the priorities or events in the information?
43. What new ideas does this information give?
44. Are the new ideas practical, and how will others view them?
45. Can the new ideas be sustained when critically assessed by others?
46. What points need further clarification, and did the information hold the receiver's attention?
47. What points could have been illustrated with examples, an anecdote, or quotation, or perhaps a fragment of recognizable literature?

The following figure is used to illustrate or diagram the concept of critical thinking:

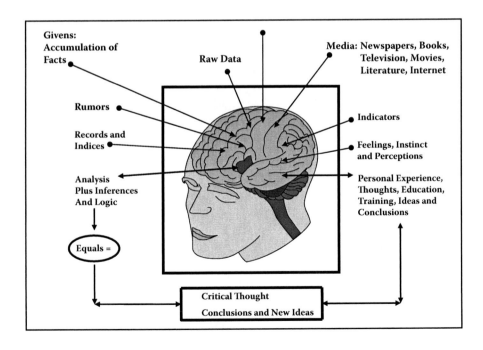

As shown in the figure, as the stimuli (or information) from a nearly endless variety of sources is received by the brain, it is mixed and churned around with the individual's questions much as water, gravel, sand, and concrete mix are blended in a rotating cement mixer. The end product is then poured out as analyzed data with deductive reasoning (inferences) and logic. As a result, the finished matter is a complete critical thought, that is, new conclusions and ideas. The new thoughts and ideas can then be recycled as fresh stimuli ad infinitum.

We are all inherently capable of critical thinking, but it is a skill that needs to be developed. Emotion and intellect are bound together in critical thinking and problem solving. Some people may look at a situation and immediately see a solution, but others may be inspired by the actions of other people in similar situations. Sometimes critical thinking is referred to as common sense or, in older terms, native horse sense. However you describe it, critical thinking is an important tool of a protective agent, a problem solver, a dreamer, and a creative artist.

DECISION MAKING

Decision making is closely related to critical thinking and anticipation. As scenarios are anticipated, decisions must be made vis-à-vis all of the whos, whats, wheres, whens, whys, and hows. The more information is available, the easier it is to forecast the probable consequences of any overlooked possibilities. An advance man should anticipate everything on a daily basis—assault, illness, injury, accident, trauma, and other activities and natural disasters that can compromise the safe environment of the protectee. His anticipation is predicated on obtaining information (intelligence gathering), analyzing data, and making the correct assumptions.

A good (successful) advance involves being aware of all consequences and obligations (anticipating problems) relating to every decision made by the advance agent. To paraphrase Sir Isaac Newton, "For every action (or inaction) there is an opposite and direct reaction (or consequence)." In other words, everything we do (or not do) and decisions we make (or do not make) have a direct consequence. According to a popular dictionary, the common meanings of *consequence* are as follows: 1. the effect, result, or outcome; 2. the conclusion reached as the result of reasoning, inference; 3. importance or significance.

There are at least eight sets of consequences that can or might occur as a result of an action (or inaction):

1. Beneficial or harmful
2. Long-term or short-term
3. Obvious or subtle
4. Instant or delayed
5. Physical or emotional
6. Intentional or unintentional
7. Moral, ethical, or legal
8. Requiring further action or no action needed

The same dictionary defines *obligation* as, "Something by which a person is bound to do by a sense of duty." When making decisions, the decision maker must consider the obligations as well as the consequences. A professional follows several factors of ethical and moral obligations. In *Thinking Critically About Ethical Issues*, fifth edition, Vincent Ryan Ruggiero[5] quoted British ethicist W. D. Ross as identifying six moral obligations:

1. Reparation (making amends for the wrongs we have done to someone else)
2. Gratitude (showing appreciation for what someone has done for us)
3. Self-improvement (learning, education, training)
4. Justice (equal treatment for all without bias or prejudice)
5. Beneficence (doing good for the sake of doing good)
6. Nonmaleficence (not doing harm to others)

In expressing the "first principle of moral philosophy," Ruggiero quotes Mortimer Adler. "We ought to desire what is really good for us and nothing else." Of course, an extension of that phrase is, "We ought to desire what is really good for others and nothing else." In decision making and considering all the consequences and obligations, a decision maker (a professional protection agent) might consider what is good for his protectee and nothing else. The agent's number one obligation is the health and well-being of his protectee, but being locked into what is good for his protectee and nothing else eliminates consideration and feeling for the people around them. Thus, a consequence of that attitude is possible animosity toward the agent, his agency, and the protectee. Therefore, a protective agent, while considering what is good for his protectee in terms of security, must also consider what is good and right for others. It is a delicate balance, but a professional agent, in dealing with a variety of personalities, will have developed enough people skills to address the issue of "what is good for all." His decisions will be based on obligations but tempered with consideration of all consequences.

A good decision maker, especially a professional, does not "shotgun" his approach. He zeros in on it, giving it just the right spin in an original and thoughtful manner. Creative thinking and decisive decision making are as important to protective agents as they are to judges, lawyers, police officers, politicians, and executives. In many circles, decision making is portrayed as "thinking on your feet," being mentally flexible enough to instantly find a solution to a problem, eliminate a predicament, or defend his position.

Decision making is not a precise science, and it is not really an art. It does not depend on a particular talent except the ability to anticipate the effects of an action taken or not taken. It often takes moral courage to make a decision and abide by it, regardless of the fallout or what others may think. But life is a matter of decisions, and the professional protection agent must make decisions that could have life or death implications. He measures the consequences of his action or inaction and acts accordingly to do the right thing.

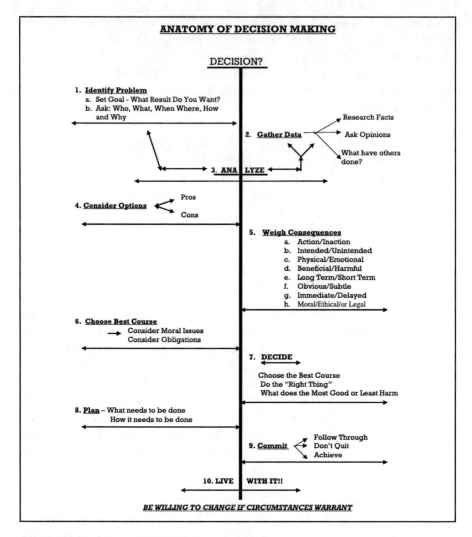

ANATOMY OF DECISION MAKING

DECISION?

1. **Identify Problem**
   a. Set Goal - What Result Do You Want?
   b. Ask: Who, What, When Where, How and Why

2. **Gather Data**
   → Research Facts
   → Ask Opinions
   → What have others done?

3. **ANALYZE**

4. **Consider Options**
   → Pros
   → Cons

5. **Weigh Consequences**
   a. Action/Inaction
   b. Intended/Unintended
   c. Physical/Emotional
   d. Beneficial/Harmful
   e. Long Term/Short Term
   f. Obvious/Subtle
   g. Immediate/Delayed
   h. Moral/Ethical/or Legal

6. **Choose Best Course**
   → Consider Moral Issues
   Consider Obligations

7. **DECIDE**
   Choose the Best Course
   Do the "Right Thing"
   What does the Most Good or Least Harm

8. **Plan** – What needs to be done
   How it needs to be done

9. **Commit**
   → Follow Through
   Don't Quit
   Achieve

10. **LIVE WITH IT!!**

BE WILLING TO CHANGE IF CIRCUMSTANCES WARRANT

PROFESSIONAL VERSATILITY

A professional practitioner of close personal protection needs to be versed in subjects beyond the theory, concepts, and exercise of occupational protection/security requirements. A professional protection agent is a good businessman and a student of history, psychology, sociology, emergency medical services, the arts, etiquette, and protocol. He should be competent in communication (spoken and written) and possibly speak a second language (but it is not enough to simply *speak* a second language, it is necessary to be convincing) and understand its grammar, vocabulary, and cultural origins. He should study related liberal arts subjects such as the humanities and social sciences. Such a diverse education can best be obtained in accredited schools, colleges, and universities. It is the responsibility of universities to ensure that students get the best possible education, meet high standards, and are challenged to make the most of their potential.

I am driven by my own passion for knowledge and selfishly believe everyone else should strive to set his educational and career goals as high as possible. I want people to think, learn, and analyze—to use their brains to the fullest capacity in anticipation of the future. We are, after all, creating the future. Albert Einstein said, "The imagination is a great thing... you can't predict the future, but you can create it." What kind of future will it be if we do not utilize all our powers of learning, thinking, analysis, creativity, and imagination? We cannot continue to live day to day in the present by thinking in ways we have thought in the past. We must look to the future with our "today" thoughts. I am a futurist and believe that the only way to see a bright future is to think in terms of the future and project our thoughts and ideas in that direction. We gather all the learning of the past, combine it with the progress of today, and create the future through education, training and experience.

It is incumbent upon university administrations, faculty, and students to work as a team to address the highest elements of ethics, academia, and experience. They must be innovative and make breakthroughs that keep us a step in front of our enemies, who are earning their own degrees and aim to destroy our freedoms and impose their own world vision on us. I firmly believe that, if we are to maintain freedom and liberty, we must use our intellectual power as well as flexing our muscles. Consequently, the "bar of learning" must be set high if we are to turn out the very best and most capable students and practitioners.

While grades are an important measurement, they do not answer the question, "Did you learn anything?" If students can complete their courses and honestly say they have learned something, then we have made great inroads toward professionalization. If they cannot, then in some way we have failed to meet our goals and have let our students down. When students interview for jobs, create their own businesses, or put their names on reports, they are representing themselves, their university, their ideals, and perhaps their country. As such, they should be highly professional and act as our best ambassadors.

Instructors need to make classes challenging enough to be worthy of the respect that comes with the earned degree. But the coursework must be realistic so students will excel by becoming engrossed in the subject seeking more data, information, and facts. This leads to new ideas, conclusions, and innovations. Universities should demand that faculty members prepare class material that challenges students with realistic as well as theoretical material. Clinical child psychologist Maureen Neihart, coauthor of the book, *The Social and Emotional Development of Gifted Children,* said,

> Children who earn good grades and high praise with relative ease may not learn how to try hard and to persevere when things are difficult. They can come to equate their academic success with innate intelligence and fail to understand the role that effort plays in achievement. When schoolwork finally becomes demanding, they are often in for a rude awakening and may lack the determination and self-confidence to succeed. The best lesson takes place when you have to reach and have supports to make that grab. We improve when we work at the edge of our competence; not when we stay in our comfort zone.[6]

Universities adopting programs that lead to professionalism in the protective-intelligence services should work to instill in each of their students the passion to seek and reach for that "extra something."

Students should look past so-called security experts who might chide them for getting a college education that consists of "book-learned theory." Such people may doubt the value of a university program dealing with close personal protection, intelligence, and counterterrorism, but with education, training, and experience comes professionalization. Students will feel confident in what they have learned from the university as well as what was passed to them from their predecessors. They will understand that they do not have all the answers, but their ideas, opinions, and innovations are worthy, and they can make great contributions to world security.

I am offended by what is called the "dumbing down" of America. I feel a real ethical obligation to push (and pull) students, faculty, and practitioners to realize their full potential. We humans have a tendency to take the easiest route to the finish line, and as a result we have "lazy minds." I believe if people are forced to use their brains, they will continue to become more educated, motivated, and intelligent. As a result, someone will be innovative and make the breakthroughs we seek. If our opponents stay one step ahead by challenging themselves (and even sacrificing their lives), we will always be playing catchup. Someone out there, perhaps a student, faculty member, or protection-intelligence specialist, has the answers we need; we need to continue asking the questions.

I have often asked, "Is our role as educators to graduate as many people as possible, or is it to raise their thinking ability to face tough challenges?" I believe that if we ask the right questions, we as professionals in the field, as well as being educators, can use our own critical thinking skills and problem-solving experience to come up with new thoughts, ideas, and improvements. That should be our ultimate goal.

Some believe that, if presented with difficult material, students will be scared off or lose confidence. Many concerned professional educators and practitioners suspect that this is the reason for much of the "dumbing down" of curricula in this country. It proceeds from the mistaken notion that by making "success" easier to obtain, confidence is built more quickly. But training that is intentionally difficult enhances graduates' competence and provides an honestly acquired self-confidence. Therefore, my bias tends to be toward leading students to professionalism by challenging them with something they believed to be a step beyond their abilities. It is a thin line, made all the more difficult by the nature of the evolving profession. But administration, faculty, and students must walk that thin line and come out of the fire stronger and more professional.

The founder of Henley-Putnam University, Mr. Nirmalya Bhowmick, has stated, "Executive protection (national security) is much more than just standing around, waiting and reacting; we must be prepared to meet any challenge long before ever being presented with it. Our responsibility, our obligation, our duty at H-P is to prepare ourselves and our students for the future before it is presented to us as the challenges of the present."

Success in close personal protection is measured in terms of being able to say, at the end of each day, that the person you are charged with protecting is alive and sleeping safely and soundly at home, in his own bed. Professionalism can be measured in terms of consistent excellence, unfailing success, and superior performance.

Performance is based on personality, confidence, natural ability, education, training, and experience. Qualitative experience involves modifying and improving what is actually done, not simply creating more of the same. Quantitative experience means obtaining the same experience over and over again. For the professional close protection specialist, experience inspires continuous change and the search for a better, more efficient way. Quality of experience means open-ended learning, critical thinking, and imagination.

In close personal protection, as in most professions, there are several layers of professionalism. The difference is not only among the different levels but also among individuals. The following diagram illustrates the various levels of protection professionals. The higher the level, the greater the qualitative experience and professionalism required.

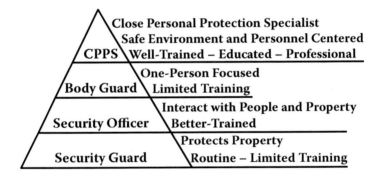

PROTECTION TRAINING

TRAINING AREAS

An experienced close protection specialist should have training in the following areas:

Advance planning
Antiambush drills
Armed and unarmed defensive tactics
Communications–written, oral, and nonverbal
Criminal and terrorist tactics
Electronic security
Emergency medical response and CPR
Escape and evasive driving techniques
Firearms and safety
Fire safety and fire fighting techniques
Intelligence analysis
Legal aspects of the use of force
Map reading and navigation

Physical fitness
Physical security
Protocol and etiquette
Surveillance detection
Threat assessment and risk analysis
Threat recognition

TRAINING FOR CERTAINTY

It is true that we train for certainty and to recognize the unusual. Training gives us the proper response for survival in a hostile environment or a spontaneous and critical situation. Often, there is no time to think, calculate, or wonder; we must counter instantaneously. When someone pulls a weapon, our training should give us the mental discipline to remain calm and to respond appropriately. Physical training should prepare us to disarm the person or to take evasive action. Training (often through mental and physical repetition) gives us the muscle memory to take action without taking the time to pass an image from the eye to the brain, recognize it, form a response, and translate the response into action. Training creates mental shortcuts and simulates real-life experience, allowing us to arrive at decisive action more quickly because the brain has already "visited" this or a similar scenario and does not need to take the time to process a solution. Training with reality and the usual teaches us to recognize things that are unusual, do not fit, or are out of place and do not belong. It also provides the ability to recognize the unexpected and the otherwise unrecognizable.

We also train for uncertainty. In unfamiliar circumstances, when things develop too quickly for rational thought, we perform mental gymnastics and take all the shortcuts that were developed through training experience. We associate the present event with familiar conditions simulated in training, thus fashioning a practical solution.

SCENARIO SIMULATION TRAINING

It is very important that a protection professional maintain sidearm expertise. Many agencies require quarterly or semiannual qualification as a minimum. Some agencies, including the Secret Service, require that all agents attend the firing range on a monthly basis. In addition to shooting, an agent practices timed drawing and firing, and shooting under simulated conditions. To increase the stress factor, a Secret Service agent is required to run a timed quarter mile in a business suit and street shoes, then assume a position alongside a moving "limousine. While street noise, music, and shouting is blared over a loudspeaker, he must recognize a potential attacker, draw, and shoot accurately within a specified time. Points are deducted for drawing against and hitting an innocent bystander.

One private security agency in Los Angeles requires all protection agents to be able to draw and "kill" two targets at a seven-yard distance in less than two seconds while dressed in a business suit. The agents are not allowed to work until they have attained that level of proficiency. They are also required to shoot at varying times of day and under differing lighting conditions, such as full daylight, dusk, and darkness—illuminating the target with a flashlight or silhouetting him against the night sky. The correct protective shooting posture is to be in an upright position with the arms extended, elbows slightly relaxed, and the "off" hand supporting the gun hand. This position provides a greater degree of protection to a protectee, who would be shielded behind the agent.

Practicing realistic events provides an agent with the confidence and knowledge that, should a situation arise, he would be capable of quickly and accurately rendering the necessary defensive firepower to negate the problem. The firing range is also the place to test other equipment such as a holster, to determine its correct placement.

One presidential protection agent had a favorite holster that he felt was a good one because it was comfortable. In spite of the admonitions of the rangemaster that the holster was not particularly suited for his type of work and was inappropriate for fast drawing and shooting, he defended its use based entirely on the way it felt. As the agent was going through his timed drawing and firing phase, his weapon did not clear the holster. The holster came loose from its attachment on the belt and was still holding the gun when the agent began firing. The holster was blown about 15 feet into the air and torn into three parts. As the rangemaster reiterated, in life-threatening situations, practicality is better than comfort.

All too often, police are involved in a potential shooting situation where, "We were afraid for our lives." In a recent shooting incident in southern California, two officers shot and killed a 19-year-old girl for brandishing a knife at them. Allegedly, she had been forcefully raped the night before, was very emotionally upset, and was engaged in an argument with her mother when the officers arrived. Reportedly, the mother had minor cuts where the girl had struck at her. The officers commanded her several times to drop the knife. When she failed to obey, they shot her in the upper torso, as their department training required.

Both officers stated they were afraid for their lives. Not being there and relying only on news accounts, it is easy (and wrong) to second guess the officers. One cannot even blame the officers for reacting as they did when facing a person holding a dangerous and deadly weapon. The blame, if any, must be placed with the training the officers received. They should have received scenario training including unarmed defense and the proper use of a baton against an edged weapon. If they had "visited" a similar realistic scenario in training, they may not have had to resort to firing fatal shots against an emotionally upset girl who had suffered terrible mental and physical trauma hours before.

Facing our fears in realistic training settings enables us to cope with the real danger when it occurs. Perhaps if the officers had faced their fears in a training session they would have been able to overcome the "we were afraid for our lives" syndrome and used tactics that would have ended the situation without gunfire. In the philosophic words of Bruce Lee, When fear is removed, the arrogance of uncertainty is dispelled. Therefore, it is no longer necessary to prove yourself in any form of combat. By learning how to fight, you learn how not to fight.... No excessive action is needed. Just keep your body and mind relaxed to deal with the outside emergency.[7]

In other words, in a time of emergency, we should fall back on and count on our training to help us deal with the situation.

Many agencies require their agents to participant in "working the principal" or "attack on the principal" drills. These "what-if" situations consist of practicing protectee movements in correct formations and positions that would protect the principal in a harmful situation. Different scenarios are visualized that simulate real-life circumstances, such as assault by a single assassin or several dissidents. The practice includes working in both friendly crowds and hostile environments with objects being thrown at the protectee and his entourage.

One scenario enacted in a training session was impressive in its innovation and realism. The training session was being held in a hotel in central Mexico. The VIP, with the protective team working in a diamond formation, entered a covered colonnade and walked toward a conference room. An aggressor dressed as a hotel cleaning woman walked toward the team and VIP and appeared disinterested in their progress. She approached a soda vending machine and inserted a coin. The soda dropped down with a distinctive clunk just as the VIP approached from the other direction. The protective team quickly visually scanned her and felt no threat as they passed by. The woman reached into the machine to retrieve her soda as the VIP passed her. Instead of removing a soda, she pulled a .45 from the machine and shot the VIP in the back.

This type of practice fulfills many objectives. By simulating an actual scenario, the participants can rehearse their anticipated reactions (or inactions) when an actual event transpires. It eliminates mistakes and the process of thinking then reacting. Practicing something over and over and seeing then results the reduces reaction time to that of an instinctive movement. It also highlights any weaknesses that must be corrected in the protective ring. Real-life simulation answers any questions a participant might have about his job and what is expected. It further brings confidence and a closer feeling of teamwork to the entire protective detail, because members know that each person understands his role. At the end of each practice session (which can be videotaped), the protective agents should participate in a self-critique of the exercise. That will reinforce the correct methods of response and strengthen instinct, hopefully eliminating mistakes when under actual attack.

PROTECTION EDUCATION—EDUCATING FOR UNCERTAINTY

A professional close protection specialist should have higher education in the following areas:

1. History (U.S. history, world history and cultures, and perhaps aspects of military history)
2. Sociology (norms, roles, race, prejudice and bias, social issues and cultures)
3. Psychology (cognitive, abnormal, behavioral, and social and organizational)
4. Natural and physical science
5. English and perhaps a second language (grammar, creative writing, and literature)

6. Political science and government, including constitutional law
7. Philosophy, critical thinking, and ethics
8. Music and art history and appreciation

Formal education in liberal arts, social science, hard sciences, and math bolsters functional training. A personal resume that includes higher education offers proof that the person is capable of abstract thinking, has the ability to "imaginate," and can solve problems that have not been previously encountered or anticipated.

The education of a protection agent never stops. Not a day should go by without learning something new, even if he has been in the business for 20 years. Each protectee is different. New circumstances develop, and some old methods may not be valid for that particular protectee. A protectee may have a personal preference for certain procedures, or he may have suggestions that he believes to be relevant to his security. Often, the suggestions have considerable merit and should not be disregarded offhand.

There was an *assistant to the special agent in charge (ASAIC)* of the Presidential Protective Division of the Secret Service who routinely made it a point to approach all "new" agents, often as early as 7:00 A.M., and inquire of them, "What did you learn new today?" Woe to the agent who could not think of anything and simply answered "nothing." The ASAIC then would begin a series of questions that the agent should be able to answer. If he could not do so, it was highly suggested and in his best interest to have the answers during the next encounter!

Other courses of study and recreational reading that a protection agent should make a part of his ongoing education include U.S. history, world history, cultures and civilizations, English (grammar and writing), a second language, sociology, psychology, courses in human relations and manners or etiquette, executive protection courses and books, accounts of previous assassination attacks and terrorist activity, and various newspapers and magazines.

It is important to study historical and contemporary assassination attacks, because a contemporary attack is often similar to a previous assault. For example, while Ferdinand Marcos was in office as the president of the Philippines, his wife, Imelda, was speaking at a local meeting. As she was greeting people in a reception line, a man with a bandage wrapped over his hand stood waiting. When the man reached the first lady, he suddenly removed the bandage and attempted to stab her with a long knife. Only her quick reflexes and some martial arts training saved her. She suffered only minor cuts on her hands as she defended herself. That assassination attempt was patterned after the assassination of U.S. President William McKinley in 1901.

Many assassination attempts on American presidents and others are similar in that the assassin fired his handgun from a crowd while standing a few rows back. There is a lesson in every terrorist act, every kidnapping, and every assassination— even unintentional injury such as the death of Princess Diana. A professional protection agent will study all aspects of an incident, learn from it, and avoid making similar mistakes.

"FOUR Is" OF PROFESSIONALISM AND SUCCESS

Intelligence, integrity, interpersonal skills, and imagination are four criteria necessary for a professional protection agent. The "four Is," as they have become known, are inherently human characteristics, but they are developed by education and training. It is a given that a certain degree of intelligence is requisite for graduation from an institution of higher learning. Intelligence is something all persons are born with; education raises the intelligence quotient and hones the ability to solve problems, meet unforeseen challenges, analyze data, and reason logically and deductively.

Integrity, as a component of character, was discussed in a previous chapter. Integrity may be natural born, but it is developed as part of a person's personality and education. Education gives exposure to various ethical and moral issues that are necessary for advancements in integrity and progress toward personal and professional success.

Some people are gifted and have good interpersonal skills from the moment they begin cognitive reasoning. For the rest of us, these skills must be learned through interaction with other people of all socioeconomic, political, and religious strata. Nowhere is an opportunity to learn interpersonal skills more readily available than through exposure to and interaction with others. Interpersonal skill education begins in kindergarten or preschool, continues through high school and college, and never ends.

Imagination is developed in very young children, usually around the age of two, or when they begin developing cognitive skills. Sadly, however, the imagination often becomes stagnant in an adult. It is a "toy" that does not belong in the adult's world of work, relationships, and idealism. But to a professional, imagination is extremely important, giving him the ability to see things in another perspective or dimension; to see things others do not see.

OTHER COMPONENTS OF PROFESSIONALISM AND SUCCESS

RESPECT AND RESPONSIBILITY

In a profession such as close personal protection, it is a given imperative to follow three Rs.

- *Respect for self.* Confidence (not overconfidence), demeanor, and trust in oneself are evident in a professional who has matured and grown in his field. "One who excels as a warrior does not appear formidable. One who excels in fighting is never aroused in anger. One who excels in defeating his enemies does not join issues. One who excels in employing others humbles himself before them."[8]
- *Respect for others.* "Respect is an important value. Treat all persons with whom you come into contact with dignity and respect, they could be someone's mother, sister, father, or brother, and they deserve to be treated with respect as a person."[9]
- *Responsibility for all your actions.* When you realize you have made a mistake, take immediate action to correct it. We all have, to varying degrees, a conscience that tells us when we have done something wrong.

MENTAL STABILITY—DEALING WITH STRESS

Stress is a constant companion of a successful professional. An experienced agent finds ways to effectively deal with it and works well under stress. But everyone has his limits and must recognize when the pressure of "walking a high tightrope" is beginning to exact its toll. Human nerves are like a rubber band that stretches beyond its original shape and capability until it suddenly snaps. The person doing the stretching must know the stretch limits and stop before the breaking point. He must do the same with his psyche. There are many ways of dealing with the daily stress of being responsible for the life and well-being of another human. To name a few: take time off and get away from the rigor; exercise; have a firm support base; discuss your anxieties with a professional counselor; and so on. One wrong way to avoid dealing with the stress is to turn to alcohol or drugs. Instead of being uplifting, this will start a downward spiral that is more than difficult to stop and worse than the stress.

EYE FOR DETAIL

Constant alertness is important; always be vigilant and on the lookout for anything and everything. "No stone too small to look under; no rock to heavy to move, no boulder too large to search around." Paying attention to the fine details (but not necessarily micromanaging) assures that all aspects, contingencies, and circumstances are covered, allowing no room for failure.

DECISIVENESS

Hemming and hawing, or telling someone, "I'll get back to you on that," leads to a no-confidence vote from subordinates, clients, and peers. A person who desires to be successful must know what he wants, make decisions with confidence, and trust that his judgment is correct.

INCLINATION TOWARD ACTION

Nothing is ever accomplished by "sitting on your hands" or "waiting for Charlie." To quote the character "Patches" O'Houlihan in the movie *Dodgeball* (2004), "You have to grab it [life] with two hands and hump it into submission." Do something; do not wait for others before you take action. Action stirs the juices and gets things done; it creates energy. In the words of the old veteran drill sergeant, "Move, move, move!"

FLEXIBILITY

Rigidity causes things to break. There is a story of a proud, old oak tree that had stood for ages with roots deep into the ground, never moving, never bending. Beside him was a young sapling with roots just beginning to dig deep into the earth. As the wind blew, the young tree waved backed and forth, first in one direction, then the next. This irritated the old tree. He told the sapling, "Stop that constant moving. Can't you see I'm trying to rest and uphold the dignity of the forest?" The younger tree replied, "Bending with the wind allows for greater range and keeps you young and alive." The old oak looked down upon the sapling with a haughty attitude, "har-rumphed," and went back to his old ways of standing straight and rigid.

A wind and rainstorm arrived in the deep woods. The rain lashed the trees, and the wind created a great force against them. The sapling, being flexible, bent and withstood the wind and rain. The old oak, unable to be flexible, could not resist the wind. As the rain pooled around the base of the tree, its roots loosened their grip in the earth. Slowly but surely, the mighty oak began a tipping and decline that caused it to uproot and come crashing down. When the storm was over, the old tree lay dying on the forest floor while the young tree continued to grow and flourish in the wind.

ADAPTS WELL TO ANY GIVEN SITUATION

The only constant that does not change is change. Change constantly plays against human social conditions. As related above, flexibility is a requisite for survival. To endure in a "dog-eat-dog" world, one must learn to adapt quickly to changing climates. This is a variation of the Darwinian theory of evolution. Those who do not adapt are soon obsolete. As the old saying goes, "If you are not making history, you become history."

ABILITY TO IMPROVISE

Emergencies happen when we least expect them. We cannot always be prepared for everything that is thrown at us. We may not have the correct tools, or we have not made sufficient allowances for the things that can occur. A professional does not stand in place wringing his hands and cussing the gods for their disruption of his purpose. He will immediately take necessary corrective action and will create a tool or be creative with whatever is at hand to remedy the situation. He is flexible and capable of "thinking on his feet."

COURAGE

A leader (protective agent) must have confidence in himself and those who support him. That confidence springs from having the courage to lead, innovate, stand up for unpopular causes and beliefs, take risks and face down danger, meet moral and physical challenges, and stand alone when others retreat.

STAMINA, STRENGTH, COORDINATION

To be truly successful, a professional must possess stamina, strength, and coordination. These are physical attributes of professional athletes, of course, but they are also very important attributes of every successful professional in nearly every human endeavor. This is another reference to the "survival of the fittest." It takes all three characteristics to endure the tests that a professional must pass. A sign was spotted one day in a local barbershop. It read, "Life is full of tests, some just count more than others." A person who can endure the marathon and go the distance will succeed in the end.

SUMMARY

Professionalism and success mean being well versed in the security profession. With new threats and technology come new challenges for a protection agent to conquer. Potential protectees, now more than ever, require experienced professionals who are well versed in the overall security field to conduct a host of tasks that require special skills. Many corporations and private individuals have come to realize a need for professionals who know how to provide industry-specific security. This means that security professionals are asked to come up with plans and procedures that address specific problems and create viable solutions to security threats and issues. Being well versed in several areas of protection has advantages for all.

It means better knowledge and skill. An employer or client will see that his protector is a professional who can speak intelligently about security and many other topics while providing the best possible service. It shows that a professional can do more than "stand and wait" as a deterrent. Being well versed in many aspects of security allows the professional to point the client in the appropriate direction and offer some specifics on other security issues if he has requirements that lie outside the protective agent's expertise.

A protective agent should be experienced, trained, and educated in several aspects of security and academic fields, because a complete security knowledge base, in conjunction with scholarly education, will allow for better client coverage. The protective agent who is an expert in only one area may have a few potentially fatal flaws in his protective program. His lack of knowledge can lead to mistakes. The agent's circles of protection may be ineffective if he based them on an incomplete picture of the threat against the client, if he did not use proper techniques to gather and analyze intelligence, or if he failed to make a complete threat assessment.

A comprehensive knowledge of security is essential for successful protection of a protectee, even if some areas are only rudimentarily understood. An agent must be able to look at a problematic situation and set up a complete protection package for the client. If more specialized knowledge is needed, it can be obtained, but it is important that the "generalist" protective agent know enough to complete most assignments without bringing in outside assistance. More importantly, various time elements may dictate that a job needs to be done quickly, and calling in a specialist might be impractical. A protective agent needs to know how to adapt to situations on the fly, whether it is dealing with workplace violence or performing technology-based surveillance.

Being knowledgeable in several aspects of security and keeping current with new training allows quick responses to threats and more versatile planning. It will also give the protective agent an idea of his limits, which in itself is an important factor in protecting a client. A general knowledge of several aspects of security is not only important, it is essential for today's security professional. The ever-changing world and the need to provide complete protection to a client makes a continuing study of the industry invaluable in the field. The quick decisions that may save a principal's life could depend on that small understanding of even a seemingly unimportant detail.

REVIEW QUESTIONS

1. Explain the concept of *mundancy of excellence* as it relates to a protective agent.
2. In your own words, define *professional*.
3. How does attitude reflect on the protection agent?
4. Define the "four Is" of professionalism and success.
5. Stress is a constant companion of a protective agent. Give examples of different sources of stress and explain how an agent should deal with it.
6. What roles do education and training play in becoming a professional?
7. Define (in your own words) *critical thinking* and explain why a protective agent must engage in it.
8. What does *strength through education* mean to you?
9. Describe the decision-making process.
10. Why should a protective agent's education and training include *scenario training*?
11. What does it mean to say, "We train for certainty and educate for uncertainty"?

NOTES

1. This word does not officially exist. However, it is descriptive of making excellence mundane or routine.
2. Forsyth, Frederick. *The Day of the Jackal*. New York: Viking Press, 1971.
3. Slogan of the Henley-Putnam University (courtesy of Sheldon Greaves, Ph.D. and chief academic officer).
4. www.henley-putnam.edu
5. Ruggiero, Vincent Ryan. *Thinking Critically about Ethical Issues*, 5th ed. Mountain View, CA: Mayfield Publishing, 2001.
6. Dr. Valerie Ulene, 2006. "The High Price of Easy School Work." *Los Angeles Times*, September 4, F-4.
7. Philosophy of Wing Chun, courtesy of the Los Angeles Traditional Wing Chun Kung Fu Academy.
8. Ibid.
9. Philosophy of Dale L. June, as taught in university-level classes, "Introduction to Police Work."

17 Dynamics of Protective Team Building

To lead people, walk beside them and ask for their best leaders.

Sun Tzu

A boss creates fear, a leader confidence. A boss fixes blame, a leader corrects mistakes. A boss knows all, a leader asks questions. A boss makes work drudgery, a leader makes it interesting. A boss is interested in himself or herself, a leader is interested in the group.

Russell H. Ewing

TEAMWORK

"One for all and all for one," the motto of Alexander Dumas' *The Three Musketeers*, exemplifies the concept of teamwork, with everyone working together to accomplish mutual goals. Teamwork is like a finely tuned machine with all parts working in cohesion. If one part breaks down, the other parts must either take up the burden or fail.

Continuing the *Three Musketeers* analogy, the important requisite is loyalty and dedication to the team and team goals. The philosophy of "win as a team, fail as a team" is a formula for success with, the key phrase being "as a team." Winning teams are composed of individuals who use their personal skills for the best interest of the team and do not take advantage of the team effort for individual advancement, glory, or recognition. Dedication calls for each team member to practice self-discipline to uphold the standards demanded of everyone and, if necessary, to make personal sacrifices for the team effort.

To have a winning team, high goals and standards are set, enforced, and lived. Mediocrity is unacceptable. To succeed, one needs a hunger to win and a fear of failure, coupled with faith in fellow team members. In the protective services, the team must operate as one integrated unit and not let failure enter the game, because failure is a life-or-death proposition. If a team member fails, falls out, or in any way is unable to carry out his assignment, another team member must step up to fill the position and complete the team mission.

A team works together for the same purposes and goals, with each member performing his role for the greater good of the whole. One team member can anticipate the movements, and even thinking, of his partners. Members are able to communicate (a key ingredient in teamwork) using nonverbal means. A slight cocking of the head, a rolling of the eyes, or a small flick of a finger can mean, "Look over there, that person bears watching." A team member must be able to recognize those subtle movements.

Effective teamwork requires clear and concise communication between members. It doesn't matter if the team is made up of two or twenty agents, good communication and teamwork are just as important as using the proper tactics and techniques. The protectee and the protector must also use good teamwork. Communication is very important in their relationship. The protector can only protect the protectee if he knows everything about the protectee and his affairs. The protector will need an itinerary in advance, so he can plan all driving routes, plus information regarding the protectee's daily activities. A good protector and his team can provide proper security for the protectee and adapt to any type of situation. In the personal protection field, teamwork is essential to operational success.

Training is important when working with a team. If you train only for protect yourself and do not train to work and communicate with those engaged in the conflict, the odds of failure increase. Therefore, when a team is formed, it should train together as a team. The training should include scenarios that deal with situations of all types. Good team members will communicate with each other, and everyone will know his responsibility during an event. A good team will also listen to and follow directions from the team leader. If something goes wrong during an event, everyone will know what to do. It will become automatic. If you do not have proper training and good communication, each person may want to "do his own thing," become a "loose cannon," and put the protectee at risk.

IMPORTANCE OF TEAMWORK

In any position that requires the coordinated effort of two or more people, a high degree of cooperation and teamwork is necessary to achieve a common goal or mission. Teamwork is often the make-or-break element in any project and the cause of failure in achieving a goal.

As society and jobs become more complicated, more people and outside sources are typically required to achieve a common goal and mission. The more people involved, the more complicated and complex—and yet essential—teamwork becomes. In a high-profile protective mission, the complexity and integration of many personnel elements will increase dramatically, calling for sophisticated teamwork, with everyone working synchronously.

At times, teamwork is easier said than achieved. Team members often have their own hidden agendas and personal needs that affect developing and establishing an effective team. Developing an effective team involves many elements, but establishing leadership is the key to creating a common focus. Other elements crucial to establishing and maintaining an effective team are

1. To have a clear goal and challenging objective. This provides a common focal point for the team.
2. To have competent, knowledgeable, and professional team members. Without these individuals' specific experience, expertise, and professionalism, the goal would not be attainable, and it would be difficult to have all players work in unison.

3. To get a commitment from all involved. Without that commitment, individuals may focus on their own needs, wants, and desires.
4. To enlist outside individuals or groups in a supportive role. Often, complicated goals and tasks require support from outside individuals or groups. Without these people working with you, your resources are limited.
5. To ensure that everyone on the team is a team player, working toward the common goal. This is the glue that holds everything together. Without it, people lose their focus on the common goal and act as individuals.

Sometimes personal protection requires the combined effort of many people, some of whom will perform tasks that place them in the background where they are not readily visible. Even so, the entire group should be aware of and appreciate their efforts. This holds especially true for advance work, countermeasures, and risk assessment.

Personal protection brings ordinary people together to accomplish an extraordinary task involving people of high stature and class who are nevertheless helpless. The task can be quite demanding. The protected individuals may not see or understand the individual efforts that go into protecting them.

In the end, teamwork is critical and crucial to any team desiring success. Successful teamwork means having the team reach their desired goal; that shared goal creates the team.

Whoever is assigned to a particular position must stay with the job and avoid straying into someone else's area of responsibility. Otherwise, an area of vulnerability is opened, compromising the total team effort. One team member supports another. While concentrating on a particular position, a team player is also aware of what is happening around his fellow mates. If needed, he will provide appropriate assistance. He must be knowledgeable in the responsibilities of other team members and capable of responding when called upon to fill in for another member. He will be eager to assist his fellow agents.

A good team member does not complain or grouse about having to spend long hours in a hallway or empty room for no apparent purpose. On the other hand, a good team leader does not assign the least desirable positions to the same member every time.

Teamwork in personal protection is important to both the protectee and the protection specialists themselves. Each member of a close protection team brings different strengths and weaknesses to the table, and each balances out the others. A team that has practiced together can provide more effective coverage to a protectee. A protection team, whether made up of two or ten people, should be cohesive and remember that all are present for the same reason and using the same playbook. Consistent protection is facilitated when team members know each other well and have practiced together.

The protection specialist needs to be consistent in his techniques. Consistency includes staying with the principal even when his activities are apparently inconsequential. Do not forbid him to go anywhere without you but then let him go alone for ice in a hotel. A one-man operation may occasionally slip up in this area, but a team should not; different team members can accompany the principal at different times.

A close protection specialist must always be aware of the world around him. He must notice the little things that most people would miss. This means detecting anything that seems out of place. "If it does not belong, it must be wrong." A team brings extra eyes and a wider range of sensory perception than any individual can provide.

If a team is not accustomed to working together, the result can be disastrous for the principal. If team members react as if working alone, making decisions independently and acting alone, confusion can ensue and safety will be jeopardized. This is why the team must have set goals and standards. Each person must know what to do in any situation to keep the protectee safe. Each team member must be comfortable and reliable in his position.

We cannot overlook, however, that there is one untrained member in any team: the principal. He is a member of the team in the sense that he must be aware of the situation and provide input. Although security can never be 100 percent perfect, if team members are not on the same page, security is further compromised.

It is beneficial if team members have different experience, expertise, and skills, and come from diverse backgrounds. One team member might have a background in psychology and experience in dealing with hostile subjects. Another might have experience in surveillance, wiretapping, or photographic specialties. There may be someone who has connections in law enforcement and is able to arrange police support when needed. Another person could be an expert in threat assessment. Success is virtually guaranteed with such diverse backgrounds and everyone working together as a team.

Successful teamwork requires team members who are dedicated to their jobs. The agents need to be dependable and reliable. If a team member says he is going to do something or be somewhere, he must follow through. Members must understand that there are times to relax and times to be serious and alert.

Teamwork is very important in protective services. Without teamwork, you cannot protect the principal. If individuals on a team communicate well and work together, they have an excellent chance for success.

Agents on a team should all be volunteers, and they should train together. This way, each member will understand the others' strengths and weaknesses and provide balance. The team will give better coverage by keeping one member at the side of the principal at all times while others attend to other aspects of security.

A protective agent must work closely with the principal. The principal and agent must maintain an open line of communication so that both know what is happening. The team concept even improves the principal's reaction time in an emergency, because he can participate in safety procedures. The team should also include the principal's family members and staff. They can be incorporated into the concentric circles of protection if kept apprised of the situation by meeting with them regularly.

TEAM BUILDING

Assembling a winning team begins with the selection of team personnel. Even the best manager in the world will fail if his team members do not have talent, training, experience, and a will to win. Selecting the best team means finding individuals with talent, motivation, and desire. It is not always the person with the most talent who brings "backbone" to a team; it can be someone who has average talent but a great deal of desire, heart, and intensity.

People responsible for finding the best talent include human resources, scouts, and current team members. They (as well as the working team) must be innovative thinkers and students of human interaction. People who work in a particular field soon encounter others who possess similar skills and aspirations. Agents on a protective team always should be on the lookout for outsiders who would be assets to the group. The team leader should identify people who have special skills and attributes that would benefit the group and add to the "chemistry."

Ideally, team members will all be volunteers who are there by choice. A misfit who does not want to be on the team and does not function as a team member should be weeded out as soon as possible. Someone who is apathetic and will not accept personal responsibility can be the weak link that leads to disaster. He should be immediately reassigned. New members must be quickly assimilated and given responsibilities and authority equal to those of the old-timers. Everyone must learn his position and role on the team and be supportive of others. The sooner this is accomplished, the sooner the team will succeed.

A team is constantly being watched, judged, evaluated, and criticized or complimented by everyone who has an interest in it. The team leader is responsible for training and motivation. He sets an example by his leadership. There is a story of General Eisenhower explaining leadership concepts. He pulled a string from his pocket and instructed a subordinate to push it. When the string went nowhere and began folding in on itself, Eisenhower is reported to have said, "Gentlemen, leadership is like that string, it cannot be pushed, but it can be pulled or led. The same holds true for leading men."

A good team leader gets to know his men—their competencies, weaknesses, how they react under duress, how they handle responsibility, and whether they have personal problems. He treats them with respect and does not let them fall into mediocrity. He encourages and challenges them to improve themselves through training and to strive for their personal best. He ensures that each team member practices accountability and encourages other team members. He convinces the team to work with and for each other in the interest of all.

Each team member expresses good fellowship by spending off-duty time with teammates and getting to know them. Communication is a free-flowing process of keeping others informed of developments and changes. A climate of trust cannot exist when members engage in backstabbing second-guessing, or "Monday-morning quarterbacking." Constructive criticism helps members to improve their performance and "keep the edge." When presented in a manner that does not create defensiveness, criticism of others (and oneself) allows weaknesses to be examined and resolved, making the team even stronger. Each team member must get to know his teammates and help them reach personal and team goals.

TEAM PLAYER

In his book, *The 17 Qualities of a Team Player*,[1] John C. Maxwell identified the following attributes:

1. Adaptable (able to adjust to changing circumstances, personnel, and assignments)
2. Collaborative (works well with others)
3. Committed (dedicated to the proposition of the mission or goal)
4. Communicative (communication being at the heart of a collaborative effort)
5. Competent (reliable, capable, knowledgeable, experienced, and skilled)
6. Dependable (like a faithful dog—steady, trusty, and staunch)
7. Disciplined ("It's not for me to question why, but to do or die"; self-disciplined)
8. Enlarging (brings and gives added value)
9. Enthusiastic (energizing with vigor, liveliness, and force)
10. Intentional (making every action count, not making five moves when one will do)
11. Mission-conscious (focused on the job at hand)
12. Prepared (can handle any situation, emergency, or routine)
13. Relational (views teammates as brothers, partners, "one for all, all for one")
14. Self-improving (devoted to becoming better, faster, smarter)
15. Selfless (no "self" in teamwork)
16. Solution-oriented (a solution to every problem)
17. Tenacious (persevering; a "bulldog" not willing to give up)

Teams and individual team players strive for consistency and cross-training, including physical fitness and mental toughness, so they will understand every aspect of the team assignment and how each team member will react under given circumstances. Teams that defeat their opponents exhibit stamina, reliability, and perspective. They will back up others when needed and sacrifice their own interest to support others.

SUMMARY

Individuals on a team must be cohesive, work together toward the same goals, pay attention to the team process, and make sure that they make a difference. This makes the difference between success and failure. By definition, a team is made up of more than one. A team is the melding of individuals to reach common goals and meet the highest possible standards.

REVIEW QUESTIONS

1. Explain the difference between a *boss* and a *leader*.
2. What does the quote, "one for all and all for one," mean to a protection agent?
3. Fully explain the role of communication to a team of protection agents.
4. Describe the importance of teamwork in a protective situation.
5. Your protective assignment requires building a team of agents; how would you make your choices?
6. To be successful, a team must consist of *team players*. What does this term mean to you? Describe what it means to be a team player.

NOTE

1. Maxwell, John C. *The 17 Essential Qualities of a Team Player.* Nashville, TN: Thomas Nelson Publishers, 2000.

18 Terrorism

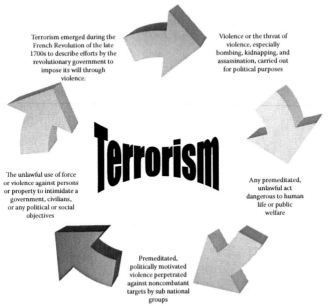

Terrorism emerged during the French Revolution of the late 1700s to describe efforts by the revolutionary government to impose its will through violence.

Violence or the threat of violence, especially bombing, kidnapping, and assassination, carried out for political purposes

The unlawful use of force or violence against persons or property to intimidate a government, civilians, or any political or social objectives

Any premeditated, unlawful act dangerous to human life or public welfare

Premeditated, politically motivated violence perpetrated against noncombatant targets by sub national groups

Diagram by Crystal Franco – Student, American InterContinental University/Los Angeles/ CA, 2006

You can discover what your enemy fears most by observing the means he uses to frighten you.

American philosopher Eric Hoffer

While nothing is easier than to denounce the evildoer, nothing is more difficult than to understand him.

Fyodor Mikhailovich Dostoevsky

The purpose of terror is to terrorize!

Carlos Marighella

He could have been any college student. Open texts and notebooks scattered around the living room, a college pennant was pinned to the wall, and a few empty beer bottles and a pizza box with one hard, dry piece of pizza sat near the oversized chair facing the television. He sat at his computer desk working on some last minute document. Checking his watch, he closed his computer and grabbed a light jacket while tossing down a small cup of cold coffee and picking up a half-eaten bologna sandwich he stuffed into his mouth as he ran out the door.

A quick stop at a local pharmacy gave him everything he needed: hair grooming cream and conditioner, skin-softening oil, toothpaste, soap, cosmetics, and *shampoo—everything necessary for personal hygiene and grooming. The friends who would be accompanying him on his trip also made similar purchases. When the airplane reached cruising altitude, the friends would combine their entirely innocent materials and await the chemical reaction, turning the simple concoction into a deadly explosion, causing the plane to erupt and burst into flames.*

In a few minutes he was at the airport. His flight was on time, and he had just enough time to check in and board before the airplane pulled away from the ramp. In a few minutes, the plane would reach cruising altitude, and the lives of all 260 people on the plane, and many thousands more on the ground would, end in a fiery collision. It would be over quickly. It would require only as long as it took him and three others to commandeer the plane and turn it into a fuel-laden bomb. There were no second thoughts. His personal sacrifice in the name of God was small, for when his job was finished he would be in Paradise.

• • •

Both sides claim to be acting according to the will of God.

Abraham Lincoln (1862)

To spread the most fear and shock, victims must feel that nothing and no one is immune. In this, Osama bin Laden and others of his ilk have been more than successful. They have killed thousands and frightened millions! Timothy McVeigh chose his target well to produce the most shock value. He struck in the heartland of America. The targeted building was important not so much for its strategic value as it was for its seemingly safe location and the widespread fear the explosion initially caused.

Potential terrorist targets do not necessarily have to be of strategic or tactical importance; they may be selected more for the symbolism and shock value. For example, national landmarks, traditional treasures, museums, military or veteran's hospitals, and so on make excellent objects for a terrorist attack. Unibomber Theodore Kaczynski and the Washington area snipers spread fear by selecting victims at random, and the same can be said of terrorists. Inhumanity, random selection, and attacks on safe targets have a "stone thrown into the pond" effect as ripples of fear rapidly spread outward.

After the skyjacking of four commercial airliners and the subsequent bombing of the World Trade Center and Pentagon, "terrorism" was on everyone's lips and mind. As a gross generalization, it is safe to say that most people have no real understanding of the concept of terrorism except that it generates fear as a consequence of some deplorable deed. From September 11, 2001, forward, fear provides a constant reminder that terrorism is successful, even if the perpetrators are killed. The belief, "It could never happen to me," has now been translated to, "It could easily have been me," or "Will I be next?" We now realize that terror can, and will, strike close to home.

Through the 1970s to the mid-1990s, America was familiar with terrorist acts only through news accounts taken with the evening meal or over the morning cup of coffee. Terrorism was considered far removed from the day-to-day routine of an American family. Aside from being momentarily horrified (yet fascinated) by a breaking terrorist event such as an airline hijacking, the shooting and killing of the athletes at the 1972 Olympic games, or the kidnapping of the OPEC oil ministers in 1975, terrorism to America was a problem unrelated to real life.

Those events led to inconvenient searches at airports and public buildings but, to Americans, terrorism was not a big problem. It was thought to be of real concern only to corporate giants whose personnel were assigned to dangerous places where the locals resented their so-called "exploitation of the masses."

But terrorism (if we include guerrilla warfare) has really been around for a long, long time. During the American Revolution, Francis Marion, the "Swamp Fox," utilized terrorist tactics in guerrilla warfare against the British around Charleston, South Carolina. When the enemy was least expecting it, Marion and his men, often made up of only a few experienced frontiersmen, would suddenly attack a British patrol or detachment, killing several of the "redcoats" and causing fear and confusion among the king's soldiers. They would as quickly disappear back into the swamps.

But we do not have to go so far back in time to find terrorism in American history. From right after the Civil War until the present day, organizations like the Ku Klux Klan have used terrorism against all who oppose their ethnocentricity and racist ideals. Striking in the dark of night, white-robed and hooded Klansmen would sweep down on a black person's house, business, settlement, or even a lone individual and burn, loot, and kill. Behind them they left ruin, violent death, and fear. As a message, the raiding Klansmen would place a burning cross on the lawn of the frightened or (most often) tortured and dead or dying victim. Extremely painful acts, including disembowelment, castration, hanging, burning, and drawing and quartering emphasized the message. To this day, crosses are left burning with the same intent of instilling fear in primarily black-dominated churches and communities.

It is generally accepted that the current wave of terrorist fear in the world is rooted in the 1970s. The decade was laced with airline skyjackings, kidnappings, bombings, and hostage taking. In 1971, in response to the growing number of airline skyjackings and to alleviate a nation's anxiety about flying, President Nixon ordered the formation of an anti-skyjacking group. Less than 48 hours after Nixon signed the executive order, federal agents known as sky marshals were in the air, flying on all international flights to and from the United States. At the same time, upgraded security measures such as passenger screening, baggage searches, and stricter procedures were instituted at all airports. After the plane takeovers in September 2001, the sky marshal program was reinvented with armed, highly trained professional undercover antiterrorist men and women.

In 1972, the Black September group, an offshoot of a splinter religious sect, attacked the Munich Olympics, resulting in the death of eleven Israeli athletes. The once peaceful games were changed forever, and fear will always haunt the games. Any nation hosting the Olympics will spend billions of dollars on security, and athletes and attendees are subjected to countless security processes and screenings.

Not only did the incidence of terrorism increase exponentially, the brazenness of each incident became ever more shocking and terrible. With each incident, popular apprehension and fear grew. Today, air travelers are subjected to very strict screening procedures and are not allowed to bring carry-on bags containing some simple personal hygiene and grooming articles or even bottles of drinking water.

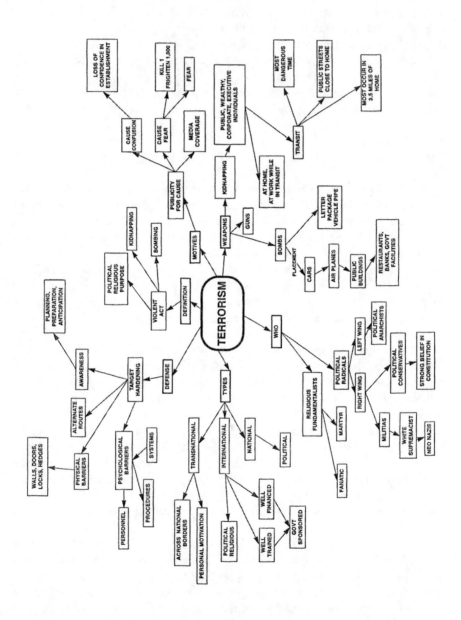

DEFINING TERRORISM AND TERRORISTS

Terrorism is customarily defined as "a violent (criminal) act usually committed for political or religious purposes with the intent to spread fear and intimidation to the noninvolved citizenry." The primary problem with any common definition is that, although it refers to intentional violence to cause fear, intimidation, or coercion, there is no specific reference to the actual nature of the criminal acts. But it is certain that intentional violence to spread fear will always be the method of choice for those who wish to influence or destroy institutions with whom they disagree.

There is no one authoritative definition of terrorism. Terrorism is often viewed as a double-edged sword. To quote a tired old terrorism-related cliché, "One man's patriot is another man's terrorist." This means that terrorism depends on which side of the issue one takes while doing the viewing. But to better grasp what terrorism means to the protection specialist, comprehension of several definitions is required.

Terrorism is violence for... effect..., not primarily, and sometimes not at all, for the physical effect on the actual target but rather for its dramatic impact on the audience.

Brian Jenkins, internationally renowned terrorism expert

Terrorism is the threat or use of violence for political purposes by individuals or groups, whether acting for or in opposition to established governmental authority, when such actions are intended to shock or intimidate victims.

National Foreign Assessment Center

Terrorism is violent criminal behavior designed primarily to generate fear in the community, or a substantial segment of it, for political purposes.

***Disorders and Terrorism,* National Advisory Committee on Criminal Justice Standards and Goals, Law Enforcement Assistance Administration (1976)**

Terrorism is the calculated use of violence or the threat of violence to attain goals: political, religious, or ideological in nature. This is done through intimidation, coercion, or instilling fear. Terrorism involves a criminal act that is often symbolic in nature and intended to influence an audience beyond the immediate victim.

U.S. Army Regulation 190-52, *Countering Terrorism and Other Major Disruptions on Military Installations*

Rex A. Hudson, a social sciences researcher, defines a terrorist action as "the calculated use of unexpected, shocking, and unlawful violence against noncombatants (including, in addition to civilians, off-duty military and security personnel in peaceful situations) and other symbolic targets perpetrated by a clandestine member(s) of a subnational group or a clandestine agent(s) for the psychological purpose of publicizing a political or religious cause and/or intimidating or coercing a government(s) or civilian population into accepting demands on behalf of the cause."[1]

A good working definition of terrorism, while falling far short of being all-inclusive, becomes a violent act usually committed for political or religious purposes with the intent to spread fear and intimidation to the uninvolved citizenry. The violent acts primarily fall into the criminal categories of bombings, assassinations, hijackings and skyjackings, hostage-taking and barricading, kidnapping, armed assaults and ambushes, arson, mob violence, and robberies. In other words, terrorism can be seen as the calculated use of violence or the threat of violence to attain a goal, usually with a political or religious reference. It often includes a criminal act with violent intent and is aimed at a specific public.

Because of the political or religious aspect of the definitions of terrorism a violent criminal act lacking those threads had not been previously considered as terrorism even though all the other criteria such as media attention and intimidation of others outside the actual target was present. That aspect of terrorist definition has been reconsidered and reevaluated. In the new world of terrorist violence and threats, many states have made it illegal to make what are defined as "terrorist threat statements." By merely uttering, "I am going to kill you" as one 17-year-old Los Angeles girl did while arguing with a bunch of friends, she was arrest and charged with "making a terrorist threat."

With the addition of the criminal act or rather a series of similar violent acts and social moivations, terrorism is not, and has not been, something that happends only "overseas" as in the Mid-East, Eruope or the politically unstable Southern Hemisphere. Terrorism has become a violent criminal act perperated for social, political, or religious significance resulting in wide spread media attention and popular intimidation and is as American and as old as teh Boston Tea Party.

There are three characteristics that distinguish true terrorism. The first is that the terrorist must have either the means or the percieved potential for violence. Violence is the determining factor that results in terrorism. Without the capacity to instill fear through violence, terror becomes a non-factor. The second is that there is an impartial frame of reference to the violence. The perpetrator must have a mental acceptance of being capable of performing the violent act. He must act cooly and without remorse for his deed and show no hesitation as though the violent act was an extension of his personality, ideology, and belief.

The third characteristic is perhaps what separates a mere violent criminal act from a true terrorist act. The terrorist *intends* to spread fear and confusion beyond the intended victim. A criminal act alone (or even a series of crimes such as serial killings or rapes) has tremendous potential for spreading fear. But there is no actual intent to spread fear beyond the victim; that comes as an unintended consequence. In addition, in a "simple" criminal act, there is *no intent to attract media attention* as in a terrorist act.

TERRORISM'S NEW FACE

As a result of recent terrorist acts, including the events of September 11, a new form of terrorism is rapidly growing in the world's trouble spots. In fact, this is a new form of unconventional warfare. Gone is the notion of opposing armies engaged in traditional tactics—nation vs. nation, or national alliances against a rogue nation or dictator. Future wars will be fought against nondescript entities led by aggressive and charismatic "high priests" or disenfranchised ideologues. Wars involving terrorist activities engage fewer personnel, with amorphous or secret lines of command and

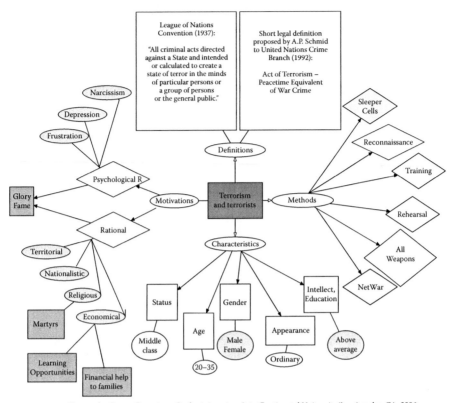

Diagram by Gayane Boysnian – Student, American InterContinental University/Los Angeles, CA, 2006

control. Bin Laden and others have proven that a small, dedicated group of fanatics can bring towering nations to bear.

TERROR'S STEALTH WEAPON—SUICIDE BOMBERS!

> No historian would deny that the part played by crimes committed for personal motives is very small compared to the vast populations slaughtered in unselfish loyalty to a jealous god, king, country, or political system… the ravages caused by individual self-assertion are quantitatively negligible compared to the number slain out of a self-transcending devotion to a flag, a leader, a religious faith, or political conviction. Man has always been prepared to die for good, bad, or completely harebrained causes.
>
> **Arthur Koestler[2]**

Just a few short years ago, who could have imagined that a terrorist, ideologue, or *anyone* would deliberately blow himself up to deliver his deadly message? That is because many lessons of history have been forgotten (e.g., Vietnamese Buddhist monks turning themselves into human torches, Algerian independence fighters in their war for independence from France in the 1950s, the kamikaze pilots of Japan in the closing days of World War II, early assassins, and even the Christian martyrs).

Today, suicide bombers are common in certain countries of the Middle East and other war-ravaged areas of the world. But the United States and other Western nations, not being psychologically prepared for such an attack, would be shocked into paralysis if even one suicide bomber detonated himself in any of a million crowded domestic locations. It could be a crowded dance floor in a popular night spot, on a packed subway at 5:00 p.m., or any place great numbers of people are present. To set off a roadside improvised explosive device (IED) on a crowed freeway would cause horror, fear, and psychological damage far beyond the explosion site. It is difficult to imagine the fear that would result from a terrorist guerrilla-type suicide bombing campaign in the United States.

Many ideological terrorists do not seek to influence the political process; instead, they consider themselves at war with their target organization. Their goals are not to gain political power but to spread as much fear as they can, as widely as possible. Therefore, such terrorists are willing to commit kamikaze-style attacks such as becoming human bombs or carriers of infectious diseases. They are willing to die in an attempt to destroy government infrastructure or military targets or to paralyze a frightened civilian population. This is the new face of terrorism. There is no sure defense against suicide bombers. Spreading fear and anxiety makes the victimized audience feel impotent, change their ways, and surrender essential liberties (e.g., freedom of movement) in the name of security. Fear is the greatest weapon.

Ariel Merari of Tel Aviv University defined suicide terrorism as "intentionally killing oneself for the purpose of killing others, in the service of a political of ideological goal."[3] Professor Merari was able to isolate and identify several personality traits typical of suicide attackers. "They possess weak personalities; are socially marginalized; are subject to rigid, concrete thinking; and demonstrate low self-esteem…. They have often cited four motivating factors: national humiliation, religion ('to do God's will'), personal revenge, and admittance to paradise in the afterlife."[4]

Other researchers have established similar theories of suicide bomber motivations:

- *Religious martyrdom*. This motivation also includes what has been described as "overzealous fanatics" seeking "Heavenly glory" by invoking the will of God as a directive to rid the world of nonbelievers. This involves a philosophy of, "There is but one God, and he is my God; my God is better than yours, and if you don't believe in my God, you are a nonbeliever, and God has ordered all nonbelievers to be killed and sent to Hell." They do not view themselves as suicide bombers but as seeking self-chosen martyrdom.
- *Making a political statement*. Wars cannot be won against an idea philosophy or belief. Belief in a certain political issue drives some adherents to radical actions. These include the IRA hunger strikers of the late 1970s and early 1980s, the English suffragists, and early Japanese samurai. In an attempt to win worldwide public support, Palestinian refugees have resorted to suicide bombing attacks against Israel in an attempt to win political concessions.

- *Pay to family (economic).* It is widely known that the families of suicide bombers, especially those supported by Saddam Hussein and Osama Bin Laden, received monetary rewards for their "brave, patriotic" efforts.
- *Glory and fame.* A "wall of heroes" displays the photograph of the "martyred," and news coverage of the "brave actions against the enemy" are spread throughout the world.
- *Psychological impact.* Especially in the Western world, suicide bombing is not seen from the same psychological viewpoint as in the Middle or Far East. To the Western mind, suicide bombing is murder in the first degree. It spreads fear and intimidation, leaving survivors (and the unaffected populace) feeling weak and impotent.
- *Violence for effect.* Suicide bombing destroys morale and the willingness to continue resisting, causes chaos, and shows the reigning government to be ineffectual and incapable of protecting its citizens.

NOT SO STEREOTYPICAL—FEMALE SUICIDE BOMBERS

The stereotype exploited by terrorists is that women are gentle, submissive, and nonviolent. Women evade most terrorist or criminal profiles, because they are perceived as wives and mothers and victims of war-torn societies, not bombers. But terrorist organizations are increasingly employing women to carry out the deadliest attacks! It is erroneous (maybe chauvinistic) to believe that terrorists would refrain from using women as suicide bombers simply because of some old-fashioned belief in chivalric ideals or that it is simply not something a woman would do. But it is indisputable that women have been widely embraced within international jihadist circles. On November 9, 2005, Belgian Muriel Degauque served as an al-Qaeda suicide bomber in Baqubah, shattering the myth that only Middle Eastern females would take a religious or political cause to the extreme of murder in the name of God. It is not beyond the range of imagination that terrorists will recruit mentally handicapped teenagers and other disabled persons as suicide bombers.

RECOGNIZING SUICIDE BOMBERS

Experience has shown that suicide bombers do not walk around with a sign around their neck advertising, "I am a suicide bomber and proud of it." A few commonalities have been observed, but not enough to lump together and classify as a *profile*. An astute protection agent must be aware of indicators signifying that a person may be a suicidal bomber. A suicide bomber

- May be depressed or hopeless, or manically happy
- May be armed with explosives and pressure-release switch
- May be sweating
- May be wearing oversized clothing (to cover explosives) or carrying a backpack
- May be shaved bald to show a "clean spirit" to God
- Can be of any age (but usually 12 to 25)

- May be of either sex
- Will see himself as a victim, not an aggressor
- Will see himself as at war

A suicide bomber's package, usually stowed in a briefcase, backpack, handbag, or wrapped around his body in a vest, contains an explosive device and such items as nails, marbles, and steel ball bearings. When the electrical circuit is completed, the explosion will hurl the shrapnel in all directions at 1,000 feet per second, analogous to hordes of angry Africanized honey bees swarming from a disturbed hive.

MAKING OF A TERRORIST

Professor Marc Sageman, a forensic psychiatrist at the University of Pennsylvania and a CIA case officer in Afghanistan from 1987 to 1989, has developed a sound sociological theory of how a person becomes a terrorist through the concept of religion.

> A socially aloof individual, perhaps new to the area, joins others in a place of worship. After meeting similar individuals there, they begin to socialize. Initially, they convene to share a common faith and similar interests, but later their association assumes an increasingly radical essence. At this point, attachment to the group trumps other considerations and affects perception, and the individual feels obligated to participate in terrorist activity out of loyalty to the group.[5]

In alluding to the causes of crime to social conditions and peer influence, Sageman's theory is very similar to those of many other sociologists and criminology researchers.

Therese Hesketh, of the Institute of Child Health at University College, London, and Zhu Wei Xing, of China's Zhejian Normal University, published a paper[6] in the *Proceedings of the National Academy of Sciences* and warned of the "perils of gender imbalance." The paper recognized aspects of Professor Sageman's theory. They warned, "In cultures that favor male babies, sex-ratio imbalances could destabilize society because more men will remain unmarried, raising the risks of antisocial and violent behavior." The authors called for "measures to reduce sex selection and an urgent change in cultural attitudes or dire consequences could follow.... When single young men congregate, the potential for more organized aggression is likely to increase substantially, and this has worrying implications for organized crime and terrorism."

IMPROVISED EXPLOSIVE DEVICES

IEDs have become a routine hazard, resulting in many deaths in Iraq. Terrorists and insurgent groups have readily adopted IEDs as a quick and inexpensive way to cause death, destruction, and fear. The explosive material is hidden in a pile of rocks or placed in a container that could be a trash bag, cardboard box, or other roadside debris, or even under or inside a dead animal or human being. An example of a simple explosive device is a 105-mm round wired to a battery and detonated from an observation post atop a ridge or small berm. Normally, a second or third IED is set nearby just in case the first one fails to make the kill. A series of IEDs may be setup to cause a chain reaction that causes enormous damage.

BOMBINGS, GUNS, AND ASSASSINATIONS

A terrorist attack usually begins with bombing, shooting, or assassination. Bombing is the most common tactic. The bomb is popular because it is cheap and easy to make, has a variety of uses, and is difficult to detect and trace after the event.

Assassination is the oldest of terrorist tactics. The targets are often predictable and vulnerable. A properly planned and executed ambush seldom fails and is the basis of most assassination plots. Usually, a vehicle or motorcade is forced to a stop where the attackers can use explosives and machine-gun fire to attack and kill all personnel in the motorcade. After the assassination, the terrorist group generally claims credit. Arson and firebombing are utilized to destroy and disrupt such targets as public utilities, political headquarters, abortion clinics, and economic or industrial targets such as shops, factories, and hotels.

Hijackings and skyjackings are commonly employed to raise funds, attract attention, and spread fear about flying. The hijacking of vehicles can be an indicator of activities to come. Kidnapping, hostage taking, and barricading are violent terrorist acts that can occur singly or as a series of acts. The kidnappers commonly confine the victim to a secret hideaway while ransom demands are made. In a hostage scenario, the hostage taker will confront the authorities and openly hold the victim for ransom, political and/or religious concessions, or acknowledgment of perceived grievances and correction of social wrongs.

Unable to achieve their unrealistic goals by conventional means, international terrorists attempt to send an ideological or religious message by terrorizing the general public. Through the choice of targets, which are often symbolic or representative of the targeted nation, terrorists attempt to create a huge public impact on their targeted enemies with the act of violence, despite their limited material resources. In doing so, they hope to demonstrate that targeted governments cannot protect their own citizens or, by assassinating a specific victim, that they can teach the general public a lesson about espousing viewpoints or policies antithetical to their own.[7]

IS MODERN TERRORISM A FORM OF GUERRILLA WARFARE?

Carlos Marighella was a Brazilian revolutionary, assassinated in Sao Paulo, Brazil, on November 4, 1969. In addition to his actions as a revolutionary, he was a prolific writer. He wrote intensely to support his theories and the practice of guerrilla warfare in the "liberation" of Brazil. His *Minimanual of the Urban Guerrilla* has become a training bible and classic mandatory reading for those engaged in the business of urban guerrilla warfare and those who oppose authority. Marighella summarizes terrorism as follows. "The purpose of terror is to terrorize. The use of terror, even killing the victim, is deliberate and dispassionate, carefully engineered for theatrical effect and involves extensive planning and rehearsal."

Labor unions and organized crime have long engaged in what today would be described as terrorist schemes to "send a message" or to win certain concessions. For

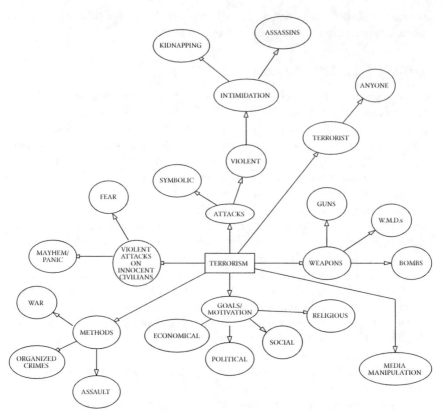

Diagram by Luis Ramirez – Student, American InterContinental University/Los Angeles, CA, 2006

centuries, dead bodies have sent messages. Gangsters refined the issue, and terrorists adopted the scheme. Message generators, in terrorist terms, are the body count or the immediate human victims of the terrorist violence. Witness the number of arsons, bombings, kidnappings, and violent deaths among opposing factions from the early 1900s through prohibition, the labor movement, and the rise of the drug culture. The role of traditional organized crime has now given way to waves of street violence and fear. Drive-by shootings are an everyday occurrence, and citizens are afraid to venture into their own neighborhoods.

Elements of terrorism are common to all the closed societies—the congested ghettos of poor, hardworking immigrants such as the Chinese, Italians, Russians, and others who have been crowded together in cities like New York and San Francisco. Terror tactics such as extortion, fear, and intimidation have been common among inhabitants of refugee communities since the great migrations began in the 1880s.

Since the mid-1970s, Vietnamese refugees (boat people) have settled in southern California, Cuban refugees have found homes in the Miami area, and Russians have located in Los Angeles and New York. Each wave of migration has brought similar versions of terrorism.

A common form of terrorism experienced by immigrants has been violence (i.e., threats, beatings, bombings, arson, and killings) to intimidate and frighten the honest, hardworking citizens into paying for protection or insurance. A thug or group of strong arms will contact a business owner or shop operator and collect a monthly or weekly premium. If no money is forthcoming, the victim can expect to be beaten, bombed, or burned. It is a simple refrain, but terror can be a powerful force inasmuch as the victims will pay and fear to cooperate with legal authorities.

For nearly 20 years, large cities in America have seen a rise in a particularly brutal terrorist crime: home invasion, robbery, and kidnapping. In such cases, small groups of vicious criminals gain entrance to a home through force, intimidation, or trickery. Often they kidnap, terrorize, and hold the homeowner for ransom while other members of the gang rob the victim's bank or business.

During the turbulent anti–Vietnam War protests of the late 1960s and early 1970s, many incidents could realistically be termed terrorist. Public buildings were seized, banks were burned and, in one highly publicized case, a famous newspaper heiress was kidnapped. The girl, Patty Hearst, was singled out because she was more vulnerable than other potential targets (e.g., her parents). The kidnapping group, which called itself the Symbionese Liberation Army (SLA), was led by a former convicted felon known as "Cinque." He took the name from an African slave who lead a mutiny aboard a slave ship in 1839. After kidnapping the heiress, the SLA, following a common terrorist strategy of humiliation, criticism, and torture, brainwashed her into participating in several bank robberies, allegedly to fund their antigovernment movement.

The "army" consisted of fewer than 20 individuals, but their activities were considered terrorist. Their violent actions (which resulted in the death of six members in a burning building during a two-hour shootout with 500 local and federal officers in south central Los Angeles) were calculated to generate maximum publicity and spread fear beyond their victims. They utilized a series of safe houses where they received comfort and care from sympathizers.

Celebrities and VIPs have felt the sting of terrorist-like activities from predatory fans. These *stalkers* are more than an inconvenience. Actress Rebecca Schaffer was killed by a fan who stalked her for a long time, as was John Lennon. An ever-growing number of celebrities are becoming victims of crazed fans who invade their lives. Victims become fearful of every telephone call, every approach by a stranger, and even moving shadows. Everywhere the victim goes, the stalker is sure to follow.

Every corporate executive and high-ranking employee, and in many instances all employees, is a potential victim of workplace violence. Sometimes, threats have left the targeted individual or corporation fearful to the point of incompetence. Workplace violence can range from vengeance planned by one disgruntled employee to violent labor disputes involving many employees.

Los Angeles has become known as the capital city of bank robberies. The three most violent and terror-filled methods of robbing a bank have become the most popular among the robbers. The number one method is for a group of heavily armed robbers, usually numbering three or more, to burst into a bank, take it over, and demand cash. There is no limit to the violence the robbers will inflict, including physical assault (e.g., blows to the head and body of a woman teller, kicking male employees in the groin) and even random shooting of bystanders.

The second method is for a gang of armed robbers to kidnap the bank employees as they arrive for work and force them to open the vault and automated teller machines. The same violent actions as in the first method can be expected. The third method has already been mentioned; the home invasion robbery in which they take over someone's home, assault him, and hold him hostage while others rob the bank. In some cases, the victim is taken to the bank and used as a hostage. These methods are extremely violent, often resulting in death. This is extremely frightening and traumatic to bank employees and customers.

To better understand and appreciate domestic terrorism and countermeasures for combating it, the protection specialist must examine terrorism on the world stage.

TERRORIST MOTIVATION

Men and women commit to a terrorist organization out of a deep, often fanatical, conviction that they are fighting to correct political, religious, social, economic, ideological, geopolitical, or even historical wrongs. Out of their fervor to establish the perceived rightful order, they are willing to make any sacrifice and commit any act, regardless of its moral or legal consequences or popular acceptance. In April 1986, a Jordanian terrorist sent his pregnant Irish girlfriend to Israel on an El-Al flight, promising to meet her there to be married. Unknown to her, he had hidden a bomb in a false bottom to her carry-on luggage. Fortunately, his plan to blow up the airliner in midair was upset when Heathrow security personnel discovered the bomb.

A terrorist is willing to enforce obedience to the movement's leadership using torture and death. It has been proven time after time that a terrorist will willingly sacrifice his life, and the lives of those around him, for his cause.

A terrorist act is calculated to generate publicity for the movement and arouse admiration and emulation. To that end, terrorism becomes theater, choreographed and staged as a media event. The bolder and more heinous the event, the greater the news coverage. Sadly, the escalating violence and dramatic coverage ("details and film at eleven") create a callousness in the world audience, with the result that each succeeding act must be more dramatic and attention grabbing than the last.

In a November 1997, attack in Luxor, Egypt, six "religiously driven and inspired" gunmen rounded up a group of Japanese, Swiss, German, and British tourists and ordered them to kneel. The terrorists then methodically slaughtered 58 of them. When the killing spree was over, the killers sang and danced among the corpses and mutilated the bodies by hacking off ears and noses. One body was slit open and a religious propaganda pamphlet jammed inside it. One of the proclaimed demands of the terrorists was the release of Sheik Omar Abdel Rahman, the aged and blind cleric who is serving a life sentence for masterminding the World Trade Center bombing in February 1993.

The effectiveness of a terrorist attack is measured by the reactions of the people beyond the targeted victim and his immediate circle. The terrorist act would have no major significance without coverage by newspapers and television. This coverage helps spread general confusion and fear, which is the terrorists' objective.

Immediately after the Oklahoma City bombing, authorities rushed to build up security at all federal buildings and airports. In many polls, Americans have indicated that they are willing to give up certain individual freedoms, fought for in past wars and guaranteed by the Constitution, to ensure safety against terrorist attacks. The public reaction after the bombing was general outrage and confusion. Until the person responsible for the attack was arrested and identified as a former American soldier, it was suspected that a foreigner, probably from the Middle East, was responsible. Although an American carried out the attack, it didn't take long for "professional" terrorists in other parts of the world to note the mass hysteria in its aftermath. The target could not have been better selected, because it was a stab at America in the heartland. And because more people were killed in the Oklahoma City bombing than in the World Trade Center attack two years earlier, it created more fear. The event vividly demonstrated that America (and the rest of the world) is highly vulnerable to the confusion, fear, and chaos that terrorism creates. As the late Chairman Mao, head of the Chinese Communist Party, said, "Kill one, frighten a thousand."

Terrorism seeks to create a loss of confidence in the established order and demoralize the population, weakening its confidence in central authority and instilling fear and support of the "revolutionary movement." The terrorist group also hopes to provoke authorities into excessively harsh and repressive measures that alienate the population and undermine support of the establishment. The stepped-up security measures instituted after the Oklahoma City bombing are neither harsh nor repressive, but the fact that it is now more difficult to travel about without being searched and monitored attests to the effectiveness of terror. Although such measures have become necessary and accepted, they are inconvenient and generate some resentment.

The terrorists also hope to discredit and demoralize authorities and show them to be ineffective. As a terrorist movement grows, reacting to it becomes increasingly costly in terms of money and human life. This can result in public demands for the abandonment of counteroffensive actions. Bit by bit, the populace is won over, either by force, fear, intimidation, or a belief in the movement. Established authority is weakened by a loss of trust and confidence and becomes unable to respond effectively.

Many terrorist organizations do not consider a mission to be a failure even if many or all participants are killed or captured. They consider themselves successful if they receive wide media coverage and the ensuing fear and panic somehow change the established order.

The Luxor, Egypt, slaughter is a perfect example. After the killing was over, the six attackers fled into the desert, where they were trapped and killed. They did not win the freedom of Sheik Omar Abdel Rahman, but they focused attention on their new brand of terrorism and increased concerns about the safety of tourists in Egypt.

Another vivid example is the terrorist raid on the 1972 Munich Olympics. The Black September group raided the Olympic village, killed several athletes, and took many others hostage. In the ensuing conflict, five of the eight terrorists were killed. This incident will be remembered as a highly successful terrorist raid because of the after effects. Since that time, hosting the "peaceful" Olympic games has required billions of dollars and virtually immeasurable hours to prevent a recurrence.

MEDIA–TERRORIST RELATIONSHIP

There is a strange symbiotic relationship between terrorists and the news media. A free people need a guaranteed free press to keep them informed of current events. The First Amendment to the U.S. Constitution provides that guarantee. Terrorism covets publicity and needs a propaganda platform. Extensive coverage of a terrorist event provides the information the public needs and seeks, but it also highlights the terrorists' ability to create havoc and airs their ideology, philosophy, and demands. We must ask, "Is it possible to provide news coverage of the horror and tragedy of terrorism without becoming an unwitting propagandist for the terrorists?"

If the press were enjoined from providing unrestricted coverage of a terrorist event, that would constitute one of the biggest victories that terrorists could ever hope to achieve. They would be successful in forcing democracies to adopt the repressive restrictions of dictatorships. But the other side of the double-edged sword is that publishing the full details of terrorist incidents can (and often does) encourage "copycat" acts.

Whether to broadcast or publish interviews with terrorists is a difficult and controversial question for journalists. By broadcasting an interview, the media is most definitely publicizing the organization and its manifesto, thus becoming a partner in the spread of the propaganda. But such an interview can be a good source of intelligence for antiterrorist organizations—and for a protection agent who is conducting a risk analysis to ensure the safety of his protectee.

It has been stated that terrorism is theater. Television is the terrorists' medium of choice, as their acts are played out on a worldwide stage. In that regard, television is not a nonpartisan observer, simply reporting a story. With cameras and reporters in place during a terrorist incident, television becomes a tool of the terrorists and a part of the story.

There are indications that terrorists are increasingly skillful in the use of, and motivated by, publicity. With the proliferation of camcorders, terrorist organizations can easily and inexpensively provide news organizations with television-ready footage. This includes messages from organization leaders, interviews with kidnapped victims, and vivid recordings of executions. Terrorists are well educated in the art of press manipulation and quite skilled in organizing press conferences and handling requests for interviews.

A protection specialist should develop skills in analyzing information obtained through media coverage, consider motivations, and identify potential targets. This will give him an edge when making risk assessments and planning security coverage.

FINANCING TERRORISM

Any government, whether it is a democracy, monarchy, or dictatorship, needs a lot of money to finance its programs and defense. A terrorist operation also has a great demand for funds to supply and support the organization and its cause. We have observed that two things, expenses and imagination, limit the protection specialist. The terrorist has only one limit: imagination! No terrorist attack is even contemplated until it has been completely funded. Some terrorist activities are designed to attract money. Capital is regularly generated through terrorist acts. Kidnapping for ransom is one popular income source, and bank robbery often brings in large sums. Many "popular" terrorist organizations raise money via donations from sympathizers. Some organizations, such as the Irish Republican Army (IRA) and the Palestine Liberation Organization (PLO), sent emissaries to the United States to hold public fundraisers and to solicit donations from supporters coast to coast.

Extortion and threats have created many donors. Selling "insurance" to guarantee the safety of people and businesses has been effective in communities where people are as fearful of the authorities as they are of the terrorist groups. Many organizations, such as the "narco-terrorists" of Central and South America and Southeast Asia, can raise all the money they need from the sale of illicit drugs. The high demand for drugs makes it easy.

Ironically, terrorism can be relatively inexpensive. A few perpetrators with inexpensive (or stolen) small arms and improvised explosives can create disruptions that affect whole nations. That is the way many revolutions (including the American one) are started. As the movement grows, so does the need for more money.

TERRORIST WEAPONS

The greatest of the terrorist weapons are beyond physical measure. The first is the element of surprise, which gives terrorists the initial advantage. The attackers choose the time, place, and circumstance. They control the who, what, when, where, why, and how. They are well trained and organized and prepare for all contingencies. Their targets are often undefended or have a weak attitude toward security. Violence, speed, and surprise characterize terrorist attacks. They happen swiftly and without warning, giving the target and its defenders no time to effectively respond unless they are mentally prepared.

The second esoteric weapon has been mentioned—the element of fear. Fear caused by the sudden appearance of a group of gun-wielding, shouting, cursing, and violent terrorists can be totally debilitating. There may be gunfire, explosives, fire, and smoke. Even people who are highly trained in combative situations may be stricken, at least momentarily, with fright or surprise, rendering them helpless and giving the advantage to the attackers.

The standard and more familiar type of weapons includes handguns, rifles, light automatic weapons, hand grenades, and improvised explosives. Guns, of course, are the primary weapons. The selection ranges from semiautomatic pistols to fully automatic assault weapons. The AK "Bullpup" and similar weapons are very effective because they are short, compact, and have a rapid fire rate and large ammunition capacity. The MAC-90 is also very effective. It is an assault-type weapon, compact and yet capable of firing several rounds per minute.

Explosives are weapons of mass destruction. Strategically placed and timed, they are effective in killing many people at once. They also instill fear in the broad populace. Bombing is the most common tactic. The bomb is popular because it is cheap and easy to produce, has variable uses, and is difficult to trace after the event. Bombs can be delivered easily and simply, and many types of bombs exist. Among them are letter bombs, package bombs, vehicle bombs, pipe bombs, and firebombs.

Bombs can be thrown from moving cars or planted virtually anywhere. They are placed in cars, airplanes, public buildings, government facilities, and in the mail, as well as under streets and overpasses. Because of their easy placement, a protection agent and other security personnel should always be aware that a bomb could be waiting anywhere it could threaten the protectee and his entourage.

The terrorist use of nuclear weapons has become a chilling matter for governments and antiterrorist organizations, especially with their easy availability as a result of the collapse of the Soviet Union. But the threat of nuclear weapons, while still very much a concern, has taken a back-burner position to the havoc that could be wrought by a new generation of terrorists who have access to chemical and biological weapons. Terrorist-sponsoring countries such as Iraq, Libya, North Korea, and China are known to have manufactured enough germ warfare components to infect and kill everyone on Earth.

A Japanese terrorist organization, the Aum Shinrikyo, used nerve gas in a strike on the Tokyo subway system in 1995, killing a dozen people. The group was later determined to be building a reserve of anthrax and botulism toxin as well. In the United States, there is evidence that leftists and right-wing extremists may be quietly obtaining a repository of deadly chemicals and germs.

Another disease that can bring intense suffering and death is also a likely candidate for germ warfare, and several nations are suspected of harboring the deadly toxin. The disease, smallpox, was declared eradicated in 1982. Since that time, an entire generation has grown without being vaccinated against this killer. Smallpox has killed entire civilizations in the past; its reintroduction could again cause pain, death, and chaos.

Protection specialists must acquaint themselves with the possibility of a biological or chemical attack and prepare accordingly. Sterile breathing gear, gas masks, and protective clothing should be readily accessible. Agents should be familiar with antidotes such as atropine, which must be administered as a preventive inoculation or within minutes after exposure.

Kidnapping is a favorite weapon of terrorists. They use kidnapping as a twofold tool; it is both a weapon and a fund-raiser. As a weapon, it spreads fear and intimidation. Governments, corporations, and individuals will spend millions to protect against kidnapping. The focus of terrorist kidnappings are powerful and wealthy (or perceived wealthy) individuals, corporate executives, and individuals whose kidnapping will result in ransom payments or news headlines. A terrorist kidnapping will likely result in a demand for the release of imprisoned terrorists or "political prisoners," a lifting of government sanctions, or other concessions. In addition, a kidnapping often involves a demand for a large amount of cash for the safe release of the victim. Kidnappings are sometimes the result of "takeovers," with the victims being held as hostages. More often, however, a kidnapping victim is an individual snatched from a public street, typically within 3.5 miles of his home.

As a weapon, a kidnapping can be as effective as all the guns and bombs because of the fear and publicity it induces. When the kidnappers have acted with audacity and success and a community, or even a government, begins to wonder who is next, the result is truly rewarding to the terrorist.

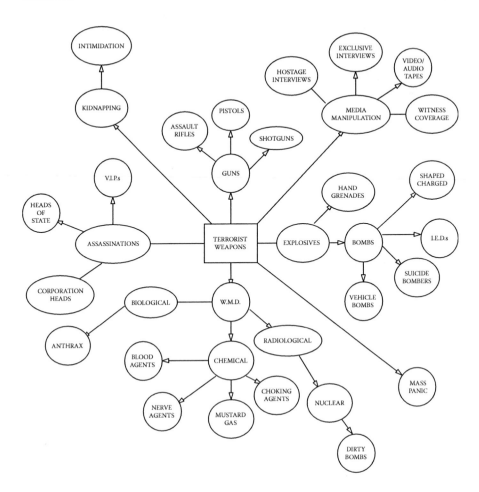

Diagram by Luis Ramirez – Student, American InterContinental University/Los Angeles, CA, 2006

WHO ARE THE TERRORISTS?

For purposes of anticipating and defending against terrorist activity, the protection specialist must recognize three classifications of terrorists for purposes of "profiling." Although basic strategies are used in all planned responses, it is important to know the psychology or mind-set of potential antagonists. A particular protectee will be more susceptible to attack from one type of threat than another. For example, he may have no value as a political hostage or religious target, but to a criminal opportunist, the protectee may be a perfect target for robbery, extortion, or kidnapping. Therefore, the executive protection specialist must recognize and prepare against the crusader, criminal, or crazy.

The stereotypical crusading terrorists are ideologically motivated. That is, they are inspired by political or religious beliefs. Either way, the terrorist is an extremist. As a political activist, he is radical in his beliefs and is defined as a right-wing ultraconservative or a left-wing anarchist or revolutionary. Or he may be a fervent religious fundamentalist. He may be a fanatic who envisions himself as a messenger or tool of God, or he may see himself as a martyr who is willing to die for his faith and cause.

An ultraconservative political terrorist has a firm belief that the individual rights of a free people take precedence over an established central government. He may be a member of a quasi-military group such as an independent militia. He may be a white neo-Nazi or "skinhead" supremacist following a racist doctrine. On the other hand, he may be an antiabortionist who believes in the "right to life" and will use bombs and arson to enforce that belief. A new word to describe some terrorists has come into use: *eco-terrorist*. These people have been known, for example, to place large spikes in trees to jam the chain saws of lumberjacks, possibly causing serious injury or death.

The political anarchist is an ultraleftist who is extremely radical and believes that no government is better than any government. Anarchists have committed many political assassinations around the world. Anarchy was especially popular during the period of 1880 to 1914, when the leaders of several national governments were assassinated. The anarchist movement is still active, although less vocal and dynamic than the 1960s and 1970s radicals who attempted to topple many governments in many nations, including the United States. But they still have aspirations of living without any government. The far left is also against corporate "exploitation of the people " and views capitalism as something that should be abolished.

The attack at Luxor took religious terrorism to a new level of depravity. Wanton killing in the name of God's purpose and believing they are accountable only to God leads terrorists to assume that their chosen creed defines the only correct way of life. To forfeit their life for religious ideals is a worthwhile sacrifice and a sure path to the gardens of Paradise.

The criminal terrorist will commit terrorist acts for personal gain rather than ideological reasons. Perhaps a drug kingpin believes that assassinating a particular political figure will enhance his standing with the cartels of Asia and South America. Or the criminal terrorist may participate in a highly lucrative robbery or kidnapping for ransom. Whatever his motivation, he chooses a target for personal gain rather than for a cause.

Every day, the White House receives letters addressed to the U.S. president from religious zealots who proclaim that God will remove the president, the cabinet, and his staff of heretic followers. To a rational mind, most of the letters are rambling discourses that make no sense. The sources of this material constitute the third category of terrorist concern—the crazies. Of course, each letter is forwarded to the Secret Service for investigation. But the president is not the only target of the crazies. Any public figure, corporate executive, or wealthy (or perceived wealthy) person is susceptible to the fixations of a psychologically disturbed individual. Yigal Amir is one religious crazy who conducted a "God approved, directed, and influenced" assassination. In 1996, he assassinated Israeli Prime Minister Yitzhak Rabin. The killing was not for a specific political or religious purpose; as Amir explained, he was only acting as God's instrument.

Many terrorists may fall into all three categories: crusader, criminal, and crazy. As a profile, the terrorist has many of the attributes of the potential assassin, the serial killer, and the vengeful employee. He may be a loner, an orphan or a neglected child, or a righteous perfectionist. Such people will join a group or cause with which they identify. They seek recognition for themselves as well as for the cause. They are usually seriously psychotic, with one manifested goal: to bring attention to their skewed purpose. They are willing to use violent means to achieve their warped ends and are willing, even eager, to die for the belief and recognition as a martyr.

The typical terrorist is an unmarried male (although terrorism is an equal opportunity employer, made up of 30 to 40 percent women) in his twenties or thirties, usually with an urban upbringing. He is above average in intelligence, having attended college and obtained at least a bachelor's degree. Coming from a middle-class or upper middle-class background, he may speak more than one language. His political philosophy leans heavily toward Marxism, and his religious tendency is to the very conservative orthodox. He will readily adapt to changes in his environment and is able to hide easily among the populace by living "underground" and assuming new identities.

The executive protection specialist should know whether his protectee is a potential target of national, transnational, or international terrorists. Each level of terrorism has similar motives, but the interest in a potential target is key.

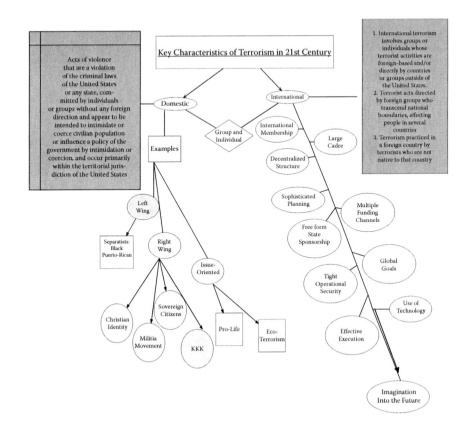

Diagram by Gayane Boysnian – Student, American InterContinental University/Los Angeles, CA, 2006

TERRORISM IN THE TWENTY-FIRST CENTURY

A national terrorist operates within only one nation and has no global or international aspirations. This type of terrorist can include the stalker and criminal elements as well as the political and religious fanatics of the left and right. It may also include antiabortionists or right-to-lifers, militant environmentalists, and animal rights activists. The targets of his interest may be considered vulnerable mostly on a regional or local level.

A transnational terrorist operates across national borders. His motivations are personal, yet he is a passionate supporter of the doctrine of the organization to which he belongs. His belief in the cause is so strong that he is willing, even eager, to die as a martyr. His targets of interest are usually on a grand scale, or his activities will be spectacular enough to generate significant international attention. The transnational terrorist will participate in skyjackings and/or downing of commercial airliners with explosives, kidnapping of high-level executives, assassinations, and unprovoked attacks like the attack on the tourists in Luxor, Egypt. His activities are designed and orchestrated as a statement intended to send a message to the widest audience possible.

An international terrorist is an operating arm of and controlled by a sovereign government and represents that state's interest. This type of terrorist has no personal interest or belief in the cause; rather, he is simply following orders of the directive governmental faction. He is often considered a mercenary, a soldier of fortune, selling his services to any government or quasi-government willing to pay his salavry and expenses. He is well financed and highly trained. His targets usually are of strategic interest to his employing government. His activities are intended to influence the attitude and behavior of a specific group, such as an opposing government, regardless of national boundaries.

Nothing brought the fear of twenty-first century terrorism home to most North Americans like the 2001 airplane-bomb attack on the World Trade Center and Pentagon. Presages of that horrific event were provided by the bombing of the federal building in Oklahoma City by former U.S. soldier Timothy McVeigh and the 1993 bombing of the World Trade Center by Middle Eastern religious terrorists. Those events brought death and destruction and held worldwide media attention, generating fear as the American public awoke to the dawning of the twenty-first century, looked around, and saw terrorism in the front yard and the "green, green grass of home." Until then, terrorism, to the average American, was something done only by religious fanatics in the Middle East or political radicals of Europe, Asia, and Africa.

In war, as brutal, savage, and uncivilized as it is, participants usually adhere to certain rules of engagement. Terrorism, on the other hand, knows no bounds and violates at least two precepts: the targets and ancillary victims are noncombatants, and the terrorist weapons are indiscriminate (i.e., bombs, bullets, and arson). Anyone in the immediate vicinity may easily become a victim, because "bombs don't discriminate," bullets don't care whose flesh is torn, and fire will burn if given fuel and oxygen.

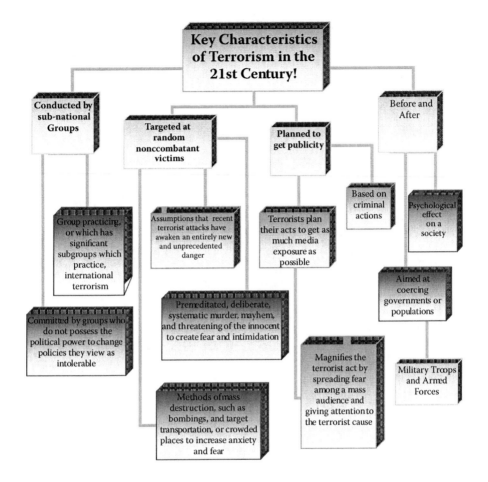

SUMMARY

Victims of terrorism may be children in a classroom, innocent travelers on an airplane or ocean liner or at a tourist attraction, businessmen, political leaders and diplomats, industrialists, and military personnel. Anyone is a potential target, and everyone can be a victim. A populace (especially those who are responsible for the safety and survival of others) must contemplate the possibilities of a terrorist attack and prepare accordingly. It is each person's responsibility to prepare for emergencies such as natural disasters, as do many people and communities. But preparing for a terrorist incident seems to be so esoteric that few people recognize the need.

Terrorist tactics will continue to evolve to conceive new ways to commit violence. Persons providing protective services have a duty and responsibility to gain a thorough understanding of the factors, goals, and motivation of persons and groups who intend to embarrass, injure, kidnap, or assassinate a protectee. The defense against terrorism begins with research and knowledge regarding the groups and activities that may threaten a principal or organization. The protective specialist must develop intelligence resources that will provide any information that could adversely impact the safety and well-being of a protectee. It is important to know how groups or individuals have carried out previous attacks and by what means. All the data is analyzed as part of the risk assessment. The higher the degree of probability and likelihood of terrorist disruption, the higher should be the degree of anticipation, planning, and preparation.

REVIEW QUESTIONS

1. Explain the statement, "Terrorism is theater."
2. What is meant by, "Terrorism is doomed to failure, but in certain respects it has been successful."
3. Why has terrorism been relatively limited in the United States? Detail several ways the United States is vulnerable to terrorism.
4. What should be the role of the press/news media with regard to terrorism and what (if any) restrictions should be placed on media representatives?
5. What is considered "the most dangerous time of your life," and how does that relate to terrorism, executive protection, or personal safety?
6. What advice would you give a loved one planning a trip to a foreign country?
7. Why is it important to read the newspaper and newsmagazines and watch or listen to broadcast news? After all, most of the news stories concern crime in the street and world problems, which are far removed from your lifestyle and neighborhood. What should you look for and how can you use the information?
8. Describe some modern methods of domestic terrorism, that is, terrorism on American soil.
9. Why should an executive protection agent develop sources of intelligence information regarding terrorist activity? What should he look for? What does he do with the data?

NOTES

1. Hudson, Rex A. *The Sociology and Psychology of Terrorism: Who Becomes a Terrorist and Why?* Washington, DC: Federal Research Division, Library of Congress, 1999, http://lcweb.loc.gov/rr/frd/.
2. Quoted in LeShan, Lawrence, *The Psychology of War.* Chicago: Noble Press, 1992, 83.
3. "Analyzing Terror: Researchers Study the Perpetrators and the Effects of Suicide Terrorism." *National Institute of Justice Journal* 254, 8.
4. Ibid., 10.
5. Ibid.
6. Hesketh, Therese, and Wei Xing, Zhu. Abnormal Sex Ratios in Human Populations: Causes and Consequences, *PNAS 103*: 36. 13271–13275. (2006)
7. Hudson, Rex A. *The Sociology And Psychology Of Terrorism.*

19 Kidnapping and Bombs!

A tale of abduction and things that go "boom" in the night!

There was martyrs in old times, that suffered death rather than give up the particular graft they enjoyed....

O. Henry, "The Ransom of Red Chief"

Kidnapping and bombs, as they relate to a protectee, are of special primary importance to a protection agent. Kidnapping of an executive or key employee or bombing of the workplace will have an adverse effect on the business and personnel. In addition to his regular protective duties, which include defending against kidnapping and preventing the placement of bombs, a protection agent is often called upon to assist in formulating antikidnapping and bomb-threat procedures.

KIDNAPPING

It was the Christmas holiday weekend in Tijuana, Mexico, an easy walk from the border at San Diego, California. An American businessman left his house at the regular time of about 9:00 A.M. and began his usual trip to the office, a few miles away. Suddenly, just a few blocks from his house, he was set upon by a group of men and forced into a car. His abduction was swift and little noticed. In a few hours, his family and business were notified of the victim's situation, and a $250,000 ransom was demanded for his safe return. The business, headquartered in Cincinnati, Ohio, furnished the money and, as the ransom was delivered, police provided surveillance and followed the person who picked up the ransom. As he arrived at the kidnapper's headquarters, the police moved in, took the kidnappers into custody, and successfully rescued the poor, frightened businessman. The unusual aspect of that kidnapping was the successful and safe return of the victim, the apprehension of the kidnappers, and recovery of the ransom money.

Tijuana is located less than twenty miles from downtown San Diego. It is a city of over a million people and is very "Americanized." American tourists, day trippers, businessmen, and even American teenagers who go there on weekends to enjoy a night of partying wrongly feel a sense of safety and security and that nothing untoward could render them victims of anything as unseemly as kidnapping. The aforementioned businessman had lived and worked in Tijuana for some time and had established a lifestyle there. As he left home, he was merely following his daily routine.

If he had been reading the daily newspaper (even a copy of the San Diego newspaper), he might have realized that kidnapping has become a cottage industry—a fast way to make large amounts of money as well as a common method of making political demands. He would also have realized that, as a foreign businessman, he was a likely victim. But he was lulled by a false sense of security. He could see the United States from his window, and Tijuana was so Americanized. He never could have been more wrong. It nearly cost him his life and his company $250,000.

Kidnapping is the physical taking of a person by force, fear, or fraud to a hidden place. It is normally accompanied by extortion—a demand for money or political concessions. Victims are usually public figures, wealthy individuals or people of perceived wealth, corporate executives, children, or young adults; anyone can be a target for kidnapping. Most kidnappings have occurred on public streets within 3.5 miles of the victim's home.

There are several reasons why kidnappings occur so close to home. Being in very familiar surroundings, the intended victim tends to be more relaxed and is only minimally aware of activity around him. He is usually preoccupied with thoughts of anything but personal security. The kidnap scenario totally surprises him. Even as it develops, he is slow in recognizing that it could be happening in his friendly neighborhood. He probably is living in an area where it is impossible to take an alternative route away from home. His normally leaves home at the same time every day.

The potential victim and his accompanying protective agent(s) must be continually alert for any unusual, potentially menacing activity in the vicinity. Even though he is in familiar surroundings, he must continue his vigilance. Often, a protective group will begin to relax as the motorcade begins to approach the home area. The agents are tired after being in a constant state of readiness. "What could happen so close to home?" becomes an understood, unasked question, and an attitude of "routine as usual" supersedes the alert status. Leaving a safe compound, estate, or home in the morning also engenders the attitude that "nothing could go wrong so early in the morning." A kidnapper will strike when your guard is down.

Kidnapping can be a way of attracting attention to a cause, righting a wrong (such as inducing a political prisoner exchange), demanding social change, or obtaining a ransom. For whatever purpose, kidnapping is on a worldwide upswing because of social and political volatility, especially in Third World countries.

Criminal justice experts, criminologists, and social scientists have identified three categories of kidnappers. The classifications may often overlap but, for general purposes, the types of kidnappers are as follows:

1. *The political kidnapper or terrorist.* This group includes religious, ethnic, and racial fanatics who act for the usual reasons of attracting publicity for their cause and achieving some political goal. American businesses abroad have often caused a feeling of exploitation in the indigenous population. The locals believe they are being taken advantage of through tax advantages granted by the host country and low wages paid by the company. Certain dissident groups have reacted to this actual or imagined exploitation by kidnapping corporate executives and making extortionate demands. The kidnapping is intended to force the government or the targeted entity (usually a foreign business) to implement some change or act. Terrorist kidnappings

are usually undertaken with multiple objectives, which include money, publicity, and the disruption of the legitimate operation of a business.

2. *The mentally disturbed or mentally ill.* Usually a psychopath, this type of kidnapper is extremely dangerous because of his unpredictability, instability, and irrationality. He might kidnap in retaliation for having been fired from his job, to address a real or imagined grievance that was not resolved to his satisfaction, or just in response to an imagined or real insult. Sometimes a mentally ill person, without any comprehensive motive, will kidnap or even kill innocent corporate personnel as a means of gaining fame and a feeling of power. This type has become increasingly common since the late 1980s and is responsible for many injuries and deaths in the workplace.

3. *The criminal kidnapper.* He is usually interested only in making a large sum of money quickly or force compliance with some demand. This type of kidnapper may not be as dangerous as the other two, as he is apt to be rational, and his only desire is monetary payment or his freedom in return for the safe release of the victim.

ESTABLISHING KIDNAP AND EXTORTION POLICY

A policy should be established that provides guidelines for handling a kidnapping attempt directed against a protectee. A protection specialist may be called on to aid in devising a procedural plan for such incidents. These guidelines should spell out specific policy relative to paying ransoms and other details. Particular emphasis should be placed on naming appropriate responsibilities and assigning authority for crisis decisions. Provisions should also be made for the uninterrupted conduct of business. Contingency plans should be frankly discussed with the potential victim, his family, and business associates regarding what should be done in the event of a kidnapping. Contingency plans should be reviewed on a regular basis, and certain code words should be created and understood by those most vulnerable to kidnapping. In the event a principal or a family member is kidnapped, code words and duress signals can be useful for sending hidden messages if the kidnappers force the victim to communicate with the outside world.

When discussing kidnap scenarios, certain decisions must be made in advance. One of the most important concerns whom to notify if an executive, celebrity, or other VIP is taken. This decision depends partly on the nature of the threat (or actual crisis) and the content of the communications from the perpetrators. A terrorist group staging a spectacular kidnapping will often communicate directly with the news media to ensure maximum publicity. Obviously, in this instance, there is no additional danger to the victim if the agent contacts appropriate law enforcement agencies directly and immediately.

On the other hand, an individual or group of criminals effecting a covert kidnapping for ransom, in their initial contact, may demand secrecy under penalty of death. In this extreme case, the crisis manager (director of security, protection specialist, or other designee) should send a prearranged signal to the Federal Bureau of Investigation (in the United States) or the proper agency in another country. It is usually best to discreetly alert the proper authorities despite any warnings received from the kidnappers. In this situation, no other agency or individuals should be notified. The victim's home and family could very well be under surveillance and the telephone monitored. At the very least, it can be expected that the kidnapper will redial the contact number several times after his initial communication to see if the line is busy (to determine if authorities are being notified in spite of his warning). Kidnap situations between these two extremes demand caution and judgment in notifying the predetermined personnel and authorities.

Other considerations are as follows:

1. Is a ransom to be paid?
2. Is the full amount to be paid, or will there be negotiations?
3. If there are to be negotiations, what are the limits?
4. How is the cash to be raised?
5. Is the money to be marked? If so, how?
6. Who will deliver the ransom?
7. Should there be a rescue/arrest attempt when payment is made? (Note that this is often the best time or only opportunity to intervene.)

HOSTAGE AND KIDNAP NEGOTIATIONS

A skilled, experienced, professional hostage negotiator must conduct hostage negotiations. The key to successful negotiations is communication between the negotiator, hostage taker, and corporate representatives or law enforcement authorities. A professional negotiator must understand the mental state of the hostage taker. Time is on the side of the negotiating team, so negotiations must not be hurried or seemingly in a state of panic. Negotiations must be done in a calm, collected manner. As part of kidnap/hostage contingency planning, expert negotiators must be identified and able to respond on very short notice. They must be familiar with the background of the victim, how the situation developed, and corporate policies regarding the circumstances. The negotiators must have authority (working with the crisis management team and police) to make decisions and must be able to convey this to the hostage taker.

Corporate executives, celebrities, VIPs, and other likely kidnapping targets should consider kidnapping as a real possibility. Executive protection programs should be planned, programmed, and implemented with special attention to prevention and preparedness. In the absence of a formal executive protection plan that includes protective agents, advance personnel, and so forth, a potential victim can do several things to deter a possible kidnapping. It is recommended that they follow standard target-hardening procedures and maintain a low-profile personal lifestyle. They should

1. Keep their names off mailboxes and front doors.
2. Have their home telephone numbers unlisted.
3. Stay out of the newspaper social columns.
4. Vary their daily routines, time of departures and arrivals, routes of travel, and so on.

5. Install security alarm systems.
6. Report threatening telephone calls and letters.
7. Look out for surveillance, being suspicious of "census takers," "lost tourists," and others.
8. Compile personal profiles on potential targets and their families. Maintain basic, everyday security procedures and alertness, and keep records that include physical descriptions, photographs, and medical histories that may be useful to authorities in case of a kidnapping or other emergency. Lock the files in a secure safe or vault.
10. Conduct liaison with local law enforcement and the FBI representatives to learn their polices and determine what help they can provide in an emergency.
11. Attempt to determine or predict how family and staff will react in a stressful emergency situation.
12. Form a crisis management team.
13. Create written contingency plans, and have them on file, for bomb threats, kidnappings and other hostage situations, and other terrorist actions.
14. Brief and train personnel in the ways, motives, and goals of terrorist groups.

These are only minimal target-hardening measures. The protection agent should develop further contingency plans and obtain the cooperation of the key inner-circle personnel to make the business and living environment as safe and free from adverse activities as possible. Living and working in high-threat areas demands very close attention to the details of target hardening, threat assessment, and preventive measures. The best way to avoid paying ransom with a life or money is to make the target unappealing or unreachable.

BOMBS AND BOMB THREATS

To the uninitiated or uninformed, a bomb may be visualized as a six-pack of dynamite wrapped with wire and having a fuse and perhaps a clock attached to it. But a metal soap dish, a thermos bottle, a cigarette package, a shoebox, beer cans, or any of thousands of containers can hold a bomb. Explosive devices come in all shapes, sizes, and containers. What really makes a bomb frightening is the fact it can be placed in anything, anywhere, and does not discriminate in whom it hurts, maims, or kills.

Protection personnel and others who could be exposed to a bomb in any way—as victims, targets, or bomb searchers—should be familiar with bombs: how they are made, delivered, and exploded. In some areas of the world, explosive devices are common tools of terrorism and political unrest. The makings of a bomb are readily available. The Oklahoma City bombing enlightened the whole world about the explosive power of simple fertilizer and motor fuel. In some instances, military ordinance (explosive material) has been stolen or bought on the black market. Commercial explosives, used at construction sites, are often stolen or purchased from munitions and explosives dealers. A bomber can readily make explosives by simply following recipes obtained from underground bomb cookbooks or literature in a public library. A bright student with a minimal education in high school chemistry can make a bomb.

Homemade bombs are especially dangerous because of the way they are made. A bomb maker is limited by his knowledge of explosives, supplies, tools, and targets. There will be variations in design and manufacture. Therefore, when an unexploded bomb is found, there can be no set procedures for rendering it safe. Only highly trained and experienced bomb disposal specialists or explosive ordinance disposal (EOD) personnel must be allowed to handle any suspicious device that could be a bomb. Protection agents should never attempt to defuse a bomb or move it to a "safer" area.

Explosive devices must contain at least two things: an explosive substance and something to make it explode. The explosion is initiated by one of three methods: (1) time, (2) motion, or (3) remote control. The most common type of bomb initiator is a burning fuse. The length of the fuse determines the burn time. But this type of bomb, because of the burning fuse, is seldom the device of choice when the target is other than a construction site or rock quarry. A timing device such as a watch or clock controls a mechanical-delay bomb. When a clock's hand reaches a specified point on the clock face, contact with an electrical source (usually a small battery) causes the initiator (an electrical blasting cap) to ignite the explosive charge.

Motion-initiated bombs (often called booby traps) are set off when an article is moved, causing a connection to be broken or brought into contact and sending a current to the igniter. Mousetraps and similar devices make excellent initiators because of their sensitivity to movement. This type of bomb is secreted in packages, books, automobiles, and other locations.

Remotely initiated bombs are rigged so that the explosive device is set off using a remote control similar to a garage door opener or television channel selector.

BOMB DELIVERY

Bombs are delivered and placed in the target area by several surreptitious means. Most commonly, one or more perpetrators gain access to the area by posing as maintenance personnel, vendors, clients, or other legitimate visitors. A bomb may be hand delivered and personally placed by the bomber in the exact position desired or to prevent premature firing.

The bomb that blew up Pan American flight 103 over Lockerbie, Scotland, in 1988 (killing 259 passengers and injuring 11 others on the ground) was thought to have been secreted in a cassette recorder. Either a passenger unknowingly carried it aboard the plane, or a ground technician placed it aboard. It is now standard procedure at all airports to remind the public to avoid leaving any luggage unattended. If unattended luggage is observed, the public is asked to report it, and police or airport authorities will confiscate it. The public is also asked to not carry any luggage for anyone not flying on the same flight and to refuse any packages from strangers.

Receptionists and other personnel who come into contact with visitors should be cautioned to watch for individuals who appear to "forget" a briefcase or other package. If a visitor ignores a reminder and persists in leaving the object behind, it could be a bomb and should be treated accordingly.

Sometimes bombs are delivered in the mail or by a package delivery service. Any suspicious package or letter should be treated as a potential bomb. Package and letter bombs can be easily delivered and accepted without suspicion during periods when packages are expected, such as Christmas or birthdays. If a return address is unfamiliar or a package or letter appears unusual in any way, it should be suspect.

Letter bombs are often identifiable because they are slightly thicker and/or heavier than the usual brochures and advertising packets. On occasion, they have been described as smelling like almonds or shoe polish. In addition, some irregularities may be discerned by very lightly touching the flat surfaces. A spring release or a mercury switch usually detonates the devices when the envelope is opened or its contents are removed. Therefore, incoming mail to offices and executives' homes can be considered potentially dangerous. Anything of a suspicious origin or appearance should not be dumped in water, tossed or handed around, or opened until it has been x-rayed or fluoroscoped and declared benign by qualified personnel.

Bombs, of course, may be dropped from planes, thrown from moving vehicles, or projected by cannons. Anything can contain a bomb, and its delivery is a simple matter. For example, an explosive device packed inside a metal soap dish can easily be attached to the undercarriage of a car, on or near the gas tank. The small packet of explosive material causes a secondary explosion as the gas tank erupts in flames and quickly engulfs the car and occupant. The person placing the device simply walks past the car and, while barely slowing down, merely slaps it in place with attached magnets. This type of device is ignited by a blasting cap and remote control. Timothy McVeigh delivered his bomb in a rented truck that he parked adjacent to the federal building.

VEHICLE BOMBS

The U.S. Bureau of Alcohol, Tobacco, Firearms and Explosives developed the following explosion and evacuation distance tables.

MINIMUM EVACUATION DISTANCE

- At this range, a life-threatening injury from blast or fragment hazards is unlikely.
- However, non–life threatening injury or temporary hearing loss may occur.

HAZARD RANGES

- These are based on open, level terrain.
- Minimum evacuation distance may be less when explosion is confined within a structure.

FALLING GLASS HAZARD

- Range is dependent on line-of-sight from explosion source to window.

- Hazard is from falling shards of broken glass.

EXPLOSION CONFINED WITHIN A STRUCTURE

- May cause structural collapse or building debris hazards.
- May include vehicle and/or environmental debris.

VEHICLE BOMBS' DESCRIPTION

COMPACT SEDAN

- *Maximum explosives capacity (in trunk)*—500 kg (227 kg)
- *Lethal air blast range*—100 ft (30 m)
- *Minimum evacuation range*—1,600 ft (457 m)
- *Falling glass hazard*—1,250 ft (301 m)

FULL-SIZED SEDAN

- *Maximum explosives capacity (in trunk)*—1,000 lb (455 kg)
- *Lethal air blast range*—125 ft (38 m)
- *Minimum evacuation range*—1,750 ft (534 m)
- *Falling glass hazard*—1,750 ft (534 m)

PASSENGER OR CARGO VAN

- *Maximum explosives capacity*—4,000 lb (1818 kg)
- *Lethal air blast range*—200 ft (61m)
- *Minimum evacuation range*—2,750 ft (838 m)
- *Falling glass hazard*—2,750 ft (838 m)

SMALL BOX VAN (14 FOOT BOX)

- *Maximum explosives capacity*—10,000 lb (4545 kg)
- *Lethal air blast range*—300 ft (91m)
- *Minimum evacuation range*—3,750 ft (1143 m)
- *Falling glass hazard*—3,750 ft (1143 m)

BOX VAN OR WATER/FUEL TRUNK

- *Maximum explosives capacity*—30,000 lb (13,636 kg)
- *Lethal air blast range*—460 ft (137 m)
- *Minimum evacuation range*—6,500 ft (1982 m)
- *Falling glass hazard*—6,500 ft (1982 m)

SEMI-TRAILER

- *Maximum explosives capacity*—60,000 lb (27,273 kg)
- *Lethal air blast range*—600 ft (183 m)

- *Minimum evacuation range—7,000 ft (2134 m)*
- *Falling glass hazard—7,000 ft (2134 m)*

REMINDER

- One mile = 5,280 ft
- One mile = 1,600 m

A semi-trailer load of explosives can create a falling glass and debris hazard over a range of 1.5 miles.

BOMB PROTECTION AND EVACUATION

Fences, locks, security barriers, and properly trained security personnel are all deterrents to a bomber. But if an unexploded bomb is discovered, the best protection is distancing oneself from the area as quickly as possible. Every corporate installation must have bomb evacuation procedures in place. The evacuation procedures are the same as for any other emergency. To effect an evacuation, it is often best to treat it as a fire drill and have all personnel leave the building in a quick and orderly manner.

Employees should be advised that management needs their cooperation; self-restraint and calm should be emphasized. All fireproof filing cabinets are to be closed and locked. Doors and windows should be left open to disperse the blast effect and reduce the fragmentation and shattering commonly associated with a confined blast. Electronically operated office machines and appliances should be disconnected if time and the situation permit. Only purses, coats, and readily accessible, sensitive and important papers should be taken during an evacuation. Evacuating personnel should leave the building as quickly and orderly as possible, using the most direct route, and move to an area as far removed from the potential danger as possible. Planners should make sure the area is sufficiently distant, includes barriers, and is large enough that people will not be in close proximity to glass windows or other large objects that could shatter. Additionally, they should ensure that the evacuation site is a safe and secure area where a secondary bomb could not be secreted.

If a bomb is located, activate evacuation procedures. The area must be secured and the bomb removal and disposal specialists notified. If a bomb explodes, normal emergency and medical procedures should be implemented immediately.

BOMB THREAT PROCEDURES

RECEIVING THE THREAT

Policies and procedures regarding bomb threats and searches should be familiar to all personnel at the site of the bomb threat. A bomb threat may be a hoax, or it may be a warning from an actual bomber. The hoax caller will generally give neither a reason for the bomb nor a specific location. However, no threatening call can be ignored. The serious-threat caller probably does not want people harmed, or he would not make the warning call. Unless the caller knows the direct telephone number of a specific employee, he will call in his threat or warning on the general telephone number at the main reception desk or telephone operator's console. Threats are most commonly received this way.

SWITCHBOARD OPERATOR INSTRUCTIONS

It is essential that the operator remains calm and obtains as much information as possible from the caller. A standard checklist for recording the details of the threat should be readily available to operators, receptionists, and others in a position to receive the threat. They should be familiar with its contents and be prepared to write down everything stated by the caller. The call recipient should start a new checklist each time the person calls. He should be cautious to avoid volunteering any information about the offices or personnel.

Immediately upon hearing the caller's threat or demand, the person handling the incoming threat should signal a nearby person to call the building security office, contact the police and fire departments, or follow the predetermined course of action as prescribed by the company emergency plan. A sample bomb threat report form appears at the end of this chapter.

SEARCHES

Evacuation is not necessarily the first course of action to be taken after every bomb threat; in some instances, it may not even be the safest course. Unless the caller gives the location of the bomb, searching before evacuation is sometimes a safer and better alternative. Bombs are often planted in passageways or near entrances and exits where the bomber has easy access. Evacuation could amass a large number of employees in these danger areas. For this reason, it may be safer to conduct a search rather than to evacuate.

The personnel working in each area should conduct searches. They are most familiar with anything that is out of place or does not belong. The rule of thumb when searching for a bomb is to look for anything that does not belong or is not recognized. Any suspicious object should remain exactly as is and not touched or moved. Only qualified bomb disposal personnel should examine it.

As each area is cleared by a search, the information should be recorded so that no area is overlooked. It is the area that is not checked that will explode. Also, after clearing an area, personnel should remain there until an "all clear" is sounded for the entire building. Otherwise, they might wander into an uncleared, unsafe area. Make notifications and communications through the switchboard telephone system or by using a runner. Two-way radios such as walkie-talkies must not be used at any time during a bomb threat. If a remotely controlled explosive device has been placed in the area, the radio transmission could detonate it.

A protection agent preparing a site for a protectee's visit must search all areas in the vicinity of the visit prior to the protectee's arrival. The area should be cleared of all personnel not involved in the search. When the search is complete, the area should be secured and the entrance of all personnel monitored. If circumstances dictate that a complete search cannot be made (e.g., if the protective personnel arrive with the protectee), a cursory search will be conducted. As the protective agents move with the protectee or wait in a "standby" position such as their assigned post, they will look for any suspicious item that could be a bomb.

CRISIS MANAGEMENT

The term *crisis management* means a planned, efficient response to any event that may significantly disrupt corporate operations. It is a process by which an organization reacts to any major event that could have an adverse effect on the personnel, property, reputation, or financial welfare of the company. Crisis management is clearly a function of management but involves anyone who may have the expertise, skill, or knowledge to help deal with the emergency. A protection agent or manager is an important figure in the overall planning and operation of crisis management when the crisis involves bomb threats, kidnap/extortion threats, and terrorist activities.

If an organization has no existing emergency plan, the protection manager should recommend that a crisis management team, plan, and policy be established. The crisis team should have the authority to implement necessary emergency management procedures and should disseminate appropriate information to other employees. Crisis policy formulation should include anticipation of all likely scenarios, planning ways to prevent or respond to the event, and preparation of required special instructions, information, training, equipment, media policy, and management policies, and so on.

The executive protection manager should work with the administration's designee in organizing the company's crisis management team (CMT) and take appropriate measures, including training and response testing. Team members should be chosen very carefully and have a record of company loyalty and a demonstrated ability to work long hours under stress and fatigue. The principal executive officer or protectee generally appoint the members of the crisis management team, which most likely will include the chief of staff or top assistant, the director of human resources, and others. But the executive protection manager should have considerable input in terms of qualifications and selection of team personnel.

The crisis management team must be available to devote full time and attention to the tasks of dealing with authorities, the news media, the business, and members of the victim's family, as well as participating in negotiations with kidnappers/extortionists. The CMT members should be absolutely loyal, discreet, and calm under stress, and should possess extraordinarily good judgment. In short, the CMT personnel should be persons corporate management would trust with their lives.

In the case of an emergency requiring evacuation of the corporate offices and work areas (i.e., discovery of a bomb) the CMT may include the switchboard operator and one primary and one alternate floor supervisor per floor.

The CMT should not, for obvious reasons, include any of the following:

1. Persons who do not operate well in stress situations or who cannot interface well with fellow employees
2. Employees who have competing career goals
3. Individuals who may have health problems

Members of the CMT should receive semiannual briefings from the executive protection manager regarding responsibilities in the event of a bomb threat, executive kidnapping, fire, hostage situation, major crime, or other crisis situations. "Other crisis" situations include natural disasters and job actions by employees. The briefing should include evacuation procedures, operation of fire-fighting equipment, emergency first aid, and corporate policy relating to situations demanding particular pre-arranged management decisions (e.g., terrorism, kidnapping/extortion). Tests of the procedures and updated recommendations should be made regularly. All team members should be given a copy of an emergency plan (prepared by the executive protection office) and should become familiar with its contents. The executive protection manager, working with an administration designee, should assume responsibility for updating, modification, and changes as necessary in the emergency plan and for briefing all company employees as appropriate.

SUMMARY

The role of a protection agent (or manager) is not limited to the prevention of a kidnapping or bombing incident. His role becomes very important in advising management in formulation of proper policy in the event that a kidnapping or bombing is anticipated or carried out. As a member of a crisis management team, he should be familiar with procedures that will limit the damage and allow a smooth recovery. In a few words, he should anticipate an adverse action, plan to prevent it, and prepare for the resolution and control of any ensuing havoc.

REPORT OF BOMB THREAT

Record the exact language of the threat.
"Please repeat the message. I was interrupted."
"When will it explode?"
"Where did you put it?"
"What will cause it to explode?"
"Which floor is it on?"
"Why did you do this?"
"There are people in the building."
"What does it look like?"

REMARKS

Voice on the phone: Male_____ Female_____ Child_____ Accent_____
Intoxicated/slurred_____ Speech impediment_____ Age_____
Background noises:
     Music_____ Airplane_____ Traffic_____ Talking_____
Machinery_____ Typing_____ Other_____
Do not discuss the call with anyone else. Report call immediately.
To: _____ Date: _____
Time: _____ Call received by: _____
Have a Nice Day.

REVIEW QUESTIONS

1. Why should one attempt escape quickly, with minimal engagement with a kidnapper or terrorist?
2. Describe the psychological mind-set of a potential victim that could cause him to quickly and meekly surrender. How can he become a victim "within sight" of his home?
3. Explain the differences in types of kidnappers. How do they overlap?
4. Is it better to evacuate and have professionals conduct a bomb search after a telephoned bomb threat, or is it better to not evacuate and have the people who work in the area conduct the search? Give some pros and cons of each school of thought.
5. Why is it not always the best policy to evacuate a building following a bomb threat?
6. Describe how a bomb search should be conducted.
7. What is a crisis management team, and what is crisis management?
8. Who should be on a crisis management team? Why should people with competing career goals or people in poor health not be on a crisis management team?

20 Staying Alive!

Balance is Happiness.
Eye of the Tiger;
Heart of the Rose.

Sifu Eric Oram

LIFE IS SIMPLY A MATTER OF BALANCES AND CIRCLES

Aristotelian philosophy and ancient Chinese thinking teach us that everything has a direct opposite; day and night, white and black, male and female, good and evil, attacker and victim, yin and yang. This is the balance of nature. Everything must be balanced. When a person is feeling out of sorts, a little sick, it is because something in his body is out of balance. The balance must be restored before the person begins feeling well again. To gain that balance, the human immune system and chemistry must go in a complete cycle and return to homeostasis (normal).

In defensive tactics, staying balanced and performing tactical maneuvers in a circular manner (the "wax on, wax off" concept of Mr. Miagi, in the *Karate Kid* movies) will deflect blows and break holds, allowing for offensive strikes and countermeasures. Even the strength and power of a bigger opponent can be neutralized by turning his force, energy, and momentum back onto him with circular movements and drawing him off balance. There is nothing magical or secretive about ancient martial arts. Basic physics tells us that for every action there is an equal reaction. Using angles, force, and the opponent's own forward movement against him will result in him flaying helplessly into the air, while the intended victim moves from a defensive position into an offensive attack (turning the circle against the aggressor). A punch or block that strikes only air wastes movement, timing, and energy and leaves the puncher or blocker open to counterattack by the victim. "Turning the circle" means learning to adapt to the situation and maneuvering your body to give yourself the best possible advantage.

DEFENSIVE TACTICS AND SELF-DEFENSE MEASURES FOR THE PROTECTIVE AGENT

The will to survive an attack must be uppermost in a victim's mind. Fight back against the odds. Turn the tables. Get up off the ground. Seize the initiative. Take every advantage. Kick. Punch. Scratch. Bite. Don't give up!

You don't bleed. You don't hurt. You're going to make it. You are not fighting just for yourself. You are fighting to see the kids again, to go home, to be with the ones you love.

If your attacker knocks your teeth loose, spit them out or swallow them and keep punching. Don't let them waste you in some stinking alley!

The above survival code is known as the "Peace Officer's Survival Creed," written by unknown police officers for police officers. It is succinct and very dramatically to the point. Staying alive can depend on how well the victim is mentally prepared and fights back.

STAYING ALIVE AS AN ATTACK VICTIM

AWARENESS

Be alert and aware of your surroundings at all times. A street or barroom attacker will choose targets who appear weak and vulnerable. Looking like a victim invites an attack. A person being attacked cannot wait until he is blind-sided and hit to begin his defense. Defense begins the instant the victim observes impending danger. It may be seeing the "hard eyes" of an adversary watching his victim. The eyes and eyebrows become narrowed and focused on every move of his intended target. The forehead becomes furrowed with anger, disgust, or contempt. He watches his victim's body language and demeanor, looking for the opportune time to strike.

When he thinks the timing is right, the attacker moves toward the person he is attacking ("bridging the gap") and either engages him in argument prior to launching the attack or, most likely, he strikes with a hard, sneaky, straight overhand right to the victims face. It may be a straight jab or a looping roundhouse.

SUDDENNESS, SURPRISE, AND VIOLENCE

Haven't you heard this before? Physical attacks (or *assaults* as they are usually incorrectly termed in newspapers) may take the surprised victim with such suddenness that he does not have time to mentally focus on the attack. The violence of the attack will most often render him defenseless or confused. Being fully awake and aware may give the surprised victim a few precious hundredths of a second to adjust to the violence directed toward him.

An aware victim will not be taken by surprise and should be able to instantly respond, perhaps avoiding the punch entirely or making it a glancing blow. If an attack is recognized and is immediate, the victim should react instantly to deflect the punch or take offensive action. The potential victim must keep his wits about him and have his body ready to react at all times. He cannot afford to wonder, "What did I do to make this guy mad at me?"

LASER-MINDED INTENT

Self-defense gives no time for wonderment. The intention of the attacker is known—he wants to rip his victim's head off! The victim must have an intention of his own. His intention is to vanquish his attacker and to survive. At that particular moment, the victim must realize that the time is *now*—not a second before or a second later, but now! His intention must be focused strictly on the moment; he must react to the attack with his conscious mind overwhelmingly focused on his intention to control the attacker and to survive the attack. A person under attack must not hesitate. His reaction time and forming of his intent must coincide with the instantaneous recognition of the attack. Creating a pinpoint, laserlike intention means ridding the mind of everything except response to the attack. A wandering mind or unfocused mind can experience 100 million conflicting thoughts or interference from other stimuli. This in turn slows a human's reaction time and leads to self-doubt, loss of confidence, tentative action, and failure to adequately defend against the attacker.

SELF-DEFENSE

Self-defense begins with the individual protection agent in his program of physical fitness, sleep patterns, diet, and alertness training. A physically fit agent commands respect and leaves little doubt as to who is the commanding presence. With regard to hand-to-hand fighting, it is the individual responsibility of the protection agent to train in gyms and develop appropriate skills. A protection agent, like a uniformed police officer, is often the target of individuals who, for whatever reason, feel they must test the combative skills of the officer. Many types of measures and tactics are available for personal defense, ranging from judo, karate, kickboxing, and other martial arts to the use of firearms, batons, and chemical agents. But just being experienced in martial arts is not sufficient. What works in a gym may not be so effective in the street, where there are no rules, referees, or time-outs. Never underestimate the opponent. He may have more experience, skills, and strength.

RECOGNIZING AND REACTING TO AN ATTACK

It has been estimated that the average barroom fight lasts only three seconds or less. This is because the sudden attack knocks the victim off his feet or backward into bystanders and (1) as he is recovering, other people intervene to end the fight, or (2) the blow is so devastating that the victim needs a second to "shake it off," after which it is too late, and the attacker will have moved in for the finishing blow or kick. Commensurate with this estimated length of a barroom fight, it has been estimated that the average assault in the street lasts a mere 15 seconds. This does not offer the victim much time to react or to form a defense. Recognition of the pending attack should require no longer than it takes for the eyes to see something and send a message to the brain, and for the brain to react with an adrenaline dump that prepared the body for "fight or flight." This response takes only hundredths of a second.

The person being attacked prepares for the assault by observing, studying, and listening to the attacker. He studies face and hand movements; nothing can happen until the attacker begins to raise his hands or moves into striking distance. If the attacker begins the fight with a verbal assault, the victim should study him and watch for telltale movements such as a clenching of the fists or feet moving into a fighting stance (in which the feet are approximately at shoulder length apart, with one foot slightly in front and to the side of the other). While the attacker is talking or shouting, he will not be attacking. The victim should listen to what the attacker is saying and how he says it. This will be a tip-off to the next move—physical attack. As soon as he shuts up, the attack begins almost immediately.

The "deer caught in the headlights" syndrome, or becoming frozen in place, is the effect of the adrenaline dump. With an attacker bridging the gap (usually with profanity or perhaps shouting), the human reaction is to respond spontaneously with a fight-or-flight reflex. There is a moment's hesitation (the freeze) while the brain sorts through all the stimuli and directs the body to react as it has been conditioned—either to fight or run. The victim cannot afford to wait those precious thousandths of a second. Response and intent must be reflexive.

It is very important to be physically ready for a fight and know how to protect yourself and others. Being mentally ready for any circumstance is equally important. Even if your body is physically ready to fight, you will fail if you are not mentally prepared. When you recognize that violence is imminent, take note of objects in the vicinity, and in your pockets, that could be utilized as weapons: pencils, pens, dirt and rocks, bottles, briefcases, purses, and so on. One person was said to have carried a pocket full of sand or pepper to throw into an attacker's face. A rolled-up newspaper or magazine makes an excellent weapon for jabbing or slapping. The more you practice scenarios and drills, the better prepared you will be for any attack.

You do not have to have typical weapons (e.g., a gun, knife, or other type of edge weapon) to be a human lethal weapon. As long as you have the heart, will, and knowledge of how to use your body as a weapon or turn other items into a weapon, you should be able to overcome most challenges that confront you. For example, you can use a pen as a stabbing instrument into the eyes, up the nose, or into the throat, ears, or solar plexus. If you use your imagination during an altercation, you can turn everyday things into weapons to incapacitate the bad guys if the circumstances warrant the use of deadly force. If you know your body and what it is capable of doing during a physical altercation, you will be more prepared to handle the physical altercations and able to escape major injuries or death. The human body is loaded with natural weapons.

Since the dawn of mankind, man has needed to protect himself from nature, beasts, and other men. In doing so, man developed his knowledge and understanding of the weapons with which he was created. These weapons are elementary in nature but still require an understanding of how they work and their uses. Essentially, the "naked human" remains combat ready by having an understanding of human anatomy and how appendages developed over time can be utilized as weapons. These weapons should only be used as a last resort, with a knowledge and understanding of the damage they can cause, their liabilities, and available alternatives.

"The naked human is combat ready" concept simply refers to the body parts God gave us for self-defense. These weapons are our heads, hands, feet, legs, arms, knees, elbows, teeth, and nails. These appendages can be used in a variety of ways, but using them effectively requires a basic knowledge of how they work and a no-nonsense kill or be killed attitude. The naked human being is combat ready, despite not having what are commonly thought of as weapons at hand. While not as flashy as the claws of a cat or the teeth of a dog, the human being's weapons can be just as dangerous when used properly.

The weapons of a human begin with his head and extend to his toes; the crown of the skull can be used to butt an opponent in vulnerable places such as the nose. The arms and hands have a plethora of weapons, including knuckles for punching, the flat of the hand for slapping, and the fingers for jabbing. We also have the forearm for whacking and blocking and nails for scratching and gouging. The most devastating weapon on the arms, however, is the elbow. The elbow is extremely powerful and can deliver a fight-ending blow. Knees, the shin, and the instep and heel of the foot can also be devastating weapons. The human being comes equipped with teeth for biting. Even without a traditional weapon in hand, a human is still formidable.

Most people begin discovering these weapons, whether on the playground or when playing with a sibling, when they are children. However, as human beings grow, they become reluctant to use these weapons. That is why most people who are confronted on the street feel helpless. They have these weapons at their disposal, but their brain is not ready to use them.

The body of a human comes "locked and loaded, ready for battle." The brain inhabiting that body makes the difference between who fights and who does not. All too often, people utilize these personal weapons without knowing their full potential, or exploit them out of context when an alternative would have been preferred. It is knowing where to kick, punch, hit, bite, or pull that makes unarmed persons lethal when necessary. By being able to use your body as a weapon makes you combat ready. When fighting, always remember to try to be the first one to give punches or use weapons, and make sure they are faster and harder than what you receive. Do not try to get fancy. To distract the opponent, do something that is out of place, unexpected, or disgusting, such as "hacking up a real goober" and spitting it into his eyes. Once the fight is engaged, keep it simple and use well-directed, effective punches, strikes, and kicks. Don't be afraid to use dirty tactics, such as punching or kicking in the groin, gouging the eyes, biting, scratching, and hair pulling. Use all your strength and fight like your life depends on it, because it probably does. Try to end the fight as soon as possible, because the longer the fight goes on, the greater your chances of being hurt or killed.

Having had the opportunity and experience of dealing with people, having been placed in dangerous, life-threatening situations, and having practiced martial arts, I have had a chance to see first hand the ramifications of the use of these weapons and the damage it can cause. One night, I was grabbed around the neck in a very strong headlock. The attacker began to crank up the pressure, forcing my face into his chest. I wrapped my arms around him so he could not move away, opened my mouth, and gave him a very strong bite on his breast. Both of his hands released as he completely opened his arms nearly in a spread-eagle fashion. While he was still trying to recover from the bite and the accompanying shock, I proceeded to render him harmless.

Having had these experiences, I firmly believe that anyone using these appendages as weapons has a responsibility to know their limitations and liabilities. They are not infallible but, when used with good judgment and appropriate timing, they are effective enough to discourage and stop the attacker. One word of caution: the level of force used must be "reasonable and necessary." A person using any level of violence must be able to articulate the totality of circumstances in those terms.

Anything that is not reasonable and necessary is viewed with disfavor by prosecutors, the courts, insurance companies, and liability lawyers. And attorneys for the aggrieved would be more than happy to attempt to turn the facts from reasonable and necessary to excessive.

There are defined escalation levels of necessary and reasonable force (see chapter 13) but, in a sudden attack, the first two levels of *discussion* and *argument* are skipped. Thus the assault moves directly into the third level, the *physical fight* or *attack*. A protective agent may be sitting or standing in a very calm and relaxed state when he must suddenly shift into a full fight-for-your-life situation.

A good first line of defense is to understand the levels of the escalation of violence. First is discussion. In a color code of threat awareness, this level is considered to be the "blue, calm and cool" stage. The second level is argument, or the orange stage. Voices begin to get louder; body temperature begins to rise along with the blood pressure, respiration, and pulse. At this point, it would seem that the winner of the argument will be the one who yells louder and defeats his opponent with the volume, tenor, and tone of his voice. Reason and logic are lost. It is said, "You cannot reason with an unreasonable person." Of course, an "unreasonable person" is commonly defined as someone who refuses to agree with you. That person is always the one who is unreasonable; it is never you.

As temperatures and blood pressure rise, so do the temper and anger level. This, then, becomes the third level of violence, the "hot, red stage" or actual physical attack or fight. The person who can no longer hold his temper is burning red and seeing only the fire of his rage. He lashes out (usually with a stealthy, overhand right-hand), and the fight is on.

Level four is the employment of nonlethal weapons. Weapons are anything the fighters can pick up, throw, or use to bludgeon. At this point, the fight has taken a very serious turn and will end only when one or both parties are defeated and unable to continue to fight. The color code of danger has now turned to a very dark red. The fifth and final stage is color coded black. This is the engagement of lethal weapons. The fight is now to the death.

As the levels of violence escalate, one overriding caveat must be borne in mind. The level of force to use, even in self-defense, must always be limited to what is considered reasonable and necessary. Reasonable and necessary force is the force an average and prudent person would engage to protect himself. Anything beyond the articulation of reasonable and necessary is excessive force and may lead to criminal charges. Excessive force is the next step beyond reasonable and necessary. Force must be escalated in the proper sequence of stages; anything else will be excessive. Levels cannot and must not be skipped.

OFFENSIVE WEAPONS

Picture a human being standing naked and bare handed. Weaponless? Hardly! Long before sticks and stones, a person was equipped with natural weapons. Those weapons are still a part of him and can be used in a number of ways. Let us enumerate the human body's weapons:

- *Brain*. Always be ready for a physical response, but first attempt to outthink the attacker and either de-escalate the threat or convince him that he is placing himself in serious danger.
- *Head*. To be used for butting.
- *Mouth*. Teeth for biting (any place); talk—words are powerful and can be a very strong psychological weapon, especially when used in conjunction with humor and reason.
- *Shoulders*. Hitting and striking.
- *Elbows*. Hitting and striking.
- *Forearm*. Hitting and striking.
- *Hand*. Fist and knuckles for hitting; knife hand for striking; flat of hand for slapping; heel of hand for punching and striking; "hammer" fist for striking; backhanded punch.
- *Fingers*. For poking into eyes, ears, throat, and nose; also for strangling, grasping, and tearing; used as a "spear hand," fingers can rupture a throat or injure eyes.
- *Fingernails*. For scratching.
- *Wrist*. The back of the wrist bone is effective when used in a "backhand" strike.
- *Knees*. Hitting and striking.
- *Shin bone*. For striking.
- *Heel*. Stomping, striking, and "ax kicking."
- *Ball of foot*. Kicking.

VULNERABILITIES

Now let us imagine where the human body is vulnerable to the same human weapons:

- *Head*. Skull can be cracked or broken; brain concussion.
- *Hair*. Pulled.
- *Temple area*. Soft spot between the eyes and ears.
- *Eyes*. Gouged, punched.
- *Ears*. Pulled, slammed with flat of hand to cause air pressure pain in ears and head. Fingers can be pushed into them, causing eardrum damage and other damage to cartilage.
- *Nose*. To be punched, pulled, and twisted. Also, fingers can be rammed up the nostrils.
- *Lips*. Can be punched, pulled, and twisted.
- *Teeth*. Can be knocked out.
- *Jawbone*. Dislocated or broken.
- *Throat*. Choking, strangulation, crushed, grasped and pulled; good area to bite! Go for the jugular!
- *Back and side of neck*. Twisted or hit.
- *Collar Bones*. Can be broken with a closed hand (hammer fist) strike.
- *Solar plexus*. Area at center of chest, just under the breast bone; damage can be done to the breathing diaphragm.

- *Ribs.* Kicked or punched (especially lower rib area).
- *Shoulders.* Dislocated.
- *Elbows.* Hyperextended or broken.
- *Wrists.* Hyperextended or broken.
- *Fingers.* Hyperextended or broken and bitten.
- *Stomach.* The "soft underbelly."
- *Groin.* Kicked, pulled, or punched.
- *Knees.* Hyperextended or broken.
- *Shin bone.* Scraped, kicked, and broken.
- *Foot.* Stomped.
- *Toes.* Stomped.
- *Spinal column.* Kicked.
- *Kidney area.* Located just above the rear hip area; can be kicked or punched, causing trembling shock to the body.
- *Shoulder blades.* Middle of back; can be kicked, struck with a fist or knife hand between them.

Knowing the human anatomy provides for always being armed and ready. It is the application of the given weapons and knowing where to hit, strike, punch, kick, bite, or pull that makes an unarmed man lethal. Each kick, punch, or strike should be delivered simultaneously with a short, loud "kiup" or yell. The kiup is an explosive release of breath from the lower chest. This causes the muscles to tighten, increasing the delivery power and psychologically intimidating the opponent.

ENVIRONMENTAL WEAPONS

Environmental weapons are things that are within reach and not usually intended to be used as weapons but can easily be turned into lethal instruments. These range from rocks and dirt on the ground to car doors swinging open with force to nearly anything that can be hurled, swung, or jabbed. If it can be reached, picked up, and used to cause injury or death, it can be considered a weapon. One high-ranking former undercover agent spoke of a time when he had no weapon to defend himself against a pair of attackers. There was a cat near where the agent was, sitting on a couch. He grabbed the cat and threw it into the face of one of the attackers. Cats have the ability to land with their claws extended. As that attacker was dealing with the cat clinging to his face and scratching at his eyes, the agent took on the other attacker and subdued him then turned his attention to the first attacker and quickly ended the fight with an accurately placed chop.

IMPROVISED WEAPONS

No one should ever be without a weapon. Nearly anything (including a cat) can be turned into a device for inflicting pain or death. A small pamphlet or several sheets of paper can be rolled tightly into a stick to be used for jabbing or slashing. A full soda can or a bar of soap in a sock becomes a lethal club. A ballpoint pen or pencil can be used as an effective stabbing tool if jabbed into the eyes, ears, or throat. A toothbrush can also be used as a stabbing weapon. A spray can of oven cleaner makes a terrific mace. With a little imagination and practical application, turning everyday things into weapons is a fairly simple process that could conceivably save a life.

CONTROLLING THE CIRCUMSTANCES UNDER STRESS

A personal attack begins before the first fist is thrown. As a discussion turns into an argument, the stress or power of the situation exerts tremendous pressure on the target of the aggressor. The first, but perhaps most difficult, step is to understand the situation and remain calm. Talk in a low, cool and reasonable manner. If possible, move to the step of deescalating, defusing, or calming the situation. Use humor if appropriate. Engage the attacker in conversation and talk. It may be necessary to move into a defensive position, placing the feet in a protective stance (shoulder-length apart, with one foot a few inches in front and to the side of the other) and hands raised to chest level with the palms pointing outward. This is an easily recognizable body language sign that says, "I don't want any trouble, but I can and will defend myself." When the hands are clenched into a fist or the palms are turned inward, this is like waving a red flag in front of a raging bull. The opponent has no choice but to charge. The challenge has now been turned to him.

At this point, if the aggressor moves into the victim's personal space, usually within arm's length, the victim should strike first, hard, and fast with a heel of the hand thrust upward into the attacker's upper lip and nose, with a follow-through to disable the attacker and end the attack.

STAYING ALIVE AS A HOSTAGE—HOSTAGE RESPONSE

Of course, none of us ever plans on becoming a victim of a kidnapping or being held hostage. But it does happen. The natural response when taken captive is to resist and to hurt and kill as many of your captors as possible while making a "great escape." That works only in the movies and if you are Chuck Norris, Jackie Chan, or Vin Diesel.

The moment of capture is a very critical point. The initial and natural reaction of the victim is to cry out for help and attempt to escape, but it may be useless while under the influence of fear, disbelief, and shock. To fight back and attempt to escape against overwhelming odds most often results in critical injury to the victim. Recognition of the reality of the situation must quickly replace fear, shock, and disbelief for the victim to regain composure. Once subdued or captured, the victim should assure his captors of his intention to cooperate and must be psychologically prepared to deal with discomfort and pain inflicted by ropes or other restraints and to be subjected to blindfolds or hoods, gags, or drugs.

After capture, an escape attempt should not be made unless it has been carefully calculated to ensure the best possible odds for success. The victim should avoid making provocative or threatening remarks and avoid discussing politics and religion. The hostage-takers may be unstable individuals who react explosively or become violent and abusive. The victim must strive to portray himself as a human being with the same feelings, emotions, and body parts as the captors. If the victim is able to break any stereotype the kidnappers may have of him, they may develop empathy for him. In most situations, we may expect the kidnappers to physically abuse and control the victim. They will frequently threaten death or some form of humiliation meant to punish and provoke. Some examples are being blindfolded, beatings with broom handles, being stripped naked or locked in a dark closet, having a sharp knife pulled across the throat, and whatever other frightening or degrading things the captors can conjure up.

Many terrorist kidnappers attempt to psychologically dominate their victims. It is crucial for the victim to resist only their psychological assaults. The victim should not attempt to fight back or struggle physically. No matter how reasonable the captors may appear on the surface, they cannot be trusted to behave normally, and their actions may be unpredictable. The victim should not panic. He should maintain calm (at least on the surface) and be alert to situations that can be exploited to his advantage.

As difficult as it will be, a disciplined mind and body can learn to cope with the harsh reality of abduction. A victim must discipline his mind to quickly establish a daily routine that includes exercise, cleanliness, and mental agility (memory, solutions to hypothetical mathematical problems, writing music, and so on). A victim's greatest psychological enemy is his own despair and fear.

Use of memory keeps a mind sharp. It can be useful to recall happier times, to "travel" to more pleasant surroundings, and to imagine oneself liberated and free. Another mind-sharpening tool is to remember details about your surroundings and the abductors. Prisoners have found ways of retaining some rudimentary way of telling time, even if it's just a scratch on the wall to represent a day. The captive must not reject food given by the captors, no matter how repulsive it may appear. To reject food will only confirm the terrorist stereotype of an aristocrat. The terrorist wants to keep the victim alive, and the food he feeds the victim will not kill him, even though it may be as unappetizing as rice garnished with meat (maggots). Physical strength is needed to maintain mental stability.

Very often, the hostage will be subjected to humiliation such as being stripped naked, urinated and defecated on, not being allowed to use toilet facilities, and other insults. The victim should keep in mind that the humiliation is known only to the captors and that, although they can force him to submit to physical humiliation, they cannot degrade his mind unless allowed to do so. Humiliation that cannot be physically resisted can always be psychologically resisted. The victim must not allow himself to be provoked by captors and must never bow his mind to their will.

Drugs may be used to create disorientation or decrease the hostage's resistance to the kidnapper's questions. Many drugs are effective (the placebo effect) because the victim believes they will work. Drugs can eventually be flushed or dried out of the system. If an addiction is induced, it can be overcome with good rehabilitation. The victim should answer his abductor's questions as truthfully as he can but answer slowly, weighing the implications of his words and resisting attempts to manipulate his answers for use against him.

A sense of humor should be maintained, even though it may seem harsh and unrealistic. Humor depends on objectivity. If it can be maintained, it will help preserve mental stability and may impress the kidnappers with the victim's humanity. When confronted by an armed abductor, the victim should never turn his back to the kidnapper. Face to face, the hostage is a "person" to the abductor. If the back is turned or the victim's head is covered with a hood, the abductor may be less inhibited about shooting him, because he sees the victim not as a human but as a dehumanized object.

A mental note can be taken of all movements, including times in transit, direction, distances, speeds, landmarks along the way, special odors, and sounds such as transportation, bells, construction, and so on. Note should also be taken of the characteristics of the abductors, their habits, surroundings, and speech mannerisms and who they contact.

A hostage should comply with the instructions of the abductors to whatever extent possible. He must not discuss what actions his family, friends, company, or government may take. The hostage must always remember that the primary objective of his family, government, and business associates will be to secure his safe return as quickly as possible.

If a hostage retrieval attempt is made, shooting, shouting, swearing, explosions, and general chaos will occur with suddenness, surprise, and violence similar to that of the initial capture. The hostage must not make any sudden moves, such as trying to run away, except to drop to the ground, lie as flat as possible, and await instructions or assistance from the rescuers.

After the rescue the victim can expect a period of readjustment to freedom. During his captivity he was dependent on his captors for everything including food, some comfort, even his very life. This is a form of "institutionalization" and the longer a person is subjected to such conditions, the more he depends upon his captors until a point is reached that the victim begins to feel a sense of security even community with his "masters." Readjustment to freedom may result in post traumatic stress syndrome, isolation from loved ones, mental confusion, an inability to make decisions or reason rationally, depression, anger and social inhibitions or *faux paux*.

SUMMARY

In fighting for survival, there are no rules, no fighting fair. It is "anything goes." "Expect no quarter and give none." Survival means fighting hard, fast, and using all available weapons. If there are any rules, there is only one—a "golden rule": "Give unto your opponent faster and harder than he gives unto you, and give it first." Giving is better than receiving.

Imagination and necessity are the only limitations on what can be considered weapons. Anything to incapacitate the enemy is permissible if the circumstances warrant using deadly force. Some of the devices and weapons, and the manner of using them, as described above may seem brutal to many. But in the reality of fighting for your life, the cardinal rule is to use anything in any manner that will render your enemy helpless before he hurts or kills you.

A good rule of thumb to remember when your life is at risk is to end the fight in your favor as quickly as possible. The longer the fight continues, the greater are your odds of getting hurt, beaten, or killed.

If taken hostage, the victim must adapt to his environment, as uncomfortable, demeaning, and psychologically threatening as it may be. Mind games, memory, and routine physical activity including personal hygiene are important for survival.

During a rescue attempt, the victim should immediately lie prone on the floor and await instructions from the rescuers.

REVIEW QUESTIONS

1. Why does staying alive depend on being mentally prepared?
2. Explain the balances and circles concept in nature and self-defense.
3. Describe the now of laser-minded intent.
4. Articulate reasonable and necessary force.
5. When does reasonable and necessary force become excessive force?
6. What weapons does a naked human always have at his disposal?
7. What are a human's physical vulnerabilities?
8. What are environmental weapons, and how can everyday household items be turned into lethal weapons?
9. Try to picture yourself as a newly captured hostage. How do you see yourself reacting? How should you react?
10. What is the golden rule of survival in a fight?

21 Of Dragons...and Other Things

We are all the sum of the stories told of our lives—the stories we tell ourselves and the stories told by others.

"Would you take a bullet for someone?" He didn't know!

We all have our dragons.

Dennis McCarthy, U.S. Secret Service

Conventional wisdom says that dragons exist only in fantasy. The snarling, fire-breathing, four-legged, winged reptilian creature of folklore, known for guarding great hoards of treasure and devouring young maidens and knights who were brave enough to challenge him, disappeared long ago into the mists of the ages (or a child's maturation into adulthood). But if you have awakened from a restless sleep, breathing heavily, sweating, and feeling a fear that something terrible has happened or will happen and there is nothing you can do to prevent it, you have been visited by a dragon! The fear is usually associated with a responsibility that weighs so heavily that it is lived in the unconscious mind in dreams of reality, worry, concern, and anxiety.

The burden of anxiety is such that what does not exist, or has not happened, nevertheless can seem real. These dreams, these nightmares, are very common to people who work in high-risk occupations, for example, firefighters, police, and protection agents. They are called anxiety dreams.

In one dream, a shadowy figure steps from the pressing crowd. He has a gun and, as everything shifts to slow motion, fire comes from the gun. A bullet, rotating slowly and ripping the air, is seen going directly toward the heart of the protectee (who is never fully recognized). Although he is only a step or two away, for the protective agent it is too far. He yells "no!" and leaps forward to place himself between the protectee and the bullet. But he can never quite get there. Sometimes the dream stops and begins over again. Sometimes the dream continues as the agent sees the protectee grabbing his chest or throat as blood slowly begins to spread red all over the scene. The crowd (in somber tones of black and white, as though attending a funeral in the rain) quietly closes around the fallen body as sympathetic do-nothing onlookers. The agent, as if he no longer exists, is seen standing aside from the crowd, still leaping forward and frantically yelling "no!"

In another version, the protection agent is seen attempting to explain to everyone in the crowd, around the body, that he did everything possible to prevent the tragedy, but each person looks at him and slowly turns away. The agent grabs a bystander by the arm to force him to listen, but the agent, who is crying and begging, cannot be heard. The onlooker turns and walks slowly away as the scene fades into a heavy, London-like fog. The dream ends as the agent stands there, whispering a cry, "I tried... I tried...." He wakes up.

A third version has the agent face to face with the attacker. He can only see the attacker's gun and the flame and smoke coming from the barrel. He pulls his own gun in slow motion and tries to shoot the attacker. But the trigger will not pull back. He grabs the gun with both hands, but there is not enough strength to pull the trigger. If the trigger does work, the bullet flies very slowly and turns in very deliberate rotations, never quite getting to the target.

There are other versions. Sometimes it is a replay of a mistake that was made or something that was overlooked in the planning, preparation, and anticipation stages that could have had bad results if a stalker or someone with harmful intent had taken advantage of the circumstance.

A very common dragon is complacency. Day after day, night after night, even year after year, routines and assignments begin to run together. Each assignment is different as each day is different, but in the overall picture, there becomes a pattern of sameness that leads to an attitude that results in little mistakes. No one notices, but the high level of alertness and awareness begins to slip a notch, reactions are not as quick, and suspicions are rationalized rather than examined. Then one day, when the protection agent has been lulled into a feeling of self-satisfaction that his protective efforts are being rewarded with no adverse activity and he just mindlessly goes about his duties, picking up an inflated paycheck every week or two, the complacency dragon bites! It may be an assassination attempt, a kidnapping, or a bomb placed in an area that should have been checked. Or it could simply be an intruder who very easily walked undetected through a checkpoint that should have stopped him. The breach of the protective circle, with luck, may be only embarrassing, but it could very well have tragic results. An assassin can decide when, where, and whom to attack. In that case, the dragon grows into the mother of all unfriendly dragons—the consequences and guilt of a dead protectee.

The details of a lost protectee will haunt a protective agent for a long time, maybe a lifetime. There was not an agent in Dallas, Texas, on November 22, 1963, that did not believe, for the rest of his life, that if he had done just "one more thing" or been "just a little faster" or "just a little more alert," President Kennedy would not have been killed. Investigation after investigation always concluded that everything was done that could realistically have been, given all the circumstances. The protective agents were fully alert; they had properly prepared for and anticipated harmful intent. However, in spite of their total effort, the events of that day unfolded with the successful and tragic assassination of the president. For many years, even the rest of a lifetime, the dragon of self-doubt and second-guessing continued to follow those dedicated agents who felt personal responsibility for the unavoidable.

The dragon of carelessness seems to hang as an inevitable offspring of shortcuts taken in the interest of time, fatigue, disinterest, or bad attitude. Carelessness plays to the strength of the unknown risk. A protective agent is also hindered and influenced by moral and psychological considerations that inhibit instant, impulsive action. Even if he is fully alert and primed for action, having no personal qualms about killing, he must evaluate every factor and decide if the circumstance legally justifies the degree of force necessary to resolve the state of affairs. Whenever a vital element of the protection shield is overlooked, waived, or forgotten, it places the entire protection program in a position of vulnerability.

There are two lesser dragons that should not actually be considered as such; more accurately, they are just human foibles. But like dragons, if not overcome, they can grow into major concerns to a protection agent. The first is a feeling of loneliness. A protection agent often spends hours at a time by himself. Manning a post at some secluded position, maybe not seeing another person for the entire shift, can lead to boredom, feelings of being the only person in that sector of the universe, and thoughts of, "What the heck am I doing in a place like this at this ungodly hour?" To that scenario, add darkness and cold, and loneliness closes in. If the position is remote, as in a forest or large estate, every noise is startling, and an active imagination can allow the unknown source of the noise to grow to unwarranted dimensions. That leads to the second foible or "baby dragon," fear.

Fear has its genesis in the unknown. Standing alone in the darkness, just listening for sounds and imagining a terrorist creeping up, can generate a certain degree of fear that if not held in check can cause irrational behavior. Fear must be overcome and controlled. In the words of former first lady Eleanor Roosevelt, "You gain strength, courage, and confidence by every experience in which you stop to look fear in the face."

There is a story of a protective agent (a young soldier), assigned to a high-ranking military person in Europe, who allowed his imagination to get just a little out of control. The position was somewhat removed from the usual activities of the household, and the closest neighbor was far enough away that his house lights were not visible. It was at the intersection of a road used only by the few residents who lived in the area and a long winding driveway bordered with shrubbery and large overhanging trees. A slight chilling wind was blowing, and the full moon was intermittently covered with dark clouds. When the protective agent's relief came to him out of the dark at about 3:00 A.M., the soldier was seen whirling a long stick around as he continued turning in circles. His explanation was that he did not want anything (especially vampires) creeping up on him. Well, nothing did creep up on him (especially vampires). It was recommended that the young soldier get a few days of rest and maybe wear a string of garlic around his neck.

Fear can play games with a protective agent's imagination and is at its peak when the assignment requires a walking around the estate or premises during the late, dark hours of night. Why did that shadow move? What is that noise? Listen as the agent walks over the gravel driveway or through the wet grass. An intruder can hear him coming and jump him as he passes the interloper's hiding place. If the agent walks with a flashlight to light the way, an intruder will know the agent is coming and can wait in ambush to spring his deadly surprise. Is that a cat or 'possum, maybe a deer in the bushes making that moving noise, or is it a person?

Patrolling an estate is better done without a light, if practical, while walking as quietly as possible and taking a wide turn around the corners of the house. It is best to stay in the shadows and move within the darkness. The movement should be slow and deliberate, utilizing all the senses including listening and smelling. A stationary post is less frightening, because the sounds and shadow movement, caused by wind in the trees, soon become familiar. The agent can blend into his surroundings with his eyes accustomed to the darkness, and he can detect any unusual movement or noise before the noise source is aware of his presence.

The single most frequently asked question of close personal protection agents and potential agents is, "Would you take a bullet for (the protectee)?" That question goes directly to the bottom of the motivations for an executive protection agent. It cannot be effectively answered with a simple yes or no. Most assuredly, if the answer is a definite no, then the agent is in the wrong business. By definition, if everything hits the fan, the role of close personal protection includes the possibility of being in harm's way.

EMOTIONAL INTELLIGENCE

Emotional dragons can and have derailed many promising protective service careers. Knowing and understanding the importance of emotions and their role in our lives is critical in developing characteristics and skills that are essential in social living. The benefits of emotional intelligence include enhancement of critical thinking, the ability to develop emotional detachment (attachment), and establishment of healthy boundary systems. To understand the importance of developing emotional intelligence in protective services, it is crucial to understand that emotions play important roles in how people confront worldly challenges with varying degrees of accuracy, efficiency, and success. Dr. Reuven Bar-On, a psychologist with Multi-Health Systems in Canada, identified five components and the related competencies for each component relative to emotional intelligence:

1. Intrapersonal skills (self-awareness, assertiveness, self-regard)
2. Interpersonal skills (empathy, interpersonal relationship, and social responsibility)
3. Cognition–orientation (problem solving, testing reality, and flexibility)
4. Stress management (stress tolerance and impulse control)
5. Affect (optimism and happiness)

Some researchers and sociologists believe emotional intelligence is a critical factor in such areas as

- Decision making
- Leadership
- Strategic and technical breakthroughs
- Open and honest communication
- Trust
- Teamwork
- Creativity and innovation

A listing of emotions a protective agent must be aware of would include anger, depression, fear, empathy, love, infatuation, anxiety, and hate. Some social and psychological researchers have divided emotional intelligence into five broad areas that summarize a number of specific skills and behaviors vital in protective services. The five areas are

1. Knowing one's own emotions
2. Managing one's own emotions
3. Motivating oneself
4. Recognizing emotions of others
5. Handling relationships with others

UNDERSTANDING ONESELF AND THE EMOTIONAL PRICE

Knowing that an assassin's bullet may change the course of history or end a protective agent's life at any moment is always at the back of an agent's mind, but it is a thought he cannot allow to linger. That is indeed another type of dangerous dragon. Thinking about that bullet will cause an agent to hesitate, perhaps to the detriment of his protectee and himself. Overthinking the inherent dangers and emotional roller coaster ride of living in a dangerous occupation may result in no reaction or extreme overreaction.

> Police officers (protective agents) themselves do not necessarily emphasize the peril associated with their work when questioned directly and may even have well developed strategies of denial. The element of danger is so integral to an officer's (agent's) work that explicit recognition might induce emotional barriers to work performance.[1]

Realistically, no one can predict how he will react under the circumstances. But he must be mentally prepared for the possibility of intentionally placing his body between the attacker and the protectee. That is exactly what Special Agent Larry Buendorf did to disarm Lynette Fromme when she pointed the .45 at President Ford. Videotape of the assault on President Reagan by John Hinckley shows very clearly that Special Agent Timothy McCarthy pushed the president aside and deliberately turned his own body to cover him, intentionally taking a bullet into his own stomach. Similar action must be an instinctive reaction developed through intensive training, practice, mental programming, visualization, and emotional intelligence. If the reaction must be thought out and emotions overcome (fear, panic, uncertainty, and

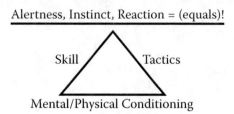

Alertness, Instinct, Reaction = (equals)!

Skill   Tactics

Mental/Physical Conditioning

doubt) during an incident, then the preventive action will be too late. Total alertness, instinct, and reaction form the three sides of an equilateral triangle. All sides are of identical importance to the whole, and the omission of any element leaves a potentially lethal gap. Mind and body conditioning, skill, and tactics must be cast into a combined, coordinated effort of reaction.

Until it happens, we cannot predict how we will react in an emergency when there is sudden shouting, shoving, shooting, explosions, and so on. We can only prepare ourselves mentally and hope the action will be the correct one.

> Police officers (protective agents) begin to develop perceptual shorthand to identify certain kinds of people as symbolic assailants (i.e., a person who uses speech, dress, and gestures that the police have come to recognize as a prelude to violence). The police (and protective agents) are trained to be suspicious and aware of potential danger.[2]

An inspirational message on a community church's outdoor message board seemed to catch the flavor of that particular dilemma of a protection agent with a word of encouragement: "Courage is to never let your actions be influenced by your fears!"

Regardless of one's political leanings, religious beliefs, and civil rights and racial concerns, all of which may conflict with or run counter to the protectee's, the protection agent is duty bound and has a professional requirement and moral obligation to take every step necessary to protect the life of his principal. If that means intentionally stepping between an assassin's bullet and the protectee, then that is how it must be! The dragon of self-doubt and unknown human reflex will always be lurking until it is faced under actual conditions.

On the other hand, if a protective agent fails to take necessary protective action, or if he dives for cover leaving the protectee completely exposed to the harmful activity, he then probably will have to face two dragons. One is possible legal liability for failing to provide best-faith efforts to fulfill his contract. The second is more serious and personal. After answering to all the inquiring commissions, panels, and boards, he must answer to himself! A very famous quote is appropriate to that dragon: "A hero dies only once, a coward dies a thousand deaths."

"Would you take a bullet" is a highly personal question that must be answered by the individual when it counts most. We can only hope the answer (as the body reacts instinctively) is the right one.

TEMPTATIONS

Most protectees live in a world that is completely different from the life of the protective agent. Many times, they live and play in what is considered "the fast lane." That could mean shopping sprees on the world's most expensive street, Rodeo Drive, in Beverly Hills; night clubbing in New York, London, Paris, or Cannes; or gambling and gaming in Las Vegas. Wherever it may be, and whatever the activity, the protection agent is there, side by side or in close proximity to all the glitter, lights, and so-called glamour. And the temptations! Day after day, night after night of being among the free-spending, hard-drinking playboys and playmates of the world makes it easy for the protective agent to be seduced into believing he is part of that world. What harm can come from buying a suit or two at a boutique in Beverly Hills (where the price of a suit is in the thousands of dollars), playing a few hands of baccarat, or sipping a drink or two in a night club? There probably is not much harm, if done at the agent's own expense and on his own time. But when it begins to erode time that would be better spent performing his assigned duties, if it results in debt that he cannot afford, or if it is done at the protectee's expense, then there is a serious problem.

After a week, a month, or consecutive assignments in the world of free spenders, luxury, and "anything goes," the protective agent must eventually return to his real world of mortgages, yard work, wife and family, budgets, and humdrum. For many, the transition is extremely difficult, especially when the invoices for the suits and the gambling debt collectors arrive. Maybe the late-night hours, lack of sleep, and use of alcohol begin to collect their toll. Without a foot firmly embedded in reality, it is very easy to lose perspective and quickly burn out.

Even for those who do not especially work in the fast lane, there are complications and temptations that can be just as seductive. How about the agent who spends his time in the company of the high-powered corporate executive who makes deals, puts together corporate mergers, and is a force on Wall Street? The agent overhears conversations and is exposed to privileged and confidential information. Based on his observations and hearing, he purchases or sells stock. That is called *insider trading* and is illegal.

It might be his proximity to power, his professional, self-confident and polite manner, or the fact that he walks a thin line of possible danger, but there is something about a protective agent that seems to be attractive to members of the opposite sex. Call them groupies, roadies, or whatever, but there are always those who will attempt to charm him for their own unfulfilled fantasies or even miscreant purposes. Some are brazen enough to appear at the agent's hotel room door in the middle of the night and seek to bestow special favors. Others, while the agent is very much occupied in shielding the protectee in a tight crowd situation, will make eye contact with the agent, lean warmly and openly against him, and slip a note with her name and telephone number into his pocket. She may whisper in his ear for him to call her when he is off duty. This can all be very tempting and flattering, especially to a young and inexperienced agent, but it is a danger dragon in an angel's disguise. The complications that can arise from a liaison of that nature have a very high potential for disaster!

Obviously, there is a health and safety risk. In addition, an illicit late night dalliance may hinder the agent's performance on an early morning shift or cause a momentary loss of concentration at a very critical time. This, of course, could very well be the intent of the provocateur. Not to be forgotten is the possibility of extortion, blackmail, wheedling for an opportunity to be introduced to the protectee, or an invitation to a special function. One favor begets another, *quid pro quo*; nothing is ever for nothing. A dream angel can quickly turn into a nightmare devil. The person who was so flattering and generous could be mentally or emotionally unstable and begin stalking the agent, following and calling him, writing letters, sending gifts, and becoming a potential threat to the effectiveness of the agent. Not to be overlooked, and a real possibility, the person may be a "front," seeking intelligence information that later could place the protectee in jeopardy or cause serious embarrassment to him or the agent and his organization.

An agent must be alert to the possibility that he is being used and decline such gracious invitations. It is not the person of the agent that attracts the attention. Rather, as he must keep in mind, it is his uniform, his position, his close association with power, influence and danger. He must guard against the wiles and wishes of those who would impose themselves for other-than-honorable purposes.

DRAGONS OF PERSONAL PROBLEMS

"Personal protection is a single man's job" is a sentiment that has been expressed many times. The hours are long and unusual. It is very common to work twelve hours or more in one day. In private protection business, twelve-hour days are considered the norm. Most protective assignments have rotating shifts, meaning that an agent may work a few days on the day shift, double back and work a midnight shift for a few days, then get off early in the morning and double back again to work the afternoon shift. With a schedule like that, it is very difficult to maintain a stable routine or regular family life.

Many wives will patiently endure it for a while, being left alone at night, night after night, and sometimes weeks on end, never knowing for sure if her husband will be home tomorrow or on the road to another exciting and exotic place. He tells her that someday he will return to those places with her, because he wants to share them with her. He believes it. She does not.

Of course, the day he returns from spending thirty days on the road, living out of a suitcase and eating meals at junk-food franchises and hotel restaurants, the wife will want to go out to dinner, because she has not been anywhere for a month or more. The agent wants a good home-cooked meal and sleep in his own bed or in front of the television. His sleep is often punctuated by dreams of his anxiety dragons. The readjustment for both partners begins to take a toll over the years. She wants to talk about the kid's latest cold, but he is thinking about the last road trip or planning the next. A few years of the uncertainty, instability, and temptations faced by both eventually lead to a drifting apart. She is raising the kids; he (she thinks) is raising hell. His off-duty companions may be loneliness and emptiness shared with patrons of whatever bar is close to his hotel, as he seeks solace in the piano bar or raunchy country-western saloon. As the kids get older, her attention is diverted outside the home activities. Eventually, she really does not care if or when he comes home, and maybe hopes he will not. He would rather be at work. His body may be at home, but his mind is always preoccupied with concern for his protectee. She has discovered new interests, new activities, and developed new friends she does not want to share. When they should be looking forward to grandchildren, they are seeking a divorce.

In the protection profession, personal relationships are extremely difficult to maintain. There will always be something, work related, that needs attention. He may be enjoying a day off with the family, perhaps going to Disneyland, or leaving to take his wife to a wedding anniversary dinner when the telephone rings. Someone could not make it to work because of illness; the protectee needs him in twenty minutes. Whatever the crisis, whatever the time, he responds, and his personal life takes a back seat. An agent must keep a suitcase, sufficient for at least a day or two, packed and ready. His briefcase contains whatever is required to sustain him for long shift hours under varying weather conditions.

But if it is so bad—psychologically, physically, and personally—why do people do it? Why is it such a rewarding profession? What makes it worth the price of admission? Why do agencies like the Secret Service have thousands of applicants every year and private companies have no difficulty recruiting personnel?

There are probably no simple answers. Each person has his own reasons and motivations. It may be the prestige, the power, the opportunity for travel to places he has only imagined, or the fortuity to walk among presidents, royalty, and celebrities. It could be the money. But in the final analysis, there is only one reason: they are all dedicated to one principle. They have a sincere impetus (albeit it perhaps a repressed desire) to help those who, although powerful and wealthy, cannot defend themselves against the incursions of those who would seek to deprive them of their wealth, power, and position, or even their lives. Those in the protection profession are the ones who "helped the little old lady cross the street," stooped to help an injured animal, or took on the schoolyard bully to defend a lesser fellow. It is probably the reason why former Boy Scouts, police, and military personnel find their way into the profession; they are accustomed to helping others and placing themselves between the person at risk and the immediate danger, regardless of their personal safety. And, yes, an agent would suffer the dragons and take a bullet for someone else.

TIPS AND ADVICE

Putting someone else's concerns, demands, and life before his own does not necessarily mean an agent must make personal sacrifices beyond what is naturally and physically possible. Some things are merely a matter of common sense, but to be aware of them in advance is to forestall unnecessary anxiety. There is no pain more agonizing or stress inducing than to be standing a post of duty, unable to leave or wait for a relief agent to arrive, when the pressures of Mother Nature begin to circulate in the lower abdominal region. What to do?

Anyone ever caught in a similar situation can have sympathy, but there is really no easy solution. One might hope for a close-by facility and an opportunity to quickly make use of it without compromising the security of the post. The best approach is to attempt to avoid the situation. At every opportunity, when a facility is available, an agent should take advantage of the moment before going on post. He should also avoid highly fibrous foods such as nuts, and multigrain cereals and breads, before going on duty. Excessive liquids should also be avoided. In other words, go to the bathroom whenever there is an opportunity, whether necessary or not, and do not eat foods or drink liquids that have a purgative effect. If diarrhea may be a problem, alert the supervisor to send a relief as soon as requested, and keep an antidiarrhea medication readily available.

It should be no surprise that an agent is often called upon to work continuously throughout the day or night with no opportunity to partake of a proper meal. It is highly advisable for an agent to keep a sandwich in his pocket. It is a good idea to have a small snack such as a sandwich (nothing with meat, mayonnaise, or anything that will spoil) and a bottle of water or soda in the briefcase. Some people prefer to catch a candy bar on the run. This will give a quick burst of energy and assuage the "hungries" for a while, but there is no nutritional value in a candy bar, so it provides only empty calories. It is recommended that a high-nutrition food bar, like the ones physical fitness advocates eat, be made a part of the standard equipment. They can easily be kept in a jacket pocket and readily available when needed. The food bars are high in nutritional calories and have a proper balance of the right vitamins and minerals. One bar and a bottle of water can maintain a person for several hours. Many kinds of high-nutrition, high-energy food bars are available, and most major food stores have made them readily accessible, and they are inexpensive.

Another natural and physical stress an agent routinely encounters is the lack of proper sleep and rest. Because of the hectic lifestyle of the protective agent, he may have little time or opportunity to obtain his full requirement of sleep. Furthermore, because of the intrusion of stress and anxiety, he may suffer from sleep deprivation. Sleep is a natural healer and refresher.

In Shakespeare's *Macbeth,* act 2, scene 2, after he has assassinated the sleeping King Duncan, Macbeth finds he cannot sleep but sums up its sweet reward:

Sleep that knits up the raveled sleeve of care,
The death of each day's life, Sore labour's bath,
Balm of hurt minds, great Nature's second course,
Chief Nourisher in life's feast.

A protective agent must know to "get what you can, when you can" and to rest when given the opportunity. He can and should learn the art of instant and total relaxation, a kind of self-hypnosis. Practitioners of hypnosis say that two hours of total relaxation is the equivalent of eight hours of regular sleep. Whenever given a relief break, an agent should sit down, raise his feet, place them on a footrest or low table, close his eyes, and concentrate on closing out all sound and thoughts from his mind. Beginning with his toes, he begins to relax his body until he reaches his neck, shoulders, and head. A few moments of total relaxation without actually sleeping will refresh the person for a while—long enough to make it until the next break. It is possible to learn to unconsciously tell when the break is over and "wake up."

Many long-distance travelers and busy people have learned to take their rest and sleep while traveling. Many are asleep as soon as they fasten their seatbelt on a plane.

It takes practice, but a little rest and a nap can work wonders when enduring the long days and nights of a protective agent.

A major debilitating factor to a protection agent is the lower back pain caused from many hours of constant standing. A proper sleeping position will alleviate most of the pain. The sleeping person should be on his side, in a semifetal or curled position. The head should rest on a pillow that is not too soft, too large, or too small. Another pillow should support the small of the back, and a third pillow should be stuffed between the knees. He should keep one leg about three-quarters straight and the other bent into a comfortable position at the knee. This position allows the back muscles to rest and relax. When pain is present, a 20-minute ice pack on the small of the back area relieves the inflammation and brings some relief. Also, a proper pair of shoes with solid support helps in taking pressure off the back while standing.

An out-of-town trip may arise with little notice. An executive protection agent is expected to respond and be ready to travel, sometimes on the next plane. He should keep his clothes cleaned, pressed, and ready to go as a matter of routine. He should have ample clothing available and not have to worry about going to the cleaners to pick up his suits or having insufficient clothes in readiness. If going out of town overnight or on a short trip of a day or two, he should plan on at least one extra suit, shirt, and pair of underwear. A good rule of thumb is that if the trip is scheduled for one day, take enough for three days. If the trip is for three days, take clothing for five days, and so on. Sometimes the overnighters turn into extended trips. A safe maximum is to prepare for seven to nine days. On one occasion, the president went to his vacation home on a Friday night, intending to return two days hence, on the following Sunday night. Everyone, including staff, Secret Service agents, and the White House press corps, carried enough clothing for the weekend. As circumstances changed, the weekend trip became a two-week stay. People were scrambling to find clean clothes.

Traveling for extended periods of time can have unexpected ancillary problems that must be remembered and addressed in advance. For example, bills must be paid. Sometimes, because he is away from home for long periods of time, a protective agent (especially if he is single) may not even receive an invoice until it is long past due. When his mortgage or rent payment comes due, the bank or landlord does not want to hear about "being out of town." Where can he safely park his car for a month or two if he does not have a garage? Who is going to take care of the lawn or pet? How about stopping delivery of the daily newspaper or having the mail held at the post office until he returns?

FRUSTRATIONS

When a new assignment begins, it is somewhat like a honeymoon period. The protectee listens intently to the protective agent and readily takes his advice regarding all security matters. On the other hand, the protective agent makes an extra effort to please and impress his client. As familiarity settles in and the threat level lowers, the relationship of the protectee and the agent at times can become strained.

The protectee may feel the protective agent is being overly cautious, maybe inflating the threat level just to maintain his position. The protectee begins to wonder if it is really necessary to have someone following and accompanying him everywhere he goes. Perhaps he may feel the relationship is becoming too close, with the protective agent involved in all his activities. He then begins making little changes, expecting and telling the agent to handle more and more nonsecurity related duties (e.g., giving instructions to the gardener, picking up the laundry, making trips to the post office, and so on). To whatever extent possible, the protective agent should diplomatically try to avoid becoming involved in the personal life of the protectee.

As the agent finds he is performing fewer and fewer protective duties, he may realize he is simultaneously taking on duties that have no direct relationship to his position as protection agent. Placed in that position, an agent can begin to develop a resentment of the protectee, and his frustration builds. He is too professional to complain and yet cannot refuse, because he feels a personal responsibility toward the protectee. A protective agent should be perfectly clear to himself and the protectee, right from the very beginning, that because of the nature of his protective responsibility, he cannot position himself to be an intermediary for the household or business staff. When the working relationship is maintained on a strictly professional basis, sustaining the proper employer–employee relationship is much easier and minimizes the frustration level.

Another source of petty frustration to the protective agent can be, for example, taking the protectee's wife and/or family shopping or for a beauty salon appointment. Providing protection to the wife and family are very important elements of the protection responsibility. However, the degree of difficulty is compounded by the frustration of having to wait in a hair salon or to look busy and interested in a department store. Out of respect to the agent, whom she feels must know everything, the wife may seek his opinion regarding the quality or value of a purchase. The opinion sought may be well out of the agent's experience or knowledge, yet he is expected to answer all of her questions while remaining alert to any possible approach of a dangerous or interfering person. He may be more familiar with shopping a "blue-light special" than with shopping in the most expensive store in the city and understand that, for value, the wife could find the same item at a much lower price at a more generic store. It is none of the agent's business how much a protectee is paying for an item, but it can be frustrating to know the purchaser is being cheated and be unable to prevent it.

As the day wears on, and the wife/shopper isn't exactly sure what she wants to buy or where she wants to go, the frustration level of the agent begins to override his professionalism. Not that he does not like being with the protectee's wife and providing his protective service; he merely becomes frustrated with being in a situation he dislikes and cannot control. As they drive along the street, the protectee's wife may suddenly say, "Stop here!" or "Turn down this street!" Then she will say, "Why didn't you stop?" or "Why didn't you turn?" Then he must explain about the closely following traffic and being unable to stop or turn so suddenly, being in the wrong lane, and so on. On such occasions, it is best to just "grin and bear it," make a turn around the block, and stop or turn as directed.

PROFESSIONALISM AND A FEW LAST WORDS

This is not the final chapter. That will be written by each and every person who assumes the role of paladin: a defender of the weak and less capable; of the rich and powerful who, only by reason of their position or wealth, are the targets of political and religious enemies or sociopaths who prey on and stalk their victims for their own demented reasons. The information contained herein is not a know-it-all or end-all complete ultimate guide to close personal protection. As stated at the beginning, this is only an introduction, intended to highlight some of the expectations, dangers, and critical aspects inherent to the profession. Yet, with this information, hopefully, some mistakes on the job and in the personal life of the protection agent will be eliminated, and he will have a long professional career in an exciting business. It could even save a life.

The many dragons we have mentioned in this book are as real and close as the next nightmare or the next anxiety-disturbed sleep. The dragons are our fears, anxieties, and personal foibles. A purposeful effort was made to paint as dark a picture as possible about close personal protection and the dragons we face. If we know what is lurking around the next corner, we can either prepare ourselves or take the easy route and avoid them entirely by not engaging in close personal protection.

By opting out of the personal protection adventure, a person also misses the rich rewards and benefits derived from using his skills, intelligence, and personal character to benefit public figures, celebrities, and VIPs who are threatened by persons or groups who would interlope into their lives and affairs. Close personal protection is not about money, glory, fame, or prestige. It is about knowing, when you go home at the end of a rigorous assignment, that a protectee is still alive and safe because of the expertise of a few unselfish, dedicated, hard-working people who are willing to stand in harm's way for a person or institution. And you are a part of the few.

Presidential protection is about being on an airliner as it flies low over the Lincoln Memorial, banks over the Washington Monument, and levels out and lands safely at Washington's Ronald Reagan National Airport. It is catching glimpses of the White House, the Capitol, Arlington National Cemetery, and all the symbols of America's glory, freedom, and strength. In moments like these, with the thrill experienced no matter how often one lands in Washington, one realizes the importance of his role in maintaining a constant vigilance over the elected leaders.

Presidential protection is about walking into the White House, spending hours walking and standing where history is discussed in hushed tones, as the smell of hickory smoke from the many fireplaces fills the air and grandfather clocks tick away the centuries. One can feel the presence of Jefferson, Jackson, Lincoln, Truman, Eisenhower, Kennedy, and many others. Here, history is truly alive, and if you listen carefully while standing post near the East Room or the State Dining Room, especially late at night, you can hear its echo.

Close personal/executive protection is also about corporate America. It is providing a safe environment for the "captains of industry" as they go about the daily business of piloting the economy, nurturing manufacturing, or planning new avenues of entertainment. It is about making sure that people in such sensitive positions of power do not have to worry about some crazy or criminal activity that would endanger them, their families, or businesses.

Close personal protection is about making sure that the young, attractive television star or the domestic violence victim can go home safely at night, knowing that her protective agents will provide a safe barrier against the stalker, the victimizer, and the beater.

Close personal protection is knowing that all has been done that can be done to provide a safe, secure environment for those at risk and that they are safe for one more day. Executive protection is intrinsically rewarding. It is about being willing to make the personal sacrifices, fight the dragons, and, yes, to take a bullet.

Be aware, be alert; stay safe, stay alive!

FINAL SUMMARY

KEEP A SAFE, SECURE ENVIRONMENT

Detect–Disrupt–Deter

1. Detect. Attacks may be similar, but they are also different. Look for surprises.
2. Disrupt. Take action. Do something!!!
3. Deterrence works!
4. Have a "game face."
5. Look like "readiness."
6. Be confident.

Be a Professional!!
- What are you doing wrong?
- What are you doing right?
- How can *you* make it better?
  - Stay alert!!
  - Stay alive!!
  - Keep your protectee alive!!
  - Fight and conquer your dragons.

Life is full of exams, but some count more than others. The final exam in protective services comes at that one instant when all instinct, reflexes, experience, education, and training are put to the test. Are you ready for it, and would you take a bullet for someone else? *Think!*

FINAL REVIEW QUESTIONS

1. What are anxiety dreams?
2. What stresses are so powerful that they cause anxiety dreams?
3. As a personal protection agent, what fears most often have to be overcome?
4. Explain, "Courage is never to let your actions be influenced by your fears."
5. Discuss the temptations of a protection agent. How should he deal with them?

6. Why is executive protection sometimes referred to as a "single person's job"?
7. What are some personal aspects of the executive protection agent's life that must be addressed as he engages in his chosen occupation?
8. What tips and advice should a protection agent keep in mind?
9. How should a person be physically and mentally prepared for his role as a close personal protection agent?
10. What particular lessons were learned from each of the assassination cases discussed in this book?
11. Professionalism is amorphous by definition. What does it mean to a protection agent?
12. In personal protection, how do the rewards outweigh the risks and sacrifices?
13. Would you intentionally step in front of a bullet for another person? Perhaps someone you do not personally like?
14. Given a controversial application of technology (e.g., electronic monitoring of a potential attacker), discuss the application.
15. Discuss legal problems and ethical considerations arising from the presence of protective personnel in areas where the person being protected instigates or participates in a violent or illegal action.
16. Discuss the potential conflicts of interest a police officer may encounter while working off duty as a private protection agent.
17. Identify the differences and similarities of police work and close personal protection.
18. Fully explain "getting too close to the person being protected" and the role of personal feelings in close personal protection.
19. Given a controversial principle of protection (e.g., how much protection is adequate and when adequate becomes excessive), describe the parameters of good judgment when addressing issues of adequate protection.
20. Explain the importance of private protective agencies, training, and education.
21. Describe the role of close personal protection in the hierarchy of protective services.
22. Describe the partnership between private entities and public agencies in the world of personal protection.
23. Identify a historical group or agency responsible for protecting government and/or religious figures, describing the methods of providing the protective service and the degree of duty, loyalty, and dedication of the protectors.
24. Describe the duty, loyalty, and dedication required of a private protection specialist.
25. Given a recent or anticipated development in the protective sciences, prepare a written forecast of the future of private security services.
26. Prepare a scenario that exemplifies how modern methods of private protection differ from government methods.
27. Present an example of the evolution of private protection and compare it with a similar evolution of governmental entities.
28. Present an outline acknowledging historical methods and mistakes to be avoided by a protection specialist.

29. In terms of protective–security services, address a historical protective entity and its relationship with modern private protection agencies.
30. Trace the evolution of modern private protective services from its roots in the mid-1800s to current times. A time-line concept should be used.
31. Discuss the temptations facing a personal protection agent. How should he deal with them?
32. What are some personal aspects of the executive protection agent's life that must be addressed as he engages in his chosen occupation?
33. What common-sense personal tips and advice should a protection agent keep in mind?
34. What specific lessons were learned from each of the presidential assassination cases?
35. Professionalism means different things to different occupations. What does it mean to a close personal protection agent?
36. In close personal protection, how do the rewards outweigh the risks and sacrifices?
37. Discuss the whistle-blower ramifications and/or ethical responsibilities of protective personnel related to safety violations by the protectee's business or organization that could potentially harm other employees but are unrelated to the safety of the person being protected.
38. What does it mean to have strict personal honesty and integrity?
39. Prepare a scenario that shows how modern methods of private protection differ from government methods.
40. In terms of protective-security services, address working the principal protocols.
41. How would you react to the following scenario? Your protectee goes to a nightclub where he drinks heavily and becomes intoxicated. He also meets "the one true love of my life," a complete stranger. He insists on taking the willing lady to his home for the remainder of the night. He also insists that he drive his own car with you, the protective agent, following in a second car.

Personal Protection - The Strength of the Shield; Sensitivity of the Rose[©]

NOTES

1. Skolnick, Jerome, *Justice Without Trial: Law Enforcement in a Democratic Society.* New York: Macmillan, 1994. Quoted in Burns, Ronald G., and Crawford, Charles E. *Policing and Violence.* Englewood Cliffs, NJ: Prentice-Hall, 2002, 93.
2. Burns and Crawford, *Policing and Violence.*

Appendix A

Close Personal Protection Team Member Self-Assessment Survey

Protection team members must understand their teammates—what motivates them, why they want to be on the team, their mental and physical attributes, and so forth. Practitioners asking and answering these questions will become more aware of what it means to be a professional close protection specialist. If individuals on a team are cohesive, work together for the same goals, give attention to the team or group process, and make sure they, themselves, make a difference, that will make the difference between success and failure. By definition, a *team* means more than one. A team is individuals melding together to reach high goals and to work for the common welfare with set standards that each must accomplish.

This survey, touching on many levels of awareness of the personal choices and decisions required by a protection agent, can also be utilized in the hiring interview and team selection processes.

Please answer the following questions as completely and sincerely as you can, in your own words.

1. Why are you doing this type of work?
2. Are you aware of the dangers, stressors, and risks? Name five.
3. What is your level of education and training?
4. Why did you select such a potentially dangerous career?
5. Why should a client think he can trust you with his life?
6. Why do you want to protect someone?
7. Would you be willing to sacrifice your life to save someone else's? Why?
8. Would you "take one (make sacrifices) for the team"? Yes or no, and explain.
9. Could and would you intentionally step into the line of fire or harm's way for someone you might not even like? Explain.
10. Can you take direction without asking why or needing an explanation?
11. In considering your motivations for doing this type of work, list your first five motivators (or reasons) in order of priority.
12. If you had to list ten motivators, where would you rank the monetary rewards? Why?
13. At what price would you "sell" your integrity?
14. Why did you choose this profession?
15. What is the most satisfying part of this career?

16. How do you handle the stress of the job?
17. Do you consider the stress as a problem? Explain.
18. Do you have a passion for this career? Explain.
19. Are you a team player? Why do you think so?
20. Do you enjoy reading and sitting quietly?
21. Are you able and willing to work long hours, perhaps miss meals, and not expect extra compensation? Explain.
22. What does to serve and protect mean to you?
23. Do you expect expressions of appreciation from others?
24. Are you good at working toward solving problems with others?
25. How good are you at building relationships with others? With persons you do not like or often disagree with?
26. Are you imaginative in preparing for emergencies?
27. Do you have good communication skills?
28. Do you enjoy heavy exercise?
29. Are you good at analyzing changing circumstances?
30. Are you able to see and quickly recognize and react in emergency situations?
31. Have you ever been in a life-or-death situation? Explain.
32. Do you enjoy doing things that are risky or dangerous? Explain.
33. Do you participate in exercise or workout programs? Why or why not?
34. What do you do for relaxation?
35. Would you volunteer for an assignment even if it meant working under hazardous conditions?
36. If you saw a fellow team member engaged in an illegal or unethical act, what would be your response? What is the right thing to do?
37. Do you have a strong support base (family, friends, and others) that agrees with your choice of career?
38. In another lifetime, would you have wanted to be a knight, samurai, and warrior? Why?
39. Do you constantly need excitement, and do you get bored easily?
40. Can you sit or stand in one place for hours with no external stimuli?
41. Can you see fellow team members as family?
42. Would you make serious sacrifices for your fellow team members—even your life?
43. Does it matter if others on your team are receiving more compensation than you for the same job?
44. How do you entertain yourself in moments where there is nothing happening?
45. What does "all for one, one for all" mean to you?
46. Do you have a tendency to want to learn every aspect of your job and the jobs of your teammates, or do you wish to specialize in certain aspects that apply only to your position? Explain.
47. What does character mean to you?
48. What does professionalism mean to you?
49. Do you tend to seek compatibility with others, or do you prefer to work alone?
50. Do you have a good sense of comedy, and can you see the humor in absurd or difficult situations?

Appendix B

Terrorist Advance Checklist

NECESSARY CHARACTERISTICS OF SPECIAL OPERATIONS[1]

1. A security plan for the operation (e.g., members, weapons, apartments, documents)
2. An operational tactical plan

A special operation must have stages. These stages are integrated and inseparable, otherwise, the operation would fail. These stages are

1. Research (reconnaissance) stage
2. Planning stage
3. Execution stage

FIRST STAGE—RESEARCH

In this stage, precise information about the target is collected. The target may be a person, a place, or (when attempting to assassinate an important target) a personality. It is necessary to gather all information related to that target, such as

- His name, age, description (photos), residence, social status.
- His work (type and place of employment and duties).
- Time of his departure to work and return.
- The routes he takes (whether he alternates routes, and whether the alternate routes are used on a routine basis).
- What are his vulnerabilities, and where and for how long will he be exposed?
- How and where he spends his recreational or "off" time and with whom.
- The names of his friends, relatives, visitors, their addresses, descriptions, etc.
- The car(s) he owns or has access to (full descriptions including places of maintenance).
- Does he drive or have a driver (driving experience and knowledge of area).
- His wife's work (type, place, and duties) and whether he visits her there.
- Her name, age, description (photos), residence, driving habits and patterns.
- His children (names and ages and descriptions, photos) and whether he visits their school.

- Does he have a girlfriend (name, age, description, photos)? What is her address, and when does he visit her there?
- Any physical ailments and the name and address of his doctor.
- What stores, restaurants, theaters, churches, etc., does he frequent?
- What are his recreational sports, and where does he participate in them?
- Places where he spends his vacations and holidays.
- Is he armed?
- How many guards does he have?
- How well trained and disciplined are his guards? What are the guards' routines?

From the Outside

- His house entrances, exits, walls, gates, vegetation, windows, open spaces, swimming pools, and other barriers such as furniture, lighting, gravel driveways.
- Surrounding streets and alleys.
- CCTV cameras and detection devices.
- Police and nearby government agencies or embassies and consulates.
- Demographic and economic characteristics of the area.
- Characteristics of the area (residential, leveled, industrial, rural, isolated, trees, physical, and psychological barriers).
- Traffic congestion times and railroad crossing times.

From the Inside

- Ways of sneaking into his house.
- Amount and location of lighting.
- Number of people inside (servants, family, guests, and their routines).
- Number of floors and rooms (safe rooms—location and equipment).
- Telephone lines and location of switchboard or telephone wiring room.
- Electrical lines into and out of the location.
- Number and location of guard posts and names and routine of guards.

In other words, the people, the timings, the entrances and exits, heating and air conditioning ducts, electrical maintenance, facilities, emergency response, parking, the weather, placement of the sun... everything!

Before the Operation

1. The operation should be appropriate to the participants' physical, mental, and moral abilities and capabilities.
2. The participants should be selected from volunteers, not draftees.
3. Roles should be distributed according to the members' physical, mental, and moral abilities.
4. Any needed equipment should be brought to the place of the operation in a timely fashion and should be placed in a convenient location.

5. The members should be well disguised and placed in a location close to that of the operation.
6. Shortly before the operation, reconnaissance should be repeated to confirm that nothing new has occurred.
7. The operation members should not be told about the operation until shortly before executing it so as to avoid leaking information about it.
8. Weapons should be tested prior to their use in the operation.
9. The place and time should be suitable for the operation.
10. When using a pistol or rifle, a bullet should be already placed in the firing chamber.

SECOND STAGE—PLANNING

After receiving information about the target, the operation, a plan is created. The operation's tactical plan should consider the following:

- Type of required weapons
- Number of required members and their training
- An alternative to the original plan
- Type of operation from a tactical perspective (It is a silent or loud elimination operation?)
- Time specified for the execution of the operation
- The target of the operation (Is it one individual or many?)
- Team meeting place prior to execution of the operation
- Team meeting place after execution of the operation
- Securing withdrawal of the team after the execution and routes of withdrawal
- Difficulties the team may encounter

THIRD STAGE—EXECUTION

To discover any unexpected element detrimental to the operation, it is necessary, prior to execution of the operation, to rehearse it in a place similar to that of the real operation. The rehearsal may take place shortly before the execution. Then the operation is executed in the place and time specified. After execution of the operation, a complete evaluation is made. At the end, a full report is given to the commanders of the organization.

AFTER THE OPERATION

1. The operation should be completely evaluated in terms of advantages and disadvantages.
2. Each member of the operation should be evaluated according to his assigned role.
3. Each member who succeeded in his role should be rewarded, and each member who was weak or slack in his role should be dismissed.
4. Hiding or sending abroad those who executed the operation.

5. Hiding the weapons used in the operation in a location difficult to find by the security apparatus.
6. Burning any documents, maps, or drawings related to the operation. Removal of all traces of burning them.
7. Defending members who participated in the operation and were captured, and taking care of their families.
8. The party that performed the operation should not be revealed.
9. No signs that might lead to the execution party should be left at the operation's location.

NOTE

1. Al-Qaeda training manual.

Appendix C

Protective Agent Advance Checklist

The following is an example of a protective agent's advance checklist. It may not be complete, but it will suffice as a guide or roadmap to a successful advance. A checklist is to be used as an elementary reference only and is not intended to be an "answer all." It is expected that an advance agent will modify and edit any recommended checklist to match his own particular needs. A checklist should be used when conducting an advance because of the stress and pressure of the high-level responsibility. "No stone too small to turn over or rock too large to look under, and nothing to overlook."

A.   THINGS TO DO BEFORE DEPARTING FOR AN ASSIGNMENT
1.   Obtain name and telephone number of contact person.
2.   Call contact person and make arrangements for meeting.
   a.   Who is the host committee?
   b.   Special dress requirements, if any
   c.   Types of expenses authorized
   d.   All pertinent phone numbers
   e.   Special requirements of principal
      •   Medical
      •   Personal
      •   Dietary
3.   Determine types of functions principal will be attending, pack or dress accordingly.
4.   Conduct office indices and records check for previous advance reports to a particular location.
5.   Check any special equipment including communications that might be required.
6.   Check weather forecast for the area to be visited.
7.   Conduct research of location to be visited (know local situation—history, location, political influence, crime and violence).
8.   Determine billing arrangements—estimate amount of funds needed for the assignment.

B.   PRINCIPAL
1.   Who is the principal?

    a. Be able to recognize principal and members of his family and staff.

    b. Know the principal's itinerary.

    c. What time does he arrive?

    d. What time does he depart?

    e. Where is he visiting?

    f. What type of transportation is to be used?

    g. Who is providing?

    h. Who are the drivers or pilots?

    i. What is their training?

    j. Phone numbers?

    k. Language considerations.
- Will an interpreter be needed for the principal?
- Will an interpreter be needed for the security detail?

    l. Medical problems of the principal or members of his party.

    m. Amount of baggage expected.

C.   ARRIVAL AT SITE OR CITY OF VISIT

1. Observe the general layout of the airport.
2. Obtain a good map of the area and orient yourself in general terms.
3. Obtain rental vehicle.
4. Proceed to your hotel and observe:
   a. Traffic conditions
   b. Road conditions
   c. General topography
   d. Landmarks
   e. Time and distance
   f. Check into hotel and note:
      - Parking areas
      - Lobby configuration
      - Elevator locations
      - Service elevators
      - Areas of congestion
      - Restaurant locations
      - Other amenities
5. Contact your home office.
   a. Tell them where you are and how to contact you.
   b. Inquire as to any changes.
   c. Obtain messages.
   d. Check in with your home office at least once per day.
6. Make preliminary telephone contact with
   a. The local contact for the visit (host)
   b. The hotel
      - Resident manager, reservations manager, or assistant manager
      - Have reservations been made for security detail as well as principal's party

- Number of agents authorized per room
- If other than a hotel, is there adequate room to lodge the security detail and to set up a command post

c. Auto rental agency or limousine company, if vehicles are needed Drivers and/or pilots
- Where are they staying?
- Contact numbers?

d. Police
- Intelligence
- Threat assessments
- Dangerous persons file
- Motorcade advice
- Special problems
- Road construction or closings
- Special events
- Emergency and nonemergency direct telephone numbers

D.   SITE SURVEYS

The investigation and resultant plans of security for a given location generally involve all security measures taken at a place to be visited by the principal. Identify undesirable elements and physical hazards, taking necessary action to reduce risk or harm to the principal. Conducting a site survey is comparable to any complete, thorough, professional criminal investigation; looking for clues of countersurveillance or adverse activity, but primary attention is given to factors either embarrassing or harmful to the principal.

1. Contact person(s) in charge of the area or site (key contact person).
   a. Building manager or owner
   b. Evaluate area where event is to occur
   c. Consider the time that the principal will be exposed
   d. Examine factors that are difficult to control
      - Crowds
      - Location
      - Press sites
      - Items outside the secured area
      - Vehicles parked near by
      - Building across the street
      - Woodlands and parks
      - Curious passers-by
      - Bridges, overpasses, tunnels, manholes, parked cars
2. Check all travel times and distances involved.
3. Check and evaluate all emergency data.
   a. Emergency phone numbers
   b. Equipment on hand
   c. Emergency escape routes
   d. Extra motorcade
   e. Panic bars, stairwells, locks, all doors, etc.

4. Decide on identification
    a.   Security team members
    b.   Principal's staff
    c.   Others in entourage
    d.   Host committee
    e.   Press area
    f.   General public and general holding room
5. Determine personnel and logistical needs
    a.   Establish security posts
    b.   Route surveys
    c.   Determine safety hazards
    d.   Improper lighting
    e.   Inadequate emergency exits
    f.   Overcrowding
    g.   Faulty equipment
    h.   Elevators (lock down elevators, make one express; others stop on floor below)
    i.   Podium, lectern, lighting, microphones, visual aids, chairs, etc.
    j.   Delay problems that could hinder rapid movement of principal
6. Preventive measures
    a.   Provide buffer zones between principal and public
    b.   Control of limited access areas
    c.   Screening of all things entering a secured area after a sweep
    d.   Change and control untenable situations
    e.   Control movement of the principal
    f.   Reduce principal's exposure
    g.   Effect continuity of security
    h.   Health hazards
        • Smoke
        • Fumes
        • Water
        • Food
        • Heating and air conditioning
        • Electric blankets, grounded lamps, etc.

E.   TYPES OF SECURITY SURVEYS
    1. Airports
    2. Ballrooms
    3. Auditoriums
    4. Hotels
    5. Coliseums (stadiums)
    6. Private residence
    7. Office buildings, factories, etc.
    8. Routes of travel
    9. Outdoor activities

F.   BASIC PERIMETER SECURITY THEORY
1. Where is the principal?
   a.   Home
   b.   Work
   c.   Airplane
   d.   Parade
   e.   Golf course
   f.   Sports event
2. Who else is at that location?
   a.   Immediate family
   b.   A few trusted friends
   c.   General public
   d.   Members of government
   e.   Spectators at a sporting event
   f.   Other persons who attract controversy or have high-risk profiles
3. Was there advance notice?
   a. Publicity
   b. Press
   c. Invitations
4. What time of day?
5. Weather conditions (direction of the sun)
6. Proximity of people to the principal
   a.   Banquet
   b.   Golf tournament
   c.   Parade, handshaking, reception
7. What intelligence do you have?
   a.   General
   b.   Specific
8. How will the "rings of protection" be deployed?

G.   THINGS TO CONSIDER WHILE DEVELOPING PLANS
1. What technical equipment do you need, have access to, or can get to your location?
   a.   Portable alarm systems
   b.   CCTV (cameras and monitors)
   c.   Bullet proof vests
   d.   Armored limos
   e.   Global positioning systems
   f.   Computers
   g.   Bomb and metal detectors
   h.   Night vision equipment
   i.   Communications equipment
   j.   Firearms
2. What is the lay of the land?
   a.   Tall buildings
   b.   Mountains

    c.   Flat fields
    d.   Woodlands with brush and shrubs
    e.   Ocean, lake, or river
3. How many people are available for post standing and other assignments?
    a.   How well trained are they?
    b.   How experienced are they?
4. What is the time frame for preparation?
5. How much protection will the principal require?

H. HOTEL ADVANCE

Walk and learn the hotel prior to meeting with the hotel staff. If you have special requests, meet with the hotel manager. If the visit requires the special services of housekeeping, food service, security, and so forth, set up a meeting with the hotel manager and department heads. (Meet all at the same time.) Have your requests printed and hand out in the presence of the hotel manager. It is important to have solutions to their objections.

Principal's Suite
  Conduct a thorough examination of the suite.
1. The principal's suite should be located away from the elevators and stairwells.
2. Know what is above, below, and adjacent to the suite.
3. Attempt to occupy these rooms with the protective detail or staff.
4. The suite should not be accessible from common balconies or fire escapes.
5. The suite should not be accessible from adjacent buildings.
6. It is recommended that the suite be located above the first and below the sixth floor.
7. Rooms with a false ceiling or other areas where listening devices or explosives could be concealed should be avoided.
8. Special needs or request should be verified. King-size bed, bar, VCR, video games, refrigerator, color scheme, cleanliness, view, etc.

Command Post
1. The command post should be close but not next to the principal's suite.
2. Should be located between the general traffic areas and the principal's suite.

Hotel Services
1. Determined the location and availability of all hotel services.
2. Have room service and all deliveries for the principal's suite delivered to the command post or agent's room for inspection and delivery.
3. Command post or agent should order the principal's food without disclosing to the kitchen the intended recipient.

Fire System
1. How does it work?
2. When was the alarm activation last tested?
3. Is the report verified before sounding the alarm?
4. You are not planning on staying during an alarm.
5. Check fire equipment on floor. Fire extinguishers, water hoses, emergency exits.

Other Hotel Advance Considerations
1. Has the hotel been announced as the temporary residence?
2. Is the main function of the principal at the hotel where the principal is staying?

Hotel Advance
1. Meet with:
   a. Resident manager
   b. General manager
   c. Determine who will be your working contact
   d. Get names, hotel, and home phone numbers of all main people
   e. General manager
   f. Head chef
   g. Food and beverage manager
   h. Catering (room service)
   i. Room reservation manager
   j. Banquet manager
   k. Head housekeeper
   l. Chief hotel telephone operator
   m. Security manager
   n. Day and night manager
   o. Concierge
   p. Public relations manager
   q. Transportation manager
   r. Maintenance and engineering manager
   s. House physician

Make a thorough examination of the principal's suite
1. Location and security problems
   a. What is above and below?
   b. What is on either side?
   c. Choose suite far removed from elevators and stairwells
   d. Access to suite from lobby
   e. False ceilings
   f. Age of building and floor level
   g. Isolated area
   h. No common balconies
   i. No exposure to adjacent buildings
   j. Are there curtains and/or blinds to cover windows
   k. No outside fire escape vulnerabilities
   l. Is the suite more than one level?

      m. Determine command post location; same floor, close proximity
         to the suite
  2.   Selecting rooms
     a. Rooms for the balance of the principal's party and security
        detail should be:
        • Above, below, and beside the principal's suite.
        • Take the whole floor or wing of suites if possible.
        • If possible get the names of other guest within the
          perimeter.
        • Check rooms for problems.

Meeting with room reservation manager
  1. Block rooms—one secured area.
  2. Arrange billings.
  3. Obtain suite and command post keys.
  4. Arrange to preregister.
  5. Arrange to have all reserved room keys at the command post on
     arrival.
  6. Arrange to check bills after departure of party.
  7. Arrange for extra standby rooms.
  8. Arrange to have beds removed from the command post.
  9. Any other special arrangements.

Meeting with assistant manager and security chief.
  1. Request names and birthdates of people who will need access to
     the suite. Keep list to a minimum. Post the list in command post.
     Always accompany them into the suite.
     a. Room service
     b. Waiters, caterers
     c. Maids
     d. Bell captain, bellboys
     e. Valet
     f. Baggage handlers
  2. Request blocked parking areas for vehicles—preferably in view of
     the parking attendant, guard, etc.
  3. Know how to operate the elevators. Request express elevators for
     arrivals and departures.
  4. Get the phone numbers for the persons who will operate the
     elevators.
     a. When were elevators last inspected?
     b. Who will respond to stuck elevators?
  5. Arrange to order food service through one or two contacts.
     a. Always have food delivered to the command post or staff per-
        son's room.
     b. Arrange for tips.
  6. Arrange baggage handlers with carts for arrivals and departures.
  7. Determine emergency power source and emergency lighting.
  8. If possible get a radio from hotel security or their radio frequency.

9. Always have alternative exits and entrances.
10. Arrange coffee, soft drinks, and midnight snacks for command post.
11. Ascertain hotel staff and services available. Get names and numbers.
    a. Masseuse
    b. Barber or beautician
    c. Shoeshine, laundry, or dry cleaning
    d. Clothing store
    e. Drugstore
    f. Health club
    g. Get copies of all hotel restaurant menus.
    h. Ascertain room service hours—have them extended if necessary.
    i. Arrange for gifts, packages, etc., to be delivered to the command post.
    j. Obtain floor plan and diagrams of hotel for command post.
12. Ascertain when they last had a fire inspection—inspect it yourself.
13. Ask to see copies of the security incident reports or at least get an idea of the types of security problems they have had in the past.
14. Find out what other events are scheduled to take place at the hotel.
15. Check stairwells for lighting, obstacles, doors, etc.
16. Do not list the principal's suite number as belonging to him.
17. Brief hotel operators on how to handle calls to the principal's suite.
    a. Do not reveal suite number.
    b. Route all calls via staff, then to the command post—not to the suite directly.
    c. Advise command post of threat or bomb calls.
18. Ascertain if hotel security is armed, how to contact them, how to identify them, their training, and when they make their rounds.
19. Determine hotel's policy as to demonstrators, hecklers, and people who interfere with guests.
20. Know the best nearby hospitals and its routes.
21. Ascertain who will greet the principal—photographers?
22. Make sure the greeting is inside, preferably on the suite floor.
23. Can the principal have kitchen privileges?
24. Keep good records of people who have helped you out and later send thank you notes.
25. Select agent post
    a. Checkpoints
    b. Suite post
    c. Command post
    d. Roving patrols
    e. Surveillance

I.   COMMAND POST EQUIPMENT
1. Equipment
    a. Radios, chargers, and batteries—flashlights
    b. Fire extinguisher
    c. Gas mask or fire/smoke escape mask
    d. Shoulder weapons
    e. Medical kit
    f. Keys to the principal's suite
    g. Vehicle keys and locations
    h. Itinerary
    i. General instructions
    j. Special Instructions
    k. Motorcade configurations
    l. Emergency telephone numbers
    m. Hospitals (maps, route directions, telephone numbers, doctors on duty)
    n. Fire department (representative and telephone numbers of contacts)
    o. Police department (representative and telephone numbers of contacts)
    p. Ambulance service (paramedics and physicians)
    q. Room assignment list
    r. Telephone list of all contacts
    s. Name lists of all authorized personnel
    t. Diagrams of site
    u. Intelligence information
    v. Route maps to all locations to be visited by principal
    w. Alternative routes
    x. Emergency hospital and evacuation information
    y. Principal's dossier
    z. Forms for agents
    aa. Posted fire evacuation routes and plan with diagrams of hotel

J.   ROUTE SURVEY
Route surveys need to include the following information:
1. . Considerations in choosing routes
    a. What is the date and time that the route is to be used?
    b. Holidays—different traffic flow
    c. Weekends—different traffic flow
    d. If near factories, government buildings, schools, major entertainment facilities
    e. What are the shift changes or when crowds are released?
    f. Train tracks
    g. Bridges, tunnels
    h. Overpasses, underpasses
    i. Construction areas

      j.   Special events, parades, demonstrations, sporting events

      k.   Parks and wooded areas

      l.   Number of intersections, stop lights, and stop signs

      m. Number of buildings and windows

      n.   Storage areas, mail boxes, sidewalk obstructions

      o.   Pedestrian traffic

      p.   Hospitals, police stations, fire stations, medical facilities, etc.

2. Detailed routes should be completed with accompanying map or route cards.

3. Alternative routes in detail with accompanying maps or route cards.

4. Time and date survey must be conducted.

K.   **AIRPORT SECURITY SURVEYS**

1. Persons to contact

    a. Airline service representative

- Is there a private airline VIP room or club available for your principal's use?
- Determine the gate where the flight will be arriving and departing.
- Arrange for principal to board last and have priority deboarding.
- Make arrangements for the principal and security teams' baggage to be loaded last and taken off first.
- Make special menu arrangements.
- Make special seating arrangements.

    b. Airport police/security representative/airport authority

- Obtain a layout of the terminal
- Find the locations of:
  1. Restrooms
  2. Medical facilities
  3. Telephones
  4. Gift shops, restaurants
  5. Duty-free shopping
  6. Shoeshine
  7. Barber
  8. Departure gates and VIP lounges

    c. Arrange for escort privileges in restricted areas.

    d. Arrange for plane-side boarding and deboarding of principal.

    e. Arrange for motorcade parking.

    f. Obtain whatever intelligence information available on possible threats.

    g. Arrange assistance in clearing customs and immigration.

2. Identify the location of the nearest hospital.

3. Complete primary and alternative route surveys to and from the airports.

4. Have a contingency plan in the event that the scheduled flight is cancelled.
5. Arrange for plane security if travel is by private plane.

L.   BANQUETS, BALLROOMS, AND AUDITORIUMS

1. Contact the host or sponsor and get the following information:
    a. Who is the banquet manager, caterer, facility manager, and host committee?
        •   Obtain phone numbers, including off-hours numbers. Also give them your contact numbers.
    b. Obtain a diagram or blueprint of the facility and a diagram and seating chart for the function.
2. Note evacuation routes, location of alarms and fire-fighting apparatus, and access control points.
3. Arrange to have awards, trophies, etc., inspected and/or mailed to your principal at a later date.
4. How is admission to be handled?
    a. Open, general, or reserved tickets?
    b. What is the price of admission, and what do the tickets look like?
    c. Invitation only. Are invitations serialized and registered?
    d. Are guest checked off as they arrive?
    e. Are substitutions permitted or possible?
    f. Where are the access control points, and who will man them?
    g. Will the facility be providing security at the event? If so get details.
    h. What is the itinerary of the event, and what part does your principal play?
    i. Will the lights go out at anytime during the event—movies, slides, etc.?
    j. Check the seating arrangement. Who is around your principal?
        •   Arrange for seating for the agents.
    k. Will there be media coverage?
        •   Who is responsible for handling the media?
        •   Make sure they are channeled into a secure area, check press passes.
        •   Assign one room as a media/press room for interviews.
        •   TV crews may have problems because of the amount of equipment. A good working knowledge of their needs, shots, lighting, access, etc., is very helpful.
    l. Who is responsible for backstage areas and security?
        •   Who has backstage privileges?
        •   Who issues and checks backstage passes?
    m. Who is responsible for utilities, air conditioning, hearing, lighting, etc.?
        •   Is there an engineer on site and on duty?
        •   Are the control panels lockable and tamper proof?

     n. What dress will be required?
- Business attire, black tie, etc.

     o. Is there an arrival point for the principal?
- Can you bypass the main access point?

     p. Can you get vehicles close to the stage for bussing/debussing?
- Where will vehicles be parked?
- Is there security for the vehicle during the event?
- Where can you stash a backup vehicle?

     q. Holding room and secured rest rooms?

     r. What type of stage is it?
- Foldable?
- Make sure that the stage, tables and chair legs and supports are fully extended and locked to prevent injury or embarrassment.
- Are there loose wires?
- What type of curtains? Are they secure?
- Look overhead for potential hazards—check catwalks.
- Look under the stage for potential hazards—trap doors.
- Check the stage for nails, loose carpets, etc.
- What types of barriers are around the stage? Plants, trees, velvet ropes, etc.

     s. Post selection
- Do agents have good observation perspectives?
- Meals? Will the agents be relieved for eating?

     t. Who are the waiters for the head table?
- When were they hired?
- Arrange for the waiters serving the head table to be provided with special pins, scarves, etc., for identification.
- Get names and addresses of head table staff and all other waiters if possible.

5. Physically walk the layout of the facility.
     a. Note dark areas near stairways, walkways, etc. Bring a flashlight for dark areas that your principal may be moving through.
     b. Look for and check out vending machines along the route.
     3. Look for places person(s) could hide or doorways that could be opened suddenly—including doors marked "Electric Danger, Do Not Enter."

6. Note the location of medical facilities and the location of the nearest hospital.

7. Prepare for possible demonstrations, and be aware that many large outside demonstrations are diversions to draw resources away from a demonstrator who may sneak inside the event.

M. RESTAURANTS
1. Obtain the following information and note the location of:
     a. Telephones
     b. Restrooms

      c.   Emergency exits—note where emergency exits open to
      d.   Kitchen
      e.   Parking
      f.   Fire extinguishers

2. Prepare a diagram of the locations of the above.
3. Select safe seating (away from doorways, windows, etc.).
   a. If you have a choice, select a table with easy access to side exit, and ask if you can enter the restaurant from that side.
   b. An agent will usually not sit at the same table as the principal, but sit at a table providing a good view of the access points and possible paths of attack to the principal.
4. Check for access control and have an agent near each point if possible.
5. Obtain a copy of the menu for the principal in advance.
6. If possible, avoid going through kitchens with the principal as kitchens have many hazards such as slippery floors, etc.
7. Whenever possible and practical, call in the team member's food order before arriving. (Order food that can be easily prepared, eaten quickly and is not messy.)
   a. Arrange for team members to be served before the principal.
   b. Make sure to feed your drivers.
      - They should not eat sitting inside the vehicles, as they could spill, and the odor will linger.
   3. Arrange for billing and tipping to be taken care of early by a team member.

H. Make sure that the maitre d', chef, head waiter, waiter, bus staff, and wine steward are properly tipped.
I. Notify other team members of any change in plans, next destination, and when the client will depart.
J. Notify the drivers well in advance of departure so that they can have the vehicles warmed up and in position for pickup.

N.   OUTDOOR EVENTS

1. Check for the following information:
   a. What is the weather forecast?
      - What is the impact of bad weather?
   b. Will there be a tent or other covered area?
      - If so, are all line, fasteners, pegs, and poles secured?
      - How will the covered area be exited?
      - What will you do if it collapses or is tampered with?
      - Are there outdoor space heaters?
        1. Are they secured and won't tip over?
        2. When will they be turned on?
        3. Are the heaters gas, oil, or electric?

O.   TEAM MOVEMENT—ON FOOT OR VEHICLE

1. Consider the following:

     a. Is movement formal or informal?

     b. Is the route or time predictable?

     c. Is the route the shortest one possible?

     d. Does it provide minimum exposure?

     e. Is there an alternative route available?

     f. Where are the danger points?

     g. What is the best evacuation route in the event of an emergency?

     h. Is there a safe area available?

     i. Where is the nearest medical facility, and what is the best route to it?

     j. Are there any physical hazards such as construction sites, bad footing, vicious dogs, overhead balconies, etc.?

     k. What types of formations are best suited for the movement?

     l. Are barriers needed for crowd control?

     m. What support is available or needed from other security/law enforcement services?

     n. Number, type, and location of security posts.

     o. Is there direct communications with the command post and the site or motorcade?

     p. What special equipment will be needed?

     q. How many people will accompany the principal during movements?

P. TEAM BRIEFING

  1. Team leader

The team leader is responsible for the team briefing after receiving all necessary information. In some circumstances, the advance man is responsible for the briefing. The briefing is an exercise in coordination around the principal's schedule.

  2. Team briefing format

     a. Roll call

     b. Introduction (Make sure everyone on the team knows each other by name and recognition.)

     c. Introduce supervisors and other key personnel

     d. Principal

       • Name, title, how addressed

       • Picture of principal and family members, staff

       • Reason for visit

       • Biographic data on principal

       • Medical history of principal

         1. Blood type

         2. Allergies

         3. Health problems

         4. Special requirements or equipment needed

         5. Is a personal physician traveling with principal?

     e. Itinerary for visit

       • Supervisors should be given copies

       • Arrival times and locations

       • Departure times and locations

- Traveling party entourage or accompanying staff—others in party, their titles and responsibilities
- Name of the contact person

f. Security in party
  - Is principal traveling with his own security?
    1. Are they armed?
    2. How many?
    3. How are they identified?
    4. Where will they ride in the motorcade?
    5. Who is in charge of the principal's security team?
    6. Who has final responsibility for the principal?

g. Intelligence and threat assessment
  - General intelligence
  - Specific intelligence
  - Countersurveillance

h. EOD operations

i. Detail operations
  - Close protection detail
  - Post assignments
    1. Report time
    2. Relief/quit time

j. Communications
  - Radio frequencies
  - Telephone numbers
    1. Land lines
    2. Cellular telephones
    3. Car phones
  - Pagers
  - Code words
    1. Ten codes
    2. Duress codes
    3. Passwords
    4. Route codes
    5. Hand signals

k. Identification
  - Lapel or other security identification pins
  - Descriptions
  - Other staff members
  - Event staff
  - Host committee
  - Visitors
  - Law enforcement and security (armed and unarmed)

l. Transportation

m. Location of safe areas
  - Holding rooms

n. Logistics and administration

    o. Special instructions
    p. Attachments
- Route sheets
- Route cards
- Maps
- Diagrams and drawings
- Photos
- Telephone numbers

Appendix D

Transportation Advance Checklist

Below is a checklist for preparing a transportation advance. This checklist is intended to help an advance agent become familiar with the routes of travel and to fill land transportation requirements.

A. Things to Know
 1. Obtain name and telephone number of contact person.
 2. Call contact person and make arrangements for meeting.
 3. Who is the principal? Be able to recognize him or her as well as members of his family and staff.
 4. Know the principal's itinerary.
 5. What type of transportation is to be used?
 6. Who is providing?
 7. Who are the drivers and what is their training?
 8. Phone numbers?
 9. Language considerations—will an interpreter be needed for the driver?
B. Arrival at Site or City of Visit
 1. Obtain a good map of the area and orient yourself in general terms.
 2. Obtain rental vehicle (if necessary). Do not survey the routes in a recognizable vehicle or one that will be driven by the protectee.
 3. Proceed to your hotel and observe:
    a. Traffic conditions
    b. Road conditions
    c. General topography
    d. Landmarks
    e. Time and distance
    f. Areas of congestion
C. Check into Hotel, Note:
 1. Parking areas
 2. Elevator locations
 3. Service elevators
 4. Restaurant locations
 5. Other amenities
 6. Make preliminary telephone contact with
    a. Auto rental agency or limo company if vehicles are needed
       1. Drivers—who are they? Qualifications?

    b.   Contact numbers?
2. Police
    a.   Intelligence
    b.   Motorcade advice
    c.   Special problems
    d.   Road construction or closings
    e.   Special events
    f.   Emergency and non-emergency direct telephone numbers
    g.   Examine factors that are difficult to control
         1.   Crowds
         2.   Location
         3.   Press sites
         4.   Items outside the secured area
         5.   Buildings across the street
         6.   Woodlands and parks
         7.   Curious passersby
         8.   Bridges, overpasses, manholes, parked cars
    h.   Check all travel times and distances involved
D. Things to Consider While Developing Plans
    1. What is the lay of the land?
        a.   Tall buildings
        b.   Mountains
        c.   Flat fields
        d.   Woodlands with brush and shrubs
        e.   Ocean, lake, or river
E. Equipment in Vehicle
    1. Radios, chargers, and batteries
    2. Flashlights
    3. Fire extinguisher
    4. Gas mask or fire/smoke escape mask
    5. Shoulder weapons
    6. Medical kit
    7. Itinerary
    8. General instructions
    9. Special instructions
    10. Motorcade configurations
    11. Emergency telephone numbers
        a.   Hospitals (maps, route directions, telephone numbers, doctors on
             duty)
        2.   Fire department (representative and telephone numbers of
             contacts)
        c.   Police department (representative and telephone numbers of
             contacts)
        d.   Ambulance service (paramedics and physicians)
    12. Room assignment list
    13. Telephone list of all contacts

14. Name lists of all authorized personnel
15. Diagrams of site
16. Intelligence information
17. Route maps to all locations to be visited by principal
18. Alternative routes
19. Emergency hospital and evacuation information
20. Global positioning systems
21. Computers
22. Communication equipment

F. Route Surveys
   1. Considerations in choosing routes:
      a. Time and distance between sites
      b. What is the date and time that the route is to be used?
      d. Holidays—different traffic flow
      d. Weekends—different traffic flow
      e. If near factories, government buildings, schools, major entertainment facilities, what time are the shift changes or when crowds are released?
      f. Train tracks (times of train crossings)
      g. Bridges, tunnels, overpasses, underpasses
      h. Construction areas
      i. Special events, parades, demonstrations, sporting events
      j. Parks and wooded areas
      k. How many intersections, stop lights, and stop signs?
      l. Number of buildings and windows
      m. Storage areas, mail boxes, sidewalk obstructions
      n. Pedestrian traffic
      o. Hospitals, police stations, fire stations, medical facilities, etc.
   2. Detailed routes should be completed with accompanying map or route cards.
   3. Determine alternative routes in detail with accompanying maps or route cards.

G. Team Movement
   1. Consider the following:
      a. Is movement on the record or off the record?
      b. Is the route or time predictable?
      c. Is the route the shortest one possible?
      d. Does it provide minimum exposure?
      e. Is an alternative route available?
      f. Where are the danger points?
      g. What is the best evacuation route in the event of an emergency?
      h. Is there a safe area available?
      i. Where is the nearest medical facility, and what is the best route to it?
      j. Are there any physical hazards such as construction sites, bad footing, vicious dogs, overhead balconies, etc.

k. Survey report attachments
- Route sheets
- Route cards
- Maps
- Diagrams and drawings
- Photos
- Telephone numbers

l. Inspect and search the vehicle before starting the assignment.

m. Check the vehicle after the protectee gets out to determine if he left anything behind.

SUMMARY OF VEHICLE SAFETY TIPS

The designated driver of the principal's vehicles should strictly adhere to the following points:

- Stay with the vehicle at all times. Never leave it unattended. If you must leave, keep it in a secure area and have someone you can trust watch it.
- When in motion, keep the vehicle's windows rolled up at all times and keep the doors locked.
- Keep the gas tank full at all times, and refill when it reaches half a tank (this may reduce the explosive hazard if attacked, or prevent running out of fuel at a critical moment).
- Use various refueling stations (avoiding patterns).
- Physically inspect the vehicle and tires. Make sure there is enough air pressure in the tires and that nothing has been placed under the tire to puncture it. Always check to make sure nobody is hiding in the back seat even though you have been watching the car the whole time.
- Do not stop to aid disabled vehicles. To be of assistance, call road service or the police for them.
- Remain in the vehicle with the engine running, windows up and the doors locked if involved in a minor accident. Have the other party follow you to a police station if he wants to report the incident.
- Always vary routes of travel. Generally keep to well-traveled roads. Avoid alleys and dead ends.
- Be present during all auto repairs and modifications.
- Keep a hidden key in the car.
- Do not touch unusual wires or objects protruding from the vehicle. Call for assistance.
- On multilane highways, stay in the middle or far left lane to prevent being run into a ditch or off the road.
- Avoid any suspicious roadblocks. Do not stop.
- When stopping at an intersection, do not stop at the line. Allow for maneuvering room, and do not stop so that you are door to door with the car next to you.

- Develop and use a system of signals to let your principal know when it is safe to enter the car. During times of duress, honk the horn, turn on the alarm, and flash the lights on and off to attract attention.
- Always check mirrors. Pay particular attention to motorcycles or scooters coming from behind (especially if the passenger on the back of the bike is facing backward).
- Avoid parking the car unattended on any street at night.
- Mentally note safe havens as you drive (police stations, fire stations, hospitals, government buildings, public areas, etc.).
- Always be alert to surveillance.
- Always use seat belts when the vehicle is in motion.
- If under attack, crouch down in the seat to make a smaller target, and have the passengers lay on the floor.
- Have the car keys ready in hand when approaching the vehicle, and do not be carrying packages, briefcases, etc., in the other.
- When driving, observe in front of the vehicle and up the road for unusual hazards, vehicles, etc.
- If suspected of being followed, do not drive home or to the office, but do drive to a safe haven such as a public shopping center, police, or fire department, etc.

SELECTION, MODIFICATION, MAINTENANCE, AND INSPECTION OF VEHICLES

A.   Vehicle Selection
   1.   When selecting a vehicle, a decision must be made more in favor of security features than esthetic wants. There are three basic security criteria that must be considered in selecting a car for the protectee.
      a.   Low profile. No easily identifiable sports models or luxury cars. No gaudy colors, markings, or distinctive insignia. It should be a vehicle common to the area and easily blend into the general motoring environment. Consideration should be given to crashworthiness and safety.
      b.   Good protection from tampering and break-in attempts. The car should have locking gas caps, hood, and trunk locks, tamper-proof door locks, and (when possible) undercarriage metal covering. The doors should be constructed in a manner to prevent jimmying with a lock pick or Slim Jim.
      c.   Excellent defensive driving characteristics. Consideration should be given to four-wheel-drive vehicles, excellent cornering and turning ability, high pickup and acceleration, wide-angle interior mirrors, and adjustable exterior mirrors.
B. Modifications (Added Security Options)

1. Obviously, the first option to consider is, should the car be armored? That depends on the expense, profile of the protectee, and the threat level and his wishes.
   a. An armored car has advantages like being bullet resistant, able to withstand "accidental" impact, and cannot be easily broken into.
   b. There are obviously disadvantages like the expense, the weight of the vehicle, the necessity for heavy duty and powerful engine and batteries, specialty tires, etc.
2. Mechanical options—subtle, but necessary, mechanical options may be added to provide an extra amount of security.
   a. High-intensity headlights and backup lights
   b. High-powered engine
   c. Power disc brakes and specialty tires for better handling
   d. Heavy-duty suspension
   e. Heavy-duty and reinforced front and rear bumpers
   f. Antitheft tamper alarms
   g. Heavy-duty battery(s) and ignition system
   h. Reliable communication system
   i. Heavy-duty hood, trunk, and gas well locks
   j. Locking wheel covers

C. Maintenance

Beyond question, the maintenance of the vehicle is extremely important. It should be fueled whenever, or before, the tank gauge nears the halfway mark (a "topping off" is always recommended). The oil should be changed and joints lubricated according to the manufacturer's recommendations. Minor tune-ups should be regularly scheduled with an overall tune-up done according to the manufacturer's recommendations. A few known and trusted mechanics should be selected to perform maintenance on the vehicle, with each being randomly assigned maintenance duties. Accurate records must be kept of all the maintenance activity. Records should include date and time, the mechanic's name and location, what work was completed, parts replaced, and recommendations for future maintenance.

D. Inspections

1. Maintenance and safety. Before the vehicles are put into service each day, they should be checked and double-checked for maintenance and safety. The following should be checked and determined to be at readiness:
   a. All lights, including interior
   b. All electrical equipment including commercial radios and communication gear
   c. Fuel and oil, brakes, fluids, battery, tire pressure, (including spare tire), ancillary equipment
   d. Heater and air conditioner
   e. Cleanliness
   f. Tamper alarms
   g. Any specialty equipment

PROTECTING AGAINST AND SEARCHING FOR CAR EMPLACED BOMBS, MECHANICAL SABOTAGE, AND SIGNS OF TAMPERING

A.   Parking and Vehicle Security
  1. Park vehicle in well-lighted areas or in a secured garage.
  2. Install tamper alarms and paging system to notify owner or driver
      a. The paging battery transmission may prematurely set off an electronic blasting device, maybe injuring or killing the placer of the bomb.
  3. Install remote starting devices.
  4. Install chicken wire into the exhaust pipe.
      a. Should not be too thick to impede exhaust flow
      b. Should not be easily seen or removed

B. Preliminary Search
  1. Preparation of the vehicle
      a. Prior to usage of the vehicle by the protectee
          • Have the vehicle "detailed" with a good washing and waxing—interior and exterior.
          • Leave nothing on the seats or floor. Keeping the exterior and interior of the vehicle clean (engine steam cleaned often) will help detect signs of tampering.
          • Photograph the exterior, interior, and undercarriage (from all sides and angles— distant and close up).
          • Document all dents, scratches, dings, loose wires, etc.
      b. The photos and documents should be maintained up to date and stored in an easily accessible location for reference when searching the vehicle.
  2. The walk-around
      a. Before entering or touching the vehicle,
          • Look for footprints, disturbed soil, or other telltale signs in the vehicle's vicinity.
          • Examine the vehicle from all angles looking for fingerprints, oil smudges, tool marks, etc., especially near doors, windows, hood and trunk, and the gas intake lid. Also look for places where the vehicle may have been wiped clean of fingerprints, smudges, etc.
          • Be sure the doors are still locked and the windows fully closed.
          • Look at the undercarriage and wheel wells. Look for things that don't belong (i.e., hanging wires, metal attachments). A long-handled inspection mirror and a small flashlight are very handy tools for undercarriage inspections.
          • Check inside the exhaust pipe and wheel covers.
  3. The interior search
      a. If everything on the exterior looks normal, carefully open the door and look for loose wires, strings, and foreign objects under the

        seats, dash, glove box, and radio and communication equipment. Be aware for signs of an explosive device.

b.   Open the trunk and hood and closely check the engine department and all spaces in the trunk. Do not overlook the gas intake well.

Appendix E

Glossary of Terms

Advance. Preparations and arrangements made prior to and in anticipation of a protectee's arrival. There are two kinds: (1) security advance relating to matters of protectee security, and (2) staff or political advance pertaining to nonsecurity arrangement.

Advance agent. The executive protection agent is responsible for making security arrangements at a site to be visited by the protectee.

Advance car. A security vehicle that precedes the motorcade by approximately two to five minutes. Usually driven by a local police officer or agent with an agent passenger and used to identify potential problem areas and looks for probable attack or ambush situations. Has direct communication to the command post and protectee's limousine. Also known as "pilot car."

Advance survey. An inspection of a particular area that will be the site or location of a protectee visit, looking for vulnerabilities, points of ingress and egress, facilities, parking, security post number and location, anything that could impact the safe arrival and departure of the protectee.

After-action report. Also known as "final survey report." A narrative form report written as soon as possible after the event or completion of the assignment. Relates the highlights, unusual incidents, contact telephone numbers, and changes in the original survey or advance report. It emphasizes any difficulties encountered and their solution and makes recommendations for future similar assignments or visits to the same location.

Agent. The term or title for a security person assigned to a protective detail, providing for the safety and security of a protectee.

Alarm system. A series of sensors detecting movement or the presence of an intruder and sends a signal to a central panel resulting in notification of the intrusion by a loud screeching horn or a silent signal of a flashing light.

Armored car. A vehicle reinforced with bulletproof or protective material rendering it capable of withstanding minor attacks. Most often limited to the protectee's vehicle.

Baggage team (or agent). The protective services agent(s) responsible for the safe conduct of the protectee's and entourage luggage from the pickup point to the actual loading onto a plane or other conveyance and the safe retrieval and delivery of it at the final destination.

Blending in. Being inconspicuous. Providing protective services without being obvious or obtrusive.

Body armor. Protective gear usually worn in known high-threat situations. Bulletproof vest.

Bodyguard. A nonprofessional providing personal security to an individual. Outdated term. Now referred to as an executive protection agent or personal protection specialist.

Bugs/bugging. Hidden listening devices or video recorders covertly placed to gain information about a principal or business.

Bump. A tip or gratuity given as extra compensation in appreciation for an agent's endeavors on behalf of the protectee. Very common among many foreign clients. Not allowed to government employees.

Bump frisk. Casually or "accidentally" bumping into or brushing against a person to feel for a concealed weapon or other object.

Call sign. A code name used during radio communications.

Caller: A potential threat. Person who makes telephone calls to warn, threaten, or harass a protectee. (*See letter writer.*)

Chase car. Also known as follow-up or follow-up car. The security vehicle directly behind the protectee's limousine. Used as a support vehicle. (*See follow-up car.*)

Check point. A manned or monitored post to control access to restricted areas limited to authorized persons only.

Choke point. Not to be confused with checkpoint. A narrow passageway. A point where a protectee is most vulnerable.

Client. The person being protected; the person who pays the bills. (*See principal; protectee.*)

Close proximity. The area immediately close to the protectee. Within the protectee's inner circle.

Command post. Centralized location and communication center where all information and equipment for a protective detail is coordinated and disseminated. Usually staffed by senior or experienced personnel with authority to make decisions.

Common sense. Using your brain; ordinary, usual; practical, workable, suitable; good sense, intelligibility; good judgment, reasonable decision-making, discretion.

Concentric circles of security. The rings of security set up around the protectee and in his environment. Should consist of a minimum number of three. Includes people, procedures, and equipment.

Confidence. Self-assured. Trusting. Maintaining entrusted information to one's self. A basic requirement of an executive protection agent.

Confidentiality. Keeping certain matters secret.

Corporate/family structure. The personnel, staff, and immediate family of the protectee and his business.

Countermeasures. An electronic sweep and physical search of a premises or business, including telephone line for listening devices and video surveillance (antibugging). Preventive action in anticipation of an attack. Procedures taken to thwart any adverse activity.

Cover and evacuate. The immediate response to a protectee in the instance of a present danger. Protective agents shield the person of the protectee with their own bodies and remove him to a safer location away from the danger.

Covert action or operation. Undercover activities. Action taken in secret.

Crisis management team. Designated personnel with specific duties and responsibilities during an emergency situation such as a terrorist attack, kidnapping of corporate personnel, natural disasters, or any other catastrophic condition disrupting the natural flow of business.

Detail. A team working for the protection of a client. (Details vary in size according to the threat level and protectee profile.) (*See protective detail; team.*)

Detail leader. The senior ranking agent or the agent in charge of the protective assignment. Usually works in close proximity to the protectee.

Discretion. Using good judgment in the best interest of the protectee. Sometimes connotes secrecy or confidentiality.

Dragon. Anxiety dreams. Worry about the safety of the protectee. Things that can go wrong and come back and haunt the agent.

Dress down. Dressing sans suit. Wearing casual dress.

Dress up. Wearing a suit or tuxedo.

Duress code or signal. A silent alarm sent by the protectee annunciated in the command post to be responded to as an emergency situation by protective agents. A secret specific word spoken or written in the instance of trouble as part of a plan to alert others to the danger or threat. Sometimes secretly written in a kidnap note by the victim.

EOD. Explosive ordinance disposal. The bomb squad. Those who remove or neutralize a potential explosive device.

Escape route. A secondary or predetermined avenue of escape to safety in case of an emergency during the course of an event or motorcade. Evacuation. (*See cover and evacuate.*)

Escorts. An outdated term for bodyguard, may be armed or unarmed. A term applied to accompanying security cars in and parallel to a motorcade. A convoy of security vehicles.

Etiquette. Socially accepted behavior and manners. Will vary greatly in different countries and cultures. (*See protectee protocol.*)

Event site. Any location for a scheduled affair of the protectee; the place to visited by the protectee.

Executive protection cocktail. A nonalcoholic drink carried by an executive protection agent while blending into a social gathering or party.

Executive protection specialist (or agent). A professional trained in the fine art of providing a secure environment to a protectee. A knowledgeable individual with expertise in all aspects of close personal protection.

Final survey report. *See after-action report.*

Follow-up car. A special vehicle with protective agents and equipment assigned to drive immediately behind the principal's car. Used to provide defensive measures for the principal's limousine. (*See chase car.*)

Formation. The positioning of the agents working in close proximity to the protectee on a walking movement.

Hardening the target. Making a potential attacker's center of interest more difficult to penetrate or a defensive posture incorporating technological systems, procedures, and awareness.

Hardware. The weapons used on a protective detail. The equipment comprising an alarm system including closed circuit television, monitors, control panel, and computers. May be a reference to a gun or weapon (as in "carrying hardware").

Heater or roscoe. Old-fashioned slang terms for a handgun.

High profile. Obvious security, maximum protection, a show of force. A well-known, highly placed, or controversial person.

High threat level. Verified threats likely to occur; possible imminent danger to the protectee. Requires full alert, total awareness, and maximum close protection.

Holding room. A specific secured room at an event site expressly reserved for the private use of the protectee. Used for refreshment, private telephone conversations, private meetings, lavatory, and final preparation before making initial public appearance at the event.

Hostage. A person taken against his will and being held in lieu of satisfaction of demands by the kidnapping source.

Hostage negotiator. A person skilled, trained, and experienced in securing the safe release of hostages.

Identification pins. Small pins worn on the lapel by protective team members for instant recognition and identification purposes. Size, color, design, and positioning change with the assignment.

Imagination. Creative ability; ideas!!!!; resourcefulness; analytical; ensuring that you account for all significant consequences; utilize reasoning, logic, experience, and training; ability to ask and answer "what if?"

Inspection. A walk-through examination of areas of particular interest.

Inspection mirror. A small mirror and flashlight attached to a long handle allowing an agent or inspector to search for bombs or listening and recording devices under a vehicle or in hard-to-reach places.

Intelligence. Analyzed data with conclusions and projections obtained from raw information relative to the safety and concern of the protectee. Two types—strategic and tactical (*see definitions under those headings*).

Kidnapping. The forceful taking of a person against his will to a secret place and to be held for ransom or settlement of demands.

KRI. Kidnapping and ransom insurance, usually purchased by large corporations for their key and vital personnel. Very expensive.

Law of unintended consequences. A totally unexpected and surprising result of a planned action.

Lead car. The vehicle immediately ahead of the protectee's vehicle. Usually a marked police car driven by a local police officer with the senior advance agent.

Letter bomb. A letter- or folder-size envelope containing an explosive charge that detonates upon breaking the seal or removing the contents.

Letter writer. A potential threat. Usually produces a prolific amount of incomprehensible writings and drawings. Usually of a radical religious nature. Sends letters as warnings, threats, and harassment. (*See caller.*)

Loose cannon. An agent who is not necessarily a team player and follows his own rules; very likely to disregard proper protocol.

Low profile. Protective agents are not obvious; blending into the crowd.

Low threat level. No actual threats or indications of potential threats; unknown or unrecognized protectee.

Medium threat level. The most common type of protective detail; potential danger but no actual threats received or determined; possible harassment telephone calls or letters.

Mental or mental case. A "person of interest" who is experiencing psychiatric problems.

Mind-set. A person's mental attitude; frame of reference.

Motorcade. A formally organized group of cars traveling in a controlled manner; may consist of three or more cars; formal motorcade aligned as: pilot or scout car, lead car, principal's car, follow-up car, staff car, press, or other necessary vehicles, tail car.

Movement. The principal changing locations; traveling or moving from one location to another.

Observation. The process of seeing, recognizing, and reacting.

Off duty. Not in a work-related status.

Off the air. Not in radio communication; radio is turned off.

Overt operation. Opposite of covert; in plain view; high profile.

Packing. Carrying a concealed weapon.

Panic button. A device carried by or placed within reach of a protectee to be utilized in the event of an emergency requiring immediate response by the protective agents. Transmits a silent alarm to a central location or to an agent's receiver to alert him of the emergency.

Person of interest. A person who may pose a threat to the protectee.

Personal protection specialist. A person highly educated and trained in the profession of close personal protection. Executive protection specialist.

Personal security agent. Individual providing close proximity protection to a protectee. This position is usually assumed by the detail leader or senior agent.

Physical barrier. Anything forming a barricade that prevents direct access. It may be a door, a wall, smash resistant glass, trees, etc.

Pilot car. A marked police car usually proceeding the motorcade by approximately a quarter mile. It scans the area for potential immediate problems such as obstructions, dangerous activity, etc.

Point man. The person assuming the lead in a protective movement formation; protects the principal in the frontal area.

Political or staff advance. Advance nonsecurity arrangements for the principal involving scheduling, social and political functions, press media arrangements, etc. (*See advance.*)

Portfolio. A confidential case file of the protectee: includes pertinent information and photos. Also referred to as principal's file.

Post. An area of responsibility established to form a part of the security network. Also known as a security post. May be a fixed surveillance post, a checkpoint, a roving post, or special assignment.

Post orders. Specific instructions regarding the operation of a security post.

Press area. Specific designated area for members of the working press. Only credentialed press members are allowed into this area.

Principal. The person receiving the close personal protection; the protectee; the client.

Principal car. The vehicle designated to carry the principal.

Private sector. Not government agency related; private firms or individuals providing protective services; private enterprise, may be an individual or a major corporation.

Professional. A highly educated and trained agent dedicated to providing the very best protective services available. Knowledgeable in every aspect of his business.

Profile. A thumbnail sketch; a synopsis; a quick reference to the risk potential; the way a person, a situation, or a protective detail is viewed.

Protectee. The person receiving the protection, the client, the principal. (*See principal.*)

Protectee protocol. Accepted and recommended behavior and attitude toward the protectee, his family, staff, business, and property. (*See protocol.*)

Protection. Security of a protectee; prevention of any harm to the protectee; includes his home, travel, and work environments.

Protective detail. The overall name given to the group of agents assigned to provide protective services to a client. The general name given to a protective responsibility.

Protective intelligence. P.I.; data, information, rumor regarding potential threats to the protectee.

Protective intelligence car. On a large scale, protectee movement for a protective intelligence car containing at least one protective agent and a local plainclothes police officer is assigned to the approximate area of the event to respond to and resolve any activity that could involve possible threats or disruptions.

Protector. The person providing the protective service. (*See executive protection specialist; personal protection specialist.*)

Protocol. A set of rules or codes that dictates social behavior in official dealings and certain circles; correct procedures for displaying the flag, receiving high-ranking political figures, etc. Medical protocol defines specific procedures for attending medical emergencies.

Psychological barriers. Those barriers that consist of alarm systems, electric-eye beams, gravel driveways, open spaces, etc. They can be intruded upon, but an intruder risks being detected.

Push. Rotating posts; post relief.

Risk analysis/assessment. An evaluation of the information and intelligence available and the potential problems and degree of danger posed by those who would do harm to a protectee. A process evaluating potential hazards and the degree of likelihood of occurrence.

Risk factor. The elements consisting of the potential danger and the probability of its occurrence.

Roger. Radio transmission acknowledgment.

Route car. A mobile team of executive protection agents (possibly with a plain-clothes police officer), usually in an unmarked car, canvassing the protectee's motorcade route for traffic problems, crowd buildup, buildings that could house a possible problem, or any obstruction that might provide an impediment to the progress of the protectee. (*See advance car.*)

Route survey. The selection of primary and alternate routes the principal will travel; includes time (at various times of day) and distance, directions, anticipated traffic problems, locations of emergency medical facilities.

Routine. Repetitious activity performed at the same time in a usual manner, a set unvaried schedule, a habit.

Sabotage. A purposeful and deliberate act to cause damage to the property of another; actions designed to counter the efforts of a protective detail.

Safe room. A reinforced secure room easily and quickly accessible to the principal and his family in case of emergency. Generally equipped with emergency rations, lighting, and communications.

Secure area. A location that has been surveyed and cleared of unauthorized persons and objects and is continuously secured by establishing security post assignments around the location.

Security advance. Prior arrangements of a security related nature in anticipation of the arrival of a protectee. (*See advance.*)

Security perimeter. An established boundary that involves the placement and utilization of security personnel, alarms, barricades, and other devices to provide protection, surveillance, and intelligence information. The area and the people within the perimeter have been cleared for security purposes.

Security post. *See post.*

Security room. A break or relief room for security related personnel, including protective agents, police, fire department personnel, and paramedics.

Security survey. A vital venue examination and analysis to determine the current security status and ascertain steps for improvement.

Security vulnerability. An assessment of existing areas of potential weaknesses and determining the degree of defenselessness and liability.

Site survey. A security inspection, advance, and subsequent security plans for a given or specific location. (*See advance.*)

Staff advance. *See political advance.*

Stalker. A person who constantly pursues and preys on the attention or affection of another against his will. Usually a predatory type person.

Strategic intelligence or planning. Information and planning for a long-range time factor. (*See intelligence.*)

Surveillance. The act of watching and monitoring the activities of another.

Sweep. A prescribed and specific method of searching an area for explosive devices or electronic listening or surveillance apparatus.

Tactical intelligence or planning. Intelligence and planning for immediate use. (*See intelligence.*)

Tail car. The last car in a motorcade, usually a marked police car.

Tail man. Agent protecting the back of a protectee while in a protective movement formation.

Team. A group of agents working together to provide protective services to a protectee. (*See detail; protective detail.*)

Team leader. *See detail leader.*

Ten-minute medicine. Emergency medical response providing life support (CPR) for the critical ten minutes. Checking airway, breathing, and circulation and taking appropriate action.

Terrorism. A violent act, usually bombing or kidnapping, for political or religious purposes. Terror created by others, directed toward a principal and his family or business for the purpose of causing major disruption and problems.

Terrorist. One who participates in a terrorist activity for political, religious, or ideological purposes.

Threat level. *See risk analysis assessment risk factor.*

Thumb peel. The specific method of disengaging a firm holding handshake with the principal.

Touch down. The actual instant the protectee's airplane lands or touches down.

Venue. The event site.

Visual protection area. The area assigned to each agent in a protective detail that provides protection with a minimum amount of head movement, that is, near a speaker's platform, facing the audience.

Wheels up. The time a protectee's airplane officially departs or leaves the ground.

Working the principal. Being in close proximity to the principal and providing protective services.

Worthy of confidence and trust. A primary requisite for a protective agent. Can be entrusted with top secret information, money, and valuable possessions.

Zone car. Mobile teams assigned to specific areas (zones) adjacent to a motorcade route or visit site for the purpose of surveillance and intelligence.

Zone or "zoning." Specific sectors of an alarm system independent of other sectors for purpose of easy identification of location when an alarm is initiated. Also used to provide capability to disable portions of the system while allowing the remainder of the system to remain active.

Index

A

intermittent rage disorder, 133–34
isolation, 134
June, Dale, L., 125
Kennedy, J.F., 125
major depressive episode, 134–35
paranoia, 135
power syndrome, 133
protective intelligence investigation, 128–29
psychological perspectives, 130–35
schizophrenia, 135
weapons, talk about, 128
written threat analysis, 136–38
    ending, 137–38
    jargon, 137
    motivation, 137
    topic, 137
    voice/tenor/tone, 136
Image as knight, protective agent, 270
Imagination, 104–5
Improvised explosive devices, 338–39
Improvised weapons, 374–75
Inclination toward action, 317
Indicators of possible ambush attack, recognizing, 217–21
Industrial espionage, theft, 189–93
Industrial targets, arson/bombings, 339
Inner directedness, 257
Innocent guilty, 60–62
Insanity, motivation and, 39
Integrity, 262, 288–91
    defined, 289
Intelligence, advance security survey report, 113
Intelligence analyst, 129–30
Intermittent rage disorder, 133–34
Isolation, 134
Itinerary, advance security survey report, 113

J

Jenkins, Brian, 333
June, Dale, L., 15, 125, 141
Justice, 262, 287

K

Kant, Immanuel, 283
Kennedy
    J.F., 125
    John F., 301
Kidnap negotiation, 356–57
Kidnapping, 353–66
Kindliness, 262
King, Jr, Dr. Martin Luther, 261
Knights, 271
    protective agents, chivalry of, 79
Knowledge, 268
Koestler, Arthur, 335

L

Lanes, changing, 208
Laser-minded intent, 368–69
Law enforcement code of ethics, 292
Leadership, 257
Lee, Bruce, 21, 295
Legal consequences, 249–50
Legal insanity, motivation and, 39
Legal issues, 241–54
Legal restrictions, 245–46
Lethal weapons, use of, 249
Lickona, Thomas, 262
Life of individual, investment in, 36
Limitations, knowing, 267–68
Lincoln A., 101
    Abraham, 330
Logistics, advance security survey report, 113
Loyalty, 262, 268, 288
Luggage, 175

M

Major depressive episode, 134–35
Managerial qualities, 256–58
Maps, role in security process, 110
Marighella, Carlos, 329
Maslow, Abraham, 23–24
McCarthy, Dennis, 379
Media, terrorist relationship, 344
Media relations, 277–79
Medical emergencies, 229–31
Medical kit, 238–39
Medicine, 229–40
Mental agility, 259
Mental illness, assassination, myth regarding, 73
Mentally disturbed individual, 355
Minimum evacuation distance, 359
Miranda rights, 276
Mirror effect, 116–18
Mirror image, 116
Motivation, protectee's, 36
Motives of threatening person, 38–39
    economic, 39
    legal insanity, 39
    political, 39
    psychological insanity, 39
    religious, 39
    revenge, 39
Murrow, Edward R., 291

N

Natural disease, human-made disasters, 193
Need for security, understanding, 23
Needs hierarchy, Maslow's, 23–24
Non-lethal weapons, use of, 249